KB177719

최신 개정 교과서 완벽 반영

기출로적중
해커스
중학영문법

★★★
베스트셀러
★★★

- 중학 내신 기출 빅데이터 반영
- 실전 · 서술형 문제로 내신 완벽 대비
- 예비고를 위한 영문법 기본 완성

워크북+해설집+문법 암기리스트/단어 암기장 제공

워크북

해설집

문법 암기리스트 + 단어 암기장

해커스북 HackersBook.com

- 본 교재 문제 해석 파일
- 서술형 대비 영작/해석 워크시트
- 단어 암기장 MP3
- 문법 암기리스트+단어 암기장 PDF
- 3학년 교과서 대표 문법 한 눈에 보기

3학년

YES24 중고등참고서 베스트셀러 중학영어 문법 분야(2020년 11월 2주 주별 베스트 기준)

해커스 교재는
다릅니다

펼쳐 보면 느껴집니다

단 한 줄도 배움의 공백이 생기지 않도록
문장 한 줄마다 20년이 넘는
해커스의 영어교육 노하우를 담았음을

덮고 나면 확신합니다

수많은 선생님의 목소리와
정확한 출제 데이터 분석으로 꽉 찬
교재 한 권이면 충분함을

해커스북 중·고등
HackersBook.com

기출로 적중

해커스 중학영문법

과 함께하면

점수가 확 오르는 이유!

기출 분석으로 완벽히 적중시키니까!

1 전국 중학교 내신
기출문제 빅데이터
철저히 분석 및 반영

2 최신 개정 교과서의
모든 문법 포인트
빠짐없이 반영

중학영문법
1학년

중학영문법
2학년

중학영문법
3학년

촘촘한 훈련으로 확실히 내 것이 되니까!

3 중간·기말·서술형
실전문제로
내신 완벽 대비

4 암기리스트·단어 암기장
+워크북으로
반복 훈련 가능

기출로 적중 해커스 중학영문법 시리즈를 검토해주신 선생님들

경기

강상훈	평촌비상에듀학원
김원덕	올림피아드학원
박윤정	이지베스트학원
최승복	오른어학원
최지영	다른영어학원

서울

김가영	송정중학교
박유정	반포중학교
박은혜	송파중학교
박정은	대청중학교
양세희	양세희수능영어학원

이계윤	씨앤씨학원
이유빈	잉글리쉬&매쓰매니저학원
이혜원	대청중학교
정혜은	용곡중학교
최다빈	최강영어

해커스 어학연구소 자문위원단 3기

강원

박정선	잉글리쉬클럽
최현주	최쌤영어

경기

강민정	김진성열정어학원
강상훈	평촌RTS학원
강지인	강지인영어학원
권계미	A&T+ 영어
김미아	김쌤영어학원
김설화	업라이트잉글리쉬
김성재	스윗스터디학원
김세훈	모두의학원
김수아	더스터디(The STUDY)
김영아	백송고등학교
김유경	벨트어학원
김유경	포시즌스어학원
김유동	이스턴영어학원
김지숙	위디벨럽학원
김지현	이지프라임영어학원
김해빈	해빛영어학원
김현지	지앤비영어학원
박가영	한민고등학교
박영서	스윗스터디학원
박은별	더킹영수학원
박재홍	록키어학원
성승민	SDH어학원 불당캠퍼스
신소연	Ashley English
오귀연	루나영어학원
유신애	에듀포커스학원
윤소정	ILP이화어학원
이동진	이룸학원
이상미	버밍엄영어교습소
이연경	명품M비온드수학영어학원
이은수	광주세종학원
이지혜	리케이온
이진희	이엠원영수학원
이충기	영어나무
이효명	갈매리드앤톡영어독서학원
임한글	Apsun앞선영어학원
장광명	엠케이영어학원
전상호	평촌이지어학원
전성훈	훈선생영어교실
정선영	코어플러스영어학원
정준	고양외국어고등학교
조연아	카이트학원
채기림	고려대학교EIE영어학원
최지영	다른영어학원
최한나	석사영수전문
최희정	SJ클쌤영어학원
현지환	모두의학원
홍태경	공감국어영어전문학원

경남

강다희	더(the)오르다영어학원
라승희	아이작잉글리쉬
박주언	유니크학원
배송현	두잇영어교습소
안윤서	어썸영어학원
임진희	어썸영어학원

경북

권현민	삼성영어석적우방교실
김으뜸	EIE영어학원 옥계캠퍼스
배세왕	비케이영수전문고등관학원
유영선	아이비티어학원

광주

김유희	김유희영어학원
서희연	SDL영어수학학원
송수일	아이리드영어학원
오진우	SLT어학원수학원
정영철	정영철영어전문학원
최경옥	봉선중학교

대구

권익재	제이슨영어
김명일	독학인학원
김보곤	베스트영어
김연정	달서고등학교
김혜란	김혜란영어학원
문애주	프렌즈입시학원
박정근	공부의힘pnk학원
박희숙	열공열강영어수학학원
신동기	신통외국어학원
위영선	위영선영어학원
윤창원	공터영어학원 상인센터
이승현	학문당입시학원
이주현	이주현영어학원
이헌욱	이헌욱영어학원
장준현	장쌤독해종결영어학원
주현아	민샘영어학원
최윤정	최강영어학원

대전

곽선영	위드유학원
김지운	더포스둔산학원
박미현	라시움영어대동학원
박세리	EM101학원

부산

김건희	레지나잉글리쉬 영어학원
김미나	위드중고등영어학원
박수진	정모클영어국어학원
박수진	지니잉글리쉬
박인숙	리더스영어전문학원
옥지윤	더센텀영어학원
윤진희	위니드영어전문교습소
이종혁	진수학원
정혜인	엠티엔영어학원
조정래	알파카의영어농장
주태양	솔라영어학원

서울

Erica Sull	하버드브레인영어학원
강고은	케이앤학원
강신아	교우학원
공현미	이은재어학원
권영진	경동고등학교
김나영	프라임클래스영어학원
김달수	대일외국어고등학교
김대니	채움학원
김문영	창문여자고등학교
김상백	강북세일학원
김정은	강북뉴스터디학원
김혜경	대동세무고등학교
남혜원	함영원입시전문학원
노시은	케이앤학원
박선정	강북세일학원
박수진	이은재어학원
박지수	이플러스영수학원
서승희	함영원입시전문학원
신지웅	강북세일학원
양세희	양세희수능영어학원
우정용	제임스영어앤드학원
이박원	이박원어학원
이승혜	스텔라영어
이정욱	이은재어학원
이지연	중계케이트영어학원
임예찬	학습컨설턴트
장지희	고려대학교사범대학부속고등학교
정미라	미라정영어학원
조민규	조민규영어
채가희	대성세그루영수학원

울산

김기태	그라티아어학원
이민주	로이아카데미
홍영민	더이안영어전문학원

인천

강재민	스터디위드제이쌤
고현순	정상학원
권효진	Genie's English
김솔	전문과외
김정아	밀턴영어학원
서상천	최정서학원
이윤주	트리플원
최예영	영웅아카데미

전남

강희진	강희진영어학원
김두환	해남맨체스터영수학원
송승연	송승연영수학원
윤세광	비상구영어학원

전북

김길자	맨투맨학원
김미영	링크영어학원
김효성	연세입시학원
노빈나	노빈나영어전문학원
라성남	하포드어학원
박재훈	위더스수학지앤비영어학원
박향숙	STA영어전문학원
서종원	서종원영어학원
이상호	나는학원
장지원	링컨더글라스학원
지근영	한솔영어수학학원
최성령	연세입시학원
최혜영	이든영어수학학원

제주

김랑	KLS어학원
박자은	KLS어학원

충남

김예지	더배움프라임영수학원
김철홍	청경학원
노태겸	최상위학원

충북

라은경	이화윤스영어교습소
신유정	비타민영어클리닉학원

최신 개정 교과서 완벽 반영

기출로 적중 해커스 중학영문법

3학년

이 책을 검토해주신 선생님들

강상훈 경기 평촌비상에듀학원 / **김가영** 서울 송정중학교 / **김원덕** 경기 올림피아드학원 / **박유정** 서울 반포중학교 / **박윤정** 경기 이지베스트학원

박은혜 서울 송파중학교 / **박정은** 서울 대청중학교 / **양세희** 서울 양세희수능영어학원 / **이계윤** 서울 씨앤씨학원 / **이유빈** 서울 잉글리쉬&매쓰매니저학원

이혜원 서울 대청중학교 / **정혜은** 서울 용곡중학교 / **최다빈** 서울 최강영어 / **최승복** 경기 오른어학원 / **최지영** 경기 다른영어학원

목차

CHAPTER 5 부정사

CHAPTER 6 동명사

CHAPTER 7 분사

CHAPTER 8 명사와 대명사

목차

구성 미리 보기

○ 시험에 나온, 또 나올 **기출 적중 문법 POINT 학습**

기출 적중 POINT

최신 개정 교과서와 전국 내신 기출 빅데이터에서 뽑아낸 문법 포인트를 빠짐없이 학습할 수 있습니다.

핵심 문법 사항

내신 시험 대비에 꼭 필요한 문법 사항을 명쾌한 설명과 예문을 통해 정확하게 이해할 수 있습니다.

심화 문법 TIP

어렵지만 실제 내신 시험에서 출제된 적이 있는 문법 사항을 학습하여 고난도 문제에 대비할 수 있습니다.

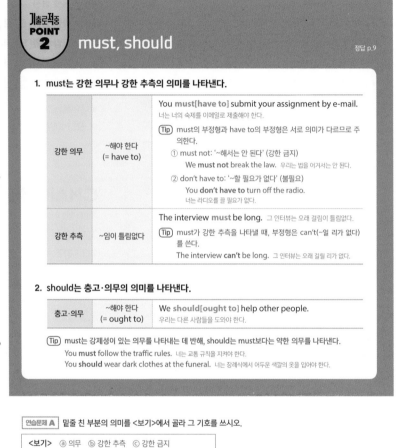

기출문제적중 POINT 2 must, should

정답 p.9

1. must는 강한 의무나 강한 추측의 의미를 나타낸다.

강한 의무	~해야 한다 (= have to)	You **must[have to]** submit your assignment by e-mail. 너는 너의 숙제를 이메일로 제출해야 한다. **Tip** must의 부정형과 have to의 부정형은 서로 의미가 다르므로 주의한다. ① must not: '~해서는 안 된다' (강한 금지) We **must not** break the law. 우리는 법을 어겨서는 안 된다. ② don't have to: '~할 필요가 없다' (불필요) You **don't have to** turn off the radio. 너는 라디오를 끌 필요가 없다.
강한 추측	~임이 틀림없다	The interview **must** be long. 그 인터뷰는 오래 걸림이 틀림없다. **Tip** must가 강한 추측을 나타낼 때, 부정형은 can't(~일 리가 없다)를 쓴다. The interview **can't** be long. 그 인터뷰는 오래 걸릴 리가 없다.

2. should는 충고·의무의 의미를 나타낸다.

충고·의무	~해야 한다 (= ought to)	We **should[ought to]** help other people. 우리는 다른 사람들을 도와야 한다.

Tip must는 강제성이 있는 의무를 나타내는 데 반해, should는 must보다는 약한 의무를 나타낸다.
You **must** follow the traffic rules. 너는 교통 규칙을 지켜야 한다.
You **should** wear dark clothes at the funeral. 너는 장례식에서 어두운 색깔의 옷을 입어야 한다.

연습문제 A 밑줄 친 부분의 의미를 <보기>에서 골라 그 기호를 쓰시오.

<보기> ⓐ 의무 ⓑ 강한 추측 ⓒ 강한 금지

1 She <u>must</u> be careful not to make the same mistake again. [   ]

2 Brian <u>must</u> be excited about his upcoming competition. [   ]

3 People <u>must</u> not drive too fast near schools and kindergartens. [   ]

4 Sumin <u>must</u> be tired after finishing the marathon. [   ]

5 Mark <u>must</u> be upset because his team lost the soccer game. [   ]

6 People <u>must</u> not touch hair dryers with wet hands. [   ]

7 The chef <u>must</u> cook faster because a lot of people are waiting. [   ]

연습문제 B 괄호 안에서 알맞은 것을 <u>모두</u> 고르시오.

1 We (must / have to) hurry because the train is about to leave.

2 The dog is barking, so there (must / should) be a stranger at the door.

3 You (must not / don't have to) wake up early tomorrow because you don't go to work on Saturdays.

4 People (must not / don't have to) leave any trash in the park.

5 You (must / don't have to) be really hungry as you skipped breakfast.

6 I (must / have to) return the books to the library today.

7 Mr. Smith (must not / doesn't have to) eat anything before his medical checkup.

8 George is good at speaking French, so he (must not / doesn't have to) take this class.

9 They (can't / ought to) be at the concert because they weren't able to purchase tickets.

10 You (must not / should not) interrupt someone who is speaking.

연습문제 C 다음 그림을 보고 should와 괄호 안의 말을 활용하여 문장을 완성하시오.

1   2   3   4

1 You _____ your hands before having dinner. (wash)

2 You _____ on the phone loudly in the hospital. (talk)

3 She _____ the bed every morning. (make)

4 He _____ harder if he wants to get a good grade. (study)

기출 적중문제

다음 밑줄 친 must의 쓰임과 <u>다른</u> 것은?

Everyone <u>must</u> wear their seatbelts during the flight.

① You <u>must</u> sign your name on this form.
② He <u>must</u> be very good at singing as he used to be a singer.
③ All participants <u>must</u> bring their ID cards.
④ You and I <u>must</u> arrive at the airport before 10 o'clock.
⑤ I <u>must</u> finish my homework by tomorrow.

must는 강한 의무와 강한 추측이라는 두 가지 의미를 가지고 있어요.

연습문제

다양한 유형과 많은 양의 연습 문제를 통해 문법 사항을 암기 하지 않고도 자연스럽게 이해 할 수 있습니다.

기출 적중문제

빈출 포인트가 적용된 실전 문 제를 풀어보며 실제 내신 시험 의 출제 방식을 미리 경험해볼 수 있습니다.

기출 해결 TIP

빈출 포인트가 적용된 실전 문 제의 해결 TIP을 통해 실제 내 신 시험에서의 정답 적중률을 높일 수 있습니다.

○ 체계적으로 시작하는 **기초 문법**

<< 중학영문법을 이해하기 위해 꼭 알아야 하는 기초 문법이 정리되어 있어 문법 실력이 부족한 학생들도 영문법을 체계적으로 학습할 수 있습니다.

○ 서술형 평가에 강해지는 **서술형 대비 문제**

<< 다양한 유형의 서술형 대비 문제를 풀어보며 서술형을 강조하는 최근 내신 평가 트렌드에 대비할 수 있습니다.

○ 정답 적중률을 높이는 **중간·기말고사 실전 문제**

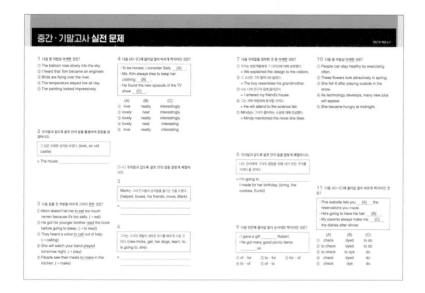

<< 전국 내신 기출문제의 빈출 유형과 문법 포인트가 반영된 객관식·주관식 문제를 풀어보며 실제 내신 시험에서의 정답 적중률을 높일 수 있습니다.

○ 학습 효과를 더욱 높이는 **워크북과 부록**

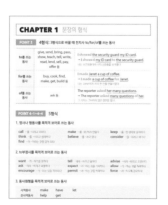

워크북

풍부한 양의 추가 문제를 풀면서 부족한 부분을 파악하고 보완할 수 있습니다.

문법 암기리스트

교재에 수록된 문법 사항 중 꼭 암기해야 할 사항을 언제 어디서나 학습할 수 있습니다.

단어 암기장

교재에서 사용된 중학 필수 단어 및 표현을 암기하며 어휘력을 향상할 수 있습니다.

기초 문법 ⚽

영어 문법, 그 기초부터 알고 들어가자!

본격적인 학습 전에, 영어 문법의 기초가 되는 8품사, 문장 성분, 구와 절에 대해 배워보도록 해요!

1 문장 성분 영어 문장을 만드는 요소

영어에서 문장을 구성하는 여러 요소들을 **문장 성분**이라고 해요. 문장 성분은 문장 안에서의 역할에 따라 구분돼요.

① 주어와 동사

The package(주어) + **arrived**(동사). 소포가 도착했다.

하나의 문장을 만들기 위해서는 주어와 동사가 반드시 필요해요. 위 문장의 The package처럼 **동작이나 상태의 주체가 되는 말**을 주어라고 하고, 우리말의 '누가, 무엇이'에 해당해요. arrived처럼 **주어의 동작이나 상태를 나타내는 말**을 동사라고 하고, 우리말의 '~이다, ~하다'에 해당해요.

② 목적어

I(주어) + ate(동사) + **some sandwiches**(목적어). 나는 약간의 샌드위치를 먹었다.

위 문장에서 동사 ate 다음에 내가 먹은 대상인 some sandwiches가 왔어요. 이렇게 **동사가 나타내는 동작의 대상이 되는 말**을 목적어라고 해요. 목적어는 주로 동사 뒤에 오며, 우리말의 '누구를, 무엇을'에 해당해요.

③ 보어

This movie(주어) + was(동사) + **sad**(주격 보어). 이 영화는 슬펐다.
It(주어) + made(동사) + me(목적어) + **cry**(목적격 보어). 그것은 나를 울게 만들었다.

첫 번째 문장의 sad는 주어 This movie가 어땠는지 보충 설명해주고 있고, 두 번째 문장의 cry는 목적어 me의 상태를 보충 설명해주고 있어요. 이렇게 **주어나 목적어를 보충 설명해주는 말**을 보어라고 해요.

④ 수식어

That boy(주어) + **playing soccer**(수식어) + is(동사) + **very**(수식어) + handsome(보어).
축구를 하고 있는 저 소년은 매우 잘생겼다.

위 문장의 playing soccer와 very는 문장에서 반드시 필요하지 않은 부가적인 요소이지만, 문장의 의미를 더 풍부하게 해주고 있어요. 이렇게 **문장 안에서 다른 문장 성분이나 문장 전체를 꾸미는 말**을 수식어라고 해요.

CHECK-UP

다음 문장의 밑줄 친 부분의 성분을 쓰세요.

1 He <u>studies</u> Korean history. [   ] 2 Dan became <u>an actor</u>. [   ]
3 <u>Playing chess</u> is my hobby. [   ] 4 Linda has lost <u>her wallet</u>. [   ]
5 Mom let me <u>watch</u> TV. [   ] 6 Penguins live <u>in Antarctica</u>. [   ]
7 I'm looking at <u>a painting</u>. [   ] 8 The <u>tall</u> man is my uncle. [   ]

정답 1 동사 2 보어 3 주어 4 목적어 5 보어 6 수식어 7 목적어 8 수식어

2 8품사 영어 문장의 재료

영어 단어는 기능과 성격에 따라 8가지로 분류할 수 있으며, 이를 **8품사**라고 해요.

① 명사

Ben knows that **Seoul** is the **capital** of **Korea**. Ben은 서울이 한국의 수도라는 것을 안다.

명사는 **우리 주위에 있는 모든 것에 붙여진 이름**으로, 문장 안에서 주어, 목적어, 보어로 쓰여요.

② 대명사

Mark and his friends went to the concert. **They** enjoyed themselves.
Mark와 그의 친구들은 콘서트에 갔다. 그들은 즐거운 시간을 보냈다.

대명사는 앞에 나온 명사를 반복해서 쓰지 않기 위해 **명사를 대신해서 쓰는 말**로, 문장 안에서 주어, 목적어, 보어로 쓰여요.

③ 동사

I **want** to buy a hat. I **will go** to the mall soon. 나는 모자를 사기를 원한다. 나는 곧 쇼핑몰에 갈 것이다.

동사는 **사람, 동물, 사물 등의 동작이나 상태를 나타내는 말**이에요.

④ 형용사

She has a **long** and **curly hair**. **Her hair** is **black**.
그녀는 길고 곱슬곱슬한 머리를 가지고 있다. 그녀의 머리는 검은색이다.

형용사는 **명사와 대명사를 꾸며서 성질이나 상태를 나타내는 말**로, 문장 안에서 보어나 수식어로 쓰여요.

⑤ 부사

The stars **are shining brightly**. They are **very pretty**. 별들이 밝게 빛나고 있다. 그것들은 매우 예쁘다.

부사는 **동사, 형용사, 다른 부사, 또는 문장 전체를 꾸미는 말**로, 문장 안에서 수식어로 쓰여요.

⑥ 전치사

I met my friend **on the street after school**. He was waving **at me**.
나는 방과 후에 길에서 나의 친구를 만났다. 그는 나에게 손을 흔들고 있었다.

전치사는 **명사나 대명사 앞에 와서 시간, 장소, 방향, 방법 등을 나타내는 말**이에요.

⑦ 접속사

I would like **potato soup**, **salad**, **and coffee**. 나는 감자 수프, 샐러드, 그리고 커피를 원한다.
Liam doesn't know that I lied to him. Liam은 내가 그에게 거짓말을 한 것을 모른다.

접속사는 단어와 단어, 구와 구, 절과 절을 연결해주는 말이에요.

⑧ 감탄사

Ouch! I fell down the stairs! 아야! 나는 계단에서 굴러 떨어졌어!

감탄사는 기쁨, 놀람, 슬픔과 같은 다양한 감정을 표현해주는 말이에요.

Tip 1. 하나의 단어가 여러 가지 품사로 사용될 수 있어요.
   I don't feel **well**(형용사). (→ I의 보어로 사용된 형용사) 나는 몸이 좋지 않다.
   I can't concentrate **well**(부사). (→ 동사 concentrate를 꾸미는 부사) 나는 잘 집중할 수 없다.

2. 약간의 형태 차이로 품사가 달라지는 단어가 있어요.
   The doctor gave me some **advice**(명사). 의사는 나에게 약간의 조언을 줬다.
   He **advised**(동사) me to drink more water. 그는 나에게 더 많은 물을 마시라고 조언했다.

CHECK-UP

다음 문장의 밑줄 친 부분의 품사를 쓰세요.

1 This <u>book</u> is <u>very</u> <u>popular</u>.
    [   ] [   ] [   ]

2 <u>We</u> ate pizza <u>and</u> <u>drank</u> coke.
    [   ]   [   ] [   ]

3 <u>Oh</u>! You can't smoke <u>in</u> the <u>building</u>.
    [   ]   [   ] [   ]

4 I <u>always</u> <u>keep</u> my room <u>clean</u>.
    [   ] [   ]   [   ]

정답 | 1 명사 / 부사 / 형용사 2 대명사 / 접속사 / 동사 3 감탄사 / 전치사 / 명사 4 부사 / 동사 / 형용사

3 구와 절 말 덩어리

두 개 이상의 단어가 모여 하나의 의미를 나타내는 말 덩어리를 **구**나 **절**이라고 해요. 구는 at midnight 처럼 주어와 동사를 포함하지 않고, 절은 because she is sick처럼 주어와 동사를 포함해요. 구와 절은 단어보다 길이만 길지만, 문장 안에서 명사, 형용사, 부사 역할을 할 수 있어요.

① 명사 역할

명사 역할을 하는 명사구와 명사절은 문장 안에서 명사처럼 주어, 목적어, 보어로 쓰여요.

명사구   **Being polite to others** is important. <주어> 다른 사람에게 공손한 것은 중요하다.

명사절   I'm not sure **if the store is open today**. <목적어> 나는 그 가게가 오늘 열었는지 확실하지 않다.

② 형용사 역할

형용사 역할을 하는 형용사구와 형용사절은 형용사처럼 명사나 대명사를 꾸며요.

형용사구   The **actor** in the movie is famous.   그 영화 속의 배우는 유명하다.

형용사절   Carl is the **boy** who broke the window.   Carl이 창문을 깬 그 소년이다.

③ 부사 역할

부사 역할을 하는 부사구와 부사절은 부사처럼 동사, 형용사, 다른 부사, 또는 문장 전체를 꾸며요.

부사구   Brandon usually **goes** to bed **at midnight**.   Brandon은 보통 자정에 잔다.

부사절   Mina **is** absent **because she is sick**.   미나는 아프기 때문에 결석했다.

CHECK-UP

다음 문장의 밑줄 친 부분이 해당하는 것을 고르세요.

1   He lives in the house <u>with large pool</u>.   (형용사구 / 형용사절)
2   I believe <u>that health is the most important thing</u>.   (명사구 / 명사절)
3   We enjoy <u>playing soccer</u> in the field.   (명사구 / 부사구)
4   Close all the windows <u>before you go out</u>.   (형용사절 / 부사절)

정답   1 형용사구   2 명사절   3 명사구   4 부사절

CHAPTER 1
문장의 형식

Josh likes ice cream. Josh는 아이스크림을 좋아한다.
주어   동사   목적어

위 문장은 주어 **Josh**, 동사 **likes**, 목적어 **ice cream**으로 이루어진 완전한 문장이에요. 완전한 문장에는 필수적인 문장 요소가 포함되어야 하는데, 주어와 동사는 반드시 필요하며 동사의 성격에 따라 보어나 목적어가 필요하기도 해요. 이렇게 동사가 어떤 문장 요소를 필요로 하는지에 따라 다섯 가지로 **문장의 형식**이 나뉘어요.

기출로 적중 POINT

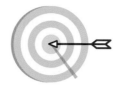

내신 100점 적중!
기출 출제율

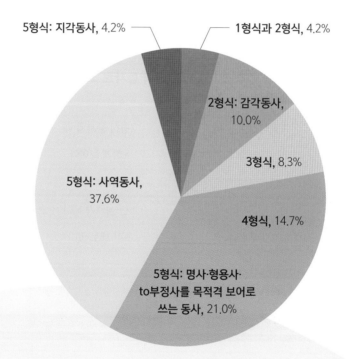

5형식: 지각동사, 4.2%

1형식과 2형식, 4.2%

2형식: 감각동사, 10.0%

3형식, 8.3%

4형식, 14.7%

5형식: 사역동사, 37.6%

5형식: 명사·형용사·to부정사를 목적격 보어로 쓰는 동사, 21.0%

TOP 1 **5형식: 사역동사 (37.6%)**
문장 안에서 사역동사의 쓰임을 묻는 문제가 자주 출제된다.

TOP 2 **5형식: to부정사를 목적격 보어로 쓰는 동사 (21%)**
to부정사가 목적격 보어 자리에 쓰이는 동사를 묻는 문제가 자주 출제된다.

TOP 3 **4형식 (14.7%)**
4형식 문장의 어순을 묻는 문제가 자주 출제된다.

1형식과 2형식

1. 1형식 문장은 「주어 + 동사」의 형태로, 수식어구가 함께 쓰이기도 한다.

Jenny **arrived**. Jenny가 도착했다.

The baby **sleeps** <u>in a bed</u>. 그 아기는 침대에서 잔다.
　　　　　　　　수식어구

(Tip) 수식어구는 1~5형식 문장에 모두 쓸 수 있으며 문장 형식에 영향을 미치지 않는다.

2. 2형식 문장은 「주어 + 동사 + 주격 보어」의 형태로, 주어를 보충 설명하는 주격 보어를 가진다. 주격 보어 자리에는 명사나 형용사가 올 수 있다.

They **are** my brothers. 그들은 나의 형제이다.

The song **became** popular. 그 노래는 인기 있어졌다.

3. 다음 동사들은 의미에 따라 주격 보어 없이 1형식 동사로 쓰이기도 하며, 주격 보어와 함께 2형식 동사로 쓰이기도 한다.

	1형식 동사일 때	2형식 동사일 때
appear	나타나다	~하게 보이다
grow	자라다(증가하다)	~하게 되다
fall	떨어지다	~한 상태가 되다
stay	머무르다	~한 채로 있다

1형식　My uncle **appeared** on the stage. 나의 삼촌이 그 무대 위에 나타났다.

2형식　He **appeared** nervous yesterday. 그는 어제 긴장한 것처럼 보였다.

[연습문제] 다음 문장의 동사에 동그라미를 치고 주격 보어가 있는 경우 주격 보어에 밑줄을 치시오. 그 후, 문장이 1형식인지 2형식인지 고르시오.

1 They became parents last week. (1형식 / 2형식)

2 Communication matters in a relationship. (1형식 / 2형식)

3 My sister suddenly appeared on television. (1형식 / 2형식)

4 The cactus grows in the desert. (1형식 / 2형식)

5 She didn't fall asleep till 3 A.M. last night. (1형식 / 2형식)

6 I stayed at his house yesterday. (1형식 / 2형식)

7 He doesn't stay angry for more than an hour. (1형식 / 2형식)

8 All the fruits in this box appear ripe enough. (1형식 / 2형식)

POINT 1-2 2형식: 감각동사

정답 p.2

1. **감각동사는 '~하게 보이다/들리다, ~한 냄새가 나다, 맛이 나다, 느낌이 들다' 같이 감각을 나타내는 2형식 동사로, 감각동사의 주격 보어 자리에는 주로 형용사가 온다.**

look	sound	smell	taste	feel

   He **looks** handsome. 그는 잘생겨 보인다.
   This blanket **feels** soft. 이 담요는 부드러운 느낌이 든다.

   (Tip) 감각동사의 주격 보어 자리에는 부사가 올 수 없다.
   Her voice **sounds** (~~beautifully~~, **beautiful**). 그녀의 목소리는 아름답게 들린다.

2. **감각동사 뒤에 명사가 오는 경우 전치사 like와 함께 「감각동사 + like + 명사」의 형태로 쓴다.**

   It **sounds like** a good plan. 그것은 좋은 계획처럼 들린다.
   The orange **smelled like** a lemon. 그 오렌지는 레몬 같은 냄새가 났다.
   Luna **looks like** a high school student. Luna는 고등학생처럼 보인다.

연습문제 괄호 안에서 알맞은 것을 고르시오.

1 The child looked (unhappy / unhappily) because of his broken toy.

2 All the songs by the artist (sound / sound like) very similar.

3 The actor feels (comfortable / comfortably) with his role in the movie.

4 The salad we had this morning didn't taste (fresh / freshly).

5 The rug in my house smelled (awful / awfully).

6 Hawaii (looks / looks like) a nice place to visit during our vacation.

7 The tea (tastes / tastes like) more bitter than I expected.

8 You will look (wonderful / wonderfully) in your new dress.

9 Her plan of traveling around Europe (sounds / sounds like) a good idea.

10 The restaurant's new dish tasted (delicious / deliciously).

11 Jisu (felt / felt like) confident in his homemade cookies.

12 The new shampoo at the store (smells / smells like) roses.

13 It (sounds / sounds like) a true story, but, actually, it is not.

1. **3형식 문장은 「주어 + 동사 + 목적어」의 형태이다. 목적어는 동사의 대상이 되는 말로, 목적어 자리에는 명사나 대명사가 올 수 있다.**

   She **met** **her friend** last week. 그녀는 지난주에 그녀의 친구를 만났다.
   　　　　　목적어

   He didn't **remember** **me**. 그는 나를 기억하지 못했다.
   　　　　　　　목적어

2. **다음 3형식 동사들은 우리말 해석과 달리 전치사를 함께 쓰지 않는다.**

about을 함께 쓰지 않는 동사	explain ~에 대해 설명하다　　discuss ~에 대해 논의하다 mention ~에 대해 언급하다
with를 함께 쓰지 않는 동사	match ~와 어울리다　　contact ~와 연락하다 marry ~와 결혼하다　　resemble ~와 닮다
to를 함께 쓰지 않는 동사	reach ~에 도달하다　　enter ~에 들어가다　　attend ~에 참석하다

   I'll **explain** ~~about~~ **the problem.** 나는 그 문제에 대해 설명할 것이다.
   My grandfather **married** ~~with~~ **my grandmother** 50 years ago.
   나의 할아버지는 50년 전에 나의 할머니와 결혼하셨다.
   We **reached** ~~to~~ **the top** of the mountain. 우리는 그 산의 정상에 도달했다.

연습문제 밑줄 친 부분이 어법상 맞으면 O를 쓰고, 틀리면 바르게 고쳐 쓰시오.

1 You should <u>explain</u> what happened today. → _____

2 Didn't he <u>enter to</u> the classroom? → _____

3 Gary <u>went with</u> his friend to buy a new bike. → _____

4 She <u>resembles with</u> her mother more than her sister does. → _____

5 Don't <u>mention about</u> my secret to other people. → _____

6 He will <u>attend to</u> Mr. Kim's class next semester. → _____

7 My new coat does not <u>match</u> my pants. → _____

8 I need to <u>reach</u> the airport before 10 A.M. → _____

9 Mark wanted to <u>contact with</u> Lisa, but he couldn't. → _____

10 Kate <u>ran to</u> the restaurant where she was meeting her family. → _____

POINT 3 4형식

1. 4형식 문장은 「주어 + 동사 + 간접 목적어(~에게) + 직접 목적어(-을)」의 형태로, 두 개의 목적어를 가진다. 4형식 동사는 '~에게 -을 (해)주다'라는 의미를 가지는 경우가 많아서 수여동사라고 한다.

I **bought** <u>my daughter</u> <u>a new doll</u>. 나는 나의 딸에게 새로운 인형을 사줬다.
　　　　　　간접 목적어　　　직접 목적어

He **lent** <u>me</u> <u>a charger</u>. 그는 나에게 충전기를 빌려줬다.
　　　　간접 목적어　직접 목적어

2. 4형식 문장은 동사에 따라 전치사 to/for/of를 사용하여 3형식 문장으로 바꿀 수 있다.

> 4형식　주어 + 동사 + <u>간접 목적어(~에게)</u> + <u>직접 목적어(-을)</u>
>
> 3형식　주어 + 동사 + <u>직접 목적어(-을)</u> + **전치사 to/for/of** + <u>간접 목적어(~에게)</u>

to를 쓰는 동사	give, send, bring, pass, show, teach, tell, write, read, lend, sell, pay, offer 등	I **showed** <u>the security guard</u> <u>my ID card</u>. → I **showed** <u>my ID card</u> **to** <u>the security guard</u>. 나는 보안요원에게 나의 신분증을 보여줬다.
for를 쓰는 동사	buy, cook, find, make, get, build 등	I **made** <u>Janet</u> <u>a cup of coffee</u>. → I **made** <u>a cup of coffee</u> **for** <u>Janet</u>. 나는 Janet에게 커피 한 잔을 만들어줬다.
of를 쓰는 동사	ask 등	The reporter **asked** <u>her</u> <u>many questions</u>. → The reporter **asked** <u>many questions</u> **of** <u>her</u>. 그 기자는 그녀에게 많은 질문을 했다.

연습문제 A 밑줄 친 부분의 역할을 <보기>에서 골라 그 기호를 쓰시오.

<보기>　ⓐ 간접목적어　ⓑ 직접목적어

1 Kelly sent <u>me</u> a special necklace.　[　　　]

2 The sun gives a plant <u>the energy</u> it needs.　[　　　]

3 She teaches students <u>math</u>.　[　　　]

4 He often writes <u>his grandparents</u> letters.　[　　　]

5 My uncle paid the cashier <u>$200</u>.　[　　　]

6 The chef cooked <u>the customers</u> a delicious meal.　[　　　]

연습문제 B 빈칸에 to, for, of 중 알맞은 것을 쓰시오.

1 Please find some plates _____ us.

2 I'll sell my old bicycle _____ anyone who needs it.

3 Mr. Brown built a tree house _____ his nephew last year.

4 I bought a ticket to the opera _____ Diana.

5 His support gave confidence _____ me.

6 The police asked a few simple questions _____ the thief.

7 She passed the ball _____ James in gym class.

연습문제 C 다음 3형식 문장은 4형식 문장으로, 4형식 문장은 3형식 문장으로 바꿔 문장을 완성하시오.

1 The carpenter made a table for the man.
→ The carpenter made _____.

2 My grandmother used to read me fairy tales.
→ My grandmother used to read _____.

3 Jack showed her his new guitar.
→ Jack showed _____.

4 She gave a bunch of flowers to me.
→ She gave _____.

5 The woman asked me a favor.
→ The woman asked _____.

6 I brought him some books about history.
→ I brought _____.

기출 적중문제

다음 중 어법상 어색한 것은?

① My parents gave me a goodnight kiss.
② Could you send some pictures of your dog to me?
③ Mr. Kim offered me a ride to school.
④ He told my sister some funny jokes.
⑤ She showed the beautiful palace the visitors.

4형식 문장은
「주어 + 동사 + 간접 목적어
(~에게) + 직접 목적어(-을)」
의 형태예요.

기출로적중 POINT 4-1 5형식

정답 p.2

> 5형식 문장은 「주어 + 동사 + 목적어 + 목적격 보어」의 형태이다. 목적격 보어는 목적어를 보충 설명해주는 말로, 목적격 보어 자리에는 동사에 따라 명사, 형용사, to부정사, 동사원형, 분사가 올 수 있다.
>
> 명사   My grandfather **calls me Nicky**. 나의 할아버지는 나를 Nicky라고 부른다.
>   목적어 목적격 보어
>
> 형용사   The snow **made my new shoes dirty**. 눈이 나의 새 신발을 더럽게 만들었다.
>   목적어   목적격 보어
>
> to부정사   My mom **told me to clean** the room. 나의 엄마는 나에게 방을 청소하라고 말했다.
>   목적어 목적격 보어
>
> 동사원형   I **let my friend use** my computer. 나는 내 친구가 나의 컴퓨터를 사용하도록 허락했다.
>   목적어   목적격 보어
>
> 분사   I **got my wallet stolen**. 나는 나의 지갑을 도난당했다.
>   목적어   목적격 보어

연습문제 | <보기>와 같이 다음 문장의 목적어에는 동그라미를 치고, 목적격 보어에는 밑줄을 치시오.

> <보기>   Today's hot weather made (me) uncomfortable.

1   They found the movie boring.

2   Daily exercise helps our minds stay healthy.

3   The teachers considered Maggie a good student.

4   He let his daughter ride in the front seat.

5   Yesterday, I heard my little sister talking about the story's ending.

6   I consider my cat cute even though she is overweight.

7   They called their first dog Milo.

8   Sujin has her ears checked by the doctor regularly.

9   My mom allowed me to play with my friends after dinner.

10   Kathy asked me to do the laundry tomorrow.

11   My brother finds that video game fun, but I disagree with him.

12   I got my headphones repaired at the electronics shop.

13   She wanted me to close the door.

14   The heavy traffic made us late for the concert.

5형식: 명사·형용사·to부정사를 목적격 보어로 쓰는 동사

정답 p.2

1. 다음 동사들의 목적격 보어 자리에는 명사나 형용사가 온다.

call ~를 -이라고 부르다	make ~를 -로/하게 만들다	keep ~을 -한 상태로 유지하다
think ~를 -이라고 생각하다	believe ~를 -라고 믿다	consider ~을 -이라고 여기다
find ~가 -이라는 것을 알게 되다		

Lisa calls him a hero. Lisa는 그를 영웅이라고 부른다.

Eating chocolate makes me happy. 초콜릿을 먹는 것은 나를 행복하게 만든다.

(Tip) 5형식 문장의 목적격 보어 자리에는 부사가 올 수 없다.

The battle scenes **kept** the movie (~~interestingly~~, **interesting**).
전투 장면들이 그 영화를 흥미롭게 유지했다.

2. 다음 동사들의 목적격 보어 자리에는 to부정사가 온다.

want ~가 -하기를 원하다	tell ~에게 -하라고 말하다
advise ~에게 -하라고 조언하다	ask ~에게 -하라고 요청하다
expect ~가 -하는 것을 기대하다	allow ~가 -하는 것을 허락하다
encourage ~가 -하는 것을 격려하다	permit ~가 -하는 것을 허락하다
force ~가 -하도록 강요하다	

The librarian wants the students to read more books.
그 사서는 학생들이 더 많은 책을 읽기를 원한다.

The neighbor asked Sean to be quiet at night.
그 이웃은 Sean에게 밤에 조용히 해달라고 요청했다.

연습문제 A 밑줄 친 부분이 어법상 맞으면 O를 쓰고, 틀리면 바르게 고쳐 쓰시오.

1 He found the song <u>wonderfully</u>. → _____

2 Mrs. Kim believes her son <u>honest</u>. → _____

3 All the snow on the ground will make us <u>late</u>. → _____

4 My older sister tries to keep my room <u>cleanly</u>. → _____

5 Some parts of the documentary made me <u>sadly</u>. → _____

6 I don't understand why my friend thinks Matt <u>gently</u>. → _____

7 He considers giving speeches <u>difficult</u>. → _____

연습문제 B 우리말과 같도록 괄호 안에서 가장 알맞은 것을 고르시오.

1 그 음악은 나를 활기차게 만들었다.

= The music made me (energetic / energetically).

2 나의 엄마는 나에게 오늘 집에 있으라고 말했다.

= My mom told me (to stay / stay) home today.

3 그녀는 그녀의 개를 Hector라고 부른다.

= She calls (Hector her dog / her dog Hector).

4 이 뜨거운 물병은 나의 손을 따뜻하게 유지했다.

= This hot water bottle kept my hands (warm / warmly).

5 그 감독은 아이에게 공을 더 세게 차라고 조언했다.

= The coach advised the child (kicking / to kick) the ball harder.

연습문제 C 우리말과 같도록 괄호 안의 말을 활용하여 문장을 완성하시오.

1 우리는 그에게 버스를 타라고 말했다. (him, take, tell)

= We _____ a bus.

2 나의 엄마는 나에게 더 자주 운동하라고 조언했다. (exercise, advise, me)

= My mom _____ more often.

3 지수는 더 많은 사람들이 그녀의 생일 파티에 오기를 원했다. (come, want, more people)

= Jisu _____ to her birthday party.

4 나의 형과 나는 우리 아빠가 어린이날에 우리와 노는 것을 기대했다. (play, expect, our dad)

= My older brother and I _____ with us on Children's Day.

5 나는 Susan에게 마감일을 나에게 상기시켜 달라고 요청했다. (ask, remind, Susan)

= I _____ me of the deadline.

기출 적중문제

다음 그림을 보고 괄호 안의 말을 알맞게 배열하시오.

_____

_____ (allowed, she,

borrow, to, her skateboard, me)

5형식: 사역동사

1. **사역동사는 '~가 -하게 하다'라는 의미의 5형식 동사로, 사역동사의 목적격 보어 자리에는 동사원형이 온다.**

make	have	let

   The teacher **made** us **take** a quiz. 그 선생님은 우리가 퀴즈를 보게 했다.
   She **had** me **paint** the wall. 그녀는 내가 그 벽을 페인트칠하게 했다.
   He'll **let** you **know** the truth. 그는 네가 사실을 알게 해줄 것이다.

2. **준사역동사 help와 get**

   ❶ help가 '~가 -하는 것을 돕다'라는 의미로 쓰일 때는 목적격 보어 자리에 동사원형과 to부정사가 모두 올 수 있다.
   I **helped** my mom **(to) carry** her bags. 나는 나의 엄마가 그녀의 가방들을 옮기는 것을 도왔다.

   ❷ get이 '~가 -하게 시키다'라는 의미로 쓰일 때는 목적격 보어 자리에 to부정사가 온다.
   Seho **got** me **to feed** his cat. 세호는 내가 그의 고양이에게 먹이를 주게 시켰다.

   (Tip) 사역동사·준사역동사의 목적어와 목적격 보어의 관계가 수동이면 목적격 보어 자리에는 과거분사가 온다.
   Joseph had **his bicycle repaired**. Joseph은 그의 자전거가 수리되게 했다.
   I will get **my dog washed**. 나는 나의 강아지가 씻겨지게 할 것이다.

연습문제 괄호 안의 말을 활용하여 빈칸에 알맞은 말을 쓰시오.

1 The nice weather will make people _____ outside. (go)

2 Dad won't let me _____ by myself. (travel)

3 My music director got me _____ the song. (practice)

4 A cup of hot chocolate will help you _____ warm. (stay)

5 The band's new album made me _____ a big fan. (become)

6 He got them _____ a story. (write)

7 The singer had the crowd _____ their hands. (wave)

8 Mr. Jones helped the students _____ their exams. (pass)

9 Andy had us _____ the information in class. (share)

10 I got my younger sister _____ the volume of the TV. (lower)

기출로적중 POINT 4-4

5형식: 지각동사

정답 p.3

지각동사는 '~가 -하는 것을 보다/듣다, ~한 냄새가 나다/느낌이 들다'라는 의미의 5형식 동사로, 지각동사의 목적격 보어 자리에는 동사원형이나 V-ing형이 올 수 있다.

| see | watch | hear | listen to | smell | feel |

I **heard** Jessica **talk** on the phone. 나는 Jessica가 전화로 이야기하는 것을 들었다.
She **saw** a stranger **walking** around here. 그녀는 낯선 사람이 이곳 주변에서 걷고 있는 것을 봤다.
↳ 목적격 보어 자리에 V-ing형이 오면 진행 중인 동작이 강조된다.

(Tip) 지각동사의 목적어와 목적격 보어의 관계가 수동이면 목적격 보어 자리에는 과거분사가 온다.
Minjae heard **his name called**. 민재는 그의 이름이 불리는 것을 들었다.

연습문제 괄호 안에서 알맞은 것을 고르시오.

1 They saw me (to stand / standing) next to the building.

2 He heard his older brother (practiced / practicing) his speech in the other room.

3 She listened to the rain (fall / fallen) on the roof.

4 I watched him (running / to run) up and down the street.

5 Andrew felt the wind (to blow / blow) against his face.

6 I smelled something (burning / to burn) when I came home.

7 The children watched the magician (to perform / perform) magic tricks.

8 The actor heard his director (to shout / shouting) loudly.

9 She listened to the birds (sing / sung) outside the window this morning.

10 She saw her friends (to study / studying) together at the library.

11 I felt my heart (beating / to beat) fast when I saw Rachael for the first time.

12 I watched some kids (play / to play) soccer in the field.

13 They saw Sam (dance / danced) to the music in the hallway.

 **기출 적중문제**

우리말과 같도록 괄호 안의 말을 활용하여 문장을 완성하시오.

나는 나의 아빠가 문을 두드리는 것을 들었다. (hear, my dad, knock, on the door)

= I _____

5형식 지각동사의 목적어와 목적격 보어의 관계가 능동이면 목적격 보어 자리에는 동사원형이나 V-ing형이 와요.

A 밑줄 친 부분이 어법상 맞으면 O를 쓰고, 틀리면 바르게 고쳐 쓰시오.

1 Everyone should stay <u>calmly</u> in emergency situations.　→ _____

2 You <u>look</u> a teddy bear in your new sweater.　→ _____

3 He will <u>attend to</u> his friend's birthday party tomorrow.　→ _____

4 I cooked pancakes <u>to</u> my little sister.　→ _____

5 The teacher asked a favor <u>to</u> his colleague.　→ _____

6 Jane had the cat <u>to come</u> into her house.　→ _____

7 The tennis player felt sweat <u>running</u> down his cheek.　→ _____

B 다음 그림을 보고 괄호 안의 말을 활용하여 문장을 완성하시오. (단, 과거시제만 사용하시오.)

1 A boy just _____. (the museum, enter)

2 The waiter _____ to the woman. (the menu, explain)

3 I _____ by phone. (contact, my teacher)

4 The cloud in the sky _____. (look, a cat)

5 The soap _____. (smell, a fresh apple)

6 She _____ with her friend. (discuss, the new book)

C 다음 3형식 문장은 4형식 문장으로, 4형식 문장은 3형식 문장으로 바꿔 쓰시오.

1 I gave Sora my new home address.

→ _____

2 Mr. Smith bought his daughter a used car.

→ _____

3 We brought some books to Claire.

→ _____

4 I showed him my new baseball bat.

→ _____

5 I found some new toys for the children.

→ _____

6 The man sent the video to the police.

→ _____

D 다음 문장에서 틀린 부분을 바르게 고쳐 완전한 문장을 쓰시오.

1 Please let me to know how many students will come to volunteer.

→ _____

2 Dr. Lee wanted to help people remembering things better.

→ _____

3 She heard the boys to fight each other in the playground.

→ _____

4 I saw a child to chase after a butterfly.

→ _____

5 He had his dog train by a specialist a few years ago.

→ _____

6 The firefighters are respected because they keep people safely.

→ _____

7 The museum didn't permit visitors taking photographs.

→ _____

중간 · 기말고사 실전 문제

1 다음 중 어법상 <u>어색한</u> 것은?

① The balloon rose slowly into the sky.
② I heard that Tom became an engineer.
③ Birds are flying over the river.
④ The temperature stayed low all day.
⑤ The painting looked impressively.

2 우리말과 같도록 괄호 안의 말을 활용하여 문장을 완성하시오.

> 그 집은 오래된 성처럼 보였다. (look, an old castle)

= The house _____.

3 다음 밑줄 친 부분을 바르게 고치지 <u>못한</u> 것은?

① Mom doesn't let me <u>to eat</u> too much ramen because it's too salty. (→ eat)
② He got his younger brother <u>read</u> the book before going to sleep. (→ to read)
③ They heard a voice <u>to call</u> out for help. (→ calling)
④ She will watch your band <u>played</u> tomorrow night. (→ play)
⑤ People saw their meals <u>to make</u> in the kitchen. (→ make)

4 다음 (A)~(C)에 들어갈 말이 바르게 짝지어진 것은?

> · To be honest, I consider Sally ___(A)___ .
> · Ms. Kim always tries to keep her clothing ___(B)___ .
> · He found the new episode of the TV show ___(C)___ .

	(A)	(B)	(C)
①	love	neatly	interestingly
②	lovely	neat	interestingly
③	lovely	neatly	interestingly
④	lovely	neat	interesting
⑤	love	neatly	interesting

[5-6] 우리말과 같도록 괄호 안의 말을 알맞게 배열하시오.

5

> Mark는 그의 친구들이 상자들을 옮기는 것을 도왔다. (helped, boxes, his friends, move, Mark)

= _____
_____

6

> 그녀는 그녀의 개들이 새로운 묘기를 배우게 시킬 것이다. (new tricks, get, her dogs, learn, to, is going to, she)

= _____
_____

7 다음 우리말을 영작한 것 중 어색한 것은?

① 우리는 방문객들에게 그 디자인에 대해 설명했다.

= We explained the design to the visitors.

② 그 소년은 그의 할머니와 닮았다.

= The boy resembles his grandmother.

③ 나는 나의 친구의 집에 들어갔다.

= I entered my friend's house.

④ 그는 과학 박람회에 참석할 것이다.

= He will attend to the science fair.

⑤ Mindy는 그녀가 좋아하는 소설에 대해 언급했다.

= Mindy mentioned the novel she likes.

8 우리말과 같도록 괄호 안의 말을 알맞게 배열하시오.

나는 은비에게 그녀의 생일을 위해 내가 만든 쿠키를 가져다 줄 것이다.

= I'm going to _____
I made for her birthday. (bring, the cookies, Eunbi)

9 다음 빈칸에 들어갈 말이 순서대로 짝지어진 것은?

· I gave a gift _____ Robert.
· He got many good picnic items _____ us.

① of – for   ② to – for   ③ for – of

④ to – of   ⑤ of – to

10 다음 중 어법상 어색한 것은?

① People can stay healthy by exercising often.

② These flowers look attractively in spring.

③ She fell ill after playing outside in the snow.

④ As technology develops, many new jobs will appear.

⑤ She became hungry at midnight.

11 다음 (A)~(C)에 들어갈 말이 바르게 짝지어진 것은?

· This website lets you ___(A)___ the reservations you made.
· He's going to have his hair ___(B)___ .
· My parents always make me ___(C)___ the dishes after dinner.

	(A)	(B)	(C)
①	check	dyed	to do
②	to check	dyed	to do
③	to check	to dye	do
④	check	dyed	do
⑤	check	dye	do

While walking past the music room yesterday, I heard Charles ⓐto sing a song. I was amazed because I found his voice very ⓑsweetly. I ⓒmentioned about his ability to my friends. Tomorrow, I'm going to ask him ⓓjoin our band as a singer. I want him ⓔprepare for the talent show with us. (A) 나는 그가 우리 밴드를 유명하게 만들 수 있다고 생각한다. (can, make, our band, he, popular)

12 위 글의 밑줄 친 ⓐ~ⓔ를 바르게 고치지 <u>못한</u> 것은?

① ⓐ to sing → singing

② ⓑ sweetly → sweet

③ ⓒ mentioned about → mentioned

④ ⓓ join → joining

⑤ ⓔ prepare → to prepare

13 위 글의 밑줄 친 우리말 (A)와 같도록 괄호 안의 말을 알맞게 배열하시오.

= I think that _____.

14 다음 중 어법상 바른 것을 <u>모두</u> 고르시오.

① Did you have your hair to cut recently?

② Let me finishing my food first.

③ She told me to get my ticket from the counter.

④ The doctor let the patient to go home.

⑤ My grandmother had me make a cup of coffee.

15 다음 중 어법상 바른 것의 개수는?

ⓐ Linda had her younger sister washed her hands regularly.

ⓑ I heard the doorbell to ring.

ⓒ We asked the principal to change our summer uniform.

ⓓ Do you feel nervous about your performance tonight?

① 0개　　　② 1개　　　③ 2개

④ 3개　　　⑤ 4개

16 다음 대화의 빈칸에 들어갈 수 있는 것을 <u>모두</u> 고르시오.

A: Excuse me, do you know how to get to Gangneung Beach?

B: Sure, I'll _____.

① show the path you

② show the path you to

③ show you the path

④ show to the path you

⑤ show the path to you

17 다음 밑줄 친 부분을 바르게 고치지 <u>못한</u> 것은?

① Jeff passed the ball <u>of</u> Minsu. (→ to)

② My uncle made a toy train <u>to</u> me. (→ for)

③ He bought the tickets to the amusement park <u>of</u> us. (→ for)

④ Is it OK if I ask a favor <u>to</u> you? (→ of)

⑤ My parents paid taxes <u>of</u> the government. (→ for)

18 우리말과 같도록 괄호 안의 말을 알맞게 배열하시오.

> 선생님은 우리에게 그 시험에 대한 정답을 줬다. (the test, gave, the teacher, for, us, the answers)

= _____

_____

19 다음 (A)~(C)에 들어갈 말이 바르게 짝지어진 것은?

> · You should stay _____(A)_____ in the library.
> · He considered his roommate's comment _____(B)_____.
> · The man became _____(C)_____ over time.

	(A)	(B)	(C)
①	quietly	rudely	strongly
②	quiet	rudely	strong
③	quiet	rude	strong
④	quiet	rude	strongly
⑤	quietly	rude	strongly

[20-21] 우리말과 같도록 괄호 안의 말을 활용하여 문장을 완성하시오.

20

> 그녀는 우리가 시를 외우도록 강요했다. (force, memorize, us, a poem)

= She _____ .

21

> 의사는 그에게 패스트푸드를 먹는 것을 중단하라고 조언했다. (him, advise, stop)

= The doctor _____
eating fast food.

[22-23] 다음 대화를 읽고 괄호 안의 말을 활용하여 문장을 완성하시오. (단, 과거시제만 사용하시오.)

22

> *Lucy*: Dad, can I go to the concert tonight?
> *Dad* : What time does the concert start?
> *Lucy*: It starts at 8 P.M.
> *Dad* : OK, but remember to call me when the concert ends.
> *Lucy*: I will! Thank you, Dad.

→ Lucy's dad _____ to the concert tonight. (go, permit, her)
Also, he _____ to call him. (remember, tell, her)

23

> *Jim* : Mom, can I use your computer?
> *Mom*: Why do you want to use it?
> *Jim* : I want to play computer games.
> *Mom*: Did you finish your homework?
> *Jim* : Not yet. I'm going to finish it after I play computer games.
> *Mom*: You can use it, but you have to finish your homework first.

→ Jim's mom _____ her computer. (allow, use, him)
However, she _____ his homework first. (finish, expect, him)

24 다음 중 4형식 문장은 3형식으로, 3형식 문장은 4형식으로 바르게 바꾼 것은?

① Mina asked me an unusual question today.
   → Mina asked an unusual question to me today.
② We built a new house for our dog.
   → We built a new house our dog.
③ I passed the store clerk my credit card.
   → I passed my credit card to the store clerk.
④ My grandfather bought me a book about career choices.
   → My grandfather bought a book about career choices to me.
⑤ I'm about to write an e-mail to my cousin.
   → I'm about to write an e-mail my cousin.

[25-26] 다음 문장에서 틀린 부분을 바르게 고쳐 완전한 문장을 쓰시오.

25

The whole audience fell silently once the play started.

→ _____

_____

26

My voice sounds strangely today because I'm sick.

→ _____

_____

27 다음 중 어법상 어색한 것은?

① I think Susan looks healthy enough.
② This laptop computer seems like a new one.
③ The birthday cake we made tastes like fantastic.
④ He sounds like a careful driver who never breaks any traffic rules.
⑤ The tomato soup smelled tasty.

28 우리말과 같도록 괄호 안의 말을 알맞게 배열하시오.

소셜 미디어는 사람들이 서로 쉽게 연락하는 것을 돕는다. (social media, people, helps, each other easily, contact)

= _____

_____

29 다음 중 어법상 어색한 것을 모두 고른 것은?

① My older brother used to call me Little Richard.
② Foreign food festivals allow you experiencing other cultures.
③ Tim heard a dog barking outside his house.
④ They found the device useful for cleaning.
⑤ The bad weather made the city delayed the ceremony.

30 다음 빈칸에 공통으로 들어갈 알맞은 전치사를 <보기>에서 골라 쓰시오.

<보기> to for of

· Yoonho cooked lunch _____ me.
· The mayor built a new park beside the river _____ children.

31 다음 중 어법상 바른 것은?

① He entered to the building.
② They resemble with each other.
③ She must attend to the lecture after lunch.
④ When did your sister marry her husband?
⑤ Jason explained about his situation.

[32-33] 괄호 안의 말을 활용하여 문장을 완성하시오.

32

Ms. Rose permitted me _____ books about Korean history in the library. (look for)

33

The school expects its students _____ _____ in the contest. (participate)

34 다음 (A)~(C)에 들어갈 말이 바르게 짝지어진 것은?

· I will show the hotel room ___(A)___ you.
· Can you get a towel ___(B)___ me on your way back?
· Don't ask any questions ___(C)___ him until the end of his speech.

	(A)	(B)	(C)
①	to	for	for
②	of	for	of
③	to	for	of
④	of	to	of
⑤	to	to	for

35 다음 중 어법상 바른 것끼리 묶인 것은?

ⓐ We will discuss the problems later.
ⓑ He mentioned about a review test.
ⓒ Your shoes match your shirts perfectly.
ⓓ Did you contact Subin on Monday?
ⓔ In summer, the temperature here reaches to almost 40°C.

① ⓐ, ⓑ, ⓒ　　② ⓐ, ⓒ, ⓓ　　③ ⓑ, ⓒ, ⓓ
④ ⓑ, ⓓ, ⓔ　　⑤ ⓒ, ⓓ, ⓔ

36 다음은 지호의 부모님이 지호에게 지키라고 한 규칙들을 정리한 표이다. 괄호 안의 말을 활용하여 문장을 완성하시오. (단, 과거시제만 사용하시오.)

규칙 1	자기 전에 일기 쓰기
규칙 2	토요일마다 방 청소 하기

(1) Jiho's parents _____
_____. (have, write in, him, a diary, before bed)

(2) Jiho's parents _____
_____. (tell, his room, him, every Saturday, clean)

37 다음 중 주어진 문장과 문장의 형식이 같은 것은?

> I make my older brother angry sometimes.

① Betty usually studies hard.
② My dog looks curious.
③ Keith brought me some food to eat.
④ Parents give their children hugs.
⑤ I allowed him to use my laptop.

38 다음 중 어법상 바른 것은?

① Let me give some important tips of you.
② Don't forget to lend me your calculator.
③ Hailey offered snacks everyone.
④ Would you find a red pen to me?
⑤ My dad taught chess of me when I was little.

39 우리말과 같도록 괄호 안의 말을 활용하여 문장을 완성하시오.

> 나는 여행사에 전화해서 나의 티켓이 취소되게 했다.
> (cancel, my ticket, get)

= I called the travel agent and _____
_____.

[40-41] 다음 우리말을 알맞게 영작한 것을 고르시오.

40

> 우리는 쓰레기를 버리지 않음으로써 환경을 깨끗하게 유지할 수 있다.

① We can keep our environment cleaning by not littering.
② We can keep our environment clean by not littering.
③ We can keep clean our environment by not littering.
④ We can keep cleaning our environment by not littering.
⑤ We can keep our environment cleanly by not littering.

41

> 선생님은 그들이 놀이터에서 축구를 하는 것을 보았다.

① The teacher saw them playing soccer on the playground.
② The teacher saw them to play soccer on the playground.
③ The teacher see them play soccer on the playground.
④ The teacher see them playing soccer on the playground.
⑤ The teacher saw them played soccer on the playground.

42 다음 밑줄 친 부분을 바르게 고치지 <u>못한</u> 것은?

① Jaemin helped me <u>solving</u> the problem yesterday. (→ to solve)

② Tonight, you may see Nancy <u>to play</u> the lead role in the performance. (→ play)

③ He listened to people <u>to shout</u> in the stadium. (→ shouting)

④ Mr. Kim let his daughter <u>to buy</u> what she wanted. (→ buy)

⑤ This is the first time I saw him <u>to raise</u> his hand during the math class. (→ raised)

43 다음 중 어법상 어색한 것은?

① The children want him to understand them.

② I expect the weather to turn cold and windy tomorrow.

③ He made me to do extra exercises today.

④ Ms. Choi heard Jinwoo whispering to me during the test.

⑤ She felt a hand tapping on her shoulder.

44 다음 중 어법상 바른 것은?

① I believed him lazily before.

② He made Jim to be the team leader.

③ He rarely calls his cat to Fluffy.

④ People consider the author's new book amusingly.

⑤ Carl found his chair uncomfortable.

45 다음 (A)~(C)에 들어갈 말이 바르게 짝지어진 것은?

> · I had my computer ___(A)___ today.
> · The hotel made us ___(B)___ before 11 A.M.
> · Don't let the dog ___(C)___ on the new bed.

	(A)	(B)	(C)
①	fix	to check out	jump up
②	fixing	to check out	jump up
③	fixed	check out	jump up
④	fixed	check out	jumping up
⑤	fix	check out	jumping up

46 다음 글의 밑줄 친 ⓐ~ⓔ 중 어법상 어색한 것을 찾아 기호를 쓰고 바르게 고쳐 쓰시오.

> The other day, my dad ⓐ<u>brought a book to me</u>. It was about a girl. She ⓑ<u>looked very ordinary</u>, just like other teenagers. However, she was very special. She began to do volunteer work when she was seven years old. It ⓒ<u>made me think</u> about myself because I had never thought of volunteering. The little girl ⓓ<u>encouraged me begin</u> to volunteer. Now my friends and I ⓔ<u>teach English to elementary school students</u>.

→ _____

CHAPTER 2
시제

Jiho **studied** Chinese two years ago. 지호는 2년 전에 중국어를 공부했다.
Jiho **will study** Chinese next year. 지호는 내년에 중국어를 공부할 것이다.

동사 study(공부하다)의 형태를 studied(공부했다), will study(공부할 것이다)로 바꿔 지호가 중국어를 공부한 시점을 나타냈어요. 이렇게 동사의 형태를 바꿔 행동이나 사건이 발생한 시간을 표현하는 것을 **시제**라고 해요.

기출로 적중 POINT

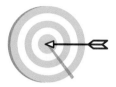

내신 100점 적중!
기출 출제율

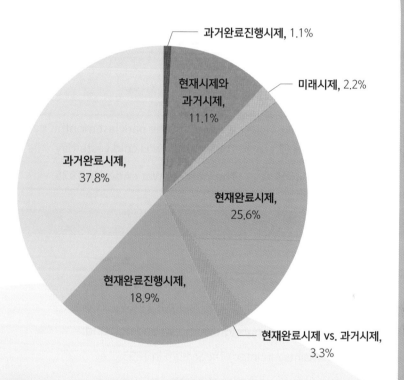

과거완료진행시제, 1.1%

현재시제와 과거시제, 11.1%

미래시제, 2.2%

과거완료시제, 37.8%

현재완료시제, 25.6%

현재완료진행시제, 18.9%

현재완료시제 vs. 과거시제, 3.3%

TOP 1 **과거완료시제 (37.8%)**
주어진 상황과 맥락에 맞게 과거완료시제를 쓰는 문제가 자주 출제된다.

TOP 2 **현재완료시제 (25.6%)**
현재완료시제의 의미와 형태를 묻는 문제가 자주 출제된다.

TOP 3 **현재완료진행시제 (18.9%)**
주어진 상황과 맥락에 맞게 현재완료진행시제를 쓰는 문제가 자주 출제된다.

현재시제와 과거시제

정답 p.5

1. 현재시제는 다음과 같을 때 쓴다.

현재의 상태를 나타낼 때	I **live** in Seoul with my family. 나는 나의 가족과 함께 서울에 산다.
현재의 습관이나 반복되는 일을 나타낼 때	Paul **goes** for a walk after a meal. Paul은 식사하고 난 후에 산책을 한다. She **gets** up at 7 A.M. every day. 그녀는 매일 아침 7시에 일어난다.
일반적·과학적 사실이나 속담·격언을 말할 때	The Earth **revolves** around the Sun. 지구는 태양 주위를 공전한다. Blood **is** thicker than water. 피는 물보다 진하다.

(Tip) 확실히 정해진 시간표나 일정표 상의 일을 말할 때는 현재시제로 미래의 일을 나타낼 수 있으며, 이때 가까운 미래를 나타내는 부사(구)가 주로 함께 쓰인다.

The movie **starts** in 15 minutes. 그 영화는 15분 후에 시작할 것이다.

2. 과거시제는 다음과 같을 때 쓴다.

과거의 동작이나 상태를 나타낼 때	We **went** to the park last month. 우리는 지난달에 그 공원에 갔다. The weather **was** cold yesterday. 어제 날씨가 추웠다.
역사적 사실을 나타낼 때	The Vietnam War **ended** in 1975. 베트남 전쟁은 1975년에 끝났다.

연습문제 괄호 안에서 알맞은 것을 고르시오.

1 My younger brother and I still (share / shared) a room at home.

2 They didn't know that peanuts (grow / grew) underground.

3 Edvard Munch (paints / painted) *The Scream* in 1893.

4 Our refrigerator (uses / used) a lot of energy last summer.

5 It is said that the early bird (gets / got) the worm.

6 The doctor said aloe vera (works / worked) well to soothe the skin.

7 I (was / am) in the library with my friend last night.

8 Jihoon and his little sisters (play / played) card games every Saturday.

9 Helen (twist / twisted) her ankle a week ago.

10 Lisa couldn't recognize me because she (loses / lost) her glasses.

11 I (take / took) a taxi at 7 P.M. yesterday.

12 Even today, my dad still (enjoys / enjoyed) watching hockey.

POINT 2 미래시제

정답 p.5

미래시제는 「will + 동사원형」 또는 「be going to + 동사원형」의 형태이다.

❶ 「will + 동사원형」은 다음과 같을 때 쓴다.

미래의 사실이나 미래에 일어날 일	The letter **will arrive** tomorrow. 그 편지는 내일 도착할 것이다. He **won't be** back this month. 그는 이번 달에 돌아오지 않을 것이다. (Tip) 이때 「will + 동사원형」은 「be going to + 동사원형」으로 바꿔 쓸 수 있다.
미래의 일에 대한 주어의 의지	I'**ll tell** you the truth. 나는 너에게 사실을 말할 것이다. (말할 것이라는 주어의 의지)
말하는 시점에 결정한 미래의 일	The phone is ringing. I'**ll get** it. 전화가 울리고 있다. 나는 그것을 받을 것이다. (말하는 시점에 받기로 결정함)

❷ 「be going to + 동사원형」은 다음과 같을 때 쓴다.

미래의 사실이나 미래에 일어날 일	It **is going to rain** soon. 곧 비가 올 것이다. We **are not going to attend** the field trip next week. 우리는 다음 주 현장 학습에 참가하지 않을 것이다. (Tip) 이때 「be going to + 동사원형」은 「will + 동사원형」으로 바꿔 쓸 수 있다.
말하는 시점 전에 이미 하기로 결정한 미래의 일	They **are going to move** to another town this weekend. 그들은 이번 주말에 다른 동네로 이사할 것이다. (말하는 시점 전에 이미 이사하기로 결정함)

(Tip) 「be about to + 동사원형」은 '~하려는 참이다'라는 의미로, 예정된 일을 막 하려는 상황을 나타낸다.
Jack **is about to** take a shower. Jack은 샤워를 하려는 참이다.

연습문제 괄호 안의 말을 활용하여 다음 문장을 미래시제로 바꿔 쓰시오.

1 The boxer fights again. (be going to)

→ _____ this September.

2 She does volunteer work in the city. (will)

→ _____ next week.

3 Thomas doesn't pick us up. (be going to)

→ _____ tomorrow.

4 I don't send Minsu another message. (will)

→ _____ tonight.

5 He buys his mother's birthday present. (be about to)

→ _____ .

POINT
3-1 현재완료시제

1. **현재완료시제는 「have/has + p.p.」의 형태이며, 과거에 발생하여 현재까지 영향을 미치는 일을 나타낼 때 쓴다.**

과거 ────────────────→ 현재

I **have lived** in Paris since last year. 나는 작년 이후로 파리에서 살아왔다.
I **have visited** this restaurant once. 나는 이 식당을 한 번 방문해본 적이 있다.

2. **현재완료시제의 부정형은 「have/has + not + p.p.」이며, 의문문은 「Have/Has + 주어 + p.p. ~?」의 형태이다.**

부정문 He **hasn't left** school yet. 그는 아직 학교를 떠나지 않았다.
의문문 **Have** you **met** Amanda before? 너는 전에 Amanda를 만난 적이 있니?

3. **현재완료시제는 완료, 경험, 계속, 결과의 의미로 쓰인다.**

완료	~했다	I **have already** finished my homework. 나는 이미 숙제를 끝마쳤다. (Tip) 함께 자주 쓰이는 부사(구): already, yet, just, lately, recently 등
경험	~해본 적이 있다	I **have been** to Africa **before.** 나는 전에 아프리카에 가본 적이 있다. (Tip) 함께 자주 쓰이는 부사(구): before, once, ~ times, ever, never 등
계속	~해왔다	Minsu **has known** Jane **for** five years. 민수는 Jane을 5년 동안 알고 지내왔다. (Tip) 함께 자주 쓰이는 부사(구): for, since, how long ~? 등
결과	~해버렸다 (지금은 ~이다)	Tim **has lost** his bag on the bus. Tim은 버스에서 그의 가방을 잃어버렸다. (지금은 가방이 없다.)

(Tip) 「have/has been to」는 경험을 나타내고, 「have/has gone to」는 결과를 나타낸다.
He **has been to** Russia. 그는 러시아에 가본 적이 있다.
He **has gone to** Russia. 그는 러시아로 가버렸다. (지금은 이곳에 없다.)

연습문제 **A** 괄호 안의 말을 활용하여 현재완료시제 문장을 완성하시오.

1 I _____ a new camera recently. (buy)

2 I'm surprised to hear that he _____ a house. (build)

3 How long _____ the scientists _____ earthquakes? (study)

4 _____ you ever _____ to Australia before? (be)

5 The director _____ several movies since she started her career. (make)

6 Keith _____ to Seattle to meet his cousin. (go)

7 How many times _____ you _____ a horse? (ride)

8 _____ Mike _____ a letter from Jacob? (receive)

9 The man _____ friends lately because of his bad attitude. (lose)

10 The music festival at the park _____ yet. (start)

11 I'm so tired because I _____ on this train for more than three hours. (be)

12 Richard _____ his skateboard, so he doesn't have it anymore. (sell)

13 He _____ this mountain with his dad before. (climb)

14 I _____ making kimchi with my grandmother already. (try)

연습문제 B 괄호 안에서 밑줄 친 부분의 쓰임을 고르시오.

1 Has your older brother <u>composed</u> a song before?   (완료 / 경험 / 계속)

2 The yogurt <u>has gone</u> bad.   (경험 / 계속 / 결과)

3 I <u>have taken</u> this art class for three years.   (경험 / 계속 / 결과)

4 My father <u>has completed</u> a marathon.   (완료 / 경험 / 계속)

5 I can't believe that they <u>have torn</u> their photos.   (경험 / 계속 / 결과)

6 Cindy <u>has been</u> to museums in Korea several times.   (완료 / 경험 / 계속)

7 <u>Have</u> you already <u>read</u> today's newspaper?   (완료 / 경험 / 계속)

8 They <u>have painted</u> pictures together since they got married.   (완료 / 경험 / 계속)

9 We are the only ones who <u>have</u> never <u>visited</u> the island.   (완료 / 경험 / 계속)

10 How long <u>has</u> Elizabeth <u>been</u> the queen of England?   (경험 / 계속 / 결과)

기출 적중문제

우리말과 같도록 괄호 안의 말을 알맞게 배열하시오.

나는 지난달부터 매일 운동을 해왔다. (every day, since, I, last month, exercised, have)

= _____

현재완료시제 vs. 과거시제

정답 p.5

현재완료시제와 과거시제의 차이는 다음과 같다.

현재완료시제	과거시제
과거 → 현재	과거 ● 현재
과거에 발생하여 현재까지 영향을 미치는 일을 나타낸다.	과거에 발생하고 완료된 일을 나타내며, 현재에 대한 정보는 나타나지 않는다.
Kelly **has worked** here for three months. Kelly는 3개월 동안 여기에서 일해왔다. (현재까지 여기에서 일하고 있음)	Kelly **worked** here three months ago. Kelly는 3개월 전에 여기에서 일했다. (현재 여기에서 일하는지 알 수 없음)
과거의 특정한 시점(last ~, yesterday, ~ ago, when 등)을 나타내는 말과 함께 쓸 수 없다.	과거의 특정한 시점(last ~, yesterday, ~ ago, when 등)을 나타내는 말과 함께 쓴다.
Martin **has visited** London **before**. Martin은 전에 런던에 방문해본 적이 있다.	Martin **visited** London **last summer**. Martin은 지난 여름에 런던을 방문했다.

연습문제 괄호 안에서 알맞은 것을 고르시오.

1 She (didn't try / hasn't tried) making noodles until now.

2 NASA (has launched / launched) Apollo II in 1969.

3 I (traveled / have traveled) across the country every year since I was a boy.

4 Minho (didn't look / hasn't looked) very happy when I saw him this morning.

5 I (didn't study / haven't studied) Chinese since I came back from China.

6 (Have you seen / Did you see) Emily's new sneakers last night?

7 She (has taught / taught) poetry since she graduated from university.

8 (Did Jane do / Has Jane done) all her biology homework yet?

9 Junho (didn't watch / hasn't watched) the opening ceremony last week.

10 My little sister (didn't eat / hasn't eaten) meat since she was young.

11 (Did Lewis meet / Has Lewis met) him at the mall yesterday?

12 I (haven't heard / didn't hear) anything from Ben for a month.

13 Sujin (won / has won) the international badminton tournament last year.

14 The student (hasn't been / wasn't) late once since the class began.

현재완료진행시제

> 현재완료진행시제는 「have/has + been + V-ing」의 형태이며, 과거에 발생한 일이 현재도 계속 진행 중임을 강조한다.
>
> The men **have been eating** dinner for two hours.   그 남자들은 두 시간 동안 저녁을 먹고 있다.
> (= The men began to eat dinner two hours ago. They are still eating dinner.)
>   그 남자들은 두 시간 전에 저녁을 먹기 시작했다. 그들은 여전히 저녁을 먹고 있다.
>
> He **has been practicing** his speech since 7 P.M.   그는 오후 7시부터 그의 연설을 연습하고 있다.
> (= He started practicing his speech at 7 P.M. He is still practicing it.)
>   그는 오후 7시에 그의 연설을 연습하기 시작했다. 그는 여전히 그것을 연습하고 있다.

연습문제 A 우리말과 같도록 괄호 안의 말을 활용하여 현재완료진행시제 문장을 완성하시오.

1 그녀는 2시부터 숲 속을 걷고 있다. (walk)

= She _____ in the forest since 2 o'clock.

2 나의 어머니는 50분 동안 그 뉴스에 대해 이야기하고 있다. (talk)

= My mother _____ about the news for 50 minutes.

3 George는 한 시간 동안 만화를 그리고 있다. (draw)

= George _____ a cartoon for an hour.

4 나는 두 달 동안 레몬 나무를 키우고 있다. (grow)

= I _____ a lemon tree for two months.

5 유리와 나는 오전 11시부터 이 문제에 대해 논의하고 있다. (discuss)

= Yuri and I _____ this problem since 11 A.M.

6 그 예술가는 네 시간 동안 조각상을 깎고 있다. (carve)

= The artist _____ a statue for four hours.

연습문제 B 두 문장의 의미가 같도록 현재완료진행시제 문장을 완성하시오.

1 I started to play the drum this afternoon. I am still playing it now.

= I _____ since this afternoon.

2 Mr. Kim began fixing his computer two hours ago. He is still fixing it.

= Mr. Kim _____ for two hours.

3 She began recording a new movie last Friday. She is still recording it.

= She _____ since last Friday.

4 Her little brother began learning to dance a month ago. He is still learning to dance.

= Her little brother _____ for a month.

5 Carol and Jessie began chatting on the phone this morning. They are still chatting on the phone.

= Carol and Jessie _____ since this morning.

6 We started to prepare for the exam five hours ago. We are still preparing for it.

= We _____ for five hours.

7 The pirates began searching for the treasure ten years ago. They are still searching for it.

= The pirates _____ for ten years.

8 Peter began writing a romance novel three months ago. He is still writing it.

= Peter _____ for three months.

연습문제 C 밑줄 친 부분이 어법상 맞으면 O를 쓰고, 틀리면 바르게 고쳐 쓰시오.

1 He <u>was studying</u> ethics from 2018. → _____

2 They <u>were making</u> dessert since 6 o'clock. → _____

3 He <u>was sleeping</u> in his room at midnight last night. → _____

4 They <u>have been tried</u> to understand the rule for two hours. → _____

5 Betty <u>has chatting</u> with her friends since this evening. → _____

6 I <u>was watching</u> this video clip since 1 P.M. → _____

7 They <u>were decorating</u> the Christmas tree when I came back home. → _____

8 Chris <u>has been stood</u> in the line from early morning. → _____

9 She <u>has been thinking</u> about the tricky question for 20 minutes. → _____

10 We <u>have been waited</u> for you since 12 o'clock. → _____

11 I <u>have been working</u> as a doctor since I was 28. → _____

기출 적중문제 🎯

다음 중 어법상 바른 것을 모두 고르시오.

① Michael is working on the assignment since Tuesday.

② My older sister hasn't been doing the household chores for two weeks.

③ The boy has singing the same song since breakfast.

④ My grandmother is wearing that ring for 65 years.

⑤ The patient hasn't been taking his medicine since last week.

> since와 for는 현재완료시제와 자주 함께 쓰여요.

POINT 5 과거완료시제

정답 p.6

1. 과거완료시제는 「had + p.p.」의 형태이며, 특정 과거 시점을 기준으로 그 시점 이전에 발생한 일이 그 시점까지 영향을 미칠 때 쓴다.

특정 과거 이전의 시점   특정 과거 시점   현재

The rain **had** already **stopped** when the class ended.
특정 과거 시점

그 수업이 끝났을 때 비는 이미 그쳐 있었다.

The house **had been** empty for five months until we rented it.
특정 과거 시점

그 집은 우리가 그곳을 빌리기 전까지 5개월간 비어있었다.

2. 과거완료시제도 현재완료시제와 동일하게 완료, 경험, 계속, 결과의 의미로 쓰인다.

완료	~했었다	He **had** already **woken** up when his alarm clock rang. 그의 알람 시계가 울렸을 때 그는 이미 깨어 있었다.
경험	~해본 적이 있었다	I **had met** Angela **before** she joined the writing club. 나는 Angela가 글쓰기 동아리에 가입하기 전에 그녀를 만나본 적이 있었다.
계속	~해왔었다	She **had lived** here **for** three years until she got a job. 그녀는 직장을 얻기 전까지 여기에 3년 동안 살아왔었다.
결과	~해버렸었다	The train **had left** the platform when I reached the station. 기차는 내가 그 역에 도착했을 때 승강장을 떠나버렸었다.

(Tip) 「had + p.p.」는 과거에 일어난 두 개의 일 중 먼저 일어난 일을 나타내기 위해 쓰일 수 있다. 이때 두 개의 일 중 먼저 일어난 일을 '대과거'라고 한다.

Laura **found** the jacket that her younger sister **had lost** in the theater.
과거   대과거

Laura는 그녀의 여동생이 영화관에서 잃어버렸던 재킷을 찾았다.
(Laura의 여동생이 재킷을 잃어버린 일이 Laura가 재킷을 찾은 일보다 먼저 발생함)

연습문제 A   괄호 안에서 알맞은 것을 고르시오.

1   Nancy (has / had) never kept a diary before she went to elementary school.

2   After Tom had gone to the countryside, we (can't / couldn't) see him anymore.

3   They (hasn't / hadn't) taken their medicine until the nurse came.

4   He (has / had) been ill for five days, so he couldn't play soccer last Saturday.

5   His presentation had just finished when we (enter / entered) the room.

6 Although the doctor had treated Patrick, he (is / was) still sick.

7 My uncle (has / had) traveled to the Middle East once before he turned 20.

8 She (becomes / became) a teacher after she had overcome many difficulties.

9 By the time his parents (return / returned), he had already washed the dishes.

10 He hadn't learned English until he (go / went) to Australia.

11 I (has / had) completed my work when my friend called me.

연습문제 B 다음 그림을 보고 <보기>의 말을 활용하여 문장을 완성하시오.

| <보기> | draw | leave | come | make |

1

2

3

4

1 Paul asked his friends to look at the picture he _____.

2 He realized that he _____ his bag in the train.

3 Minho and I _____ inside the house before the rain started.

4 They ate the pizza that they _____ by themselves.

기출 적중문제 🎯

다음 빈칸에 들어갈 알맞은 것은?

> I _____ to brush my teeth before I went to sleep.

① forget   ② forgets
③ has forgotten   ④ am forgetting
⑤ had forgotten

기출로 적중 POINT 6 과거완료진행시제

정답 p.6

과거완료진행시제는 「had + been + V-ing」의 형태이며, 특정 과거 시점을 기준으로 그 이전에 발생한 일이 그 시점에도 계속 진행 중이었음을 강조한다.

I **had been waiting** for 20 minutes <u>when Jason arrived at 3 o'clock.</u>
특정 과거 시점

Jason이 3시에 도착했을 때 나는 20분 동안 기다리고 있었다.

(= I was waiting for 20 minutes. Then Jason arrived at 3 o'clock.)
나는 20분 동안 기다리고 있었다. 그때 Jason이 3시에 도착했다.

She **had been watching** TV for two hours <u>before her baby cried.</u>
특정 과거 시점

그녀의 아기가 울기 전까지 그녀는 두 시간 동안 TV를 보고 있었다.

(= She was watching TV for two hours. Then her baby cried.)
그녀는 두 시간 동안 TV를 보고 있었다. 그때 그녀의 아기가 울었다.

CHAPTER 2 시제 해커스 중학영문법 3학년

연습문제 우리말과 같도록 괄호 안의 말을 활용하여 완료진행시제 문장을 완성하시오.

1 Jessica는 오늘 아침부터 그 벽을 페인트칠하고 있다. (paint)
= Jessica ＿＿＿＿＿＿＿＿＿＿＿ the wall since this morning.

2 내가 태어났을 때 나의 부모님은 캐나다에서 3년 동안 살고 있었다. (live)
= My parents ＿＿＿＿＿＿＿＿＿＿＿ in Canada for three years when I was born.

3 눈이 오기 시작했을 때 그 소년들은 두 시간 동안 야구를 하고 있었다. (play)
= The boys ＿＿＿＿＿＿＿＿＿＿＿ baseball for two hours when it started to snow.

4 우리는 하루 종일 사진을 찍고 있다. (take)
= We ＿＿＿＿＿＿＿＿＿＿＿ pictures for a whole day.

5 나의 형은 샤워를 하기 전에 50분 동안 뛰고 있었다. (run)
= My older brother ＿＿＿＿＿＿＿＿＿＿＿ for 50 minutes before he took a shower.

6 그녀는 대구로 이사 가기로 결정했을 때 서울에 한 달 동안 머물고 있었다. (stay)
= She ＿＿＿＿＿＿＿＿＿＿＿ in Seoul for a month when she decided to move to Daegu.

7 엄마가 돌아왔을 때 아빠는 한 시간 동안 싱크대를 고치기 위해 노력하고 있었다. (try)
= Dad ＿＿＿＿＿＿＿＿＿＿＿ to repair the sink for an hour when Mom came back.

8 David는 최근 그의 학업에 집중하지 않고 있다. (focus)
= David ＿＿＿＿＿＿＿＿＿＿＿ on his studies lately.

9 내가 문을 두드렸을 때 그들은 그 계획에 대해 논의하고 있었다. (discuss)
= They ＿＿＿＿＿＿＿＿＿＿＿ the plan when I knocked on the door.

Chapter 2 시제 **49**

서술형 대비 문제

A 다음 그림을 보고 괄호 안의 말을 활용하여 문장을 완성하시오.

1

2

5 o'clock   now

3

4

last month   now

1 I _____ a photographer for several years before I became a painter. (be)

2 I am studying right now. I _____ since 5 o'clock. (study)

3 My older sister _____ table tennis with her friend yesterday. (play)

4 I _____ in the morning every day since last month. (exercise)

B 우리말과 같도록 괄호 안의 말을 알맞게 배열하시오.

1 우리는 전에 화산에 대한 다큐멘터리 영화를 시청한 적이 있다. (watched, have, the documentary film, we)
= _____ about a volcano before.

2 그녀는 그녀가 어른이 되기 전까지 해외로 여행 가본 적이 전혀 없었다. (had, traveled, never, she, abroad)
= _____ before she became an adult.

3 Andrew는 최근에 그의 우산을 잃어버렸다. (lost, Andrew, his umbrella, has)
= _____ recently.

4 화재경보기가 울렸을 때 그 학생들은 한 시간 동안 학교에 있었다. (at school, had, the students, been)
= _____ for an hour when the fire alarm rang.

5 나의 남동생은 대학교에 가기 전까지 시를 써본 적이 없었다. (my younger brother, a poem, hadn't, written)
= _____ before he went to university.

6 그는 세 달 동안 지구 온난화에 대해 조사해왔다. (researched, he, global warming, has)

= _____ for three months.

7 나는 나의 인생에서 여러 번 상을 받아왔다. (won, have, I, awards)

= _____ several times in my life.

8 내가 그 체육관에 도착했을 때, 나의 친구들은 이미 집에 가버렸었다. (already, had, home, gone, my friends)

= When I arrived at the gym, _____ .

9 그들은 제주도를 방문하기 전까지 유람선을 타본 적이 없었다. (taken, a cruise, hadn't, they)

= _____ before they visited Jejudo.

10 내가 그를 지난달에 본 이후로 그는 살이 쪘다. (has, weight, he, gained)

= _____ since I saw him last month.

11 수미는 어제 나와 싸운 이후로 나의 전화를 받지 않고 있다. (hasn't, my calls, answered, Sumi)

= _____ since she fought with me yesterday.

C 우리말과 같도록 괄호 안의 말을 활용하여 완료진행시제 문장을 완성하시오.

1 Smith씨는 두 시간 동안 스캐너를 사용하고 있다. (use the scanner)

= Mr. Smith _____ for two hours.

2 그의 아들은 20분 동안 울고 있다. (cry)

= His son _____ for 20 minutes.

3 내가 방으로 들어오기 전까지 그들은 서로 말하지 않고 있었다. (talk to each other)

= They _____ until I entered the room.

4 Jessica는 2012년부터 피아노를 배우고 있다. (learn the piano)

= Jessica _____ since 2012.

5 그녀의 여동생이 그녀를 불렀을 때 그녀는 한 시간 동안 자고 있었다. (sleep)

= She _____ for an hour when her younger sister called her.

6 John은 한 달 전에 팔이 부러졌기 때문에, 최근에 수영을 하지 않고 있다. (swim)

= Because John broke his arm a month ago, he _____ lately.

7 관리인이 들어왔을 때 Hailey의 배드민턴 동아리는 연습을 하고 있었다. (practice)

= Hailey's badminton club _____ when the manager came in.

8 나는 열 살 때부터 매일 우유 한 잔을 마시고 있다. (drink a glass of milk)

= I _____ every day since I was ten.

CHAPTER 2 시제 해커스 중학영문법 3학년

중간·기말고사 실전 문제

1 다음 중 어법상 <u>어색한</u> 것은?

① Andy went to the hospital last weekend.
② We will go to a café for breakfast tomorrow.
③ Our science teacher seemed so happy yesterday.
④ My friend visits Beijing last year.
⑤ The teacher told me that Mozart died in 1791.

2 어법상 바른 것끼리 짝지어진 것은?

ⓐ I was bringing my dad a newspaper every morning.
ⓑ Mr. Han used to tell us, "Even a stopped clock is right twice a day."
ⓒ The Sun is a source of energy for plants on Earth.
ⓓ Jiho learned how to play this song on the piano last month.
ⓔ My teacher said that Mt. Everest was 8848 meters high.

① ⓐ, ⓑ   ② ⓐ, ⓒ   ③ ⓑ, ⓒ
④ ⓑ, ⓒ, ⓓ   ⑤ ⓒ, ⓓ, ⓔ

3 다음 중 어법상 <u>어색한</u> 것은?

① She swam in the pool yesterday.
② Internet service spread rapidly across the country.
③ He won't participate in fundraising activities last month.
④ Jane and her older sister share their secrets all the time.
⑤ The teacher taught the students about the solar system.

4 다음 ⓐ~ⓒ 중 어법상 <u>어색한</u> 것을 찾아 기호를 쓰고 바르게 고쳐 완전한 문장을 쓰시오.

ⓐ My dad buys me an ice cream cake every Saturday.
ⓑ The train from Yeosu arrives soon.
ⓒ We're going to a soccer practice last Thursday.

_____ → _____
_____

5 우리말과 같도록 괄호 안의 말을 활용하여 대화를 완성하시오.

A: May I give you a ride to school today?
B: No, thanks. <u>나는 학교로 가는 버스를 막 잡으려는 참이야.</u> (catch, about, the bus to school)

= I _____ .

6 밑줄 친 부분을 바르게 고치지 <u>못한</u> 것은?

> A: Tina, what will you ⓐdid tonight?
> B: I ⓑhad dinner with Sandy after school. Why?
> A: I ⓒwatched the movie tonight. I was hoping you would come with me.
> B: Oh, but I already promised to meet Sandy.
> A: It's OK. I ⓓhave gone to the movie by myself.
> B: Maybe we could go with Sandy. I'm about ⓔcalling Sandy. I'll ask if she wants to.
> A: Oh, that sounds like a great plan.

① ⓐ did → do
② ⓑ had → will have
③ ⓒ watched → am going to watch
④ ⓓ have gone → went
⑤ ⓔ calling → to call

7 다음 중 어법상 <u>어색한</u> 것의 개수는?

> ⓐ She has wrote a novel since last year.
> ⓑ She has heard about the movie many times.
> ⓒ I have bought a new computer a week ago.
> ⓓ The bicycle that I has fixed yesterday broke down again.
> ⓔ Have you already seen the new history teacher?

① 1개   ② 2개   ③ 3개
④ 4개   ⑤ 5개

8 다음 중 밑줄 친 부분의 용법이 나머지 넷과 <u>다른</u> 것은?

① Mom <u>has</u> just <u>come</u> home from work.
② He <u>has</u> already <u>finished</u> a bowl of cereal.
③ <u>Has</u> that rock band <u>released</u> a new album recently?
④ The shipping company <u>hasn't delivered</u> my box yet.
⑤ Joseph <u>has been</u> to Daejeon several times.

9 다음 밑줄 친 부분의 용법과 같은 것은?

> One of my best friends <u>has participated</u> in a marathon once.

① Mirae <u>has been</u> in the library for two hours.
② She <u>has never eaten</u> Taiwanese food before.
③ They <u>have studied</u> Spanish since last year.
④ Ann <u>has lost</u> the watch her father gave her.
⑤ We <u>have played</u> on the national team for three years.

10 다음 중 어법상 바른 것은?

① I have been to Rome in 2015.

② Has he already done all his work when you went to school?

③ He had had enough time to clean the house before his parents got home.

④ He has been sick for two days when I visited him.

⑤ She has completed her assignment two days ago.

11 괄호 안의 말을 활용하여 빈칸에 알맞은 말을 쓰시오.

I ⓐ_____(hear) about the new mayor from my mother yesterday. She said that they grew up together in Busan. He ⓑ_____(do) many nice things to help people since he became a politician. She thinks he will be a great mayor.

12 두 문장의 의미가 같도록 현재완료진행시제 문장을 완성하시오.

The artist started painting this picture when he moved into his new studio, and he is still painting it.

= The artist _____

since_____.

[13-14] 다음 표를 보고 표에 나온 표현을 활용하여 빈칸에 알맞은 말을 쓰시오.

13

10:00 A.M.	Minju started waiting for her friend Sophia at the post office.
11:00 A.M.	Sophia arrived at the post office. Minju was still waiting for Sophia.

→ Minju _____ _____ _____ for Sophia for an hour when Sophia _____ at the post office.

14

5:30 P.M.	My father began to make jam with my little brother.
6:00 P.M.	I came home. My father and my little brother were still making jam.

→ When I _____ home, my father and my little brother _____ _____ _____ _____ for 30 minutes.

15 다음 중 어법상 어색한 것은?

① He bought a house in Seoul after he had sold his old house.

② Mina and I have been best friends since we were kids.

③ I had never gotten a good score on a math test until last semester.

④ My mom has fallen asleep by the time I got home.

⑤ Karen told me she had volunteered on a farm for two months.

[17-18] 두 문장의 의미가 같도록 빈칸에 알맞은 말을 쓰시오.

17

> She started to work as a librarian in 2013, and she still works as a librarian now.
> = She _____ _____ as a librarian since 2013.

18

> He began making clothes many years ago, and he still makes clothes now.
> = He _____ _____ clothes for many years.

16 다음 밑줄 친 ⓐ~ⓔ 중 어법상 어색한 것을 찾아 기호를 쓰고 바르게 고쳐 쓰시오.

> A: Have you ⓐseen that new action movie *Star Heroes* yet?
> B: No, I ⓑdidn't. Is it good?
> A: I ⓒwatched it last Thursday. It ⓓwas great.
> B: I ⓔhaven't been to the cinema for a long time. I will go to see *Star Heroes* this weekend, I think.
> A: You won't regret it!

_____ → _____

19 다음 우리말을 알맞게 영작한 것은?

> 나의 언니는 오늘 아침부터 같은 곡을 흥얼거리고 있다.

① My older sister is humming the same melody since this morning.

② My older sister hummed the same melody since this morning.

③ My older sister had hummed the same melody since this morning.

④ My older sister has been humming the same melody since this morning.

⑤ My older sister had been humming the same melody since this morning.

20 다음 중 어법상 바른 것의 개수는?

> ⓐ My younger brother has been decorating his room for an hour.
> ⓑ They received an award for a film that they has worked on.
> ⓒ The movie has already begun when we sat down in the theater.
> ⓓ Yunsu was upset because he had missed the last subway of the day.
> ⓔ The thieves had taken all the jewelry before the police arrived.

① 1개   ② 2개   ③ 3개
④ 4개   ⑤ 없음

21 괄호 안의 말을 활용하여 빈칸에 알맞은 말을 쓰시오.

> Betty joined the fitness club and started to take fitness classes six weeks ago. She ⓐ＿＿＿＿＿＿(learn) how to do yoga since then. Over the past few weeks, she ⓑ＿＿＿＿＿＿(lose) some weight.

[22-23] 다음 글을 읽고 주어진 질문에 답하시오.

> My older sister ①has been learning to play the violin since she ②has been seven years old. From the time she was in high school, she (A) has practiced the violin every day. At first, I ③hated hearing her practice. She couldn't play the songs well so there ④were often missed notes interrupting the melodies. But now, she plays beautifully and ⑤has even performed in concerts several times. I'm so proud of her.

22 위 글의 밑줄 친 (A)와 용법이 같은 것은?

① She has never tried learning taekwondo.
② He has just eaten at a Mexican restaurant with his friends.
③ How long have you used this camera?
④ John has already fixed my old computer.
⑤ Has your father gone to Italy on a business trip?

23 위 글의 밑줄 친 ①~⑤ 중, 어법상 어색한 것을 찾아 번호를 쓰고, 바르게 고쳐 쓰시오.

＿＿＿＿ → ＿＿＿＿＿＿＿＿＿

24 다음 중 어법상 바른 것은?

① Have you been eaten lunch with him until now?

② We have been study history since 9 o'clock.

③ I've been wear glasses since I was six years old.

④ They have been waiting for a train to Sejong since 6 P.M.

⑤ Suji has been written in her diary for an hour.

25 다음 빈칸에 들어갈 알맞은 것은?

> When my friends and I got there, many people _____ the festival.

① leave

② leaving

③ have left

④ have been leaving

⑤ had left

26 우리말과 같도록 주어진 <조건>에 맞게 문장을 완성하시오.

> Mike는 여기로 이사 온 이후로 우리 학교에서 영어를 가르치고 있다.

<조건>

1. 현재완료진행시제를 사용하시오.
2. 7단어로 쓰시오.
3. teach, at our school을 활용하시오.

= Mike _____

_____ since he moved here.

27 다음 글을 아래와 같이 바꿔 쓸 때, 본문에 나온 단어를 활용하여 빈칸에 알맞은 말을 쓰시오.

> This morning, my mom entered my room to wake me up as usual. However, I got up before that. I went to school and had lunch. Then, I took a math test.

→ Today, I _____ _____

_____ before my mom entered my room to wake me up. At school,

I _____ a math test after

I _____ _____ lunch.

[28-29] 두 문장의 의미가 같도록 현재완료진행시제 문장을 완성하시오.

28

> We started talking about our exam at breaktime, and we are still talking about it.
>
> = We _____
>
> since breaktime.

29

> Claire began to work on her science homework on Wednesday. She is still working on it.
>
> = Claire _____
>
> _____ since
>
> Wednesday.

30 괄호 안의 말을 활용하여 질문에 대한 대답을 쓰시오.

A: How long has Jessica been taking swimming lessons?

B: She _____

_____ .

(take, swimming lessons, 5 years, for)

31 다음 우리말과 같도록 빈칸에 들어갈 말이 순서대로 짝지어진 것은?

우리가 인천 국제 공항에 도착했을 때, 그 비행기는 이미 이륙해버렸었다.

= When we _____ at Incheon International Airport, the plane _____ .

① arrived – has already takes off
② had arrived – has already taken off
③ arrived – is already taking off
④ arrived – had already taken off
⑤ had arrived – already took off

32 다음 빈칸에 들어갈 말을 <u>모두</u> 고르시오.

She has waited for the letter _____ .

① yesterday   ② for five days
③ three days ago   ④ last evening
⑤ since last week

33 다음은 Alex와 Iris가 경험해본 것을 나타낸 표이다. 표를 보고 현재완료시제 문장을 완성하시오.

	Alex	Iris
study cooking	O	X
work in restaurants	O	O

Alex has studied cooking, but Iris _____ . However, both Alex and Iris _____

_____ .

34 다음 (A)~(C)에 들어갈 말이 바르게 짝지어진 것은?

Let me tell you about my best friend, Justin. He is a good soccer player. He ___(A)___ soccer since he was a little boy. He ___(B)___ a defender for a long time before his coach offered him the chance to play as a striker in one game. Last year, he ___(C)___ the MVP award at our city's middle-school soccer tournament. His dream is to become the captain of the national soccer team.

	(A)	(B)	(C)
①	played	has been	had won
②	has played	has been	had won
③	has played	had been	won
④	played	had been	won
⑤	has played	had been	had won

[35-37] 우리말과 같도록 괄호 안의 말을 활용하여 완료시제 문장을 완성하시오.

35

Austin은 도시락을 가져오지 않았었다는 것을 깨달았다. (realize, bring)

= Austin _____ that he _____ _____ his lunch box.

36

그 소방관들은 이틀 동안 잠을 못 잤었기 때문에 매우 피곤해 보였다. (seem, sleep)

= The fire fighters _____ very tired because they _____ for two days.

37

그는 그 기차를 놓치고 난 후 다른 티켓을 예약했다. (book, miss)

= He _____ another ticket after he _____ the train.

38 다음 그림을 보고 <보기>의 말을 활용하여 빈칸에 알맞은 말을 쓰시오.

<보기>	eat	buy

I hour ago	30 minutes ago

My younger brother and I _____ the strawberry cake that my mother _____ at my favorite cake shop.

39 다음 중 어법상 바른 것은?

① We have been studying for an hour before Sumin came into the classroom.

② Tom wanted to take a rest, but he hasn't finished his math homework.

③ I have lived in China for five years until I came back to Korea.

④ They hadn't yet drunk soda before the movie started.

⑤ They were exhausted because they have been working all day.

40 괄호 안의 말을 활용하여 대화를 완성하시오.

A: _____
on this website before? (buy, ever, clothes)

B: Yes, I have. This website sells various products at reasonable prices.

41 다음 빈칸에 들어갈 말이 순서대로 짝지어진 것은?

Mary _____ in the drama club's plays since last year, and her older brother _____ in the drama club's plays until he was 18 years old.

① acted – acted
② acted – had acted
③ has acted – acted
④ has acted – had acted
⑤ had acted – has acted

42 다음 문장에서 어법상 어색한 부분을 찾아 쓰고 바르게 고쳐 쓰시오.

Jinsu had hurt his arm while skiing a few days ago.

_____ → _____

43 다음 그림을 보고 <보기>의 단어를 활용하여 빈칸에 알맞은 말을 쓰시오.

30 minutes ago	Now

<보기> dance   begin

The performers ⓐ_____
to dance on the stage 30 minutes ago, and they are still dancing. The performers ⓑ_____
on the stage for 30 minutes.

44 다음 밑줄 친 부분을 바르게 고치지 못한 것은?

① Tyson has created a model of the solar system for the science fair last weekend. (→ created)
② Lily had been thinking of learning the guitar until she had heard someone playing the cello. (→ has heard)
③ My little brothers had been building the fence since Thursday. (→ have been building)
④ Marie Curie wins two Nobel Prizes in physics by the time she was 44. (→ had won)
⑤ Mrs. Yoon had taught the origins of World War II since last semester. (→ has been teaching)

[45-47] 우리말과 같도록 괄호 안의 말을 활용하여 완료시제 문장을 완성하시오.

45

> 그녀는 그녀의 친구가 그녀에게 보드 게임을 사준 이후로 그것을 해본 적이 없다. (play)

= She _____ that board game since her friend bought it for her.

46

> 진호는 이전에 하키를 하는 것을 시도해보았고, 그것이 매우 흥미롭다는 것을 알게 되었다. (try)

= Jinho _____ playing hockey before, and he found it very interesting.

47

> 그 오케스트라는 그가 합류했을 때 세 시간 동안 함께 연습하고 있었다. (practice)

= The orchestra _____ together for three hours when he joined.

CHAPTER 3
조동사

Paul exercises every day. Paul은 매일 운동한다.
Paul **should** exercise every day. Paul은 매일 운동해야 한다.

'Paul은 매일 운동한다.'라는 문장에 조동사 **should**(~해야 한다)가 포함되어 'Paul은 매일 운동해야 한다.'라는 문장이 됐어요. 이렇게 다른 동사와 함께 쓰여 여러 가지 의미를 더하는 동사를 **조동사**라고 해요.

기출로 적중 POINT

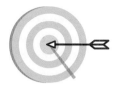

내신 100점 적중!
기출 출제율

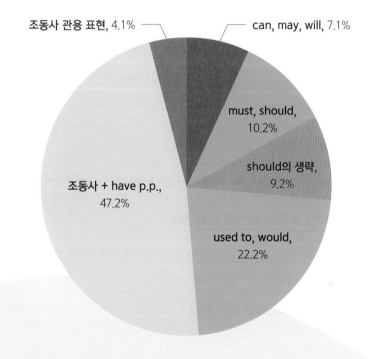

조동사 관용 표현, 4.1%

can, may, will, 7.1%

must, should, 10.2%

should의 생략, 9.2%

조동사 + have p.p., 47.2%

used to, would, 22.2%

TOP 1 **조동사 + have + p.p. (47.2%)**
「조동사 + have + p.p.」의 형태와 쓰임을 묻는 문제가 자주 출제된다.

TOP 2 **used to, would (22.2%)**
would와 used to의 쓰임을 구별하는 문제가 자주 출제된다.

TOP 3 **must, should (10.2%)**
must와 should의 의미와 쓰임을 묻는 문제가 자주 출제된다.

can, may, will

1. can은 능력, 가능, 허가, 요청, 추측의 의미를 나타낸다.

능력	~할 수 있다 (= be able to)	John **can[is able to]** run 50 meters in 7 seconds. John은 50미터를 7초 이내에 달릴 수 있다.
가능	~할 가능성이 있다	Miracles **can** happen anytime. 기적은 언제든 일어날 가능성이 있다.
허가	~해도 된다	You **can** use my scissors. 너는 나의 가위를 사용해도 된다.
요청	~해주겠니?	**Can** you answer the phone? 전화를 받아주겠니?
추측	~일 리가 없다	Our goal **can't** be met. 우리의 목표는 이루어질 리가 없다. That **can't** be Matt. Matt is much taller. 저 사람은 Matt일 리가 없다. Matt은 훨씬 더 키가 크다.
	~일 수도 있다	He **could** be at home. He said he was going home an hour ago. 그는 집에 있을 수도 있다. 그는 한 시간 전에 집에 가고 있는 중이라고 말했다.

(Tip) could는 can의 과거형으로 쓰이거나 can보다 정중한 요청을 나타낸다.

He **could[was able to]** swim fast when he was young. 그는 어렸을 때 빠르게 수영할 수 있었다.
Could you give me some advice, please? 저에게 조언을 해주시겠습니까?

2. may는 허가나 약한 추측의 의미를 나타낸다.

허가	~해도 된다	You **may** eat a piece of cake. 너는 케이크 한 조각을 먹어도 된다.
약한 추측	~일지도 모른다	We **may** need boxes. 우리는 상자가 필요할지도 모른다.

(Tip) might는 may보다 불확실한 추측을 나타낸다.

She **might** have a cold or the flu. 그녀는 감기나 독감에 걸렸을지도 모른다.

3. will은 미래, 의지, 요청의 의미를 나타낸다.

미래	~할 것이다 (= be going to)	I **will[am going to]** enter high school next year. 나는 내년에 고등학교에 입학할 것이다.
의지	~하겠다	We **will** always tell the truth. 우리는 항상 진실을 말하겠다.
요청	~해주겠니?	**Will** you open the door? 문을 열어주겠니?

(Tip) would는 will보다 정중한 요청을 나타낸다.

Would you please be quiet? 조용히 해주시겠습니까?

연습문제 A 괄호 안에서 알맞은 것을 <u>모두</u> 고르시오.

1 (Can / Will) you tell Adam to give me a call?

2 You (can / may) come to my house if you want.

3 Children know how to use computers, so it (can't / will) be difficult.

4 Sam's story about his grandparents (could / might) be true.

5 (May / Can) you help me solve this tricky puzzle, please?

6 Joseph (can / is able to) do more than 100 push-ups in one session.

연습문제 B 우리말과 같도록 괄호 안의 말을 활용하여 문장을 완성하시오.

1 네가 뉴욕에 방문하면 우리에게 엽서를 보내주겠니? (send)

= _____ us a postcard when you visit New York?

2 우리는 학급 견학으로 박물관에 갈지도 모른다. (go)

= We _____ to a museum for a class trip.

3 유미는 그녀의 계획이 변경된다면 나에게 알려줄 것이다. (let)

= Yumi _____ me know if her plan is changed.

4 그는 성실하지 않기 때문에 좋은 학생일 리가 없다. (be)

= He _____ a good student, as he is not diligent.

5 스트레스는 다양한 건강 문제를 유발할 가능성이 있다. (cause)

= Stress _____ various health problems.

6 너는 수업 후에 너의 숙제를 제출해도 된다. (turn in)

= You _____ your assignment after class.

7 그는 어려운 수학 문제들을 몇 초 이내에 풀 수 있다. (solve)

= He _____ difficult math problems in seconds.

8 그녀는 오늘 오후에 공항에 갈 것이다. (go)

= She _____ to the airport this afternoon.

기출 적중문제

다음 대화의 밑줄 친 우리말과 같도록 괄호 안의 말을 활용하여 영작하시오.

> A: I heard that Kathy is in London now.
> B: <u>그녀는 해외에 있을 리가 없다.</u> (be, overseas) I just saw her at the mall.

= _____

1. must는 강한 의무나 강한 추측의 의미를 나타낸다.

강한 의무	~해야 한다 (= have to)	You **must[have to]** submit your assignment by e-mail. 너는 너의 숙제를 이메일로 제출해야 한다. (Tip) must의 부정형과 have to의 부정형은 서로 의미가 다르므로 주의한다. ① must not: '~해서는 안 된다' (강한 금지) We **must not** break the law. 우리는 법을 어겨서는 안 된다. ② don't have to: '~할 필요가 없다' (불필요) You **don't have to** turn off the radio. 너는 라디오를 끌 필요가 없다.
강한 추측	~임이 틀림없다	The interview **must** be long. 그 인터뷰는 오래 걸림이 틀림없다. (Tip) must가 강한 추측을 나타낼 때, 부정형은 can't(~일 리가 없다)를 쓴다. The interview **can't** be long. 그 인터뷰는 오래 걸릴 리가 없다.

2. should는 충고·의무의 의미를 나타낸다.

충고·의무	~해야 한다 (= ought to)	We **should[ought to]** help other people. 우리는 다른 사람들을 도와야 한다.

(Tip) must는 강제성이 있는 의무를 나타내는 데 반해, should는 must보다는 약한 의무를 나타낸다.
You **must** follow the traffic rules. 너는 교통 규칙을 지켜야 한다.
You **should** wear dark clothes at the funeral. 너는 장례식에서 어두운 색깔의 옷을 입어야 한다.

연습문제 **A** 밑줄 친 부분의 의미를 <보기>에서 골라 그 기호를 쓰시오.

<보기> ⓐ 의무 ⓑ 강한 추측 ⓒ 강한 금지

1 She <u>must</u> be careful not to make the same mistake again.　　　　　[　　　]

2 Brian <u>must</u> be excited about his upcoming competition.　　　　　[　　　]

3 People <u>must not</u> drive too fast near schools and kindergartens.　　　[　　　]

4 Sumin <u>must</u> be tired after finishing the marathon.　　　　　[　　　]

5 Mark <u>must</u> be upset because his team lost the soccer game.　　　[　　　]

6 People <u>must not</u> touch hair dryers with wet hands.　　　　　[　　　]

7 The chef <u>must</u> cook faster because a lot of people are waiting.　　　[　　　]

연습문제 B 괄호 안에서 알맞은 것을 <u>모두</u> 고르시오.

1 We (must / have to) hurry because the train is about to leave.

2 The dog is barking, so there (must / should) be a stranger at the door.

3 You (must not / don't have to) wake up early tomorrow because you don't go to work on Saturdays.

4 People (must not / don't have to) leave any trash in the park.

5 You (must / don't have to) be really hungry as you skipped breakfast.

6 I (must / have to) return the books to the library today.

7 Mr. Smith (must not / doesn't have to) eat anything before his medical checkup.

8 George is good at speaking French, so he (must not / doesn't have to) take this class.

9 They (can't / ought to) be at the concert because they weren't able to purchase tickets.

10 You (must not / should not) interrupt someone who is speaking.

연습문제 C 다음 그림을 보고 should와 괄호 안의 말을 활용하여 문장을 완성하시오.

1  **2**  **3**  **4**

1 You _____ your hands before having dinner. (wash)

2 You _____ on the phone loudly in the hospital. (talk)

3 She _____ the bed every morning. (make)

4 He _____ harder if he wants to get a good grade. (study)

기출 적중문제

다음 밑줄 친 <u>must</u>의 쓰임과 <u>다른</u> 것은?

Everyone <u>must</u> wear their seatbelts during the flight.

① You <u>must</u> sign your name on this form.
② He <u>must</u> be very good at singing as he used to be a singer.
③ All participants <u>must</u> bring their ID cards.
④ You and I <u>must</u> arrive at the airport before 10 o'clock.
⑤ I <u>must</u> finish my homework by tomorrow.

must는 강한 의무와 강한 추측이라는 두 가지 의미를 가지고 있어요.

should의 생략

제안, 주장, 요구, 명령의 동사 뒤에 오는 that절의 동사 자리에는 「should + 동사원형」이 오며, 이때 should는 생략할 수 있다.

suggest 제안하다	recommend 추천하다	insist 주장하다	request 요청하다
require 요구하다	demand 요구하다	order 명령하다	

I **suggested** that Janet **(should) be** the class president.
나는 Janet이 반장이 되어야 한다고 제안했다.

He **insisted** that we **(should) report** the lost wallet to the police.
그는 우리가 그 분실된 지갑을 경찰에 신고해야 한다고 주장했다.

연습문제 | 우리말과 같도록 괄호 안의 말을 활용하여 빈칸에 쓰시오.

1 Mike는 모두가 핼러윈 파티에 변장을 하도록 요구했다. (demand, dress up)

= Mike _____ that everyone _____ for the Halloween party.

2 나는 Amy가 그 후식을 맛봐야 한다고 제안했다. (suggest, try)

= I _____ that Amy _____ the dessert.

3 그 학교는 모든 학생들이 교복을 착용해야 한다고 요구한다. (require, wear)

= The school _____ that all the students _____ a school uniform.

4 우리는 그들이 그 상품을 우리에게 돌려줘야 한다고 요청했다. (request, return)

= We _____ that they _____ the product to us.

5 그 보호 단체는 우리가 자연환경을 보호해야 한다고 주장한다. (insist, protect)

= The conservation group _____ that we _____ the natural environment.

6 판사는 모두가 법정을 떠나야 한다고 명령했다. (order, leave)

= The judge _____ that everyone _____ the courtroom.

 기출 적중문제

다음 중 어법상 바른 것을 <u>모두</u> 고르시오.

① She recommended that I wore comfortable clothes.
② They recommended that I deal with the broken computer first.
③ He recommended that they cleaning up their own mess.
④ You recommended that I to eat healthy food.
⑤ We recommended that he check his answers again.

제안, 주장, 요구, 명령의 동사 뒤에 오는 that절의 동사 자리에 should가 생략되더라도 반드시 동사 원형이 와야 해요.

POINT 4 used to, would

1. used to는 과거의 습관이나 상태를 나타낸다.

과거의 습관	~하곤 했다	Helen **used to** go to church when she was young. Helen은 그녀가 어렸을 때 교회에 가곤 했다. I **didn't use to** eat onions, but I like them now. 나는 양파를 먹지 않곤 했지만, 지금은 그것들을 좋아한다.
과거의 상태	~이었다	There **used to** be a bridge here two years ago. 2년 전에는 여기에 다리가 있었다.

(Tip) used to와 형태가 비슷하지만 의미가 다른 표현

① 「**be used to + 동사원형**」: ~하는 데 사용되다

This knife **is used to cut** bread. 이 칼은 빵을 자르는 데 사용된다.

② 「**be used to + V-ing/명사**」: ~에 익숙하다

I **am used to eating** spicy food. 나는 매운 음식을 먹는 것에 익숙하다.
I **am used to the hot weather**. 나는 더운 날씨에 익숙하다.

2. would는 과거의 습관을 나타낸다.

과거의 습관	~하곤 했다	We **would** go camping every summer when we were children. 우리는 아이였을 때 매년 여름에 캠핑을 가곤 했다.

(Tip) would는 과거의 상태를 나타낼 수 없다.

James (~~would~~ / **used to**) be short, but he is tall now. James는 키가 작았지만, 현재 키가 크다.

연습문제 A 괄호 안에서 알맞은 것을 고르시오.

1 There (were used / used) to be dinosaurs in the world.

2 She (is used / used) to climb mountains with her grandfather.

3 My dad used to (carrying / carry) me on his shoulders when I was little.

4 There (would / used to) be more babies in the country, but fewer are born now.

5 My older sister (is used / used) to staying up all night to study for tests.

6 A long time ago, there (used to / would) be many palaces in Korea.

7 This machine is used to (pump / pumping) air into the ball.

8 The mayor of the city (is used / used) to be a police officer.

9 Yerim and I used to (go / going) to the lake to take a walk.

10 He is used to (jog / jogging) in the early morning.

연습문제 B 밑줄 친 부분이 어법상 맞으면 O를 쓰고, 틀리면 바르게 고쳐 쓰시오.

1 She adopted a dog that used to <u>guided</u> blind people. → _____

2 I am used to <u>visiting</u> my grandparents on the holidays. → _____

3 They aren't used to <u>spend</u> so much money on trips. → _____

4 Heaters are used to <u>keeping</u> us warm in winter. → _____

5 He is used to <u>take</u> the bus to the gym every day. → _____

6 The statue <u>would</u> be in the park before it was moved to the museum. → _____

7 We didn't <u>use</u> to study in the library, but these days we study there. → _____

8 My aunt <u>is used to</u> work at a department store when she was in her 20s. → _____

9 I heard Julie <u>used to</u> be a gymnast and once competed in the Olympics. → _____

10 We are used to <u>watch</u> a movie at least three times a week. → _____

연습문제 C 우리말과 같도록 used to와 괄호 안의 동사를 활용하여 문장을 완성하시오.

1 나의 할머니께서는 나에게 맛있는 수프를 만들어 주시곤 하셨다. (make)
= My grandmother _____ me a delicious soup.

2 Sally는 매일 두 시간 동안 자전거를 타는 데 익숙하다. (ride)
= Sally _____ a bicycle for two hours every day.

3 나는 야구를 많이 하지 않곤 했지만, 요즘 그것을 즐겨 한다. (play)
= I _____ baseball a lot, but I enjoy it these days.

4 Jake는 학교 합창단 소속이었지만, 그만둬야 했다. (be)
= Jake _____ in the school choir, but he had to quit.

5 공기 청정기는 공기 중의 미세 먼지를 걸러내는 데 사용된다. (filter)
= Air purifiers _____ fine dust from the air.

기출 적중문제

두 문장의 의미가 같도록 빈칸에 알맞은 말을 쓰시오.

My family lived in a house with a swimming pool, but now we live in an apartment.
= My family _____ _____ _____ in a house with a swimming pool.

조동사 + have + p.p.

정답 p.9

「조동사 + have + p.p.」의 형태로 과거 사실에 대한 추측이나 후회·유감을 나타낼 수 있다.

약한 추측	may[might] + have p.p.	~했을 수도 있다
강한 추측	must + have p.p.	~했음이 틀림없다
	can't + have p.p.	~했을 리가 없다
후회·유감	should + have p.p.	~했어야 했다 (하지만 하지 않았다)
	could + have p.p.	~했을 수도 있었다 (하지만 하지 않았다)

I **may[might] have sent** the wrong file. 나는 잘못된 파일을 보냈을 수도 있다.

That tree on the road **must have fallen** during the storm.
도로에 있는 저 나무는 폭풍우 중에 쓰러졌음이 틀림없다.

The neighbors **can't have moved** already. 그 이웃들은 벌써 이사했을 리가 없다.

You **should have asked** me before throwing it away.
너는 그것을 버리기 전에 나에게 물어봤어야 했다.

We **could have traveled** abroad, but we stayed home.
우리는 해외여행을 갔을 수도 있었지만, 집에 머물렀다.

연습문제 A | 괄호 안에서 알맞은 것을 고르시오.

1 They (must / could) have given us more useful information, but they didn't.

2 We (might / should) have passed the store, so we should turn around.

3 You (should / can't) have called me if you needed help.

4 You (could / shouldn't) have revealed his secrets, but you didn't.

5 My keys (may /should) have fallen out of my pocket while I was running.

6 She (must / should) have been on vacation as she got sunburned.

7 I thought I saw Hyunsu at the mall, but it (can't / might) have been somebody else.

8 We (can't / should) have worn shorts today because it's hot.

9 He (must / can't) have lifted the sofa by himself because he isn't strong enough.

10 He (should / shouldn't) have overslept because it made him late for school.

11 Yujin (must / shouldn't) have studied hard to get such a good grade.

12 My family (could / can't) have stayed at that hotel, but we decided to go outside.

13 Since she is an honest kid, she (can't / must) have lied to her teacher yesterday.

연습문제 B 우리말과 같도록 괄호 안의 말을 활용하여 문장을 완성하시오.

1 그녀는 Tom의 실수에 대해 화내지 말았어야 했다. (be)

= She _____ angry about Tom's mistake.

2 나는 뜨거운 커피 대신에 아이스티를 마셨어야 했다. (drink)

= I _____ an iced tea instead of a hot coffee.

3 내가 가장 좋아하는 밴드가 이미 새 앨범을 녹음했을 수도 있다. (record)

= My favorite band _____ a new album already.

4 나는 수영장에서 수영했을 수도 있었지만, 대신 바다에 갔다. (swim)

= I _____ in the pool, but I went to the beach instead.

5 민호가 전화를 받지 않고 있으므로 그가 그의 전화기를 꺼놓은 것이 틀림없다. (turn off)

= Minho _____ his phone because he isn't answering.

6 불이 꺼져 있으므로 그들은 아직 그들의 집에 도착했을 리가 없다. (get)

= They _____ to their house yet because the lights are off.

연습문제 C <보기>의 조동사를 사용한 「조동사 + have + p.p.」와 괄호 안의 말을 활용하여 문장을 완성하시오.

<보기> must   can't   should

1 They _____ lunch at the new Italian restaurant because it is not open today. (eat)

2 The blue wall doesn't go well with the kitchen. You _____ it pink. (paint)

3 I can hear my friends' voices downstairs. They _____. (arrive)

4 Mr. Smith _____ quietly not to wake up the baby. The baby is still asleep. (walk)

5 Inho is very happy today. He _____ some good news. (receive)

6 He _____ to the festival because he was ill. (go)

기출 적중문제

다음 글의 밑줄 친 우리말과 같도록 괄호 안의 말을 활용하여 문장을 완성하시오.

> I hurt Larry's feelings, but I didn't tell him I was sorry. 나는 그에게 사과했어야 했다. (apologize)

= I _____ to him.

기출로 적중 POINT 6 조동사 관용 표현

정답 p.10

다음은 자주 사용되는 조동사 관용 표현이다.

would like + 명사 ~을 원하다	I **would like a room** with a balcony. 나는 발코니가 있는 방을 원한다. (Tip) 부정형: wouldn't like
would like to + 동사원형 ~하고 싶다	I **would like to play** tennis. 나는 테니스를 치고 싶다. (Tip) 부정형: wouldn't like to
would rather + 동사원형 (차라리) ~하겠다	I **would rather visit** Spain than France. 나는 프랑스보다 차라리 스페인을 방문하겠다. (Tip) 부정형: would rather not
may well + 동사원형 (~하는 것도) 당연하다	They **may well think** so. 그들이 그렇게 생각하는 것도 당연하다. (Tip) 부정형: may well not
may as well + 동사원형 ~하는 편이 좋다	You **may as well try** the new program. 너는 새로운 프로그램을 시도해보는 편이 좋다. (Tip) 부정형: may as well not
had better + 동사원형 ~하는 것이 낫다	You **had better save** the money. 너는 돈을 저축하는 것이 낫다. (Tip) 부정형: had better not

연습문제 우리말과 같도록 괄호 안의 말을 활용하여 문장을 완성하시오.

1 나는 Sharon과 대화를 나누고 싶다. (have)

= I _____ a conversation with Sharon.

2 우리는 우리 제품들의 가격을 낮추는 것이 낫다. (lower)

= We _____ the prices of our products.

3 Diana가 그녀의 반에서 최고의 학생인 것도 당연하다. (be)

= Diana _____ the best student in her class.

4 나는 나의 낡은 전화기를 수리하는 것보다는 차라리 새로운 전화기를 사겠다. (buy)

= I _____ a new phone than have my old one repaired.

5 너는 진수에게 그 숙제에 대해 질문하는 편이 좋다. (ask)

= You _____ Jinsu about the homework.

6 그녀는 그녀의 새 전자레인지에 대한 설명서를 원한다. (a manual)

= She _____ for her new microwave oven.

A 밑줄 친 부분이 어법상 맞으면 O를 쓰고, 틀리면 바르게 고쳐 쓰시오.

1 You <u>must have practiced</u> a lot since you have passed the speaking test. → _____

2 I <u>would like to see</u> you at the baseball stadium at 5 P.M. → _____

3 There <u>is used to be</u> a gas station on the corner. → _____

4 The government recommended that teenagers <u>avoided</u> eating fast food. → _____

5 You <u>may as well taking</u> a seat. → _____

6 We <u>ought put</u> trash in the trash can. → _____

7 The teacher requested that Beth <u>come</u> to school early. → _____

8 You <u>had better drinking</u> a lot of water, especially in the summer. → _____

9 The food <u>must have spoiled</u> as it smells bad. → _____

10 Our class <u>can have visited</u> that exhibit, but we went to another one. → _____

11 Joe <u>must have believed</u> what his friends said since he always trusts them. → _____

B 다음 그림을 보고 must와 괄호 안의 말을 활용하여 대화를 완성하시오.

1   **2**   **3**

1 *A*: You _____ in the library. (run)
   B: Sorry. I will walk slowly.

2 *A*: The virus can spread through coughing and sneezing.
   B: Everyone _____ a mask. (wear)

3 *A*: Tom slept on the couch for five hours after coming back home from the gym.
   B: He _____ very tired that day. (be)

C 두 문장의 의미가 같도록 「조동사 + have p.p.」를 활용하여 문장을 완성하시오.

1 It's not possible that they completed the test already.

= They _____ the test already.

2 We are sorry that we didn't bring our towels and swimsuits.

= We _____ our towels and swimsuits.

3 It's uncertain whether she watched the play yesterday with her friends.

= She _____ the play yesterday with her friends.

4 It was not permitted for you to speak during the exam.

= You _____ during the exam.

5 I am sure that the clothes I ordered last week were delivered.

= The clothes I ordered last week _____ .

6 It was a bad idea for me to skip lunch today.

= I _____ lunch today.

7 It's certain that Ms. Miller paid the electric bill on time.

= Ms. Miller _____ the electric bill on time.

D 우리말과 같도록 괄호 안의 말을 알맞게 배열하시오.

1 Jenny가 그 영화를 무서워하는 것도 당연하다. (scared, may, by, the movie, well, Jenny, be)

= _____

2 나는 스키보다는 차라리 스케이트를 타러 가겠다. (go, rather, skating, I, than, would, skiing)

= _____

3 나는 나의 남동생이 이 공연을 원한다고 생각한다. (my younger brother, think, would, I, this show, like)

= _____

4 그는 그의 재선 운동을 포기하는 편이 좋다. (reelection campaign, his, well, as, give up, he, may)

= _____

5 그 고객은 예약을 하고 싶어 한다. (make, to, the customer, like, a reservation, would)

= _____

6 너는 너의 자리를 그 노인에게 권하는 것이 낫다. (to, offer, better, you, the elderly man, had, your seat)

= _____

1 다음 밑줄 친 can과 의미가 같은 것은?

> I can speak English and three other languages.

① may　　　　② am able to
③ should　　　④ had better
⑤ am going to

2 우리말과 같도록 괄호 안의 말을 알맞게 배열하시오.

> 만약 네가 프랑스를 방문한다면, 너는 스위스
> 도 방문하는 편이 좋다. (as, you, visit, may,
> Switzerland, well)

= If you visit France, _____
_____, too.

3 다음 우리말과 같도록 빈칸에 알맞은 말을 고르시오.

> 내일 아침에 눈이 많이 올지도 모른다.
> = It _____ snow heavily tomorrow
>   morning.

① used to　　② will　　　③ may
④ should　　　⑤ must

4 다음 대화의 밑줄 친 Can과 의미가 같은 것은?

> A: Can I use your computer to check
>   my e-mail?
> B: Sure. It's right over there on the desk.

① May　　　② Will　　　③ Do
④ Must　　　⑤ Should

5 다음 중 어법상 어색한 것은?

① Could we buy a new sofa for the lounge?
② Sean must finish his assignment today.
③ I had better pack my bags now.
④ Children ought read books to gain
   knowledge.
⑤ You should go to the gym regularly.

6 다음 빈칸에 공통으로 들어갈 알맞은 것은?

> · My friends _____ come here to
>   practice baseball in the spring.
> · I _____ like a chicken burger and
>   some cheese sticks, please.

① can　　　② could　　　③ may
④ might　　　⑤ would

7 다음 밑줄 친 Can과 의미가 같은 것은?

> Can I choose the menu for dinner tonight?

① We couldn't hear what the speaker was saying.
② You can't bring food or drink into the museum.
③ The clinic can't be closed yet.
④ Could you call me after the class ends?
⑤ I could not see very far because of the thick fog.

9 다음 우리말을 알맞게 영작한 것은?

> 사람들은 이 정원 안에서 꽃들을 꺾으면 안 된다.

① People must not pick the flowers in this garden.
② People would not pick the flowers in this garden.
③ People could not pick the flowers in this garden.
④ People might not pick the flowers in this garden.
⑤ People do not have to pick the flowers in this garden.

10 두 문장의 의미가 같도록 빈칸에 알맞은 말을 쓰시오.

> Mr. Brown was a famous musician, but now he is not.
> = Mr. Brown _____ _____ _____ a famous musician.

8 다음 대화의 밑줄 친 우리말과 같도록 괄호 안의 말을 이용하여 빈칸에 알맞은 말을 쓰시오.

> A: Should I get you a ticket for the concert?
> B: No. 너는 나에게 그것을 사줄 필요가 없어. (buy)
> A: Why is that?
> B: I bought one yesterday.

= You _____ _____ _____ _____ me one.

11 다음 중 밑줄 친 부분의 의미가 나머지 넷과 다른 것은?

① We must submit the report by tomorrow.
② You must arrive here by noon.
③ Those shoes must be very expensive.
④ Must I pay extra to get a front row seat?
⑤ You must return the book by next week.

12 다음 빈칸에 공통으로 들어갈 알맞은 것은?

A: _____ I ask you a favor?
B: Sure. What is it?
A: Would you feed my cat while I'm on my vacation?
B: No problem. I _____ do that!

① will ② must ③ can
④ might ⑤ should

13 다음 빈칸에 들어갈 말이 순서대로 짝지어진 것은?

· I _____ find a good novel to read.
· You _____ talk on the phone during the movie.

① would like – should
② would like – should not
③ would like to – should
④ would like to – should not
⑤ would like to – must

14 다음 글의 밑줄 친 ⓐ~ⓔ 중 어법상 어색한 것을 찾아 기호를 쓰고 바르게 고쳐 쓰시오.

Next year, I ⓐwill graduate from middle school and start high school. I think I will need more money than I get currently. I ⓑmight need to buy school supplies, or I ⓒmay want to buy more snacks. I ⓓcould also want to do more things with my friends. I ⓔought ask my parents for an increase in my allowance.

_____ → _____

15 <보기>의 말을 모두 사용하여 대화를 완성하시오.

<보기> would rather like to would

A: What do you want to eat tonight?
B: I ⓐ_____ eat pizza for dinner tonight. How about you?
A: I don't feel like pizza. I ⓑ_____ _____ have sushi.
B: OK. Then let's order some.

16 다음 중 어법상 어색한 것은?

① This detergent is used to wash dishes.
② Brad used to play basketball when he was younger.
③ We didn't use to be interested in photography.
④ I am used to get up very early in the morning.
⑤ Mina used to buy milk every day.

17 다음 글의 빈칸에 들어갈 말이 순서대로 짝지어진 것은?

If you go to the amusement park, you have to know a few things about the park. For instance, some rides require you to be a certain height. You _____ find another ride so you don't waste your time in line. There are a lot of other rides without height restrictions. Also, food and drinks are really expensive in the park. You _____ bring your own snacks and drinks so you can save some money.

① could not – don't have to
② may as well – don't have to
③ may as well – should
④ cannot – should not
⑤ cannot – should

18 다음 밑줄 친 may와 의미가 다른 것은?

The teacher said I <u>may</u> use a calculator when I solve the problems.

① We <u>may</u> need a new camera.
② People <u>may</u> take pictures inside the church.
③ <u>May</u> we take our dogs with us?
④ You <u>may</u> eat the sandwich after washing your hands.
⑤ <u>May</u> I borrow your stapler?

19 괄호 안의 말을 활용하여 문장을 완성하시오.

People _____(use, to) take many international trips, but now it's very common.

20 다음 글을 읽고 밑줄 친 우리말과 같도록 주어진 <조건>에 맞게 문장을 완성하시오.

Some people are superstitious. In Germany, it is considered bad luck to wish someone a happy birthday before their birthday. They believe that saying happy birthday early can cause something bad to happen to the person. So in Germany, <u>당신은 당일에 생일 축하한다고 말하는 것이 낫다.</u>

<조건>
1. 10단어로 쓰시오.
2. had better, the right day, happy birthday, say, on을 활용하시오.

= _____
_____

21 <보기>의 조동사를 사용한 「조동사 + have + p.p.」와 괄호 안의 말을 활용하여 문장을 완성하시오.

<보기> should   must

(1) John is still not here. He _____
_____(get) lost.

(2) Jake _____(yell) at us. We didn't do anything wrong.

22 다음 빈칸에 들어갈 말이 순서대로 짝지어진 것은?

> · You had _____ call Jack until his exam is finished.
> · You may as well _____ some sleep now and study tomorrow.

① better not – getting
② better not – to get
③ better not – get
④ not better – to get
⑤ not better – get

[23-24] 우리말과 같도록 괄호 안의 말을 활용하여 문장을 완성하시오.

23

> 너는 수요일까지 이 쿠폰을 사용하는 것이 낫다.
> (better, by Wednesday, this coupon, use)

= _____

_____

24

> 우리는 이곳에 우리의 자전거를 두면 안 된다.
> (should, our bicycles, leave, here)

= _____

_____

25 괄호 안의 말을 활용하여 대화를 완성하시오.

> A: Where was your home when you were young?
> B: I ⓐ_____(use, live) in an apartment near the Hangang Park in Seoul.
> A: Did you go to the park a lot?
> B: Yes. I ⓑ_____(would, go) to the Hangang every weekend.
> A: Wow! That sounds like a lot of fun.
> B: It was. We ⓒ_____ (use, fly) kites there.

26 다음 빈칸에 알맞은 말을 <보기>에서 한 번씩만 골라 쓰시오.

> <보기> might   used to   had to

(1) We _____ be quiet in the auditorium last night.

(2) When I was little, there _____ be many things to play with.

(3) Laura _____ write an e-mail to her parents if she isn't busy.

27 다음 (A)~(C)에 들어갈 말이 바르게 짝지어진 것은?

- That new movie may have ___(A)___ out in theaters already.
- James ___(B)___ have failed the test because he's the smartest person I know.
- She ___(C)___ have gone outside because her bag isn't in her room.

	(A)	(B)	(C)
①	came	might	shouldn't
②	come	can't	shouldn't
③	came	can't	must
④	come	can't	must
⑤	came	might	must

[28-29] 우리말과 같도록 괄호 안의 말을 활용하여 문장을 완성하시오.

28

지호는 해돋이를 보기 위해 우리가 일찍 일어나야 한다고 제안했다. (suggest, get up, we, that, early)

= Jiho _____
_____ to see the sunrise.

29

그 학생들은 그들의 숙제를 끝마치기 위해 교실에 남아야 한다고 주장했다. (insist, that, stay, they, in the classroom)

= The students _____
_____ to complete their homework.

30 괄호 안의 말을 활용하여 대화를 완성하시오.

A: Katie _____
(must, late) for her appointment yesterday.
B: What makes you think so?
A: I saw her running out the door.

31 다음 우리말을 영작한 것 중 어색한 것은?

① 우리는 다음 달에 이 음악 축제에 가야 한다.
= We should go to this music festival next month.
② 그가 그의 아들을 자랑스러워 하는 것도 당연하다.
= He may well be proud of his son.
③ 나는 축구를 하느니 차라리 테니스를 치겠다.
= I would rather play tennis than play soccer.
④ 우리는 환경에 좋은 것들을 사는 편이 좋다.
= We may as well buy things that are good for the environment.
⑤ 그들은 오후 12시까지 집을 떠났을 리가 없다.
= They should not leave the house by 12 P.M.

32 다음 중 짝지어진 두 문장의 의미가 <u>다른</u> 것은?

① Must we do all the renovations this weekend?
= Do we have to do all the renovations this weekend?
② I will bake a cake for the party.
= I am going to bake a cake for the party.
③ You can use my phone to send a message.
= You may use my phone to send a message.
④ He can't be here because he is in Chicago now.
= He is not able to be here because he is in Chicago now.
⑤ Alan should solve the problem today.
= Alan ought to solve the problem today.

33 다음 글을 읽고 괄호 안의 말을 활용하여 혜지가 그녀의 오빠에게 할 말을 완성하시오.

Hyeji was on holiday in Australia with her family. They were staying in a large hotel with a pool. Hyeji's older brother decided to read his book by the pool. He did not tell anyone where he was going. Hyeji and her family thought he was missing and called hotel security. The guard found him reading quietly by the pool. In this situation, what would Hyeji say to her older brother?

Hyeji: You _____ _____

_____ without writing a note.
(should, leave)

34 다음 문장과 의미가 같은 것은?

It is impossible that he bought a new cell phone because he has no money.

① He had to buy a new cell phone.
② He may well buy a new cell phone.
③ He must have bought a new cell phone.
④ He can't have bought a new cell phone.
⑤ He should have bought a new cell phone.

[35-36] 우리말과 같도록 괄호 안의 말을 활용하여 문장을 완성하시오.

35

그녀는 어젯밤에 밤을 새지 말았어야 했다. (stay)

= She _____ up last night.

36

Tim은 오늘 아침에 비행기를 놓쳤음이 틀림없다. (miss)

= Tim _____ the flight this morning.

[37-38] 두 문장의 의미가 같도록 use를 활용하여 문장을 완성하시오.

37

My grandmother and I would go to the market to purchase fruits every Saturday.

= My grandmother and I _____ _____ to purchase fruits every Saturday.

38

I was afraid to talk to people, but now I'm not.

= I _____ to talk to people.

39 다음 (A)~(C)에 들어갈 말이 바르게 짝지어진 것은?

· Somin suggested that I ___(A)___ a new laptop since I need one for next semester.
· The children insisted that Michael ___(B)___ bullying the other kids.
· The woman demanded that the store ___(C)___ her a refund.

	(A)	(B)	(C)
①	get	stops	give
②	get	stop	gave
③	get	stop	give
④	got	stops	gave
⑤	got	stop	give

40 다음 글의 밑줄 친 ⓐ~ⓔ 중 어법상 어색한 것을 두 군데 찾아 기호를 쓰고 바르게 고쳐 쓰시오.

My family lived in Vietnam 10 years ago. When we were there, I was ⓐused to have a lot of free time. I ⓑused to exercise a lot when I didn't have anything else to do. In Da Nang, we ⓒwould take trips to the beach every day after school, so I was ⓓused to swimming in the ocean. Now that we are living in Seoul again, I don't get as much physical activity. I'm thinking of buying some fitness equipment that can ⓔbe used to getting fit again.

(1) _____ → _____

(2) _____ → _____

41 다음 중 자연스럽지 <u>않은</u> 대화를 <u>모두</u> 고른 것은?

① A: Sorry, I'm late. I didn't wake up on time this morning.
   B: You should have slept late.
② A: I'm looking for Doris. Have you seen her?
   B: No. She may have already gone home.
③ A: My older brother won the piano contest.
   B: Wow. He can't have practiced really hard.
④ A: I was busy yesterday because I had to move.
   B: I didn't know that. You could have asked me to help.
⑤ A: Do you think Roy has replied to our e-mail yet?
   B: He can't have replied yet. It's 2 A.M. there.

42 우리말과 같도록 주어진 <조건>에 맞게 문장을 완성하시오.

> 그녀는 나의 이웃이었지만, 이제 그녀는 다른 동네에 산다.

> <조건>
> 1. would 또는 used to 중 하나를 골라 활용하시오.
> 2. be, my neighbor를 활용하시오.

= She _____, but now she lives in a different town.

43 다음 빈칸에 들어갈 말이 순서대로 짝지어진 것은?

> · My younger sister is allergic to peanuts. She _____ have eaten the peanut ice cream.
> · Hojin didn't turn around when I called him. He _____ have been using his earphones.

① should - must
② should - can't
③ can't - must
④ can't - should
⑤ can't - can't

[44-45] 두 문장의 의미가 같도록 빈칸에 알맞은 말을 쓰시오.

44

> It is possible that I dropped my ring on my way home, but I'm not sure.
> = I _____ _____ _____ my ring on my way home.

45

> I'm sorry we didn't keep calm during the emergency training.
> = We _____ _____
> _____ calm during the emergency training.

46 다음 대화를 읽고 밑줄 친 우리말과 같도록 괄호 안의 말을 활용하여 빈칸에 알맞은 말을 쓰시오.

> A: How do I use the school computer system?
> B: (A) 너는 먼저 로그인을 해야 한다. (ought, log in)
> A: But I don't have a username or a password.
> B: In that case, (B) 너는 사서에게 너를 위해 그것들을 만들어 달라고 요청해야 한다. (ask, should)
> A: I'll do that. Thanks.

(A) You _____ _____ _____
_____ first.
(B) you _____ _____ the librarian
to make them for you.

47 다음 중 문맥상 <u>어색한</u> 것은?

① I used to like drawing with a pencil, but now I like painting with oil paints more.

② I didn't use to light candles because I didn't like the smell. But now I light them.

③ I would listen to a song at night before bed when I was young.

④ I didn't see Sophia much last year because we used to be in different classes.

⑤ He would be shy when he was younger.

48 다음 글을 읽고 괄호 안의 말을 활용하여 빈칸에 알맞은 말을 쓰시오.

Today, I was supposed to meet my teacher to talk about my science project. I scheduled a meeting with her after fifth period. I was five minutes late, but she wasn't in her office. I was worried that I ⓐ_____ _____ _____(might, miss) her. But she ⓑ_____ _____ _____ (must, forget) about our meeting. She didn't show up for 45 minutes.

CHAPTER 4
수동태

Jane **took** the picture.   Jane이 그 사진을 찍었다.
The picture **was taken** by Jane.   그 사진은 Jane에 의해 찍혔다.

'Jane이 그 사진을 찍었다.'라는 문장에서는 주어인 Jane이 사진을 찍는 동작을 하고 있어요. 이렇게 주어가 동작을 하는 행위자가 되는 것을 **능동태**라고 해요. 반면에, '그 사진은 Jane에 의해 찍혔다.'라는 문장에서는 그 사진이 주어가 되어 Jane에 의해 찍히는 동작을 당하고 있어요. 이렇게 주어가 동작을 당하는 대상이 되는 것을 **수동태**라고 해요.

기출로 적중 POINT

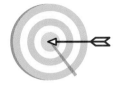

내신 100점 적중!
기출 출제율

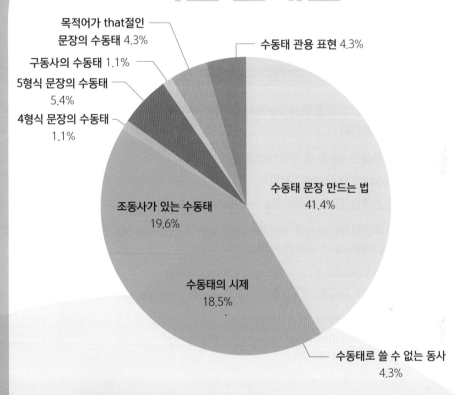

목적어가 that절인
문장의 수동태 4.3%

구동사의 수동태 1.1%

5형식 문장의 수동태
5.4%

4형식 문장의 수동태
1.1%

조동사가 있는 수동태
19.6%

수동태 관용 표현 4.3%

수동태 문장 만드는 법
41.4%

수동태의 시제
18.5%

수동태로 쓸 수 없는 동사
4.3%

TOP 1 **수동태 문장 만드는 법 (41.4%)**
수동태의 형태를 묻는 문제가 자주 출제된다.

TOP 2 **조동사가 있는 수동태 (19.6%)**
조동사가 있는 수동태의 형태를 묻는 문제가 자주 출제된다.

TOP 3 **수동태의 시제 (18.5%)**
완료형 수동태를 활용하여 영작하는 문제가 자주 출제된다.

기출로적중 POINT 1 수동태 문장 만드는 법

1. 수동태 문장은 아래와 같은 방법으로 만든다.

> ① 능동태 문장의 목적어를 주어 자리로 보낸다. 목적어가 인칭대명사인 경우 목적어를 주격으로 바꾼다.
>
> ② 능동태 문장의 동사를 「be동사 + p.p.(과거분사)」의 형태로 바꾼다. 이때 be동사는 수동태 문장 주어의 인칭과 수에 일치시키고, 능동태 문장의 시제를 그대로 쓴다.
>
> ③ 능동태 문장의 주어를 「by + 목적격」의 형태로 바꾼다. 이때 능동태 문장의 주어가 people, we와 같은 일반 사람이거나 언급할 만큼 중요하지 않은 경우 「by + 목적격」은 생략할 수 있다.

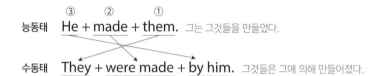

능동태 He + made + them. 그는 그것들을 만들었다.

수동태 They + were made + by him. 그것들은 그에 의해 만들어졌다.

2. 수동태 문장의 부정문과 의문문은 be동사가 있는 문장을 부정문과 의문문으로 만드는 것과 같은 방법으로 만든다.

❶ 수동태 문장의 부정문: be동사 뒤에 not을 쓴다.

The book **was** written by Sarah. 그 책은 Sarah에 의해 쓰였다.

→ The book **was not** written by Sarah. 그 책은 Sarah에 의해 쓰이지 않았다.

❷ 수동태 문장의 의문문: be동사와 주어의 순서를 바꾼다. 의문사가 필요한 경우 의문사를 문장 맨 앞에 쓰고 be동사와 주어의 순서를 바꾼다.

This pasta **was cooked** by a famous chef. 이 파스타는 유명한 요리사에 의해 요리되었다.

→ **Was** this pasta **cooked** by a famous chef? 이 파스타는 유명한 요리사에 의해 요리되었니?

Penicillin **was discovered** by Fleming. 페니실린은 Fleming에 의해 발견되었다.

→ **When was** penicillin **discovered** by Fleming?
언제 페니실린이 Fleming에 의해 발견되었니?

연습문제 A 다음 능동태 문장을 수동태 문장으로 바꿔 쓰시오.

1 My aunt makes ginger tea every morning.

→ _____ by my aunt every morning.

2 Our tennis club uses this court on Sundays.

→ _____ by our tennis club on Sundays.

3 My classmates planted these trees last week.

→ _____ by my classmates last week.

4 The man operated a lighthouse on the coast.

→ _____ by the man.

5 On the ranch, the worker feeds the cows.

→ On the ranch, _____ by the worker.

6 The school will rent the convention center.

→ _____ by the school.

연습문제 B 다음 문장을 괄호 안의 지시대로 바꿔 쓰시오.

1 The living room was cleaned by my dad. (부정문으로)

→ _____ by my dad.

2 Pork dishes are served in the restaurant. (의문문으로)

→ _____ in the restaurant?

3 The movie is liked by Ms. Lee's children. (부정문으로)

→ _____ by Ms. Lee's children.

4 All the windows were closed before you left. (의문문으로)

→ _____ before you left?

5 The wall of the church was painted by Leonardo da Vinci. (부정문으로)

→ _____ by Leonardo da Vinci.

6 Her old computer was donated to the charity. (when 의문문으로)

→ _____ to the charity?

기출 적중문제 🎯

다음 우리말을 알맞게 영작한 것은?

① 그 도둑들은 경찰에 의해 잡혔다.

= The thieves were catch by the police.

② 그 연구는 과학자들에 의해 검토되지 않았다.

= The study didn't reviewed by scientists.

③ 그 계획은 많은 사람들에 의해 의논되었다.

= The plan was discussed by many people.

④ 그 바이올린은 그 박물관에 의해 소유된다.

= The violin is owned to the museum.

⑤ 다리는 그 회사에 의해 건설되었다.

= A bridge was building by the company.

수동태 문장은
「주어 + be동사 + p.p.(과거분사)」
의 형태예요.

1. 목적어를 가지지 않는 1형식·2형식 동사는 수동태로 쓸 수 없다.

1형식   The bus (was arrived, **arrived**) at the station. 그 버스가 정류장에 도착했다.

2형식   Jenny (was remained, **remained**) calm. Jenny는 계속 평정심을 지켰다.

(Tip) 다음은 수동태로 쓸 수 있을 것 같지만 수동태로 쓸 수 없는 1형식·2형식 동사이다.

> arrive   remain   stay   happen   appear   disappear

(Tip) 다음은 의미와 형태를 혼동하기 쉬운 동사들로, 목적어를 가지지 않는 동사는 수동태로 쓸 수 없음에 주의한다.

수동태를 쓸 수 없는 동사	수동태를 쓸 수 있는 동사
rise – rose – risen 오르다	raise – raised – raised 키우다
lie – lay – lain 눕다, 놓여있다	lay – laid – laid 눕히다, 놓다
fall – fell – fallen 떨어지다	fell – felled – felled 넘어뜨리다

She (was risen, **was raised**) in the city. 그녀는 도시에서 키워졌다.
The baby (was lain, **was laid**) on the bed. 아기가 침대에 눕혀졌다.

2. 목적어를 가지는 동사 중에서도 상태를 나타내는 동사는 수동태로 쓸 수 없다.

> resemble 닮다   fit 적합하다   lack 부족하다   cost 비용이 들다   have 가지다

Mark **resembles** his father. (O) Mark는 그의 아버지를 닮았다.
His father **is resembled** by Mark. (X)

연습문제 괄호 안에서 알맞은 것을 고르시오.

1   The meal (costs / is cost) $12 per person.

2   The unfortunate accident (happened / was happened) unexpectedly.

3   The kite (rose / was risen) high in the sky.

4   A friend of mine (appeared / was appeared) on television once.

5   The dog (was risen / was raised) on a farm.

6   The area (was lacked / lacked) enough rain for many plants.

7   Linda's plane (arrived / was arrived) over an hour ago.

8   Many people (remained / was remained) after the concert was over.

9   The blanket (was lain / was laid) across the bed.

10   I was worried because my passport (disappeared / was disappeared).

기출로 적중 POINT 3 · 수동태의 시제

정답 p.12

수동태의 시제는 be동사가 있는 문장과 같이 be동사로 시제를 나타낸다.

❶ 단순시제

현재	am/is/are + p.p.	Bananas **are grown** in tropical regions. 바나나는 열대 지역에서 재배된다.
과거	was/were + p.p.	This huge statue **was built** in 1455. 이 거대한 조각상은 1455년에 세워졌다.
미래	will + be + p.p.	Dinner **will be prepared** soon. 저녁식사가 곧 준비될 것이다.

❷ 진행시제

현재진행	am/is/are + being + p.p.	The brochures **are being printed** now. 그 책자들은 지금 인쇄되는 중이다.
과거진행	was/were + being + p.p.	The elevator **was being repaired**. 그 엘리베이터는 수리되는 중이었다.

❸ 완료시제

현재완료	have/has + been + p.p.	This phone **has been used** since last year. 이 전화기는 작년부터 사용되어 왔다.
과거완료	had + been + p.p.	The TV **had been fixed** when I arrived. 내가 도착했을 때 그 TV는 수리되어 있었다.

연습문제 A 다음 능동태 문장을 수동태로 바꿔 쓰시오.

1 A postal worker brings the mail every afternoon.

→ The mail _____ by a postal worker every afternoon.

2 Benjamin has grown carrots since he was 20.

→ Carrots _____ by Benjamin since he was 20.

3 Our teacher will provide the necessary study materials.

→ The necessary study materials _____ by our teacher.

4 The school is not accepting applications now.

→ Applications _____ by the school now.

5 Many teenagers loved Nicky's first movie.

→ Nicky's first movie _____ by many teenagers.

6 He had locked the door before we arrived.

→ The door _____ by him before we arrived.

7 The band is playing her favorite song right now.

→ Her favorite song _____ by the band right now.

8 The researchers will estimate the world's 2100 population.

→ The world's 2100 population _____ by the researchers.

9 Lightning has struck the tall tree.

→ The tall tree _____ by lightning.

10 She was sorting items in the garage all weekend.

→ Items _____ by her in the garage all weekend.

11 The gardener has watered all of the plants in the front yard.

→ All of the plants in the front yard _____ by the gardener.

연습문제 B 우리말과 같도록 괄호 안의 말을 활용하여 문장을 완성하시오.

1 몇 분 후에 디저트가 제공될 것이다. (will, serve)

= Desserts _____ in a few minutes.

2 그 조리법은 그 요리사에 의해 작년부터 개발되어 왔다. (have, develop)

= The recipe _____ by the chef since last year.

3 진호가 도착했을 때 그 창문은 깨져 있었다. (have, break)

= The window _____ when Jinho arrived.

4 어제 그 연설이 끝난 후 긴 토론이 그 학생들에 의해 열렸다. (hold)

= A long discussion _____ by the students after the speech yesterday.

5 지금 몇몇 소프트웨어가 설치되고 있기 때문에 네트워크가 작동이 안 된다. (be, install)

= The network is down because some software _____ now.

기출 적중문제 🎯

다음 문장을 수동태로 바꿔 쓰시오.

> Carl has composed more than ten songs.
>
> → _____
>
> _____

> 능동태 문장을 수동태 문장으로
> 바꿀 때, 동사는 수동태
> 문장의 주어의 인칭과 수에
> 일치시켜야 해요.

기출로적중 POINT 4 조동사가 있는 수동태

정답 p.13

조동사가 있는 수동태는 조동사와 be동사가 있는 문장과 같은 방법으로 만든다.

❶ 조동사가 있는 수동태는 「조동사 + be + p.p.」 형태로 쓴다.

We **can protect** the environment. 우리는 환경을 보호할 수 있다.

→ The environment **can be protected**. 환경은 보호될 수 있다.

You **must return** the book tomorrow. 너는 그 책을 내일 반납해야 한다.

→ The book **must be returned** tomorrow. 그 책은 내일 반납되어야 한다.

❷ 조동사가 있는 수동태 문장의 의문문은 「조동사 + 주어 + be + p.p. ~?」 형태로 쓴다.

The milk **should be kept** in the refrigerator. 그 우유는 냉장고에 보관되어야 한다.

→ **Should** the milk **be kept** in the refrigerator? 그 우유는 냉장고에 보관되어야 하니?

The film **will be released** next week. 그 영화는 다음 주에 개봉될 것이다.

→ **Will** the film **be released** next week? 그 영화는 다음 주에 개봉될 것이니?

연습문제 | 다음 능동태 문장을 수동태로 바꿔 문장을 완성하시오.

1 You should take your smartphone to the repair shop.

→ Your smartphone _____ to the repair shop.

2 Dr. Park will conduct the chemistry experiment.

→ The chemistry experiment _____ by Dr. Park.

3 You must enter the password to open the file.

→ The password _____ to open the file.

4 You should put the cup on the shelf.

→ The cup _____ on the shelf.

5 People can solve these problems.

→ These problems _____ by people.

6 We should leave her alone for a while.

→ She _____ alone for a while.

7 I can finish the assignment within this week.

→ The assignment _____ within this week.

8 You may use oil instead of butter when making this dish.

→ Oil _____ instead of butter when making this dish.

4형식 문장의 수동태

정답 p.13

1. 4형식 문장은 목적어가 2개이므로 각 목적어를 주어로 하는 두 가지 형태의 수동태 문장을 만들 수 있다. 이때 직접 목적어가 주어인 수동태 문장의 경우 간접 목적어 앞에 **to/for/of** 중 하나를 쓴다.

Matt gave **Sam helpful advice**. Matt은 Sam에게 유용한 조언을 해주었다.
　　　　　　간접 목적어　　　직접 목적어

간접 목적어가 주어 → **Sam was given helpful advice** by Matt.
　　　　　　　　　　　Sam은 Matt에 의해 유용한 조언을 받았다.

직접 목적어가 주어 → **Helpful advice was given to Sam** by Matt.
　　　　　　　　　　　유용한 조언이 Matt에 의해 Sam에게 주어졌다.

2. 직접 목적어가 주어인 수동태 문장에서 대부분 간접 목적어 앞에 전치사 to를 쓰지만, 동사에 따라 전치사 for나 of를 쓰기도 한다.

to를 쓰는 동사	give, send, bring, show, teach, tell, write, read, lend, pay, sell, offer
for를 쓰는 동사	make, buy, cook, get, find, build, choose, fix
of를 쓰는 동사	ask, inquire, require, request

The new robot **was shown to** an audience by him.
그 새로운 로봇이 그에 의해 관중들에게 보여졌다.

A birthday cake **was made for** Minsu by me. 생일 케이크가 나에 의해 민수에게 만들어졌다.

Many questions **were asked of** us by the reporter.
많은 질문들이 그 기자에 의해 우리에게 물어졌다.

(Tip) send, bring, write, read, make, buy, cook, get 등의 동사가 사용된 4형식 문장의 경우 주로 직접 목적어를 수동태 문장의 주어로 쓴다.

My father sent me **a present**. 나의 아버지가 나에게 선물을 보냈다.
→ **A present** was sent to me by my father. 선물이 나의 아버지에 의해 나에게 보내졌다.

연습문제 A | 괄호 안에서 가장 알맞은 것을 고르시오.

1 A storybook was read (to / of) the children by the teacher.

2 The new sofa was bought (for / to) us by my aunt.

3 A free gift was offered (to / of) Danny by the shop.

4 Writing an article for the school magazine is required (for / of) Chris by the editor.

5 A calculator was lent (to / of) Nancy by her friend.

6 A scarf was made (for / of) Haley by Sujin.

7 The location of the Eiffel Tower was inquired (to / of) me by an old couple.

8 The costumes were chosen (for / to) the performers by the director.

9 Some letters were written (of / to) all of the children in the school.

10 A big meal was cooked (for / of) our family by my neighbor.

연습문제 B 다음 능동태 문장을 수동태로 바꿔 쓰시오.

1

I gave my grandmother some flowers.

→ My grandmother _____

by me.

→ Some flowers _____ by

me.

2

The salesclerk showed the woman a diamond ring.

→ The woman _____ by

the salesclerk.

→ A diamond ring _____

by the salesclerk.

3

The teacher taught the students Math.

→ The students _____ by

the teacher.

→ Math _____ by the

teacher.

4

A tourist asked me the direction of the train station.

→ I _____ by a tourist.

→ The direction of the train station _____

_____ by a tourist.

기출 적중문제

다음 중 어법상 바른 것을 <u>모두</u> 고르시오.

① The old television was sold to Mr. Black.

② The evidence was shown of the police.

③ A bracelet was bought to Carol.

④ My mom made a new sweater of my younger sister.

⑤ A textbook was given to him by me.

5형식 문장의 수동태

1. **목적격 보어가 명사, 형용사, to부정사, 분사인 5형식 문장을 수동태 문장으로 만들 때는 목적격 보어를 「be동사 + p.p.」 뒤에 그대로 쓴다.**

   We **elected** him **student representative**. 우리는 그를 학생 대표로 선출했다.

   → He **was elected student representative**. 그는 학생 대표로 선출되었다.

   Cathy **found** the book **interesting**. Cathy는 그 책이 흥미롭다고 생각했다.

   → The book **was found interesting** by Cathy. 그 책은 Cathy에 의해 흥미롭다고 생각되었다.

   They **asked** her **to give** a speech. 그들은 그녀에게 연설을 해달라고 요청했다.

   → She was **asked to give** a speech. 그녀는 연설을 해달라고 요청받았다.

   People **observed** the soldiers **marching**. 사람들은 그 군인들이 행진하는 것을 목격했다.

   → The soldiers **were observed marching**. 그 군인들은 행진하는 것이 목격되었다.

2. **목적격 보어가 동사원형인 5형식 문장을 수동태 문장으로 만들 때는 동사원형을 to부정사로 바꾼다.**

   My mom **made** me **stop** crying. 나의 엄마는 내가 우는 것을 멈추게 했다.

   → I **was made to stop** crying by my mom. 나는 나의 엄마에 의해 우는 것이 멈춰졌다.

   I **saw** James **play** soccer. 나는 James가 축구하는 것을 보았다.

   → James **was seen to play** soccer by me. James는 나에 의해 축구하는 것이 보여졌다.

연습문제 다음 능동태 문장을 수동태로 바꿔 문장을 완성하시오.

1 My dad painted our house yellow.

→ Our house ＿＿＿＿＿＿＿＿＿＿＿＿＿＿＿＿＿＿＿ by my dad.

2 She asked me to do the dishes.

→ I ＿＿＿＿＿＿＿＿＿＿＿＿＿＿＿＿＿＿＿ by her.

3 Yejin's classmates considered Yejin a good friend.

→ Yejin ＿＿＿＿＿＿＿＿＿＿＿＿＿＿＿＿＿ by Yejin's classmates.

4 He saw a deer jump across the stream.

→ A deer ＿＿＿＿＿＿＿＿＿＿＿＿＿＿＿＿＿ by him.

5 The judge made the man pay a fine.

→ The man ＿＿＿＿＿＿＿＿＿＿＿＿＿＿＿＿＿ by the judge.

6 Michael heard Anna sing on the stage.

→ Anna ＿＿＿＿＿＿＿＿＿＿＿＿＿＿＿＿＿ by Michael.

구동사의 수동태

정답 p.13

두 개 이상의 단어로 이루어진 구동사를 수동태로 쓰는 경우, 동사만 「be동사 + p.p.」의 형태로 쓰고 나머지 부분은 동사 뒤에 그대로 쓴다.

take care of ~를 돌보다	→	**be taken** care of ~가 돌보아지다
pick up ~를 태우다	→	**be picked** up ~가 태워지다
look down on ~를 무시하다	→	**be looked** down on ~가 무시되다
turn on ~을 켜다	→	**be turned** on ~이 켜지다
put off ~을 미루다	→	**be put** off ~이 미뤄지다
laugh at ~를 보고 비웃다	→	**be laughed** at ~가 비웃어지다
set up ~을 세우다	→	**be set** up ~이 세워지다
turn down ~을 거절하다	→	**be turned** down ~이 거절되다
make use of ~을 이용하다	→	**be made** use of ~이 이용되다
speak to ~에게 말을 걸다	→	**be spoken** to ~에게 말이 걸어지다

I **took care of** my younger sister yesterday. 나는 어제 나의 여동생을 돌봤다.
→ My younger sister **was taken care of** by me yesterday.
나의 여동생은 어제 나에 의해 돌보아졌다.

He **looked down on** my friend. 그는 나의 친구를 무시했다.
→ My friend **was looked down on** by him. 나의 친구는 그에 의해 무시되었다.

연습문제 두 문장의 의미가 같도록 문장을 완성하시오.

1 He turned on the stove to make noodles.

= The stove _____ by him to make noodles.

2 She puts off the house chores frequently.

= The house chores _____ by her frequently.

3 Everyone laughed at Edward when he told his story.

= Edward _____ by everyone when he told his story.

4 Marie picked up Ben from the airport.

= Ben _____ by Marie from the airport.

5 The residents set up the neighborhood committee last month.

= The neighborhood committee _____ by the residents last month.

6 People make use of smartphones everywhere around the world.

= Smartphones _____ by people everywhere around the world.

목적어가 that절인 문장의 수동태

정답 p.13

목적어가 that절인 문장은 두 가지 형태의 수동태 문장으로 만들 수 있다.

❶ that절 전체를 수동태 문장의 주어로 쓰는 형태: that절 전체가 주어 자리에 오면 주어가 길어지므로, 가주어 it을 주어 자리에 쓰고 that절은 수동태 동사 뒤에 쓴다.

People **know** that the news story was fake. 사람들은 그 보도 기사가 가짜였다는 것을 안다.
→ **That the news story was fake is known.**
→ **It is known** that the news story was fake. 그 보도 기사가 가짜였다는 것은 알려져 있다.
  가주어   진주어

❷ that절의 주어를 수동태 문장의 주어로 쓰는 형태: that절의 주어를 주어 자리에 쓰고 that절의 동사를 to부정사로 바꾼다.

People **say** that onions prevent cancer. 사람들은 양파가 암을 예방한다고 말한다.
→ **Onions** are said to prevent cancer. 양파는 암을 예방한다고 말해진다.

연습문제 │ 다음 능동태 문장을 수동태 문장으로 바꿔 문장을 완성하시오.

1 They thought that the test would be difficult.

→ It _____.

2 Everyone said that the information was outdated.

→ The information _____.

3 People believe that spirits live in natural objects.

→ It _____.

4 They report that polar bears are suffering due to the hot weather.

→ Polar bears _____ due to the hot weather by them.

5 People know that Neil Armstrong walked on the moon.

→ It _____.

6 People say that eating too much salt raises blood pressure.

→ Eating too much salt _____.

7 We expected that the coach would praise us for a good game today.

→ It _____ for a good game today by us.

8 People thought that the painting was destroyed in a fire long ago.

→ The painting _____ in a fire long ago by people.

정답 p.13

다음은 자주 사용되는 수동태 관용 표현이다.

be known as	~으로서 알려져 있다	be made of	~으로 만들어지다 (재료 성질이 변하지 않음)
be known to	~에게 알려져 있다	be made from	~으로 만들어지다 (재료 성질이 변함)
be known for	~으로 유명하다	be interested in	~에 흥미가 있다
be filled with	~으로 가득 차 있다	be remembered for	~으로 기억되다
be covered with	~으로 덮여 있다	be disappointed at	~에 실망하다
be pleased with	~에 기뻐하다	be used to + 동사원형	~을 하는 데 사용되다
be satisfied with	~에 만족하다	be supposed to + 동사원형	~을 하기로 되어 있다

Our house **is made of** bricks. 우리의 집은 벽돌로 만들어졌다.
I **am satisfied with** my grade. 나는 나의 성적에 만족한다.

(Tip) 「be used to + 동사원형」과 형태는 비슷하지만 의미가 다른 표현
 ① 「used to + 동사원형」: ~하곤 했다
   They **used to drink** tea after lunch. 그들은 점심 이후에 차를 마시곤 했다.
 ② 「be used to + V-ing」: ~에 익숙하다
   He **is used to waking** up early in the morning. 그는 아침에 일찍 일어나는 것에 익숙하다.

연습문제 괄호 안에서 알맞은 것을 고르시오.

1 The master key is used (to / at) open all locks in the building.

2 The pancakes are filled (by / with) nuts and berries.

3 Her parents are interested (by / in) collecting stamps.

4 Paris is known (as / to) the City of Light.

5 My father was pleased (in / with) his gray suit.

6 The bus was supposed (to / in) arrive at 4:30 P.M.

7 Kim Yuna is remembered (to / for) her wonderful skating skills.

8 We were disappointed (at / to) the design of the new tablet computer.

9 The paper in the notepad is made (from / of) wood.

10 Benny's hands are covered (for / with) dust and mud.

11 Daegu is known (for / to) its hot and humid weather.

서술형 대비 문제

A 밑줄 친 부분이 어법상 맞으면 O를 쓰고, 틀리면 바르게 고쳐 쓰시오.

1 The festival <u>was held</u> by the city government.　　　→ _____

2 The video application <u>is enjoyed</u> by the young.　　　→ _____

3 The washing machine <u>is being repairing</u> by the repair person now.　→ _____

4 The order <u>has delivered</u> already.　　　→ _____

5 Jeremy <u>was risen</u> by his grandmother when he was a kid.　→ _____

6 The distribution of donated clothing <u>was done</u> by volunteers.　→ _____

7 A basketball <u>was brought</u> by Eunji.　　　→ _____

8 Should the assignment <u>given</u> to the teacher by Friday?　→ _____

9 The groceries <u>were lay</u> on the counter by my mom.　→ _____

B 다음 문장을 수동태로 바꿔 쓰시오.

1 The chefs prepare each meal for customers.
→ Each meal _____ for customers.

2 Charles hasn't revised the essay on Shakespeare.
→ The essay on Shakespeare _____.

3 The scientists developed this technology last year.
→ This technology _____ last year.

4 Jiho is organizing a party for his friend who is moving.
→ A party _____ for his friend who is moving.

5 The pianist will play the famous song in the concert.
→ The famous song _____ in the concert.

6 The photographer has uploaded the pictures to the school's Web page.
→ The pictures _____ by the photographer.

7 She made these brownies and cookies for her daughter.
→ These brownies and cookies _____ for her daughter.

8 His many talents may shock his parents.
→ His parents _____.

C 다음은 Brooks Catsup Bottle에 대한 글이다. 괄호 안의 동사를 활용하여 빈칸에 알맞은 말을 쓰시오.

Collinsville, Illinois, is ⓐ_____(know) the Brooks Catsup Bottle, which claims to be the largest ketchup bottle in the world. It is ⓑ_____(make) steel and located on the side of the road near the town. The ketchup bottle is a water tank and is ⓒ_____(fill) water, which it supplies to a local factory. The tourists who visited were ⓓ_____(please) the attraction. And many people now stop to visit the 21-meter ketchup bottle during trips.

D 다음 문장을 괄호 안의 지시대로 바꿔 쓰시오.

1 Harry turned down the opportunity to study abroad. (수동태 문장으로)

→ _____

2 People say that luck comes to those who look after it. (luck이 주어인 수동태 문장으로)

→ _____

3 We know that fruits are helpful for our bodies. (fruits가 주어인 수동태 문장으로)

→ _____

4 They thought that Mount Everest was impossible to climb. (it이 주어인 수동태 문장으로)

→ _____

5 People believed that the Earth was flat. (the Earth가 주어인 수동태 문장으로)

→ _____

6 Calvin takes care of the elderly neighbor. (수동태 문장으로)

→ _____

7 France gave America the Statue of Liberty. (the Statue of Liberty가 주어인 수동태 문장으로)

→ _____

8 Jordan helped me move the heavy boxes. (수동태 문장으로)

→ _____

9 Daniel sent me a gift on my birthday. (a gift가 주어인 수동태 문장으로)

→ _____

중간·기말고사 실전 문제

1 다음 중 수동태로 바꿀 수 <u>없는</u> 것을 <u>모두</u> 고르시오.

① She has most of her money in a savings account.
② The villagers in this region make their huts from palm leaves.
③ Jenny threw a stone into the river.
④ This magazine provides a lot of information.
⑤ Carl appears angry because of the long wait time.

2 다음 중 수동태로 바르게 바꾼 것은?

① They know that luxury products are expensive.
→ Luxury products are known to have been expensive.
② Everyone says that oranges prevent colds.
→ Oranges are saying to prevent colds.
③ We expect that Sunho will become a lawyer.
→ It is expected to Sunho will become a lawyer.
④ They believe that society is getting more equal.
→ Society is believed to get more equal.
⑤ People reported that the popular toy was sold out.
→ It was reported that the popular toy was sold out.

3 우리말과 같도록 괄호 안의 말을 활용하여 문장을 완성하시오.

> 그 기차는 엔진 문제 때문에 지연되었다. (delay)

= The train _____ because of engine problems.

4 다음 문장을 수동태 문장으로 바꿔 쓰시오.

> Researchers found many insect species in the Amazon rainforest.
>
> → _____
> _____ by researchers.

[5-6] 두 문장의 의미가 같도록 문장을 완성하시오.

5

> He never speaks until someone speaks to him.
> = He never speaks until he _____
> _____.

6

> The citizens make use of this bicycle path.
> = This bicycle path _____
> _____.

7 다음 중 어법상 어색한 것은?

① The players were trained by a newly hired coach.
② Many islands were discovered by Christopher Columbus.
③ Serious injuries can be prevented by wearing seatbelts.
④ Only one piece of candy was remained in the jar.
⑤ Fortune-tellers are asked about the future.

8 우리말과 같도록 주어진 <조건>에 맞게 문장을 완성하시오.

그 뮤지컬은 국립 극장에서 공연되는 중이다.

<조건>
1. 현재진행시제로 쓰시오.
2. the musical, play를 활용하시오.

= _____ in the National Theater.

9 다음 중 어법상 어색한 것은?

① The computer should be fixed today.
② The mail has to be sent before noon.
③ The bowls were put in the cupboard by the cooks.
④ This special opportunity must not be missed.
⑤ Those library books should organize on the shelf by the employees.

10 괄호 안의 말을 알맞게 배열하여 문장을 완성하시오.

The garden party _____ _____ every May. (by, held, is, the neighbors)

11 다음 문장을 수동태로 바르게 바꾼 것을 모두 고르시오.

The fitness center will give members a 50 percent discount.

① Members will be given a 50 percent discount by the fitness center.
② Members will be given to a 50 percent discount by the fitness center.
③ A 50 percent discount will be given members by the fitness center.
④ A 50 percent discount will be given for members by the fitness center.
⑤ A 50 percent discount will be given to members by the fitness center.

12 다음 우리말을 알맞게 영작한 것은?

그 파일들은 기술자에 의해 복구되었다.

① A technician was recovering the files.
② The files recovered by a technician.
③ The files were recovering by a technician.
④ A technician was recovered the files.
⑤ The files were recovered by a technician.

[13-15] 우리말과 같도록 괄호 안의 말을 활용하여 문장을 완성하시오.

13

새로운 다리가 내년에 한강 위에 지어질 것이다. (build)

= A new bridge _____ over Hangang next year.

14

그 범인은 어제 경찰에 의해 잡혔다. (catch)

= The criminal _____ by the police yesterday.

15

찰리 채플린의 코미디는 수십 년 동안 보여져 왔다. (show)

= Charlie Chaplin's comedies _____ _____ for decades.

16 다음 문장을 수동태로 바꿔 쓰시오.

The store doesn't offer that type of wallet.

→ _____

_____

17 우리말과 같도록 괄호 안의 말을 알맞게 배열하시오.

나는 나의 친구들에 의해 침착하게 있으라는 말을 들었다. (calm, I, to, was, by, told, stay, my friends)

= _____

18 다음 중 문장의 태를 잘못 바꾼 것은?

① Mr. Cho grows pears at the farm.
  → Pears are grown at the farm by Mr. Cho.
② Julie didn't commit the crime.
  → The crime wasn't committed by Julie.
③ Jim brought me a cute puppy.
  → A cute puppy was brought for me by Jim.
④ I have stored the letters in this drawer.
  → The letters have been stored in this drawer by me.
⑤ They translated the book from Korean to Russian.
  → The book was translated from Korean to Russian by them.

19 우리말과 같도록 괄호 안의 말을 활용하여 문장을 완성하시오.

사막에서는 선글라스가 쓰여야 한다. (have to, wear)

= Sunglasses _____ in the desert.

20 다음 문장을 수동태로 바꿔 쓰시오.

> The postal service doesn't deliver dangerous goods.
>
> → _____
>
> _____

21 다음 우리말을 알맞게 영작한 것은?

> 자동차는 독일에서 1880년대부터 운전되어왔다.

① Cars have been drove in Germany since the 1880s.
② Cars have being drove in Germany since the 1880s.
③ Cars have been driven in Germany since the 1880s.
④ Cars have been driving in Germany since the 1880s.
⑤ Cars have being driven in Germany since the 1880s.

22 다음 밑줄 친 부분을 바르게 고친 것을 <u>모두</u> 고르시오.

> ⓐ The country <u>does not</u> visited by tourists due to safety issues.
>   (→ is not)
> ⓑ The movie <u>was resembled</u> something I read in a book. (→ resembled)
> ⓒ The butter is <u>been melted</u> in the pan.
>   (→ being melt)
> ⓓ The price of gasoline will <u>raise</u> in June. (→ be risen)

① ⓐ, ⓑ
② ⓐ, ⓒ
③ ⓑ, ⓓ
④ ⓑ, ⓒ
⑤ ⓒ, ⓓ

23 우리말과 같도록 괄호 안의 말을 활용하여 빈칸에 쓰시오.

> Justin은 아프리카 문화에 흥미가 있다. (interest)

= _____ _____ _____

_____ African culture.

24 다음 빈칸에 들어갈 말이 순서대로 짝지어진 것은?

> · A toy robot was bought _____ the kid by Mr. Lee.
> · Instructions were given _____ the students by the teacher.

① for – to
② of – to
③ for – of
④ of – for
⑤ to – for

25 다음 중 문장의 태를 바르게 바꾼 것은?

① Dana lent me an umbrella.
  → An umbrella was lent me by Dana.
② She heard someone knock on the door.
  → Someone was hearing to knock on the door by her.
③ Matthew told me to take a look at his notes.
  → I was told take a look at Matthew's notes by him.
④ The members put off the movie club meeting until next week.
  → The movie club meeting was put off the members until next week.
⑤ Many people don't know his real name.
  → His real name isn't known by many people.

26 다음 중 밑줄 친 부분이 어법상 어색한 것은?

① Textbooks for school were gotten <u>for</u> the kids by Ms. Choi.

② A hundred dollars is paid <u>to</u> the driver by the bus company every day.

③ Burritos are being cooked <u>for</u> all the guests.

④ The address was asked <u>of</u> me by the mailman.

⑤ Balloons were brought <u>of</u> the children by the clown.

27 다음 문장을 가주어 it을 사용한 수동태 문장으로 바꿔 쓰시오.

> Everyone thought that the choir was magnificent.
> → It _____
> _____ .

28 다음 중 밑줄 친 부분이 어법상 어색한 것은?

① Allison's new dress <u>is made of</u> delicate silk.

② Her face <u>was filled with</u> excitement when she got off the plane.

③ My family <u>is satisfied for</u> the new interior decoration.

④ This restaurant <u>is known for</u> its fried noodles.

⑤ The student information <u>is supposed to</u> be protected by a password.

29 다음 두 문장의 의미가 같도록 문장을 완성하시오.

> The teacher made Jane memorize at least 30 vocabulary words a day.
> = Jane _____
> _____ .

30 다음 중 문장의 태를 잘못 바꾼 것은?

① He was asked to join our golf team by me.
> → I asked him to join our golf team.

② The reporter called Terry a hero.
> → Terry was called a hero by the reporter.

③ I saw a small bird fly over Jeff's house.
> → A small bird was seen to fly over Jeff's house by me.

④ David helped me prepare lunch.
> → I was helped preparing lunch by David.

⑤ Sunlight makes tomatoes grow faster.
> → Tomatoes are made to grow faster by sunlight.

31 우리말과 같도록 괄호 안의 말을 알맞게 배열하시오.

> 그는 그의 친구들에 의해 컴퓨터에 관한 전문가로 여겨진다. (an, considered, expert, he, is)

= _____ on computers by his friends.

32 다음 빈칸에 들어갈 말이 순서대로 짝지어진 것은?

- He saw a mysterious creature jump over the fence.
  → A mysterious creature was seen _____ over the fence by him.
- Sujin heard the wind blowing through the grass.
  → The wind was heard _____ through the grass by Sujin.

① to jump - blown
② to jump - blowing
③ to jump - blow
④ jumping - blown
⑤ jumped - blowing

33 다음 글의 밑줄 친 ⓐ~ⓔ 중 어법상 <u>어색한</u> 것을 찾아 기호를 쓰고 바르게 고쳐 쓰시오.

I read a story called *The Last Leaf*. It ⓐ<u>was written</u> by O. Henry. The main character was an artist suffering from an illness. From her window, she could see a tree. She thought that her life ⓑ<u>was connected</u> to the last leaf on the tree. When it ⓒ<u>was fallen</u> due to the heavy winds, she would die. She ⓓ<u>was use to</u> spending her days watching that leaf. But it never dropped, as it turned out to ⓔ<u>be made of</u> paint. Her friend had painted it on the wall, saving her life.

(1) _____ → _____
(2) _____ → _____

34 다음 John의 일기를 보고 지문에 나온 단어를 활용하여 문장을 완성하시오.

Date: Monday, October 30
Weather: Cloudy
I made a huge mistake today. I thought today was Halloween! I went to school all dressed up, and my friends laughed at me for my Superman costume. I was so embarrassed!

→ John _____ for his Superman costume by his friends.

35 괄호 안의 말을 알맞게 배열하여 문장을 완성하시오.

The loud music _____ my brother. (on, turned, by, was)

36 다음 중 문장의 태를 잘못 바꾼 것은?

① We will preserve the land for future generations.
→ The land will be preserved for future generations by us.

② The instructor is teaching the members of the class how to swim.
→ The members of the class are being taught how to swim by the instructor.

③ The pirates buried the treasure in a cave.
→ The treasure was buried in a cave by the pirates.

④ Ms. Lee got the little kid a new hat.
→ A new hat is got for the little kid by Ms. Lee.

⑤ An engineer is updating the computer right now.
→ The computer is being updated by a technician right now.

37 다음 중 어법상 어색한 것은?

① A mailbox was installed on the wall.
② I was glad to hear that a nanny would be hired sometime soon.
③ The television has been broken last week.
④ In recent years, stress has been linked to various diseases.
⑤ Old water pipes in my neighborhood are being replaced with new ones.

38 다음 빈칸에 들어갈 알맞은 것은?

> A journey across the Pacific _____ in one month by the captain.

① could be completed
② could complete
③ could be completing
④ could being completed
⑤ could been completed

39 다음 글의 빈칸에 공통으로 들어갈 알맞은 것은?

> Today is Christmas Day. This morning, I found a gift box under my small Christmas tree. The box was covered _____ pink wrapping paper. My brother and I opened it together. The box was filled _____ our favorite candies and chocolates. We were both very pleased _____ the gift.

① with   ② to   ③ by
④ in   ⑤ at

40 다음 중 어느 빈칸에도 들어갈 수 없는 것은?

> · We are supposed _____ be home already.
> · Eric is interested _____ professional wrestling.
> · My new coat is made _____ leather.
> · He was disappointed _____ the weather.

① of   ② for   ③ to
④ in   ⑤ at

41 우리말과 같도록 괄호 안의 말을 활용하여 빈칸에 쓰시오.

크로아티아는 아름다운 해변들로 유명하다. (know)

= Croatia _____ _____
_____ its beautiful beaches.

42 다음 문장을 수동태로 바르게 바꾼 것을 모두 고르시오.

People say that blood is thicker than water.

① Blood is said to be thicker than water.
② Blood is said that thicker than water.
③ It is said that blood is thicker than water.
④ It says that blood is thicker than water.
⑤ People are said that blood is thicker than water.

43 괄호 안의 말을 알맞게 배열하여 문장을 완성하시오.

Robert _____
his family. (to, Bobby, as, known, is)

44 다음 중 어법상 어색한 것을 모두 고르시오.

① A map of Ulleungdo was given to us by the tour guide.
② A box of fresh doughnuts was bought to us by Rachel.
③ The puppet was made to dance on the stage.
④ My request for help turned down by Brad.
⑤ The news website was set up by a group of professional web designers.

45 다음 문장을 주어진 지시대로 바꿔 쓰시오.

The teacher divided the class into two sections.

(1) 수동태 문장으로
→ _____
_____

(2) 수동태 부정문으로
→ _____
_____

(3) 수동태 의문문으로
→ _____
_____

CHAPTER 5
부정사

To read a book is my hobby.　책을 읽는 것은 나의 취미이다.

I have a book **to read**.　나는 읽을 책을 가지고 있다.

I went to a library **to read** a book.　나는 책을 읽기 위해 도서관에 갔다.

동사 read 앞에 to가 붙어 '읽는 것', '읽을', '읽기 위해'라는 의미를 나타냈어요. 이렇게 동사 앞에 to를 붙인 「to + 동사원형」의 형태를 to부정사라고 하며, to부정사는 문장 안에서 명사·형용사·부사 역할을 할 수 있어요.

기출로 적중 POINT

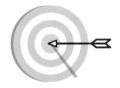

내신 100점 적중!
기출 출제율

to부정사의 형태와 용법, 4.0%

명사적 용법: 주어와 보어로 쓰이는 to부정사, 14.3%

to부정사의 의미상의 주어, 19.1%

too ~ to, enough to, 9.0%

명사적 용법: 목적어로 쓰이는 to부정사, 24.8%

부사적 용법, 10.3%

형용사적 용법: be동사 + to부정사, 1.4%

명사적 용법: 의문사 + to부정사, 13.7%

형용사적 용법: 명사·대명사 수식, 3.4%

TOP 1 명사적 용법: 목적어로 쓰이는 to부정사 (24.8%)
to부정사가 목적어로 쓰이는 동사를 묻는 문제가 자주 출제된다.

TOP 2 to부정사의 의미상의 주어 (19.1%)
to부정사의 의미상의 주어를 쓰는 경우 「for + 목적격」 형태와 「of + 목적격」
형태를 구별하는 문제가 자주 출제된다.

TOP 3 명사적 용법: 주어와 보어로 쓰이는 to부정사 (14.3%)
to부정사가 주어와 보어로 쓰인 문장의 어순과 형태를 묻는 문제가 자주 출제
된다.

to부정사의 형태와 용법

정답 p.16

1. **to부정사는 「to + 동사원형」의 형태이다. to부정사의 부정형은 to 앞에 not을 붙인 「not to + 동사원형」이다.**

   To study math is difficult. 수학을 공부하는 것은 어렵다.
   Jinsu decided **not to stay** home. 진수는 집에 머물지 않기로 결정했다.

2. **to부정사는 문장 안에서 명사·형용사·부사 역할을 한다.**

명사적 용법	명사처럼 문장의 주어·목적어·보어로 쓰인다. **To lie** is a bad thing. 거짓말하는 것은 나쁜 것이다. I hope **to get** a better grade. 나는 더 좋은 점수를 받는 것을 희망한다. His dream is **to receive** a gold medal. 그의 꿈은 금메달을 받는 것이다.
형용사적 용법	형용사처럼 명사·대명사를 수식하거나 보어로 쓰인다. It is an easy **question to answer**. 그것은 대답하기 쉬운 질문이다. Peter appeared **to be** in a good mood. Peter는 기분이 좋아 보인다.
부사적 용법	부사처럼 동사·형용사·부사·문장 전체를 수식하는 데 쓰인다. He **studied to pass** the test. 그는 시험을 통과하기 위해 공부했다. This oven is **easy to use**. 이 오븐은 사용하기 쉽다. She was nice **enough to help** me. 그녀는 나를 도와줄 만큼 착했다. **To build** a fence, **I need some tools**. 울타리를 만들기 위해서, 나는 몇몇 도구가 필요하다.

연습문제 밑줄 친 to부정사의 쓰임을 <보기>에서 골라 그 기호를 쓰시오.

<보기> ⓐ 명사적 용법 ⓑ 형용사적 용법 ⓒ 부사적 용법

1 To pay taxes is an important duty for all citizens. [   ]
2 Mary woke up early to go to church. [   ]
3 He brought me some snacks to eat. [   ]
4 The author's plan is to write three new novels next year. [   ]
5 I was disappointed not to hear the news. [   ]
6 I want someone to talk to about my concerns. [   ]
7 We agreed to help the old woman next door. [   ]
8 She wore gloves not to hurt her hands while gardening. [   ]
9 He didn't buy the book because he already had books to read. [   ]

POINT 2-1 명사적 용법: 주어와 보어로 쓰이는 to부정사

정답 p.16

1. **to부정사는 명사처럼 주어로 쓰이며, '~하는 것'의 의미이다. to부정사가 쓰인 주어는 항상 단수 취급한다.**

   To raise pets **is** hard. 애완동물을 키우는 것은 어렵다.
   To make brownies **takes** time. 브라우니를 만드는 것은 시간이 걸린다.

   (Tip) to부정사구가 주어 자리에 와서 주어가 길어진 경우, 주어 자리에 가주어 it을 쓰고 to부정사구를 문장 맨 뒤로 보낼 수 있다.
   To swim in the ocean is dangerous. 바다에서 수영하는 것은 위험하다.
   = **It** is dangerous **to swim in the ocean**.

2. **to부정사는 명사처럼 주어와 목적어를 보충 설명하는 보어로 쓰인다.**

   주격 보어   **My goal** is **to run** my own restaurant. 나의 목표는 내 소유의 음식점을 운영하는 것이다.
   목적격 보어 He advised **Jane** **to eat** vegetables. 그는 Jane에게 채소를 먹으라고 조언했다.

연습문제 | 밑줄 친 to부정사의 쓰임을 <보기>에서 골라 그 기호를 쓰시오.

<보기>   ⓐ 주어   ⓑ 주격 보어   ⓒ 목적격 보어

1 To design musical costumes is Amy's job.   [   ]

2 He doesn't want his friends to know about his science test score.   [   ]

3 Bella's dream is to become a flight attendant.   [   ]

4 It is hard to keep my white shoes clean every day.   [   ]

5 Jake's idea was to find a part-time job over the summer vacation.   [   ]

6 My dad allows me to use his laptop on weekends.   [   ]

7 Mina's plan was to travel to Spain for her holiday.   [   ]

8 It is annoying to catch a taxi when traffic is bad.   [   ]

9 I told my mom to wait outside.   [   ]

10 The teacher encouraged the students to focus during the class.   [   ]

11 To spend time with friends makes me happy.   [   ]

12 The doctor's advice was to go to bed as early as possible.   [   ]

13 The manager told the visitors to stand in line.   [   ]

14 It is useful to learn a foreign language these days.   [   ]

15 Sora asked us to read the passage quickly.   [   ]

1. to부정사는 명사처럼 목적어로 쓰인다.

He planned **to fix** his old bicycle. 그는 그의 오래된 자전거를 고치는 것을 계획했다.

They hope **to see** a full moon tonight. 그들은 오늘 밤 보름달을 보기를 바란다.

2. 다음 동사들은 to부정사를 목적어로 쓴다.

want	promise	fail	wish	plan	choose
decide	agree	learn	need	hope	expect
refuse	aim	manage			

I **want to buy** a new coat. 나는 새로운 코트를 사기를 원한다.

Can you **promise to come** to my birthday party?
너는 나의 생일 파티에 올 것을 약속할 수 있니?

Sujin **decided to go** to the theater. 수진이는 영화관에 가기로 결정했다.

연습문제 A 우리말과 같도록 괄호 안의 말을 활용하여 문장을 완성하시오.

1 사람들은 때때로 어떠한 노력 없이 무언가를 배우기를 기대한다. (expect, learn)

= People sometimes _____ something without any effort.

2 나는 이 자전거를 James에게 팔기로 결정했기 때문에 그에게 전화할 것이다. (sell, decide)

= Because I _____ this bicycle to James, I will call him.

3 우리는 병원에 계신 나의 삼촌을 방문하기로 정했다. (visit, choose)

= We _____ my uncle in the hospital.

4 우리 기관은 부모님을 잃은 아이들을 도와주는 것을 목표로 한다. (aim, help)

= Our agency _____ kids who have lost their parents.

5 나의 친구들과 나는 토요일에 만나는 것에 동의했다. (meet, agree)

= My friends and I _____ on Saturday.

6 당신은 저에게 그 과제에 대한 구체적인 세부사항들을 말씀해주셔야 합니다. (need, tell)

= You _____ me the specific details about the assignment.

7 그는 다음 주 주말에 그의 할머니를 방문하기를 원한다. (want, visit)

= He _____ his grandmother next weekend.

8 나는 너에게 빌렸던 책을 돌려주는 것을 약속한다. (return, promise)

= I _____ the book that I borrowed from you.

9 나의 남동생은 언젠가 우주 비행사가 되기를 바란다. (hope, become)

= My little brother _____ an astronaut one day.

10 우리는 오늘 오후에 공원에 소풍 가기로 계획했다. (plan, have)

= We _____ a picnic at the park this afternoon.

연습문제 B 다음 그림을 보고 <보기>와 괄호 안의 말을 활용하여 문장을 완성하시오. (단, 과거시제를 쓰시오.)

<보기> refuse   wish   fail   learn   choose   manage

1 We _____ at the airport on time. (arrive)

2 The boy _____ by practicing with a coach. (swim)

3 My baseball team _____ the game. (win)

4 He _____ the test because he didn't study hard. (pass)

5 Ben _____ her an umbrella. (lend)

6 Jessie _____ fish instead of steak. (order)

기출 적중문제

다음 중 어법상 바른 것은?

① She refused reading science fiction when she was young.

② The researcher managed to translate the ancient language.

③ The bird failed to building a nest under my roof.

④ The organization aims reduce air pollution.

⑤ Mr. Ryan decided to performing magic tricks for the children.

명사적 용법: 의문사 + to부정사

「의문사 + to부정사」는 명사처럼 주어, 목적어, 보어로 쓰이며, 의문사에 따라 '무엇을, 어떻게, 어디서, 어느 것을, 언제, 누구를[누구에게] ~할지'를 의미한다.

what 무엇을	where 어디서	when 언제		
how 어떻게	which 어느 것을	who[whom] 누구를[누구에게]	+	to부정사 ~할지

주어 **Where to stay** on vacation is an important consideration.
휴가 중에 어디서 머물 것인지는 중요한 고려 사항이다.

목적어 I don't know **where to catch** a bus. 나는 버스를 어디서 타는지 모른다.

보어 My concern is **how to start** my project. 나의 걱정은 나의 과제를 어떻게 시작할지이다.

(Tip) 「의문사 + to부정사」는 「의문사 + 주어 + should + 동사원형」으로 바꿔 쓸 수 있다.

Steven forgot **when to submit** his application. Steven은 그의 신청서를 언제 제출할지 잊어버렸다.
= Steven forgot **when he should submit** his application.

연습문제 | 우리말과 같도록 괄호 안의 말을 활용하여 문장을 완성하시오.

1 점심 식사로 무엇을 먹을 것인지는 항상 어려운 결정이다. (eat)

= _____ for lunch is always a difficult decision.

2 Roy는 체육관에 언제 갈지에 대해 생각하는 중이다. (go)

= Roy is thinking about _____ to the gym.

3 너는 나에게 그 로봇을 어떻게 조립하는지 가르쳐 줄 수 있니? (assemble)

= Can you teach me _____ the robot?

4 나의 엄마는 내가 로마로 여행하는 동안 누구에게 전화할지 나에게 말해주었다. (call)

= My mom told me _____ during my trip to Rome.

기출 적중문제

다음 우리말을 알맞게 영작한 것을 <u>모두</u> 고르시오.

나는 수업 후에 그에게 무엇을 말할지 잊었다.

① I forgot what tell to him after the lecture.
② I forgot what to tell him after the lecture.
③ I forgot what telling him after the lecture.
④ I forgot what I should tell him after the lecture.
⑤ I forgot what I telling him after the lecture.

「의문사 + to부정사」와 「의문사 + 주어 + should + 동사원형」은 서로 바꿔 쓸 수 있어요.

기출로적중 POINT 3-1 | 형용사적 용법: 명사·대명사 수식

정답 p.16

1. to부정사는 형용사처럼 명사나 대명사를 수식하는 데 쓰이며, '~할'의 의미이다. 이때 to부정사는 명사나 대명사를 뒤에서 수식한다.

It is **time to have** lunch. 이제 점심 먹을 시간이다.

I need **someone to support** me. 나는 나를 지지해줄 누군가가 필요하다.

2. to부정사가 수식하는 명사나 대명사가 전치사의 목적어인 경우 to부정사 뒤에 반드시 전치사를 쓴다.

The kid has **a toy to play with**. 그 아이는 (가지고) 놀 장난감이 있다.

She found **someone to take care of** while volunteering.

그녀는 봉사활동을 하는 동안 돌볼 누군가를 찾았다.

(Tip) to부정사가 수식하는 명사나 대명사가 전치사의 목적어로 쓰인 to부정사 표현

a chair to sit on (위에) 앉을 의자	someone to talk to 말할 누군가
a house to live in (안에) 살 집	someone to take care of 돌볼 누군가
paper to write on (위에) 쓸 종이	a toy to play with (가지고) 놀 장난감
a pen to write with (가지고) 쓸 펜	a spoon to eat with (가지고) 먹을 숟가락

연습문제 | 우리말과 같도록 괄호 안의 말을 활용하여 문장을 완성하시오.

1 우리의 건물에는 페인트칠할 방이 하나 더 있다. (room, paint)

= There is one more _____ in our building.

2 David는 그의 문제에 대해 말할 누군가가 필요하다. (someone, talk)

= David needs _____ about his problem.

3 그녀는 편지를 쓸 펜을 원했다. (a pen, write)

= She wanted _____ for a letter.

4 나는 택시 대신 지하철을 탈 계획에 동의했다. (the plan, take)

= I agreed with _____ the subway instead of the taxi.

5 그는 일주일 동안 살 집을 빌렸다. (a house, live)

= He rented _____ for a week.

6 그들은 그들의 여행을 위해 방문할 곳을 결정했다. (somewhere, visit)

= They decided on _____ for their trip.

형용사적 용법: be동사 + to부정사

정답 p.16

「be동사 + to부정사」는 예정, 가능, 의무, 운명, 의도의 의미를 나타낸다.

예정	~할 예정이다 (= will, be going to)	Mark **is to graduate** in February. Mark는 2월에 졸업할 예정이다.
가능	~할 수 있다 (= can)	The paintings **are to be seen** here. 그 그림들은 여기에서 볼 수 있다.
의무	~해야 한다 (= must, have to)	We **are to respect** our elders. 우리는 노인을 공경해야 한다.
운명	~할 운명이다 (= be destined to)	The Roman Empire **was to fall**. 로마 제국은 멸망할 운명이었다.
의도	~하려고 하다 (= intend to)	If you **are to succeed**, you must set a goal first. 성공하려고 한다면, 너는 먼저 목표를 설정해야 한다.

연습문제 <보기>와 같이 두 문장의 의미가 같도록 「be동사 + to부정사」를 활용하여 문장을 완성하시오.

> <보기> Fred has to clean his room.
> = Fred _is to clean_ his room.

1 Romeo and Juliet were destined to die at the end of the play.
= Romeo and Juliet _____ at the end of the play.

2 If they intend to beat their competitor, they must work together.
= If they _____ their competitor, they must work together.

3 She is going to see the dentist next week about her toothache.
= She _____ the dentist next week about her toothache.

4 A police officer could be found near the entrance.
= A police officer _____ near the entrance.

5 Students have to finish their work by Thursday.
= Students _____ their work by Thursday.

6 If you intend to stay healthy, you must exercise regularly.
= If you _____ healthy, you must exercise regularly.

7 Henry will take an exam for college.
= Henry _____ an exam for college.

POINT 4 부사적 용법

정답 p.16

1. to부정사는 부사처럼 동사, 형용사, 부사, 문장 전체를 수식하는 데 쓰인다.

동사 수식	All players should **practice to win**. 모든 선수들은 우승하기 위해 연습해야 한다.
형용사 수식	The biology textbook is **difficult to read**. 그 생물학 교과서는 읽기에 어렵다.
부사 수식	I jumped high **enough to touch** the ceiling. 나는 천장에 닿을 만큼 충분히 높이 뛰었다.
문장 전체 수식	**To get** a perfect score, **Tom** studied hard. 만점을 받기 위해서, Tom은 열심히 공부했다.

2. to부정사가 부사처럼 쓰일 때 다양한 의미를 나타낸다.

목적	~하기 위해	목적을 나타내는 경우 to대신 in order to나 so as to를 쓸 수 있다. He goes to the library **to read**. 그는 독서하기 위해 도서관에 간다. = He goes to the library **in order to[so as to] read**. I lied **not to tell** the secret. 나는 비밀을 말하지 않기 위해 거짓말했다. = I lied **in order not to[so as not to] tell** the secret.
감정의 원인	~해서, ~하니	주로 감정을 나타내는 형용사(happy, sad 등) 뒤에 쓰인다. We are happy **to meet** you. 우리는 너를 만나서 기쁘다.
판단의 근거	~하다니	주로 추측을 나타내는 조동사(must, can't 등)와 함께 쓰인다. She must be kind **to help** the patients. 환자들을 돕다니 그녀는 친절한 것이 틀림없다.
결과	(…해서 결국) ~하다	주로 grow up, live 등과 함께 쓰인다. He grew up **to become** a teacher. 그는 자라서 선생님이 되었다.
형용사 수식	~하기에	The machine is safe **to use**. 그 기계는 사용하기에 안전하다.

연습문제 A <보기>와 같이 to부정사를 이용하여 다음 두 문장을 한 문장으로 연결하시오.

> <보기> I wanted to buy snacks. I went to the supermarket.
> → I went to the supermarket *to buy snacks*.

1 Cindy wanted to learn Spanish. She signed up for a Spanish class.

→ Cindy signed up for a Spanish class _____.

2 Molly will eat some spicy food for dinner. She will stop by a Korean restaurant.

→ Molly will stop by a Korean restaurant _____.

3 He lived. He saw his grandchildren graduate from high school.

→ He lived _____.

4 She thought of such creative solutions. She must be smart.

→ She must be smart _____.

5 He constantly argues with his friends. He can't be nice.

→ He can't be nice _____.

6 Both teams were ready. They would begin the soccer game.

→ Both teams were ready _____.

7 They won the first prize in the competition. They were delighted.

→ They were delighted _____.

연습문제 B 다음 밑줄 친 부분의 의미를 <보기>에서 골라 그 기호를 쓰시오.

<보기>	ⓐ 목적(~하기 위해)	ⓑ 감정의 원인(~해서, ~하니)
	ⓒ 판단의 근거(~하다니)	ⓓ 결과((…해서 결국) ~하다)

1 Ms. Kim must be generous to donate to the orphanage.   [   ]

2 I grew up to become a loving wife and mother.   [   ]

3 To make cupcakes, I should buy some flour and butter.   [   ]

4 You must be smart to speak three different languages.   [   ]

5 Chris was annoyed to discover that his bag had been stolen.   [   ]

6 The whale lived to be 90 years old.   [   ]

7 The fruit must be spoiled to smell so bad.   [   ]

8 She was surprised to hear about the upcoming event.   [   ]

9 The marathon runners must register to run in the race.   [   ]

기출 적중문제

주어진 문장의 밑줄 친 to부정사와 쓰임이 같은 것은?

> He can't be selfish to share all of his food.

① He sometimes wears glasses to look smart.
② I waited for two hours to see the movie.
③ We have to check whether the mountain is safe to hike on.
④ She must be lucky to win the big match.
⑤ The documentary was edited to reduce its length.

판단의 근거를 나타내는 to부정사는 주로 추측을 나타내는 조동사(must, can't 등)와 함께 쓰여요.

POINT 5 · too ~ to, enough to

정답 p.16

1. 「too + 형용사/부사 + to부정사」는 '…하기에 너무 ~한/~하게'라는 의미로, 「so + 형용사/부사 + that + 주어 + can't/couldn't + 동사원형」으로 바꿔 쓸 수 있다.

   My cat is **too** fat **to** run. 나의 고양이는 달리기에 너무 뚱뚱하다.
   = My cat is **so** fat **that it can't run**. 나의 고양이는 너무 뚱뚱해서 달릴 수 없다.

2. 「형용사/부사 + enough + to부정사」는 '…할 만큼 충분히 ~한/~하게'라는 의미로, 「so + 형용사/부사+ that + 주어 + can/could + 동사원형」으로 바꿔 쓸 수 있다.

   Minsu is small **enough to hide** in the closet. 민수는 옷장에 숨을 만큼 충분히 몸집이 작다.
   = Minsu is **so** small **that he can hide** in the closet.
   민수는 충분히 몸집이 작아서 옷장에 숨을 수 있다.

연습문제 다음 두 문장의 의미가 같도록 문장을 완성하시오.

1 Harry is so tired that he can't work on his painting today.
= Harry is _____ on his painting today.

2 The tea is hot enough to burn someone's tongue.
= The tea is _____ someone's tongue.

3 She is too busy to help me with my homework.
= She is _____ me with my homework.

4 The politician was so popular that he could win the election.
= The politician was _____ the election.

5 The slogan is too long to fit on the paper.
= The slogan is _____ on the paper.

6 The man was strong enough to lift the heavy weights.
= The man was _____ the heavy weights.

7 The apples are so ripe that they can be sold at the grocery store.
= The apples are _____ at the grocery store.

8 You are so young that you can't drive a car.
= You are _____ a car.

9 The cheetah was so fast that it could catch the zebra.
= The cheetah was _____ the zebra.

CHAPTER 5 부사 해커스 중학영문법 3학년

to부정사의 의미상의 주어

정답 p.17

1. **to부정사의 의미상의 주어는 to부정사의 동작 주체이며, to부정사의 의미상의 주어가 문장의 주어나 목적어와 다른 경우 의미상의 주어를 다음과 같이 쓴다.**

   ❶ 대부분의 경우: 「for + 목적격」의 형태로 to부정사 앞에 쓴다.

   It is difficult **for me to remember** people's faces.
   내가 사람들의 얼굴을 기억하는 것은 어렵다.

   I bought a bicycle **for my younger sister to use**. 나는 나의 여동생이 사용할 자전거를 샀다.

   ❷ 사람의 성격·태도를 나타내는 형용사와 쓰인 경우: 「of + 목적격」의 형태로 to부정사 앞에 쓴다.

kind	nice	rude	selfish	silly	generous
bad	clever	cruel	polite	thoughtful	stupid
wise	honest	foolish	careful	careless	

   It is **kind of her to donate** for the homeless. 노숙자들을 위해 기부하다니 그녀는 친절하다.
   It was **silly of you to lift** the desk alone. 그 책상을 혼자 들다니 너는 어리석었다.

2. **to부정사의 의미상의 주어가 people, we, they와 같이 일반 사람인 경우 의미상의 주어를 생략할 수 있다.**

   It is necessary **(for people) to have** confidence. (사람들이) 자신감을 가지는 것은 필수적이다.
   It is best **(for us) to be** helpful. (우리가) 도움이 되는 것이 최고이다.

연습문제 A 괄호 안에서 가장 알맞은 것을 고르시오.

1 It is easy (for / of) me to write in Korean.

2 It is polite (for / of) you to come and greet me.

3 Wasn't that careless (for / of) her to lose her passport?

4 It was thoughtful (for / of) you to send a letter to your grandmother.

5 It is too cold (for / of) me to play basketball in the park this afternoon.

6 The problem with the car was easy (for / of) the mechanic to fix.

7 It was selfish (for / of) Brian to move the furniture without asking his roommate.

8 It was wise (for / of) Mina to listen to others carefully.

9 It is safe (for / of) people to swim in this lake.

10 There was nothing (for / of) them to do when they arrived.

연습문제 B 우리말과 같도록 괄호 안의 말을 활용하여 빈칸에 쓰시오.

1 Kevin이 칠판을 보는 것은 어려웠다. (hard, see, Kevin)

= It was _____ the black board.

2 얕은 수영장으로 뛰어들다니 그들은 어리석었다. (foolish, them, dive)

= It was _____ into the shallow pool.

3 수미가 버스를 제시간에 타는 것은 중요하다. (important, take, Sumi)

= It is _____ the bus on time.

4 나는 그가 환불을 받는 것은 불가능할 것이라고 생각한다. (impossible, him, get)

= I think it would be _____ a refund.

5 그런 방식으로 행동하다니 너는 무례했다. (rude, act, you)

= It was _____ like that.

6 나에게 너의 실수를 말하다니 너는 매우 정직했다. (inform, you, honest)

= It was very _____ me of your mistake.

7 그 배우는 그가 이 역할을 맡은 것은 행운이었다고 말했다. (him, lucky, get)

= The actor said that it was _____ this role.

8 아이들이 그들의 부모님과 솔직하게 대화하는 것은 바람직하다. (desirable, kids, talk)

= It is _____ openly with their parents.

9 그는 아이들이 이해하기에 그 책이 쉽다는 것을 알아냈다. (understand, easy, children)

= He found the book _____ .

10 교통 규칙을 따르는 것은 필요하다. (necessary, follow)

= It is _____ the traffic rules.

11 나의 모든 친구들은 투표하는 것이 중요하다고 생각한다. (important, vote)

= All my friends think it is _____ .

기출 적중문제 🎯

다음 빈칸에 들어갈 말이 순서대로 짝지어진 것은?

· It was difficult _____ her to catch the bug.

· It is nice _____ him to help his young brother.

① for – to ② to – for ③ of – of

④ of – for ⑤ for – of

A 밑줄 친 부분이 어법상 맞으면 O를 쓰고, 틀리면 바르게 고쳐 쓰시오.

1 The Amazon Rainforest is very <u>dangerous to explore</u>. → _____

2 The coach will tell us <u>what do</u> before noon. → _____

3 It is <u>important of me</u> to make my parents happy. → _____

4 I put on sunscreen <u>not to get</u> a sunburn. → _____

5 Robin needs <u>a spoon to eat</u>. → _____

6 The flower shop <u>is to expand</u> its service to another city. → _____

7 Fall is the best season <u>to go</u> on a picnic in a park. → _____

8 The school needs <u>someone to teach</u> music lessons. → _____

9 It was very <u>kind for you</u> to give directions to the traveler. → _____

10 To write songs <u>take</u> a lot of talent. → _____

B 우리말과 같도록 괄호 안의 말을 활용하여 문장을 완성하시오.

1 그는 아이들에게 어떻게 자전거를 타는지 보여주었다. (ride, a bike)
= He showed the kids _____.

2 Robert는 30분 이내로 올 것을 약속했다. (promise, come)
= Robert _____ within 30 minutes.

3 그녀는 그녀의 고양이와 함께 살 집을 찾았다. (a house, live)
= She found _____ with her cat.

4 우리는 손님들에게 간식과 음료를 제공할 예정이다. (provide, be)
= We _____ snacks and drinks for the guests.

5 너는 질병의 위험을 최소화하기 위해 운동을 해야 한다. (minimize, exercise)
= You should _____ the risk of disease.

6 나의 친구들은 오늘 방과 후에 영화를 보러 갈 예정이다. (watch, be)
= My friends _____ a movie after school today.

7 제가 당신의 이름을 어디에 서명할지 보여줄게요. (sign, your name)
= Let me show you _____.

C 다음 그림을 보고 괄호 안의 말을 활용하여 문장을 완성하시오.

1  2  3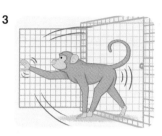

1 It was _____. (his friend, nice, him, help)

2 It was _____ on the escalator. (dangerous, the boy, run)

3 It was _____ the cage. (the monkey, clever, unlock)

D 두 문장의 의미가 같도록 문장을 완성하시오.

1 The woman was so fast that she could set a world record.

   = The woman was _____.

2 He has no idea what to show Amy.

   = He has no idea _____.

3 This lotion is mild enough to be used on a baby's skin.

   = This lotion is _____.

4 She was too hungry to continue working.

   = She was _____.

5 My alarm goes off so loudly that it can wake me up in the morning.

   = My alarm goes off _____.

6 My older sister thinks that I am so lazy that I can't answer her messages.

   = My older sister thinks that I am _____.

7 He wants to find out how to spend money wisely.

   = He wants to find out _____.

8 My family took photos to make our family album.

   = My family took photos _____.

중간·기말고사 실전 문제

1 우리말과 같도록 괄호 안의 말을 활용하여 문장을 완성하시오.

> 혜리는 그 고양이에게 먹이를 주기로 결정했다.
> (decide, feed, the cat)

= Hyeri _____.

2 다음 빈칸에 들어갈 말이 순서대로 짝지어진 것은?

> · I want my neighbors _____ the
>   music late at night.
> · Did you tell your cousin _____ us at
>   the mall?

① turn off – meet
② turn off – to meet
③ to turn off – meet
④ to turn off – to meet
⑤ to turn off – meeting

3 다음 우리말을 알맞게 영작한 것을 <u>모두</u> 고르시오.

> 나는 너무 스트레스를 받아서 그 과제를 시작할 수 없다.

① I am too stressed to start the assignment.
② I am too stressed not to start the assignment.
③ I am too stressed start the assignment.
④ I am so stressed that I can't start the assignment.
⑤ I am so stressed that I can start the assignment.

4 다음 중 어법상 <u>어색한</u> 것을 <u>모두</u> 고르시오.

① It was not easy of me to move this box.
② It is very kind of you to invite me.
③ The problem is too difficult for me to handle.
④ It was impossible for him to understand the foreign language.
⑤ It was careless for her to say that to you.

[5-6] 두 문장의 의미가 같도록 문장을 완성하시오.

5

> To prevent natural disasters is important.
> = It _____ natural disasters.

6

> Many people leave their home early to avoid traffic.
> = Many people leave their home early _____ avoid traffic.

7 다음 문장에서 어법상 <u>어색한</u> 부분을 찾아 쓰고 바르게 고쳐 쓰시오.

> All our club members expect winning this competition.

_____ → _____

8 다음 빈칸에 들어갈 알맞은 것은?

> The teacher asked me _____ my
> phone in class.

① not use   ② use not
③ not to use   ④ use not to
⑤ not to using

9 다음 두 문장의 의미가 같도록 문장을 완성하시오.

> The guide told the tourists where they
> should go.
> = The guide told the tourists _____
> _____ .

10 다음 대화의 (A)~(C)에 들어갈 말이 바르게 짝지
어진 것은?

> A: Do you know which flowers are
>   easiest to grow?
> B: Not really. Are you planning ___(A)___
>   a garden?
> A: No. I just want something for my
>   balcony. But I can't decide ___(B)___ .
> B: If you want ___(C)___ some ideas, you
>   could visit a garden center.

	(A)	(B)	(C)
①	to start	where to plant	getting
②	starting	what to plant	to get
③	to start	what to plant	to get
④	starting	where to plant	getting
⑤	to start	what to plant	getting

[11-12] 다음 글을 읽고 주어진 질문에 답하시오.

> Ants live together in a large group
> called a colony. Different ants have
> different jobs. Most ants work ⓐto
> gather food. They spend their days
> looking for something to eat. When they
> find it, they carry it back to the nest.
> (A) 다른 개미들은 둥지를 지킬 커다란 몸을 가지
> 고 있다. (large bodies, the nest, protect)
> They act like soldiers and fight other
> insects. A few ants stay inside the nest.
> Their job is to care for the eggs.

11 위 글의 밑줄 친 ⓐ의 용법과 같은 것은?

① Do you have a spoon for me to eat with?
② To work as a doctor has always been my
   dream.
③ They are looking for a nice place to stay.
④ She went back home to do the laundry.
⑤ Jason found a way to contact her.

12 위 글의 밑줄 친 우리말 (A)와 같도록 괄호 안의 말
을 활용하여 문장을 완성하시오.

= Other ants have _____
_____ .

13 다음 중 밑줄 친 to부정사의 용법이 나머지 넷과 다른 것은?

① I'm going to Paris to see the Eiffel Tower.
② Oliver was surprised to meet his friend from his hometown.
③ He must be tired to stay up all night.
④ If you want to get a good job, you must study hard.
⑤ The lawyer was excited to win the trial.

14 우리말과 같도록 괄호 안의 말을 배열할 때 세 번째에 오는 것을 쓰시오.

우리는 정오에 떠날 예정이다. (to, noon, at, are, leave, we)

→ _____

15 다음 우리말을 알맞게 영작한 것을 모두 고르시오.

Billy는 나에게 고장 난 의자를 어떻게 고치는지 보여줬다.

① Billy showed me what to fix the broken chair.
② Billy showed me what I should to fix the broken chair.
③ Billy showed me how fixing the broken chair.
④ Billy showed me how to fix the broken chair.
⑤ Billy showed me how I should fix the broken chair.

16 다음 빈칸에 들어갈 말이 순서대로 짝지어진 것은?

· To buy a house to live _____ takes a lot of effort.
· Hyunji gave her puppy a toy to play _____.

① in - to   ② in - at   ③ in - with
④ on - to   ⑤ on - with

17 우리말과 같도록 괄호 안의 말을 활용하여 문장을 완성하시오.

Robert Peary는 역사상 첫 번째로 북극점에 도달하는 것을 해냈다. (manage, the North Pole, reach)

= Robert Peary _____
_____ for the first time in history.

18 다음 빈칸에 들어갈 말이 나머지 넷과 다른 것은?

① We went to the forest in order _____ look for wild raspberries.
② We aim _____ finish setting up the campsite before lunch.
③ The winter jacket you gave me was _____ big to wear.
④ More people today choose _____ live in the city.
⑤ I told my parents about my plan _____ study abroad.

19 우리말과 같도록 괄호 안의 말을 활용하여 문장을 완성하시오.

> 셜록 홈즈 영화에는 해결할 새로운 미스터리들이 항상 있다. (solve, new mysteries)

= There are always _____
in Sherlock Holmes movies.

[20-21] 다음 글을 읽고 질문에 답하시오.

> Mr. Roper feels it is important ⓐto get along with his neighbors. (A) To become friends with him is not difficult. He always wants ⓑto help people. For example, one day my dad didn't turn his car's lights off. Mr. Roper knocked on our door ⓒtelling my dad. Also, he taught me how ⓓto use a lawn mower. It was so nice ⓔfor him to help my dad and me.
>
> *lawn mower 잔디 깎는 기계

20 위 글의 밑줄 친 ⓐ~ⓔ 중 어법상 어색한 것을 찾아 기호를 쓰고 바르게 고쳐 쓰시오.

(1) _____ → _____

(2) _____ → _____

21 위 글의 밑줄 친 (A)와 의미가 같도록 주어진 <조건>에 맞게 문장을 완성하시오.

> <조건>
> 1. 가주어 it을 사용하시오.
> 2. become, easy를 활용하시오.

= _____
friends with him.

22 다음 빈칸에 들어갈 말로 어색한 것은?

> It was _____ for the team to win the match.

① critical　　　　② wise
③ impossible　　④ necessary
⑤ important

23 다음 밑줄 친 to부정사의 용법이 같은 것끼리 묶인 것은?

> ⓐ She wishes to live in a large house.
> ⓑ Can you give me a knife and fork to eat with?
> ⓒ Everyone deserves the right to vote.
> ⓓ Kevin went to a park to watch birds.
> ⓔ He hopes to go to an art school.

① ⓐ, ⓑ　　　② ⓐ, ⓓ　　　③ ⓑ, ⓒ
④ ⓒ, ⓔ　　　⑤ ⓓ, ⓔ

[24-25] 다음 문장에서 어법상 어색한 부분을 찾아 쓰고 바르게 고쳐 쓰시오.

24

> My younger brother refused apologizing for breaking my phone.

_____ → _____

25

> I gave the students paper to write.

_____ → _____

26 다음 중 어법상 바른 것은?

① To learn to drive a car is Gary's goal.
② It was difficult me to fix your computer.
③ The siren is too loud be heard
   2 kilometers away.
④ The baby's heart beat too strongly
   enough to surprise the doctor.
⑤ It was honest for Minseo to admit her
   fault.

27 다음 밑줄 친 to부정사와 용법이 같은 것을 <u>모두</u>
고르시오.

Mark gave his dad a pen <u>to write</u> with as
a present.

① I had a chance <u>to meet</u> a famous singer.
② John is looking for someone <u>to talk</u> to
   about his grades.
③ The doctor's advice is <u>to take</u> some
   medicine for a week.
④ Chloe agreed <u>to join</u> the volunteer
   program with me.
⑤ It is necessary <u>to fix</u> the radio for my
   grandfather.

28 다음 중 어법상 <u>어색한</u> 것은?

① Alice must be hungry to eat three
   doughnuts.
② Dave promised his mother not buying
   games anymore.
③ The mango is too delicious for me to stop
   eating.
④ My teacher advised me to review the
   textbook more often.
⑤ It would be great to give a watch as a gift.

[29-30] 다음 글을 읽고 질문에 답하시오.

To the Bill & Jack Bookstore:

I am writing this letter ⓐ<u>to complain</u>
about the package you sent me. I
visited your website ⓑ<u>order</u> the book
Romeo and Juliet last week. However,
the book cover was too dirty ⓒ<u>touching</u>.
(A) Moreover, the letters in the book
were so small that they couldn't be
identified. I was also disappointed ⓓ<u>to
find</u> out that the book was
nonrefundable. Please tell me how we
can deal with this problem as I really
want ⓔ<u>to get</u> a refund.

Sarah Johnson

29 위 글의 밑줄 친 ⓐ~ⓔ 중 어법상 <u>어색한</u> 것을 찾
아 기호를 쓰고 바르게 고쳐 쓰시오.

(1) _____ → _____
(2) _____ → _____

30 위 글의 밑줄 친 (A)와 의미가 같도록 <조건>에 맞
게 문장을 완성하시오.

<조건> too를 포함하시오.

= Moreover, the letters in the book were

_____.

31 우리말과 같도록 괄호 안의 말을 배열할 때 다섯
번째에 오는 것은?

그 수영장은 수영하기에 너무 붐볐다. (to, in, too,
swim, swimming, the, crowded, pool,
was)

① in   ② pool   ③ was
④ too   ⑤ crowded

32 주어진 문장과 의미가 같은 것은?

> To finish this homework will be easy for me.

① It was easy for me to finish this homework.
② It is easy of me to finish this homework.
③ It will be easy of me to finish this homework.
④ It is easy for me to finish this homework.
⑤ It will be easy for me to finish this homework.

33 다음 밑줄 친 부분의 용법과 같은 것은?

> I was excited <u>to go</u> to the theater.

① My mother told me <u>to clean</u> my room.
② You are <u>to go</u> straight home after class.
③ It is hard for me <u>to write</u> in a journal every day.
④ The new mall next to the hospital is <u>to open</u> next week.
⑤ Jane was glad <u>to meet</u> her old friend.

34 우리말과 같도록 주어진 <조건>에 맞게 영작하시오.

> 그에게 돈을 빌려주다니 나는 어리석었다.

> **<조건>**
> 1. 9단어로 쓰시오.
> 2. 가주어 it을 사용하시오.
> 3. foolish, lend, money를 활용하시오.

= _____

_____

35 두 문장의 의미가 같도록 문장을 완성하시오.

> The man was so tall that he could reach the top shelf.
> = The man was _____ the top shelf.

36 다음 빈칸에 들어갈 말이 순서대로 짝지어진 것은?

> · Wasn't that old computer too slow _____ you to use?
> · It was polite _____ that man to open the door for us.

① of – to   ② of – for   ③ for – for
④ for – of   ⑤ to – of

37 우리말과 같도록 괄호 안의 말을 활용하여 문장을 완성하시오.

> 나는 불꽃놀이를 보기 위해 밖으로 나갔다. (go outside, watch)

= I _____ the fireworks.

CHAPTER 6
동명사

I like **drawing** cartoons. 나는 만화를 그리는 것을 좋아한다.

'그리다'라는 의미의 동사 draw를 V-ing형으로 바꿔 '그리는 것'이라는 의미를 나타냈어요. 이렇게 동사가 V-ing형으로 쓰여 문장 안에서 명사 역할을 하는 것을 **동명사**라고 해요.

기출로 적중 POINT

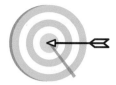

내신 100점 적중!
기출 출제율

동명사의 형태와 쓰임,
24.0%

동명사 관용 표현,
34.8%

동명사를 목적어로
쓰는 동사,
18.4%

동명사와 to부정사를
모두 목적어로 쓰는 동사,
22.8%

TOP 1 **동명사 관용 표현 (34.8%)**
동명사 관용 표현의 의미와 형태를 묻는 문제가 자주 출제된다.

TOP 2 **동명사의 형태와 쓰임 (24%)**
동명사의 형태와 쓰임을 묻는 문제가 자주 출제된다.

TOP 3 **동명사와 to부정사를 모두 목적어로 쓰는 동사 (22.8%)**
목적어로 동명사를 쓸 때와 to부정사를 쓸 때의 의미가 다른 동사를 묻는
문제가 자주 출제된다.

동명사의 형태와 쓰임

정답 p.19

1. **동명사는 V-ing의 형태이다. 동명사의 부정형은 동명사 앞에 not이나 never를 붙인 「not[never] + V-ing」의 형태이다.**

   Helping other people is meaningful. 다른 사람들을 돕는 것은 의미 있다.
   The doctor advised **not[never] eating** greasy food.
   그 의사는 기름진 음식을 먹지 않는 것을 조언했다.

2. **동명사는 문장 안에서 명사처럼 주어·목적어·보어로 쓰인다.**

주어	**Exercising** with my friends **is** fun. 나의 친구들과 함께 운동하는 것은 재미있다. **Buying** snacks **makes** me happy. 간식을 사는 것은 나를 기쁘게 한다. └→ 동명사가 쓰인 주어는 항상 단수 취급한다.
목적어	She **enjoys shopping** for baking materials. 그녀는 제빵 재료를 사는 것을 즐긴다. 동사의 목적어 Jack is interested **in watching** movies. Jack은 영화를 보는 것에 흥미가 있다. 전치사의 목적어
보어	My hobby is **growing** plants. 나의 취미는 식물을 기르는 것이다.

연습문제 우리말과 같도록 동명사와 괄호 안의 말을 활용하여 문장을 완성하시오.

1 집 안에서 너의 신발을 신지 않아줘서 고마워. (wear, your shoes)
= Thank you for _____ in the house.

2 책을 읽는 것은 윤수가 방과 후에 하기 좋아하는 것이다. (read, books, be)
= _____ what Yunsu likes to do after school.

3 베트남 음식점에 점심 먹으러 가는 것이 어떠니? (go, for lunch)
= How about _____ at the Vietnamese restaurant?

4 충분한 잠을 자지 않는 것은 너의 건강을 해치는 방법 중 하나이다. (get, enough sleep, be)
= _____ one of the ways to ruin your health.

5 내가 정말 좋아하는 것은 학기 초에 새로운 사람들을 만나는 것이다. (meet, new people)
= What I really like is _____ at the beginning of the semester.

6 Jack은 새 스마트폰을 사달라고 그의 부모님을 설득하는 것을 시도했다. (persuade, his parents)
= Jack tried _____ to buy him a new smartphone.

POINT 2 동명사의 의미상의 주어

정답 p.19

동명사의 의미상의 주어는 동명사의 동작 주체이다. 동명사의 의미상의 주어가 문장의 주어와
다른 경우 보통 「소유격 + V-ing」의 형태로 의미상의 주어를 나타낸다.

I don't mind **his opening** the window. 나는 그가 창문을 여는 것을 신경 쓰지 않는다.
I like **Jessie's singing** for me. 나는 Jessie가 나를 위해 노래 부르는 것을 좋아한다.

(Tip) 동명사의 의미상의 주어가 무생물 명사 또는 부정대명사인 경우 소유격으로 쓸 수 없으므로 목적격으로 쓴다.

I look forward to **the movie** being released. 나는 그 영화가 개봉하기를 기대한다.
He worried about **all of them** arriving late. 그는 그들 모두가 늦는 것을 걱정했다.

연습문제 | <보기>와 같이 두 문장의 의미가 같도록 문장을 완성하시오.

<보기> I respect that my little sister tries her best.
　　　 = I respect *my little sister's trying her best* .

　　　 He is certain that his dad received the letter.
　　　 = He is certain of *his dad's receiving the letter* .

---

1 I always enjoy that he cooks dinner for me.
= I always enjoy _____ .

2 I felt sorry that my mom lost her bag at the store.
= I felt sorry for _____ .

3 She was proud that Billy won a trophy at the science contest.
= She was proud of _____ .

4 Jim is aware that Daniel plays the piano well.
= Jim is aware of _____ .

5 I was annoyed that a child made a noise.
= I was annoyed by _____ .

6 He doesn't like that his older sister eats her food loudly.
= He doesn't like _____ .

7 Mr. Lee was disappointed that his son failed his math exam.
= Mr. Lee was disappointed at _____ .

8 Nancy is grateful that her friend helps her study.
= Nancy is grateful for _____ .

1. **동명사의 시제가 문장의 시제와 같거나 미래를 나타내는 경우 단순형인 「V-ing」를 쓰고, 동명사의 시제가 문장의 시제보다 이전인 경우 완료형인 「having + p.p.」를 쓴다.**

단순형	V-ing	I like **reading** short stories. 나는 단편 소설을 읽는 것을 좋아한다. She is sure of **winning** the contest tomorrow. 그녀는 내일 대회에서 우승하는 것을 확신한다.
완료형	having + p.p.	Jacob apologized for **having missed** my call. Jacob은 나의 전화를 받지 못했던 것에 대해 사과했다.

2. **동명사의 의미가 능동인 경우 능동형인 「V-ing」를 쓰고, 동명사의 의미가 수동인 경우 수동형인 「being + p.p.」를 쓴다.**

능동형	V-ing	He considered **moving** to France next year. 그는 내년에 프랑스로 이사 가는 것을 고려했다.
수동형	being + p.p.	Emily is certain of **being accepted** into college. Emily는 대학 입학이 받아들여질 것으로 확신한다.

연습문제 우리말과 같도록 괄호 안의 말을 활용하여 문장을 완성하시오.

1 나의 언니는 두 시간 동안 기다렸던 것에 화가 났다. (wait)

= My older sister is angry about _____ for two hours.

2 그녀는 한국을 대표하도록 선택된 것을 자랑스러워 한다. (choose)

= She is proud of _____ to represent Korea.

3 준수는 그의 키에 대해 질문을 받는 것에 싫증이 났다. (ask)

= Junsu is tired of _____ about his height.

4 그는 어제 농구 경기에서 규칙을 어겼던 것을 부인한다. (break)

= He denies _____ the rules in the basketball game yesterday.

5 몇몇 아이들은 심지어 겨울에도 양말 신는 것을 싫어한다. (wear)

= Some kids hate _____ socks even in winter.

6 나는 그날 Lisa와 이야기하는 것을 피했다. (talk)

= I avoided _____ to Lisa that day.

7 그 달리기 선수는 초보자에게 졌던 것을 인정하지 않는다. (defeat)

= The runner does not admit _____ by a rookie.

기출로적중 POINT 4 동명사를 목적어로 쓰는 동사

정답 p.19

다음 동사들은 동명사를 목적어로 쓴다.

enjoy	avoid	finish	keep	mind	admit	practice	suggest
quit	deny	imagine	resist	dislike	postpone	consider	recommend

My older brother **practices playing** soccer every day. 나의 형은 매일 축구하는 것을 연습한다.
I **finished climbing** to the top of the mountain. 나는 그 산의 꼭대기까지 오르는 것을 마쳤다.

(Tip) 동명사를 목적어로 쓰는 동사의 목적어 자리에 to부정사는 쓰지 않는다.
Most owls **avoid** (~~to hunt~~, **hunting**) in the daytime. 대부분의 부엉이는 낮에 사냥하는 것을 피한다.

연습문제 | 우리말과 같도록 괄호 안의 말을 활용하여 문장을 완성하시오.

1 그는 탄산음료 마시는 것을 끊었다. (quit, drink)
= He _____ soda.

2 나는 점심 이후에 낮잠을 위해 집에 가는 것을 제안했다. (suggest, go)
= I _____ home for a nap after lunch.

3 그녀는 큰 무대에서 공연하는 것을 상상할 수 없다. (imagine, perform)
= She _____ on a big stage.

4 선생님은 그녀의 학생들에게 쪽지시험을 내기로 결심했다. (decide, give)
= The teacher _____ her students a pop quiz.

5 의사는 점심 이후까지 그의 환자를 만나는 것을 연기할 것이다. (postpone, meet)
= The doctor _____ his patient until after lunch.

6 나는 언젠가 파리에 사는 것을 바란다. (hope, live)
= I _____ in Paris one day.

기출 적중문제

다음 글에서 어법상 어색한 부분을 두 군데 찾아 쓰고 바르게 고쳐 쓰시오.

I recommend to visit La Tomatina, a tomato
festival in Spain. People enjoy throw tomatoes at
each other, and it is really fun.

(1) _____ → _____
(2) _____ → _____

POINT 5 — 동명사와 to부정사를 모두 목적어로 쓰는 동사 정답 p.19

다음 동사들은 동명사와 to부정사 둘 다 목적어로 쓸 수 있다.

❶ 목적어로 동명사를 쓸 때와 to부정사를 쓸 때의 의미가 같은 동사

start	begin	love	like	hate	continue	prefer	intend

We **began painting[to paint]** our house yesterday.
우리는 어제 우리의 집을 페인트칠하는 것을 시작했다.

Hyeju **likes writing[to write]** letters to her friends.
혜주는 그녀의 친구들에게 편지를 쓰는 것을 좋아한다.

❷ 목적어로 동명사를 쓸 때와 to부정사를 쓸 때의 의미가 다른 동사

forget	동명사	(과거에) ~한 것을 잊다	He **forgot taking** the medicine. 그는 약을 먹은 것을 잊었다.
	to부정사	(미래에) ~할 것을 잊다	He **forgot to take** the medicine. 그는 약을 먹을 것을 잊었다.
remember	동명사	(과거에) ~한 것을 기억하다	I **remembered calling** her. 나는 그녀에게 전화한 것을 기억했다.
	to부정사	(미래에) ~할 것을 기억하다	I **remembered to call** her. 나는 그녀에게 전화할 것을 기억했다.
regret	동명사	~한 것을 후회하다	I **regret informing** you of the problem. 나는 너에게 그 문제를 알린 것을 후회한다.
	to부정사	~하게 되어 유감이다	I **regret to inform** you of the problem. 나는 너에게 그 문제를 알리게 되어 유감이다.
try	동명사	(시험 삼아) ~해보다	She **tried lifting** the box. 그녀는 시험 삼아 그 박스를 들어올려 보았다.
	to부정사	~하려고 노력하다	She **tried to lift** the box. 그녀는 그 박스를 들어올리려고 노력했다.

Tip 「stop + 동명사」(~하는 것을 멈추다)에서 동명사는 stop의 목적어이며, 「stop + to부정사」(~하기 위해 멈추다)에서 to부정사는 부사적 용법으로 쓰여 목적을 나타낸다.
Danny **stopped cleaning** his desk. Danny는 그의 책상을 치우는 것을 멈췄다.
Danny **stopped to clean** his desk. Danny는 그의 책상을 치우기 위해 멈췄다.

연습문제 A 괄호 안에서 알맞은 것을 <u>모두</u> 고르시오.

1 Helen loves (visiting / to visit) her grandparents' home in downtown Miami.

2 They resisted (opening / to open) the box on the table.

3 Some people dislike (spending / to spend) money on things they don't really need.

4 The sunflowers continued (growing / to grow) until they were two meters tall.

5 I practiced (diving / to dive) every day in the pool.

6 The children started (singing / to sing) on the school bus.

연습문제 B 우리말과 같도록 괄호 안의 말을 활용하여 문장을 완성하시오.

1 나는 수업에 나의 과학책을 가져가야 하는 것을 잊었다. (forget, bring)

= I _____ my science book to class.

2 그녀는 그 서랍에 그녀의 전화기를 둔 것을 기억하지 못했다. (remember, put)

= She didn't _____ her phone in the drawer.

3 그는 그의 시계를 고치려고 노력했지만, 그것을 할 수 없었다. (try, fix)

= He _____ his watch, but he couldn't do it.

4 나는 처음으로 비행기를 탄 것을 절대 잊지 못할 것이다. (forget, take)

= I will never _____ an airplane for the first time.

5 Alice는 어젯밤에 늦게 잔 것을 후회한다. (regret, go)

= Alice _____ to bed late last night.

6 아무도 그 오븐에서 피자를 꺼내야 하는 것을 기억하지 못했다. (remember, take)

= No one _____ the pizza out of the oven.

7 나의 여동생은 그녀의 손목을 다쳤기 때문에 테니스 치는 것을 멈췄다. (stop, play)

= My younger sister _____ tennis because she hurt her wrist.

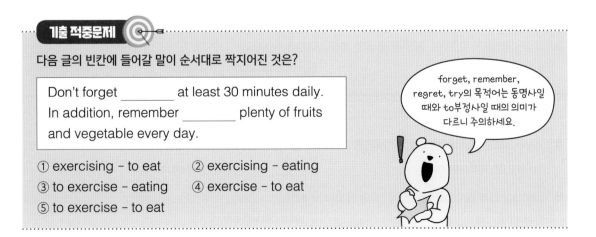

기출 적중문제

다음 글의 빈칸에 들어갈 말이 순서대로 짝지어진 것은?

> Don't forget _____ at least 30 minutes daily.
> In addition, remember _____ plenty of fruits and vegetable every day.

① exercising – to eat   ② exercising – eating

③ to exercise – eating   ④ exercise – to eat

⑤ to exercise – to eat

forget, remember, regret, try의 목적어는 동명사일 때와 to부정사일 때의 의미가 다르니 주의하세요.

동명사 관용 표현

정답 p.19

1. 다음은 전치사의 목적어로 동명사를 쓰는 관용 표현이다.

be afraid of + V-ing ~하는 것을 두려워하다
be good at + V-ing ~을 잘하다
be interested in + V-ing ~하는 것에 흥미가 있다
be used to + V-ing ~하는 것에 익숙하다
be tired of + V-ing ~하는 것에 싫증이 나다
be sorry for + V-ing ~하는 것에 대해 유감이다
feel like + V-ing ~하고 싶다
by + V-ing ~함으로써, ~해서

How[What] about + V-ing? ~하는 게 어때?
look forward to + V-ing ~하는 것을 기대하다
end up + V-ing 결국 ~하게 되다
thank … for + V-ing ~에 대해 …에게 감사하다
when it comes to + V-ing ~하는 것에 관한 한
dream of + V-ing ~하는 것을 꿈꾸다
on + V-ing ~하자마자

(Tip) 동명사 관용 표현에 쓰인 to는 to부정사가 아닌 전치사 to이므로 뒤에 동사원형을 쓰지 않는다.
Peter was looking forward to (live, **living**) in the city. Peter는 그 도시에 사는 것을 기대하고 있었다.

2. 다음은 동명사를 쓰는 관용 표현이다.

be worth + V-ing ~할 가치가 있다
be busy + V-ing ~하느라 바쁘다
cannot help + V-ing ~하지 않을 수 없다
have difficulty[trouble] + V-ing ~하는 것에 어려움[문제]이 있다

go + V-ing ~하러 가다
It is no use + V-ing ~해도 소용 없다
spend + 시간/돈 + V-ing ~하는 데 시간/돈을 쓰다

연습문제 A 우리말과 같도록 동명사 관용 표현과 괄호 안의 말을 활용하여 문장을 완성하시오.

1 나는 축구 연습 후에 간식을 먹지 않을 수 없다. (eat)

= I ＿＿＿＿＿＿＿＿＿＿＿＿＿＿＿ snacks after soccer practice.

2 그는 많은 사람들 앞에서 말하는 것을 두려워한다. (speak)

= He ＿＿＿＿＿＿＿＿＿＿＿＿＿＿＿ in front of a lot of people.

3 그녀는 이집트에 방문하는 것과 낙타를 타는 것을 기대한다. (visit)

= She ＿＿＿＿＿＿＿＿＿＿＿＿＿＿＿ Egypt and riding on a camel.

4 네가 바꿀 수 없는 것들에 대해 걱정해도 소용 없다. (worry)

= ＿＿＿＿＿＿＿＿＿＿＿＿＿＿＿ about things you cannot change.

5 초록색 버튼을 눌러서 기계를 켜라. (press)

= Turn on the machine ＿＿＿＿＿＿＿＿＿＿＿＿＿＿＿ the green button.

6 Henry는 그의 왼쪽 귀로 듣는 것에 어려움이 있다. (hear)

= Henry ＿＿＿＿＿＿＿＿＿＿＿＿＿＿＿ with his left ear.

7 집에 도착하자마자 나는 부엌에서 이상한 냄새가 나는 것을 알아챘다. (arrive)

= _____ home, I noticed there was a weird smell in the kitchen.

8 나는 수영하는 것에 관한 한 실내 수영장을 선호한다. (swim)

= I prefer an indoor pool _____ .

연습문제 B | 다음 그림을 보고 <보기>와 괄호 안의 동사를 활용하여 문장을 완성하시오.

<보기>	go + V -ing	how about + V -ing	be good at + V -ing
	be busy + V -ing	be tired of + V -ing	be used to + V -ing

1

2

3

4

5

6

1 _____ pizza for lunch? (have)

2 My mom _____ the plants in the garden now. (water)

3 She _____ to her little brother's boring stories. (listen)

4 Susan _____ her own clothes and accessories. (design)

5 I _____ with my parents yesterday. (camp)

6 My younger sister _____ her bike yet. (ride)

기출 적중문제 🎯

다음 중 어법상 어색한 것은?

① She ended up buying a product she had never tried before.

② The sunrise over the beach was worth watching.

③ I feel like going for a walk in the park this afternoon.

④ He was used to studying with other students.

⑤ Are you interested at going to the museum tomorrow?

A 밑줄 친 부분이 어법상 맞으면 O를 쓰고, 틀리면 바르게 고쳐 쓰시오.

1 Speaking to people in other countries <u>are</u> rather easy today. → _____

2 I don't mind <u>my little brother's using</u> my laptop. → _____

3 He got praised <u>for having helped</u> his neighbors last month. → _____

4 <u>Being eaten</u> too much sugar can cause health problems. → _____

5 My favorite thing about summer vacation is <u>having not</u> classes. → _____

6 My nephew does not <u>like treating</u> like a baby. → _____

7 <u>Becoming an astronomer was</u> my dad's childhood dream. → _____

8 She was surprised <u>at inviting</u> to the concert. → _____

9 <u>Writing songs are</u> not an easy task. → _____

B 우리말과 같도록 <보기>와 괄호 안의 말을 활용하여 문장을 완성하시오.

<보기>	enjoy	continue	forget	postpone	try	dislike	begin

1 그녀는 그녀의 여동생과 영화 보러 가는 것을 즐긴다. (go to the movies)
= She _____ with her younger sister.

2 그는 다음 주에 요가 수업을 듣기 시작할 것이다. (take yoga lessons)
= He will _____ next week.

3 Chris는 강한 냄새 때문에 마늘 먹는 것을 싫어했다. (eat garlic)
= Chris _____ because of the strong smell.

4 대호는 오늘 아침에 재즈 음악을 들어 보았다. (listen to jazz music)
= Daeho _____ this morning.

5 나는 어젯밤 나의 휴대폰을 충전해야 하는 것을 잊었다. (charge my cell phone)
= I _____ last night.

6 나의 형은 내년에 프랑스어 공부하는 것을 계속할 것이다. (study French)
= My older brother will _____ next year.

7 우리는 태풍 때문에 하와이에 가는 것을 미뤘다. (go to Hawaii)
= We _____ because of a typhoon.

ⓒ 우리말과 같도록 괄호 안의 말을 알맞게 배열하시오.

1 Brian은 수학 문제를 푸는 것을 잘한다. (solving, is, at, math problems, good)
= Brian _____ .

2 나의 아빠는 종종 주말 동안 낚시를 하러 간다. (fishing, weekends, during, goes)
= My dad often _____ .

3 오늘 밤 연극에 와 주셔서 감사합니다. (for, coming, you, thank)
= _____ to the play tonight.

4 민호는 학교의 토론팀에 들어가는 것에 흥미가 있다. (interested, the school's debate team, in, joining, is)
= Minho _____ .

5 나의 가족은 다음 달에 너를 만날 것을 기대한다. (to, you, meeting, forward, looks)
= My family _____ next month.

6 제빵사들은 결혼식 케이크를 장식하느라 바쁘다. (the wedding cake, busy, are, decorating)
= The bakers _____ .

7 그녀는 그의 생일 파티를 놓친 것에 대해 유감이다. (is, birthday party, missing, his, for, sorry)
= She _____ .

8 그는 언젠가 스페인으로 여행가는 것을 꿈꾸었다. (one day, Spain, traveling, of, dreamed, to)
= He _____ .

ⓓ 다음 글의 빈칸에 괄호 안의 말을 활용하여 알맞은 말을 쓰시오.

Jenna loves volleyball!

ⓐ_____(play) volleyball at the Olympics ⓑ_____(be) Jenna's goal. Her coach thinks ⓒ_____(she) playing is good enough. However, she worries about not ⓓ_____(have, start) training earlier. To make up for this, she practices daily. Hopefully, Jenna's wish will come true.

Sarah's problem

ⓔ_____(on, arrive) at school, Sarah noticed that she ⓕ_____(forget, bring) her textbook. She ⓖ_____(consider, ask) her mother to bring it, but there was not enough time. Therefore, she ended up ⓗ_____(share) the book with her classmate sitting next to her.

중간 · 기말고사 실전 문제

1 다음 빈칸에 들어갈 말이 순서대로 짝지어진 것은?

> · The chore I dislike most is _____ out the garbage.
> · Texting to friends _____ not allowed during class.

① taking – are   ② taking – is
③ took – is   ④ took – are
⑤ taken – is

2 다음 중 밑줄 친 부분이 어법상 <u>어색한</u> 것을 <u>모두</u> 고르시오.

> ①<u>Listen</u> to music is fun. However, many people don't like ②<u>to hear</u> the same songs repeatedly. For them, the key to finding new music is ③<u>using</u> streaming services. These services analyze listener preferences, and recommend similar songs. So all you need to do is ④<u>to listen</u> to the songs suggested by the service. Having access to new songs ⑤<u>make</u> it more entertaining because there is always something new.

3 우리말과 같도록 괄호 안의 말을 활용하여 문장을 완성하시오.

> 나는 예지에게 나의 숙제를 도와달라고 부탁했던 것을 인정했다. (ask, Yeji, admit, I)

= _____ to help
me with my homework.

4 다음 우리말을 알맞게 영작한 것은?

> 그는 보여지는 것을 피하기 위해 나무 뒤에 숨었다.

① He hid behind a tree avoid to be seen.
② He hid behind a tree to avoid being seen.
③ He hid behind a tree to avoid seeing.
④ He hid behind a tree to avoid been seen.
⑤ He hid behind a tree to avoid to be seen.

5 다음 (A)~(C)에 들어갈 말이 바르게 짝지어진 것은?

> · I couldn't resist _____(A)_____ the gift before my older brother got home.
> · We will continue _____(B)_____ after lunch.
> · Mr. Jenkins forgot _____(C)_____ me copies of the pictures he took, so I don't have them yet.

	(A)	(B)	(C)
①	opening	working	sending
②	to open	working	to send
③	opening	to work	sending
④	opening	to work	to send
⑤	to open	working	sending

6 다음 우리말을 영작한 것 중 어색한 것은?

① 너는 언제 태권도 연습하는 것을 시작했니?
   = When did you start practicing taekwondo?

② 그는 그 책상 위에 그의 안경을 올려놓은 것을 잊었다.
   = He forgot putting his eyeglasses on the desk.

③ 그녀는 냉동실에서 고기를 꺼내야 하는 것을 기억했다.
   = She remembered to take the meat out of the freezer.

④ 그들은 그 프로젝트를 금요일까지 완료하려고 노력할 것이다.
   = They will try to finish the project by Friday.

⑤ 나는 그 배드민턴팀을 위해 시험을 본 것을 후회하지 않는다.
   = I don't regret to try out for the badminton team.

7 다음 글의 밑줄 친 ⓐ~ⓔ 중 어법상 어색한 부분을 세 군데 찾아 기호를 쓰고 바르게 고쳐 쓰시오.

The purpose of the police force is ⓐprevent crime. However, ⓑaccomplishing this task can be difficult. Stopping crime ⓒmean officers need to have control over people. But many community members worry about ⓓgiving them too much power. They feel that ⓔnot limit officers' authority can lead to abuses.

(1) _____ → _____
(2) _____ → _____
(3) _____ → _____

8 다음 빈칸에 들어갈 알맞은 것은?

비닐 봉투가 환경에 미치는 영향 때문에, 나는 그것들을 사용하는 것을 멈췄다.
= Because of plastic bags' impact on the environment, I've stopped _____ them.

① not using
② to use
③ using
④ used
⑤ use

[9-10] 다음 대화의 밑줄 친 우리말과 같도록 괄호 안의 말을 활용하여 영작하시오.

9

A: Carl, 다음 주말에 스키 타러 가는 게 어때?
   (next weekend, ski, go, how)
B: That's a great idea. I'd love to go.

= _____
_____

10

A: Do you want some more of this chicken curry?
B: No, thanks. 나는 매운 음식을 먹는 것에 익숙하지 않아. (eat, spicy food, use)

= _____
_____

11 다음 글의 밑줄 친 부분이 어법상 어색한 것은?

①Seeing handmade blankets reminds me of my grandmother. Her favorite hobby was ②quilting. Turning scraps of fabric into beautiful blankets ③was her talent. I even remember ④she winning awards for it. I wish I had her skill. I tried ⑤doing it once, but the final result was not as good as hers.

*scrap 종이 옷감의 조각

12 다음 중 어법상 어색한 것은?

① We dream of opening our own restaurant someday.
② Do you mind waiting at the café for me?
③ Dentists recommend to brush your teeth three times a day.
④ Jason started to snore loudly once he fell asleep.
⑤ The Chicago Tigers kept beating higher-rated teams.

13 다음 대화를 읽고 괄호 안의 말을 활용하여 빈칸에 알맞은 말을 쓰시오.

Minji : You used my computer yesterday, didn't you?
Yunsu: No, I didn't.

→ Yunsu denied _____ _____ _____. (use, Minji's computer)

14 우리말과 같도록 괄호 안의 말을 활용하여 영작하시오.

Nick은 시험 삼아 일주일 동안 고기를 먹지 않는 것을 해봤다. (try, eat, meat, for a week)

= _____

15 다음 (A)~(C)에 들어갈 말이 바르게 짝지어진 것은?

· We intend ___(A)___ for a solution to the problem at the next meeting.
· Please stop ___(B)___ with your phone in class because it is too noisy.
· My friends finished ___(C)___ the movie.

	(A)	(B)	(C)
①	to look	playing	to watch
②	looking	to play	watching
③	to look	playing	watching
④	looking	playing	to watch
⑤	to look	to play	watching

16 <보기>의 말을 활용하여 빈칸에 알맞은 말을 쓰시오.

<보기> cook   watch   provide

Masterchef is one of the world's most popular television shows. There are versions of it in 40 countries. The show is famous because people enjoy ⓐ_____ cooks compete. They also like to practice ⓑ_____ the dishes from the show. This is possible because the show has begun ⓒ_____ its recipes online.

17 다음 문장에서 어법상 어색한 부분을 찾아 쓰고 바르게 고쳐 쓰시오.

> Janet postponed to write a script for the musical that she will take a role in.

_____ → _____

18 다음 중 어법상 바른 것의 개수는?

> ⓐ Andy can't imagine to leave his hometown for college.
> ⓑ You should continue taking the medicine even after you begin to feel better.
> ⓒ We plan arriving before the ceremony starts.
> ⓓ Doris is considering taking French lessons from next month.
> ⓔ I can't quit playing video games every day.

① 1개　　② 2개　　③ 3개
④ 4개　　⑤ 5개

19 괄호 안의 말을 활용하여 빈칸에 알맞은 말을 쓰시오.

> A: Hi, Jen. Could you do me a favor? I forgot ⓐ_____(say) that I have an appointment with my doctor today. I need someone to tell the teacher why I won't be in class.
> B: Oh, I can notify him for you.
> A: Thanks so much.
> B: No problem. Just remember ⓑ_____(ask) me for the assignments later.

20 다음 대화의 밑줄 친 부분이 어법상 어색한 것은?

> A: Samantha, can you finish ①making our slide show by this afternoon?
> B: Sure. I'll try ②to get it done by then.
> A: Great! You'll need to send it to Laura for ③edit when you finish.
> B: Um... I keep ④losing her e-mail address. Do you know what it is?
> A: No, but ⑤finding it in the student directory shouldn't be hard. Just search for Laura Lieu.
> B: OK. I'll check that.

21 다음 우리말을 영작한 것 중 어색한 것은?

① 나의 엄마는 호두 파이를 만드는 것을 좋아한다.
   = My mom likes making walnut pies.
② Mark는 잠들지 않을 수 없었다.
   = Mark couldn't help fall asleep.
③ 그녀는 비가 그친 후에 산책하러 갈 것이다.
   = She will go strolling after it stops raining.
④ 그는 결국 혼자 그의 숙제를 하게 되었다.
   = He ended up doing his homework by himself.
⑤ 저 로봇 청소기는 구매할 가치가 있다.
   = That robotic vacuum cleaner is worth purchasing.

22 다음 빈칸에 들어갈 알맞은 것은?

> Nahee feels sorry that she ignored Tyler's message last night.
> = Nahee feels sorry for _____ Tyler's message last night.

① ignore   ② ignored
③ have ignored   ④ having ignored
⑤ being ignored

[23-24] 다음 글을 읽고 주어진 질문에 답하시오.

Luke's worry

@Hiking is my favorite hobby. I always have fun when I spend time ⓑwalk up mountain paths and enjoying the fresh air. I like ⓒto do it whenever I can. Unfortunately, studying ⓓtake up all my time now. I study every single day. I hate ⓔmissing out on my hobby. I don't know what to do. How can I find time to participate in my hobby?

Diane's advice

(A) 일주일에 한번은 휴식을 취하려고 노력하는 게 어때?

23 위 글의 밑줄 친 @~ⓔ 중 어법상 어색한 부분을 두 군데 찾아 기호를 쓰고 바르게 고쳐 쓰시오.

(1) _____ → _____
(2) _____ → _____

24 위 글의 밑줄 친 우리말 (A)와 같도록 <보기>의 말을 활용하여 영작하시오.

> <보기>   take, try, how about, a break

= _____ once a week?

25 다음 중 어법상 어색한 것은?

① I'm tired of taking the bus to school every morning.
② Rosa is interested in touring the old city.
③ You can get a discount on ice cream by using this coupon.
④ Thanks for coming to my birthday party today.
⑤ It is no use to recycle when you don't reduce your plastic use.

26 다음 글의 밑줄 친 ⓐ~ⓔ를 바르게 고친 것은?

When I was young, I loved ⓐpractice the piano. I looked forward ⓑto go to my lessons after school. However, I don't enjoy ⓒplay anymore. I have even considered ⓓtaking not lessons next year. Unfortunately, my mother keeps ⓔtell me that I have to stick with it.

① ⓐ practice → to practicing
② ⓑ to go → going
③ ⓒ play → to play
④ ⓓ taking not → not taking
⑤ ⓔ tell → to tell

27 우리말과 같도록 괄호 안의 말을 활용하여 문장을 완성하시오.

Dennis는 어제 발생한 사고에 대해 알고 있는 것을 부인했다. (deny, know)

= Dennis _____ about the accident that happened yesterday.

28 다음 빈칸에 들어갈 말이 순서대로 짝지어진 것은?

· Michael imagined _____ his graduation speech without any mistakes.
· I was busy _____ my homework when the phone suddenly rang.

① give - doing
② to give - doing
③ giving - to do
④ to give - do
⑤ giving - doing

29 다음 중 어법상 바른 것끼리 묶인 것은?

ⓐ I prefer to read printed books rather than e-books.
ⓑ Dan postponed to go to the market because he had too much homework.
ⓒ When it comes to sing, Katie is the best I know.
ⓓ The team is having difficulty to win a championship.
ⓔ I recommend going to Taiwan for your summer vacation.

① ⓐ, ⓑ
② ⓐ, ⓔ
③ ⓑ, ⓒ
④ ⓑ, ⓓ
⑤ ⓓ, ⓔ

30 두 문장의 의미가 같도록 빈칸에 알맞은 말을 쓰시오.

We are sorry that we lost your luggage.
= We _____ you that we lost your luggage.

31 다음 글의 밑줄 친 ⓐ~ⓔ 중 어색한 부분을 두 군데 찾아 기호를 쓰고 바르게 고쳐 쓰시오.

I really look forward to ⓐwatch the new movie, *Peter Cottontop*. I am interested in ⓑcomparing the movie with its book series. I remember ⓒto be a huge fan of the books when I was in elementary school. I loved ⓓreading them in my free time. The author was good at ⓔcreating realistic fantasy situations. But I'm sure it won't be easy for the director to recreate them.

(1) _____ → _____
(2) _____ → _____

32 다음 중 어법상 어색한 것은?

① Do you mind my turning off the heater?
② I dislike she watching sad movies.
③ His winning the tournament surprised the world.
④ She is aware of her son's lying about his grades.
⑤ Classmates are tired of Jimmy's spreading rumors.

33 다음 우리말을 영작할 때 빈칸에 들어갈 알맞은 것은?

그 요리사는 그의 손님들에게 비난을 받는 것을 두려워한다.
= The chef is afraid of _____ by his guests.

① criticize
② criticizing
③ be criticize
④ criticized
⑤ being criticized

34 다음 중 어법상 바른 것의 개수는?

ⓐ Learning to follow a budget is an important life skill.
ⓑ Respecting other people make you a nice person.
ⓒ The best thing about camping is see so many wild animals.
ⓓ Never experiencing failure might not be good for you.
ⓔ Making international calls these days cost much less than in the past.

① 1개
② 2개
③ 3개
④ 4개
⑤ 5개

35 다음 대화의 빈칸에 들어갈 알맞은 것은?

A: Why did Susan call the police?
B: On _____ the door, she realized someone had broken into her house.

① open
② opened
③ has open
④ opening
⑤ to open

36 다음 우리말을 알맞게 영작한 것은?

> 나는 Richard가 도서관에 있었던 것이 기억나지 않는다.

① I don't remember Richard to be at the library.
② I don't remember Richard be at the library.
③ I don't remember of Richard being at the library.
④ I don't remember Richard's to be at the library.
⑤ I don't remember Richard's being at the library.

37 다음 글의 밑줄 친 부분이 어법상 어색한 것은?

> Have you ever imagined ①living in another country? Millions of people try ②moving abroad each year. And their reactions are diverse. Some regret ③deciding to relocate. They find ④leaving their friends and family to be too difficult. However, others adjust well and forgot ⑤to have worries about their choice soon after they move.

38 다음 우리말을 영작할 때 빈칸에 들어갈 알맞은 것은?

> 나는 나의 휴대폰으로 소셜미디어 앱을 확인하는 데 너무 많은 시간을 쓴다.
> = I spend too much time _____ social media apps on my cell phone.

① to checking
② checked
③ to check
④ checking
⑤ check

[39-40] 다음 글을 읽고 주어진 질문에 답하시오.

> Hey Charlie,
>
> Can you do me a favor? Today is your uncle Tom's birthday. I need to buy him a birthday cake. However, I am too busy (A) _____ at the office all day. Do you mind (B) _____ up a cake for me? I know you dislike (C) _____, but I really need your help. Since it's on your way home from school, ⓐI recommend that you go to Keller's Bakery. I'm sorry for (D) _____ at the last minute. I'll see you at home. Thanks!
>
> Love,
> Dad

39 <보기>의 말을 활용하여 빈칸에 알맞은 말을 쓰시오.

> <보기> shop   pick   work   ask

(A) _____   (B) _____
(C) _____   (D) _____

40 위 글의 밑줄 친 ⓐ를 주어진 <조건>에 맞게 바꿔 쓰시오.

> <조건>
> 1. 동명사를 포함하시오.
> 2. 7단어로 쓰시오.
> 3. suggest를 활용하시오.

→ _____

41 다음 중 어법상 어색한 것은?

① I look forward to trying the new Singaporean street food stand.

② I don't mind spending money buying the new headphones.

③ I had trouble finding the book I was looking for.

④ I dislike to eat the same thing repeatedly.

⑤ I feel like taking a nap for a few hours.

43 다음 대화의 빈칸에 들어갈 알맞은 것은?

> A: Did you buy bread and lettuce?
> B: Sorry, I didn't. I forgot _____ them.

① buy　　　② buying　　　③ bought

④ to buy　　⑤ to buying

42 다음 글의 밑줄 친 ⓐ~ⓔ 중 어색한 부분을 세 군데 찾아 기호를 쓰고 바르게 고쳐 쓰시오.

> Our teacher said she hates ⓐhearing the phrase, "I can't." She suggested ⓑto say, "I can't yet." She said the difference is small but important. Saying "yet" means that we won't quit ⓒto try. It shows that we will continue ⓓworking towards our goal. At first, I thought she was being silly. However, I took her suggestion. Now, I regret ⓔnot change my thinking earlier.

(1) _____ → _____

(2) _____ → _____

(3) _____ → _____

44 다음 중 어법상 어색한 것은?

① A: Why did you leave your phone at home?

　B: I cannot help playing games when I have it.

② A: Why don't you come to Thailand with us?

　B: I want to, but I'm afraid of taking an airplane.

③ A: I feel like eating something different today.

　B: How about trying the new Greek restaurant?

④ A: Are you buying that phone?

　B: No. I would end up to spend too much.

⑤ A: I have difficulty seeing. Can I sit in the front?

　B: Sure, just take that empty seat.

[45-47] 우리말과 같도록 괄호 안의 말을 활용하여 문장을 완성하시오.

45

> 집에 도착하자마자, 나는 샤워를 했다. (arrive home, on)

= _____, I took a shower.

46

> 나는 그런 추운 나라에서 사는 것이 익숙하지 않다. (live, use)

= I _____ in such a cold country.

47

> 나는 그 새로운 책이 읽을 가치가 있다고 생각하지 않는다. (read, worth)

= I don't think the new book is _____ _____.

CHAPTER 7
분사

Yeonji is watching the **flying** bird. 연지는 날고 있는 새를 보고 있다.

'날다'라는 의미의 동사 fly를 V-ing형으로 바꿔 '날고 있는'이라는 의미를 나타냈어요. 이렇게 동사가 V-ing형이나 V-ed형으로 쓰여 형용사 역할을 하는 것을 **분사**라고 해요.

기출로 적중 POINT

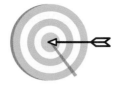

내신 100점 적중!
기출 출제율

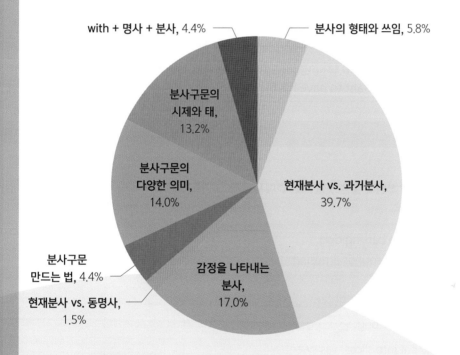

with + 명사 + 분사, 4.4%

분사의 형태와 쓰임, 5.8%

분사구문의 시제와 태, 13.2%

분사구문의 다양한 의미, 14.0%

분사구문 만드는 법, 4.4%

현재분사 vs. 동명사, 1.5%

감정을 나타내는 분사, 17.0%

현재분사 vs. 과거분사, 39.7%

TOP 1 **현재분사 vs. 과거분사 (39.7%)**
명사와 분사의 관계에 따라 현재분사와 과거분사를 구별하는 문제가 자주 출제된다.

TOP 2 **감정을 나타내는 분사 (17%)**
감정을 나타내는 분사가 수식하거나 보충 설명하는 대상에 따라 현재분사와 과거분사를 구별하는 문제가 자주 출제된다.

TOP 3 **분사구문의 다양한 의미 (14%)**
문맥에 맞는 알맞은 형태의 분사구문을 쓰는 문제가 자주 출제된다.

분사의 형태와 쓰임

정답 p.22

분사는 V-ing(현재분사)나 V-ed(과거분사)의 형태로, 형용사처럼 명사를 수식하거나 문장 안에서 보어로 쓰인다.

명사 수식	형용사처럼 명사를 수식한다. 분사가 단독으로 쓰이면 명사 앞에서 명사를 수식하고, 분사가 구를 이루어 쓰이면 명사 뒤에서 명사를 수식한다. We looked after the **crying baby**. 우리는 우는 아기를 보살폈다. **The cookies left** on the table are yours. 식탁 위에 남겨진 쿠키들은 너의 것이다.
보어	형용사처럼 주어나 목적어를 보충 설명하는 보어로 쓰인다. **The history class** seems **interesting**. 그 역사 수업은 흥미로워 보인다. I got **interested** in the class. 나는 그 수업에 흥미를 가졌다. Billy saw **his dad taking** pictures. Billy는 그의 아빠가 사진을 찍고 있는 것을 보았다. Billy didn't want to have **his picture taken**. Billy는 그의 사진이 찍히는 것을 원하지 않았다.

연습문제 밑줄 친 부분의 쓰임과 같은 것을 <보기>에서 골라 그 기호를 쓰고, 수식하거나 보충 설명하는 대상에 동그라미를 치시오.

<보기> ⓐ Look at the barking dog.
ⓑ The musical sounds amusing.

1 She hugged her smiling daughter. [　　　]
2 I was surprised by the bug. [　　　]
3 The pineapple cut into slices was sweet. [　　　]
4 Sally had her house painted. [　　　]
5 We saw a bear swimming in the lake. [　　　]
6 The new action movie seems exciting. [　　　]
7 He opened the gift wrapped in red paper. [　　　]
8 I heard someone singing outside. [　　　]
9 He read a novel written by George Orwell. [　　　]
10 My dad felt exhausted after he exercised. [　　　]
11 There are a few children playing at the park. [　　　]
12 Yeonsu was distracted by the talking student. [　　　]

기출로적중 POINT 2 현재분사 vs. 과거분사

정답 p.22

현재분사는 능동·진행의 의미를 나타내고, 과거분사는 수동·완료의 의미를 나타낸다.

현재분사(V-ing)	과거분사(V-ed)
능동 (타동사의 현재분사) ~하는, ~하게 만드는	수동 (타동사의 과거분사) ~된, ~당한
명사와 분사의 관계가 능동이면 현재분사를 쓴다. I watched the **exciting** play. 나는 신나는 연극을 보았다. **The play** was very **exciting**. 그 연극은 매우 신났다.	명사와 분사의 관계가 수동이면 과거분사를 쓴다. He found his **stolen** wallet. 그는 그의 도난당한 지갑을 찾았다. **My wallet** was **stolen** at the park. 나의 지갑은 그 공원에서 도난당했다.
진행 (자동사의 현재분사) ~하고 있는	완료 (자동사의 과거분사) ~한, ~된
Look at the **running** boy. 달리고 있는 소년을 봐라. We saw **the boy running**. 우리는 소년이 달리고 있는 것을 봤다.	I picked up the **fallen** leaves. 나는 떨어진 나뭇잎을 주웠다. Some leaves have **fallen** in the garden. 약간의 나뭇잎이 정원에 떨어졌다.

연습문제 A 괄호 안에서 알맞은 것을 고르시오.

1 She mashed the (cooking / cooked) potato.

2 The people (skiing / skied) down the mountain look small.

3 The exhibition looks (amazing / amazed).

4 The situation was so (embarrassing / embarrassed) that I had to run away.

5 The machine kept the plants (watering / watered).

6 I sent my (breaking / broken) computer to a shop for repairs.

7 The concert was (satisfying / satisfied).

8 The people rescued the bird (catching / caught) in the trap.

9 She complained about the (ticking / ticked) clock during the test.

10 There are some customers (waiting / waited) in front of the restaurant.

11 He saw the kitten (sleeping / slept) on the couch.

12 Jisun heard the kid (shouting / shouted) outside.

13 The earthquake left many homes (damaging / damaged).

14 The thief stole a statue (carving / carved) by a famous artist.

1 *A*: Did you hear that _____? (news, surprise)

   B: No. I missed it.

2 *A*: I heard that ice fishing is very popular here.

   B: Yes. In the winter, hundreds of tents are set up on the _____. (lake, freeze)

3 *A*: Who is that _____? (man, wave at us)

   B: Oh, that's my father.

4 *A*: Where is my report? I printed it yesterday.

   B: Is it that _____ on the table? (paper, fold)

5 *A*: Were you the first person in line for the concert tickets?

   B: No. There were tons of _____ when I arrived. (people, wait in line)

1 너는 비명을 지르는 소년을 보았니? (scream, boy)

   = Did you see the _____?

2 그 박물관은 미켈란젤로에 의해 그려진 몇 개의 스케치들을 소장하고 있다. (paint, sketches, by Michelangelo)

   = The museum owns several _____.

3 한수가 그 문 옆에 서 있는 남자이다. (guy, stand, next to the door)

   = Hansu is the _____.

4 나의 아빠는 비행하고 있는 항공기들의 사진을 찍는 것을 좋아한다. (fly, airplanes)

   = My dad likes taking pictures of _____.

5 지난달에 출간된 그 소설은 베스트셀러가 되었다. (last month, publish, the novel)

   = _____ became a best seller.

기출 적중문제

다음 빈칸에 들어갈 말이 나머지 넷과 다른 것은?

① This house was _____ in 1940.

② The girl _____ the sandcastle is my little sister.

③ They _____ a cabin in the woods three years ago.

④ The nest _____ by the bird is large.

⑤ The town has many churches _____ of stone.

> 능동·진행이면 현재분사를 쓰고, 수동·완료이면 과거분사를 써요.

감정을 나타내는 분사

정답 p.22

1. **감정을 나타내는 분사가 수식하거나 보충 설명하는 대상이 감정을 일으키는 주체인 경우 현재분사를 쓰고, 감정을 느끼는 대상인 경우 과거분사를 쓴다.**

   It was a **surprising** result. 그것은 놀라운 결과였다. (결과 = 놀라운 감정을 일으키는 주체)
   He was **surprised** at the result. 그는 그 결과에 놀랐다. (그 = 놀란 감정을 느끼는 대상)

2. **다음은 감정을 나타낼 때 자주 사용되는 분사이다.**

현재분사(~한 감정을 느끼게 하는)		과거분사(~한 감정을 느끼는)	
surprising	놀라게 하는	surprised	놀란
amazing	놀라게 하는	amazed	놀란
disappointing	실망스럽게 하는	disappointed	실망스러워하는
boring	지루하게 하는	bored	지루해하는
confusing	혼란스럽게 하는	confused	혼란스러워하는
embarrassing	당황스럽게 하는	embarrassed	당황해하는
shocking	충격을 주는	shocked	충격을 받은
depressing	우울하게 하는	depressed	우울해하는
exhausting	지치게 하는	exhausted	지친
amusing	즐겁게 하는	amused	즐거운
exciting	신나게 하는	excited	신이 난
thrilling	흥분하게 하는	thrilled	흥분한
worrying	걱정하게 하는	worried	걱정하는
pleasing	기쁘게 하는	pleased	기뻐하는
satisfying	만족스럽게 하는	satisfied	만족스러워하는
frightening	겁나게 하는	frightened	겁이 난
impressing	감동하게 하는	impressed	감동한
moving	감동하게 하는	moved	감동한
relaxing	편하게 하는	relaxed	편안한
interesting	흥미롭게 하는	interested	흥미로워하는
fascinating	황홀하게 하는	fascinated	황홀해하는

괄호 안의 동사를 알맞은 형태로 바꿔 빈칸에 쓰시오.

1 (relax)　　① Going to the spa is _____ to Jenny.

② Jenny feels _____ when she goes to the spa.

2 (embarrass)　① The child made his parents _____.

② The child's behavior was _____ to his parents.

3 (excite)　　① The circus was _____.

② My family was _____ by the circus.

4 (disappoint)　① He was _____ because he didn't win the competition.

② Not winning the competition was _____ to him.

우리말과 같도록 <보기>의 단어를 활용하여 빈칸에 쓰시오.

<보기>　shock　confuse　satisfy　impress　exhaust

1 그 시험의 지시 사항들은 나를 혼란스러워하게 했다.

= The instructions of the test made me _____.

2 그 신문의 주요 뉴스는 그것을 읽은 모든 사람들에게 충격을 주었다.

= The headline on the newspaper was _____ to everyone who read it.

3 나의 남동생은 공원에 간 이후에 지쳐 보였다.

= My little brother looked _____ after going to the park.

4 나의 엄마는 내가 나의 성적이 올랐다고 말했을 때 감동했다.

= My mom was _____ when I told her my grade had improved.

5 진호는 새로운 베트남 식당에서 만족스러운 저녁 식사를 했다.

= Jinho had a _____ dinner at the new Vietnamese restaurant.

기출 적중문제

다음 글의 밑줄 친 ⓐ~ⓔ 중 어법상 어색한 것을 찾아 기호를 쓰고 바르게 고쳐 쓰시오.

I attended a speech ⓐgiven by a Nobel Prize winner. She told an ⓑinteresting childhood story. She gave a ⓒmoved speech and encouraged us not to give up hope. The audience was ⓓfascinating by her ⓔamazing speech.

감정을 일으키면 현재분사를 쓰고, 감정을 느끼면 과거분사를 써요.

(1) _____ → _____

(2) _____ → _____

현재분사 vs. 동명사

정답 p.22

현재분사와 동명사는 둘 다 V-ing 형태이지만 쓰임이 다르다.

현재분사	동명사
명사를 수식하여 능동·진행(~하는, ~하고 있는)의 의미를 나타낸다. There is a **sleeping** dog. 자고 있는 개가 있다.	명사를 수식하여 명사의 용도·목적(~하기 위한)을 나타낸다. I bought a new **sleeping** bag. 나는 새 침낭을 샀다. (sleeping bag ≠ 자고 있는 가방)
보어로 쓰인다. The drone looks **interesting**. 그 드론은 흥미로워 보인다. I saw him **studying** in the library. 나는 그가 도서관에서 공부하고 있는 것을 봤다.	주어나 보어로 쓰인다. **Writing** in a journal is meaningful. 일기를 쓰는 것은 의미 있다. My hobby is **playing** baseball. 나의 취미는 야구를 하는 것이다.
be동사와 함께 진행시제를 만든다. Jacob is **drinking** orange juice. Jacob은 오렌지 주스를 마시고 있다.	동사나 전치사의 목적어로 쓰인다. Emily enjoys **listening** to the music. Emily는 음악을 듣는 것을 즐긴다. I'm afraid of **swimming** in the sea. 나는 바다에서 수영하는 것을 무서워한다.

연습문제 밑줄 친 부분의 쓰임과 같은 것을 <보기>에서 골라 그 기호를 쓰시오.

<보기>　ⓐ Do you know the man <u>wearing</u> the blue jeans?
　　　ⓑ I always wear my <u>running</u> shoes when I exercise.

1 Everyone laughed at the video of the <u>sneezing</u> panda. 　　[　　]

2 He enjoys <u>playing</u> chess with his grandfather. 　　[　　]

3 I saw a very <u>interesting</u> movie about rainforests last night. 　　[　　]

4 Some of my classmates are <u>taking</u> extra classes after school. 　　[　　]

5 The chef uses <u>baking</u> powder to make her cookies rise. 　　[　　]

6 The new roller coaster at the amusement park seems <u>thrilling</u>. 　　[　　]

7 <u>Traveling</u> is much cheaper now than it was in the past. 　　[　　]

8 He is good at <u>managing</u> a lot of work efficiently. 　　[　　]

9 My grandmother needs a <u>walking</u> stick when she goes outside. 　　[　　]

분사구문 만드는 법

1. 분사구문은 「부사절 접속사 + 주어 + 동사」 형태의 부사절을 분사를 이용하여 부사구로 바꾼 것이다.

① ② ③ ~~Because they tried~~ their best, they won. **Trying** their best, they won. 최선을 다했기 때문에, 그들은 이겼다.	① 부사절 접속사를 생략한다. ② 주절과 부사절의 주어가 같은 경우 부사절의 주어를 생략한다. ③ 부사절의 동사를 V-ing형으로 바꾼다.

~~When I~~ **opened** the window, I saw a bird.

= **Opening** the window, I saw a bird. 창문을 열었을 때, 나는 새를 보았다.

(Tip) 분사구문의 부정형은 분사 앞에 not이나 never를 붙여 만든다.

Because I **didn't like** that show, I changed the channel.

= **Not[Never] liking** that show, I changed the channel.

그 방송을 좋아하지 않았기 때문에, 나는 채널을 바꿨다.

2. 분사구문의 의미를 분명하게 하기 위해 부사절 접속사를 생략하지 않을 수 있다.

After ~~she~~ **ate** dinner, she went upstairs.

= **After eating** dinner, she went upstairs. 저녁을 먹고 나서, 그녀는 위층으로 갔다.

3. 분사구문 맨 앞이 「Being + 과거분사」의 형태인 경우 Being은 생략할 수 있다.

~~Since the child~~ **was** left alone, he began to cry.

= **(Being) Left** alone, the child began to cry. 혼자 남겨졌기 때문에, 그 아이는 울기 시작했다.

4. 부사절의 주어와 주절의 주어가 다른 경우 부사절의 주어를 생략하지 않고 분사구문 맨 앞에 쓴다.

~~While Sam~~ **washed** the dishes, I cleaned the room.

= **Sam washing** the dishes, I cleaned the room.

Sam이 설거지를 하는 동안, 나는 방을 청소했다.

연습문제 A 두 문장의 의미가 같도록 분사구문을 이용하여 문장을 완성하시오. (단, 부사절의 접속사를 생략하시오.)

1 While he listened to the music, he ate an ice cream.

= _____ , he ate an ice cream.

2 Because he didn't forget her birthday, he bought a present.

= _____ , he bought a present.

3 Because I was injured in training last week, I couldn't join the soccer game.

= _____ , I couldn't join the soccer game.

4 While he boarded the train, he waved at his family.

= _____ , he waved at his family.

5 When she lived in France, she taught English to the students.

= _____ , she taught English to the students.

6 Since he was put in prison, he was no longer a threat.

= _____ , he was no longer a threat.

7 Since my older sister cooked dinner, I set the table.

= _____ , I set the table.

연습문제 B 우리말과 같도록 괄호 안의 말을 활용하여 문장을 완성하시오. (단, 부사절의 접속사를 생략하시오.)

1 길을 찾으면서, 길을 잃은 등산객은 몇 시간 동안 숲을 돌아다녔다. (look)

= _____ for the trail, the lost hiker walked around the forest for hours.

2 강의 수위를 높게 만들면서, 그 태풍은 둑을 따라 늘어선 집들을 침수시켰다. (cause)

= _____ the river to rise, the storm flooded homes along the banks.

3 운전면허증이 없기 때문에, 나는 대중교통을 이용해야 한다. (have)

= _____ a driver's license, I have to use the public transportation.

4 피카소에 의해 창작되었기 때문에, 그 예술 작품은 매우 가치있었다. (create)

= _____ by Picasso, the art work was very valuable.

5 그녀의 집을 떠날 때, 그녀는 그것의 모든 소중한 기억들을 생각해냈다. (leave)

= _____ her house, she recalled all her precious memories of it.

6 Chris가 집에 돌아왔을 때, 우리는 막 나가려던 참이었다. (Chris, come back)

= _____ home, we were about to go out.

기출 적중문제

다음 중 어법상 어색한 것은?

① Playing at the beach, I got a sunburn.
② Climbing the ladder, she nearly fell.
③ Satisfying by the gift, Paul smiled happily.
④ Stepping outside, we felt the fresh air.
⑤ Getting on the bus, I dropped my water bottle.

분사구문은 접속사에 따라 다양한 의미를 나타낸다.

의미	접속사	예문
시간	when(~할 때), while(~하는 동안), after(~한 후에), before(~하기 전에)	**When she heard** the alarm clock, she woke up. = **Hearing** the alarm clock, she woke up. 알람을 들었을 때, 그녀는 일어났다.
이유	because/since/as (~이기 때문에)	**Because we live** in the country, we know many farmers. = **Living** in the country, we know many farmers. 시골에 살기 때문에, 우리는 많은 농부들을 안다.
동시동작	while/as (~하면서)	**While I looked** at old photos, I thought of my childhood. = **Looking** at old photos, I thought of my childhood. 오래된 사진들을 보면서, 나는 나의 어린 시절에 대해 생각했다.
연속동작	and (~하고 나서)	I left home at 8 A.M., **and I reached** school at 9 A.M. = I left home at 8 A.M., **reaching** school at 9 A.M. 나는 오전 8시에 집을 떠나고 나서, 오전 9시에 학교에 도착했다.
양보	though/although (비록 ~이지만)	**Though he is** young, he is very wise. = **Though being young**, he is very wise. 비록 어리지만, 그는 매우 현명하다. (Tip) 양보를 나타내는 분사구문은 의미를 분명하게 하기 위해 주로 접속사를 생략하지 않는다.
조건	if (~라면)	**If you turn** to the left, you will find Mike's house. = **Turning** to the left, you will find Mike's house. 왼쪽으로 돌면, 니는 Mike의 집을 찾을 것이다.

(Tip) 분사구문을 접속사가 있는 문장으로 바꿀 경우 문맥에 맞는 접속사를 쓴다.
Having an important exam, I had to study until midnight.
= (~~If~~, **Since**) I had an important exam, I had to study until midnight.
나는 중요한 시험이 있었기 때문에, 자정까지 공부해야 했다.

연습문제 A   두 문장의 의미가 같도록 분사구문을 이용하여 문장을 완성하시오. (단, 부사절의 접속사를 생략하시오.)

1   When she arrived at the café, she met a friend.

= _____ , she met a friend.

2 Andy fell down the stairs, and he broke his arm.

= Andy fell down the stairs, _____.

3 Because she was confused by the question, she scratched her head.

= _____, she scratched her head.

4 While the students listened to the storyteller, none of them made a sound.

= _____, none of the students made a sound.

5 As I was given the prize, I jumped for joy.

= _____, I jumped for joy.

6 If I have enough money, I will buy those new running shoes.

= _____, I will buy those new running shoes.

7 While the researcher was digging up the site, he discovered many old pots.

= _____, the researcher discovered many old pots.

8 Since he didn't worry about the score, he played tennis to have fun.

= _____, he played tennis to have fun.

연습문제 **B** | <보기>에서 가장 알맞은 접속사를 한 번씩만 골라 두 문장의 의미가 같도록 문장을 완성하시오.

<보기> because   if   when   and

1 Leaving Korea, he promised to come back.

= _____, he promised to come back.

2 Two cars had an accident, stopping traffic for several hours.

= Two cars had an accident, _____.

3 Studying hard, you will see an improvement in your grades.

= _____, you will see an improvement in your grades.

4 Being exhausted from work, he is having a rest now.

= _____, he is having a rest now.

기출 적중문제

우리말과 같도록 분사구문과 괄호 안의 말을 활용하여 문장을 완성하시오.

우유를 마시면서, Brad는 전화 통화를 하고 있었다. (drink, milk)

= _____, Brad was speaking on the phone.

1. 분사구문의 시제가 주절의 시제와 같을 경우 「V-ing」 형태로 쓰고, 분사구문의 시제가 주절의 시제보다 이전인 경우 「Having + V-ed」 형태로 쓴다.

단순형	V-ing	**Because** she <u>felt</u> tired, she <u>didn't go</u> out. = **Feeling** tired, she didn't go out. 피곤했기 때문에, 그녀는 외출하지 않았다.
완료형	Having + V-ed	**After** he <u>had heard</u> about the news, he <u>panicked</u>. = **Having heard** about the news, he panicked. 그 소식에 대해 듣고 나서, 그는 당황했다.

2. 주절의 주어와 분사구문의 관계가 능동인 경우 「V-ing」 형태로 쓰고, 주절의 주어와 분사구문의 관계가 수동인 경우 「(Being) + V-ed」 형태로 쓴다.

능동형	V-ing	**When** I made breakfast, I burnt myself on a hot pan. = **Making** breakfast, I burnt myself on a hot pan. 아침 식사를 만들었을 때, 나는 뜨거운 팬에 데었다.
수동형	(Being) + V-ed	**Since** the table was decorated with gold, it was expensive. = **(Being) Decorated** with gold, the table was expensive. 금으로 장식되었기 때문에, 그 식탁은 비쌌다.

연습문제 A 두 문장의 의미가 같도록 분사구문을 이용하여 문장을 완성하시오. (단, 부사절의 접속사를 생략하시오.)

1 Since she took Spanish in high school, she can speak it well.

= _____, she can speak it well.

2 While I waited for my mother, I played games on my phone.

= _____, I played games on my phone.

3 Because I had been offered the chance, I joined the soccer team.

= _____, I joined the soccer team.

4 Because I don't have any free time, I can't go traveling.

= _____, I can't go traveling.

5 After he had finished his painting, he started another one.

= _____, he started another one.

6 Because she had gotten lost, she was 40 minutes late for her flight.

= _____, she was 40 minutes late for her flight.

7 As I haven't seen her, I am very curious about her.

= _____, I am very curious about her.

8 When I study by myself, I often get distracted.

= _____, I often get distracted.

연습문제 B 우리말과 같도록 괄호 안의 말을 활용하여 문장을 완성하시오.

1 아이 취급을 받았기 때문에, 동호는 화가 났다. (treat, like, a child)

= _____, Dongho got upset.

2 넘어지고 나서, 그는 그의 발목을 삐었다. (fall down)

= _____, he sprained his ankle.

3 버터로 덮여 있었기 때문에, 그 팬케이크는 맛있었다. (cover, with, butter)

= _____, the pancakes were delicious.

4 냉장고에 보관되고 나서, 피클은 몇 개월 동안 상하지 않았다. (store, in, the refrigerator)

= _____, pickles lasted for months.

5 런던에 머무르면서, 우리는 타워 브리지를 보러 갔다. (stay, in, London)

= _____, we went to see Tower Bridge.

6 모두에게 알려져 있기 때문에, 그는 붐비는 장소를 피한다. (know, to, everyone)

= _____, he avoids crowded places.

7 한 시간 넘게 줄을 서고 나서, 나는 매우 지쳤다. (stand, in, line)

= _____ for over an hour, I got very tired.

8 그 모퉁이에서 오른쪽으로 돌았을 때, 나는 그 빵집을 찾았다. (turn, right)

= _____ at the corner, I found the bakery.

기출 적중문제

다음 중 어법상 어색한 것은?

① Feeling tired, I went to bed early.

② Being late, he missed the beginning of the concert.

③ Reading a novel, she imagined being a wizard.

④ Breaking the silence, the alarm clock rang.

⑤ Surprising by the message, Amanda began to sweat.

> 주절의 주어와 분사구문의 관계가 수동인 경우 「(Being) + V-ed」형태를 써요.

with + 명사 + 분사

정답 p.23

> 「with + 명사 + 분사」는 '~가 -한 채로/하면서'의 의미로, 동시에 일어나는 상황을 나타낸다.
>
> ❶ 명사와 분사의 관계가 능동인 경우 「with + 명사 + V-ing」형태로 쓴다.
> Dave kept working **with his phone** ringing. Dave는 그의 전화기가 울리는 채로 계속 일했다.
> = Dave kept working, while his phone rang.
>
> ❷ 명사와 분사의 관계가 수동인 경우 「with + 명사 + V-ed」형태로 쓴다.
> Susan stared at me **with her arms** crossed. Susan은 팔짱을 낀 채로 나를 쳐다봤다.
> = Susan stared at me, and her arms were crossed.

연습문제 우리말과 같도록 「with + 명사 + 분사」와 괄호 안의 말을 활용하여 문장을 완성하시오.

1 민호는 그의 손을 든 채로 앉아 있었다. (raise, his hand)
= Minho was sitting _____ .

2 나는 이불에 나의 머리가 덮인 채로 잤다. (cover, my head)
= I slept _____ by a blanket.

3 그는 그의 감독이 응원해주는 채로 득점했다. (his coach, cheer)
= He scored a goal _____ .

4 나의 남동생은 그의 컴퓨터가 켜진 채로 잠들었다. (his computer, turn on)
= My younger brother fell asleep _____ .

5 그녀는 그녀의 다리가 붕대에 감긴 채로 병원을 떠나고 있다. (her leg, bandage)
= She is leaving the hospital _____ _____ .

6 나는 나의 강아지가 나를 따르는 채로 나의 자전거를 탔다. (my dog, follow)
= I rode my bicycle _____ me.

7 그녀는 창문이 닫힌 채로 공부를 하고 있었다. (close, the windows)
= She was studying _____ .

8 수지는 그녀의 팔을 흔들면서 빠르게 걸었다. (swing, her arms)
= Suji walked quickly _____ .

9 예나는 관중들이 그녀를 보는 채로 경주로를 달리고 있었다. (the crowd, watch)
= Yena was running on the track _____ her.

10 나의 엄마는 그녀의 머리를 묶은 채로 아침 식사를 준비하고 있다. (her hair, tie back)
= My mom is preparing breakfast _____ .

기출로적중 POINT 7 · 분사구문 관용 표현

정답 p.23

다음은 분사구문이 쓰인 관용 표현이다.

Generally speaking	일반적으로 말하면	Judging from	~으로 판단하건대
Strictly speaking	엄밀히 말하면	Considering	~을 고려하면
Frankly speaking	솔직히 말하면	Speaking of	~에 관해서 말한다면

Generally speaking, most people prefer sunny weather.
일반적으로 말하면, 대부분의 사람들은 화창한 날씨를 선호한다.

Judging from the schedule, it is faster to take the subway.
시간표로 판단하건대, 지하철을 타는 것이 더 빠르다.

Speaking of Yuha, she did well on her science test.
유하에 관해서 말한다면, 그녀는 과학 시험을 잘 봤다.

CHAPTER 7 분사 해커스 중학영문법 3학년

연습문제 우리말과 같도록 분사구문 관용 표현을 이용하여 문장을 완성하시오.

1 솔직히 말하면, 나는 피아노를 연주하는 것을 좋아하지 않았다.

= ＿＿＿＿＿＿＿＿＿＿＿＿＿＿＿＿＿, I never liked to play the piano.

2 일반적으로 말하면, 꽃들은 주로 7월에 풍성하다.

= ＿＿＿＿＿＿＿＿＿＿＿＿＿＿＿＿＿, flowers are usually plentiful in July.

3 여행에 관해서 말한다면, 나는 방금 뭄바이행 비행기를 예약했다.

= ＿＿＿＿＿＿＿＿＿＿＿＿＿＿＿＿＿ traveling, I just booked a flight to Mumbai.

4 그의 성적으로 판단하건대, Eric은 매우 열심히 공부했음이 틀림없다.

= ＿＿＿＿＿＿＿＿＿＿＿＿＿＿＿＿＿ his grades, Eric must have studied very hard.

5 그의 나이를 고려하면, 나의 할아버지는 매우 건강하시다.

= ＿＿＿＿＿＿＿＿＿＿＿＿＿＿＿＿＿ his age, my grandfather is in great shape.

6 엄밀히 말하면, 우리 땅의 경계는 여기에서 끝난다.

= ＿＿＿＿＿＿＿＿＿＿＿＿＿＿＿＿＿, the borders of our land end here.

7 솔직히 말하면, 어제 저녁 식사의 음식은 맛있지 않았다.

= ＿＿＿＿＿＿＿＿＿＿＿＿＿＿＿＿＿, the food at yesterday's dinner wasn't delicious.

8 그의 억양으로 판단하건대, 그는 미국인임이 틀림없다.

= ＿＿＿＿＿＿＿＿＿＿＿＿＿＿＿＿＿ his accent, he must be an American.

A 우리말과 같도록 괄호 안의 말을 활용하여 문장을 완성하시오.

1 그 요리사는 얇게 썰린 치즈와 함께 파스타를 제공했다. (slice, cheese)

= The chef served the pasta with _____ .

2 소풍을 계획하는 팀은 날씨에 대해 걱정했다. (plan, team)

= The _____ the picnic worried about the weather.

3 도난당한 모든 조각품들이 창고 안에서 발견되었다. (steal, sculptures)

= All the _____ were found in a warehouse.

4 놀이터에서 놀고 있는 학생들은 나의 친구들이다. (students, play)

= The _____ in the playground are my friends.

5 나는 나의 코트를 추위에 떨고 있는 소녀에게 주었다. (girl, shiver)

= I gave my coat to the _____ .

6 Nicole은 그녀의 어머니가 요리해 주신 음식을 먹었다. (cook, meal)

= Nicole ate a _____ by her mother.

7 문 옆에 서 있는 남자에게 방향을 물어보자. (stand, man)

= Let's ask the _____ by the door for directions.

8 나의 형과 나는 깨진 유리를 치웠다. (glass, break)

= My older brother and I cleaned up the _____ .

B 다음은 페루 과학자들의 발견에 대한 기사이다. 괄호 안의 말을 활용하여 빈칸에 알맞은 말을 쓰시오.

Scientists in Peru were ⓐ_____ (excite) to find the remains of a distant relative of whales. The bones ⓑ_____ (find) along the southern coast proved that whales once had four legs. This ⓒ_____ (amaze) discovery helped the researchers understand the history of whales. ⓓ_____ (reassemble) the bones, the scientists realized that the animal could both swim and walk. This meant the newly ⓔ_____ (discover) species was able to leave the ocean. It could go onto land to eat the plants ⓕ_____ (grow) there. ⓖ_____ (research) the species, the scientists were ⓗ_____ (fascinate) by the results. It was one of the first connections between animals ⓘ_____ (dwell) on land and modern marine mammals.

*dwell 살다
*marine mammal 해양 포유 동물

C 우리말과 같도록 괄호 안의 말을 알맞게 배열하시오.

1 나는 나의 여동생이 옆에 앉아 있는 채로 시험공부를 했다.
(studied for, with, sitting, beside me, I, an exam, my little sister)
= _____

2 그녀의 반응으로 판단하건대, 그녀는 그 선물을 좋아했다.
(she, the gift, judging from, her reaction, liked)
= _____

3 그 소년은 그의 다리를 굽힌 채로 계단에 앉아 있었다.
(with, the floor, sat on, his legs, the boy, bent)
= _____

4 음악에 관해서 말한다면, 우리는 콘서트에 가야 한다.
(to, a concert, music, we, should, speaking of , go)
= _____

D 두 문장의 의미가 같도록 분사구문을 이용하여 문장을 완성하시오. (단, 부사절의 접속사를 생략하시오.)

1 When I climbed up the mountain, I sweated a lot.
= _____, I sweated a lot.

2 As she was proven innocent, she left the jail.
= _____, she left the jail.

3 Because he hoped to get there before the train departed, he ran to the station.
= _____, he ran to the station.

4 After we had finished our work, we took a short break.
= _____, we took a short break.

5 Since I was praised by the teacher, I was proud of myself.
= _____, I was proud of myself.

6 While he cleaned his room, he discovered his family album.
= _____, he discovered his family album.

7 If you mix yellow paint and blue paint, you will get green paint.
= _____, you will get green paint.

중간 · 기말고사 실전 문제

1 다음 중 어법상 바른 것은?

① I stepped on a piece of the breaking cup and cut my foot.
② The police are looking for the stealing vehicle.
③ Please take this coffee to the man sat in the corner.
④ Is this the sculpture creating by Mr. Jackson?
⑤ There are several people helping the patients.

3 다음 중 어법상 어색한 것은?

① The dog chasing the cat is very excited.
② The man singing on the stage is my cousin.
③ The newspaper published an article writing by the journalist.
④ Apartments located near subway stations are expensive.
⑤ The girl entering the room is from China.

2 다음 글의 밑줄 친 ⓐ~ⓔ를 바르게 고친 것은?

The boy ⓐwait to see the doctor is my younger brother. ⓑPlay on the jungle gym today, he slipped and fell to the ground. He was very ⓒsurprising. Unfortunately, he now has an ⓓinjuring arm that needs to be checked out. I hope the doctor ⓔtreat him doesn't say it's broken.

① ⓐ wait → waited
② ⓑ Play → Played
③ ⓒ surprising → surprise
④ ⓓ injuring → injured
⑤ ⓔ treat → treated

4 다음 (A)~(C)에 들어갈 말이 바르게 짝지어진 것은?

· The ___(A)___ stars lit up the night sky.
· Did you offer a drink to the man ___(B)___ in the corner?
· All of the money ___(C)___ at the auction will be donated to charity.

	(A)	(B)	(C)
①	shone	stood	raised
②	shining	standing	raising
③	shone	standing	raised
④	shining	standing	raised
⑤	shone	stood	raising

5 다음 글의 밑줄 친 우리말 (A), (B)와 같도록 괄호 안의 말을 활용하여 문장을 완성하시오.

Every year, John's family goes to (A) <u>그의 할아버지에 의해 소유된 오두막</u>(by his grandfather, a cabin, own). They love spending time there because it is very peaceful and quiet. John likes to see (B) <u>숲 속에 숨어있는 동물들</u>(hide, the animals, in the forest). So far, he has seen four deer, lots of birds, and even a bear.

(A) _____

(B) _____

6 다음 빈칸에 들어갈 알맞은 것은?

I'm looking for a restaurant _____ Italian food.

① serve ② served ③ is serving
④ is served ⑤ serving

7 다음 중 밑줄 친 부분의 쓰임이 나머지 넷과 다른 것은?

① He is <u>waiting</u> in the parking lot.
② We talked about <u>going</u> to the science fair.
③ There are many people <u>exercising</u> in the park.
④ <u>Getting</u> closer to the station, the train slowed down.
⑤ I thought I heard somebody <u>calling</u> me.

8 다음 글의 빈칸에 괄호 안의 말을 활용하여 알맞은 말을 쓰시오.

Save the Earth
We should keep the environment
ⓐ_____(protect). People
ⓑ_____(interest) in saving the earth can do several things to help.
1. Using less water
2. Not using plastics
3. Buying ⓒ_____(use) products
4. Using public transportation

9 다음 중 어법상 어색한 것의 개수는?

ⓐ The room designing by Terry is really beautiful.
ⓑ I saw Peter walking home yesterday.
ⓒ Jennifer was embarrassing about falling in the street.
ⓓ The teacher caught two students cheated on the test.
ⓔ I had my uniform fixed so that it would fit better.

① 1개 ② 2개 ③ 3개
④ 4개 ⑤ 5개

[10-11] 다음 대화의 밑줄 친 우리말과 같도록 괄호 안의 말을 활용하여 문장을 완성하시오.

10

> *A*: I don't know how to make tea. Is it difficult?
> *B*: No. Just put the tea bag in 끓고 있는 물 (boil, water).

= _____

11

> *A*: Your older sister said you were in an accident.
> *B*: Yes. 자전거를 탄 남자(ride, a bike, a man) ran into me.

= _____

12 다음 (A)~(C)에 들어갈 말이 바르게 짝지어진 것은?

> · Michael's speech was very ___(A)___.
> · I was ___(B)___ by the comic book.
> · I have felt ___(C)___ for the last few weeks.

	(A)	(B)	(C)
①	shocked	amused	depressed
②	shocking	amused	depressing
③	shocked	amusing	depressed
④	shocking	amused	depressed
⑤	shocking	amusing	depressing

13 괄호 안의 말을 활용하여 대화를 완성하시오.

> *A*: That is so strange!
> *B*: What?
> *A*: _____ is wearing roller skates. (at the table, sit, the girl)

14 다음 중 분사구문으로 잘못 바꾼 것은?

① Because he didn't have a car, he took a taxi.
  → Not having a car, he took a taxi.
② Although I had lost my wallet, I still have some cash.
  → Having lost my wallet, I still have some cash.
③ Since he had not finished his homework, he could not play video games.
  → Not having finished his homework, he could not play video games.
④ If I miss the bus, I won't make it to my appointment on time.
  → Missed the bus, I won't make it to my appointment on time.
⑤ As she was influenced by her father, she decided to be a lawyer.
  → Influenced by her father, she decided to be a lawyer.

[15-16] 다음 글을 읽고 주어진 질문에 답하시오.

Local jewelry store owner Kevin Leon had a (A) 겁나게 하는 경험(frighten, experience) last week. (B) 마스크를 쓴 두 명의 남자들(two men, wear, masks) tried to rob his store. Luckily, Mr. Leon's store had security cameras. One of the thieves took his mask off by mistake. (C) 그의 얼굴이 노출된 채로(with, his face, expose), he was clearly visible in the video. ⓐHaving installed security cameras, Mr. Leon was able to catch the thieves.

15 위 글의 밑줄 친 우리말 (A)~(C)와 같도록 괄호 안의 말을 활용하여 문장을 완성하시오.

(A) _____

(B) _____

(C) _____

16 위 글의 밑줄 친 ⓐ와 바꿔 쓸 수 있는 것은?

① While he installed security cameras
② If he had installed security cameras
③ Before he installed security cameras
④ Though he had installed security cameras
⑤ Because he had installed security cameras

17 다음 중 어법상 어색한 것은?

① Protected by the big tree in the yard, the home was saved from storm damage.
② Crossing the street, the child looked both ways carefully.
③ Archaeologists discovered a hidden pyramid, proving their theory.
④ Trapping in a cage, the mouse began to panic.
⑤ With his mother watching, Juwon cleaned his room.

18 다음 문장의 밑줄 친 부분과 쓰임이 다른 것은?

The man drinking coffee under the beach umbrella is my father.

① I watched the falling snow last night.
② The phone ringing on the table is Jacob's.
③ I heard my older brother practicing the guitar.
④ John was bathing his new puppy.
⑤ The topic of the lesson is identifying plant species.

19 다음 중 밑줄 친 부분이 어법상 바른 것은?

I was really ①exciting to hear about the upcoming *StarMax* movie. This weekend I finally saw it. Unfortunately, I was very ②disappointing. The plot was ③confused, so I felt ④boring. It would be ⑤surprising to hear that anyone actually liked the movie. Science fiction movie fans should wait to check out the one that will open next month instead.

20 다음 중 어법상 어색한 것은?

① Looking through the telescope, I could see Mars.

② Taking this subway, you will reach your destination.

③ Being taken French for years, I had no trouble speaking it.

④ Reading the book, I learned a lot about history.

⑤ The team was defeated in the semifinal game, ending its dream.

21 다음 대화를 읽고 괄호 안의 말을 활용하여 대화를 완성하시오.

> A: Do you hear someone crying?
> B: Yes. It's ⓐ_____.
> (the girl, sit over there)
> A: Are you sure? She has ⓑ_____
> _____. (her face, cover)
> B: Yes. I talked to her. She is upset
> about her ⓒ_____.
> (dog, lose)

22 다음 괄호 안의 단어를 알맞은 형태로 바꿔 빈칸에 쓰시오.

> The South Korean soccer team beat Senegal in the Under-20 World Cup. The players achieved an _____(amaze) win at the last minute. I was _____ (impress) when it happened.

[23-24] 두 문장의 의미가 같도록 밑줄 친 부분을 분사구문으로 바꿔 쓰시오.

23

> As I opened my mouth to sing the song, I forgot the words.
> = _____,
> I forgot the words.

24

> After I had quit my piano lessons, I had nothing to do in the afternoon.
> = _____,
> I had nothing to do in the afternoon.

25 다음 문장에서 어법상 어색한 부분을 찾아 쓰고 바르게 고쳐 쓰시오.

> Patients are often satisfying with the results of alternative medicine.

_____ → _____

26 다음 빈칸에 들어갈 말이 순서대로 짝지어진 것은?

The city's only Greek restaurant has closed. _____ attractive advertisements, it became one of the most well-known restaurants around. However, with the restaurant _____ less money, debts began to increase rapidly.

① Used – earning   ② Used – earned
③ Using – earn   ④ Using – earned
⑤ Using – earning

27 우리말과 같도록 괄호 안의 말을 활용하여 문장을 완성하시오.

그 원숭이는 그녀의 새끼를 등에 매단 채로 나무를 오르고 있었다. (her baby, with, hang, on her back)

= The monkey was climbing the tree _____
_____ .

28 다음 문장과 바꿔 쓸 수 있는 것을 <u>모두</u> 고르시오.

Wanting to please my parents, I always try to do my best in school.

① Although I want to please my parents, I always try to do my best in school.
② As I want to please my parents, I always try to do my best in school.
③ While I wanted to please my parents, I always try to do my best in school.
④ Because I want to please my parents, I always try to do my best in school.
⑤ Before I want to please my parents, I always try to do my best in school.

[29-30] 다음 문장을 주어진 <조건>에 맞게 바꿔 쓰시오.

29

Since he knew how to solve the math problem, he got the correct answer.

<조건>
분사구문으로 바꿔 쓰시오.

= _____
_____

30

Having finished the painting, she put it in a gold frame.

<조건>
1. 부사절이 있는 완전한 문장으로 바꿔 쓰시오.
2. 접속사 when를 활용하시오.

= _____
_____

31 우리말과 같도록 괄호 안의 말을 활용하여 문장을 완성하시오.

그 소년은 그의 눈을 감은 채로 꽃의 향기를 맡았다. (with, close, his eyes)

= The boy smelled a flower _____
_____ .

32 두 문장의 의미가 같도록 밑줄 친 부분을 분사구문으로 바꿔 쓰시오.

> <u>Because the concert was over</u>,
> everyone tried to leave the arena.
> = _____,
> everyone tried to leave the arena.

33 다음 중 어법상 바른 것의 개수는?

> ⓐ A barked dog woke him up in the middle of the night.
> ⓑ The mechanic replaced the broken parts with new ones.
> ⓒ While searching for my keys, I found the watch I had lost.
> ⓓ John finished the race first, won an award.
> ⓔ Stuck in the elevator, she called the building manager.
> ⓕ The author's novel about a father's love was very moved.
> ⓖ Judging from his review, the critic hated the movie.

① 1개   ② 2개   ③ 3개
④ 4개   ⑤ 5개

[34-35] 다음 글을 읽고, 주어진 질문에 답하시오.

> Although (A) _____ (know) as a musical genius today, Beethoven had a very different reputation during his lifetime. ⓐ1700년대 후반에 비엔나에서 살았기 때문에, Beethoven knew many of history's greatest musicians, who also lived in Vienna. Unfortunately, he had negative relationships with most of them. One of the best examples of this was with his teacher Joseph Haydn. Haydn suggested that the phrase "pupil of Haydn" be added to some songs (B) _____ (produce) by Beethoven. Unfortunately, Beethoven was not (C) _____ (please) with this idea. He said that Haydn had taught him nothing.
>
> * pupil 제자, 학생

34 괄호 안의 말을 활용하여 빈칸 (A)~(C)에 알맞은 말을 쓰시오.

(A) _____
(B) _____
(C) _____

35 위 글의 밑줄 친 우리말 ⓐ와 같도록 주어진 <조건>에 맞게 빈칸에 쓰시오.

> **<조건>**
> 1. 분사구문으로 쓰시오.
> 2. live, in Vienna, in the late 1700s를 활용하시오.

= _____

36 다음 밑줄 친 부분과 바꿔 쓸 수 있는 것은?

Since she had been given an opportunity to study abroad, she got excited.

① Give an opportunity to study abroad
② Having been given an opportunity to study abroad
③ Giving an opportunity to study abroad
④ Gives an opportunity to study abroad
⑤ To give an opportunity to study abroad

[37-38] 다음 문장을 주어진 <조건>에 맞게 바꿔 쓰시오.

<조건>
1. 접속사 as와 if 중 하나를 각각 포함하시오.
2. 밑줄 친 부분을 부사절로 바꿔 쓰시오.

37

Approaching the reception desk, she saw her package.

→ ＿＿＿＿＿＿＿＿＿＿＿＿＿
＿＿＿＿＿＿＿＿＿＿＿, she saw her package.

38

Looking up, you can see the top of the mountain.

→ ＿＿＿＿＿＿＿＿＿＿＿＿＿,
you can see the top of the mountain.

[39-40] 다음 대화를 읽고 주어진 질문에 답하시오.

A: I saw a guy ⓐsold tacos outside.
B: Yes. I saw him, too. He was ⓑprepared his cart.
A: The menu ⓒdisplay on it looked great.
B: I know. (A) 그것을 읽고 난 후, 나는 정말 배고파졌어.
A: The smell of the cooked meat was ⓓamazed. I wish we had time to eat there.
B: Me too. ⓔThink about that delicious food, I'll have a hard time concentrating in class.

39 위 글의 밑줄 친 ⓐ~ⓔ를 바르게 고친 것은?

① ⓐ sold → sell
② ⓑ prepared → preparing
③ ⓒ display → displaying
④ ⓓ amazed → amaze
⑤ ⓔ Think → Thought

40 위 글의 밑줄 친 우리말 (A)를 알맞게 영작한 것을 모두 고르시오.

① Read it, I got really hungry.
② Reading it, I got really hungry.
③ After read it, I got really hungry.
④ Being read it, I got really hungry.
⑤ After I read it, I got really hungry.

41 다음 빈칸에 들어갈 알맞은 것은?

> As I had arrived at the cinema earlier than Judy, I looked at some posters while I waited for her.
> = _____ at the cinema earlier than Judy, I looked at some posters while I waited for her.

① Being arrived　　② Having arrived
③ Arrived　　　　 ④ Arriving
⑤ To arrive

42 우리말과 같도록 <조건>에 맞게 문장을 완성하시오.

> <조건>
> with, shoe laces, untie를 활용하시오.

> 그는 그의 신발끈이 풀린 채로 경주로를 달리고 있었다.

= He was running on the track _____
_____.

[43-45] 다음 대화를 읽고 주어진 질문에 답하시오.

> *Host* : Today, on *New Morning*, I will be interviewing Megan Parker, who designed the first self-driving system for cars.
> *Megan*: It's a pleasure to be invited to a program ⓐ_____(see) by so many viewers.
> *Host* : Your system is really ⓑ_____(fascinate). What was your inspiration?
> *Megan*: I have been ⓒ_____(research) about people's safety in cars for a long time. (A) 솔직히 말하면, 저는 많은 자동차 사고가 예방될 수 있다고 생각합니다. (speaking, car accidents, avoided, frankly, think, be, I, can, many)
> *Host* : Oh... So you're saying your invention will make driving safer?
> *Megan*: Yes. I built a self-driving system based on artificial intelligence, (B) 자동차를 훨씬 더 안전하게 만들면서. (the car, much safer, make) It reacts to information much faster than human drivers.
> *Host* : Wow! That's incredible. I have a few more questions about the system, which we'll get to after this commercial break.
>
> *artificial intelligence 인공지능

43 괄호 안의 말을 활용하여 빈칸 ⓐ~ⓒ에 알맞은 말을 쓰시오.

ⓐ _____

ⓑ _____

ⓒ _____

44 위 대화의 밑줄 친 우리말 (A)와 의미가 같도록 괄호 안의 말을 알맞게 배열하시오.

= _____

_____

45 위 대화의 밑줄 친 우리말 (B)와 같도록 괄호 안의 말을 활용하여 문장을 완성하시오.

= _____

46 다음 빈칸에 들어갈 알맞은 것은?

> When I arrived home, I found the door
> _____.

① unlock
② unlocked
③ unlocking
④ to unlock
⑤ unlocks

47 다음 우리말을 알맞게 영작한 것은?

> 유리는 그곳에 앉아서 다리를 꼰 채로 TV를 보았다.

① Yuri sat there and watched TV with her legs crossing.
② Yuri sat there and watched TV with her legs cross.
③ Yuri sat there and watched TV with her legs crossed.
④ Yuri sat there and watched TV with her legs having crossed.
⑤ Yuri sat there and watched TV with her legs being crossing.

48 다음 (A)~(C)에 들어갈 말이 알맞게 짝지어진 것은?

> _____(A)_____ no watch, Jacob was unsure how much time was remaining for the test. He wanted to check the clock _____(B)_____ on the back wall, but didn't want to turn around. He was nervous that his teacher would think he was trying to cheat. At last, _____(C)_____ by worrying, he raised his hand and asked the remaining time. Luckily, he still had 25 minutes.

	(A)	(B)	(C)
①	Having	located	exhausted
②	Had	located	exhausted
③	Had	locating	exhausting
④	Having	located	exhausting
⑤	Having	locating	exhausting

49 다음 대화의 밑줄 친 문장을 분사구문으로 바꿔 쓰시오.

> A: Why weren't you at the party?
> B: Because my bike was stolen, I had no way to get there.
> A: Oh, I'm sorry to hear that.
> B: It's OK. The police are looking for it.

→ _____

_____

CHAPTER 8
명사와 대명사

Mark saw **Julie** at the park. **She** was riding a **bicycle**.
　명사　　　　명사　　　　　　　　　대명사　　　　　　　　　명사

Mark는 Julie를 공원에서 보았다. 그녀는 자전거를 타고 있었다.

Mark, Julie와 같은 사람의 이름이나 bicycle과 같은 사물의 이름을 나타내는 말을 **명사**라고 해요. 그리고 앞에 나온 명사 Julie를 대신해서 뒤 문장에 나온 She와 같이 명사를 대신해서 쓰는 말을 **대명사**라고 해요.

기출로 적중 POINT

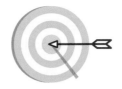

내신 100점 적중!
기출 출제율

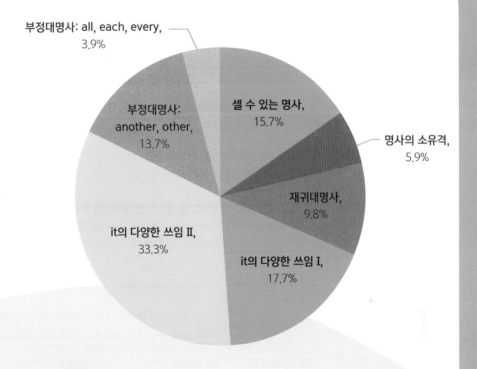

부정대명사: all, each, every, 3.9%

부정대명사: another, other, 13.7%

셀 수 있는 명사, 15.7%

명사의 소유격, 5.9%

재귀대명사, 9.8%

it의 다양한 쓰임 I, 17.7%

it의 다양한 쓰임 II, 33.3%

TOP 1 **it의 다양한 쓰임 II (33.3%)**
「It seems that ~」 구문과 to부정사를 활용한 문장을 바꿔 쓰는 문제가
자주 출제된다.

TOP 2 **it의 다양한 쓰임 I (17.7%)**
it의 다양한 쓰임을 묻는 문제와 이를 구별하는 문제가 자주 출제된다.

TOP 3 **셀 수 있는 명사 (15.7%)**
불규칙하게 변화하는 셀 수 있는 명사의 복수형을 묻는 문제가 자주 출제된다.

셀 수 있는 명사

정답 p.26

1. 셀 수 있는 명사가 단수일 때는 명사 앞에 a(n)을 붙이고, 복수일 때는 복수형으로 쓴다. 셀 수 있는 명사에는 보통명사와 집합명사가 있다.

보통명사	일반적인 사람·동물·사물을 나타내는 명사 girl, doctor, lion, insect, building, piano, computer, apple 등
집합명사	사람·동물·사물이 모인 집합을 나타내는 명사 team, family, audience, people, police 등

(Tip) team, family, audience 등의 집합명사는 의미에 따라 단수 취급하기도 하고 복수 취급하기도 한다.

My **team is** practicing for the championship game. 내 팀은 챔피언 결정전을 위해 연습하고 있다.
팀 한 무리 (단수 취급)
Many **teams compete** against each other in the tournament. 많은 팀들이 토너먼트에서 서로 겨룬다.
팀 여러 무리 (복수 취급)
The **team are** trying on their new uniforms. 그 팀은 그들의 새로운 유니폼을 입어보고 있다.
팀 구성원 개개인 (복수 취급)

(Tip) people, police 등의 집합명사는 항상 복수 취급한다.

People who exercise regularly **are** likely to live longer.
운동을 규칙적으로 하는 사람들은 더 오래 살 가능성이 있다.
The police start to track down the missing children. 경찰들이 실종된 아이들을 추적하기 시작한다.

2. 셀 수 있는 명사의 복수형은 대부분 명사에 -(e)s를 붙여 만들며, 일부는 불규칙하게 변한다.

대부분의 명사	명사 + -s	pencil – pencils	bag – bags
-s, -x, -ch, -sh로 끝나는 명사	명사 + -es	class – classes switch – switches	box – boxes dish – dishes
「자음 + o」로 끝나는 명사	명사 + -es	potato – potatoes (Tip) 예외: piano – pianos	volcano – volcanoes photo – photos
「자음 + y」로 끝나는 명사	y를 i로 바꾸고 + -es	fly - flies lady - ladies	city – cities story – stories
-f, -fe로 끝나는 명사	f, fe를 v로 바꾸고 + -es	shelf – shelves (Tip) 예외: roof – roofs	half – halves cliff – cliffs
불규칙 변화	man – men tooth – teeth ox – oxen	woman – women goose – geese mouse – mice	child – children deer – deer sheep – sheep

(Tip) 「숫자 + 하이픈(-) + 단위 표현」이 형용사처럼 쓰여 명사 앞에서 명사를 꾸밀 때는 숫자 뒤의 단위 표현을 단수형으로 쓴다.

Peter had a (two-hours, two-hour) interview. Peter는 두 시간 동안의 인터뷰를 했다.

연습문제 A 괄호 안에서 알맞은 것을 고르시오.

1 I bought a fresh (orange / oranges) from the market.

2 Jinseo's parents (get / gets) up early in the morning.

3 We have placed several (chair / chairs) in the banquet room.

4 There (was / were) lots of young people at the concert.

5 Many (family / families) are having picnics by the river today.

6 My grandfather used to catch a lot of (snake / snakes) when he was little.

7 The police (was / were) watching the crowd carefully.

8 Some new (team / teams) are participating in this week's game.

9 (A lion / Lions) are very dangerous animals.

10 People that work hard (is / are) more successful.

연습문제 B 괄호 안의 명사를 활용하여 빈칸에 알맞은 말을 쓰시오.

1 I need some _____ to put my books in. (box)

2 There are some _____ on the wall. (photo)

3 You should take your _____ off before you come in. (shoe)

4 Those _____ in the cradle are small and cute. (baby)

5 _____ are cheap and delicious. (tomato)

6 My grandfather raises lots of _____ in the countryside. (ox)

7 Usually, your wisdom _____ come in after you turn 18. (tooth)

8 Jiwoo has a nine-_____-old brother. (year)

9 The hunters were chasing after those _____ in the forest. (wolf)

10 The _____ of the houses are covered with red tiles. (roof)

11 She asked me to wash some _____. (dish)

12 Five _____ are having dinner at the restaurant. (woman)

기출 적중문제

다음 중 명사의 복수형이 바른 것을 모두 고르시오.

① goose – geese ② child – children
③ sheep – sheeps ④ deer – deers
⑤ mouse – mouses

기출로적중 POINT 2 · 셀 수 없는 명사

1. 셀 수 없는 명사는 명사 앞에 a(n)을 붙일 수 없고, 복수형으로도 쓸 수 없다. 셀 수 없는 명사에는 고유명사, 추상명사, 물질명사가 있다.

고유명사	사람, 장소, 요일, 월 등의 고유한 이름을 나타내는 명사 Alice, Mina, Seoul, China, Grand Canyon, Tuesday, November 등
추상명사	눈에 보이지 않는 추상적인 개념을 나타내는 명사 time, use, value, importance, help, wisdom, love, accident, advice 등
물질명사	일정한 형태가 없는 물질을 나타내는 명사 water, meat, cake, rice, sand, paper, trash, oxygen, paint, money 등

(Tip) 추상명사는 전치사와 함께 쓰여 형용사 또는 부사 역할을 할 수 있다.

of + 추상명사 = 형용사	of use 유용한 (=useful) of value 가치 있는 (=valuable) of importance 중요한 (=important)	of no use 쓸모 없는 (=useless) of help 도움이 되는 (=helpful) of wisdom 현명한 (=wise)
기타 전치사 + 추상명사 = 부사	by luck 운 좋게도 (=luckily) in particular 특히 (=particularly) to perfection 완벽하게 (=perfectly)	by accident 우연히 (=accidently) on purpose 고의적으로 (=purposely) with ease 쉽게 (=easily)

2. 셀 수 없는 명사는 담는 그릇이나 자른 모양 등의 단위 표현을 이용하여 수량을 나타낸다. 복수형은 단위 표현에 -(e)s를 붙여 만든다.

단위 표현	함께 쓰이는 명사	단위 표현	함께 쓰이는 명사
a glass of	water, milk, juice, wine	a bar of	chocolate, soap, gold
a cup of	tea, coffee, water	a sheet of	paper, newspaper
a bottle of	water, milk, juice, ink	a slice of	pizza, ham, cheese, bread
a can of	cola, soda, paint	a spoonful of	sugar, salt, rice
a bowl of	soup, rice, salad, cereal	a loaf of	bread
a piece of	cheese, bread, cake, paper, furniture, advice, news, information	

Would you like to drink **a cup of tea**? 너는 차 한 잔 마시길 원하니?
I ate **two bowls of salad** for breakfast. 나는 아침 식사로 샐러드 두 그릇을 먹었다.
My mom bought **four bottles of milk**. 나의 엄마는 우유 네 병을 샀다.

연습문제 A 다음 문장의 밑줄 친 명사와 종류가 <u>다른</u> 것을 고르시오.

1 Martin needs your <u>help</u>.   ① love   ② paint   ③ use

2 He is known for his <u>bravery</u>.   ① advice   ② importance   ③ money

3 The kid folded the <u>paper</u> in half.   ① tea   ② ease   ③ gold

4 Would you like to drink <u>water</u>?   ① value   ② rice   ③ cake

5 It's <u>time</u> to go outside.   ① wisdom   ② oxygen   ③ purpose

6 <u>New York</u> is the city of lights.   ① rain   ② January   ③ Tuesday

7 She picked up some <u>trash</u> in the park.   ① meat   ② sand   ③ accident

연습문제 B 괄호 안에서 알맞은 것을 고르시오.

1 Mr. Brown starts the day with a (cup / slice) of coffee.

2 My little sister had a (bar / bowl) of soup for lunch.

3 Helen gave me two (slice / slices) of pizza on a plate.

4 The couple ordered two (glasses / bars) of juice at the café.

5 Seri brought four (cans / glasses) of paint to repaint her fence.

6 There are three (loaves / bowls) of bread on the shelf.

7 The recipe said you should add two (spoonfuls / pieces) of salt.

8 Robert gave me a (sheet / piece) of advice for the interview.

9 I drank a (bottle / bottles) of water after playing soccer.

10 We carried (sheets / pieces) of furniture into the apartment.

11 My mom purchased a (bar / slice) of soap at the market.

12 I added three (bottles / slices) of ham to my sandwich.

13 Please take a (slice / sheet) of paper out of the box and put it on the desk.

14 My little brother asked for a (can / spoonful) of soda after he finished his meal.

기출 적중문제

우리말과 같도록 괄호 안의 말을 활용하여 문장을 완성하시오.
(단, 숫자는 영어로 쓰시오.)

> 나는 샐러드 한 그릇과 빵 두 덩어리를 먹고 싶다. (salad, bread)

= I would like to have _____ and
_____ .

1. 사람이나 동물을 나타내는 명사의 소유격은 명사에 -'(s)를 붙여 만든다.

단수명사	명사 + 's	**Minji's** purse 민지의 지갑 **my mother's** bag 내 어머니의 가방
-s로 끝나지 않는 복수명사		**men's** clothes 남성용 옷　**children's** books 아동용 책
-s로 끝나는 복수명사	명사 + '	**girls'** school 여학교　**Parents'** Day 어버이날

(Tip) 소유격 뒤의 명사가 반복되거나 집·상점 등을 나타내면 생략할 수 있다.
This **camera** must be **Sumi's (camera).** 이 사진기는 수미의 사진기임에 틀림없다.
What are you doing? – We're having a party at **Karen's (house).**
너희들은 뭐 하고 있니? – 우리는 Karen의 집에서 파티를 하고 있어.

2. 무생물을 나타내는 명사의 소유격은 주로 「of + 명사」로 나타낸다.

the roof **of the building** 그 건물의 지붕　　the top **of the mountain** 그 산의 꼭대기

(Tip) 시간·거리·가격·무게를 나타내는 명사의 소유격은 명사에 -'(s)를 붙여 만든다.
today's newspaper 오늘의 신문　　ten miles' distance 10마일의 거리
a dollar's worth 1달러의 가치　　three tons' weight 3톤의 무게

3. 명사 앞에 관사·지시형용사·부정형용사가 쓰였을 때는 소유격을 명사 뒤에 「of + 소유대명사/명사의 소유격」의 형태로 나타내며, 이를 이중소유격이라고 한다.

① 관사: a, an, the
② 지시형용사: this, that, these, those + 명사 + of + 소유대명사 또는 명사의 소유격
③ 부정형용사: some, any, no, …

a my friend (X) → **a friend of mine** 나의 한 친구
this his bike (X) → **this bike of his** 그의 이 자전거
Mike's some books (X) → **some books of Mike's** Mike의 많은 책

연습문제 A 우리말과 같도록 괄호 안의 말을 활용하여 영작하시오.

1 아이들의 방　= _____ (children, room)

2 Tom의 가족　= _____ (Tom, family)

3 환자들의 차트　= _____ (patients, chart)

4 사람들의 사진　= _____ (people, pictures)

5 조부모님의 집　= _____ (grandparents, house)

6 남자 화장실 = _____ (men, bathroom)

7 그 영화의 제목 = _____ (the movie, the title)

8 그 건물의 로비 = _____ (the building, the lobby)

9 두 시간의 일 = _____ (two hours, work)

10 그의 그 바지 = _____ (he, those pants)

11 개의 꼬리 = _____ (a dog, tail)

12 그 책상의 다리 = _____ (the desk, the legs)

13 Jack의 그 컴퓨터 = _____ (Jack, the computer)

연습문제 B 다음 밑줄 친 부분이 어법상 맞으면 O, 틀리면 바르게 고쳐 쓰시오.

1 The president of the country is elected every five years. → _____

2 He saw the article in yesterday's newspaper. → _____

3 You had better fix that your shirt. → _____

4 I met some friends of mine for dinner last night. → _____

5 Jina introduced me to a relative of her at the social party. → _____

6 We've taken some pictures with this camera of Mina's. → _____

7 She asked me the way to get to Mr. Smith' house. → _____

8 Tokyo is the world's most crowded city. → _____

9 I'm using my mom's this cell phone because mine is broken. → _____

10 The city skyline looks different at distance of ten miles'. → _____

11 I'm interested in hearing about any ideas of yours. → _____

12 We're going to buy twenty dollars' worth of snacks for the party. → _____

13 I really enjoyed reading this your story. → _____

14 These John's songs always lift my spirits. → _____

기출 적중문제

다음 두 문장의 의미가 같도록 문장을 완성하시오. (단, the와 of를 반드시 포함하시오.)

You can put those books on your desk.
= You can put those books on _____ .

재귀대명사

1. 재귀대명사는 인칭대명사의 소유격이나 목적격에 self/selves를 붙인 형태로, '~자신, ~자체'의 의미이다.

인칭 ＼ 수	단수	복수
1인칭	I - **myself**	we - **ourselves**
2인칭	you - **yourself**	you - **yourselves**
3인칭	he - **himself** / she - **herself** / it - **itself**	they - **themselves**

2. 재귀대명사의 용법

재귀 용법	동사나 전치사의 목적어가 주어와 같은 대상일 때 목적어 자리에 재귀대명사를 쓴다. 이때 재귀대명사는 생략할 수 없다. **I** introduced **myself** to them. 나는 그들에게 나 자신을 소개했다. **You** should be proud of **yourself**. 너는 너 자신을 자랑스러워해야 한다.
강조 용법	명사나 대명사를 강조하기 위해 강조하는 말 바로 뒤나 문장 맨 뒤에 재귀대명사를 쓸 수 있다. 이때 재귀대명사는 생략할 수 있다. **They** (**themselves**) wrote all these letters. 그들은 이 모든 편지들을 직접 썼다. = **They** wrote all these letters (**themselves**).

3. 재귀대명사의 관용 표현

by oneself 혼자서, 홀로 for oneself 스스로, 혼자 힘으로
in itself 그 자체가, 본래 enjoy oneself 즐거운 시간을 보내다
talk[say] to oneself 혼잣말을 하다 between ourselves 우리끼리의 이야기(지만)
help oneself (to ~) ~을 마음껏 먹다 make oneself at home (집에서처럼) 편히 쉬다

She created those sculptures **by herself**. 그녀는 그 조각품들을 혼자서 만들었다.
We all **enjoyed ourselves** during the vacation. 우리 모두는 휴가 동안 즐거운 시간을 보냈다.

연습문제 A | 괄호 안에서 알맞은 것을 고르시오.

1 I need to find (me / myself) a new hobby.

2 Ms. Yoon invited (us / ourselves) to her restaurant.

3 Linda bought (hers / herself) a pair of shoes.

4 We shouldn't blame (us / ourselves) because we did our best.

5 Sharon wanted to tell (me / myself) a secret.

6 I'm going to call Jack because I need to ask (him / himself) something.

7 The students decorated the auditorium (them / themselves).

연습문제 **B** 밑줄 친 부분을 생략할 수 있으면 O를 쓰고, 생략할 수 없으면 X를 쓰시오.

1 Don't play with the knife, or you may hurt <u>yourself</u>. → _____

2 The president <u>himself</u> will visit the school for the graduation ceremony. → _____

3 We heard about the robbery but did not see it <u>ourselves</u>. → _____

4 Has Jane <u>herself</u> responded to your message? → _____

5 He fell down and laughed at <u>himself</u>. → _____

연습문제 **C** 우리말과 같도록 <보기>의 표현과 괄호 안의 대명사를 활용하여 문장을 완성하시오.

<보기> in itself   help oneself   between ourselves   make oneself at home

1 민식이는 블루베리 머핀을 마음껏 먹었다. (he)

= Minsik _____ to the blueberry muffins.

2 제가 돌아올 때까지 여기서 편히 쉬세요. (you)

= Please _____ here until I get back.

3 지금부터 이 이야기는 우리끼리의 이야기로 지켜야 한다. (we)

= We should keep this story _____ from now on.

4 새로운 공연 그 자체는 나쁜 생각이 아니었다. (it)

= The new performance wasn't a bad idea _____ .

기출 적중문제

주어진 문장의 밑줄 친 재귀대명사와 쓰임이 같은 것은?

I remind <u>myself</u> to eat healthy food every day.

① Mr. Collins will repair the car <u>himself</u>.

② The actress <u>herself</u> volunteers at the charity.

③ We didn't like the hotel, but the town <u>itself</u> was nice.

④ Emily is mad at <u>herself</u> for failing the exam.

⑤ I made the advertisements for the band <u>myself</u>.

재귀대명사가 목적어 또는 주어와 같은 대상일 때는 재귀 용법이고, 재귀대명사가 명사나 대명사를 강조할 때는 강조 용법이에요.

it의 다양한 쓰임 I

정답 p.26

it은 '그것'이라는 의미의 대명사로 쓰이며, 비인칭 주어, 가주어, 가목적어로도 쓰인다.

비인칭 주어	날씨, 계절, 시간, 요일, 날짜, 명암, 거리를 나타낼 때 주어 자리에 쓰며 해석은 하지 않는다. **It**'s getting cold. 추워지고 있다. What day is **it** today? – **It**'s Monday. 오늘 무슨 요일이니? – 월요일이야.
가주어	문장의 주어 자리에 to부정사구나 명사절 등이 와서 주어가 긴 경우 주어 자리에 가주어 it을 쓰고 진주어(원래 주어)를 뒤로 보낸다. **It** is important **to go to school on time**. 학교에 제시간에 가는 것은 중요하다. **It** made me angry **that Alex ignored my message**. Alex가 내 메시지를 무시한 것이 나를 화나게 했다.
가목적어	문장의 목적어 자리에 to부정사구나 명사절 등이 와서 목적어가 긴 경우 목적어 자리에 가목적 어 it을 쓰고 진목적어(원래 목적어)를 뒤로 보낸다. He thought **it** hard **to speak in Chinese**. 그는 중국어로 말하는 것이 어렵다고 생각했다. I made **it** clear **that I couldn't go there**. 나는 내가 그곳에 갈 수 없었다는 것을 분명히 했다.

연습문제 밑줄 친 it의 쓰임과 같은 것을 <보기>에서 골라 그 기호를 쓰시오.

<보기>	ⓐ I don't know how they do it.
	ⓑ It is raining heavily outside.
	ⓒ It is necessary to buy a new chair.
	ⓓ Lucy found it easy to make an apple pie.

1 It is already 2 o'clock, so we need to start studying.　　　　　　[　　　　]

2 It is a great idea to save money whenever you can.　　　　　　[　　　　]

3 Wash and peel the carrot, and cut it into small pieces.　　　　　　[　　　　]

4 We thought it necessary to bathe the dog.　　　　　　[　　　　]

5 It is a problem that he didn't finish all his homework yet.　　　　　　[　　　　]

6 I watched the movie with Sam yesterday, and it was interesting.　　　　　　[　　　　]

7 It is dangerous to cross the road while listening to loud music.　　　　　　[　　　　]

8 It is just two kilometers from here to the airport.　　　　　　[　　　　]

9 Put it on your skin in the morning and at night.　　　　　　[　　　　]

10 The scientist considered it possible to develop a new vaccine within a month.　　[　　　　]

POINT 5-2 it의 다양한 쓰임 Ⅱ

정답 p.27

「It seems that ~」은 '~인 것 같다'의 의미이며, that절의 주어를 문장의 주어 자리에 쓰고 that절의 동사를 to부정사로 바꿔 쓸 수 있다.

It seems that Junwoo **is** happy. 준우는 행복한 것 같다.
= Junwoo **seems to be** happy.

It seemed that he **didn't know** about the accident. 그는 그 사고에 대해 모르는 것 같았다.
= He **seemed not to know** about the accident.
= He **didn't seem to know** about the accident.

연습문제 | 두 문장의 의미가 같도록 문장을 완성하시오.

1 It seems that you are a little tired.
= You _____ a little tired.

2 It seemed that somebody was in the kitchen.
= Somebody _____ in the kitchen.

3 The computer monitor seems to be broken.
= It _____ broken.

4 It seemed that there were enough seats in the stadium.
= There _____ enough seats in the stadium.

5 It seems that the television is working well now.
= The television _____ well now.

6 It seems that she knows a lot about the book.
= She _____ a lot about the book.

7 The weather seems to be getting colder these days.
= It _____ colder these days.

8 It seemed that she didn't have a camera with her.
= She _____ a camera with her.

9 It seems that the idiom is based on an old folk tale.
= The idiom _____ on an old folk tale.

10 It seemed that the town wasn't affected by the recent earthquake.
= The town _____ by the recent earthquake.

CHAPTER 8 명사와 대명사 해커스 중학영문법 3학년

부정대명사: one

정답 p.27

> **1. one은 앞에서 언급된 명사와 같은 종류이지만 다른 대상을 가리킬 때 쓴다.**
>
> Have you lost your **wallet**? I'll buy you a new **one**.
> 너의 지갑을 잃어버렸니? 내가 너에게 새것을 사줄게.
>
> I don't have any **chopsticks**. – Use these **ones**. 나는 젓가락이 하나도 없어. – 이것들을 써.
>
> (Tip) 대명사 it과 they/them은 앞에서 언급된 것과 같은 대상을 가리킬 때 쓴다.
> This is my **new bag**. I bought **it** last week. 이것은 나의 새 가방이다. 나는 이것을 지난 주에 샀다.
> I have four **books**. I'll read **them** tomorrow. 나는 책 네 권이 있다. 나는 그것들을 내일 읽을 것이다.
>
> **2. one은 일반적인 사람을 나타낼 때 쓴다.**
>
> **One** should respect other people. 사람은 다른 사람들을 존중해야 한다.

연습문제 A 밑줄 친 부분이 어법상 맞으면 O를 쓰고, 틀리면 바르게 고쳐 쓰시오.

1 My laptop broke, so I have to go buy a new <u>it</u>. → _____

2 Call your friends and invite <u>ones</u> to the hockey game. → _____

3 You can have my piece of cake if you want <u>it</u>. → _____

4 She offered me a hotdog, but I already had <u>one</u> at lunch. → _____

5 I like these jeans more than those black <u>one</u>. → _____

6 If you need a seat, there's <u>it</u> over there. → _____

연습문제 B 다음 빈칸에 알맞은 말을 <보기>에서 골라 쓰시오.

| <보기>   one   ones   it   them |

1 These flowers are beautiful. Where did you buy _____?

2 The bus was full of people, so I took the next _____.

3 I'm going to throw this cup away because of the crack in _____.

4 You said you don't like these kinds of shoes. Then what about those _____?

5 I was looking for wooden frames, but there were only plastic _____.

6 _____ should not pursue goals that are easily achieved.

부정대명사: some, any

정답 p.27

some과 any는 '어떤 것/사람들, 몇 개/사람'이라는 의미이다.

some	주로 긍정문에서 쓴다.

Some of the oranges are rotten. 그 오렌지들 중 어떤 것은 썩었다.

Jane invited **some of her friends** to her house.
Jane은 그녀의 친구 중 몇 사람을 그녀의 집으로 초대했다.

(Tip) some은 부정형용사로도 쓰일 수 있다.
There are **some stars** in the sky. 하늘에 몇 개의 별들이 있다.

any	주로 부정문과 의문문에서 쓴다.

I can't lend you money. I don't have **any** left.
나는 너에게 돈을 빌려줄 수 없어. 어떤 것도 남은 것이 없어.

Did you reply to **any of her letters**? 너는 그녀의 어떤 편지들에라도 답장했니?

(Tip) any는 부정형용사로도 쓰일 수 있다.
She doesn't have **any coins**. 그녀는 어떤 동전도 가지고 있지 않다.

(Tip) some과 any에 -thing이 붙으면 '어떤 것, 무엇'이라는 의미로 불특정한 사물을 대신하고, -one/-body가 붙으면 '어떤 사람, 누구'라는 의미로 불특정한 사람을 대신한다.

Something is wrong with my bicycle. 나의 자전거에 무언가가 잘못되었다.
I didn't buy **anything** at the shopping mall. 나는 그 쇼핑몰에서 어떤 것도 사지 않았다.
We need **someone** to lift these boxes. 우리는 이 상자들을 들 누군가가 필요하다.
Did you meet **anyone** at the park? 너는 그 공원에서 어떤 사람이라도 만났니?

연습문제 다음 빈칸에 가장 알맞은 말을 <보기>에서 골라 쓰시오.

<보기> some any something anything someone anyone

1 _____ of the sand has fallen on the floor.

2 There was _____ unusual about the man I saw.

3 I don't think _____ knows about this actor.

4 _____ of the tables in the restaurant are still dirty.

5 Has _____ here ever been to Africa before?

6 There's _____ talking on the phone loudly in the library.

7 Are _____ of the books here offered at a discounted price?

8 Carla doesn't have _____ to wear to the wedding.

부정대명사: another, other

정답 p.27

1. another, others의 쓰임

another 다른 하나, 하나 더	That candy was good. I'll have **another**. 이 사탕은 맛있었다. 나는 하나 더 먹을 것이다. (Tip) another는 단수 명사를 수식하여 '또 다른 ~'이라는 의미의 형용사로도 쓰인다. 　　　We need to buy **another** computer. 우리는 또 다른 컴퓨터를 살 필요가 있다.
others 다른 사람들/ 것들	He likes to talk with **others**. 그는 다른 사람들과 이야기하는 것을 좋아한다. (Tip) other는 복수 명사를 수식하여 '다른 ~'이라는 의미의 형용사로 쓰인다. 　　　We should help **other** people. 우리는 다른 사람들을 도와야 한다.

(Tip) the other는 '나머지 하나', the others는 '나머지 전부'라는 의미이다.
I found one sock. Where is **the other**? 나는 양말 하나를 찾았어. 나머지 하나는 어디에 있니?
I ate a slice of pizza. Who ate **the others**? 나는 피자 한 조각을 먹었어. 나머지 전부는 누가 먹었니?

2. one, another, other(s), some을 써서 여럿 중 일부를 가리킬 수 있다.

one ~, the other ··· (둘 중) 하나는 ~, 나머지 하나는 ···	There are two pens. **One** is blue, and **the other** is black. 펜 두 개가 있다. 하나는 파란색이고, 나머지 하나는 검정색이다.
one ~, another ···, the other – (셋 중) 하나는 ~, 다른 하나는 ···, 나머지 하나는 –	There are three pens. **One** is blue, **another** is red, and **the other** is black. 펜 세 개가 있다. 하나는 파란색이고, 다른 하나는 빨간색이고, 나머지 하나는 검정색이다.
one ~, the others ··· (여럿 중) 하나는 ~, 나머지 전부는 ···	There are many pens. **One** is blue, and **the others** are black. 많은 펜이 있다. 하나는 파란색이고, 나머지 전부는 검정색이다.
one ~, another ···, the others – (여럿 중) 하나는 ~, 다른 하나는 ···, 나머지 전부는 –	There are many pens. **One** is blue, **another** is red, and **the others** are black. 많은 펜이 있다. 하나는 파란색이고, 다른 하나는 빨간색이고, 나머지 전부는 검정색이다.
some ~, others ··· (여럿 중) 몇몇은 ~, 다른 사람들/것들은 ···	There are many pens. **Some** are blue, and **others** are red. 많은 펜이 있다. 몇몇은 파란색이고, 다른 것들은 빨간색이다. (그리고 파란색도 빨간색도 아닌 펜들도 있다.)
some ~, the others ··· (여럿 중) 몇몇은 ~, 나머지 전부는 ···	There are many pens. **Some** are blue, and **the others** are red. 많은 펜이 있다. 몇몇은 파란색이고, 나머지 전부는 빨간색이다.

연습문제 A 괄호 안에서 알맞은 것을 고르시오.

1 Wendy is very nice, so she gets along well with (another / others).

---

2 Some people ordered cake for dessert, while (another / others) ordered ice cream.

3 I'm still hungry after that hot dog, so I'm going to eat (another / other).

4 She is afraid of giving a presentation in front of (another / others).

5 That movie was great. Can we watch (another / other) movie?

6 If you don't like that necklace, we have (others / other) necklaces to choose from.

연습문제 B. 다음 그림을 보고 빈칸에 알맞은 말을 쓰시오.

1

2

3

4

1 The clown is juggling four balls. _____ is green, _____ is blue, and _____ are red.

2 Two people are standing next to each other. _____ is holding an umbrella, and _____ is wearing a raincoat.

3 There are four people exercising in the park. _____ is jumping rope, and _____ are jogging.

4 Of the five students in the group, _____ students are from Canada while _____ are from England.

기출 적중문제

다음 빈칸에 알맞은 말을 <보기>에서 골라 쓰시오.

<보기>   one   another   other   others

(1) Some students say that math is more important than history. _____ disagree.

(2) If you are still thirsty after that glass of water, you can have _____.

부정대명사: all, each, every

정답 p.27

부정대명사 all, each, every 뒤에 올 수 있는 명사와 동사의 형태에 주의한다.

all 모든	all (of) + 복수명사 + 복수동사	**All (of) the tickets were** sold out. 모든 티켓들이 매진되었다.
	all (of) + 셀 수 없는 명사 + 단수동사	**All (of) the food was** delicious. 모든 음식이 맛있었다.
each 각각(의)	each of + 복수명사 + 단수동사	**Each of the kids was** wearing a hat. 각각의 아이들은 모자를 쓰고 있었다.
	each + 단수명사 + 단수동사	**Each classroom has** a computer. 각각의 교실에는 컴퓨터가 있다.
every 모든	every + 단수명사 + 단수동사	**Every book has** a different ending. 모든 책에는 다른 결말이 있다.
	every + -thing/-body/-one + 단수동사	**Everybody is** having a good time. 모두가 좋은 시간을 보내고 있다.

연습문제 A | 괄호 안에서 알맞은 것을 고르시오.

1 Each (plant / plants) needs a different amount of water.

2 All of the information I received from Jinsu (was / were) wrong.

3 (Each / All) of the students has to choose a topic to write about.

4 Every (teacher / teachers) likes to spend time talking with their students.

5 (All / Each) of the participants were satisfied with the results.

연습문제 B | 우리말과 같도록 괄호 안의 말을 활용하여 문장을 완성하시오.

1 그 극장의 모든 좌석들이 비어있다. (seat, be)
= All of the _____ in the theater _____ empty.

2 지구상의 모든 생물은 생존하기 위해 음식이 필요하다. (living thing, need)
= All _____ _____ on the earth _____ food to survive.

3 모두가 민우의 생일 파티에 가기를 원한다. (want)
= Everyone _____ to go to Minwoo's birthday party.

4 이 모임에 있는 각각의 사람은 다른 목표들을 가지고 있다. (person, have)
= Each _____ in this group _____ different goals.

기출로적중 POINT 6-5 부정대명사: both, either, neither

정답 p.27

부정대명사 both, either, neither 뒤에 올 수 있는 명사와 동사의 형태에 주의한다.

both 둘 모두	both (of) + 복수명사 + 복수동사	**Both (of) the players are** exhausted. 두 선수들 모두 기진맥진하다.
either 둘 중 어느 것이든 / 누구든	either of + 복수명사 + 단/복수동사	**Either of the plans is[are]** excellent. 둘 중 어느 계획이든 훌륭하다.
	either + 단수명사 + 단수동사	**Either solution is** possible. 두 해결책 중 어느 것이든 가능하다.
neither 둘 중 어느 것도 / 누구도	neither of + 복수명사 + 단/복수동사	**Neither of the kids has[have]** a bag. 그 아이들 둘 중 누구도 가방을 가지고 있지 않다.
	neither + 단수명사 + 단수동사	**Neither answer is** correct. 두 답안 중 어느 것도 정확하지 않다.

연습문제 우리말과 같도록 both, neither, either와 괄호 안의 말을 활용하여 빈칸에 쓰시오.

1 나는 재킷이 두 벌 있지만 둘 중 어느 것도 나에게 맞지 않는다. (fit)

= I have two jackets, but _____ of them _____ me.

2 그는 두 그림들 모두가 할인한다는 소식을 듣고 놀랐다. (painting)

= He was surprised to hear that _____ of the _____ were on sale.

3 두 개의 알약 중 어느 것이든 두통을 완화하는 데에 도움을 준다. (help)

= _____ of the pills _____ relieve a headache.

4 너는 현금이나 카드로 계산할 수 있다. 두 지불 방법 중 어느 것이든 괜찮다. (be)

= You can pay by cash or card. _____ payment method _____ fine.

5 수지와 John은 이미 그들의 샌드위치를 먹어서 둘 중 누구도 배고프지 않다. (be)

= Suzy and John already ate their sandwiches, so _____ of them _____ hungry.

6 두 선생님들 모두 열심히 하는 학생들을 칭찬하신다. (teacher)

= _____ _____ praise hard-working students.

7 두 소설 중 어느 것도 독자의 관심을 끌 정도로 흥미롭지 않았다. (be)

= _____ novel _____ interesting enough to hold the reader's attention.

8 그녀는 두 학생들 모두 이야기할 권리가 있다고 말했다. (student)

= She said that _____ _____ have the right to speak.

A 밑줄 친 부분이 어법상 맞으면 O를 쓰고, 틀리면 바르게 고쳐 쓰시오.

1 My favorite characters in the cartoon are the five fat <u>mouses</u>.　→　_____

2 The chef added three <u>spoonful</u> of salt to the pasta sauce.　→　_____

3 We really enjoyed <u>ourself</u> at the music festival.　→　_____

4 He bought two <u>loaf</u> of bread at the bakery yesterday.　→　_____

5 There is an interesting <u>piece</u> of information on the website.　→　_____

6 The <u>shelfs</u> in the library are full of interesting books.　→　_____

7 My father decided to prepare <u>himself</u> a sandwich for lunch.　→　_____

8 Diane made herself <u>in home</u> when she visited my house.　→　_____

9 We used to have two <u>pianos</u>, but we sold one of them.　→　_____

B 우리말과 같도록 괄호 안의 말을 알맞게 배열하시오.

1 그 야영장이 어두워서 나는 나의 책을 읽을 수가 없었다. (at, dark, was, the campsite, it)
= _____, so I couldn't read my book.

2 너는 그 문장을 이해하지 못하는 것 같다. (not, understand, to, seem, you)
= _____ the sentence.

3 빠르고 키도 큰 축구 선수를 찾는 것은 어렵다. (difficult, is, it, a soccer player, find, to)
= _____ who is both fast and tall.

4 그들은 땅에 있는 무언가를 보고 있는 것 같았다. (that, it, were, looking, seemed, they)
= _____ at something on the ground.

5 어떤 사람들은 달에 가는 것이 불가능하다고 믿었다. (believed, impossible, people, it, some)
= _____ to go to the Moon.

6 오늘 버스가 그렇게 늦는 것은 이례적이다. (is, that, unusual, it)
= _____ the bus is so late today.

7 그녀는 런던에서 좋은 시간을 보낸 것 같다. (she, it, had, that, seems)
= _____ a great time in London.

8 그 소음은 내가 공부에 집중하는 것을 어렵게 만들었다. (made, difficult, the noise, it)
= _____ for me to concentrate on studying.

C 다음 빈칸에 부정대명사 one, some, any, another, the other 중 알맞은 것을 쓰시오.

Yesterday, I met with my friend Julia at the park. I wanted some candy, but I didn't have
ⓐ_____. She had ⓑ_____, so she gave me three pieces of fruit-flavored candy.
ⓒ_____ was shaped like a watermelon, ⓓ_____ looked like a pineapple, and
ⓔ_____ looked like a lemon. They were all delicious.

D 우리말과 같도록 괄호 안의 말을 활용하여 문장을 완성하시오.

1 각각의 방들은 욕조와 샤워실을 가지고 있다. (each, the rooms, have)

= _____ a bathtub and shower.

2 모든 제품은 6개월짜리 품질 보증서를 가지고 있다. (all, have, the products)

= _____ a six-month warranty.

3 두 남동생들 모두 음악 듣는 것을 좋아한다. (both, like, my little brother)

= _____ listening to music.

4 두 책 중 어느 것이든 너의 지식을 향상하는 데 유용하다. (either, the books, be)

= _____ useful to improve your knowledge.

5 모든 돈은 나의 은행 계좌 안에 있다. (all, be, the money)

= _____ in my bank account.

6 두 나라 중 어느 곳도 평화 조약에 먼저 서명하기를 원하지 않는다. (neither, want, the countries)

= _____ to sign the peace treaty first.

7 모든 아이들은 그 게임을 하고 싶어 한다. (all, be, the kids)

= _____ willing to play the game.

8 각각의 기계들은 다른 일련 번호를 가지고 있다. (each, have, the machines)

= _____ a different serial number.

9 모든 학생은 5분 동안 연설을 해야 한다. (every, need, student)

= _____ to give a speech for five minutes.

10 둘 중 누구도 그곳에 어떻게 가는지 모른다. (neither, know, the men)

= _____ how to get there.

중간 · 기말고사 실전 문제

1 다음 중 어법상 <u>어색한</u> 것은?

① There are four people standing in line.
② I saw some ghosts in the basement of my house.
③ All of the chairs at my school is very old.
④ Jerry took three classes during the summer vacation.
⑤ Many children were at the garden today.

2 다음 (A)~(C)에 들어갈 말이 바르게 짝지어진 것은?

· My friendship with Mark started when we were ____(A)____ boys.
· The ____(B)____ were swimming in the lake.
· My grandmother used to tell me many fun ____(C)____.

	(A)	(B)	(C)
①	ten-years-old	gooses	stories
②	ten-year-old	gooses	stories
③	ten-year-old	geese	stories
④	ten-year-old	geese	storys
⑤	ten-years-old	geese	storys

3 우리말과 같도록 괄호 안의 말을 활용하여 문장을 완성하시오.

Amy는 매우 배고팠기 때문에 시리얼 두 그릇과 초콜릿 바 세 개를 먹었다. (cereal, chocolate)

= Since Amy was starving, she ate
_____ and
_____.

4 다음 중 어법상 바른 것끼리 묶인 것은?

ⓐ Jaeho drinks a bottle of milk every morning.
ⓑ Some families with children live in the apartment building.
ⓒ I asked for an extra slices of cheese for my sandwich.
ⓓ I need a sheet of paper to write my e-mail address on.
ⓔ He showed some photoes to his friend.

① ⓐ, ⓑ, ⓒ   ② ⓐ, ⓒ, ⓓ   ③ ⓐ, ⓑ, ⓓ
④ ⓑ, ⓒ, ⓓ   ⑤ ⓑ, ⓓ, ⓔ

5 우리말과 같도록 <보기>의 말을 활용하여 빈칸에 쓰시오.

<보기>　either　neither

(1) 식탁 위에 두 가지 맛의 차가 있지만, 나는 둘 중 어느 것도 원하지 않는다.
= There are two flavors of tea on the table, but I want _____
_____ _____.

(2) 우리는 우리의 여행지에 대한 두 가지 선택지가 있다. 둘 중 어느 곳이든 재미있어 보인다.
= We have two options for our travel destination. _____ _____
_____ looks fun.

6 우리말과 같도록 주어진 <조건>에 맞게 영작하시오.

> 나의 아버지가 우리 손님들에게 편히 쉬라고 말씀하셨다.

> <조건>
> 1. my father, tell, our guest, to, make를 활용하시오
> 2. 10단어로 쓰시오.

= _____

_____

7 다음 빈칸에 공통으로 들어갈 알맞은 것은?

> · He put a _____ of cheese in his sandwich.
> · My parents decided to buy a _____ of furniture for the kitchen.
> · I have a _____ of news to tell you.

① spoonful   ② piece   ③ sheet
④ loaf   ⑤ slice

8 다음 중 밑줄 친 부분이 어법상 어색한 것은?

① Jack's sweater is thicker than that <u>one</u>.
② <u>One</u> must follow the national laws.
③ I lost my pen, so I have to buy a new <u>one</u>.
④ I want that skirt because <u>it</u> looks good on me.
⑤ I don't have a notebook, but there's <u>it</u> on that desk.

9 다음 빈칸에 공통으로 들어갈 알맞은 대명사를 쓰시오.

> · Mr. Parker was looking for a job for a long time, and now he has a good _____.
> · _____ should not worry too much about either the future or the past.

10 다음 중 밑줄 친 부분을 생략할 수 있는 것은?

① I wasn't able to lift the sofa by <u>myself</u>.
② Helen bought the cookies for <u>herself</u>.
③ She saw her brother talking to <u>himself</u>.
④ Make <u>yourself</u> at home while I get some drinks.
⑤ Leo <u>himself</u> worked as a painter when he was young.

11 다음 대화의 빈칸에 알맞은 말을 <보기>에서 골라 쓰시오.

> <보기> it they them one ones

(1) A: Do you like your new apartment?
   B: Yes. ⓐ_____ has a much larger bedroom than my old ⓑ_____.

(2) A: Which flowers will be best to give to my mother?
   B: Those purple ⓒ_____ are nice.

12 다음 중 어느 빈칸에도 들어갈 수 <u>없는</u> 것은?

> ⓐ_____ have their own mottos, and
> ⓑ_____ don't. However, there are
> many great people in history who had
> mottos and followed ⓒ_____. Do you
> have a motto? If not, why don't you try
> making ⓓ_____?

① some   ② one   ③ other
④ them   ⑤ others

13 다음 우리말을 영작한 것 중 <u>어색한</u> 것은?

① 배가 고프면 냉장고에서 컵케이크를 꺼내 마음껏 먹어
라.
= Help yourself to a cupcake from the
fridge if you are hungry.
② 이 소식을 우리끼리의 이야기로 해야 할까?
= Should we keep this news between
ourselves?
③ 나는 혼자서 나의 부모님을 위해 저녁을 차릴 수 있다.
= I can make dinner for my parents in
myself.
④ 이 문제는 그 자체로는 해결하기 어렵지 않다.
= This problem is not difficult to solve in
itself.
⑤ 나의 삼촌은 멕시코에서 즐거운 시간을 보내는 것 같다.
= My uncle seems to be enjoying himself
in Mexico.

14 다음 밑줄 친 부분의 쓰임이 같은 것끼리 묶인 것
은?

> ⓐ We have to leave now, as <u>it</u>'s already
> half past ten.
> ⓑ <u>It</u> will be challenging to learn a new
> foreign language.
> ⓒ <u>It</u>'s very windy outside, so you'd
> better not go out.
> ⓓ He finds <u>it</u> difficult to find time to see
> his friends these days.
> ⓔ They should take a taxi home, as <u>it</u> is
> too far from here.

① ⓐ, ⓑ, ⓓ   ② ⓐ, ⓒ, ⓔ   ③ ⓑ, ⓒ, ⓓ
④ ⓑ, ⓒ, ⓔ   ⑤ ⓑ, ⓓ, ⓔ

15 주어진 문장의 밑줄 친 <u>it</u>과 쓰임이 같은 것은?

> <u>It</u> is already December. We should start
> preparing for the school Christmas
> party.

① <u>It</u> is so boring to stay at home on a rainy
day.
② I find <u>it</u> hard to believe what Jason told
me yesterday.
③ <u>It</u> is my older sister's birthday.
④ Steve made <u>it</u> clear that he did not know
about the rumor.
⑤ <u>It</u> is amazing that her older brother is an
astronaut.

[16-17] 우리말과 같도록 괄호 안의 말을 활용하여 문장을 완성하시오.

16

> 그는 나에게 그의 꿈을 말해줬다. (he, a dream)

= He told me _____ .

17

> 그 건물의 꼭대기 층에는 레스토랑이 있다. (the building, the top floor)

= There's a restaurant on _____
_____ .

18 우리말과 같도록 괄호 안의 말을 알맞게 배열하시오.

> 미나는 많은 스트레스를 받을 때 혼잣말을 한다.
> (she, feels, stress, a lot of, herself, to, when, talks)

= Mina _____
_____ .

19 두 문장의 의미가 같도록 빈칸에 알맞은 말을 쓰시오.

> The river seems to be frozen.
> = It _____ _____ the river
> _____ _____ .

20 다음 중 밑줄 친 부분이 어법상 어색한 것은?

> Last autumn, ①everyone in our class went on a school trip to a bird sanctuary. I had never seen ②anything like it, so I was really looking forward to it. Some birds were flying around, and ③others were singing. I saw flamingos, cranes, and massive swans, and I even managed to feed some ducks. Some students were afraid of interacting with the birds, while ④the others enjoyed it a lot. At the end, all of us ⑤was given a cap with the bird sanctuary logo on it.
>
> *sanctuary 보호구역
> *crane 학

21 다음 (A)~(C)에 들어갈 말이 바르게 짝지어진 것은?

> · It seems that the bus ___(A)___ running late today.
> · Kids seem ___(B)___ the new movie, but adults don't enjoy it.
> · It seemed that the kittens ___(C)___ afraid of us.

	(A)	(B)	(C)
①	is	like	was
②	to be	like	were
③	is	to like	were
④	to be	to like	were
⑤	is	to like	to be

22 우리말과 같도록 괄호 안의 말을 알맞게 배열하시오.

> 그 과학자는 대지진이 곧 발생하는 것이 불가능하다고 생각한다. (a large earthquake, it, impossible, that, will happen, soon)

= The scientist thinks _____

_____.

23 다음 글에서 어법상 어색한 부분을 찾아 쓰고 바르게 고쳐 쓰시오.

> Mr. Wells has three sons. One is a teacher, another is a journalist, and other is a student.

_____ → _____

24 우리말과 같도록 괄호 안의 말을 활용하여 문장을 완성하시오.

> 나는 두 개의 샌드위치가 있지만, 둘 중 어느 것도 안에 오이가 들어있지 않다. (them, have, cucumber)

= I have two sandwiches, but _____

_____ in it.

25 다음 중 짝지어진 두 문장의 의미가 <u>다른</u> 것은?

① It seems that we need a new sofa for the lounge.
= We seem to need a new sofa for the lounge.

② It seemed that he finished the exam before anyone else.
= He seemed to finish the exam before anyone else.

③ It seemed that the baseball team practiced all day.
= The baseball team seemed to practice all day.

④ It seemed that the mufflers were not hers.
= The mufflers seemed to be hers.

⑤ It seemed that Somin was watching a movie on her phone.
= Somin seemed to be watching a movie on her phone.

26 다음 글의 밑줄 친 ⓐ~ⓔ 중 어법상 <u>어색한</u> 것을 찾아 기호를 쓰고 바르게 고쳐 쓰시오.

> · Jia is practicing the piano again. She ⓐ<u>seems like to</u> playing the piano.
> · Joseph didn't bring his homework. He ⓑ<u>seemed to be</u> feeling sad about it.
> · She doesn't want to go to the beach. She ⓒ<u>seem to think</u> it's not a good idea to go there.
> · I saw Jiho in the street. He ⓓ<u>seemed to be</u> going to a yoga class.
> · He couldn't use the elevator this morning. It ⓔ<u>seemed to be</u> broken.

(1) _____ → _____

(2) _____ → _____

27 다음 중 어법상 바른 것은?

① The hotel has no rooms, so I'll check other.

② Put some in the refrigerator and another in the freezer.

③ He ate other piece of cheese cake I was about to have.

④ I found my left shoe, but I can't find the other.

⑤ Only one of the cookies is left, because we ate others.

28 우리말과 같도록 괄호 안의 말을 알맞게 배열하시오.

두 다큐멘터리 영화 중 어느 것도 아마존 강에 관한 것이 아니다. (about, neither, the documentary films, of, is, the Amazon River)

= _____

_____

29 다음 (A)~(C)에 들어갈 말이 바르게 짝지어진 것은?

· My mother enjoys going for walks by ___(A)___ .

· My cousins and I built this tree house ___(B)___ .

· The software program updates ___(C)___ regularly.

	(A)	(B)	(C)
①	her	ourselves	itself
②	her	themselves	itself
③	herself	ourselves	itself
④	herself	themselves	himself
⑤	herself	ourselves	himself

30 다음 중 어법상 어색한 것을 모두 고르시오.

① Mike plays two computer games, and both of them are exciting.

② Are there any of those lollipops left on the table?

③ I couldn't find everything to read at the bookstore.

④ Neither students were wearing a uniform.

⑤ I don't have any cash left in my wallet.

31 우리말과 같도록 빈칸에 알맞은 부정대명사를 넣어 문장을 완성하시오.

그 화가는 자신의 작품 중 몇몇을 팔았지만, 아직 나머지 작품들 전부는 그의 작업실에 있다.

= The painter sold _____ of his paintings, but _____ are still in his workroom.

32 다음 대화의 빈칸에 알맞은 말을 <보기>에서 골라 쓰시오.

<보기> all either anything everything

A: Can I help you with ⓐ_____ ?

B: Yes. I can't decide which of these two T-shirts to buy.

A: I think ⓑ_____ of them looks good on you.

33 다음 (A)~(C)에 들어갈 말이 바르게 짝지어진 것은?

· There are two kinds of desks for sale in this store. One is small but strong, and ___(A)___ is large and grey.

· So far, my aunt has had three jobs. One was a part-time job at a book store. ___(B)___ was as a graphic designer for a small company. ___(C)___ was at an elementary school, teaching art to children.

	(A)	(B)	(C)
①	another	Other	Another
②	another	Another	Other
③	the other	Another	Other
④	the other	Another	The other
⑤	the other	Other	The other

34 다음 중 어법상 바른 것끼리 묶인 것은?

ⓐ After the students entered the classroom, the teacher gave themselves their exam papers.

ⓑ We ourselves need to check the presentation to make sure the information is correct.

ⓒ You should all get yourselves something nice from the shops.

ⓓ If you see Mike, tell himself that this present is from me.

ⓔ There is a problem with the phone battery itself rather than with the charger.

① ⓐ, ⓑ, ⓒ ② ⓐ, ⓑ, ⓓ ③ ⓑ, ⓒ, ⓓ
④ ⓑ, ⓒ, ⓔ ⑤ ⓑ, ⓓ, ⓔ

35 두 문장의 의미가 같도록 문장을 완성하시오.

It seems that Yujin is not studying at the library.
= Yujin _____
  at the library.

36 주어진 문장의 밑줄 친 one과 쓰임이 같은 것은?

One must be kind to the elderly.

① Our last history test was much harder than the previous one.
② Tim's phone broke, so he had to buy a new one.
③ One should always tell the truth.
④ Do you prefer this dress or that one on the table?
⑤ There is a blanket on the sofa and one on the bed.

37 다음 글의 빈칸에 들어갈 수 있는 것을 모두 고르시오.

A: Have you seen Eric today?
B: No, I haven't. _____.
A: That makes sense. He looked a little unwell yesterday.
B: I hope he's OK.
A: So do I.

① Eric seems not to be resting at home
② It seems that Eric is resting at home
③ Eric seems that he is resting at home
④ It seems that Eric isn't resting at home
⑤ Eric seems to be resting at home

38 다음 중 어법상 바른 것은?

① Neither flashlight work very well.
② During the ceremony, each of the children was holding a flower.
③ Every people were trying to take a picture with the famous statue.
④ I was left alone because both of my friend had gone home.
⑤ All students has to follow the new safety policy.

39 다음 밑줄 친 ⓐ~ⓔ 중 어법상 어색한 것을 찾아 기호를 쓰고 바르게 고쳐 쓰시오.

A: Look! ⓐEvery student is wearing a Halloween mask.
B: Yes. ⓑAll of them looks so real and terrifying.
A: Don't you have a Halloween mask?
B: I bought ⓒone last week, but I left ⓓit at home.
A: Oh, do you want to borrow one of mine? I brought two.
B: Sure, I'd love to. Let's ⓔenjoy ourselves.

_____ → _____

40 우리말과 같도록 주어진 <조건>에 맞게 빈칸에 쓰시오.

이 지하철 안에 있는 모든 승객들은 다른 사람들의 발을 밟지 않으려고 노력하는 것 같다.

<조건>
all, the passenger, seem, try를 활용하시오.

= _____ _____ _____
on this subway _____ _____
_____ not to step on others' feet.

41 다음 글을 아래와 같이 요약할 때 <보기>의 말을 활용하여 빈칸에 알맞은 말을 쓰시오.

Not all animals can survive in the Arctic's harsh winters. Thus, some animals migrate to avoid the cold. However, there are animals that can survive there. One is the Arctic fox. In summer, the fox's fur is brown. But when winter comes, it grows new fur. The Arctic fox's winter fur is pure white, so it is the same color as the snow around it. The fox's winter fur can warm the body, so Arctic foxes are comfortable even when the temperature is −50 degrees Celsius.

<보기> one some other others

The Arctic is too cold for _____, but _____, such as the Arctic fox, can easily survive in it.

42 다음 대화의 빈칸에 알맞은 말을 쓰시오.

A: Have you heard of an odd-eyed cat?
B: Yes, I have. But I've never seen one. Have you?
A: Yes. Actually, my cat had a kitten last month. It has odd eyes.
ⓐ_____ of her eyes is blue, and ⓑ_____ is green.
B: Your kitten sounds so cute. Can I see the kitten someday?
A: Of course you can.

CHAPTER 9
형용사와 부사

형용사 The girl has **big eyes.** 그 소녀는 큰 눈을 가지고 있다.

The girl's eyes are **big.** 그 소녀의 눈이 크다.

부사 The boy **smiled brightly.** 그 소년은 활짝 웃었다.

그냥 '눈'이라고 말하는 것보다 '큰 눈' 혹은 '눈이 크다'라고 말하면 그 소녀의 눈이 어떻게 생긴 눈인지 더 자세하게 알 수 있어요. 이렇게 사람이나 사물의 모양, 상태, 성질 등을 설명해주는 것을 **형용사**라고 해요. 그리고 그냥 '웃었다'라고 말하는 것보다 '활짝 웃었다'라고 말하면 어떻게 웃고 있는지 더 자세하게 알 수 있어요. 이렇게 형용사, 동사, 다른 부사 또는 문장 전체를 수식하여 의미를 강조하거나 풍부하게 하는 것을 **부사**라고 해요.

기출로 적중 POINT

1 • 형용사의 용법

2 • 수량형용사

3 • 부사의 역할

4 • 형용사와 형태가 같은 부사

5 • -ly가 붙으면 의미가 달라지는 부사

6 • 빈도부사

7 • 타동사 + 부사

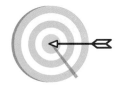

내신 100점 적중!
기출 출제율

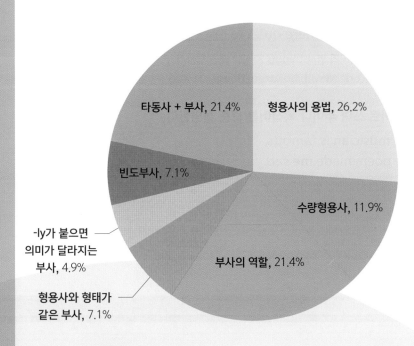

타동사 + 부사, 21.4%

형용사의 용법, 26.2%

빈도부사, 7.1%

수량형용사, 11.9%

-ly가 붙으면
의미가 달라지는
부사, 4.9%

부사의 역할, 21.4%

형용사와 형태가
같은 부사, 7.1%

TOP 1 **형용사의 용법 (26.2%)**
-thing, -body, -one, -where 등으로 끝나는 대명사와 형용사의 어순을
묻는 문제가 자주 출제된다.

TOP 2 **부사의 역할, 타동사 + 부사 (21.4%)**
부사의 형태와 역할을 묻는 문제가 자주 출제된다. 타동사 + 부사의 의미와
어순을 묻는 문제가 자주 출제된다.

TOP 3 **수량형용사 (11.9%)**
뒤에 오는 명사나 의미에 따라 (a) few와 (a) little을 구별하는 문제가 자주
출제된다.

형용사의 용법

정답 p.29

1. 한정적 용법: 명사를 수식하여 명사의 범위를 제한한다.

❶ 대부분의 명사: 형용사가 명사 앞에 온다.

A **luxurious house** is on the street. 호화로운 집이 그 거리에 있다.

She answered a **difficult question**. 그녀는 어려운 질문에 답했다.

(Tip) 「the + 형용사」는 '~한 사람들'이라는 의미로, 복수 명사처럼 쓰인다.

❷ -thing, -body, -one, -where 등으로 끝나는 대명사: 형용사가 대명사 뒤에 온다.

He found **nothing fresh** in the kitchen. 그는 부엌에서 신선한 어떤 것도 찾지 못했다.

Have you met **anybody tall** like Tim? 너는 Tim처럼 키가 큰 누군가를 만난 적이 있니?

I would like to work with **someone new**. 나는 새로운 누군가와 함께 일하고 싶다.

He didn't know of **anywhere quiet** to rest. 그는 쉴 만한 조용한 어느 곳도 알지 못했다.

(Tip) '것, 물건'이라는 의미의 명사 thing을 수식할 때는 형용사가 명사 앞에 온다.

The tree is decorated with **beautiful things**. 그 나무는 아름다운 것들로 장식되어 있다.

2. 서술적 용법: 보어로 쓰여 주어나 목적어를 보충 설명한다.

주격 보어   **The musician** is **famous**. 그 음악가는 유명하다.

목적격 보어   The poem made **me sad**. 그 시는 나를 슬프게 했다.

(Tip) 서술적 용법으로만 사용되는 형용사

afraid 무서워하는	alike 비슷한	alive 살아있는	alone 혼자인	ashamed 부끄러운
asleep 잠든	awake 깨어 있는	glad 반가운, 기쁜	pleased 기쁜	worth ~의 가치가 있는

The tiger is **awake**. (O) 그 호랑이는 깨어 있다.

It is an awake tiger. (X)

연습문제 A   괄호 안의 말을 알맞게 배열하시오.

1 My cell phone isn't a _____. (popular, brand)

2 Did you notice _____ about her hair? (special, anything)

3 I enjoy doing _____ in my free time. (puzzles, challenging)

4 I met _____ at a party yesterday. (fun, someone)

5 I'm trying to build my house _____. (somewhere, relaxing)

6 What exercises can I do to improve my _____? (physical, health)

7 Did you see _____ by the bridge? (strange, anybody)

연습문제 B 우리말과 같도록 <보기>의 형용사와 괄호 안의 말을 활용하여 문장을 완성하시오.

<보기> tall   safe   useful   soft   excited   delicious

1 그 장갑은 겨울에 유용했다. (be)

= Those gloves _____ in winter.

2 그 퍼레이드는 나를 신나게 했다. (make)

= The parade _____ .

3 그녀는 군중 속에서 키가 큰 누군가를 지목했다. (someone)

= She pointed to _____ in the crowd.

4 침대 위에 있는 그 베개는 부드러워 보인다. (look)

= The pillow on the bed _____ .

5 나는 냉장고를 맛있는 것들로 채웠다. (things)

= I filled the refrigerator with _____ .

6 그 보안 요원이 너를 안전하게 해줄 것이다. (keep)

= The security guard will _____ .

연습문제 C 괄호 안에서 알맞은 것을 고르시오.

1 The two cookies are (like / alike) in price but different in taste.

2 Look at the (asleep / sleepy) cat on the top of the piano.

3 All of the passengers were found (live / alive) after the plane crash.

4 The (scared / afraid) giraffe ran across the grassland.

5 The new novel is about a (lonely / alone) boy who lives in a cave.

기출 적중문제

다음 빈칸에 들어갈 말이 순서대로 짝지어진 것은?

· There isn't _____ in the newspaper.

· Give me _____ .

① anything interesting - something warm
② anything interesting - warm something
③ interesting anything - anything warm
④ interesting nothing - warm anything
⑤ nothing interesting - something warm

-thing, -body, -one,
-where 등으로 끝나는
대명사는 형용사가 뒤에
위치해요.

1. 다음 수량형용사는 셀 수 있는 명사의 복수형과 함께 쓴다.

many (수가) 많은	a number of (수가) 많은	a large number of (수가) 많은
a few (수가) 약간의	few (수가) 거의 없는	

Many students are studying in the library. 많은 학생들이 도서관에서 공부하고 있다.
A few candies are in my pocket. 약간의 사탕들이 나의 주머니 안에 있다.
There are **few seats** in the café. 카페에 자리들이 거의 없다.

(Tip) 「a number of + 복수명사」가 주어 자리에 쓰일 때 실제 주어는 of 뒤에 오는 복수명사이므로 복수동사를 쓰지만, 「the number of + 복수명사」가 주어 자리에 쓰일 때 실제 주어는 the number(~의 수)이 므로 단수동사를 쓴다.
  A number of wild elephants **have** died recently. 많은 야생 코끼리들이 최근에 죽었다.
  The number of wild elephants **is** falling rapidly. 야생 코끼리의 수가 급격하게 감소하고 있다.

2. 다음 수량형용사는 셀 수 없는 명사와 함께 쓴다.

much (양이) 많은	a great deal of (양이) 많은	a large amount of (양이) 많은
a little (양이) 약간의	little (양이) 거의 없는	

I had **much time** to sleep. 나는 잘 시간이 많이 있었다.
Please put **a little oil** in the frying pan. 약간의 기름을 프라이팬에 넣어 주세요.
Mr. Brown spends **little money** on shopping. Brown씨는 쇼핑에 돈을 거의 쓰지 않는다.

3. 다음 수량형용사는 셀 수 있는 명사와 셀 수 없는 명사에 모두 쓸 수 있다.

a lot of (수나 양이) 많은	lots of (수나 양이) 많은	plenty of (수나 양이) 많은
all 모든	some (수나 양이) 약간의	any (수나 양이) 약간의

(Tip) some은 주로 긍정문과 권유·요청을 나타내는 의문문에 쓰고, any는 주로 부정문과 의문문에 쓴다.
  Would you like to have **some** cereal? 너는 약간의 시리얼을 먹고 싶니?
  I didn't drink **any** water today. 나는 오늘 약간의 물도 마시지 않았다.

연습문제 A 괄호 안에서 알맞은 것을 고르시오.

1 (A few / A little) sandwiches are left on the kitchen counter.

2 There are not (much / many) people skilled enough to compete in the Olympics.

3 There are (some / a little) books on the shelf.

4 I don't have (much / a number of) energy to study today.

5 (A little / A few) customers participated in the survey.

6 Despite the cloudy weather, there were (many / much) children sitting on the beach.

7 Wonho received (much / a lot of) gifts for his birthday.

8 The researcher found (a number of / a great deal of) dinosaur bones in the ground.

9 We are expecting (a little / a few) rain tonight.

10 (Plenty of / A number of) effort was put into restoring the damaged paintings.

11 Young people today have (little / few) interest in learning how to farm.

12 She has (a large amount of / a large number of) experience volunteering at the shelter.

13 (A number of / The number of) rats living on the street has been decreasing.

연습문제 B 우리말과 같도록 <보기>의 수량형용사와 괄호 안의 말을 활용하여 문장을 완성하시오.

<보기>	a few much few a little many little

1 쇼핑몰에 아직 열려 있는 가게들이 거의 없다. (store)
= There are _____ still open in the mall.

2 Kristen은 최근에 운동할 시간이 거의 없다. (time)
= Kristen has _____ to exercise lately.

3 나의 부모님은 나에게 크리스마스 선물로 약간의 책들을 주었다. (book)
= My parents gave me _____ as a Christmas gift.

4 나는 나의 코코아에 약간의 휘핑크림을 넣는다. (whipped cream)
= I put _____ on my cocoa.

5 그는 그의 비밀을 나눌 많은 친구들이 있다. (friend)
= He has _____ to share his secrets with.

6 두 컴퓨터 간에 많은 차이는 없다. (difference)
= There isn't _____ between the two computers.

기출 적중문제

다음 문장의 빈칸에 들어갈 수 있는 것을 <u>모두</u> 고르시오.

> _____ prizes will be given to the winner of the competition.

① Many   ② Much   ③ Lots of
④ A little   ⑤ A great deal of

부사는 주로 형용사에 -ly를 붙여 만들며, 명사를 제외한 나머지 품사들과 문장 전체를 수식한다.

동사 수식	He **plays** the piano **beautifully**. 그는 피아노를 아름답게 연주한다.
형용사 수식	The new movie was **absolutely** **fantastic**. 그 새로운 영화는 굉장히 환상적이었다.
다른 부사 수식	Dana worked **extremely** **diligently** on her math homework. Dana는 그녀의 수학 숙제를 매우 성실하게 했다.
문장 전체 수식	**Surprisingly**, **there was no one at the pool**. 놀랍게도, 수영장에 아무도 없었다.

연습문제 밑줄 친 부분이 어법상 맞으면 O를 쓰고, 틀리면 바르게 고쳐 쓰시오.

1 Buying a new car is not an <u>easy</u> task.　　　　　　　→ _____

2 He sang <u>happy</u> in his room.　　　　　　　→ _____

3 With hard work, his test scores became <u>true</u> impressive.　→ _____

4 Everyone in the gallery admired the <u>lovely</u> painting.　→ _____

5 The ants worked <u>very</u> busily to collect food.　　→ _____

6 Junho was <u>still</u> tired after his workout.　　　→ _____

7 The jeweler promised me that this was a piece of <u>genuinely</u> gold.　→ _____

8 High temperatures can <u>negatively</u> affect the production of cheese.　→ _____

9 Jessica was <u>certain</u> nicely dressed on most days.　→ _____

10 <u>Hopeful</u>, the restaurant will deliver our lunch soon.　→ _____

기출 적중문제 ◎

다음 문장에서 어법상 어색한 부분을 찾아 쓰고 바르게 고쳐 쓰시오.

> We need to come up with a complete different
> solution to the problem.

_____ → _____

기출로적중 POINT 4

형용사와 형태가 같은 부사

정답 p.30

다음 단어는 형용사와 부사의 형태가 같다.

	형용사	부사		형용사	부사
late	늦은	늦게	**long**	긴, 오랜	길게, 오래
early	이른	일찍	**fast**	빠른	빠르게
close	가까운	가까이	**high**	높은	높게
near	가까운	가까이	**well**	좋은, 건강한	좋게, 잘
enough	충분한	충분히	**hard**	열심인, 어려운	열심히

The baby began to cry in the **early** morning. 그 아기는 이른 아침에 울기 시작했다.
Several guests arrived **early** for the party. 몇몇 손님들은 파티를 위해 일찍 도착했다.

(Tip) 일반적으로 부사는 형용사나 다른 부사를 앞에서 수식하지만 부사로 쓰인 enough는 형용사나 다른 부사를 뒤에서 수식한다.
This room isn't **big enough** for 20 people. 이 방은 20명의 사람들에게 충분히 크지 않다.

연습문제 밑줄 친 부분의 쓰임과 같은 것을 <보기>에서 골라 그 기호를 쓰시오.

<보기>	ⓐ The city is surrounded by <u>high</u> mountains.
	ⓑ There is a flag waving <u>high</u> in the sky.

1 We practiced <u>hard</u> for the performance. [   ]

2 The hotel is very <u>close</u> to many popular tourist attractions. [   ]

3 Smoke stayed <u>long</u> after the fire was put out. [   ]

4 After being sick for a week, I am finally <u>well</u> again. [   ]

5 The bathroom is at the end of the <u>long</u> hallway. [   ]

6 The water is hot <u>enough</u> to cause a burn. [   ]

7 People are always surprised that I can speak Japanese <u>well</u>. [   ]

8 Sandy brought <u>enough</u> blueberries for everyone. [   ]

9 That is a <u>hard</u> question to answer. [   ]

10 Wherever he went, his dog followed <u>close</u> behind. [   ]

-ly가 붙으면 의미가 달라지는 부사

정답 p.30

다음은 -ly가 붙으면 의미가 달라지는 부사이다.

close 가까이	
closely 면밀히, 밀접하게, 열심히	

late 늦게	
lately 최근에	

near 가까이	
nearly 거의	

hard 열심히	
hardly 거의 ~않다	

high 높게	
highly 매우, 대단히	

most 가장, 가장 많이	
mostly 주로, 대부분	

He got angry because the train arrived **late**. 그는 기차가 늦게 도착했기 때문에 화가 났다.
I have been writing a novel **lately**. 나는 최근에 소설을 쓰고 있다.
My kite flew **high** in the sky. 나의 연은 하늘에서 높게 날았다.
The contest is **highly** competitive. 그 대회는 매우 경쟁적이다.

(Tip) 명사에 -ly가 붙으면 형용사로 쓰인다.

Alice is a **friendly** person. Alice는 친절한 사람이다.

연습문제 | 괄호 안에서 알맞은 것을 고르시오.

1 The students listened (close / closely) as she read the story.

2 I can (hard / hardly) believe that the year is almost over.

3 Are you (near / nearly) done with your blog postings?

4 Jimin arrived (late / lately) because she overslept.

5 The desk is (most / mostly) made of marble.

6 What's the matter with you (late / lately)?

7 The squirrel climbed (high / highly) up the tree.

8 The man came (close / closely) to me and asked for directions.

9 We sat (near / nearly) to the exit, so we could leave easily.

기출 적중문제

다음 문장에서 어법상 <u>어색한</u> 부분을 찾아 쓰고 바르게 고쳐 쓰시오.

A lot of people worked hardly to make the show a success.

_____ → _____

POINT 6 빈도부사

정답 p.30

1. **빈도부사는 어떤 일이 얼마나 자주 발생하는지를 나타내는 부사이다.**

100%					0%
always	usually	often	sometimes	rarely/hardly/seldom	never
항상	보통, 대개	종종, 자주	때때로, 가끔	거의 ~않다	결코 ~않다

   The store **always** opens at noon. 그 가게는 항상 정오에 문을 연다.
   I **sometimes** play basketball with my friends. 나는 때때로 나의 친구들과 농구를 한다.
   Jisu **never** eats fast food. 지수는 패스트푸드를 결코 먹지 않는다.

2. **빈도부사는 일반동사의 앞 또는 be동사나 조동사의 뒤에 위치한다.**

   She **often goes** fishing with her dad. 그녀는 종종 그녀의 아빠와 낚시를 하러 간다.
   Watching documentaries **is usually** helpful. 다큐멘터리를 보는 것은 보통 유익하다.
   I **can hardly** understand French. 나는 프랑스어를 거의 이해하지 못한다.

연습문제 우리말과 같도록 빈도부사와 괄호 안의 말을 활용하여 문장을 완성하시오.

1 Julie는 샤워를 할 때 항상 노래를 듣는다. (listen to)
= Julie _____ music when she takes a shower.

2 나는 도서관에서 보통 내가 필요한 것을 찾을 수 있다. (find, can)
= I _____ what I need at the library.

3 나는 페루에 사는 나의 사촌들을 거의 방문하지 않는다. (visit)
= I _____ my cousins who live in Peru.

4 그 라디오 방송국은 요즘 이 노래를 종종 튼다. (play)
= The radio station _____ this song nowadays.

5 그 배우는 때때로 그의 아내와 함께 영화에 출연했다. (be)
= The actor _____ in movies with his wife.

6 그녀는 스파게티를 주문할 때 종종 미트볼을 추가한다. (add)
= She _____ meatballs when she orders spaghetti.

7 Richard는 그의 누나의 생일을 결코 잊지 않는다. (forget)
= Richard _____ his older sister's birthday.

8 우리는 복도에서 우리의 이웃들을 거의 보지 않는다. (see)
= We _____ our neighbors in the hallway.

POINT 7 타동사 + 부사

1. 다음은 자주 쓰이는 「타동사 + 부사」 표현이다.

bring up ~을 꺼내다	look up ~을 찾아보다	try on ~을 입어보다
call off ~을 취소하다	make up ~을 만들어내다, 정하다	turn down ~을 거절하다
check out ~을 확인하다	pick up ~을 줍다, ~를 태우러 가다	turn in ~을 제출하다
fill in ~을 작성하다	put off ~을 미루다	turn off ~을 끄다
find out ~을 알아내다	put on ~을 입다, 쓰다	turn on ~을 켜다
give up ~을 포기하다, 그만두다	take off ~을 벗다	wake up ~를 깨우다
hand in ~을 제출하다	throw away ~을 버리다	write down ~을 적다

Tom **picked up the trash** without hesitation.   Tom은 망설임 없이 쓰레기를 주웠다.

I have to **hand in my application** tomorrow.   나는 내일 나의 지원서를 제출해야 한다.

Look up the answer in the back of the book.   책의 뒷부분에서 정답을 찾아봐라.

2. 「타동사 + 부사」는 목적어가 명사인지 대명사인지에 따라 어순이 달라진다.

❶ 목적어가 명사인 경우, 「타동사 + 부사 + 명사」 또는 「타동사 + 명사 + 부사」의 어순으로 쓴다.

I **wrote down** my address on the paper.   나는 종이에 나의 주소를 적었다.

= I **wrote** my address **down** on the paper.

I would like to **try on those pants**.   나는 저 바지를 입어보고 싶다.

= I would like to **try those pants on**.

❷ 목적어가 대명사인 경우, 「타동사 + 대명사 + 부사」의 어순으로 쓴다.

The lights were too bright, so I **turned them off**.   불이 너무 밝아서, 나는 그것들을 껐다.

She **found it out** at last.   그녀는 결국 그것을 알아냈다.

연습문제 A | 괄호 안에서 알맞은 것을 <u>모두</u> 고르시오.

1 Please don't (throw away it / throw it away).

2 It is usual to (take off your shoes / take your shoes off) indoors in Korea.

3 Feel free to (try those coats on / try on those coats).

4 A person's age is a sensitive topic, so don't (bring it up / bring up it).

5 Dongho (made the entire story up / made up the entire story) before class.

6 John is sad because the school he wished to go to (turned down him / turned him down).

7 Don't forget to (turn on the heater / turn the heater on) when you get home.

8 The Field Museum is great, so be sure to (check out it / check it out) when you visit Chicago.

9 We tried to (find it out / find out it) ahead of time.

10 The teacher told us to (turn in our report / turn our report in) by tomorrow.

11 There was a baseball game planned yesterday, but we had to (call it off / call off it) because of rain.

연습문제 **B** 우리말과 같도록 괄호 안의 말을 알맞게 배열하시오.

1 제가 부츠를 신는 동안 기다려주시겠어요? (my boots, on, put)
= Could you wait while I _____?

2 나는 집에 가는 길에 그를 태우러 갈 수 있다. (him, up, pick)
= I can _____ on my way home.

3 당신이 교실을 떠나기 전에 불을 꺼주세요. (the lights, off, turn)
= Please _____ before you leave the classroom.

4 Betty는 낮잠에서 나를 깨웠다. (me, up, woke)
= Betty _____ from my nap.

5 모든 학생들은 그들의 시험지를 제출했다. (in, handed, their tests)
= All of the students _____.

6 이 종이에 당신의 이름을 적으세요. (your name, down, write)
= Please _____ on this paper.

7 만약 네가 단어의 의미를 알지 못한다면, 사전에서 그것을 찾아볼 수 있다. (it, up, look)
= If you don't know a word's meaning, you can _____ in the dictionary.

8 우리는 그 여행을 몇 주 동안 미뤄야 했다. (the trip, off, put)
= We had to _____ for a few weeks.

9 나는 그 행사에 참석하고 싶었지만, 주최측에서 그것을 취소했다. (called, off, it)
= I wanted to attend the event, but the host _____.

기출 적중문제

다음 중 밑줄 친 부분이 어법상 어색한 것은?

① Turn off the television when you go to bed.
② My mother picks up me after work.
③ Don't turn down friends who invite you to dinner.
④ Although I failed to achieve my goal the first time, I won't give it up.
⑤ It is important to know how to look things up on the Internet.

> 목적어가 대명사인 경우
> 「타동사 + 대명사 + 부사」
> 의 어순으로 써요.

서술형 대비 문제

A 우리말과 같도록 괄호 안의 말을 알맞게 배열하시오.

1 Nancy는 그녀의 숙제를 일찍 끝내서 기쁘다. (homework, Nancy, glad, she, finished, her, early, is, so)

= _____

2 이 신발은 신기에 충분히 편하다. (to wear, enough, are, these shoes, comfortable)

= _____

3 우리는 휴가를 갈 재미있는 어딘가를 찾았다. (somewhere, to go, found, for a vacation, fun, we)

= _____

4 Matthew는 유럽에 결코 가본 적이 없다. (to Europe, has, been, never, Matthew)

= _____

5 축구 선수들은 경기하는 동안 종종 다친다. (while, get injured, football players, playing, often)

= _____

B 우리말과 같도록 <보기 1>과 <보기 2>의 말을 한 번씩만 골라 문장을 완성하시오.

| <보기 1> little   much   a few   the number of   many   few   a little |

| <보기 2> parents   black rhinos   apples   milk   free time   food   days |

1 차에 약간의 우유를 넣으면 더 좋은 맛이 날 것이다.

= Add _____ to the tea, and it will taste better.

2 민수는 너무 많은 음식을 먹었기 때문에 배가 아팠다.

= Minsu got a stomachache because he ate too _____.

3 Ann은 너무 바빠서 자유시간이 거의 없다.

= Ann is so busy that she has _____.

4 많은 부모들은 그들의 아이들이 외국어를 배워야 한다고 느낀다.

= _____ feel that their children should learn foreign languages.

5 그 단체는 검정코뿔소의 수를 유지하기 위해 노력한다.

= The organization tries to maintain _____.

6 그는 여행을 갔지만 며칠 후에 돌아올 것이다.

= He went on a trip, but he'll be back in _____.

7 남은 사과들이 거의 없어서, 우리는 더 사야 할 것이다.

= There are _____ left, so we'll have to buy more.

C 괄호 안의 말을 알맞은 형태로 바꿔 빈칸에 쓰시오.

1 The hospital is _____ to the bakery. (near)

2 Anthony listened _____ for his name to be called. (close)

3 The baseball player threw the ball _____ in the air. (high)

4 The blanket _____ covered the bed. (most)

5 I _____ got any sleep last night. (hard)

6 My family eats dinner _____ in the evening. (late)

7 I've studied for the test very _____ over the past month. (hard)

D 우리말과 같도록 <보기>의 「타동사 + 부사」 표현과 괄호 안의 말을 활용하여 문장을 완성하시오.

<보기>　turn down　call off　write down　hand in　put off　put on　pick up

1 나는 너의 숙제를 보지 못했어. 너는 그것을 언제 제출했는지 기억하니? (it)
= I haven't seen your homework. Do you remember when you _____?

2 그 선생님은 태풍 때문에 현장 학습을 취소해야 했다. (the field trip)
= The teacher had to _____ because of the storm.

3 그는 왜 너의 초대를 거절했니? (your invitation)
= Why did he _____?

4 나의 할머니는 나를 위해 그녀의 요리법을 적어 주셨다. (her recipe)
= My grandmother _____ for me.

5 그 선수들은 비가 멈출 때까지 경기를 미뤄야 했다. (the game)
= The players had to _____ until the rain stopped.

6 바닥에 약간의 장난감들이 있어. 그것들을 주워줄 수 있니? (them)
= There are some toys on the floor. Can you _____?

7 밖이 추우니 너는 그것을 입어야 한다. (it)
= You should _____ since it is cold outside.

중간 · 기말고사 실전 문제

1 다음 중 어법상 어색한 것은?

① I'd like shiny shoes.
② She enjoys slow songs.
③ He answered the question quickly.
④ 40 people can comfortable fit in the bus.
⑤ Roses are very beautiful flowers.

2 다음 밑줄 친 ⓐ~ⓔ 중 어법상 어색한 것을 찾아 기호를 쓰고 바르게 고쳐 쓰시오.

· ⓐNobody talented entered the contest this year.
· The doctor recently told me to avoid ⓑsweet anything.
· Emma wants to go ⓒsomewhere new for lunch.
· The investigation revealed ⓓastonishing something.
· I haven't heard a ⓔthing positive about the concert.

(1) _____ → _____
(2) _____ → _____
(3) _____ → _____

3 다음 중 어법상 어색한 것은?

① John was ashamed of his bad behavior.
② Tina and her twin sister look alike.
③ He was glad to see his grandparents.
④ The alive performance was exciting to watch.
⑤ I am afraid of watching horror movies.

4 우리말과 같도록 괄호 안의 단어를 알맞게 배열하시오.

> A: What did you think of the new store manager?
> B: 나는 나이가 더 많은 누군가를 예상했어. (older, somebody, expected, I)

= _____.

5 다음 중 밑줄 친 형용사의 용법이 나머지 넷과 다른 것은?

① The boy found an <u>old</u> picture.
② <u>New</u> cars are really expensive.
③ The bridge always makes me <u>nervous</u>.
④ That was a <u>thrilling</u> action movie.
⑤ We rode a <u>giant</u> roller coaster.

6 다음 중 어법상 바른 것끼리 묶인 것은?

> ⓐ Mark heard an interestingly story from Mina.
> ⓑ The dog is sleeping peacefully.
> ⓒ James worked hardly last weekend.
> ⓓ Each chapter of the book is clearly summarized in the study guide.
> ⓔ Some animals are natural slow, which makes them easy prey for predators.
> ⓕ Most of the students showed up late because of the rain.

① ⓐ, ⓑ, ⓕ   ② ⓐ, ⓒ, ⓔ   ③ ⓑ, ⓒ, ⓓ
④ ⓑ, ⓓ, ⓔ   ⑤ ⓑ, ⓓ, ⓕ

7 다음 글의 밑줄 친 ⓐ~ⓔ 중 어법상 어색한 것을 찾아 기호를 쓰고 바르게 고쳐 쓰시오.

Minhee hated going to her violin lessons every day. She wished she could do ⓐfun something instead. One day, she asked her mother if she could take ⓑa little time off. ⓒSurprising, she said it would be OK. After a few weeks of not practicing, Minhee decided to practice ⓓsome tunes and songs on her own. Without the stress of going ⓔboring somewhere after school, playing the violin became a fun pastime.

(1) _____ → _____
(2) _____ → _____
(3) _____ → _____

8 다음 (A)~(C)에 들어갈 말이 바르게 짝지어진 것은?

· The article provided ___(A)___ opinions about the new law.
· There is ___(B)___ information about the class on the website.
· ___(C)___ baggage was left on the plane.

	(A)	(B)	(C)
①	few	little	Plenty of
②	little	few	A lot of
③	few	little	A number of
④	little	little	A lot of
⑤	few	few	A number of

[9-10] 다음 글을 읽고 주어진 질문에 답하시오.

___(A)___ energy is wasted on air conditioning every day. ⓐThis is because most of our buildings are inefficient designed. ___(B)___ changes could lower our need for air conditioning. For instance, higher ceilings would keep rooms cooler. People concerned about energy consumption should ask their builders to take ___(C)___ steps like building a higher ceiling. Well-designed buildings may not need air conditioning.

*consumption 소비

9 위 글의 (A)~(C)에 들어갈 말이 바르게 짝지어진 것을 고르시오.

	(A)	(B)	(C)
①	Many	A little	some
②	Many	A few	much
③	A lot of	A few	much
④	A lot of	A few	some
⑤	A lot of	A little	some

10 위 글의 밑줄 친 ⓐ에서 어색한 부분을 바르게 고쳐 완전한 문장을 쓰시오.

→ _____

_____

11 우리말과 같도록 괄호 안의 말을 배열할 때 여섯 번째에 오는 것을 쓰시오.

> 준호는 그의 어린 시절이 비범한 어떤 것도 아니라고 생각했다. (thought, Junho, his, nothing, was, remarkable, childhood)

→ _____

12 다음 중 어법상 바른 것의 개수는?

> ⓐ A lot of furniture is made of plastic nowadays.
> ⓑ A number of information can be found on the Internet.
> ⓒ A little facts about the case were uncovered during the investigation.
> ⓓ My mother had little time to help me with my schoolwork.
> ⓔ The number of her ancestors were brave soldiers.

① 1개   ② 2개   ③ 3개
④ 4개   ⑤ 5개

13 다음 중 밑줄 친 enough의 쓰임이 나머지 넷과 다른 것은?

① This plastic bag won't be strong <u>enough</u>.
② Is your coffee sweet <u>enough</u>?
③ The room is large <u>enough</u> for four guests.
④ He isn't tall <u>enough</u> to reach the top shelf.
⑤ I don't have <u>enough</u> money for lunch.

14 <보기>의 말을 활용하여 빈칸에 알맞은 말을 쓰시오.

> <보기> close high near

> (A) Jane bought a new laptop that cost _____ $2,000.
> (B) The meeting ended _____ to lunchtime.
> (C) We are looking for _____ qualified staff.

15 다음 빈칸에 들어갈 말로 어색한 것은?

> Today there are various reality shows covering _____ different topics.

① a lot of   ② a number of
③ plenty of   ④ much
⑤ lots of

16 다음 중 밑줄 친 부분이 어법상 바른 것은?

> Hillsdale Middle School's ①<u>annually</u> end of the year trip is coming up in two weeks. This year, all three classes will be going to Phoenix Fields Ski Resort. ②<u>Previous</u>, each class planned its own trip to a different location. However, the student council decided last year that it would be easier if everyone went to the same place for ③<u>future</u> trips. As always, students are looking forward to the trip ④<u>eager</u>. It ⑤<u>is considered usually</u> the highlight of the school year.

17 다음 빈칸에 공통으로 들어갈 알맞은 것은?

> · People in Argentina consume _____ beef.
> · Kelly read _____ books over the summer.
> · We took _____ photographs while on vacation.
> · We saw _____ deer in the forest where we were camping.

① a few   ② many
③ much   ④ a number of
⑤ a lot of

18 다음 중 어법상 어색한 것은?

① I always can rely on my older sister.
② The students sometimes clean the classroom.
③ Kevin usually studies in the library after school.
④ Do you often practice playing the piano?
⑤ Our teacher says that bullying is never acceptable.

19 다음 중 어법상 어색한 것은?

① The president spoke firmly as he discussed the need for new taxes.
② My dog hates getting wet and will never willingly take a shower.
③ Privately, Chris worries that he is not good at his job.
④ The car runs well after being repaired.
⑤ Everyone easy passed the test after taking part in the study group.

20 다음 대화의 밑줄 친 ⓐ~ⓔ 중 어법상 어색한 것을 찾아 기호를 쓰고 바르게 고쳐 쓰시오.

> A: Did you see that the Thunderbolts ⓐnarrowly won the soccer tournament?
> B: No. I don't follow sports ⓑclose these days.
> A: That's too bad. The tournament was ⓒreally exciting.
> B: I'm sure it was, but I'm far too ⓓbusily with my homework.
> A: Oh, I understand ⓔcomplete.

(1) _____ → _____
(2) _____ → _____
(3) _____ → _____

21 다음 중 밑줄 친 부분이 어법상 어색한 것은?

① Please turn the fan on in the living room.
② The city called off the event due to the lack of interest.
③ You need to put on your jacket before going outside.
④ The shoes were old, so I decided to throw away them.
⑤ Nobody is taking exams because the school put them off until Friday.

22 다음 중 어법상 바른 것끼리 묶인 것은?

ⓐ You should sometimes relax even though you have lots of work to do.
ⓑ People use rarely phone booths nowadays.
ⓒ I'll find out the solution and get back to you.
ⓓ That actor performs always good in movies.
ⓔ Your alarm is ringing. Please turn off it.

① ⓐ, ⓒ   ② ⓐ, ⓑ   ③ ⓑ, ⓒ
④ ⓒ, ⓓ   ⑤ ⓓ, ⓔ

23 다음 (A)~(C)에 들어갈 말이 바르게 짝지어진 것은?

A: Why weren't you at band practice yesterday? You ___(A)___ ever miss it.
B: I needed a break. I haven't had any free time ___(B)___ because of all my school activities.
A: I understand. It can be ___(C)___ to keep up sometimes.
B: Yes. I'm feeling much better now though.

	(A)	(B)	(C)
①	hard	late	hard
②	hardly	late	hardly
③	hardly	lately	hard
④	hardly	lately	hardly
⑤	hard	lately	hard

24 다음 중 밑줄 친 부분이 어법상 어색한 것은?

Somi couldn't ①make up her mind about what she wanted to do after graduation. So, she decided to ②put school off for a year and think about her future. Her mother suggested living in another country since she had studied French for ③nearly ten years. Agreeing to her mother's suggestion, Somi went to France. However, even though there was ④nothing wrong with the city, she just didn't like living in Paris. She moved down to Marseille, which ⑤made her happily. Now she has been living there for two months.

*Marseille 마르세유(프랑스 남부의 항구 도시)

25 다음 글의 밑줄 친 ⓐ~ⓔ 중 어법상 어색한 것을 찾아 기호를 쓰고 바르게 고쳐 쓰시오.

Every February 2, ⓐmany people turn their attention to a town in Pennsylvania for the ⓑyearly Groundhog's Day forecast. Everyone watches closely to see if the groundhog will be scared by its shadow and go back into its underground home. If it does, people say that winter will continue for six more weeks. However, if it doesn't, the cold weather will end ⓒshort. Although the ⓓannual event has no real scientific value, after a long winter, people look for any sign that a ⓔwarmly spring is coming.

*groundhog 마멋(다람쥐 과의 설치 동물)

(1) _____ → _____

(2) _____ → _____

26 다음 글의 빈칸에 들어갈 알맞은 것은?

Steven is a local weather forecaster. People _____ complain about his predictions. He says the frequent errors are not his fault because the region's weather changes quickly.

① rarely　　② hardly　　③ seldom
④ never　　⑤ often

27 다음 대화의 밑줄 친 우리말 (A)와 같도록 괄호 안의 말을 활용하여 문장을 완성하시오.

A: Are you still studying Spanish?
B: No. (A) 나는 시간이 없어서 그것을 포기했어.
　 (it, give, I, up)

= _____ because I don't have time.

28 다음 글의 밑줄 친 ⓐ~ⓔ를 바르게 고치지 <u>못한</u> 것은?

A long time ago, people didn't believe that building a flying machine was possible. While ⓐmuch people had attempted to build one, they had all failed. The task seemed impossible until the Wright brothers tried it. The brothers built a ⓑbasically plane but had trouble getting it to fly. ⓒEventual, they created a craft that flew for ⓓnear one minute. This was the first powered flight. Although the plane flew only ⓔfew times, it was a great step forward.

① ⓐ much → a great deal of
② ⓑ basically → basic
③ ⓒ Eventual → Eventually
④ ⓓ near → nearly
⑤ ⓔ few → a few

29 다음은 Emily의 일정표이다. 빈칸에 알맞은 말을 <보기>에서 골라 쓰시오.

Emily's Schedule	
Mon	Wake up at 6 A.M. Feed the dog
Tues	Wake up at 6 A.M. Feed the dog
Wed	Wake up at 6 A.M. Feed the dog
Thurs	Wake up at 6 A.M. Feed the dog
Fri	Wake up at 6 A.M. Feed the dog
Sat	Feed the dog Visit cousins
Sun	Feed the dog Visit cousins

<보기>　always　usually　sometimes

(1) Emily _____ feeds the dog.
(2) Emily _____ visits her cousins.
(3) Emily _____ wakes up at 6 A.M.

30 다음 중 어법상 <u>어색한</u> 것을 <u>모두</u> 고르시오.

① We are looking for someone hardworking for our team.
② Do you know anyone really smart?
③ Mary refuses to go dangerous anywhere near the ocean.
④ There is nothing available at the resort next week.
⑤ I found many incorrectly things in the book I read.

31 다음 중 어법상 바른 것의 개수는?

> ⓐ They called off the picnic at the last minute.
> ⓑ You must hand your essays in by tomorrow.
> ⓒ That can't be true. Did you make up it?
> ⓓ Amy turned down the internship opportunity.
> ⓔ I'll pick up you at 3:30 in front of the mall.

① 1개　　　② 2개　　　③ 3개
④ 4개　　　⑤ 5개

32 다음 빈칸에 들어갈 말이 순서대로 짝지어진 것은?

> · Do you have _____ ?
> · After hearing of the show, I _____ .

① anything healthier – checked it out
② healthier anything – checked out it
③ anything healthier – checked out it
④ healthier anything – checked it out
⑤ healthier thing – checked out it

33 다음 중 어법상 어색한 것은?

① Nari is always late for class.
② He has never been to Paris until now.
③ She usually makes tacos on Mondays.
④ We often play tennis in the park.
⑤ Their parents will help sometimes the kids with homework.

34 다음 글의 빈칸에 들어갈 알맞은 것은?

> The Internet is a great tool for research. It puts a lot of information at our fingertips. For example, I needed the address of a local restaurant. I was able to _____ with a few taps of the keyboard.

① look up it　　　② looks it up
③ look it up　　　④ look them up
⑤ look up them

35 다음 빈칸에 들어갈 말이 순서대로 짝지어진 것은?

> · When you don't like somebody's offer, _____ .
> · After you finish with your paper cup, please _____ .

① turn down them – throw away it
② turn down it – throw away it
③ turn them down – throw them away
④ turn it down – throw them away
⑤ turn it down – throw it away

36 다음 중 밑줄 친 부분의 쓰임이 나머지 넷과 <u>다른</u> 것은?

① I have to wait <u>long</u> to see the doctor.
② She arrived <u>early</u> for dinner.
③ The cat jumped <u>high</u> into the air.
④ You don't look so <u>well</u> today.
⑤ He is working <u>hard</u> to improve quality.

[37-38] 다음 대화를 읽고 주어진 질문에 답하시오.

A: You've missed ⓐa number of classes this semester.

B: I know. I've been getting sick ⓑfrequent.

A: (A) 우리는 많은 숙제가 있었어. Have you been able to keep up with your work ⓒlately?

B: Not really. I've fallen behind ⓓrecent.

A: What are you going to do then?

B: I'm not sure. I have to ⓔbring up it with my teacher.

37 위 글의 밑줄 친 ⓐ~ⓔ 중 어법상 어색한 것을 찾아 기호를 쓰고 바르게 고쳐 쓰시오.

(1) _____ → _____

(2) _____ → _____

(3) _____ → _____

38 위 글의 밑줄 친 우리말 (A)와 같도록 주어진 <조건>에 맞게 문장을 완성하시오.

<조건>
1. 현재완료시제를 사용하시오.
2. have homework를 활용하시오.

= We _____

_____ .

39 우리말과 같도록 괄호 안의 말을 알맞게 배열하시오.

나는 나의 엄마의 생일 선물로 기억할 만한 어떤 것을 사고 싶다. (want, memorable, buy, to, my, something, mom's, I, birthday present, for)

= _____

_____

40 다음 중 어법상 어색한 것의 개수는?

ⓐ I have nothing new to tell you about what happened at the party.

ⓑ I could see the entirely city from the tower.

ⓒ Thomas is actual the brother of James.

ⓓ When the sun finally set, we were touched by the beautiful view.

ⓔ John wants to go somewhere tropically for his vacation.

① 1개 　　② 2개 　　③ 3개

④ 4개 　　⑤ 5개

41 우리말과 같도록 주어진 <조건>에 맞게 빈칸에 쓰시오.

과학자들은 다이아몬드보다 더 단단한 어떤 것도 결코 발견하지 못했다.

<조건>
1. 현재완료시제를 사용하시오.
2. 알맞은 빈도부사를 사용하시오.
3. find, harder than diamond, anything을 활용하시오.

= Scientists _____

_____ _____ _____

_____ .

CHAPTER 10
비교구문

A tiger is **as big as** a lion. 호랑이는 사자만큼 크다.
A mouse is **smaller than** a fox. 쥐는 여우보다 작다.
the blue whale is **the biggest** mammal in the world.
흰긴수염고래는 세상에서 가장 큰 포유류이다.

위 문장들에서 여러 동물들의 크기를 비교하고 있는데, 이렇게 두 가지 이상의 대상을 서로 비교하는 문장을 **비교구문**
이라고 해요. 비교하는 두 대상의 정도가 비슷하거나 같음을 나타낼 때는 **원급**, 두 대상 간 정도의 차이가 있음을 나타
낼 때는 **비교급**, 셋 이상의 비교 대상 중 하나의 정도가 가장 높음을 나타낼 때는 **최상급**을 써요.

기출로 적중 POINT

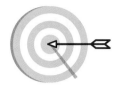

내신 100점 적중!
기출 출제율

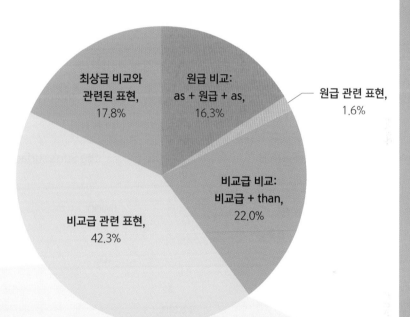

최상급 비교와
관련된 표현,
17.8%

원급 비교:
as + 원급 + as,
16.3%

원급 관련 표현,
1.6%

비교급 비교:
비교급 + than,
22.0%

비교급 관련 표현,
42.3%

TOP 1 **비교급 관련 표현 (42.3%)**
「the + 비교급, the + 비교급」을 활용하여 영작하는 문제가 자주 출제된다.

TOP 2 **비교급 비교: 비교급 + than (22%)**
비교급 비교의 올바른 형태를 묻는 문제가 자주 출제된다.

TOP 3 **최상급 비교와 관련된 표현 (17.8%)**
최상급 비교와 관련된 표현을 활용하여 최상급을 의미를 나타내는 문제가
자주 출제된다.

원급 비교: as + 원급 + as

정답 p.33

---

1. 「as + 원급 + as」는 '…만큼 ~한/하게'라는 의미로, 비교하는 두 대상의 정도가 비슷하거나 같음을 나타낸다.

   This phone is **as cheap as** my shoes. 이 전화기는 나의 신발만큼 저렴하다.

   He can run **as fast as** I can. 그는 나만큼 빨리 달릴 수 있다.

2. 「not + as[so] + 원급 + as」는 '…만큼 ~하지 않은/않게'라는 의미이다.

   This test is **not as[so] hard as** the last one. 이 시험은 지난번만큼 어렵지 않다.

   I can**not** find the answer **as[so] easily as** Jinho. 나는 진호만큼 쉽게 답을 찾을 수 없다.

연습문제 A 우리말과 같도록 <보기>의 말을 활용하여 문장을 완성하시오.

| <보기> tired   heavy   hot   cold   flat   skillfully   difficult   interesting   fluently |

1 지구의 중앙은 태양의 표면만큼 뜨겁다.

= The center of the Earth is _____ the Sun's surface.

2 나는 지우만큼 능숙하게 농구를 할 수 없다.

= I can't play basketball _____ Jiwoo.

3 그 컵 안의 물은 얼음만큼 차갑다.

= The water in the cup is _____ ice.

4 자동차는 기차만큼 무겁지 않다.

= A car is _____ a train.

5 나는 Kelly씨만큼 스페인어를 유창하게 말할 수 있다.

= I can speak Spanish _____ Mr. Kelly.

6 수학을 공부하는 것은 과학을 공부하는 것만큼 어렵지 않다.

= Studying math is _____ studying science.

7 그 산봉우리는 팬케이크만큼 납작했다.

= The mountaintop was _____ a pancake.

8 축구 경기 후 그는 Jack만큼 피곤해 보였다.

= After the soccer game, he looked _____ Jack.

9 그 앨범은 그 밴드의 지난번 것만큼 흥미롭지 않았다.

= The album was _____ the band's last one.

연습문제 B 괄호 안의 말을 활용하여 다음 두 문장을 한 문장으로 바꿔 쓰시오.

1 Minsoo can lift up to 30 kilograms. I can lift up to 30 kilograms, too. (be, strong)

→ I _____ Minsoo.

2 The book I read last month was entertaining. This book was entertaining, too. (be, entertaining)

→ This book _____ the one I read last month.

3 Siwoo can dance for 60 minutes. Junsu can dance for 60 minutes, too. (can, long, dance for)

→ Junsu _____ Siwoo.

4 He paid 40,000 won for the vase. He paid 30,000 won for the painting. (be, expensive)

→ The painting _____ the vase.

5 Peter can jump over the 2 meter bar. I can't jump over the 2 meter bar. (can, jump, high)

→ I _____ Peter can.

6 Jenny exercises twice a week. Christine also exercises twice a week. (exercise, often)

→ Christine _____ Jenny does.

7 Mary woke up at 7 P.M. Bill woke up at 8 P.M. (wake up, early)

→ Bill _____ Mary did.

8 It takes 30 minutes to get to the hotel. It takes 40 minutes to get to the airport. (be, close)

→ The airport _____ the hotel.

9 The largest shark is 18 meters long. The largest whale is 30 meters long. (be, long)

→ The largest shark _____ the largest whale.

10 Jim is 170 centimeters tall. I am 160 centimeters tall. (be, tall)

→ I _____ Jim.

11 New York City has a population of 8.3 million people. Seoul has a population of 9.7 million people. (be, crowded)

→ New York City _____ Seoul.

12 Lara has five ideas for the contest. Paul has one idea for the contest. (have, ideas, many)

→ Paul _____ Lara.

기출 적중문제

다음 중 어법상 바른 것은?

① His solution to the problem was as clever as Mr. Kim's.

② She sings so not passionately as an opera singer.

③ This bus is as not full as the last one.

④ She was not as honest so Patrick.

⑤ He is playing as loudly so the band.

원급 관련 표현

정답 p.33

1. 「배수사(twice, three times, half 등) + as + 원급 + as」는 '…보다 −배 더 ~한/하게' 라는 의미이다.

   The building is **twice as tall as** the tree. 그 건물은 그 나무보다 두 배 더 높다.
   I run **three times as quickly as** my little sister does.
   나는 나의 여동생보다 세 배 더 빠르게 달린다.

2. 「as + 원급 + as + possible」은 '가능한 한 ~한/하게'라는 의미이며, 「as + 원급 + as + 주어 + can[could]」으로 바꿔 쓸 수 있다.

   Tom held **as many** boxes **as possible**. Tom은 가능한 한 많은 상자들을 들었다.
   = Tom held **as many** boxes **as he could**. Tom은 그가 할 수 있는 한 많은 상자들을 들었다.

   You should clean up the room **as soon as possible**. 너는 가능한 한 빨리 그 방을 치워야 한다.
   = You should clean up the room **as soon as you can**.
   너는 네가 할 수 있는 한 빨리 그 방을 치워야 한다.

3. 다음은 자주 사용되는 원급 관련 관용 표현이다.

as far as ~까지, ~하는 한	as long as ~하기만 하면, ~하는 한
as good as ~나 다름없는	as often as ~할 때마다

   I will forgive you **as long as** you fix it. 나는 네가 그것을 고치기만 하면 용서해 줄 것이다.
   The author's next book is **as good as** finished. 그 작가의 다음 책은 완성된 것이나 다름없다.

연습문제 A 우리말과 같도록 괄호 안의 말을 알맞게 배열하시오.

1 로봇은 인간보다 열 배 더 빠르게 사과를 딴다. (as, ten, times, fast, as)
= A robot picks apples _____ a human.

2 그는 나보다 다섯 배 더 자주 체육관에 간다. (times, as, five, as, often)
= He goes to the gym _____ I do.

3 나는 그녀보다 네 배 더 많은 피자 조각들을 먹었다. (pizza, as, times, pieces, many, four, of, as)
= I ate _____ she did.

4 나의 일정은 너의 것보다 두 배 더 바쁘다. (busy, as, twice, as)
= My schedule is _____ yours.

5 저 기계는 다른 것보다 절반만큼 시끄럽다. (as, loud, half, as)
= That machine is _____ the other one.

연습문제 B 다음 두 문장의 의미가 같도록 빈칸에 알맞은 말을 쓰시오.

1 I tried to take my medicine as regularly as possible.

= I tried to take my medicine _____ .

2 She explained the new rule as kindly as possible.

= She explained the new rule _____ .

3 Make your frying pan as hot as possible.

= Make your frying pan _____ .

4 Many teenagers check their cell phones as frequently as possible.

= Many teenagers check their cell phones _____ .

5 Ancient Egyptians built the pyramids as high as possible.

= Ancient Egyptians built the pyramids _____ .

연습문제 C 우리말과 같도록 <보기>에서 알맞은 말을 골라 쓰시오.

<보기>   as far as   as long as   as good as   as often as

1 그 탑의 꼭대기에서, 너는 바다까지 볼 수 있다.

= From the top of the tower, you can see _____ the ocean.

2 그녀는 그녀의 숙제를 먼저 끝내기만 하면 영화를 보러 올 수 있다.

= She can come to the movies _____ she finishes her homework first.

3 그 수리공은 나의 컴퓨터가 새것이나 다름없을 것이라고 말했다.

= The repairman said that my computer would be _____ new.

4 에이브러햄 링컨은 그가 할 수 있을 때마다 그의 연설을 연습했다.

= Abraham Lincoln practiced his speeches _____ he could.

기출 적중문제

다음 우리말을 영작할 때 빈칸에 들어갈 알맞은 것은?

반 친구들과 함께 숙제를 하는 것은 혼자 하는 것보다 두 배 더
효과적이다.

= Doing homework with classmates is _____
  effective as doing it alone.

① twice as   ② two as   ③ twice so
④ two so   ⑤ twice more

'…보다 -배 더 ~한/하게'라는
의미를 나타낼 때는 「배수사
(twice, three times, half 등)
+ as + 원급 + as」를 써요.

1. 「비교급 + than」은 '…보다 더 ~한/하게'라는 의미로, 비교하는 두 대상 간 정도의 차이를 나타낸다.

   She is **older than** my younger brother. 그녀는 나의 남동생보다 나이가 더 많다.

   This bicycle is **more expensive than** that one. 이 자전거는 저것보다 더 비싸다.

   (Tip) 「less + 원급 + than」은 '보다 덜 ~한/하게'라는 의미로, 「not + as[so] + 원급 + as」로 바꿔 쓸 수 있다.

   Norway was **less cold than** Iceland. 노르웨이는 아이슬란드보다 덜 추웠다.

   = Norway was **not as[so] cold as** Iceland. 노르웨이는 아이슬란드만큼 춥지 않았다.

2. 비교급 앞에 much, even, still, far, a lot을 써서 '훨씬'이라는 의미로 비교급을 강조할 수 있다.

   She plays the piano **much better** than I do. 그녀는 나보다 피아노를 훨씬 더 잘 친다.

   He arrived **a lot earlier** than Lucy. 그는 Lucy보다 훨씬 더 일찍 도착했다.

연습문제 A 우리말과 같도록 <보기>의 말을 활용하여 문장을 완성하시오.

<보기> colorful   beautiful   small   clean   lonely   heavy

1 파란색 자동차는 빨간색 자동차보다 더 작다.

   = The blue car is _____ the red one.

2 너의 접시는 나의 것보다 더 깨끗하다.

   = Your plate is _____ mine.

3 몇몇 새들은 다른 새들보다 더 다채롭다.

   = Some birds are _____ others.

4 그 조각은 그 그림보다 더 무겁다.

   = The sculpture is _____ the painting.

5 그 소년은 이전보다 더 외롭다.

   = The boy is _____ he was before.

6 이 스카프는 너의 것보다 덜 아름답다.

   = This scarf is _____ yours.

연습문제 B 밑줄 친 부분이 어법상 맞으면 O를 쓰고, 틀리면 바르게 고쳐 쓰시오.

1 Fish tastes <u>salty</u> than meat.   → _____

2 This leather bag is <u>lighter</u> than I thought.   → _____

3 Buying a wedding dress is <u>more costly</u> than buying a hanbok. → _____

4 Renting an apartment is <u>more cheap</u> than buying a house.   → _____

5 The weather was <u>very</u> cooler than I expected.   → _____

6 Sunflowers look much <u>cheerful</u> than other flowers.   → _____

7 Dancing makes me <u>less embarrassed</u> than acting does.   → _____

8 My grandmother is <u>activer</u> than she was five years ago.   → _____

9 Racing bike tires are <u>slimmer</u> than mountain bike tires.   → _____

10 Carter sang far more <u>loudlier</u> than the other choir members. → _____

연습문제 C 두 문장의 의미가 같도록 괄호 안의 말을 활용하여 문장을 완성하시오.

1 Allan was brave enough to go on the scary ride. Brad would not go on it. (brave)
   = Allan was _____ Brad was.

2 Your hair looked a little wavy yesterday. Today, it is full of curls. (much, curly)
   = Your hair is _____ it was yesterday.

3 Rome is 2772 years old. Seoul is 2039 years old. (old)
   = Rome is _____ Seoul.

4 I was not very strong before I started boxing. Now I am very strong. (a lot, strong)
   = I have definitely gotten _____ I was.

5 I think hamburgers are tasty. However, I think sandwiches are tastier. (even, good)
   = I think sandwiches taste _____ hamburgers.

기출 적중문제

다음 글에서 어법상 어색한 부분을 찾아 쓰고 바르게 고쳐 쓰시오.

> When I started learning French, I was very bad
> at it. But now I am far advanced than anyone
> else in my class.

_____ → _____

1. 「the + 비교급 ~, the + 비교급 …」은 '~할수록 더 …하다'라는 의미이다.

   The longer you study, **the smarter** you become. 네가 더 오래 공부할수록 너는 더 똑똑해진다.
   The more books I read, **the more** knowledge I will have.
   나는 더 많은 책을 읽을수록 더 많은 지식을 얻을 것이다.

2. 「비교급 + and + 비교급」은 '점점 더 ~한/하게'라는 의미이다.

   My backpack became **heavier and heavier**. 나의 배낭은 점점 더 무거워졌다.
   The game is getting **more and more exciting**. 그 게임은 점점 더 흥미진진해지고 있다.
   ↳ 비교급이 「more + 원급」의 형태인 경우 「more and more + 원급」으로 쓴다.

3. 「배수사 + 비교급 + than」은 '…보다 –배 더 ~한/하게'라는 의미이며, 「배수사 + as + 원급 + as」로 바꿔 쓸 수 있다.

   The castle is **four times older than** the church. 그 성은 그 교회보다 네 배 더 오래되었다.
   = The castle is **four times as old as** the church.

연습문제 **A**   <보기>와 같이 다음 문장을 「the + 비교급, the + 비교급」 형태로 바꿔 쓰시오.

<보기>   When the beach is cleaner, the view becomes more beautiful. → *The cleaner the beach is, the more beautiful the view becomes.*

1 When I exercise harder, I feel more hungry.

   → _____

2 As we get older, we rely on our friends more.

   → _____

3 If the earth gets warmer, the ice in Antarctica will melt more.

   → _____

4 When you practice bowling more, it becomes easier.

   → _____

5 When you eat junk food more, your body gets more unhealthy.

   → _____

6 If you buy a train ticket earlier, the tickets are cheaper.

   → _____

연습문제 B 괄호 안의 말과 「비교급 + and + 비교급」 형태를 활용하여 문장을 완성하시오.

1 I got _____ as I watched the tragic play. (sad)

2 Taking a plane gets _____ each year. (safe)

3 The athlete ran _____ as he got closer to the finish line. (fast)

4 As the holiday approaches, my family becomes _____. (happy)

5 Mr. Lee shouted _____ while he argued with his boss. (angrily)

6 Since getting a new cell phone, I send messages _____. (often)

7 People spend _____ time in stores because they shop online. (little)

연습문제 C 우리말과 같도록 괄호 안의 말을 활용하여 빈칸에 쓰시오. (단, 숫자는 영어로 쓰시오.)

1 이 책은 점점 더 흥미로워지고 있다. (interesting)
= This book is becoming _____.

2 집이 더 작을수록 청소하기에 더 쉽다. (small, easy)
= _____ a house is, _____ it is to clean.

3 나의 새 베개는 예전 것보다 세 배 더 부드럽다. (soft)
= My new pillow is _____ my old one.

4 네 방이 더 밝을수록 너는 더 기분 좋게 느낄 것이다. (bright, pleasant)
= _____ your room is, _____ you will feel.

5 이 고추들은 일반적인 것들보다 여덟 배 더 맵다. (spicy)
= These peppers are _____ regular ones.

6 모스크바는 나의 도시보다 다섯 배 더 춥다. (cold)
= It is _____ in Moscow than in my city.

7 식료품점이 더 가까울수록 음식을 사는 것은 더 편리하다. (close, convenient)
= _____ a grocery store is, _____ it is to buy food.

기출 적중문제

우리말과 같도록 괄호 안의 말을 활용하여 문장을 완성하시오.

> 그 연구는 네가 누군가를 더 오래 볼수록 네가 그 또는 그녀를 더 좋아한다는 것을 보여준다. (long, much)

= The research shows that _____ you look at someone, _____ you like him or her.

1. 「**the + 최상급 + (명사)**」는 '가장 ~한/하게'라는 의미로, 셋 이상의 비교 대상 중 하나의 정도가 가장 높음을 나타낸다. 부사의 최상급은 the를 생략하기도 한다.

   Watermelon is **the sweetest** fruit nowadays. 수박은 요즘 가장 단 과일이다.
   He came to school **(the) earliest**. 그는 학교에 가장 일찍 왔다.

2. **원급이나 비교급을 이용하여 최상급의 의미를 나타낼 수 있다.**

the + 최상급 + 명사 가장 ~한/하게
= No (other) + 단수명사 ~ as[so] + 원급 + as (다른) 어떤 …도 −만큼 ~하지 않은
= No (other) + 단수명사 ~ 비교급 + than (다른) 어떤 …도 −보다 더 ~하지 않은
= 비교급 + than any other + 단수명사 다른 어떤 …보다 더 ~한
= 비교급 + than all the other + 복수명사 다른 모든 …보다 더 ~한

   Jihyo is **the fastest player** on the team. 지효는 그 팀에서 가장 빠른 선수이다.
   = **No (other) player** on the team is **as[so] fast as** Jihyo.
     그 팀에서 (다른) 어떤 선수도 지효만큼 빠르지 않다.
   = **No (other) player** on the team is **faster than** Jihyo.
     그 팀에서 (다른) 어떤 선수도 지효보다 더 빠르지 않다.
   = Jihyo is **faster than any other player** on the team.
     지효는 그 팀에서 다른 어떤 선수보다 더 빠르다.
   = Jihyo is **faster than all the other players** on the team.
     지효는 그 팀에서 다른 모든 선수들보다 더 빠르다.

3. **최상급 관련 표현**

one of the + 최상급 + 복수명사 가장 ~한 것들 중 하나	the least + 원급 가장 덜 ~한
at best 잘해야	at least 최소한

   He is **one of the smartest students** I know. 그는 내가 아는 가장 똑똑한 학생들 중 한 명이다.
   This is **the least expensive** way to get there. 이것은 그곳에 가기 위한 가장 덜 비싼 방법이다.

연습문제 A 우리말과 같도록 괄호 안의 말과 「the + 최상급」 형태를 활용하여 문장을 완성하시오.

1 나의 엄마에게서 받은 그 목걸이는 나의 방에서 가장 소중한 물품이다. (precious, item)
   = The necklace from my mom is _____ in my room.

2 엠파이어 스테이트 빌딩은 세계에서 가장 높은 건물들 중 하나였다. (tall, building)
   = The Empire State Building was _____ in the world.

3 연극을 보는 것은 시간을 보내는 가장 덜 흥미로운 방법이다. (interesting, way)

= Watching plays is _____ to spend time.

4 Anna는 내가 본 것 중 가장 환상적인 드레스를 입었다. (fantastic, dress)

= Anna wore _____ I have ever seen.

5 이것들은 내가 본 신발들 중 가장 더러운 것이다. (dirty, shoes)

= These are _____ that I have ever seen.

연습문제 B | 다음 문장들의 의미가 같도록 문장을 완성하시오.

1 He is the most diligent man in the office.

= _____ is _____ him in the office.

= _____ is _____ him in the office.

= He is _____ in the office.

= He is _____ in the office.

2 Albert Einstein was the most brilliant scientist.

= _____ was _____ Albert Einstein.

= _____ was _____ Albert Einstein.

= Albert Einstein was _____ .

= Albert Einstein was _____ .

3 Russia is the biggest country in the world.

= _____ in the world is _____ Russia.

= _____ in the world is _____ Russia.

= Russia is _____ in the world.

= Russia is _____ in the world.

4 Ken is the most successful person in my group of friends.

= _____ in my group of friends is _____ Ken.

= _____ in my group of friends is _____ Ken.

= Ken is _____ in my group of friends.

= Ken is _____ in my group of friends.

기출 적중문제 ◎→

우리말과 같도록 괄호 안의 말을 활용하여 문장을 완성하시오.

> 셰익스피어는 영국 문학 역사상 가장 훌륭한 작가들 중 한 명이었다. (writer, great)

= Shakespeare was _____
in the history of English literature.

서술형 대비 문제

A 다음은 여러 강의 특징을 비교하는 표이다. 괄호 안의 말을 활용하여 빈칸에 알맞은 말을 쓰시오.

강	Congo	Huang He	Mississippi	Amazon
길이	4,690 km	5,464 km	6,275 km	6,575 km
너비(최대)	16 km	35 km	19 km	48 km
깊이	250 m	80 m	61 m	100 m

1 The Amazon River is _____ _____ the Mississippi River. (long)

2 The Congo River is _____ _____ of the four rivers. (deep)

3 The Mississippi River is _____ _____ _____ _____ the Huang He River. (deep)

4 The Congo River is _____ _____ the Mississippi River. (narrow)

5 The Amazon River is _____ _____ of all. (wide)

B 두 문장의 의미가 같도록 문장을 완성하시오.

1 The cake recipe seems four times as complicated as the pie recipe.
= The cake recipe seems _____ the pie recipe.

2 The full-size SUV appears three times as safe as the mini SUV.
= The full-size SUV appears _____ the mini SUV.

3 Kate talked about cooking ten times as passionately as she talked about fishing.
= Kate talked about cooking _____ she talked about fishing.

4 Please make the soup as spicy as you can.
= Please make the soup _____.

5 Mike tied his shoelaces as tightly as possible.
= Mike tied his shoelaces _____.

6 She wanted to write her name as neatly as possible.
= She wanted to write her name _____.

7 She was not as nervous as Harry while acting on the stage.
= She was _____ Harry while acting on the stage.

C 우리말과 같도록 괄호 안의 말을 활용하여 영작하시오.

1 너는 한 행동을 더 자주 반복할수록 더 잘 수행할 것이다. (an action, repeat, frequently, well, it, perform, you)

= _____

2 그 책이 점점 더 무서워질수록 나는 점점 더 불안함을 느꼈다. (scary, get, anxious, the book, I, feel)

= _____

3 동물원은 더 흥미로울수록 더 인기 있어질 것이다. (interesting, be, a zoo, it, popular, be)

= _____

4 그 논쟁이 계속되면서, 그녀는 점점 더 화가 났다. (continue, angry, became, as, she, the argument)

= _____

5 그들의 생활 방식의 변화 때문에, 그들은 점점 더 건강해졌다. (because of, they, healthy, become, their, lifestyle changes)

= _____

6 눈이 주말 동안 점점 더 많이 내렸다. (fall, the snow, over the weekend, heavily)

= _____

D 다음 문장들의 의미가 같도록 문장을 완성하시오.

1 Carter is the most dramatic person I know.

= No _____ I know is _____ .

= No _____ I know is _____ .

= Carter is _____ than _____ I know.

= Carter is _____ than _____ I know.

2 The British Empire was the largest empire in the world.

= No _____ in the world was _____ .

= No _____ in the world was _____ .

= The British Empire was _____ than _____ in the world.

= The British Empire was _____ than _____ in the world.

3 Neptune is the furthest planet in our solar system from the Sun.

= No _____ in our solar system is _____ from the Sun.

= No _____ in our solar system is _____ from the Sun.

= Neptune is _____ than _____ in our solar system from the Sun.

= Neptune is _____ than _____ in our solar system from the Sun.

중간 · 기말고사 실전 문제

1 다음 빈칸에 들어갈 말이 순서대로 짝지어진 것은?

> The highway is less crowded on
> Saturdays than it is on Fridays.
> = The highway is _____ crowded on
>   Saturdays _____ it is on Fridays.

① as – as
② not so – as
③ not less – than
④ not much – as
⑤ not so – than

2 다음 중 밑줄 친 부분이 어법상 <u>어색한</u> 것은?

① The waiting line for the new restaurant is <u>as long as</u> the street.
② Were you <u>as confused as</u> I was when you heard the news?
③ Few animals can swim <u>as fast as</u> dolphins.
④ Mice are able to move <u>as quiet as</u> cats.
⑤ He didn't take care of this matter <u>as quickly as</u> I hoped.

3 다음 빈칸에 들어갈 수 있는 것을 <u>모두</u> 고르시오.

> The hurricane was not _____ the
> news said it would be.

① as terrible so
② as more terrible as
③ as terrible as
④ terrible than
⑤ so terrible as

4 다음 중 어법상 바른 것의 개수는?

> ⓐ Did you bring as more food as Amy for lunch?
> ⓑ Recycling is less effective than reusing an item.
> ⓒ This novel is not as interesting as the last one.
> ⓓ Singing in public is not as more embarrassing as falling over in public.
> ⓔ A birthday card is important as a birthday present.

① 5개
② 4개
③ 3개
④ 2개
⑤ 1개

5 다음 우리말을 알맞게 영작한 것은?

> 너는 사과가 오렌지보다 영양가가 덜 높다는 것을 알고 있었니?

① Did you know that apples are not as more nutritious as oranges?
② Did you know that oranges are not nutritious as apples?
③ Did you know that apples are as nutritious as oranges?
④ Did you know that apples are less nutritious than oranges?
⑤ Did you know that oranges are not as nutritious as apples?

[6-7] 다음은 John과 친구들이 유기견 보호소에서 7월 동안 봉사활동을 한 횟수를 나타낸 표이다. 괄호 안의 단어를 활용하여 문장을 완성하시오.

Month	John	Sooah	Yejun
July	5	20	5

6

Yejun visited the dog shelter _____ _____ John in July. (frequently)

7

Sooah went to the dog shelter _____ _____ John in July.
(often, four times)

8 우리말과 뜻이 같도록 할 때 빈칸에 들어갈 알맞은 것은?

우리는 공항에 제시간에 도착하기 위해 가능한 한 빠르게 운전해야 할 것이다.
= We will have to drive _____ to get to the airport on time.

① much possible
② as much possible
③ as fast as possible
④ as fast we can
⑤ as fast as we could

9 다음 대화의 밑줄 친 우리말과 같도록 괄호 안의 말을 활용하여 문장을 완성하시오.

A: I can't wait for this weekend.
B: Neither can I.
A: Do you have any plans?
B: 아니. 이번 주말에 나는 가능한 한 느긋해질 거야.
(lazy)

= No. I will be _____ this weekend.

10 우리말과 같도록 괄호 안의 말을 배열할 때 일곱 번째에 오는 것을 쓰시오.

달리기는 수영보다 세 배 더 많은 칼로리를 소모한다.
(calories, as, running, many, three, swimming, burns, as, times)

→ _____

11 다음 우리말을 알맞게 영작한 것을 모두 고르시오.

스페인으로 가는 비행은 내가 예상했던 것보다 두 배 더 오래 걸렸다.

① The flight to Spain took twice as long as I expected.
② The flight to Spain took twice as longer as I expected.
③ The flight to Spain took twice as longer than I expected.
④ The flight to Spain took twice longer than I expected.
⑤ The flight to Spain took twice as longest as I expected.

12 다음 문장에서 어법상 어색한 부분을 찾아 쓰고 바르게 고쳐 쓰시오.

> The traffic was five times heavy than usual during the holiday.

_____ → _____

13 다음 중 어법상 바른 것은?

① Turtles move slow than rabbits.
② Scientists have to think more logically as other people.
③ Which dress do you think is more attractiver, blue or purple?
④ Michelangelo's paintings are more popular than his sculptures.
⑤ Watching a drama is least entertaining than performing in a drama.

14 다음 (A)~(C)에 들어갈 말이 바르게 짝지어진 것은?

> · The experiment was as ___(A)___ as previous ones.
> · The invention of the airplane was the ___(B)___ development of the last century.
> · Even though I washed it, this shirt is ___(C)___ than my other shirt.

	(A)	(B)	(C)
①	successful	biggest	dirtier
②	more successful	bigger	dirty
③	successful	bigger	dirtier
④	successful	biggest	dirty
⑤	more successful	biggest	dirtier

15 다음 빈칸에 들어갈 말이 순서대로 짝지어진 것은?

> · Is Claire _____ than Emma? Let's measure them both.
> · The book was very detailed. Watching the movie was less _____ than reading the book.

① shorter – more interesting
② shorter – interesting
③ more short – interesting
④ more short – more interesting
⑤ more shorter – much interesting

[16-17] 다음 글을 읽고 주어진 질문에 답하시오.

> The Taj Mahal is ⓐas famous as the Eiffel Tower, but it is ⓑmuch older. The Taj Mahal is nearly 400 years old! It also took ⓒvery longer to build. Builders spent ⓓas longer as eleven years building it. However, the Eiffel Tower is ⓔeven most frequently visited than the Taj Mahal. (A) It is almost four times more popular than the Taj Mahal.

16 ⓐ~ⓔ 중 어법상 어색한 것을 찾아 기호를 쓰고 바르게 고쳐 쓰시오.

(1) _____ → _____
(2) _____ → _____
(3) _____ → _____

17 밑줄 친 (A)와 의미가 같도록 문장을 완성하시오.

= It is almost _____
_____.

18 다음 중 어법상 바른 것끼리 묶인 것은?

ⓐ The test questions got more and more hard.
ⓑ The faster the service, the more higher the cost will be.
ⓒ The smaller the home is, the easier it is to clean.
ⓓ The more dangerous a place is, the most careful we should be.
ⓔ Jobs are becoming more and more competitive these days.

① ⓐ, ⓑ   ② ⓐ, ⓓ   ③ ⓑ, ⓒ
④ ⓒ, ⓔ   ⑤ ⓓ, ⓔ

19 다음은 경이 중학교 학생들이 선호하는 여름 휴양지를 나타낸 그래프이다. 이에 대한 설명으로 옳지 <u>않은</u> 것은?

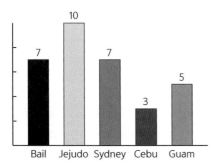

① Bali is as popular as Sydney.
② Sydney is less popular than Jejudo.
③ Jejudo is more popular than all the other vacation destinations.
④ Cebu is less popular than any other vacation destination.
⑤ Guam is more popular than Sydney.

20 다음 우리말을 영작할 때 빈칸에 들어갈 말은?

교통체증 때문에 나는 너보다 훨씬 늦게 도착할 것이다.
= Because of the traffic jam, I'm going to arrive _____ you.

① more later than   ② even latter than
③ very later than   ④ far later than
⑤ latter than

21 다음 우리말을 알맞게 영작한 것은?

네가 먹는 사탕이 더 달콤할수록, 너의 치아는 더 상할 것이다.

① The sweet the candy you eat, the damaged your teeth will be.
② The sweeter the candy you eat, the more will be damaged your teeth.
③ Sweeter the candy you eat, more damaged your teeth will be.
④ The sweeter the candy you eat, the more damaged your teeth will be.
⑤ The sweeter the candy you eat, the most damaged your teeth will be.

22 다음 빈칸에 들어갈 가장 알맞은 것은?

I think Alex is _____ at playing the piano than Tim is.

① least talented
② very less talented
③ much less talented
④ the most talented
⑤ very most talented

23 우리말과 같도록 괄호 안의 말을 활용하여 문장을 완성하시오.

> 최근 몇 년 동안 차 안의 터치 스크린은 점점 더 편리해져 왔다. (convenient)

= Touch screens in cars have become
_____ in recent
years.

24 다음 글의 밑줄 친 ⓐ~ⓔ 중 어법상 어색한 것은?

> The earth is getting ⓐwarmer and warmer each year. This is because of global warming. It is ⓑone of the most serious problems. If temperatures become 5 degrees ⓒhigher than now, many animals will suffer. So, we have to stop global warming! For example, we need to use ⓓas few items made of plastic as possible. ⓔThe lesser we use them, the more we help stop global warming.

① ⓐ   ② ⓑ   ③ ⓒ
④ ⓓ   ⑤ ⓔ

25 다음 빈칸에 들어갈 가장 알맞은 것은?

> As she followed a plant-based diet, her health became _____.

① more and more well
② better and better
③ more and better
④ more and more good
⑤ more and more better

26 다음 중 어법상 바른 것은?

① The deeper we dove, the most careful we were.
② The stronger the people are, more weight they can lift.
③ The funnier the jokes were, the loud I laughed.
④ The more amazing a sunset looks, more impressed am I.
⑤ The more useful an item is, the more commonly it can be found.

27 다음 중 짝지어진 두 문장의 의미가 같은 것을 모두 고르시오.

① I try to drink water as much as possible each day.
= I try to drink water more than I can each day.
② Plastic items are less durable than steel items.
= Steel items are not as durable as plastic items.
③ The street was 50 times as crowded as usual because of the parade.
= The street was 50 times more crowded than usual because of the parade.
④ No other diamond in the safe is rarer than that diamond.
= That diamond as rare as all the other diamonds in the safe.
⑤ When someone is more polite, they can get more respect from others.
= The more polite someone is, the more respect they can get from others.

28 다음 대화의 밑줄 친 부분을 <조건>에 맞게 바꿔 쓰시오.

> *A*: Can I bring one more friend to your party?
> *B*: Of course! <u>When we have more people, the party becomes more fun!</u>

> <조건> 「the + 비교급, the + 비교급」 구문을 사용하시오.

→ _____

_____

29 다음 중 어법상 바른 것의 개수는?

> ⓐ Taking a walk is a lot more interesting than studying a textbook.
> ⓑ We need to find a ladder as high as the ceiling to start painting.
> ⓒ I think you are as more creative as that famous musician.
> ⓓ We were not as luckier as we hoped to be in the contest.
> ⓔ I feel like time is moving ten times as quickly today as it was yesterday.

① 1개   ② 2개   ③ 3개
④ 4개   ⑤ 5개

30 우리말과 같도록 괄호 안의 말을 활용하여 영작하시오.

> 이 스웨터는 나의 겨울 옷들 중 가장 따뜻하다.
> (warm, my winter clothes, of)

= This sweater is _____

_____.

31 다음 중 어법상 바른 것끼리 묶인 것은?

> ⓐ Only bravest people can become firefighters.
> ⓑ Keeping a schedule is one of the most easy ways to organize your life.
> ⓒ Monaco has the most dense population of any country.
> ⓓ One of the most thrilling rides in Korea is at Neverland.
> ⓔ Pablo Picasso had one of the most creative minds in history.

① ⓐ, ⓑ   ② ⓑ, ⓒ   ③ ⓒ, ⓓ
④ ⓓ, ⓔ   ⑤ ⓐ, ⓔ

32 다음 밑줄 친 부분과 바꿔 쓸 수 <u>없는</u> 것은?

> The earthquake caused <u>far</u> more damage than anyone expected.

① even   ② much   ③ still
④ very   ⑤ a lot

33 두 문장의 의미가 같도록 바꿔 쓸 때 전체 문장의 아홉 번째에 오는 것은?

> As the team scored more goals, the crowd became more cheerful.
> = The more goals _____
> _____.

① the   ② more   ③ cheerful
④ crowd   ⑤ scored

34 다음 중 밑줄 친 부분이 어법상 바른 것은?

① Arnold gave <u>the more accurate</u> answer to the question of all the students.

② Mr. Simons gives <u>a small</u> amount to charity than any other member in our group.

③ Eric is <u>the tallest</u> person in our class.

④ The shopping mall in Busan is <u>the most largest</u> in the country.

⑤ What is <u>cheapest</u> drink to buy here?

35 우리말과 같도록 주어진 <조건>에 맞게 영작하시오.

> 김치는 William이 먹었던 것 중에 가장 매운 음식이다.

<조건>
1. 최상급을 활용하시오.
2. spicy food, have ever eaten을 활용하시오.

= Kimchi _____

_____.

36 다음 문장에서 어법상 어색한 부분을 찾아 쓰고 바르게 고쳐 쓰시오.

> The International Space Station is more ambitious than any other projects up to now.

_____ → _____

[37-38] 우리말과 같도록 괄호 안의 말을 알맞게 배열하시오.

37

> 네가 더 많은 긍정적인 말을 들을수록, 너는 더 행복해질 것이다. (positive words, you, hear, the, more, the, be, will, happier, you)

= _____

_____

38

> 나의 형이 더 신이 날수록, 그는 더 크게 웃었다. (more, the, my older brother, excited, was, he, louder, laughed, the)

= _____

_____

39 다음 중 어법상 바른 것은?

① Charles recently experienced the worst illness of his life.

② Going to the safari was most amazing part of the trip.

③ The store sells one of the most prettier dress I've ever seen.

④ A cell phone is one of the most useful item of all time.

⑤ Amanda rented least expensive house she could find.

40 우리말과 같도록 괄호 안의 말을 활용하여 문장을 완성하시오.

그 배우는 할리우드에서 가장 바쁜 연예인들 중 한 명이다. (busy, celebrity)

= The actor is _____
in Hollywood.

41 다음 중 의미가 나머지 셋과 <u>다른</u> 두 개는?

① Michael Phelps is greater than all the other swimmers in Olympic history.
② Michael Phelps is as great as any other swimmer in Olympic history.
③ Michael Phelps is the greatest swimmer in Olympic history.
④ No swimmer in Olympic history is greater than Michael Phelps.
⑤ Michael Phelps is not greater than other swimmers in Olympic history.

42 다음은 Michael과 친구들이 지난 한 달간 영화관에 방문한 횟수를 나타낸 표이다. 이에 대한 설명으로 옳은 것은?

Michael	Emma	Jay
3	1	7

① Michael visited the cinema more often than Jay.
② Emma visited the cinema more frequently than Michael.
③ Jay went to the cinema the least frequently.
④ Michael didn't go to the cinema as often as Emma.
⑤ Emma went to the cinema the least often.

43 주어진 문장과 의미가 같은 것은?

Many drivers are not as careful as they should be.

① Many drivers are not the most careful.
② Many drivers are as careful as they should be.
③ Many drivers are more careful than they should be.
④ Many drivers are less careful than they should be.
⑤ Many drivers should be as careful as they are.

44 다음 중 어법상 바른 것은?

① Brenda is the more skillful tennis player of all.
② This ring is more valuable than all the other one.
③ Thomas is most generous friend of all.
④ No teacher is thoughtful as Mr. Greer.
⑤ No other student is as honest as Jason.

[45-46] 다음 글을 읽고 주어진 질문에 답하시오.

Polar bears are ⓐthe largest than all the other bears on the planet. They are three times as ⓑheavier as panda bears. (A) 그들은 많은 음식을 먹을수록, 덩치가 더 커진다. (food, eat, big, grow) They have ⓒthe thickest layers of fat and fur out of all bears. Therefore, they like places that are ⓓcold than anywhere else. Unfortunately, polar bears are endangered. There are ⓔfewer than 30,000 left in the wild.

45 위 글의 밑줄 친 우리말 (A)와 같도록 괄호 안의 말을 활용하여 「the + 비교급, the + 비교급」 형태로 영작하시오.

= _____

_____

46 밑줄 친 ⓐ~ⓔ 중 어색한 것을 찾아 기호를 쓰고 바르게 고쳐 쓰시오.

(1) _____ → _____

(2) _____ → _____

(3) _____ → _____

[47-48] 다음 대화를 읽고 주어진 질문에 답하시오.

A: Who do you think is the smartest person in your family?

B: My grandfather is brighter than any other person I know. His knowledge of history is especially great.

A: I think that's common for elderly people.

B: Yes. (A) 나는 그들이 나이가 들수록 점점 더 현명해진다고 생각해. (wise)

A: That's true. Young people should really respect their knowledge.

B: I totally agree.

47 위 글의 밑줄 친 문장을 <조건>에 맞게 바꿔 쓰시오.

<조건>

1. No other로 문장을 시작하시오.

2. 비교급을 사용하시오.

= _____

_____

48 위 글의 밑줄 친 (A)와 같도록 괄호 안의 단어를 활용하여 빈칸에 쓰시오.

= I think that they become _____ _____ _____ as they age.

49 주어진 문장과 의미가 같은 것은?

> Being the president is more stressful than all the other jobs in a company.

① All the jobs are as stressful as being the president in a company.
② Being the president is as stressful as all the other jobs in a company.
③ Being the president is more stressful than any other job in a company.
④ No job is more stressful than the jobs in a company.
⑤ All the jobs in a company are more stressful than being the president.

50 다음 (A)~(C)에 들어갈 말이 바르게 짝지어진 것은?

> · The singer's ___(A)___ album got a positive review.
> · The more time I spend in a forest, ___(B)___ I become.
> · Try to hold the rope as ___(C)___ as you can.

	(A)	(B)	(C)
①	last	the calmer	tightly
②	latest	the calmer	more tightly
③	last	calmer	tightlier
④	latest	the calmer	tightly
⑤	last	the calm	tightlier

51 다음 우리말을 영작할 때 빈칸에 들어갈 알맞은 것은?

> 내가 휴가를 갈 때 나의 개를 돌봐주기만 하면, 나도 너에게 똑같이 해줄 수 있다.
> = _____ you take care of my dog when I go on vacation, I can do the same for you.

① As often as
② As soon as
③ As long as
④ As fast as
⑤ As good as

52 다음 두 문장의 의미가 같도록 빈칸에 알맞은 말을 쓰시오.

> The calculations were not as complicated as I imagined.
> = The calculations were _____ _____ I imagined.

CHAPTER 11
전치사

The vase is on the shelf. 그 꽃병은 선반 위에 있다.

명사 the shelf 앞에 **on**이 와서 '선반 위에'라는 의미를 나타냈어요. 이렇게 명사나 대명사 앞에 와서 시간, 장소, 위치, 방향 등을 나타내는 것을 **전치사**라고 해요.

기출로 적중 POINT

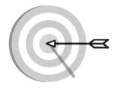

내신 100점 적중!
기출 출제율

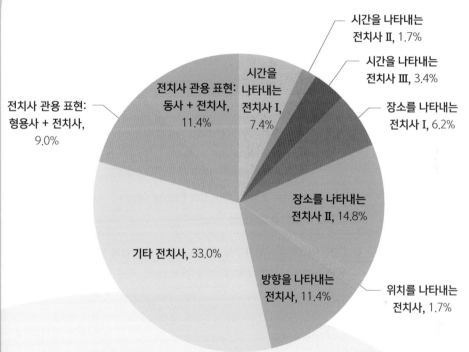

시간을 나타내는
전치사 II, 1.7%

시간을 나타내는
전치사 III, 3.4%

장소를 나타내는
전치사 I, 6.2%

전치사 관용 표현:
동사 + 전치사,
11.4%

시간을
나타내는
전치사 I,
7.4%

전치사 관용 표현:
형용사 + 전치사,
9.0%

장소를 나타내는
전치사 II, 14.8%

기타 전치사, 33.0%

방향을 나타내는
전치사, 11.4%

위치를 나타내는
전치사, 1.7%

TOP 1 **기타 전치사 (33%)**
다양한 의미를 나타내는 전치사의 의미와 쓰임을 묻는 문제가 자주 출제된다.

TOP 2 **장소를 나타내는 전치사 II (14.8%)**
장소를 나타내는 전치사 in, on, at의 쓰임을 묻는 문제가 자주 출제된다.

TOP 3 **방향을 나타내는 전치사 (11.4%),**
   전치사 관용 표현: 동사 + 전치사 (11.4%)
방향을 나타내는 전치사의 의미와 쓰임을 묻는 문제가 자주 출제된다. 「동사 + 전치사」 관용 표현의 의미와 형태를 묻는 문제가 자주 출제된다.

at, on, in은 '~에'라는 의미로 시간을 나타낸다.

	시각	**at** 1 o'clock 1시에 **at** 6:10 6시 10분에
at	시점	**at** noon 정오에 **at** midnight 한밤중에 **at** dawn 새벽에 **at** the beginning of the month 월초에
on	요일	**on** Tuesday 화요일에 **on** Friday 금요일에 (Tip) 「on + 요일s」: (요일)마다 **on** Wednesdays 수요일마다
	날짜, 기념일	**on** May 5, 2015 2015년 5월 5일에 **on** Halloween 핼러윈에 **on** my birthday 나의 생일에
in	월, 계절	**in** February 2월에 **in** winter 겨울에
	연도, 세기	**in** 2019 2019년에 **in** the 17th century 17세기에
	아침·오후·저녁	**in** the morning/afternoon/evening 아침/오후/저녁에 (Tip) 특정한 날의 아침·오후·저녁을 나타낼 때는 on을 쓴다. **on** Saturday night 토요일 밤에 **on** Christmas morning 크리스마스 아침에
	기타	**in** the past 과거에 **in** the future 미래에 (Tip) 예외: **at** present 현재에

(Tip) last, every, next와 같이 시간을 나타내는 부사구와 전치사 at, on, in은 함께 쓰지 않는다.
I took a trip to Vietnam **last year**. 나는 작년에 베트남으로 여행을 갔다.

연습문제 | 괄호 안에서 알맞은 전치사를 고르시오.

1 I will need a ride to soccer practice (at / on / in) the afternoon.

2 Many people visit Vermont to see the colorful leaves (at / on / in) autumn.

3 The clothes I ordered are supposed to arrive (at / on / in) March 2.

4 The city held a large fireworks show (at / on / in) Independence Day.

5 School was closed (at / on / in) Wednesday and Thursday because of bad weather.

6 The same bird sings next to my window every morning (at / on / in) 5 A.M.

7 Many scientists expect global warming to get worse (at / on / in) the future.

8 She makes plans (at / on / in) the beginning of the month.

9 The Japanese restaurant is usually filled with people (at / on / in) Friday night.

POINT 1-2 시간을 나타내는 전치사 Ⅱ

정답 p.37

다음은 시간을 나타내는 다양한 전치사이다.

before	~ 전에	My family usually has dinner **before** 7 o'clock. 나의 가족은 보통 7시 전에 저녁을 먹는다.
after	~ 후에	We ride bicycles each day **after** school. 우리는 방과 후에 매일 자전거를 탄다. **Tip** in 뒤에 기간을 나타내는 말이 오면 '(기간) 후에'라는 의미이다. He will buy a new bike **in two years**. 그는 2년 후에 새 자전거를 살 것이다.
from	~부터	I have classes **from** 8 A.M. every morning. 나는 매일 아침 오전 8시부터 수업이 있다. **Tip** 「from ~ to …」는 '~부터 …까지'라는 의미로 기간을 나타낸다. The Korean War lasted **from** 1950 **to** 1953. 한국전쟁은 1950년부터 1953년까지 지속되었다.
since	~ 이후로	since는 주로 완료시제와 함께 쓰여 특정 시점부터 어떤 행동이나 상황이 계속되는 것을 나타낸다. Sujin has taken a yoga class **since** last year. 수진이는 작년 이후로 계속 요가 수업을 들어왔다.
by	~까지 (완료)	by는 정해진 시점까지 어떤 행동이나 상황이 완료되는 것을 나타낸다. Martin's mom told him to clean his room **by** lunchtime. Martin의 엄마는 그에게 점심시간까지 그의 방을 청소하라고 말했다.
until	~까지 (계속)	until은 특정 시점까지 어떤 행동이나 상황이 계속되는 것을 나타낸다. The flight was delayed **until** 6 P.M. 그 비행기는 오후 6시까지 (계속) 지연되었다.

연습문제 A 다음 빈칸에 before나 after 중 알맞은 것을 쓰시오.

1 You have to wash your hands, and then you can hold the baby.

① _____ washing your hands, you can hold the baby.

② You have to wash your hands _____ holding the baby.

2 Sarah finished her homework, and then she played video games.

① Sarah finished her homework _____ playing video games.

② _____ finishing her homework, Sarah played video games.

3 I'll travel to Europe next month, and then I'll visit Africa.

① I'll visit Africa _____ traveling to Europe next month.

② _____ visiting Africa, I'll travel to Europe next month.

4 Insu took a shower, and then he started reading a book.

① Insu started reading a book _____ taking a shower.

② Insu took a shower _____ starting to read a book.

5 She listened to the radio, and then she watched a movie.

① She listened to the radio _____ watching a movie.

② _____ listening to the radio, she watched a movie.

연습문제 **B** │ 괄호 안에서 알맞은 전치사를 고르시오.

1 Shawn told his teacher that he would finish the project (by / until) Thursday.

2 Emma has played basketball (from / since) middle school.

3 Kyle has soccer practice (by / until) 8 P.M., so he'll get home late tonight.

4 I haven't been to the beach (by / since) last summer.

5 Most people work for eight hours a day (from / since) Monday to Friday.

6 The new community swimming pool will be completed (by / until) May 31.

7 (Until / Since) the beginning of her career, Susan has composed more than 100 songs.

8 Tickets for the concert will be available for purchase (from / since) August 23 on our website.

9 The street will be closed for water pipe repairs (by / until) July 1.

10 Please let me know the address (by / until) noon.

11 The company will be handing out prizes (from / since) 11 A.M.

기출 적중문제

다음 글의 빈칸에 들어갈 말이 순서대로 짝지어진 것은?

> _____ the mid-19th century, people started traveling by train. Over the years, more advanced means of transportation were introduced. For example, air travel has been common _____ the mid-20th century.

① In – for
② While – since
③ For – from
④ In – since
⑤ While – from

정답 p.37

기출로적중 POINT 1-3 시간을 나타내는 전치사 Ⅲ

for와 during은 모두 '~ 동안'이라는 의미이지만, for는 숫자를 포함한 시간 표현 앞에 오고 during은 명사 앞에 온다.

for	+ 숫자를 포함한 시간 표현	She studied **for six years** to become a doctor. 그녀는 의사가 되기 위해 6년 동안 공부했다.
during	+ 명사	Many bats sleep in caves **during** the day. 많은 박쥐들이 낮 동안 동굴에서 잠을 잔다. There was a thunder storm **during** the festival. 축제 동안 폭풍우가 쳤다. (Tip) during은 전치사로 뒤에 명사가 나오지만, while은 접속사로 뒤에 완전한 문장이 나온다. My mom talked on the phone **while** she was making pasta. 나의 엄마는 그녀가 파스타를 만드는 동안 전화 통화를 했다.

연습문제 괄호 안에서 알맞은 전치사를 고르시오.

1 Sejin plays the piano at the restaurant (for / during) three hours every night.

2 The man stopped by the bank (for / during) his lunch hour.

3 My dog was missing (for / during) two weeks before we found her.

4 I held my breath (during / while) I sank into the water.

5 Huge economic losses occurred (during / while) the Great Depression.

기출 적중문제

다음 글의 빈칸에 들어갈 말이 순서대로 짝지어진 것은?

> The Suez Canal connects the Mediterranean Sea and the Red Sea. It has been important to world trade _____ 150 years. For example, _____ the past year, nearly 19,000 ships passed through the canal.
>
> *canal 운하

for와 during은 모두 '~ 동안'이라는 의미이지만, for는 뒤에 숫자를 포함한 시간 표현이 오고 during은 뒤에 명사가 와요.

① for - while
② while - for
③ for - during
④ while - during
⑤ during - for

at, on, in은 장소를 나타낸다.

at ~에, ~에서	비교적 좁은 장소나 하나의 지점	**at** the crosswalk 횡단보도에 **at** the corner 모퉁이에
on ~에, ~ 위에	표면에 접촉한 상태	**on** the wall 벽에 **on** the road 도로에 **on** the sofa 소파 위에
in ~에, ~안에	비교적 넓은 장소나 공간의 내부	**in** Busan 부산에 **in** the forest 숲에 **in** the box 상자 안에 **in** the building 건물 안에

연습문제 다음 그림을 보고 빈칸에 at, on, in 중 알맞은 것을 쓰시오.

[1-4]

[5-8]

1 The cat is _____ the sofa.

2 He is standing _____ the window.

3 There is a picture _____ the wall.

4 A red coat is hanging _____ the closet.

5 A girl is standing _____ the bus stop.

6 Some vegetables are _____ the bag.

7 A man is sitting _____ a bench.

8 The newspaper is _____ the ground.

기출 적중문제 ◎

다음 그림을 보고 빈칸에 알맞은 전치사를 쓰시오.

There are two cars _____ the road. A man is _____ a blue car. A woman is standing _____ the crosswalk.

기출로적중 POINT 2-2 장소를 나타내는 전치사 Ⅱ

정답 p.37

at, on, in은 다양한 상황을 나타내기도 한다.

at	일상적으로 다니는 장소	**at** home 집에서 **at** school 학교에서 **at** work 직장에서 **at** the bookstore 서점에서 **at** the theater 극장에서
	행사, 모임	**at** a concert 콘서트에서 **at** a contest 대회에서 **at** a party 파티에서 **at** a meeting 회의에서
	기타	**at** the top/bottom of ~의 위/아래에 (Tip) 예외: **in** the middle of ~의 가운데에
on	길, 층	**on** the street 길 위에 **on** the second floor 2층에
	교통수단	**on** a bus 버스에 **on** a subway 지하철에 **on** a plane 비행기에 **on** a train 기차에 (Tip) 예외: **in** a car 차에 **in** a taxi 택시에
	통신수단	**on** the Internet 인터넷상에서 **on** the phone 전화로, 통화 중인
	기타	**on** the[one's] way to school 학교로 가는 길에 **on** the[one's] left/right 왼쪽에/오른쪽에
in	자연환경	**in** the sky 하늘에 **in** the ocean 바다에 **in** the world 세상에, 세계에 **in** space 우주에
	인쇄물	**in** a book 책에 **in** a newspaper 신문에 **in** a dictionary 사전에 **in** a picture 그림에
	(특정 장소에서) ~하는 중인	**in** bed 취침 중인 **in** prison 수감 중인 **in** the hospital 입원 중인
	기타	**in** half 반으로 **in** a line 한 줄로 **in** uniform 제복을 입은 **in** a hurry 서두르는 **in** danger 위험에 빠진 **in** need 어려움에 처한 **in** pencil 연필로 **in** Spanish 스페인어로

연습문제 A   괄호 안에서 알맞은 전치사를 고르시오.

1 The article (at / on / in) the newspaper about the traffic problem was convincing.

2 He folded the letter (at / on / in) half before putting it in the envelope.

3 The reporter spent a lot of time (at / on / in) a car driving around for work.

4 I eat dinner (at / on / in) home most nights, because I enjoy cooking.

5 *Sarang* means *love* (at / on / in) Korean.

6 Head down the street, and the store will be (at / on / in) the left.

7 The company decided to build a luxury hotel (at / on / in) the middle of the city.

8 (At / On / In) my way to the gym, I ran into my best friend.

9 I was thrilled to find my name (at / on / in) the top of the list of best students.

10 A jet flew overhead, writing words (at / on / in) the sky.

11 There is an empty chair (at / on / in) the right. Please take a seat.

12 If you look (at / on / in) the bottom, there is a line for signing your name.

13 Be careful not to give out too much private information (at / on / in) the Internet.

14 Joe was popular (at / on / in) work and had many friends.

15 Every year, a fundraiser is held to collect money for people (at / on / in) need.

연습문제 **B** │ 괄호 안의 말과 전치사 at, on, in을 활용하여 문장을 완성하시오.

1 There was a thick layer of snow ＿＿＿＿＿＿＿＿＿＿, so we decided not to drive. (the street)

2 Scientists found a lot of plastic ＿＿＿＿＿＿＿＿＿＿ during their research. (the ocean)

3 I talked to my cousin from New York ＿＿＿＿＿＿＿＿＿＿ this morning. (the phone)

4 The man has been ＿＿＿＿＿＿＿＿＿＿ for more than ten years. (prison)

5 We got a city-view suite ＿＿＿＿＿＿＿＿＿＿ of the hotel. (the sixth floor)

6 The tallest mountain ＿＿＿＿＿＿＿＿＿＿ is located between India and Nepal. (the world)

7 Alice forgot her science book ＿＿＿＿＿＿＿＿＿＿, so she couldn't do her homework. (school)

8 You should always wear a seatbelt when you are ＿＿＿＿＿＿＿＿＿＿. (a car)

9 Giho can't come to the party because he will be ＿＿＿＿＿＿＿＿＿＿ in Denver. (a concert)

10 The team was ＿＿＿＿＿＿＿＿＿＿ of losing the game at the last minute. (danger)

🎯 기출 적중문제

다음 중 빈칸에 들어갈 말이 나머지 넷과 다른 것은?

① Albert Einstein was born ＿＿＿＿＿ 1879.
② The man ＿＿＿＿＿ the picture is Abraham Lincoln.
③ Bob had an urgent meeting, so he left ＿＿＿＿＿ a hurry.
④ John picked up some litter ＿＿＿＿＿ his way to school.
⑤ Almost 10 million people live ＿＿＿＿＿ the city of Seoul.

POINT 3 위치를 나타내는 전치사

정답 p.37

다음 전치사는 위치를 나타낸다.

in front of	~ 앞에	There is a bus stop **in front of** my house. 나의 집 앞에 버스 정류장이 있다.
behind	~ 뒤에	He is hiding **behind** his older brother. 그는 그의 형 뒤에 숨어 있다.
over	~ (덮여 있듯이 바로) 위에	I put on a jacket **over** my pajamas. 나는 나의 잠옷 위에 재킷을 입었다.
under	~ (덮여 있듯이 바로) 아래에	My bag is **under** the desk. 나의 가방은 책상 아래에 있다.
above	~(보다) 위에	A helicopter is flying **above** city hall. 헬리콥터가 시청 위를 비행하고 있다.
below	~(보다) 아래에	The mirror is hanging **below** the light fixture. 그 거울은 조명 기구 아래에 걸려 있다.
by, next to, beside	~ 옆에	Minho sat **by[next to/beside]** me. 민호는 나의 옆에 앉았다.
near	~ 가까이에	We gathered **near** the campfire. 우리는 모닥불 가까이에 모였다.
between	~ (둘) 사이에	The post office is **between** the bank and the supermarket. 우체국은 은행과 슈퍼마켓 사이에 있다.
among	~ (셋 이상) 사이에	She is sitting **among** her classmates. 그녀는 그녀의 반 친구들 사이에 앉아 있다.

연습문제 | 다음 그림을 보고 괄호 안에서 가장 알맞은 전치사를 고르시오.

1	2	3

1 Tom raised his hand (over / under) his head.

2 There is a light hanging (under / above) the dining table.

3 The boat is passing (below / over) the bridge.

4   There are some presents (under / above) the Christmas tree.

5   The café is located (near / under) the house.

6   The book is (beside / among) the alarm clock.

7   A deer is standing (among / above) the trees.

8   The car is parked (in front of / behind) the building.

9   The lamp is (between / among) the sofa and the bookshelf.

10   The bird is flying (below / above) the forest.

11   The puppy is sleeping (under / above) the table.

12   There is a bus (behind / below) a red car on the road.

> between과 among 모두
> '~ 사이에'라는 의미이지만,
> between은 대상이 둘일 때
> 쓰고 among은 대상이
> 셋 이상일 때 써요.

기출 적중문제

우리말과 같도록 빈칸에 알맞은 전치사를 쓰시오.

많은 흰 양들 사이에 검은 양 한 마리가 있다.

= There is one black sheep _____ many white ones.

방향을 나타내는 전치사

POINT 4

정답 p.37

up	~ 위로	Sam is going **up** the stairs. Sam은 계단 위로 올라가고 있다.
down	~ 아래로	Sam is going **down** the stairs. Sam은 계단 아래로 내려가고 있다.
into	~ 안으로	He got **into** the pool. 그는 수영장 안으로 들어갔다.
out of	~ 밖으로	He got **out of** the pool. 그는 수영장 밖으로 나왔다.
onto	~ 위로	I moved the dictionary **onto** the third shelf. 나는 그 사전을 세 번째 선반 위로 옮겼다.
off	~에서 떨어져	The ball rolled **off** the bench. 그 공이 벤치에서 굴러 떨어졌다.
across	~을 가로질러	We are going to travel **across** the country next month. 우리는 다음 달에 그 나라를 가로질러 여행할 것이다.
along	~을 따라서	We walked **along** the road for a few hours. 우리는 도로를 따라서 몇 시간 동안 걸었다.
around	~ 주위에	Trees are planted **around** the house. 나무들이 그 집 주위에 심어져 있다.
through	~을 통해서	Robert ran out **through** the door. Robert는 문을 통해서 뛰어나갔다.
over	~을 넘어서	The child jumped **over** the fence. 그 아이는 울타리를 넘어서 뛰었다.
from	~으로부터	Jenny transferred to this school **from** Canada. Jenny는 캐나다로부터 이 학교로 전학을 왔다.
to	~으로, ~에	to는 주로 동사 go, come, get, return과 함께 쓰여 목적지나 도착지점을 나타낸다. I didn't want to go **to** the hospital. 나는 병원에 가고 싶지 않았다.
for	~으로, ~을 향해	for는 주로 동사 leave, start, depart, head와 함께 쓰여 가고자 하는 방향을 나타낸다. She is leaving **for** Brazil tomorrow afternoon. 그녀는 내일 오후에 브라질을 향해 떠날 것이다.
toward(s)	~쪽으로, ~을 향해	toward(s)는 주로 동사 run, walk, come, drive, turn과 함께 쓰여 움직임의 방향을 나타낸다. Amy ran **toward** the shop. Amy는 그 가게를 향해 달렸다.

CHAPTER 11 전치사 해커스 중학영문법 3학년

1  **2**  **3**

1 The snowboarder is going (into / down) the slope.

2 Mom came (down / into) the house with a bag of groceries.

3 The zookeeper had the tiger come (up / out of) the cage.

4  **5**  **6**

4 The train is going (around / through) a tunnel.

5 The children are running (toward / into) the ice cream truck.

6 The hiker climbed (up / out of) the mountain.

7  **8**  **9**

7 The bus stop is (across / through) the road.

8 Kate is jogging (along / for) the beach with her dog.

9 There are lots of beautiful flowers (around / across) the tree.

기출 적중문제

다음 빈칸에 들어갈 알맞은 것은?

The bird is returning _____ its nest with a worm in its mouth.

① off ② to ③ over
④ down ⑤ for

기출로적중 POINT 5 기타 전치사

정답 p.38

with	~와 함께	Henry likes to hang out **with** his friends. Henry는 그의 친구들과 함께 어울리는 것을 좋아한다.
	~을 가진	The boy **with** the curly brown hair is my little brother. 곱슬거리는 갈색 머리카락을 가진 소년은 나의 남동생이다.
	~을 이용해서 (도구)	She is drawing a picture **with** colored pencils. 그녀는 색연필을 이용해서 그림을 그리고 있다.
	~에 대해	I was very satisfied **with** the bread at the new bakery. 나는 새 빵집에 있는 빵에 대해 매우 만족했다.
without	~ 없이	To climb the mountain **without** preparation is dangerous. 준비 없이 그 산을 오르는 것은 위험하다.
by	~을 타고 (교통수단)	We planned to go Yeosu **by** plane instead of train. 우리는 여수에 기차 대신 비행기를 타고 가기로 계획했다. (Tip) 예외: **on** foot 걸어서
	~로 (수단)	Dogs are able to identify people **by** smell alone. 개는 오직 냄새만으로 사람들을 알아볼 수 있다.
	~에 의해	This soup is made **by** a famous chef. 이 수프는 유명한 요리사에 의해 만들어졌다.
	~(정도)로	The arrow missed the target **by** 5 centimeters. 그 화살은 5센티미터 정도로 과녁을 빗나갔다.
about	~에 대한	The speech **about** environmental pollution was interesting. 환경오염에 대한 연설은 흥미로웠다.
like	~처럼, ~같이	The children look just **like** their father. 그 아이들은 꼭 그들의 아버지처럼 생겼다.
as	~로	Pumpkins can be used **as** decorations for Halloween. 호박은 핼러윈을 위한 장식으로 사용될 수 있다.
of	~의	The cover **of** the book was pretty. 그 책의 표지는 예뻤다.
	~에 대한	The issue **of** climate change has become a hot topic. 기후 변화에 대한 문제는 화제가 되어왔다.
for	~을 위해	Alison wrote a lovely poem **for** her boyfriend. Alison은 그녀의 남자친구를 위해 사랑스러운 시를 썼다.
	~에 찬성하는	The mayor is **for** building a new expressway in the city. 그 시장은 그 도시에 새로운 고속도로를 짓는 것에 찬성한다.

against	~에 반대하는, 맞서는	I am **against** using animals for medical tests. 나는 동물들을 의학 실험용으로 사용하는 것에 반대한다.
except	~을 제외하고는	Everyone is here **except** Jacob. Jacob을 제외하고는 모두가 여기에 있다.
throughout	~ 동안 내내	It snowed heavily **throughout** Sunday morning. 일요일 아침 동안 내내 눈이 많이 왔다.
such as	~와 같은	China has many big cities, **such as** Beijing and Shanghai. 중국에는 베이징과 상하이와 같은 큰 도시들이 많이 있다.
because of (= due to)	~ 때문에	I was late today **because of**(= **due to**) a traffic jam. 나는 오늘 교통체증 때문에 늦었다.
according to	~에 따르면	**According to** the weather forecast, it will rain today. 일기예보에 따르면, 오늘 비가 올 것이다.
instead of	~ 대신	We decided to study math first **instead of** science. 우리는 과학 대신 수학을 먼저 공부하기로 결정했다.

연습문제 괄호 안에서 알맞은 전치사를 고르시오.

1 Hojin went to the beach (with / by) his family last weekend.

2 I always go to school (from / by) subway because it's faster than taking the bus.

3 The teacher told her students (like / about) the upcoming contest.

4 Jessica hopped down the sidewalk (of / like) a bunny.

5 Can I get the tuna sandwich (without / for) lettuce and tomatoes?

6 He will work (about / as) a lifeguard at the community pool this summer.

7 The cost (of / by) the phone was too high for Ron.

8 The store will have a number of promotions (as / throughout) the month.

9 I bought a wedding gift (for / about) my older sister when I was in England.

10 We stayed indoors (due to / instead of) the heat.

11 John has watched all of the *Catman* movies (for / except) the newest one.

12 We will read a part of a novel (instead of / for) a poem in today's class.

13 Students were (without / against) having their lunch periods shortened.

14 The price of corn dropped (like / by) 20 percent compared to last year.

15 Vincent van Gogh created many famous paintings, (against / such as) *Starry Night*.

16 I baked the cake (according to / such as) the directions on the box.

POINT 6-1 전치사 관용 표현: 형용사 + 전치사

정답 p.38

다음 전치사는 형용사와 함께 관용 표현을 만든다.

be good/bad at ~을 잘하다/못하다	be known for ~으로 알려져 있다
be frightened at[by] ~에 놀라다, 겁먹다	be ready for ~할/~에 준비가 되다
be surprised at[by] ~에 놀라다	be responsible for ~에 책임이 있다
be ashamed of ~을 부끄러워하다	be accustomed to ~에 익숙하다
be capable of ~을 할 수 있다	be born to ~이 될/~을 할 운명을 타고 나다
be full of ~으로 가득 차있다	be likely to ~을 하기 쉽다, ~을 할 것 같다
be jealous of ~을 시기하다	be married to ~와 결혼하다
be proud of ~을 자랑스러워하다	be similar to ~와 비슷하다
be short of ~이 부족하다	be crowded with ~으로 붐비다
be tired of ~에 싫증이 나다	be filled with ~으로 가득하다
be based on ~에 기초하다, 근거하다	be satisfied with ~에 만족하다
be crazy about ~에 빠져 있다	be absent from ~에 결석하다

CHAPTER 11 전치사 해커스 중학영문법 3학년

연습문제 괄호 안에서 알맞은 전치사를 고르시오.

1 The jar is filled (of / with) jelly beans of various flavors.

2 Hyunsoo is proud (with / of) his science fair trophy.

3 My little brother was responsible (for / of) stealing my candy.

4 He was absent (from / to) our meeting yesterday.

5 Justin is ashamed (of / with) how he spoke to his grandmother.

6 Vermeer was known (of / for) his ability to capture light in his paintings.

7 She wrote a story based (to / on) her childhood growing up in Africa.

8 My parents have been married (to / with) each other for nearly 30 years.

9 I'm not accustomed (to / for) the new layout of the maze, so I keep getting lost.

10 The robot is capable (with / of) performing many different actions at once.

11 The new phone is similar (to / of) the one that it replaced.

12 My little brother was born (to / of) play soccer.

13 Billy is crazy (about / to) taking photos with his new digital camera.

14 I was frightened (at / to) the loud noise outside.

15 We had to be ready (of / for) any problems that might happen.

16 The stadium was crowded (about / with) people for the big match.

전치사 관용 표현: 동사 + 전치사

정답 p.38

다음 전치사는 동사와 함께 관용 표현을 만든다.

apologize for ~에 대해 사과하다	belong to ~에 속하다
apply for ~에 지원하다	prefer A to B B보다 A를 더 선호하다
ask for ~을 요구하다	believe in ~을 믿다
stand for ~을 나타내다	result in (결과적으로) ~을 낳다, 야기하다
concentrate on ~에 집중하다	succeed in ~에 성공하다
decide on ~으로 정하다	divide A into B A를 B로 나누다
depend on ~을 의존하다/믿다	run into ~와 우연히 만나다
focus on ~에 초점을 맞추다	turn A into B A를 B로 바꾸다
spend A on B A를 B에 쓰다	come up with ~을 제안하다, 생각해내다
consist of ~으로 이루어지다	talk with/to ~와 대화를 나누다
die of ~으로 죽다	look after ~를 돌보다
laugh at ~을 비웃다	live by (신조/원칙)에 따라 살다

연습문제 괄호 안에서 알맞은 전치사를 고르시오.

1 I used to spend a lot of money (on / off) clothes.

2 How did you come up (about / with) this plan?

3 Not getting enough sleep can result (in / to) illnesses.

4 Jerry apologized (for / to) his bad behavior.

5 I prefer living in the country (to / for) living in a city because it's much quieter.

6 Everyone laughed (at / for) me when I fell off the stage.

7 I live (at / by) the motto "Honesty is the best policy."

8 She was surprised to run (into / about) her classmate on the street in Paris.

기출 적중문제

다음 빈칸에 들어갈 알맞은 것은?

> The dog with the red collar belongs _____ the Miller family.

① for ② of ③ to
④ in ⑤ by

POINT 6-3 전치사 관용 표현: 동사 + 명사 + 전치사

정답 p.38

다음 전치사는 동사, 명사와 함께 관용 표현을 만든다.

get rid of ~을 제거하다	take pity on ~를 불쌍히 여기다
make a fool of ~를 바보 취급하다	take part in ~에 참가[참여]하다
make use of ~을 이용하다	pay attention to ~에 관심을 갖다, ~에 주목하다
take care of ~를 돌보다	have fun with ~와 즐거운 시간을 보내다

연습문제 우리말과 같도록 문장을 완성하시오.

1 Cindy는 주말마다 동물 보호소에서 다친 동물들을 돌본다.

= Cindy _____ injured animals at the animal shelter on weekends.

2 그녀는 노숙자를 불쌍히 여겼고 그에게 여분의 잔돈을 주었다.

= She _____ the homeless man and gave him some spare change.

3 그는 지역 사회 극장에서 장기 자랑에 참가했다.

= He _____ the talent show at the community theater.

4 아파트 주민들은 바퀴벌레를 제거하기 위해서 열심히 노력했다.

= The apartment's residents worked hard to _____ the cockroaches.

5 그들은 수업 동안 그들의 선생님들에게 주목하도록 요구된다.

= They are required to _____ their teachers during class.

6 Hailey는 내가 아이를 돌보는 동안 나의 남동생과 즐거운 시간을 보냈다.

= Hailey _____ my little brother while I was babysitting.

7 우리 아빠는 항상 낡거나 고장난 전자 제품들을 이용할 새로운 방법들을 찾는다.

= My dad always finds new ways to _____ old or broken electronics.

8 그녀는 그녀의 반 친구가 그녀를 바보 취급했을 때 짜증이 났다.

= She was annoyed when her classmate _____ her.

9 오래 살기 위해서, 너 자신을 돌보는 것은 중요하다.

= In order to live a long life, it is important to _____ yourself.

10 너는 너의 휴대폰을 가지고 노는 것을 그만하고 영화에 주목해야 한다.

= You should stop playing with your cell phone and _____ the movie.

11 그녀는 연례 퍼레이드에 참가하는 것을 즐겼다.

= She enjoyed _____ the annual parade.

서술형 대비 문제

A 다음 빈칸에 알맞은 말을 <보기>에서 한 번씩만 골라 쓰시오.

<보기> in near until through at

1 We will take a field trip to Jeju Island _____ September.

2 The room is reserved _____ Friday morning.

3 Did you see the lunar eclipse _____ midnight last night?

4 My room is _____ the elevator, so it's often very noisy.

5 We can save 20 minutes if we drive _____ the tunnel.

<보기> due to according to of with for

6 He wiped the counter _____ a towel.

7 Many parents are _____ the school's plan to require students to wear uniforms.

8 Teams must have five members _____ the judge.

9 _____ an accident, there was heavy traffic on the freeway.

10 The roof _____ the house needs to be replaced.

B 밑줄 친 부분이 어법상 맞으면 O를 쓰고, 틀리면 바르게 고쳐 쓰시오.

1 Sumin was absent <u>about</u> school because of an illness.　　→ _____

2 The play is based <u>as</u> the life of a famous musician.　　→ _____

3 I hate doughnuts that are filled <u>for</u> cream and fruit.　　→ _____

4 Downtown Charlotte is full <u>of</u> small restaurants and coffee shops.　　→ _____

5 Chef Andreas is known <u>to</u> his amazing vegetarian dishes.　　→ _____

6 The power company apologized <u>for</u> the recent outage.　　→ _____

7 She came up <u>by</u> a plan to make some money during the summer.　　→ _____

8 She depends <u>to</u> her mother to bring her to school.　　→ _____

9 The apartment consists <u>of</u> two rooms, a bathroom, and a kitchen.　　→ _____

C 다음은 보물을 찾을 수 있는 방법에 대한 글이다. 다음 빈칸에 알맞은 말을 <보기>에서 한 번씩만 골라 쓰시오.

<보기> on   over   at   to   next to

How to Find the Treasure

To find the treasure, you should first go ⓐ_____ the park. After you enter the park, head for the stone bridge that crosses ⓑ_____ the stream. Once you are there, find the big tree that has some carvings ⓒ_____ it. The treasure is buried ⓓ_____ the tree. To find it, you should dig where the tree's shadow appears ⓔ_____ 3 o'clock.

D 다음은 Janet의 일기이다. 다음 그림을 보고 빈칸에 알맞은 말을 <보기>에서 한 번씩만 골라 쓰시오.

<보기> to   on   at   between   with   across   down

Janet's Diary

I had a great time ⓐ_____ the amusement park yesterday. I got to ride a huge roller coaster that was ⓑ_____ a small island. I had to walk ⓒ_____ a bridge to get there. After that, I went on a waterslide. I slid ⓓ_____ the slide, and the water felt great. The weather was really hot, so the waterslide was crowded ⓔ_____ people. Then, I went ⓕ_____ the hot dog shop ⓖ_____ the roller coaster and the waterslide to get a hot dog.

중간·기말고사 실전 문제

1 다음 중 밑줄 친 부분이 어법상 어색한 것은?

① The first airplane was invented in 1903.
② I don't like going outside alone at dawn.
③ We always have tacos at Tuesdays.
④ Karl played basketball on June 24.
⑤ Mark loves to go apple picking in fall.

2 다음 (A)~(C)에 들어갈 말이 바르게 짝지어진 것은?

School will start in September this year. It always started around August 15 ___(A)___ the past. However, the building was damaged by a storm ___(B)___ the school was on summer break. As a result, we have to wait ___(C)___ August 31 when the repairs are completed to begin the year.

	(A)	(B)	(C)
①	in	while	until
②	at	while	by
③	in	during	until
④	at	during	by
⑤	in	while	by

3 다음 빈칸에 공통으로 들어갈 알맞은 것은?

· Don't forget to go to soccer practice _____ Saturday and Sunday.
· Angela's older brother was born _____ March 26, 2003.

① in ② on ③ at
④ for ⑤ by

4 다음 문장에서 어법상 어색한 부분을 찾아 쓰고 바르게 고쳐 쓰시오.

(A) He usually goes for a jog at the morning.
(B) The doctor is not available on present.
(C) My family always meets at my grandparents' house in Friday evening.

(A) _____ → _____
(B) _____ → _____
(C) _____ → _____

5 다음 빈칸에 들어갈 말이 순서대로 짝지어진 것은?

· I will take tennis lessons _____ my vacation.
· Please return the library books _____ next Monday.

① during – until ② by – for
③ during – by ④ for – until
⑤ while – by

6 <보기>의 전치사를 한 번씩만 골라 빈칸에 알맞은 말을 쓰시오.

<보기> since during from for

· Several buildings fell ⓐ_____ the earthquake.
· I'm tired, so I will go lie down ⓑ_____ 30 minutes.
· My band has played at the Christmas party every year ⓒ_____ 2017.
· Our power was out ⓓ_____ Monday to Wednesday.

7 다음 중 어법상 바른 것의 개수는?

ⓐ I practiced the piano for three hours every night.
ⓑ We will be back from our trip until the end of August.
ⓒ The population of Paris doubled in the 17th century.
ⓓ The professor studied pyramids during 40 years in Egypt.
ⓔ We have been best friends since first grade.

① 1개   ② 2개   ③ 3개
④ 4개   ⑤ 5개

8 다음 빈칸에 공통으로 들어갈 알맞은 것은?

· There are some stools to sit _____.
· I was _____ my way to the library when I fell over.
· Someone wrote _____ the bathroom walls.

① in   ② on   ③ at
④ for   ⑤ by

9 다음 대화의 빈칸에 들어갈 전치사가 같은 것끼리 묶인 것은?

A: Hi. Is Mr. Jones in today?
B: Yes, but he is ⓐ_____ the phone now. Can I help you?
A: No. I just want to talk ⓑ_____ him ⓒ_____ something I read in his book.
B: OK. You can wait for him ⓓ_____ the sofa. He will be finished ⓔ_____ a few minutes.

① ⓐ, ⓑ   ② ⓐ, ⓓ   ③ ⓑ, ⓒ
④ ⓒ, ⓔ   ⑤ ⓓ, ⓔ

10 다음 빈칸에 들어갈 전치사가 나머지 넷과 다른 것은?

① I put some sunscreen _____ my face.
② A helicopter landed _____ the roof of the building.
③ Nancy was _____ a taxi when she got a phone call from James.
④ The hotel has a pool and fitness center _____ the 20th floor.
⑤ These days, I watch TV shows _____ the Internet.

11 다음 (A)~(C)에 들어갈 말이 바르게 짝지어진 것은?

· Please fold your test paper __(A)__ half so no one can see your answers.
· Habitat destruction is putting many plant species __(B)__ danger of going extinct.
· Many coins were found __(C)__ the bottom of the wishing well.

	(A)	(B)	(C)
①	in	in	at
②	on	at	at
③	in	at	in
④	on	at	in
⑤	in	in	on

12 다음 밑줄 친 ⓐ~ⓔ 중 어법상 어색한 것을 찾아 기호를 쓰고 바르게 고쳐 쓰시오.

I spent last weekend ⓐat Chuncheon. My family has a villa ⓑby the lake there. I had hoped to go fishing, but it was too cold. I ended up staying ⓒin the cabin most of the time. I was disappointed and wished I had just stayed ⓓat home. Next time, I will check the weather report ⓔin the Internet before I go.

(1) _____ → _____
(2) _____ → _____

13 다음 빈칸에 공통으로 들어갈 알맞은 것은?

· Bats locate things _____ sound.
· I have a baseball card signed _____ my hero.
· The fastest way to get to the museum is _____ bus.

① as   ② for   ③ over
④ by   ⑤ of

14 다음 빈칸에 들어갈 말이 순서대로 짝지어진 것은?

· The next plane leaving _____ Chicago is at 8 o'clock.
· The lady took her wallet _____ her bag to buy coffee.

① for – to   ② for – into
③ for – out of   ④ to – out of
⑤ to – into

15 다음 빈칸에 들어갈 수 있는 전치사 to의 개수는?

- You can get _____ the park if you follow this road.
- After 30 minutes, you'll need to get the cookies _____ the oven.
- A lot of fruit sold in Korean grocery stores is imported _____ the Philippines.
- Tourists often spend hours _____ looking around the Louvre in Paris.
- We decided to return _____ Lake Michigan next summer for vacation.

① 1개　　② 2개　　③ 3개
④ 4개　　⑤ 5개

17 다음 중 어느 빈칸에도 들어갈 수 <u>없는</u> 것은?

My younger brother recently joined a hockey team. He had to buy some equipment _____ a helmet and a hockey stick. The team practices every day _____ Sundays. He is very tired _____ his busy schedule. However, he is becoming a better player. His first game _____ another team is next Saturday. I hope he does well.

① except　　　② against
③ instead of　④ because of
⑤ such as

18 <보기>의 전치사를 한 번씩만 골라 빈칸에 알맞은 말을 쓰시오.

<보기>　after　down　along　from

- We took the train (A) _____ Seattle to Portland last weekend.
- The security guard searched the parking lot (B) _____ hearing a loud noise.
- Kevin slid (C) _____ the pole when he visited the fire station.
- The gardener planted flowers (D) _____ the fence.

16 우리말과 같도록 빈칸에 알맞은 전치사를 쓰시오.

그 점원은 계산대 뒤에 서 있다.

= The clerk is standing _____ the counter.

Yesterday, I went to a show. It was my best friend's first performance ⓐ_____ a professional magician. The hall was crowded ⓑ_____ people. Luckily, I sat ⓒ_____ the stage, so I could see well. He was really good. (A) <u>그는 심지어 토끼를 비둘기로 바꿨다.</u> He asked audience members to come onto the stage to take part ⓓ_____ some of the tricks.

19 위 글의 빈칸에 알맞은 전치사를 <보기>에서 골라 쓰시오.

<보기> as   near   with   in

ⓐ _____   ⓑ _____
ⓒ _____   ⓓ _____

20 위 글의 밑줄 친 우리말 (A)와 같도록 괄호 안의 말을 활용하여 문장을 완성하시오.

= He even _____.
(a rabbit, turn, a dove, into)

21 다음 문장의 밑줄 친 for와 의미가 같은 것은?

I am <u>for</u> the plan to go to Washington D.C. for our class trip.

① She got in her car and headed <u>for</u> home.
② This cream is <u>for</u> treating sunburns.
③ No one is <u>for</u> canceling the game.
④ The vet gave me some medicine <u>for</u> my cat.
⑤ The closet has a secret panel <u>for</u> hiding things.

22 다음 빈칸에 들어갈 알맞은 것은?

My friend, Jaemin, looks exactly _____ her little sister. It took me many months before I could distinguish them.

① by   ② like   ③ about
④ for   ⑤ as

23 다음 빈칸에 공통으로 들어갈 알맞은 것은?

· Emily went to the beach _____ Jessica.
· I always order my pizza _____ extra cheese.
· The city has had a lot of problems _____ electricity since the storm.

① by   ② about   ③ for
④ of   ⑤ with

24 다음 중 어느 빈칸에도 들어갈 수 <u>없는</u> 것은?

· The bowler was disappointed when he lost the tournament _____ one point.
· The student asked a question _____ Louisiana's ecosystem.
· Ms. Brown got small gifts _____ her children while she was on a trip.
· I was lucky enough to take a picture _____ last night's amazing sunset.
· David uses his computer _____ talking to his friends around the world.

① for   ② about   ③ of
④ like   ⑤ by

25 다음 빈칸에 들어갈 가장 알맞은 것은?

My family is moving to Dubai this summer. I am excited but also a little nervous. I am scared that I won't like going to school _____ my friends.

① by　　　　② for　　　　③ as
④ of　　　　⑤ without

[26-27] 다음 우리말과 같도록 알맞은 전치사를 고르시오.

26

Nick을 제외하고는 모두가 오늘 아침에 학교에 늦었다.
= Everyone was late for school this morning _____ Nick.

① with　　　　② except　　　　③ by
④ off　　　　⑤ about

27

우리는 그 공원이 문을 닫았기 때문에 이번 주말에 소풍을 갈 수 없다.
= We won't be able to have the picnic this weekend _____ the park being closed.

① without　　　　② throughout
③ about　　　　④ due to
⑤ such as

28 다음 (A)~(C)에 들어갈 말이 바르게 짝지어진 것은?

· We explored the town _____(A)_____ foot during the afternoon.
· Yejin talked _____(B)_____ an astronomer who discovered many famous stars.
· He asked me to take a picture _____(C)_____ him.

　　　(A)　　　(B)　　　(C)
① on　　　with　　　for
② on　　　at　　　about
③ in　　　at　　　for
④ on　　　with　　　about
⑤ in　　　with　　　about

29 다음 중 어느 빈칸에도 들어갈 수 <u>없는</u> 것은?

· My family moved _____ a new apartment.
· There are several kinds of cookies _____ the snack cabinet.
· The pharmacy _____ the two hospitals is always very crowded.
· The main actor's name was _____ the title on the poster.

① into　　　　② between　　　　③ in
④ above　　　　⑤ among

Teacher
I want to discuss voting today. Some people are saying that we should lower the voting age to 16. What do you think ⓐ_____ that?

Jun
I'm ⓑ_____ lowering the voting age. I don't think people in my age group know enough about politics and current events. They only know things they hear ⓒ_____ home from their parents. It would be ⓓ_____ giving an extra vote to their parents.

Jihyun
I disagree. (A) <u>나는 나이가 더 어린 사람들이 투표하게 하는 것에 찬성한다.</u> Government actions affect us, so we should be allowed to vote in elections.

30 위 글의 빈칸에 알맞은 전치사를 <보기>에서 한 번씩만 골라 쓰시오.

<보기> about like at against

ⓐ _____   ⓑ _____
ⓒ _____   ⓓ _____

31 위 글의 밑줄 친 우리말 (A)와 같도록 주어진 <조건>에 맞게 문장을 완성하시오.

<조건>
1. 전치사 한 개를 포함하시오.
2. let, vote, younger people을 활용하시오.

= I am _____ .

[32-33] 다음 빈칸에 공통으로 들어갈 알맞은 전치사를 쓰시오.

32

- Bread consists _____ flour, yeast, sugar, and water.
- The swimming pool is full _____ leaves and branches.
- Many people die _____ cancer each year.

33

- The test is always given _____ the morning.
- The school raised more than $5,000 to provide winter coats for those _____ need.
- You need to be _____ bed and get lots of sleep to recover from the injury.

34 다음 빈칸에 공통으로 들어갈 알맞은 것은?

- He uses his tablet mainly _____ a gaming device.
- She was cast _____ Snow White in the school play.
- All of the resort's guests are treated _____ kings and queens.

① off   ② as   ③ for
④ with   ⑤ except

35 다음 문장의 밑줄 친 like와 쓰임이 다른 것은?

> Children often love to eat sweets like chocolates and candies.

① I want to go somewhere fun like an amusement park this weekend.
② I want to find a new bag that looks just like my old one.
③ No one can make me laugh like my best friend, Jaeho.
④ Jane's dog likes to chase the birds that live in their backyard.
⑤ Today, car manufacturers like ours are reducing the prices of electric vehicles.

36 다음 밑줄 친 ⓐ~ⓔ 중 어법상 어색한 것을 찾아 기호를 쓰고 바르게 고쳐 쓰시오.

> · I am very proud ⓐof the perfect score I got on my math test.
> · Minsik is accustomed ⓑfrom his mother keeping his room clean.
> · She was short ⓒin breath after running up the stairs.
> · She wants a new bike that is similar ⓓto her sister's.
> · The restaurant is known ⓔabout its delicious sandwiches.

(1) _____ → _____
(2) _____ → _____
(3) _____ → _____

[37-38] 다음 빈칸에 들어갈 알맞은 것을 고르시오.

37

> Lisa is capable _____ solving math problems in high school textbooks.

① about   ② in   ③ by
④ for   ⑤ of

38

> Jason is responsible _____ the broken window.

① without   ② by   ③ for
④ from   ⑤ in

39 다음 중 밑줄 친 부분이 어법상 바른 것은?

① Our dog is bad off doing tricks.
② My aunt has been married to her husband for ten years.
③ Junhee was absent to class last week because of the flu.
④ I was crazy at swimming when I was young.
⑤ I am jealous with my friend because he is taller than me.

40

> It's been a long time since I've ridden a bicycle. It feels _____ the first time.

① as   ② about   ③ like

④ with   ⑤ by

41

> Greg had fun _____ his friends at the birthday party.

① over   ② with   ③ to

④ for   ⑤ on

42 다음 빈칸 (A)~(C)에 들어갈 말이 바르게 짝지어진 것은?

> · Suho cannot come up ___(A)___ an answer to the problem.
> · My coach believed ___(B)___ my ability to win the race.
> · I apologized ___(C)___ the rude things I said to my mother.

	(A)	(B)	(C)
①	with	in	to
②	with	on	for
③	by	in	to
④	by	on	to
⑤	with	in	for

43 다음 중 어법상 바른 것은?

① Can you divide the cake on five pieces?

② The lightning last night resulted with a fire at the school.

③ Boy Scouts live by the motto "Be prepared."

④ He is likely of succeed because of his hard work.

⑤ My father often makes dinner because he is good to cooking.

44 다음 빈칸에 들어갈 말이 나머지 넷과 다른 것은?

① The cost of the meal will depend _____ what you order.

② The movie is based _____ a true story about a famous bank robbery.

③ I can't concentrate _____ what I'm doing.

④ These trophies belong _____ the national swimming team.

⑤ The construction noise outside made it hard to focus _____ our schoolwork.

45 다음 대화의 빈칸에 들어갈 말이 순서대로 짝지어진 것은?

> A: Have you ever been to Dilly's Restaurant?
> B: Yes. My family went there _____ Thursday. Why?
> A: I am thinking of going there tomorrow.
> B: That's a great choice. It's the best restaurant _____ the city.

① for – on ② on – in ③ in – on
④ in – for ⑤ on – for

46 다음 빈칸에 들어갈 말이 나머지 넷과 다른 것은?

① I have to take care _____ my little brother.
② My father wants to get rid _____ his old car.
③ The bully made a fool _____ himself during soccer practice.
④ I hardly ever make use _____ my calculator these days.
⑤ I took pity _____ the stray dog and brought it home with me.

[47-48] 다음 글을 읽고 주어진 질문에 답하시오.

> By spending time ⓐ_____ the Internet, many people learn about unusual psychological conditions. For instance, if certain people see pictures of things ⓑ_____ random patterns of holes, (A) 그들은 그것들에 겁먹는다. According ⓒ_____ psychologists, a condition called trypophobia is responsible ⓓ_____ this feeling. These holes appear unnatural and cause people to feel uncomfortable or anxious. And people would not know about this phobia ⓔ_____ reading about it online.
>
> *trypophobia 환공포증

47 위 글의 빈칸에 알맞은 말을 <보기>에서 골라 쓰시오.

<보기> without to for on with

ⓐ _____   ⓑ _____
ⓒ _____   ⓓ _____
ⓔ _____

48 위 글의 밑줄 친 우리말 (A)와 같도록 <보기>의 말을 활용하여 문장을 완성하시오.

<보기> be them frighten

= _____.

CHAPTER 12
접속사

I bought apples **and** oranges. 나는 사과들과 오렌지들을 샀다.
단어   접속사   단어

위 문장에서 두 단어 apples와 oranges가 **and**라는 말로 연결되어 있어요. 이렇게 단어와 단어, 구와 구 또는 절과
절을 연결하는 것을 **접속사**라고 해요.

기출로 적중 POINT

내신 100점 적중!
기출 출제율

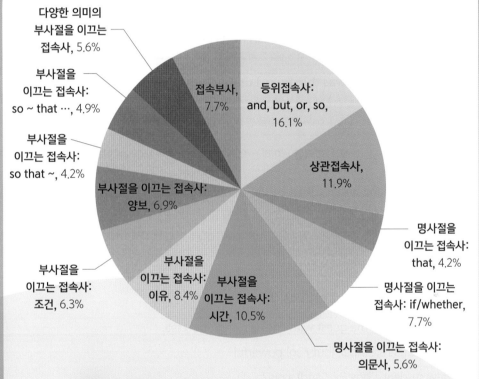

다양한 의미의 부사절을 이끄는 접속사, 5.6%

부사절을 이끄는 접속사: so ~ that …, 4.9%

부사절을 이끄는 접속사: so that ~, 4.2%

부사절을 이끄는 접속사: 양보, 6.9%

부사절을 이끄는 접속사: 조건, 6.3%

부사절을 이끄는 접속사: 이유, 8.4%

부사절을 이끄는 접속사: 시간, 10.5%

접속부사, 7.7%

등위접속사: and, but, or, so, 16.1%

상관접속사, 11.9%

명사절을 이끄는 접속사: that, 4.2%

명사절을 이끄는 접속사: if/whether, 7.7%

명사절을 이끄는 접속사: 의문사, 5.6%

TOP 1 등위접속사: and, but, or, so (16.1%)
맥락에 맞는 등위접속사를 고르는 문제가 자주 출제된다.

TOP 2 상관접속사 (11.9%)
맥락에 맞는 상관접속사를 사용하여 영작하는 문제가 자주 출제된다.

TOP 3 부사절을 이끄는 접속사: 시간 (10.5%)
시간을 나타내는 접속사의 의미와 쓰임을 묻는 문제가 자주 출제된다.

등위접속사: and, but, or, so

정답 p.41

등위접속사는 문법적으로 대등한 단어와 단어, 구와 구, 절과 절을 연결한다.

and	~과, 그리고, ~하고 나서	Jenny went to **Mexico and Peru** for a trip. Jenny는 여행으로 멕시코와 페루에 갔다. I ate **soup, salad and pasta**. 나는 수프, 샐러드, 그리고 파스타를 먹었다. She **took a shower and ate dinner**. 그녀는 샤워를 하고 나서 저녁을 먹었다.
but	하지만, 그러나	This shirt is **pretty but too small**. 이 셔츠는 예쁘지만 너무 작다. **The team won the game, but the coach is still angry.** 그 팀은 경기를 이겼지만, 감독은 여전히 화가 나있다.
or	또는, ~이거나	They will play **tennis or badminton**. 그들은 테니스 또는 배드민턴을 칠 것이다. You can **buy fresh fruits at the grocery store or order them online**. 너는 싱싱한 과일을 식료품점에서 구입하거나 그것들을 온라인에서 주문할 수 있다.
so	그래서, 따라서	**I was thirsty, so I drank a bottle of water.** 나는 목이 말라서, 물 한 병을 마셨다. (Tip) so는 절과 절을 연결할 때만 쓸 수 있다.

(Tip) 「명령문 + and ~」는 '-해라, 그러면 ~'이라는 의미이고, 「명령문 + or ~」는 '-해라, 그렇지 않으면 ~'이라는 의미이다.
Take the medicine, **and** you'll get better. 그 약을 먹어라, 그러면 너는 나아질 것이다.
Hurry up, **or** you may miss the train. 서둘러라, 그렇지 않으면 너는 기차를 놓칠 수도 있다.

연습문제 괄호 안에서 가장 알맞은 것을 고르시오.

1 My parents provided the guest with cookies (and / but) tea.

2 Tablet computers are small (but / so) powerful.

3 Is the new student a boy (or / and) a girl?

4 She put on her shoes (and / but) went for a walk.

5 Did she go to the photo studio (or / but) the restaurant?

6 He took a taxi (so / but) didn't arrive at the station on time.

7 Study hard, (or / and) you'll do well on the exam.

8 The store gave out free samples, (or / so) many people visited.

9 I normally like sweet stuff, (or / but) this smoothie has too much sugar in it.

10 Finish your meal, (or / and) you can't have dessert.

11 I cleaned the living room, my bedroom (and / but) the kitchen.

POINT 2 상관접속사

정답 p.41

1. **상관접속사는 두 개 이상의 단어가 짝을 이뤄 문법적으로 대등한 단어와 단어, 구와 구, 절과 절을 연결한다.**

both A and B	A와 B 둘 다	I like **both** baseball **and** basketball. 나는 야구와 농구 둘 다 좋아한다.
not only A but (also) B = B as well as A	A뿐만 아니라 B도	He wants **not only** money **but (also)** honor. = He wants honor **as well as** money. 그는 돈뿐만 아니라 명예도 원한다.
not A but B	A가 아니라 B	Tim studied **not** math **but** English. Tim은 수학이 아니라 영어를 공부했다.
either A or B	A나 B 둘 중 하나	**Either** I **or** she will clean the bathroom. 나와 그녀 둘 중 한 명이 화장실을 청소할 것이다.
neither A nor B	A도 B도 아닌	The movie was **neither** scary **nor** funny. 그 영화는 무섭지도 웃기지도 않았다.

2. **「both A and B」로 연결된 주어 뒤에는 항상 복수동사를 쓴다. 나머지 상관접속사로 연결된 주어의 뒤에 오는 동사는 B에 수일치시킨다.**

Both he **and** she (~~has~~, **have**) a younger sister. 그와 그녀 둘 다 여동생이 있다.
Not only Kelly **but also** her parents (~~is~~, **are**) at home now.
Kelly뿐만 아니라 그녀의 부모님도 지금 집에 있다.

연습문제 A 상관접속사를 이용하여 다음 두 문장을 한 문장으로 연결할 때 빈칸에 알맞은 말을 쓰시오.

1 Nate is American. Andrew is American, too.
→ _____ Nate _____ Andrew are American.

2 He has ridden a horse. He has ridden a camel, too.
→ He has ridden a camel _____ _____ _____ a horse.

3 She doesn't enjoy watching dramas. She doesn't enjoy reading novels either.
→ She enjoys _____ watching dramas _____ reading novels.

4 This board game can be played by four people. Or it can be played by eight people.
→ This board game can be played by _____ four _____ eight people.

5 The chess match's winner was me. Jiho lost the match.
→ The chess match's winner was _____ Jiho _____ me.

6 My town has a big playground. My town has a lake, too.

→ My town has _____ _____ a big playground _____ _____ a lake.

7 You may choose to print the picture in color. Or you may choose to print it in black-and-white.

→ You may choose to print the picture _____ in color _____ in black-and-white.

8 Seoha joined the dance club. Tony also joined the dance club.

→ _____ Seoha _____ Tony joined the dance club.

9 Jimmy has never been to the Netherlands. I have never been to the Netherlands, either.

→ _____ Jimmy _____ I have been to the Netherlands.

연습문제 B 괄호 안에서 알맞은 것을 고르시오.

1 Either my sister or I (has / have) to stay home and do the chores.

2 The cars as well as the street (is / are) covered in snow.

3 Neither the plates nor the bowl (are / is) in the cabinet.

4 The kitchen lights as well as the bedroom lamp (are / is) turned off.

5 Not the galleries but the museum (has / have) a lounge.

6 Not only the bridges but also the tunnel (are / is) under repair.

7 Both Brian and Harry (take / takes) violin lessons twice a week.

8 Either Jamie or I (have / has) to go shopping for Christmas presents.

9 Neither the teacher nor the students (is / are) satisfied with the school event.

10 The mind as well as the body (needs / need) to be trained.

11 Both Yeri and Jessica (like / likes) singing in front of crowds.

12 Not the gloves but the scarf (cost / costs) 20 dollars.

13 Not only our uncle but also our cousins (are / is) coming to visit us.

14 Both the passengers and the pilot (were / was) afraid of the storm.

기출 적중문제

다음 중 어법상 바른 것은?

① Both New York and Washington is big cities.

② He not only works diligently but also playing hard after work.

③ Either you or your friends needs to help our teacher.

④ I want to order a bowl of salad as well as a glass of milk for lunch.

⑤ A coupon as well as free gifts were provided to the new customers.

명사절을 이끄는 접속사: that

정답 p.41

1. that이 이끄는 명사절은 문장 안에서 주어·목적어·보어 역할을 한다.

주어	**That we recycle plastic** is important. 우리가 플라스틱을 재활용하는 것은 중요하다. = **It** is important **that we recycle plastic**. └→ that절이 주어로 쓰였을 때 주로 주어 자리에 가주어 it을 쓰고 진주어인 that절은 문장 뒤로 보낸다.
목적어	He noticed **(that) his phone was missing**. 그는 그의 전화기가 없어진 것을 알아챘다. └→ that절이 문장 안에서 목적어로 쓰였을 때 that은 생략할 수 있다.
보어	The problem is **that the computer is not working**. 문제는 그 컴퓨터가 작동하지 않고 있다는 것이다.

2. that은 아래와 같은 명사를 설명하는 명사절을 이끌기도 하며, 이때 that은 생략할 수 없다.

fact   truth   promise   idea   thought   news   suggestion   evidence

Remember **the fact that** health is important.
건강이 중요하다는 사실을 기억해라. (사실 = 건강이 중요하다)

I made **a promise that** I will study hard.
나는 열심히 공부할 것이라는 약속을 했다. (약속 = 나는 열심히 공부할 것이다)

연습문제 A   밑줄 친 that절의 역할을 <보기>에서 골라 그 기호를 쓰시오.

<보기>   ⓐ 주어   ⓑ 목적어   ⓒ 보어

1 It is important that you believe in yourself.   [   ]

2 I heard that John will travel abroad next summer.   [   ]

3 Scientists found that sharks have poor vision.   [   ]

4 It is shocking that he lied to his parents.   [   ]

5 The thing is that the door was locked when we arrived.   [   ]

6 It is clear that Sarah broke the vase.   [   ]

7 The bank manager noticed that some money was missing.   [   ]

8 It is sad that our soccer team lost the championship.   [   ]

9 Many people believe that children learn new languages faster than adults.   [   ]

10 Nancy's problem was that her glasses were broken.   [   ]

11 It is amazing that the climbers made it to the top of Mt. Everest.   [   ]

12 She said that the restaurant has tasty food. [   ]

13 The most surprising thing was that she won first place. [   ]

14 I guess that he forgot to call me back. [   ]

연습문제 B 우리말과 같도록 <보기>의 말과 괄호 안의 말을 알맞게 배열하시오.

<보기>	the fact	the truth	the evidence	the promise
	the idea	the news	the thought	the suggestion

1 유명 인사들이 많은 돈을 번다는 사실은 놀랍지 않다. (that, make, celebrities, money, a lot of)

= _____ is not surprising.

2 Susan은 그녀가 일찍 일어나겠다는 약속을 어겼다. (would, up, that, she, early, wake)

= Susan broke _____.

3 그 가족은 그들의 개가 실종되었다는 사실을 받아들여야 했다. (dog, that, was, their, lost)

= The family had to accept _____.

4 위험한 범죄자가 마을 안에 있다는 생각은 모두를 겁먹게 했다. (was, in the town, a dangerous criminal, that)

= _____ scared everyone.

5 우리는 우리의 비행기가 지연되었다는 소식을 들었다. (our plane, delayed, had been, that)

= We heard _____.

6 그 남자가 그 그림을 훔쳤다는 증거는 불충분하다. (the man, the painting, that, stole)

= _____ is weak.

7 우리가 경기에서 질지도 모른다는 생각은 실망스러웠다. (might, that, lose, we, the game)

= _____ was disappointing.

8 Dylan이 그 소문을 퍼뜨렸다는 의견은 거짓이다. (started, Dylan, that, the rumor)

= _____ is false.

기출 적중문제

다음 밑줄 친 that과 역할이 같은 것을 모두 고르시오.

> That Taekwondo is popular is known to everyone.

① Some people think that Ann is rude.

② That she lied to us is certain.

③ The fact is that hamburgers are not good for your health.

④ I noticed that you bought a new dress.

⑤ It is too bad that we don't have enough time.

that이 이끄는 명사절은 문장 안에서 주어·목적어· 보어로 쓰일 수 있어요.

기출로적중 POINT 3-2 명사절을 이끄는 접속사: if/whether

정답 p.41

if/whether는 명사절을 이끄는 접속사로, '~인지'의 의미이다. whether가 이끄는 명사절은 주어·목적어·보어 역할을 할 수 있지만, if가 이끄는 명사절은 동사의 목적어 역할만 할 수 있다.

주어	**Whether he trusts me** is not clear. 그가 나를 믿는지는 확실하지 않다.
목적어	Sally wonders **if[whether] the story is true.** Sally는 그 이야기가 사실인지 궁금해한다. We had a debate **on whether Tom lied.** 우리는 Tom이 거짓말을 했는지에 대해 논쟁했다. └→ 전치사의 목적어 자리에는 if가 이끄는 명사절을 쓸 수 없다.
보어	My concern is **whether she found the wallet.** 나의 관심은 그녀가 그 지갑을 찾았는지이다.

(Tip) or not은 whether의 바로 뒤에 붙여 쓸 수 있지만 if의 바로 뒤에는 쓸 수 없다.
I don't know (if, **whether**) or not Jiwoo will come to the park. 나는 지우가 공원에 올지 오지 않을지 모른다.

연습문제 밑줄 친 부분이 어법상 맞으면 O를 쓰고, 틀리면 바르게 고쳐 쓰시오.

1 <u>If</u> the festival will be held at school is not important. → _____

2 We will see <u>if</u> Michelle's choice is right. → _____

3 He wants to know <u>whether</u> there are good places to shop downtown. → _____

4 <u>If</u> the soldier survived the last attack is unknown. → _____

5 I'm not sure <u>if</u> or not I made her upset. → _____

6 The question is <u>whether</u> Mr. Kris is guilty. → _____

7 <u>If</u> the new horror movie will come out this summer is still in question. → _____

8 Rachel has to decide on <u>if</u> she will participate in the student council. → _____

기출 적중문제

다음 중 어법상 <u>어색한</u> 것은?

① Whether I can answer the phone depends on what I'm doing.

② I couldn't tell whether he was joking or not.

③ If it will snow next week is not certain.

④ My mom's worry is whether there will be enough food.

⑤ I am curious if you know what happened.

if가 이끄는 명사절은 동사의 목적어 역할만 할 수 있어요.

1. **의문사가 이끄는 명사절은 주어·목적어·보어로 쓰이며, 「의문사 + 주어 + 동사」의 형태로 쓴다.**

주어	**Why Charlie left** is unclear. 왜 Charlie가 떠났는지 불분명하다.
목적어	I forgot **when the deadline was**. 나는 마감일이 언제였는지 잊었다.
보어	The question is **how he passed the exam without studying**. 의문은 어떻게 그가 공부를 하지 않고 그 시험을 통과했는지이다.

2. **의문사가 이끄는 명사절 안에서 의문사가 주어 역할을 하는 경우, 의문사 뒤에 동사를 바로 쓴다.**

   I want to know **who sent** this package. 나는 누가 이 소포를 보냈는지 알고 싶다.
   I'm not sure **which is** the right way. 나는 어느 쪽이 맞는 길인지 확실하지 않다.

연습문제 우리말과 같도록 괄호 안의 말을 활용하여 문장을 완성하시오.

1 나는 그녀에게 내일 우리가 언제 만날 것인지 물어볼 것이다. (meet, will)

= I will ask her _____ tomorrow.

2 누가 나에게 초콜릿을 줬는지는 의문이다. (give)

= _____ me the chocolate is a mystery.

3 다음 주에 그들이 어디에 갈지 나에게 말해줄 수 있니? (will, go)

= Can you tell me _____ next week?

4 아무도 그가 어제 왜 화가 났는지 알지 못했다. (be)

= Nobody found out _____ angry yesterday.

5 그들은 누가 반장이 될지 확신하지 못했다. (be, would)

= They weren't sure _____ class president.

6 내가 어떻게 그 역에 가는지가 문제이다. (get)

= _____ to the station is the problem.

7 그녀의 걱정은 누가 그를 대신할 것인지이다. (will, replace)

= Her concern is _____ him.

8 그녀는 그녀가 어떻게 그 책꽂이를 고칠 수 있는지 찾아보았다. (fix, could)

= She looked up _____ the bookshelf.

기출로적중 POINT 4-1 부사절을 이끄는 접속사: 시간

정답 p.41

1. 다음 접속사는 시간을 나타내는 부사절을 이끈다.

when	~할 때	I was short **when** I was young. 나는 어렸을 때 키가 작았다.
before	~하기 전에	We used to hang out **before** we graduated. 우리는 졸업하기 전에 함께 어울리곤 했다.
after	~한 후에	He called me **after** he returned from his trip. 그는 그의 여행에서 돌아온 후에 나에게 전화했다.
as	~할 때, ~하면서	**As** I heard this story, I thought about my parents. 나는 이 이야기를 들었을 때, 나의 부모님에 대해 생각했다.
while	~하는 동안	Carl played a game **while** he was waiting for Sandra. Carl은 Sandra를 기다리는 동안 게임을 했다.
until/till	~할 때까지	**Until** my dad came, I had to stay there. 나의 아빠가 올 때까지, 나는 그곳에 머물러야 했다.
as soon as	~하자마자	Amy went to the library **as soon as** she arrived at school. Amy는 학교에 도착하자마자 도서관에 갔다.
since	~한 이래로	You **have changed** since we met. 너는 우리가 만난 이래로 변했다. └→ 주절에는 주로 완료시제가 쓰이고, since가 이끄는 부사절에는 　　주로 과거시제가 쓰인다.

2. 시간을 나타내는 부사절에서는 미래를 표현할 때 미래시제가 아닌 현재시제를 쓴다.

She will go to bed **after** she (~~will finish~~, **finishes**) studying.
그녀는 공부를 끝낸 후에 자러 갈 것이다.

They will buy train tickets **before** they (~~will pack~~, **pack**) their clothes.
그들은 그들의 옷을 싸기 전에 기차표를 구매할 것이다.

연습문제 A | 괄호 안에서 가장 알맞은 것을 고르시오.

1 I usually draw pictures (when / before) I have free time.

2 Minho took a nap (after / while) he set the alarm.

3 I have known her (after / since) I was ten years old.

4 He rushed home (as soon as / until) he heard the news.

5 Helen was playing with her cat (until / since) I knocked on the door.

6 My younger sister kept talking about her day (as / as soon as) we were eating dinner.

7 Cows have been important to humans (till / since) farming began.

8 Do you want to have some coffee (while / after) we're waiting for the others?

9 Make sure you write your name at the top (since / before) you turn in your assignment.

10 We will have a welcome party (after / until) she comes back.

11 Only wealthy Koreans could write and read (while / before) Hangul was invented.

12 Can you hand in the research paper (when / until) the experiment is over?

13 They will remain here (till / since) their number is called.

14 Try to fix it yourself (before / as soon as) asking for help.

15 Please give me a call (since / as soon as) you arrive.

연습문제 **B** | 밑줄 친 부분이 어법상 맞으면 O를 쓰고, 틀리면 바르게 고쳐 쓰시오.

1 Please hold your dog while I <u>will examine</u> it. → _____

2 He <u>turned</u> off the TV as soon as his favorite show was over. → _____

3 I want to see a lot of things when I <u>travel</u> in Europe. → _____

4 Nobody can enter the cafeteria until the repairman <u>will fix</u> the door. → _____

5 I won't know her name until she <u>introduces</u> herself. → _____

6 William <u>is</u> in a bad mood since he saw his report card. → _____

7 He will call his mother after he <u>will arrive</u> in Hawaii. → _____

8 Jennifer becomes emotional as she <u>reads</u> the letter from her parents. → _____

9 When I <u>will get</u> older, I will be able to go anywhere by myself. → _____

10 They <u>have been</u> at this hotel since I saw them. → _____

11 She walked her dog until she <u>became</u> tired. → _____

12 We will yell "surprise" as soon as the guest <u>entered</u> the room. → _____

기출 적중문제

빈칸에 알맞은 접속사를 <보기>에서 골라 쓰시오.

| <보기>   while   since   until |

(1) _____ he was five, he has lived in Singapore.

(2) _____ I was getting out of the car, I bumped my head.

(3) _____ it becomes sunny again, the game must be put off.

POINT 4-2 부사절을 이끄는 접속사: 이유

정답 p.42

다음 접속사는 이유를 나타내는 부사절을 이끈다.

because	~이기 때문에	We will go on a picnic today **because** the weather is nice. 날씨가 좋기 때문에 우리는 오늘 소풍을 갈 것이다.
since		She bought a gift **since** it was her mom's birthday. 그녀의 엄마의 생신이었기 때문에 그녀는 선물을 샀다.
as		**As** the light went out, we couldn't do anything. 불이 나갔기 때문에, 우리는 아무것도 할 수 없었다.
now that		People are leaving **now that** the concert is over. 콘서트가 끝났기 때문에 사람들은 떠나고 있다.

(Tip) 접속사 because 뒤에는 절이 오고, 전치사 because of 뒤에는 명사(구)가 온다.

접속사 I skipped the soccer practice **because I had a stomachache.**
나는 복통이 있었기 때문에 축구 연습을 건너뛰었다.

전치사 I skipped the soccer practice **because of a stomachache.**
나는 복통 때문에 축구 연습을 건너뛰었다.

연습문제 괄호 안에서 가장 알맞은 것을 고르시오.

1 We ordered a large pizza (because / till) we were all hungry.

2 He plays the violin at school (before / now that) he has learned how.

3 My dad cooked dinner (now that / while) I watched the TV.

4 I like that movie (as / when) its special effects are amazing.

5 They lined up early (since / before) they were excited for the parade.

6 The dog wagged his tail (because / because of) he was happy.

7 We weren't sure (because / when) the fire drill would occur.

8 Everyone is wearing coats (now that / until) the weather is cold.

9 He couldn't go surfing (because / because of) his injury.

10 The athlete played hard (because / until) she had a desire to win.

11 People must stay away from the mountain (since / because of) there was a volcanic eruption.

12 You should visit the hospital (since / after) you're sick.

13 He wants to study photography (till / now that) he has a camera.

14 They showed up late (when / as) they had gotten lost.

부사절을 이끄는 접속사: 조건

1. **다음 접속사는 조건을 나타내는 부사절을 이끈다.**

if	만약 ~한다면	**If** you visit Beijing, you can see the Great Wall. 만약 네가 베이징을 방문한다면, 너는 만리장성을 볼 수 있다. (Tip) if는 '~인지'라는 의미의 명사절 접속사로도 쓰인다. I want to know **if** I can go to the festival. 나는 내가 그 축제에 갈 수 있는지 알고 싶다.
unless (= if ~ not)	만약 ~하지 않으면	**Unless** you wear a swimsuit, you can't enter the pool. (= **If** you do **not** wear a swimsuit, you can't enter the pool.) 만약 네가 수영복을 입지 않으면, 너는 그 수영장에 들어갈 수 없다.
once	일단 ~하면	You'll enjoy the game **once** you understand all the rules. 일단 네가 모든 규칙들을 이해하면 너는 그 게임을 즐길 것이다.

2. **조건을 나타내는 부사절에서는 미래를 표현할 때 미래시제가 아닌 현재시제를 쓴다.**

   If he (~~will come~~, **comes**), I will notify you. 만약 그가 온다면, 내가 너에게 알려줄 것이다.
   Unless he (~~will catch~~, **catches**) the bus, he will not arrive on time.
   만약 그가 그 버스를 타지 않으면, 그는 제시간에 도착하지 않을 것이다.

3. **조건을 나타내는 부사절은 명령문으로 바꿔 쓸 수 있다.**

   ❶ 조건을 나타내는 부사절이 긍정문인 경우 「명령문, and ~」 형태로 바꿔 쓸 수 있다.

   If you **take a deep breath**, you'll feel better.
   만약 네가 심호흡을 한다면, 너는 기분이 좋아질 것이다.

   = **Take a deep breath**, **and** you'll feel better.
   심호흡을 해라, 그러면 너는 기분이 좋아질 것이다.

   ❷ 조건을 나타내는 부사절이 부정문인 경우 「명령문, or ~」 형태로 바꿔 쓸 수 있다.

   If you **are not careful**, you'll get hurt. 만약 네가 조심하지 않으면, 너는 다칠 것이다.

   = **Be careful**, **or** you'll get hurt. 조심해라, 그렇지 않으면 너는 다칠 것이다.

   (Tip) unless가 이끄는 부사절은 「명령문, or ~」 형태로 바꿔 쓸 수 있다.

   Unless you **keep quiet**, you'll never catch any fish.
   만약 네가 조용히 하지 않으면, 너는 절대 아무 물고기도 잡지 못할 것이다.

   = **Keep quiet**, **or** you'll never catch any fish.
   조용히 해라, 그렇지 않으면 너는 절대 아무 물고기도 잡지 못할 것이다.

연습문제 A 괄호 안에서 가장 알맞은 것을 고르시오.

1 You will know why I like this dish (unless / once) you (will taste / taste) it.

2 You can't learn a new language (if / unless) you invest time.

3 I'd like to look around the mall (if / unless) we have enough time.

4 (Once / Unless) the new exhibition (opens / will open), the museum will be crowded.

5 The police will come (unless / if) the security alarm goes off.

6 (Unless / Once) we leave the theme park, we can't go back in.

7 (Unless / If) humans (stop / will stop) throwing plastic in the ocean, whales will suffer.

연습문제 B 다음 두 문장의 의미가 같도록 빈칸에 알맞은 말을 쓰시오.

1 Unless you write it down, you will forget what the teacher said.
= Write it down, _____ you will forget what the teacher said.

2 If you don't pay close attention, you won't notice the differences between the twins.
= Pay close attention, _____ you won't notice the differences between the twins.

3 If you tell them, they will recognize the situation.
= Tell them, _____ they will recognize the situation.

4 Fix the machine first, or it will not start.
= _____ you fix the machine first, it will not start.

5 Get used to the noise, and it won't bother you anymore.
= _____ you get used to the noise, it won't bother you anymore.

6 Take good care of the piano, or it will get out of tune.
= _____ you take good care of the piano, it will get out of tune.

7 If you don't bring your ticket, you will not be allowed through the entrance.
= Bring your ticket, _____ you will not be allowed through the entrance.

기출 적중문제

다음 중 밑줄 친 if의 쓰임이 나머지 넷과 다른 것은?

① Dogs will run toward you if you whistle.
② If you know the answer, raise your hand.
③ He will understand if you explain it to him.
④ Laura wasn't sure if her little brother was still sick.
⑤ They can give you assistance if you ask them.

if가 명사절을 이끌 때는 '~인지'라는 의미를 나타내고, 부사절을 이끌 때는 '만약 ~한 다면'라는 의미를 나타내요.

부사절을 이끄는 접속사: 양보

정답 p.42

다음 접속사는 양보를 나타내는 부사절을 이끈다.

though	비록 ~이지만	The movie is great, **though** it is too long. 그 영화는 비록 너무 길지만 훌륭하다.
although		**Although** he apologized, she is still angry. 비록 그가 사과했지만 그녀는 여전히 화가 나있다.
even though		He did the laundry **even though** it was raining. 비록 비가 내리고 있었지만 그는 빨래를 했다.
even if	비록 ~일지라도	**Even if** he wins the match, he will not stop practicing. 비록 그가 그 경기를 이길지라도 그는 연습을 멈추지 않을 것이다.
while	~인 반면에	Jack is positive, **while** Tina is negative. Jack은 긍정적인 반면에 Tina는 부정적이다.
whereas		I prefer black, **whereas** my younger sister likes white better. 나의 여동생은 흰색을 더 좋아하는 반면에 나는 검은색을 선호한다.

(Tip) despite와 in spite of도 '~에도 불구하고'라는 양보의 의미이지만, 전치사이므로 뒤에 절이 아닌 명사(구)를 쓴다.

Despite the heavy traffic, I could arrive at school on time.
교통체증에도 불구하고, 나는 제시간에 학교에 도착할 수 있었다.

(= **Although** the traffic was heavy, I could arrive at school on time.)
비록 교통이 혼잡했지만, 나는 제시간에 학교에 도착할 수 있었다.

연습문제 A   밑줄 친 부분이 어법상 맞으면 O를 쓰고, 틀리면 바르게 고쳐 쓰시오.

1   The sports car is popular <u>even if</u> it is very expensive.   → _____

2   My dog likes cats <u>whereas</u> Jisu's dog doesn't like them.   → _____

3   <u>Despite</u> the cold weather, they went camping.   → _____

4   <u>In spite of</u> many tries, he couldn't score a goal.   → _____

5   She won the race <u>although</u> the bad start.   → _____

6   Jungha is my best friend <u>despite</u> I don't see her very often.   → _____

7   Some animals eat meat <u>even though</u> others eat plants.   → _____

8   <u>Even if</u> you tell them to leave now, they will stay for another hour.   → _____

9   He enjoys listening to guitar <u>whereas</u> he doesn't play one himself.   → _____

10 We'll still be proud of ourselves <u>even if</u> we lose the game.　　　　→ _____

11 The red bird laid five eggs <u>while</u> the blue one laid seven.　·　→ _____

12 <u>Despite</u> Carol is strong, she couldn't open the jar.　　　　→ _____

연습문제 B | 괄호 안의 말을 활용하여 다음 두 문장을 한 문장으로 바꿔 쓰시오.

1 I will buy a smartphone. My older brother will buy a laptop. (while)
→ I will buy a smartphone _____.

2 He wasn't tired at all. He had stayed up all night. (although)
→ He wasn't tired at all _____.

3 I will climb the mountain. It snows tomorrow. (even if)
→ I will climb the mountain _____.

4 Minsoo was satisfied. He ate only one piece of pizza. (even though)
→ Minsoo was satisfied _____.

5 I took a pill. I still have a headache. (although)
→ _____, I still have a headache.

6 The side door is for staff. The front door is for customers. (whereas)
→ The side door is for staff _____.

7 I will not go to the birthday party. I receive an invitation. (even if)
→ I will not go to the birthday party _____.

8 I like classic novels. My younger sister prefers best-selling novels. (while)
→ I like classic novels _____.

9 Karen was quite famous. Nobody recognized her. (though)
→ _____, nobody recognized her.

기출 적중문제

우리말과 같도록 괄호 안의 말을 알맞게 배열하시오.

> 비록 곰은 귀여워 보이지만 아주 위험한 동물이다. (look, they, even though, cute)

= Bears are very dangerous animals _____

_____.

부사절을 이끄는 접속사: so that ~

정답 p.42

1. 「so that ~」은 '~하기 위해, ~할 수 있도록'의 의미로, 목적을 나타내는 부사절을 이끈다.

   I organize my desk **so that** I can study. 나는 공부하기 위해 나의 책상을 정리한다.

   He turned off his cell phone **so that** he could sleep. 그는 잠들 수 있도록 그의 휴대폰을 껐다.

2. 「so that ~」은 「in order[so as] + to부정사」로 바꿔 쓸 수 있다.

   I woke up early **so that** I could go jogging. 나는 조깅하러 가기 위해 일찍 일어났다.
   = I woke up early **in order[so as] to** go jogging.

연습문제 <보기>와 같이 다음 문장을 괄호 안의 말을 활용하여 바꿔 쓰시오.

> <보기> I opened the window to feel the breeze. (so that)
>   → I opened the window *so that I could feel the breeze* .

1 I stopped the car for everyone to take photos. (so that)
   → I stopped the car _____.

2 I'll bring my comic book tomorrow in order to lend it to you. (so that)
   → I'll bring my comic book tomorrow _____.

3 Put the food on the table for people to share. (so that)
   → Put the food on the table _____.

4 Please turn off the TV for me to have a conversation with you. (so that)
   → Please turn off the TV _____.

5 He bought a hammer and some nails so that he could fix the chair. (in order to)
   → He bought a hammer and some nails _____.

6 I closed the windows to prevent mosquitoes from coming inside. (so that)
   → I closed the windows _____.

7 Belle arranged her files so that she could easily find what she needed. (so as to)
   → Belle arranged her files _____.

8 The store is offering a discount on the diamond ring so as to attract more customers. (so that)
   → The store is offering a discount on the diamond ring _____.

기출로적중 POINT 4-6

부사절을 이끄는 접속사: so ~ that …

정답 p.42

1. 「so + 형용사/부사 + that …」은 '너무 ~해서/~하게 …한'의 의미이며, 결과를 나타내는 부사절을 이끈다.

   I was **so happy that** I yelled. 나는 너무 기뻐서 소리를 질렀다.

   He solved the problem **so easily that** we were surprised.
   그가 그 문제를 너무 쉽게 풀어서 우리는 놀랐다.

2. 「so + 형용사/부사 + that + 주어 + can't」는 「too ~ to」로 바꿔 쓸 수 있다.

   She is **so exhausted that** she can't exercise. 그녀는 너무 지쳐서 운동을 할 수 없다.

   (= She is **too** exhausted **to** exercise.)

연습문제 <보기>와 같이 다음 문장을 괄호 안의 말을 활용하여 바꿔 쓰시오.

> **<보기>** The weather is cold. My car won't start. (so, that)
> → The weather is _so cold that my car won't start_ .
>
> He is young. He can't understand this article. (too, to)
> → He is _too young to understand this article_ .

1 She was curious. She read her daughter's diary. (so, that)
   → She was _____ .

2 The mouse was too fast. The cat couldn't catch it. (so, that)
   → The mouse was _____ .

3 His shoe collection is large. It can't fit in his closet. (too, to)
   → His shoe collection is _____ .

4 This elevator moves slowly. I take the stairs. (so, that)
   → This elevator moves _____ .

5 The museum is huge. I can't find the exhibit. (too, to)
   → The museum is _____ .

6 Jenny ate the ice cream quickly. She got a headache. (so, that)
   → Jenny ate the ice cream _____ .

7 The movie was boring. Half of the audience left before it ended. (so, that)
   → The movie was _____ .

다양한 의미의 부사절을 이끄는 접속사

정답 p.42

1. as가 이끄는 부사절은 다양한 의미를 나타낸다.

~할 때, ~하면서	**As** I was having dinner, he called me. 내가 저녁을 먹고 있을 때, 그가 나에게 전화했다.
~이기 때문에	He volunteered at the shelter **as** he loved animals. 그는 동물을 사랑했기 때문에 보호소에서 자원 봉사했다.
~할수록	**As** the price falls, more people want it. 가격이 내려갈수록, 더 많은 사람들이 그것을 원한다.
~처럼, ~듯이	Knowledge is power, **as** my dad said. 나의 아빠가 말했던 것처럼, 지식은 힘이다.

> **Tip** as는 '~로서, ~처럼'이라는 의미의 전치사로도 쓰이며, 이때 뒤에 명사(구)가 온다.
> **As a reporter**, she always watches news. 기자로서, 그녀는 항상 뉴스를 본다.
> Mr. Peterson dressed **as Santa Claus**. Peterson씨는 산타클로스처럼 옷을 입었다.

2. since가 이끄는 부사절은 시간이나 이유를 나타낸다.

~한 이래로	**Since** my family moved here, we have met a lot of foreigners. 우리 가족이 이곳으로 이사 온 이래로 우리는 많은 외국인들을 만났다.
~ 때문에	I can't buy the book **since** I have no money. 나는 돈이 없기 때문에 그 책을 살 수 없다.

> **Tip** since는 '~이래로'라는 의미의 전치사로도 쓰이며, 이때 뒤에 명사(구)가 온다.
> I haven't eaten cake **since my last birthday**. 나는 나의 지난 번 생일 이래로 케이크를 먹은 적이 없다.

3. while이 이끄는 부사절은 시간이나 양보를 나타낸다.

~동안	He listened to music **while** he did his homework. 그는 그의 숙제를 하는 동안 음악을 들었다.
~인 반면에	My older sister enjoys going out **while** I enjoy staying home. 나는 집에 있는 것을 즐기는 반면에 나의 언니는 밖에 나가는 것을 즐긴다.

연습문제 A 다음 밑줄 친 as의 의미를 <보기>에서 골라 그 기호를 쓰시오.

<보기> ⓐ ~할 때 ⓑ ~이기 때문에 ⓒ ~듯이 ⓓ ~할수록 ⓔ ~로서

1 As I was washing the dishes, I broke my mom's favorite plate. [   ]

2 As the speech went on, I got more and more bored. [   ]

3 As you already know, Alice cannot attend the meeting.   [   ]

4 I can't park my car here <u>as</u> no spaces are available.   [   ]

5 <u>As</u> a chef, he knew all about food.   [   ]

6 <u>As</u> I had a tough day, I should get a rest now.   [   ]

7 The band's concert started <u>as</u> I got there.   [   ]

8 <u>As</u> you may recall, the Korean War broke out in 1950.   [   ]

9 <u>As</u> time goes by, Peter gets thinner and thinner.   [   ]

10 She went to camp <u>as</u> a counselor.   [   ]

연습문제 B 우리말과 같도록 since 또는 while과 괄호 안의 말을 활용하여 문장을 완성하시오.

1 나는 서울로 이사한 이래로 Thomas를 본 적이 없다. (move)

= I haven't seen Thomas _____ to Seoul.

2 그곳에 가기 위해 비행기로 30분이 걸리는 반면에 기차로는 세 시간이 걸린다. (take)

= It takes three hours to get there by train _____ 30 minutes
by airplane.

3 그녀는 우리가 후식을 먹고 있는 동안 도착했다. (be having)

= She arrived _____ dessert.

4 그는 초여름 이래로 다이어트를 시작했다. (the beginning of summer)

= He has been on a diet _____.

5 내가 중학교를 졸업한 이래로 5년이 지났다. (graduate)

= Five years have passed _____ from middle school.

6 나는 샤워를 하는 동안 미래를 상상했다. (be taking)

= I imagined the future _____ a shower.

7 Tommy는 키가 가장 큰 학생이었기 때문에 농구를 잘했다. (be)

= _____ the tallest student, he was good at basketball.

기출 적중문제

다음 중 밑줄 친 while의 의미가 넷과 다른 것은?

① We ate chicken <u>while</u> Sally was sleeping.

② Can you please be quiet <u>while</u> I study?

③ <u>While</u> I was walking along the river, I met Hyunsu.

④ My mom likes watching dramas <u>while</u> my dad likes watching documentaries.

⑤ He had a flat tire <u>while</u> he was driving on the highway.

접속부사는 앞 문장과 뒤 문장의 의미를 자연스럽게 이어주는 역할을 하는 부사이다.

예시	for example 예를 들어 for instance 예를 들어
반대	however 그러나 on the other hand 반면에 in contrast 그에 반해서 nevertheless 그럼에도 불구하고
강조	in fact 사실 indeed 정말
전환	by the way 그런데 otherwise 그렇지 않으면 instead 대신 anyway 어쨌든
추가 설명	moreover 게다가 besides 게다가 furthermore 뿐만 아니라 in addition 게다가
결론	therefore 그러므로 thus 그러므로 as a result 결과적으로

Minju wanted to be a lawyer. **However**, she is a singer now.
민주는 변호사가 되고 싶었다. 그러나, 그녀는 현재 가수이다.
He was sick yesterday. **Therefore**, he did not come to school.
그는 어제 아팠다. 그러므로, 그는 학교에 오지 않았다.

연습문제 A   괄호 안에서 가장 알맞은 접속부사를 고르시오.

1   I started a diet last week. (For instance / However), I have gained more weight.

2   I forgot to do the homework. (Thus / Otherwise), my teacher got disappointed.

3   He likes to follow plans. (In contrast / Furthermore), his older brother likes to be spontaneous.

4   Janet is the best player on the team. (Therefore / Nevertheless), we chose her as the team captain.

5   Jungmo volunteered at the charity. (In contrast / Moreover), he donated money to it.

6   I washed the sheets two days ago. (In addition / As a result), I vacuumed the carpet.

7   You should take care of your younger brother. (Otherwise / In fact), he will mess up your room.

8   Crows usually symbolize bad luck. (On the other hand / As a result), people in some cultures believe crows represent good luck.

9   The theater has the largest screen in the city. (Otherwise / Besides), its seats are very comfortable.

10   They didn't want to work on their project. (Furthermore / Anyway), they finished it.

11   I have a lot to do tonight. (For example / Instead), I have to iron my clothes and throw out the trash.

연습문제 B 우리말과 같도록 빈칸에 알맞은 접속부사를 쓰시오.

1 경제가 정말 좋지 않다. 결과적으로, 많은 사람들이 그들의 직업을 잃었다.

= The economy is really bad. _____, many people have lost their jobs.

2 그녀는 조용하고 수줍음을 타는 사람이다. 그에 반해서, 그녀의 여동생은 말을 많이 하고 사교적이다.

= She is a quiet and shy person. _____, her little sister talks a lot and is sociable.

3 그녀는 어제 수학을 공부했다고 말했다. 사실, 그녀는 하지 않았다.

= She said she studied math yesterday. _____, she didn't.

4 나는 그 셔츠가 품절이었기 때문에 사지 못했다. 대신, 나는 티셔츠를 샀다.

= I couldn't buy the shirt because it was sold out. _____, I bought a T-shirt.

5 나의 컴퓨터가 고장 났다. 그러므로, 나는 내일 서비스 센터에 전화할 것이다.

= My computer broke down. _____, I'll call the service center tomorrow.

6 바깥의 온도는 자전거를 타기에 완벽하다. 그러나, 나는 아직 나의 자전거를 수리하지 못했다.

= The temperature outside is perfect for a bike ride. _____, I haven't repaired my bicycle yet.

7 기술이 우리의 삶을 더 편하게 만들었다. 예를 들어, 사람들은 그들의 스마트폰을 사용해 택시를 예약할 수 있다.

= Technology has made our lives more convenient. _____, people can book taxis using their smartphones.

8 너의 개에게 씹을 무언가를 남겨 주어라. 그렇지 않으면, 그는 가구를 손상시킬 것이다.

= Leave your dog something to chew on. _____, he'll destroy the furniture.

기출 적중문제 🎯

다음 글의 빈칸에 들어갈 말이 순서대로 짝지어진 것은?

People love traveling overseas. _____, not many people know which country attracts the most tourists. The answer is France! According to the UN, 89.4 million tourists visited France in 2018. _____, the number of tourists is increasing every year.

① Therefore – For example
② Therefore – Moreover
③ However – For example
④ However – Moreover
⑤ Moreover – For example

서술형 대비 문제

A 다음 밑줄 친 부분이 어법상 맞으면 O를 쓰고, 틀리면 바르게 고쳐 쓰시오.

1 Go straight for two blocks, <u>and</u> you'll see the city hall. → _____

2 Not only shirts but also a blanket <u>are</u> being dried outside. → _____

3 Either Lena or her friends <u>are</u> responsible for this accident. → _____

4 I asked him to wash the dishes and <u>cleaning</u> the carpet. → _____

5 Food is not allowed on the subway, <u>so</u> put away that bag of snacks. → _____

6 You can neither review <u>and</u> change your test after submitting it. → _____

B 괄호 안의 접속사를 이용하여 두 문장을 한 문장으로 연결하시오.

1 It is interesting. + Humans aren't the only animals that dream. (that)
→ It _____.

2 You should remind yourself. + Planning your schedule is important. (that)
→ You _____.

3 Children are told. + They should eat healthy food. (that)
→ Children _____.

4 I don't know. + Should I laugh or cry? (whether)
→ I _____.

5 I wonder. + Is there life on Mars? (if)
→ I _____.

6 The researcher wonders. + Is the product safe for babies? (if)
→ The researcher _____.

7 Have you decided? + Will you order some more dessert? (whether)
→ Have _____?

8 Can you guess? + What does this picture mean? (what)
→ Can _____?

9 I have no idea. + When will this broken door be fixed? (when)
→ I _____.

C 우리말과 같도록 괄호 안의 말을 활용하여 문장을 완성하시오.

1 파도가 그 보트를 쳤을 때 그 보트는 물로 가득 찼다. (hit, the wave, when, the boat)
= _____, the boat filled with water.

2 나는 성공할 때까지 계속 노력할 것이다. (finally, succeed, until)
= _____, I will keep trying.

3 우리가 축구 연습을 하는 동안 감독은 우리에게 조언을 해주었다. (practice, soccer, while)
= _____, the coach gave us advice.

4 만약 네가 사람들을 돕고 싶다면, 너는 의사가 되는 것이 낫다. (want, if, to help people)
= _____, you had better become a doctor.

5 비록 나는 한복을 소유하고 있지만 보통 그것을 입지 않는다. (own, a hanbok, though)
= _____, I don't usually wear it.

6 Betty가 타자를 빠르게 칠 수 있기 때문에, 그녀에게 그 키보드를 사용하게 해라. (can type, fast, as)
= _____, let her use the keyboard.

7 그는 아무도 그것을 찾을 수 없도록 보물을 땅 속에 묻었다. (it, so, no one, that, could find)
= He buried the treasure _____.

8 Vincent는 키가 너무 커서 천장에 손을 댈 수 있다. (so, that, touch the ceiling, can, he, tall)
= Vincent is _____.

9 비록 우리가 비행기를 탈지라도 그 여행은 네 시간이 걸릴 것이다. (a plane, catch, even if)
= _____, the trip will take four hours.

D 다음 빈칸에 알맞은 말을 <보기>에서 한 번씩만 골라 쓰시오.

<보기> However   Therefore   For example   In addition

In ancient times, people in Egypt depended on a big river called the Nile. The Nile flooded at the same time every year. _____, Egyptians could prepare for each flood by building dams and canals. By trapping the water, they could keep their farmland wet. Then, at the right time, they could plant various crops. _____, they grew wheat and barley. _____, the Nile provided drinking water for the cities. _____, if the Nile had too much or too little water, it became a big problem for the Egyptians.

중간 · 기말고사 실전 문제

1 우리말과 같도록 괄호 안의 말을 활용하여 문장을 완성하시오.

> 나는 사탕 한 봉지를 샀고, 그녀는 쿠키 두 상자를 샀다. (box, cookies)

= I bought a bag of candy, _____

_____.

2 다음 빈칸에 공통으로 들어갈 알맞은 것은?

> · _____ they survived the accident is quite surprising.
> · The problem is _____ no one has enough time to prepare Jimmy's party.

① because　② if　③ whether
④ but　⑤ that

3 다음 중 어느 빈칸에도 들어갈 수 <u>없는</u> 것은?

> · Admiral Yi Sun-shin won many battles _____ Geobukseons.
> · You shouldn't send text messages _____ you are talking to someone.
> · Jenny stopped eating clams _____ she was allergic to shellfish.
> · Due to traffic delays, I couldn't make it to class _____ 9 A.M.

① since　② while　③ because of
④ until　⑤ unless

4 다음 우리말을 가장 알맞게 영작한 것은?

> 새로운 형제자매가 태어날 때 몇몇 아이들은 질투를 느낄 것이다.

① Some children will feel jealous as a new sibling will be born.
② Some children will feel jealous when a new sibling is born.
③ Some children will feel jealous because a new sibling is born.
④ Some children will feel jealous before a new sibling will be born.
⑤ Some children will feel jealous although a new sibling is born.

5 다음 문장에 대한 설명이 바른 것끼리 묶인 것은?

> (A) Don't move around in the bus while it is moving. : while이 '~인 반면에'라는 의미로 사용되었다.
> (B) I'm going to wait here until the mall opens. : 시간을 나타내는 부사절에서 현재시제 opens를 사용하여 미래를 나타냈다.
> (C) She has been playing soccer since she was seven years old. : since가 '~이기 때문에'라는 의미로 사용되었다.

① (A)　② (B)　③ (C)
④ (A), (B)　⑤ (B), (C)

[6-7] 다음 빈칸에 공통으로 들어갈 알맞은 것을 고르시오.

6

· I checked the map _____ couldn't find a way out.
· This disease is serious, _____ we have a cure.

① and ② or ③ for
④ but ⑤ so

7

· Turn your assignment in by tomorrow, _____ you'll be in trouble.
· Jason either goes to a gym _____ jogs along the Hangang on weekends.

① but ② or ③ so
④ and ⑤ that

8 다음 빈칸에 들어갈 말이 나머지 넷과 <u>다른</u> 것은?

① He held the door for me _____ my hands were full.
② Jessie couldn't finish the book _____ the difficult words.
③ I didn't recognize her _____ she was wearing a mask.
④ People often get confused _____ my older brother and I look so similar.
⑤ The festival was stopped _____ there was a shortage of funding.

9 <보기>와 같이 두 문장의 의미가 같도록 문장을 완성하시오.

<보기>
Because the snail was slow, I thought it wasn't moving.
= *The snail was so slow that I thought it wasn't moving.*

(1) Because the shopping mall is popular, it is always crowded.
= _____
_____

(2) Because Paul was injured badly, he had to cancel all his appointments.
= _____
_____

10 다음 중 어법상 <u>어색한</u> 것은?

① I cooked the rice and fried the eggs.
② Pedro is Spanish, but he lives in Korea.
③ The test is over, so you can leave now.
④ I arrived at the hotel and taking a short nap.
⑤ I did most of my homework but forgot about math.

11 두 문장의 의미가 같도록 문장을 완성할 때, 빈칸에 알맞은 말을 쓰시오. (단, as를 반드시 활용하시오.)

Not only courage but also confidence was shown by Jihoon.
= _____ _____ _____
_____ _____ was shown by Jihoon.

12 다음 문장을 주어진 <조건>에 맞게 바꿔 쓰시오.

If you try to keep your promises, people will start to trust you.

<조건>
1. 명령문으로 쓰시오.
2. 12단어로 쓰시오.

→ _____

_____

13 다음 글의 빈칸에 들어갈 말이 순서대로 짝지어진 것은?

It is easy to tell the difference between butterflies and moths. Butterflies fly around in the daytime. _____, moths fly around at night. _____, butterfly wings are usually more colorful than moth wings.

* moth 나방

① In contrast – Otherwise
② In contrast – Moreover
③ However – For example
④ Therefore – Moreover
⑤ Therefore – Otherwise

14 다음 빈칸에 들어갈 수 있는 것을 <u>모두</u> 고르시오.

_____ the other team was more experienced, his team won the game.

① Although   ② Despite
③ As soon as   ④ Though
⑤ If

15 다음 중 밑줄 친 <u>as</u>의 쓰임이 나머지 넷과 <u>다른</u> 것은?

① The garage is used <u>as</u> a practice space by the band.
② I'm tired <u>as</u> I've been looking after my cousins all day.
③ Everyone should stand <u>as</u> the president will arrive soon.
④ I need to charge my phone <u>as</u> its battery is getting low.
⑤ The child can't ride a bike <u>as</u> she is too young.

[16-17] 괄호 안의 말을 알맞게 배열하여 문장을 완성하시오.

16

Peter looked for a four-leaf clover

_____.

(he, good luck, wanted, because)

17

_____,

you have to end your speech in ten minutes. (time, limited, is, since)

18 다음 중 어법상 <u>어색한</u> 것은?

① Alex is too tired to deal with the customers.
② He threw the ball so softly that every batter could hit it.
③ Kate is so smart that she got a perfect score on a difficult exam.
④ I am too nervous to sing in front of others.
⑤ Jacob is so busy person that he can't go on vacation this summer.

19 우리말과 같도록 빈칸에 알맞은 말을 쓰시오.

> 그 기계는 공간 낭비였을 뿐 아니라 전력 낭비이기도 했다.

= The machine was _____ _____ a waste of space _____ _____ a waste of electricity.

20 다음 중 밑줄 친 since의 의미가 나머지 넷과 다른 것은?

① The singer sang another song since the audience requested it.
② Eric stayed at home since he wanted to recover fast.
③ This restaurant must be good since it is full of customers.
④ Nobody has entered the cave since it was first discovered.
⑤ Children ask a lot of questions since they are curious.

21 다음 문장을 주어진 <조건>에 맞게 바꿔 쓰시오.

> If you don't apologize to your parents, you'll feel guilty.

> <조건> unless를 사용하시오.

→ You'll _____
_____ .

22 우리말과 같도록 괄호 안의 말을 활용하여 문장을 완성하시오.

> Lisa는 그녀의 단체가 대회에서 졌다는 사실을 인정했다. (the fact, her group, lose, the competition)

= Lisa accepted _____
_____ .

23 다음 글의 밑줄 친 if와 바꿔 쓸 수 있는 것은?

> Terry is known for having an excellent poker face. That means that it's hard to tell if he is telling a lie. It's best not to believe what he says.

① when   ② unless   ③ whether
④ that   ⑤ what

24 다음 중 문맥상 어색한 것은?

① It was already past the deadline when Leo finished his assignment.
② The umbrella will break if the wind blows too strongly.
③ Though he is kind and generous, he is popular among his friends.
④ The deer ran away because it was afraid of people.
⑤ I've wanted to see the exhibition since I heard about it.

25 다음 문장에서 어색한 부분을 바르게 고친 것끼리 묶인 것은?

> (A) Both Emily and I was heading to the theater. (→ am)
> (B) Neither Linda nor her friends likes physical activities. (→ like)
> (C) Either I or my brother have to stay home to take care of our dog. (→ has)
> (D) Wood as well as bricks were used to build that house. (→ was)

① (A), (C) ② (B), (C)
③ (C), (D) ④ (A), (B), (C)
⑤ (B), (C), (D)

26 다음 밑줄 친 as와 의미가 같은 것을 <보기>에서 골라 쓰시오.

<보기> when   before   because   once

(1) A crab bit my toe as I was making a sandcastle on the beach.

→ _____

(2) There are fewer tourists during the winter as sightseeing in the cold weather is difficult.

→ _____

27 다음 중 밑줄 친 that을 생략할 수 있는 것을 모두 고르시오.

① That Joe broke the window is a secret between you and me.
② She complained that the rules of the board game were unfair.
③ The truth is that too many forests have already been damaged.
④ It is obvious that Cindy is the leader of our group.
⑤ I sincerely hope that we can meet again someday.

[28-29] 우리말과 같도록 주어진 말을 알맞게 배열하시오.

28

> 너는 어제 무엇이 너의 부모님을 화나게 했는지 이해해야 한다. (what, yesterday, upset, your, parents, made)

= You should understand _____

_____ .

29

> 나는 이 가게가 언제 여는지 모른다. (this store, opens, when)

= I don't know _____ .

30 다음 글의 빈칸에 들어갈 알맞은 것을 모두 고르시오.

People should sit up straight _____ bad posture can be harmful. Many people tend to sit on their chairs with their backs bent, and it causes back problems.

① because   ② while   ③ that
④ since   ⑤ even if

31 우리말과 같도록 괄호 안의 말을 이용하여 문장을 완성하시오.

나는 내가 실수하지 않기 위해 그 설명서를 신중히 확인할 것이다. (make a mistake, I)

= I will read the instructions carefully
_____ .

32 다음 중 밑줄 친 부분이 어법상 어색한 것은?

①Before I moved to the United States last year, I couldn't speak English at all. ②Since last year, I have studied English very hard in various ways. ③For instance, I have tried to read as many English books as possible. ④In addition, I have watched a lot of English TV dramas to improve my listening and speaking skills. ⑤Besides, I am good at English now.

33 다음 중 밑줄 친 if의 쓰임이 나머지 넷과 다른 것은?

① He has to take another pill if his headache comes back.
② Remember to bring your sunglasses if you visit the Grand Canyon.
③ If anyone needs help, don't hesitate to call me.
④ I was wondering if I should arrive early to keep my reservation.
⑤ I'm sure that they will miss the train if they don't leave immediately.

34 다음 빈칸에 공통으로 들어갈 알맞은 말을 쓰시오.

· I read some articles _____ I was waiting for the bus.
· _____ my older sister is excellent at cooking, I am not.

35 다음 글의 빈칸에 들어갈 알맞은 것은?

London is full of interesting tourist attractions. _____, Big Ben, the London Tower, and the London Eye attract thousands of visitors every year.

① For example   ② In addition
③ Also   ④ On the other hand
⑤ However

36 다음 문장을 주어진 <조건>에 맞게 바꿔 쓰시오.

Be nice to people, and you will present a good image to them.

<조건>
1. 접속사 if를 사용하시오.
2. 14단어로 쓰시오.

→ _____

_____

37 다음 밑줄 친 that과 역할이 같은 것은?

It is certain that the air quality is getting worse.

① I remembered that I watched the movie before.
② That Einstein was a genius is a common belief.
③ The weather forecaster said that this summer will be hotter than before.
④ A lot of tourists know that many beautiful flowers bloom in Japan.
⑤ The problem is that we are already late for the concert.

38 우리말과 같도록 괄호 안의 단어를 활용하여 문장을 완성하시오.

나는 내가 치마를 사야 할지 또는 드레스를 사야 할지 결정할 수 없다. (should, if, a skirt, buy, a dress)

= I can't decide _____

_____.

39 다음 빈칸에 들어갈 말이 순서대로 짝지어진 것은?

Keep in mind the most important thing in sports is _____ to win _____ to play fair.

① not – but
② neither – and
③ not – so
④ either – but
⑤ either – and

40 다음 중 빈칸에 if가 들어갈 수 <u>없는</u> 것은?

① You should ask _____ choosing a different dressing for the salad costs extra.
② She wondered _____ those sandals were popular.
③ The results depend on _____ or not you try hard.
④ Let's check _____ we can fish in the lake.
⑤ Please explain _____ this method is wrong.

41 다음 우리말과 같도록 알맞은 접속사를 고르시오.

그는 그의 그림을 완성했기 때문에 그것을 벽에 걸 수 있다.
= _____ he has finished his painting, he can hang it on the wall.

① After
② Unless
③ Whether
④ If
⑤ Now that

42 우리말과 같도록 빈칸에 알맞은 접속사를 쓰시오.

> 우리는 신호등이 초록색인 동안 길을 건너야 한다.

= We should cross the street _____ the traffic light is green.

43 우리말과 같도록 다음 문장의 밑줄 친 부분을 괄호 안의 말을 활용하여 영작하시오.

> <u>만약 네가 계속 연습한다면</u>, you'll become a better trumpet player. (keep, practice)

= _____

44 다음 문장에서 어법상 어색한 부분을 찾아 쓰고 바르게 고쳐 쓰시오.

> I respect her opinion despite I don't agree with her.

_____ → _____

45 두 문장의 의미가 같도록 빈칸에 알맞은 말을 쓰시오.

> The country banned the use of plastic straws so that it could protect the environment.
> = The country banned the use of plastic straws _____ protect the environment.

46 괄호 안의 말을 알맞게 배열하여 문장을 완성하시오.

> The lava was _____ _____. (melted, that, it, so, hot, the metal)

47 우리말과 같도록 빈칸에 알맞은 말을 쓰시오.

> Kevin은 달걀 한 통을 떨어뜨렸다. 결과적으로, 그것들 중 몇 개가 깨졌다.

= Kevin dropped a carton of eggs. _____, some of them broke.

48 다음 문장의 밑줄 친 as와 같은 의미로 쓰인 것은?

> She couldn't attend the meeting <u>as</u> she had a high fever.

① Anne works <u>as</u> an editor for the newspaper.
② Sumi doesn't need a tour guide <u>as</u> she knows the area well.
③ Check the recipe regularly <u>as</u> you make the cookies.
④ The *Mona Lisa* was mysterious, <u>as</u> I thought it would be.
⑤ The liquid in the beaker turned green, <u>as</u> the scientist had predicted.

CHAPTER 13
관계사

선행사　　　　　관계절
I met a girl who is from China. 나는 중국에서 온 소녀를 만났다.

위 문장에서 **who**가 이끄는 절인 **who is from China**가 명사 **a girl**을 꾸며서 '중국에서 온 소녀'라는 의미가 됐어요. 이처럼 명사를 꾸미는 절을 관계절이라고 하고, 관계절이 꾸미는 명사를 선행사라고 해요. who처럼 두 절을 연결하는 접속사 역할을 하는 것을 **관계사**라고 하며, 관계사에는 관계대명사와 관계부사가 있어요.

기출로 적중 POINT

1 • 관계대명사의 역할과 종류

2-1 • 주격 관계대명사

2-2 • 목적격 관계대명사

2-3 • 소유격 관계대명사

3 • 관계대명사 that

4 • 관계대명사 what

5 • 전치사 + 관계대명사

6 • 관계부사의 역할과 종류

7 • 관계사의 계속적 용법

8 • 복합관계사

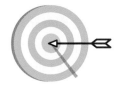

내신 100점 적중!
기출 출제율

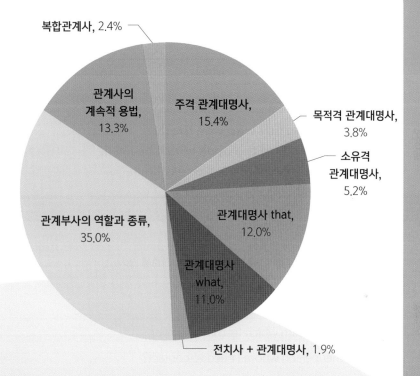

복합관계사, 2.4%

관계사의 계속적 용법, 13.3%

주격 관계대명사, 15.4%

목적격 관계대명사, 3.8%

소유격 관계대명사, 5.2%

관계대명사 that, 12.0%

관계부사의 역할과 종류, 35.0%

관계대명사 what, 11.0%

전치사 + 관계대명사, 1.9%

TOP 1 **관계부사의 역할과 종류 (35%)**
관계부사의 형태와 쓰임을 묻는 문제가 자주 출제된다.

TOP 2 **주격 관계대명사 (15.4%)**
주격 관계대명사의 역할과 선행사에 맞는 올바른 주격 관계대명사를 쓰는 문제가 자주 출제된다.

TOP 3 **관계사의 계속적 용법 (13.3%)**
「콤마(,) + 관계대명사」의 형태와 의미를 묻는 문제가 자주 출제된다.

관계대명사의 역할과 종류

정답 p.45

---

1. 관계대명사는 관계대명사절을 이끄는 접속사 역할과 대명사 역할을 한다.

She is talking to **a man**. **He** is tall. 그녀는 한 남자와 이야기하고 있다. 그는 키가 크다.

→ She is talking to **a man, and he** is tall. 그녀는 한 남자와 이야기하고 있고, 그는 키가 크다.
　　　　　　　　　접속사 + 대명사

→ She is talking to **a man who** is tall. 그녀는 키가 큰 한 남자와 이야기하고 있다.
　　　　　　　　선행사　관계대명사

2. 선행사의 종류와 문장 안에서 선행사의 역할에 따라 어떤 관계대명사를 쓸지 결정된다.

선행사　　　격	주격	목적격	소유격
사람	who	who(m)	whose
사물, 동물	which	which	whose
모두 적용	that	that	–

주격　　I know **the boy who** won the race. 나는 그 경주에서 이긴 소년을 안다.

목적격　He showed me **the book which** he liked. 그는 그가 좋아했던 책을 나에게 보여주었다.

소유격　I have **a friend whose** name is Jimin. 나는 이름이 지민인 친구가 있다.

연습문제 | 밑줄 친 부분의 쓰임을 <보기>에서 골라 그 기호를 쓰시오.

<보기>　ⓐ 주격　ⓑ 목적격　ⓒ 소유격

1 This is the walking path <u>which</u> leads to the river.　　[　　]

2 Is there another person <u>whom</u> I need to contact?　　[　　]

3 There was a man <u>whose</u> name was Siwon in the group.　　[　　]

4 Here are some of the wonderful songs <u>which</u> we wrote.　　[　　]

5 We donated to a charity <u>that</u> protects wild animals in South Africa.　　[　　]

6 I saw a girl <u>whose</u> hair is brown.　　[　　]

7 I learned about the people <u>who</u> changed the world.　　[　　]

8 We visited a house <u>whose</u> roof was covered with bushes.　　[　　]

9 I'm meeting with a friend <u>who</u> I missed so much.　　[　　]

10 Magellan was the explorer <u>that</u> first sailed around the world.　　[　　]

기출로적중 POINT 2-1 주격 관계대명사

정답 p.45

1. **주격 관계대명사는 관계대명사절에서 주어 역할을 하며, 선행사 뒤에서 문장을 연결할 수 있다. 주격 관계대명사는 선행사의 종류에 따라 who, which, that을 쓴다.**

   I know **the girl. She** is wearing a hat. 나는 그 소녀를 안다. 그녀는 모자를 쓰고 있다.
   → I know **the girl who[that]** is wearing a hat. 나는 모자를 쓰고 있는 그 소녀를 안다.
   └→ 주격 관계대명사절의 동사는 선행사에 수일치시킨다.

   The sofa feels soft. **It's** made from wool. 그 소파는 부드러운 느낌이 든다. 그것은 양털로 만들어졌다.
   → **The sofa which[that]** is made from wool feels soft.
   양털로 만들어진 그 소파는 부드러운 느낌이 든다.

2. **「주격 관계대명사 + be동사」는 생략할 수 있다.**

   The boy **(who is)** doing the laundry is Eric. 빨래를 하고 있는 소년은 Eric이다.
   All the customers **(that are)** eating in the restaurant are tourists.
   그 식당에서 식사하고 있는 모든 손님들은 관광객들이다.

연습문제 A 관계대명사를 이용하여 다음 두 문장을 한 문장으로 연결하시오.

1 Put the bottles in the green bin. It is for recycling.
   → Put the bottles in _____.

2 There are a lot of children. They live in Mark's neighborhood.
   → There are _____.

3 I found a picture. It showed my mother as a child.
   → I found _____.

4 This is a new TV model. It has many special features.
   → This is _____.

5 The mailman gave the package to the woman. She answered the door.
   → The mailman gave the package to _____.

연습문제 B 밑줄 친 부분을 생략할 수 있으면 O, 생략할 수 없으면 X를 쓰시오.

1 Meet me at the bakery <u>which is</u> across from the bank. → _____

2 Could you get me the eggs <u>that are</u> in the fridge? → _____

3 There is a local charity <u>which offers</u> free medical care. → _____

4 There was a man <u>who was</u> selling oranges on the street. → _____

1. 목적격 관계대명사는 관계대명사절에서 목적어 역할을 하며, 선행사 뒤에서 문장을 연결할 수 있다. 목적격 관계대명사는 선행사의 종류에 따라 who(m), which, that을 쓴다.

   I know **the man**. We saw **him** at church. 나는 그 남자를 안다. 우리는 그를 교회에서 봤다.

   → I know **the man** **who[whom/that]** we saw at church.
   나는 우리가 교회에서 본 그 남자를 안다.

   The items are expensive. He ordered **them**. 그 물건들은 비싸다. 그는 그것들을 주문했다.

   → **The items** **which[that]** he ordered are expensive. 그가 주문한 그 물건들은 비싸다.

2. 목적격 관계대명사는 생략할 수 있다.

   He is a classmate **(who[whom/that])** I often talk to after school.
   그는 내가 방과 후에 종종 이야기하는 반 친구이다.

   Peter wore the shirt **(which[that])** he bought at the store.
   Peter는 그 상점에서 산 셔츠를 입었다.

연습문제 | 관계대명사를 이용하여 다음 두 문장을 한 문장으로 연결하시오.

1 I am about to see some artists. I met them last month.

→ I am about to see some artists _____.

2 We need to practice the song. Ms. Johnson wrote it a few days ago.

→ We need to practice the song _____.

3 The train is coming to the platform. We can take it to Paris.

→ The train _____ is coming to the platform.

4 The young man became a famous scientist. My mother used to babysit him.

→ The young man _____ became a famous scientist.

5 There's the island. We explored it on our vacation.

→ There's the island _____.

6 Katie is a friend. I play with her every weekend.

→ Katie is a friend _____.

7 My younger sister is the person. I missed her the most while studying abroad.

→ My younger sister is the person _____.

정답 p.45

POINT 2-3 소유격 관계대명사

소유격 관계대명사는 관계대명사절에서 소유격 역할을 하며, 선행사 뒤에서 문장을 연결할 수 있다. 소유격 관계대명사는 선행사와 상관없이 **whose**를 쓴다.

Nancy is **my friend**. **Her** father is a teacher. Nancy는 나의 친구이다. 그녀의 아버지는 선생님이다.
→ Nancy is **my friend whose** father is a teacher. Nancy는 아버지가 선생님인 나의 친구이다.

I received **a headset**. **Its** sound quality is great. 나는 헤드셋을 받았다. 그것의 음질은 훌륭하다.
→ I received **a headset whose** sound quality is great. 나는 음질이 훌륭한 헤드셋을 받았다.

(Tip) 선행사가 사물일 경우 「whose + 명사」는 「명사 + of which」로 바꿔 쓸 수 있다.
I decided to buy **the dress whose color** was red. 나는 색깔이 빨간색이었던 그 드레스를 사기로 결정했다.
= I decided to buy **the dress the color of which** was red.

연습문제 관계대명사를 이용하여 다음 두 문장을 한 문장으로 연결하시오.

1 Try to choose the apartment. Its location suits you best.
→ Try to choose the apartment _____.

2 The manager apologized to the customers. Their order was late.
→ The manager apologized to the customers _____.

3 We stood in the kitchen. Its walls had been painted blue.
→ We stood in the kitchen _____.

4 The woman seemed so excited. Her invention won the competition.
→ The woman _____ seemed so excited.

5 My mom gave lotion to the little girl. Her face had turned red in the sun.
→ My mom gave lotion to the little girl _____.

기출 적중문제

다음 빈칸에 공통으로 들어갈 알맞은 것은?

· Fans lined up to meet the author _____ book was popular.
· The children _____ names were called should clean the classroom.

① which ② that ③ whose
④ who ⑤ whom

정답 p.46

1. **관계대명사 that은 선행사와 상관없이 주격·목적격 관계대명사로 쓸 수 있으며, 소유격 관계대명사로는 쓸 수 없다.**

주격   The woman **that** lives next door is an athlete.   옆집에 사는 그 여자는 운동선수이다.
         = The woman **who** lives next door is an athlete.

목적격   I read **the e-mail that** you sent.   나는 네가 보낸 이메일을 읽었다.
         = I read **the e-mail which** you sent.

(Tip) that은 명사절 접속사, 지시대명사, 지시형용사로도 쓰인다.

명사절 접속사   I heard **that** the test was too difficult.   나는 그 시험이 너무 어려웠다는 것을 들었다.
지시대명사   **That** must be a wrong answer.   저것은 오답임에 틀림없다.
지시형용사   I met **that** girl yesterday.   나는 어제 저 소녀를 만났다.

2. **선행사에 다음이 포함되는 경우 관계대명사 that을 사용한다.**

최상급/서수	David is **the tallest boy that** I have seen. David는 내가 봤던 사람 중에 가장 키가 큰 소년이다.
the same/the only/ the very	This is **the same umbrella that** we lost. 이것은 우리가 잃어버린 것과 동일한 우산이다.
-body, -thing으로 끝나는 대명사	I know **somebody that** moved to your town. 나는 너희 동네로 이사 간 어떤 사람을 안다.
all, no, little, much 등	This is **all the information that** I have. 이것이 내가 갖고 있는 모든 정보다.

연습문제 A   밑줄 친 that과 바꿔 쓸 수 있는 말을 빈칸에 모두 쓰시오.

1   Mr. Smith is a neighbor <u>that</u> we see every day.   → _____

2   This is the room <u>that</u> she wants to renovate.   → _____

3   I know teenagers <u>that</u> want to improve the world.   → _____

4   Can you suggest a shirt <u>that</u> matches these trousers?   → _____

5   The coffee shop offers discounts to customers <u>that</u> bring their own cups.   → _____

6   All of us went out to the beach <u>that</u> is crowded with people.   → _____

7   Do you remember the woman <u>that</u> Giho lent his book?   → _____

8   These are the sneakers <u>that</u> Harry got last week.   → _____

연습문제 B 밑줄 친 부분이 어법상 맞으면 O를 쓰고, 틀리면 바르게 고쳐 쓰시오.

1 Look at the mountain <u>that</u> top is covered with snow. → _____

2 The police found the very car <u>that</u> caused the accident. → _____

3 Anything <u>that</u> Suho needs will be provided by the school. → _____

4 There were no songs <u>which</u> Janice knew on the radio. → _____

5 He came back with two pots <u>that</u> handles were very long. → _____

6 This is the best Italian dish <u>that</u> I have ever eaten. → _____

7 Food is one of the many things <u>which</u> closely connect us. → _____

연습문제 C 밑줄 친 that의 쓰임과 같은 것을 <보기>에서 골라 그 기호를 쓰시오.

> <보기> ⓐ I lost the letter <u>that</u> came on Thursday.
> ⓑ The hamburger <u>that</u> I had for lunch was delicious.
> ⓒ I believe <u>that</u> all citizens should vote.
> ⓓ He realized <u>that</u> a long time ago.
> ⓔ The thief got away through <u>that</u> window.

1 My friends and I hiked in a forest <u>that</u> had many gorgeous trees. [　　　]

2 The cell phone <u>that</u> I bought yesterday is really good. [　　　]

3 I heard <u>that</u> he would join our club in May. [　　　]

4 Let's buy something to eat at <u>that</u> food truck. [　　　]

5 We need a person <u>that</u> is right for this position. [　　　]

6 You have to return the laptop <u>that</u> you borrowed last month. [　　　]

7 He told me <u>that</u> was the truth. [　　　]

8 <u>That</u> is my desk over there. [　　　]

9 I think <u>that</u> my older sister is sleeping. [　　　]

기출 적중문제

밑줄 친 that의 쓰임이 나머지 넷과 <u>다른</u> 것은?

① She realized <u>that</u> Peter was absent this morning.

② I like feeding the ducks <u>that</u> live in the pond.

③ Try to set a goal <u>that</u> you can achieve.

④ Your donation will help many people <u>that</u> need clean water.

⑤ The koala is an animal <u>that</u> only eats tree leaves.

that은 관계대명사뿐만 아니라 명사절 접속사, 지시대명사, 지시형용사로도 쓰여요.

관계대명사 what

정답 p.46

관계대명사 what은 선행사를 포함하고 있으며, '~한 것'을 의미한다. 관계대명사 what은 the thing which[that]로 바꿔 쓸 수 있다.

What he told me was a white lie.　그가 나에게 말한 것은 선의의 거짓말이었다.

= **The thing which[that]** he told me was a white lie.

The best way is **what** she suggested.　가장 좋은 방법은 그녀가 제안한 것이다.

= The best way is **the thing which[that]** she suggested.

(Tip) what은 '무엇, 무슨'이라는 의미의 의문사로도 쓰인다.
　　I don't know **what** this machine is.　나는 이 기계가 무엇인지 모른다.

(Tip) 관계대명사 what은 선행사를 포함하고 있지만, 관계대명사 that은 선행사를 포함하지 않는다. that과 what은 혼동될 수 있으니 주의한다.
　　The kids like (~~that~~, **what**) Beth made for them.　그 아이들은 Beth가 그들을 위해 만든 것을 좋아한다.
　　The kids like **the toy** (~~what~~, **that**) Beth made for them.
　　그 아이들은 Beth가 그들을 위해 만든 장난감을 좋아한다.

연습문제 │ 우리말과 같도록 괄호 안의 말을 활용하여 문장을 완성하시오.

1 그가 발견했던 것은 역사를 바꿀 것이다. (discover)

= _____ would change history.

2 너는 내가 너에게 말했던 것이 타당하다고 생각하니? (say, to)

= Do you think _____ makes sense?

3 우리가 어제 한 것은 우리가 가진 유일한 선택지였다. (do, yesterday)

= _____ was the only choice we had.

4 너는 그가 수업 동안 설명한 것을 이해했니? (explain)

= Did you understand _____ during the class?

기출 적중문제

다음 빈칸에 들어갈 말이 나머지 넷과 다른 것은?

① I need to see _____ you've been working on today.

② Comic books are _____ he reads every day.

③ My assistant does _____ I tell him to do.

④ Maria listens to _____ the teacher says.

⑤ You can choose any subject _____ you are interested in.

> 관계대명사 what은 관계대명사 앞에 선행사가 없지만, 관계대명사 that은 관계대명사 앞에 선행사가 있어요.

전치사 + 관계대명사

정답 p.46

관계대명사가 전치사의 목적어일 때, 전치사를 관계대명사절의 맨 끝이나 관계대명사 바로 앞에 쓸 수 있다.

The boy is over there. + You can borrow the book **from** him.

→ **The boy** (who/whom/that) you can borrow the book **from** is over there.
네가 그 책을 빌릴 수 있는 소년이 저기에 있다.

→ **The boy from** whom you can borrow the book is over there.
└→ 관계대명사 바로 앞에 전치사가 올 때는 목적격 관계대명사를 생략할 수 없다.

I ordered **a coffee.** + I will eat some cake **with** it.

→ I ordered **a coffee** (which/that) I will eat some cake **with.**
나는 약간의 케이크와 함께 먹을 커피를 주문했다.

→ I ordered **a coffee with which** I will eat some cake.

(Tip) 전치사 뒤에는 관계대명사 who나 that을 쓸 수 없다.
She likes the people **with** (~~who~~, **whom**) she works. 그녀는 함께 일하는 사람들을 좋아한다.
This is the house **in** (~~that~~, **which**) I lived last year. 이곳은 내가 작년에 살았던 집이다.

연습문제 | <보기>와 같이 관계대명사를 이용하여 다음 두 문장을 한 문장으로 연결하시오. (단, 관계대명사는 생략하지 마시오.)

<보기> The library will be closing. I get my books from there.
→ The library *which[that] I get my books from will be closing* .
→ The library *from which I get my books will be closing* .

1 The chef uses a special knife. He cuts fish with it.
→ The chef uses a special knife _____.
→ The chef uses a special knife _____.

2 The resort was beautiful. We spent our vacation at it.
→ The resort _____ was beautiful.
→ The resort _____ was beautiful.

3 The patient is feeling better. The nurse gave some medicine to him.
→ The patient _____ is feeling better.
→ The patient _____ is feeling better.

4 Are you going to the graduation party? We were invited to it.
→ Are you going to the graduation party _____?
→ Are you going to the graduation party _____?

1. 관계부사는 관계부사절을 이끄는 접속사 역할과 부사 역할을 하며, 장소, 시간, 이유, 방법을 나타낸다.

	선행사	관계부사
장소	the place, the city, the house 등	where
시간	the time, the year, the day 등	when
이유	the reason	why
방법	the way	how

Judy returned to **the place where** she left her bag.
Judy는 그녀의 가방을 놓고 온 장소로 돌아갔다.

I forgot **the time when** we were supposed to meet.
나는 우리가 만나기로 되어 있던 시간을 잊어버렸다.

This is <u>**the way[how]**</u> I tie my shoes. 이것은 내가 나의 신발 끈을 묶는 방법이다.
└→ the way와 how는 둘 중 하나만 쓸 수 있다.

(Tip) 관계부사의 선행사가 the place, the time, the reason과 같이 장소, 시간, 이유를 나타내는 일반적인 명사인 경우 선행사나 관계부사 중 하나를 생략할 수 있다.

I found (**the place**) **where** you bought your shoes. 나는 네가 너의 신발을 샀던 곳을 발견했다.
Can you tell me **the reason (why)** you are sad? 네가 슬픈 이유를 내게 말해줄 수 있니?

2. 관계부사는 「전치사 + 관계대명사」로 바꿔 쓸 수 있다. 이때, 전치사는 선행사에 맞게 쓴다.

where	=	in/on/at/to which	**why**	=	for which
when	=	in/on/at/during which	**how**	=	in which

This is **the place where** I study. 이곳은 내가 공부하는 장소이다.
= This is **the place at which** I study.

I want to know **the reason why** she didn't come. 나는 그녀가 오지 않은 이유를 알고 싶다.
= I want to know **the reason for which** she didn't come.

연습문제 **A** 관계부사를 이용하여 두 문장을 한 문장으로 연결하시오.

1 Do you remember the day? Your kids graduated from middle school on that day.
→ Do you remember the day _____?

2 This is the restaurant. I met my wife at this place for the first time.

→ This is the restaurant _____ .

3 The cold weather is the reason. I gained weight lately for this reason.

→ The cold weather is the reason _____ .

4 I want to know the way. John beat the video game in that way.

→ I want to know _____ .

5 The stationery shop is on this street. You can buy paints there.

→ The stationery shop _____ is on this street.

6 The day was a public holiday. I went to the park on that day.

→ The day _____ was a public holiday.

7 I asked Emily to show me the way. She makes her bread in that way.

→ I asked Emily to show me _____ .

8 Climate change is the reason. Temperatures are unstable for this reason.

→ Climate change is the reason _____ .

9 The studio is located downtown. He makes his paintings at this place.

→ The studio _____ is located downtown.

연습문제 B 괄호 안에서 알맞은 것을 고르시오.

1 I went to an island (which / where) I saw beautiful waterfalls.

2 March 1 is the day on (which / when) we move to our new apartment.

3 Don't you remember the time at (which / when) no one had a mobile phone?

4 In the past, money was often the reason (which / why) people explored the world.

5 This is the pool in (which / where) you must wear your swimming cap.

6 I really like the way (how / in which) she organizes her stuff.

7 I don't know (which / why) he left so early.

기출 적중문제

다음 중 어법상 바른 것을 <u>모두</u> 고르시오.

① I want to know the way which the computer works.

② The town where I live has many art museums.

③ Tell me what you installed the air conditioner.

④ Do you know the reason for why the Internet is so slow?

⑤ August is the month in which I go on vacation.

관계사의 계속적 용법

정답 p.46

관계사의 계속적 용법은 관계대명사가 선행사에 대해 추가적인 설명을 하는 것이며, 이때 관계사 앞에 콤마(,)를 쓴다.

❶ 계속적 용법에서 관계대명사는 who(m)와 which만 쓸 수 있고, 「접속사 + 대명사」로 바꿀 수 있다.

Ms. Stevens has a son, **who** is a painter. Stevens씨는 아들이 있는데, 그는 화가이다.

(= Ms. Stevens has a son, **and he** is a painter.)

He decorated the house, **which** looks great now.

그는 그 집을 장식했는데, 그것은 이제 근사해 보인다.

(= He decorated the house, **and it** looks great now.)

(Tip) 계속적 용법은 선행사에 대한 추가 설명을 해주고, 한정적 용법은 선행사를 수식하며 범위를 제한한다. 콤마의 여부로 둘을 구분할 수 있다.

계속적 Jay has a cousin, **who** is a dentist. Jay는 사촌이 있는데, 그는 치과의사다. (Jay의 사촌은 한 명임)

한정적 Jay has a cousin **who** is a dentist. Jay는 치과의사인 사촌이 있다. (Jay의 사촌은 한 명 이상일 수 있음)

(Tip) 계속적 용법으로 쓰인 관계대명사 which는 앞에 나온 구나 절을 선행사로 취할 수 있다.

I helped him, **which** made him happy. 나는 그를 도와주었는데, 그것이 그를 행복하게 했다.

❷ 계속적 용법에서 관계부사는 when과 where만 쓸 수 있고, 「접속사 + 부사」로 바꿀 수 있다.

We went to the beach on Friday, **when** I got an important phone call.

우리는 금요일에 해변에 갔는데, 그때 나는 중요한 전화를 받았다.

(= We went to the beach on Friday, **and then** I got an important phone call.)

I toured the museum, **where** I met Sarah. 나는 박물관을 견학했는데, 그곳에서 Sarah를 만났다.

(= I toured the museum, **and there** I met Sarah.)

연습문제 A 다음 빈칸에 알맞은 관계사를 쓰시오.

1 This is my best friend, _____ I trust more than anyone.

2 This book was written in 2018, _____ the Winter Olympics were held.

3 The car factory has many robots, _____ do most of the work.

4 The boy went to the concert hall, _____ he saw his favorite pop star.

5 I'll introduce him to my friends, _____ are coming here tonight.

6 He gave flowers to the girl, _____ made her happy.

7 This is my teacher, _____ I learned English from.

8 I went back home, _____ I took a shower before dinner.

연습문제 B 우리말과 같도록 관계사와 괄호 안의 말을 활용하여 문장을 완성하시오.

1 민주는 훌륭한 제빵사인데, 그녀 소유의 빵집을 열 계획이다. (be, a great baker)

= Minju, _____ , plans to open her own bakery.

2 나는 한 교회를 우연히 발견했는데, 그것은 백 년 전에 지어졌다. (build, 100 years ago)

= I came across a church, _____ .

3 우리는 독일에서 일주일 동안 머물렀는데, 그곳에서 우리는 많은 유적지를 방문했다. (visit, many historic sites)

= We stayed in Germany for one week, _____ .

4 나는 지난 주말에 David를 봤는데, 그때 우리는 스케이트보드를 구매했다. (purchase, skateboards)

= I saw David last weekend, _____ .

5 그 도시는 폭풍우에 타격을 받았는데, 그것이 막대한 손해를 유발했다. (cause, great damage)

= The city was hit by a storm, _____ .

6 나는 Karen과 이야기했는데, 그녀는 다음 달에 미국으로 이사를 갈 것이다. (move, to America)

= I talked to Karen, _____ next month.

7 우리는 편의점으로 갔는데, 그곳에서 나는 주스 한 병을 샀다. (buy, a bottle of juice)

= We went to a convenience store, _____ .

8 그는 나의 일을 도와주었는데, 이것이 약간의 시간을 절약해 주었다. (save, some time)

= He helped me with my work, _____ .

9 소라는 그 회사를 설립했는데, 월말에 은퇴할 것이다. (found, the company)

= Sora, _____ , will retire at the end of the month.

10 나는 나의 삼촌과 시간을 보내는 것을 즐기는데, 그는 나를 웃게 만든다. (make, laugh)

= I enjoy spending time with my uncle, _____ .

기출 적중문제

주어진 <조건>에 맞게 다음 두 문장을 한 문장으로 연결하시오.

> She tried to open the door. It was locked.

<조건>

· 1. 아래 우리말과 같은 문장을 쓰시오.

: 그녀는 그 문을 열려고 노력했는데, 그것은 잠겨있었다.

2. 9단어로 쓰시오.

3. 관계대명사와 콤마(,)를 사용하시오.

→ _____

기출로적중 POINT 8 복합관계사

1. 복합관계대명사는 「관계대명사(who(m), which, what) + ever」의 형태로, 선행사를 포함한 명사절 또는 양보 부사절을 이끈다.

복합관계대명사	명사절	양보 부사절
who(m)ever	anyone who(m) 누구든지	no matter who(m) 누구더라도
whichever	anything that 어느 것이든지	no matter which 어느 것이더라도
whatever	anything that 무엇이든지	no matter what 무엇이더라도

명사절 We will welcome **whoever** comes here. 우리는 여기 오는 누구든지 환영할 것이다.
(= We will welcome **anyone who** comes here.)

양보 부사절 **Who(m)ever** you meet, you should be polite.
네가 만나는 게 누구더라도, 너는 공손해야 한다.
(= **No matter who(m)** you meet, you should be polite.)

(Tip) whichever와 whatever는 뒤에 오는 명사를 수식하는 복합관계형용사로도 쓸 수 있다.
Sandy will give you **whichever doll** you choose. Sandy는 네가 고르는 어느 인형이든지 네게 줄 것이다.
You can listen to **whatever music** you want. 너는 네가 원하는 무슨 음악이든지 들어도 된다.

2. 복합관계부사는 「관계부사(where, when, how) + ever」의 형태로, 장소·시간·방법의 부사절이나 양보 부사절을 이끈다.

복합관계부사	장소·시간·방법의 부사절	양보 부사절
wherever	at any place (where) ~하는 어디든지	no matter where 어디서 ~하더라도
whenever	at any time (when) ~할 때마다	no matter when 언제 ~하더라도
however	in any way (that) 어떤 방법으로든	no matter how 아무리 ~하더라도

장소 부사절 You can sit **wherever** you like. 너는 네가 원하는 곳 어디든지 앉아도 된다.
= You can sit **at any place (where)** you like.

양보 부사절 **Wherever** he goes, his younger sister follows him.
그가 어디를 가더라도, 그의 여동생은 그를 따라간다.
= **No matter where** he goes, his younger sister follows him.

(Tip) 복합관계부사 however가 양보 부사절을 이끄는 경우 「however + 형용사/부사 + 주어 + 동사」로 쓴다.
However high the mountain is, I will climb to the top.
그 산이 아무리 높더라도, 나는 정상까지 오를 것이다.
= **No matter how** high the mountain is, I will climb to the top.

연습문제 A | 다음 두 문장의 의미가 같도록 복합관계사를 이용하여 문장을 완성하시오.

1 No matter which you wear, you'll look great.

= _____ , you'll look great.

2 No matter how hungry you are, you shouldn't eat junk food.

= _____ , you shouldn't eat junk food.

3 I can lend you anything that you require for the event.

= I can lend you _____ .

4 My father can fly a drone at any time when he has no work to do.

= My father can fly a drone _____ .

5 We will send an invitation to anyone whom we wish to invite.

= We will send an invitation to _____ .

6 No matter what he chooses , I will give it to him.

= _____ , I will give it to him.

7 At any place you shop, you can use this credit card.

= _____ , you can use this credit card.

연습문제 B | 괄호 안에서 알맞은 것을 고르시오.

1 Emily is rich enough to buy (whatever / however) she wants.

2 (However / Whoever) hard Sally tried, she could not beat her little sister at chess.

3 (Whichever / Whenever) I ride my bike, I wear a helmet.

4 (Whoever / Wherever) wins the game, I will be happy.

5 (Whichever / However) thirsty you are, you shouldn't drink this expired milk.

6 (Wherever / Whatever) we go for the party, I'm sure it'll be fun.

7 (Whoever / Whatever) you expect the ending to be, I'm confident you'll be surprised.

기출 적중문제

다음 중 어법상 바른 것은?

① Whatever I feel tired, I take a rest.

② You always sound beautiful whomever you sing.

③ You can order whatever you like.

④ Whoever the weather is like, we'll take a walk.

⑤ Wherever long it takes, you need to wait your turn.

Ⓐ 다음 대화의 빈칸에 알맞은 관계대명사나 관계부사를 쓰시오.

1

A: I'll show you the pictures ⓐ_____ I took.

B: Great! Are these pictures from the museum ⓑ_____ you went on your field trip?

A: Yes, they are. This is Susan about ⓒ_____ I talked the other day.

B: Oh, she is your friend ⓓ_____ is in the same class as you!

A: You're right. We are very close. We really enjoy studying together.

2

A: Is this the movie ⓐ_____ Jack wants to watch?

B: Yes. Do you remember ⓑ_____ he said about the movie?

A: No, I don't remember.

B: He said the movie has an actor ⓒ_____ is very popular in the UK.

A: I saw that in a review. Is that the reason ⓓ_____ he wanted to see the movie?

B: It's possible. Maybe Jack read the same review.

A: That's probably true.

Ⓑ 관계대명사나 관계부사를 이용하여 다음 두 문장을 한 문장으로 연결하시오. (단, 콤마(,)는 쓰지 마시오.)

1 I forgot the name of that country. It is next to Thailand.

→ _____

2 Lily is my neighbor. Everybody likes her very much.

→ _____

3 Mr. Hwang is a writer. His book became a best seller.

→ _____

4 Let me show you the way. My grandmother bakes scones in this way.

→ _____

5 This is the street. Jason said he would meet us on the street.

→ _____

6 I can still remember the day. I won the dance contest on the day.

→ _____

C <보기>와 같이 두 문장의 의미가 같도록 관계대명사나 관계부사를 이용하여 문장을 완성하시오.

> <보기> I waved at Alice, and she is my classmate.
>   = _I waved at Alice, who is my classmate._

1 The soccer players practiced on the field, and it was still wet due to the rain.

= _____

2 This is the restaurant's chef, and he has worked here for years.

= _____

3 I saw my cousin in June, and then I went to Texas.

= _____

4 She went to the store, and there she bought some potatoes.

= _____

5 I sent him a birthday card, but he didn't receive it.

= _____

D 우리말과 같도록 복합관계사와 괄호 안의 말을 활용하여 문장을 완성하시오.

1 그가 하는 말이 무엇이더라도, 그녀는 그의 말에 절대 동의하지 않을 것이다. (say)

= _____, she will never agree with him.

2 새 교재가 필요한 누구든지 교무실로 가야 한다. (need, a new textbook)

= _____ should go to the school office.

3 아무리 당신이 화가 나더라도, 폭력을 사용하는 것은 용납할 수 없다. (upset, feel)

= _____, using violence is not acceptable.

4 당신이 어디서 여행하든지 그곳에 사는 사람들에게 항상 정중하라. (travel)

= _____, always be polite to the people who live there.

5 이 박물관에 방문하는 누구든지 음성 안내를 무료로 이용할 수 있다. (visit, this museum)

= _____ can use the audio guide for free.

6 나는 시험이 있을 때마다 일찍 잔다. (have, an exam)

= _____, I go to sleep early.

7 그 가수가 아무리 유명하더라도, 그는 여전히 매우 겸손하다. (famous, the singer, be)

= _____, he is still very humble.

중간·기말고사 실전 문제

1 다음 빈칸에 들어갈 말이 순서대로 짝지어진 것은?

> · Is there anyone _____ can help me
>   with this problem?
> · You should get a special oven _____
>   cooks food quickly.

① who – which　　② that – who
③ which – that　　④ who – whose
⑤ which – which

3 관계대명사를 이용하여 다음 두 문장을 한 문장으로
연결하시오.

> This novel is about a girl. She becomes
> a brave soldier.
> → _____
>   _____

2 다음 (A)~(C)에 들어갈 말이 바르게 짝지어진 것은?

> · I met a person who ___(A)___ at that
>   company.
> · This is a good movie for people that
>   ___(B)___ romantic stories.
> · Let's find a vending machine which
>   ___(C)___ coffee and juice.

	(A)	(B)	(C)
①	work	love	sell
②	work	loves	sells
③	works	love	sell
④	works	loves	sells
⑤	works	love	sells

4 다음 두 문장을 한 문장으로 바르게 연결한 것은?

> He carried groceries for the old lady.
> Her bags were too heavy.

① He carried groceries for the old lady who
　bags were too heavy.
② He carried groceries for the old lady that
　bags were too heavy.
③ He carried groceries for the old lady
　whose bags were too heavy.
④ He carried groceries for the old lady
　which bags were too heavy.
⑤ He carried groceries for the old lady
　whom bags were too heavy.

5 다음 글의 밑줄 친 부분 중 어법상 어색한 것은?

Today is the last day of school before summer vacation. The students in our school ①who is going on vacation are very excited. I talked to my friend ②who sits beside me in class. Tomorrow, we are going to visit the water park ③that opens this weekend. We chose to go there because it has many thrilling rides ④that seem fun. I hope we have a summer vacation ⑤that lasts a long time.

6 다음 빈칸에 알맞은 말을 쓰시오. (단, that은 쓰지 마시오.)

· Tom is the roommate ⓐ_____ I have lived with for two years.
· This is the new camera ⓑ_____ Jiho bought three weeks ago.

7 다음 빈칸에 공통으로 들어갈 알맞은 것은?

· John is a friend of mine _____ hobby is playing the guitar.
· We can help the person _____ computer needs repairs.

① who ② whom ③ whose
④ that ⑤ which

[8-9] 다음 글을 읽고 주어진 질문에 답하시오.

Nikola Tesla was the person ⓐ_____ invented the type of electricity we use at home today. He invented a kind of electric current ⓑ_____ many different machines could use. This current turns on and off very quickly. (A) There are many benefits of this electrical technology. (B) It makes our lives more convenient. When you use a computer or a toaster, you are using something invented by Tesla.

8 위 글의 빈칸 ⓐ와 ⓑ에 들어갈 말이 순서대로 짝지어진 것은?

① whom - who ② who - which
③ which - who ④ who - whom
⑤ whom - which

9 관계대명사를 이용하여 밑줄 친 (A)와 (B)를 한 문장으로 연결하시오. (단, that은 쓰지 마시오.)

→ _____
_____
_____

10 다음 밑줄 친 (A)~(D)에 대한 설명이 바른 것끼리 묶인 것은?

> If you have a friend (A) who (B) want a pet, recommend that they adopt a dog or cat. Animals in a shelter (C) which (D) has no owners need love and care. This is better than getting a pet from a pet store.

> ⓐ (A)는 목적격 관계대명사 whom과 바꿔 쓸 수 있다.
> ⓑ (A)는 생략할 수 있지만, (C)는 생략할 수 없다.
> ⓒ (B)는 선행사가 a friend이므로 wants로 고쳐야 한다.
> ⓓ (C)는 주격 관계대명사로 that과 바꿔 쓸 수 있다.
> ⓔ (D)는 선행사가 a shelter이므로 has가 맞다.

① ⓐ, ⓒ   ② ⓑ, ⓓ   ③ ⓑ, ⓒ, ⓔ
④ ⓒ, ⓓ   ⑤ ⓒ, ⓓ, ⓔ

11 다음은 *The Golden Egg*를 읽고 친구들이 나눈 대화이다. 대화를 보고 관계대명사를 이용하여 문장을 완성하시오. (단, that은 쓰지 마시오.)

> *Jinseo*: I heard that it became a best seller.
> *Yeji* : Yes, right. This novel was written by a young woman.
> *Taeho* : Really? That's interesting. The book's main character reminded me of myself.

Book Review: *The Golden Egg*
(1) Jinseo: *The Golden Egg* is a book

_____.

(2) Yeji: *The Golden Egg* is a novel _____

_____.

(3) Taeho: It is a book _____

_____.

12 다음 빈칸에 공통으로 들어갈 알맞은 관계대명사를 <보기>에서 골라 쓰시오.

> <보기>   who   whose   which   that

> (A) This website is available for people _____ prefer to read the magazine online.
> (B) Have you seen the flowers _____ my neighbor planted?
> (C) That is the cutest dog _____ I have ever seen.

13 다음 밑줄 친 that과 쓰임이 같은 것은?

> These are the chairs that we have to return to the meeting room.

① I'm wearing the shoes that my dad bought me.
② Can you pass me that spoon on the table, please?
③ That is my cat over there sleeping on the couch.
④ It was very unexpected that it would rain on the weekend.
⑤ That she won the speech contest is really surprising.

14 다음 중 밑줄 친 that의 쓰임이 나머지 넷과 다른 것은?

> A: Have you heard the story ①that Michael told me yesterday?
> B: No. What happened?
> A: He told me ②that he was walking in the street and he saw Chris Evans!
> B: The actor? No way. I didn't know ③that Chris Evans was visiting our city.
> A: Michael said ④that he smiled and said hello.
> B: Wow. I'm jealous. I wish ⑤that I had seen Chris Evans too!

15 우리말과 같도록 괄호 안의 말을 알맞게 배열하시오.

> 우리에게 필요한 것은 외국 문화를 존중하는 것이다.
> (need, we, respect, cultures, foreign, what, is, to)

= _____

16 다음 빈칸에 공통으로 들어갈 알맞은 말을 쓰시오.

> · The result wasn't _____ I had expected.
> · Orange juice and milk are _____ we have in the refrigerator.

17 다음은 Theo의 일기이다. 밑줄 친 ⓐ~ⓔ 중 어법상 어색한 것을 찾아 기호를 쓰고 바르게 고쳐 쓰시오.

> Date: July 10
> Weather: Sunny
> I collected shells at Parkview Beach ⓐwhere there were shells of all different sizes. My father, ⓑwho was swimming, told us we could keep them, but we should leave any shells ⓒthat have creatures inside. At the end of the day, he double-checked ⓓthat we had found. My little brother and I each had a bucket ⓔwhich was full of shells to take home.

_____ → _____

18 다음 중 밑줄 친 what의 쓰임이 나머지 넷과 다른 것은?

① A vacation is what Jina needs at the moment.

② John was being silly, so I asked him what he was talking about.

③ What you did at camp last summer impressed everyone.

④ Students who take notes remember what they learn in class better.

⑤ What Anderson did for the charity was very generous.

19 다음 대화의 빈칸 (A)와 (B)에 알맞은 말을 쓰시오.

> Q: Do tigers still live in Korea?
> A: No. Tigers were the most famous animals (A) _____ lived in Korea, but people killed the last one around 100 years ago. This was similar to (B) _____ happened in several other countries in the world. The animals were hunted too much. But maybe they will come back one day.

20 다음 문장 (A), (B)에서 생략된 말이 들어갈 위치와 생략된 말이 바르게 짝지어진 것은?

> (A) It is one of the ⓐ shows ⓑ I recommend you ⓒ see.
> (B) He can't stop thinking about ⓓ the song ⓔ played ⓕ by the pianist last night.

	(A)	(B)
①	ⓐ, that	ⓓ, which was
②	ⓑ, that are	ⓓ, which
③	ⓑ, that	ⓔ, which was
④	ⓒ, who are	ⓔ, that
⑤	ⓒ, whom	ⓕ, that was

21 다음 ⓐ~ⓒ 중 어법상 어색한 것을 찾아 기호를 쓰고 주어진 <조건>에 맞게 바르게 고쳐 쓰시오.

> ⓐ This is a photograph of the man we met while traveling on the Amazon River.
> ⓑ Can you see the parrot sitting on his shoulder?
> ⓒ We listened to a speaker gives motivational speeches.

<조건> 관계대명사를 활용하여 쓰시오.

_____ → _____

_____

22 주어진 <조건>에 맞게 다음 두 문장을 한 문장으로 연결하시오.

> He showed us sample tools. They were made of wood.

> **<조건>** 8단어로 이루어진 문장을 완성하시오.

→ _____

_____

23 다음 빈칸 (A)와 (B)에 들어갈 알맞은 말을 <보기>에서 골라 쓰시오.

> **<보기>** that   who   whom   which

> · Politics is a subject in (A) _____ many citizens are interested these days.
> · Tomorrow, I'll have lunch with Amy, with (B) _____ I used to share my dormitory room.

24 다음 두 문장을 한 문장으로 연결할 때, 빈칸 ⓑ에 올 수 있는 것은?

> Jasmine is the woman. My uncle is getting married to her.
> → Jasmine is the woman ___ⓐ___ ___ⓑ___ ___ⓒ___ ___ⓓ___ ___ⓔ___ getting married.

① is   ② whom   ③ uncle
④ my   ⑤ to

25 다음 두 문장을 한 문장으로 바르게 연결하지 <u>못한</u> 것을 <u>모두</u> 고르시오.

> I went to a museum. I saw some of Monet's paintings in it.

① I went to a museum which I saw some of Monet's paintings in.
② I went to a museum that I saw some of Monet's paintings in.
③ I went to a museum in that I saw some of Monet's paintings.
④ I went to a museum where I saw some of Monet's paintings in.
⑤ I went to a museum in which I saw some of Monet's paintings.

26 다음 빈칸에 들어갈 말이 순서대로 짝지어진 것은?

> · On the street, I walked by my friend, _____ was on her way home.
> · Minho passed the math test, _____ he had failed twice last year.

① who – that   ② which – that
③ who – which   ④ that – which
⑤ that – that

27 다음 (A)~(C)에 들어갈 알맞은 말을 <보기>에서 한 번씩만 골라 쓰시오.

> **<보기>** who   whom   which   that

> Yesterday, I talked to my older brother, (A) _____ is a vet. He works at a clinic, (B) _____ is near his house. He helps a lot of animals (C) _____ are sick or hurt.

28 다음 @~ⓒ 중 어법상 어색한 것을 찾아 기호를 쓰고 바르게 고쳐 쓰시오.

> @ Jiwoo got a call from Suyeon, who wanted to chat about her school life.
> ⓑ I walked into the kitchen, which smelled of fresh coffee.
> ⓒ I visited China with my parents, that had never been there before.

_____ → _____

_____

29 다음 두 문장의 의미가 같도록 관계대명사를 이용하여 문장을 완성하시오.

> I practiced ice-skating all day long, and it made me too exhausted.
> = I practiced ice-skating all day long,
> _____ .

30 다음 문장에서 어법상 어색한 부분을 찾아 쓰고 바르게 고쳐 쓰시오.

> This is the spare bedroom in that my guests can stay.

_____ → _____

31 우리말과 같도록 관계대명사와 <보기>의 말을 활용하여 문장을 완성하시오. (단, that은 쓰지 마시오.)

> <보기> watch   travel   many people
> a lot   a horror movie   a person

(1) 만약 당신이 여행을 많이 다니는 사람이라면 당신의 삶은 더 신날 것임에 틀림없다.

= Your life must be more exciting if you are _____ .

(2) 그 여배우는 많은 사람들이 봤던 공포 영화에서 주연을 맡았다.

= The actress starred in _____

_____ .

32 다음 (A)~(C)에 들어갈 말이 바르게 짝지어진 것은?

> · That was the year ___(A)___ I moved from Seoul to London.
> · This is the field ___(B)___ my team used to practice soccer.
> · Do you know the reason ___(C)___ they like history so much?

	(A)	(B)	(C)
①	when	where	how
②	when	when	why
③	when	where	why
④	where	when	why
⑤	where	where	how

33 다음 중 어법상 바른 것끼리 묶인 것은?

ⓐ This is where we have to wait if we want to catch a taxi.
ⓑ My favorite vacation was last winter when I went skiing for the first time.
ⓒ I wanted to find out the reason how the sky looks blue.
ⓓ Do you remember the spot where we had a picnic last year?
ⓔ That's the folder where you should keep all your important files in.

① ⓐ, ⓑ, ⓒ   ② ⓐ, ⓑ, ⓓ   ③ ⓑ, ⓒ, ⓓ
④ ⓑ, ⓒ, ⓔ   ⑤ ⓑ, ⓓ, ⓔ

34 다음 ⓐ와 ⓑ에 들어갈 알맞은 말을 <보기>에서 골라 쓰시오.

<보기> where   when   why   how

The first time I tried scuba diving, I was very frightened. I was in an area ⓐ_____ many fish were swimming all around me. But I was too busy focusing on breathing to look at them. Later, my teacher taught me ⓑ_____ I could breathe naturally underwater. Now, I love scuba diving.

35 다음 두 문장의 의미가 같도록 빈칸에 알맞은 관계부사를 쓰시오.

You should visit the museum. The new exhibit is opening there.
= You should visit the museum _____ the new exhibit is opening.

36 다음 중 괄호 안의 말을 밑줄 친 부분과 바꿔 쓸 수 없는 것을 모두 고르시오.

① I want to hear about how you came up with this amazing plan. (→ the way)
② Did you buy this coat in the shop in which I used to work? (→ where)
③ Luna was born in the year when the World Cup Games were held. (→ in which)
④ He asked me to show him what I made this morning. (→ for which)
⑤ My younger brother's missing toy is the reason why he cried all day. (→ at which)

37 다음 ⓐ~ⓔ 중 빈칸에 들어갈 관계사가 같은 것끼리 묶인 것은?

· Is this the town golf course at ⓐ_____ your dad plays golf?
· That is the restaurant ⓑ_____ Mr. Park works.
· Thailand is a country ⓒ_____ you can try lots of different types of food.
· My uncle built a house last year, ⓓ_____ is not far from here.
· Could you tell me the place in ⓔ_____ I should park my car?

① ⓐ, ⓑ, ⓒ   ② ⓐ, ⓑ, ⓓ   ③ ⓐ, ⓓ, ⓔ
④ ⓑ, ⓒ, ⓓ   ⑤ ⓒ, ⓓ, ⓔ

38 다음 두 문장의 의미가 같도록 알맞은 관계사를 활용하여 문장을 완성하시오.

(1)
> Did you think about the thing which Jacob wants to do on the weekend?
> = Did you think about _____ _____ on the weekend?

(2)
> This is the spot at which my husband proposed to me.
> = This is the spot _____ _____ to me.

39 다음 (A)~(C)에 들어갈 말이 바르게 짝지어진 것은?

> · This is the class in __(A)__ students are taught about design.
> · February is the month __(B)__ I always want to go to a warm country.
> · Let me show you the bookstore __(C)__ I worked during university.

	(A)	(B)	(C)
①	which	when	where
②	which	when	which
③	which	where	where
④	where	that	which
⑤	where	that	where

40 다음 두 문장의 의미가 같도록 복합관계사를 활용하여 문장을 완성하시오.

(1)
> Anything that you want to do today is fine with me.
> = _____ is fine with me.

(2)
> At any time when you get angry, try to take deep breaths before you speak.
> = _____ , try to take deep breaths before you speak.

41 다음 빈칸에 들어갈 복합관계사가 같은 것끼리 묶인 것은?

> ⓐ _____ you need my help, just ask me.
> ⓑ _____ participates in the event will be rewarded with a present.
> ⓒ You can visit me _____ it is convenient.
> ⓓ _____ she stops by the bakery, she always buys a strawberry cake.
> ⓔ _____ cold the weather becomes, she won't turn on the heater.

① ⓐ, ⓑ, ⓒ ② ⓐ, ⓒ, ⓓ ③ ⓑ, ⓒ, ⓓ
④ ⓑ, ⓓ, ⓔ ⑤ ⓒ, ⓓ, ⓔ

42 다음 중 밑줄 친 부분을 생략할 수 <u>없는</u> 것은?

① The students were impressed by the concert <u>which</u> they went to.
② Jennifer ate the dinner <u>that</u> her mother had made for her.
③ I tried to find the woman to <u>whom</u> the package was sent.
④ I bought tickets for the concert <u>that is</u> taking place this week.
⑤ The man <u>whom</u> she met was very nice to everyone.

43 다음 밑줄 친 what과 쓰임이 같은 것은?

> This radio program is <u>what</u> I enjoy listening to.

① May I ask <u>what</u> you did last night?
② Please tell me <u>what</u> your secret is.
③ <u>What</u> he wants is to take some rest.
④ Can you check <u>what</u> we have in the fridge?
⑤ She told us <u>what</u> happened during the meeting.

44 다음 중 괄호 안의 말을 밑줄 친 부분과 바꿔 쓸 수 <u>없는</u> 것은?

① She bought a book, <u>which</u> is popular for its amazing characters. (→ and it)
② You may do the things <u>that</u> you'd like to do while in New York. (→ which)
③ I don't know the reason <u>for which</u> she hates me. (→ why)
④ <u>No matter who</u> talks to him, he'll never listen. (→ Whoever)
⑤ You can take home <u>anything that</u> you like. (→ wherever)

[45-46] 우리말과 같도록 빈칸에 알맞은 관계사를 쓰시오.

45

> 지수가 아침 식사로 먹었던 것은 맛이 너무 단 크림 도넛이었다.

= _____ Jisu ate for breakfast was a cream doughnut _____ taste was too sweet.

46

> 그 경기장이 있었던 장소에 지어진 병원은 이제 문을 닫았다.

= The hospital _____ was built on the site _____ the stadium used to be is now closed.

CHAPTER 14
가정법

If I **had** a cell phone, I **would call** him immediately.
만약 내가 휴대폰을 가지고 있다면, 그에게 즉시 전화할 텐데.

'만약 내가 휴대폰을 가지고 있다면, 그에게 즉시 전화할 텐데.'라며 현재 휴대폰이 없어서 즉시 전화할 수 없지만, 만약 휴대폰을 가지고 있다면 즉시 전화할 것이라고 가정하여 말하고 있어요. 이렇게 사실과 반대되거나 실현 가능성이 매우 낮은 일을 가정하여 말하는 것을 **가정법**이라고 해요.

기출로 적중 POINT

1	• 가정법 과거와 가정법 과거완료
2	• 혼합 가정법
3	• 가정법을 직설법으로 바꾸는 법
4	• if를 생략한 가정법
5	• Without 가정법
6	• I wish 가정법
7	• as if[though] 가정법

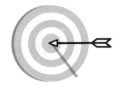

내신 100점 적중!
기출 출제율

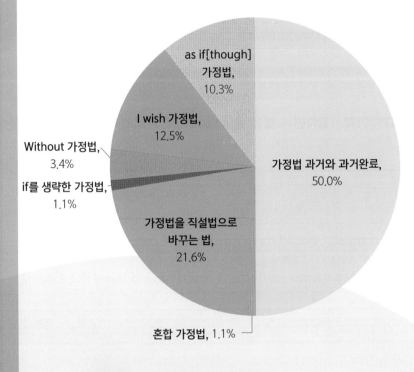

as if[though] 가정법, 10.3%

I wish 가정법, 12.5%

Without 가정법, 3.4%

if를 생략한 가정법, 1.1%

가정법 과거와 과거완료, 50.0%

가정법을 직설법으로 바꾸는 법, 21.6%

혼합 가정법, 1.1%

TOP 1 **가정법 과거와 과거완료 (50%)**
가정법 과거를 활용하여 영작하는 문제가 자주 출제된다.

TOP 2 **가정법을 직설법으로 바꾸는 법 (21.6%)**
접속사가 사용된 문장을 가정법으로 바꿔 쓰는 문제가 자주 출제된다.

TOP 3 **I wish 가정법(12.5%)**
I wish 가정법의 형태를 묻는 문제가 자주 출제된다.

가정법 과거와 가정법 과거완료

정답 p.50

1. 가정법 과거는 '만약 ~한다면 …할 텐데'의 의미로 현재의 사실과 반대되거나 실현 가능성이 매우 낮거나 없는 일을 가정할 때 쓴다.

If	+	주어	+	동사의 과거형 (be동사는 were)	~,	주어	+	would, could should, might	+	동사원형	…

└─────────── if절 ───────────┘　　└─────────── 주절 ───────────┘

If I **went** into space, I **would be** very excited.　만약 내가 우주에 간다면, 정말 신날 텐데.

If I **didn't have** plans, I **might visit** Jinsu.　만약 내가 계획이 없다면, 아마 진수를 방문할 텐데.

If he **were** here, I **could ask** him.　만약 그가 여기에 있다면, 나는 그에게 물어볼 수 있을 텐데.

　　　└→ if절의 be동사는 주어에 상관없이 were을 쓴다.

(Tip) 가정법은 실현 가능성이 매우 낮거나 없는 경우에 사용하고, 조건문은 실현 가능성이 있는 경우에 사용한다.

　가정법　If she **came** here, we **would have** a party for her.
　　　　만약 그녀가 여기에 온다면, 우리는 그녀를 위해 파티를 할 텐데. (그녀가 올 가능성이 매우 낮거나 없음)

　조건문　If she **comes** here, we **will have** a party for her.
　　　　만약 그녀가 여기에 온다면, 우리는 그녀를 위해 파티를 할 것이다. (그녀가 올 가능성이 있음)

2. 가정법 과거완료는 '만약 ~했다면 …했을 텐데'의 의미로 과거의 사실과 반대되는 일을 가정할 때 쓴다.

If	+	주어	+	had + p.p.	~,	주어	+	would, could should, might	+	have + p.p.	…

└─────────── if절 ───────────┘　　└─────────── 주절 ───────────┘

If I **had won** the contest, I **would have donated** the prize money.
만약 내가 그 대회에서 이겼다면, 상금을 기부했을 텐데.

If I **hadn't played** video games yesterday, I **could have passed** the exam.
만약 내가 어제 비디오 게임을 하지 않았다면, 그 시험을 통과할 수 있었을 텐데.

연습문제 A 괄호 안에서 알맞은 것을 고르시오.

1 If you (move / moved) closer to school, you wouldn't have to wake up early in the morning.

2 If we weren't late, we (will walk / could walk) slowly.

3 If we (had practiced / practiced) more, we might not have lost the game.

4 If you had requested me, I (would give / would have given) you the data yesterday.

5 If she (had returned / returned), I would prepare a welcome gift for her.

6 If she goes to New York next week, she (will view / would view) the Statue of Liberty.

7 If the chef (paid / had paid) attention, he wouldn't have burned the dish.

8 If I had gone to the doctor, I (wouldn't be / wouldn't have been) so sick last night.

9 If I (get / got) a new couch, I will choose a green one.

연습문제 B 우리말과 같도록 괄호 안의 말을 활용하여 문장을 완성하시오.

1 만약 내가 돈이 있다면, 새 배낭을 살 텐데. (have, buy)

= If I _____ the money, I _____ a new backpack.

2 만약 그가 그녀의 편지를 받았다면, 그녀에게 답장했을 텐데. (receive, reply)

= If he _____ her letter, he _____ to her.

3 만약 밖에 있는 가로등이 너무 밝지 않다면, 나는 잠이 들 수 있을 텐데. (be, fall)

= If the streetlight outside _____ so bright, I _____ asleep.

4 만약 그녀가 한가했다면, 네가 이 퍼즐을 완성하는 것을 도울 수 있었을 텐데. (be, help)

= If she _____ free, she _____ you complete this puzzle.

5 만약 내게 기회가 주어진다면, 나는 외국에서 공부할 텐데. (give, study)

= If I _____ the opportunity, I _____ in a foreign country.

6 만약 나무가 전기선에 쓰러지지 않았다면, 정전은 일어나지 않았을 텐데. (fall, occur)

= If a tree _____ on the power line, the blackout _____.

7 만약 더 따뜻하다면, 나는 수영장에 갈 텐데. (be, go)

= If it _____ warmer, I _____ to the swimming pool.

8 만약 네가 너의 우산을 사용했다면, 폭풍우에 젖지 않았을 텐데. (use, get)

= If you _____ your umbrella, you _____ wet in the storm.

9 만약 John이 그의 숙제를 끝낸다면, 우리와 함께 공원에 올 것이다. (finish, come)

= If John _____ his homework, he _____ to the park with us.

기출 적중문제

다음 우리말을 알맞게 영작한 것은?

> 내가 너라면, 물 한 병을 가져올 텐데.

① If I am you, I would bring a bottle of water.
② If I were you, I would bring a bottle of water.
③ If I was you, I will bring a bottle of water.
④ If I were you, I will bring a bottle of water.
⑤ If I had been you, I will bring a bottle of water.

가정법 과거에서 if절의 be동사는 주어에 상관없이 were을 써요.

혼합 가정법은 '만약 (과거에) ~했다면 (지금) …할 텐데'의 의미로 과거의 사실과 반대되는 일이 현재까지 영향을 미치는 상황을 가정할 때 쓴다.

| If | + | 주어 | + | had + p.p. | ~, | 주어 | + | would, could should, might | + | 동사원형 | … |

└─────── if절 ───────┘ └─────── 주절 ───────┘

If you **had helped** me yesterday, I **wouldn't work** today.
만약 네가 어제 나를 도와줬다면, 나는 오늘 일하지 않을 텐데.

If I **hadn't missed** the train, I **could be** at home now.
만약 내가 기차를 놓치지 않았다면, 지금 집에 있을 수 있을 텐데.

(Tip) 혼합 가정법의 주절에는 now, today, this time과 같이 현재를 나타내는 수식어구가 주로 쓰인다.

If I **had worn** a jacket, I **wouldn't be** cold **now**. 만약 내가 재킷을 입었다면, 지금 춥지 않을 텐데.

연습문제 우리말과 같도록 괄호 안의 말을 활용하여 문장을 완성하시오.

1 만약 그의 팔이 부러지지 않았다면, 오늘 우리와 놀 수 있을 텐데. (break, play)

= If he _____ his arm, he _____ with us today.

2 만약 네가 조심했다면, 너의 전화기는 지금 수리될 필요가 없을 텐데. (be, need)

= If you _____ careful, your phone _____ to be repaired now.

3 만약 네가 어제 나를 도와주지 않았다면, 나는 오늘 피곤할 텐데. (help, tired)

= If you _____ me yesterday, I _____ today.

4 만약 경찰이 도둑을 잡지 않았다면, 우리는 지금 안심할 수 없을 텐데. (catch, feel)

= If the police _____ the thief, we _____ safe now.

5 만약 내가 나의 가방에 코트를 챙겼다면, 지금 따뜻할 텐데. (pack, be)

= If I _____ a coat in my bag, I _____ warm now.

6 만약 우리가 카드를 가져왔다면, 지금 게임을 할 수 있을 텐데. (bring, play)

= If we _____ some cards, we _____ a game now.

가정법을 직설법으로 바꾸는 법

정답 p.50

가정법 문장은 접속사 because, as, since, so를 사용하는 직설법 문장으로 바꿔 쓸 수 있다.

가정법 과거	if절과 주절의 과거시제를 현재시제로 바꾸고, 긍정·부정을 뒤바꾼다. If I **didn't have** a fever, I **could go** to the beach. 만약 내가 열이 나지 않는다면, 바닷가에 갈 수 있을 텐데. = **Because[As/Since]** I **have** a fever, I **can't go** to the beach. 나는 열이 나기 때문에, 바닷가에 갈 수 없다. = I **have** a fever, **so** I **can't go** to the beach. 나는 열이 나서, 바닷가에 갈 수 없다.
가정법 과거 완료	if절과 주절의 과거완료시제를 과거시제로 바꾸고, 긍정·부정을 뒤바꾼다. If you **had arrived** on time, we **wouldn't have been** late. 만약 네가 제시간에 도착했다면, 우리는 늦지 않았을 텐데. = **Because[As/Since]** you **didn't arrive** on time, we **were** late. 네가 제시간에 도착하지 않기 때문에, 우리는 늦었다. = You **didn't arrive** on time, **so** we **were** late. 네가 제시간에 도착하지 않아서, 우리는 늦었다.
혼합 가정법	if절의 과거완료시제를 과거시제로, 주절의 과거시제를 현재시제로 바꾸고, if절과 주절의 긍정·부정을 뒤바꾼다. If you **had bought** the flour yesterday, we **could make** the cake now. 만약 네가 어제 그 밀가루를 샀다면, 우리는 지금 케이크를 만들 수 있을 텐데. = **Because[As/Since]** you **didn't buy** the flour yesterday, we **can't make** the cake now. 네가 어제 그 밀가루를 사지 않기 때문에, 우리는 지금 케이크를 만들 수 없다. = You **didn't buy** the flour yesterday, **so** we **can't make** the cake now. 네가 어제 그 밀가루를 사지 않아서, 우리는 지금 케이크를 만들 수 없다.

연습문제 A 다음 가정법 문장을 직설법 문장으로 바꿔 쓰시오.

1 If I remembered Christine's e-mail address, I could send her a note.

→ As _____ .

2 If I had known the deadline, I wouldn't have made other plans.

→ Because _____ .

3 If Angela knew how to sew, she could make herself a dress.

→ As _____ .

4 If you had come at 3 P.M., you would have seen my parents.

→ Since _____ .

5 If she had studied for today's quiz, she wouldn't have failed it.

→ Because _____.

6 If Tom had exercised regularly, he wouldn't be out of shape now.

→ Since _____.

연습문제 B 다음 두 문장의 의미가 같도록 문장을 완성하시오.

1 As Minsu is not good at soccer, he can't join the soccer team.

= If _____, he could join the soccer team.

2 If the tickets weren't already sold out, I could go to the concert.

= Since the tickets are already sold out, _____.

3 Because the book is so interesting, I can't put it down.

= If _____, I could put it down.

4 If Clara had a bus card, she could transfer free of charge.

= _____, so she can't transfer free of charge.

5 If I had been invited, I would have gone to his birthday party.

= Since _____, I didn't go to his birthday party.

6 As it started to snow, the baseball game was delayed.

= If _____, the baseball game wouldn't have been delayed.

7 If you had told Mina about the contest, she would have signed up for it.

= Because _____, she didn't sign up for it.

8 If you had washed your shirt in cold water, it wouldn't look faded now.

= As _____, it looks faded now.

9 You didn't stop eating when you got full, so you feel uncomfortable now.

= If you had stopped eating when you got full, you _____.

기출 적중문제

다음 밑줄 친 부분을 직설법 문장으로 바꿔 쓰시오.

Last week, I really messed up my budget. If I hadn't spent all of my money on snacks, I wouldn't be broke now. I can't even afford to buy the pencils I need.

→ _____, so

_____.

기출로적중 POINT 4 if를 생략한 가정법

정답 p.50

가정법에서 if절의 동사가 were이거나 「had p.p.」의 형태인 경우, if를 생략하고 if절의 주어와 were/had의 위치를 바꿔 「Were/Had + 주어」의 형태로 쓸 수 있다.

가정법 과거   **If I were** a bird, I would fly high in the sky.
만약 내가 새라면, 하늘을 높이 날 텐데.
→ **Were I** a bird, I would fly high in the sky.

If he weren't a singer, he wouldn't join a band.
그가 가수가 아니라면, 밴드에 가입하지 않을 텐데.
→ **Were he not** a singer, he wouldn't join a band.

가정법 과거완료   **If he had** taken a taxi, he wouldn't have missed the show.
만약 그가 택시를 탔다면, 그 공연을 놓치지 않았을 텐데.
→ **Had he** taken a taxi, he wouldn't have missed the show.

If I hadn't eaten dinner, I would have had dinner with you.
만약 내가 저녁을 먹지 않았다면, 너와 함께 저녁을 먹었을 텐데.
→ **Had I not** eaten dinner, I would have had dinner with you.

연습문제   다음 가정법 문장을 if를 생략한 가정법 문장으로 바꿔 쓰시오.

1   If I were an architect, I would build an amazing castle.

→ _____, I would build an amazing castle.

2   If you hadn't been at the party, we wouldn't have enjoyed it.

→ _____, we wouldn't have enjoyed it.

3   If he were here, he would make us clean the kitchen.

→ _____, he would make us clean the kitchen.

4   If Adam had spent more time on the painting, it wouldn't have looked bad.

→ _____, it wouldn't have looked bad.

5   If she hadn't followed the rules, she would have been punished.

→ _____, she would have been punished.

6   If I were as fast as a cheetah, I could win the race.

→ _____, I could win the race.

7   If she hadn't known how to use this oven, she couldn't have baked cookies.

→ _____, she couldn't have baked cookies.

8   If you had bought a good quality speaker, your music wouldn't have sounded bad.

→ _____, your music wouldn't have sounded bad.

기출로적중 POINT 5 Without 가정법

가정법 If절의 위치에 「Without + 명사」의 형태가 올 경우, '~가 없다면/없었다면'의 의미이다.

❶ 「Without + 명사, 가정법 과거」는 '~가 없다면 …할 텐데'의 의미로, 이때 「Without + 명사」는 「But for + 명사」 또는 「If it were not for + 명사」로 바꿔 쓸 수 있다.

| Without | + | 명사 | , | 주어 | + | would, could should, might | + | 동사원형 |

Without his advice, I **would make** a mistake. 그의 충고가 없다면, 나는 실수를 할 텐데.

→ **But for** his advice, I **would make** a mistake.

→ **If it were not for[Were it not for]** his advice, I **would make** a mistake.
   └→ 「If it were not for ~」에서 if를 생략하여 「Were it not for ~」로도 쓸 수 있다.

❷ 「Without + 명사, 가정법 과거완료」는 '~가 없었다면 …했을 텐데'의 의미로, 이때 「Without + 명사」는 「But for + 명사」 또는 「If it had not been for + 명사」로 바꿔 쓸 수 있다.

| Without | + | 명사 | , | 주어 | + | would, could should, might | + | have + p.p. |

Without your efforts, I **would have failed**. 너의 노력이 없었다면, 나는 실패했을 텐데.

→ **But for** your efforts, I **would have failed**.

→ **If it had not been for[Had it not been for]** your efforts, I **would have failed**.
   └→ 「If it had not been for~」에서 if를 생략하여 「Had it not been for ~」로도 쓸 수 있다.

연습문제 A 우리말과 의미가 같도록 괄호 안의 말을 활용하여 문장을 완성하시오.

1 소방관들이 없었다면, 그것은 큰 문제가 될 수 있었을 텐데. (be)
= Without firefighters, it _____ a big problem.

2 그 지도가 없다면, 우리는 길을 잃을 텐데. (get lost)
= Without the map, we _____.

3 일기예보가 없다면, 우리는 다가오는 태풍에 관해 알지 못할 텐데. (know)
= But for the weather report, we _____ about the upcoming storm.

4 그의 농담이 없었다면, 우리는 많이 웃지 않았을 텐데. (laugh)
= Without his jokes, we _____ a lot .

5 나의 휴대폰 알람이 없었다면, 나는 제시간에 일어나지 못했을 텐데. (wake up)
= Without my cell phone alarm, I _____ on time.

6 중력이 없다면, 우리는 땅 위에 서있지 못할 텐데. (be able to)

= But for gravity, we _____ stand on the ground.

7 선생님의 강의와 설명이 없었다면, 나는 그 시험을 통과할 수 없었을 텐데. (pass)

= But for the teacher's lectures and explanations, I _____ the test.

8 기차가 없었다면, 우리가 여기에 오는 것은 불가능했을 텐데. (be)

= Without the train, getting here _____ impossible for us.

연습문제 B 다음 두 문장의 의미가 같도록 if를 사용하여 문장을 완성하시오.

1 Without water, animals couldn't live.

= _____, animals couldn't live.

2 But for my mother's rules, I could stay out at night.

= _____, I could stay out at night.

3 Without the dark curtains, my room would be brighter.

= _____, my room would be brighter.

4 Were it not for the air conditioner, we would suffer in the hot weather.

= _____, we would suffer in the hot weather.

5 Had it not been for Josh, my team would have lost the game.

= _____, my team would have lost the game.

6 But for Derek's help, I wouldn't have been able to complete my history project .

= _____, I wouldn't have been able to complete my history project.

7 But for your warning, I would have stepped on the broken glass.

= _____, I would have stepped on the broken glass.

8 Without the lifeguard, I would have drowned.

= _____, I would have drowned.

기출 적중문제 🎯

두 문장의 의미가 같도록 문장을 완성하시오.

> Had it not been for Elizabeth, the play wouldn't have been touching.
>
> = Without _____
>
> _____ .

1. 「I wish + 주어 + 동사의 과거형」은 '~하면 좋을 텐데'의 의미로 현재 실현 가능성이 매우 낮거나 없는 일을 소망할 때 쓴다.

   I wish I **were** an astronaut. 내가 우주 비행사라면 좋을 텐데.
   └→ be동사는 주어에 상관없이 were를 쓴다.

   I wish I **knew** how to swim. 내가 수영하는 법을 알면 좋을 텐데.

   (Tip) 「I wish + 주어 + 동사의 과거형」은 「I'm sorry (that) + 주어 + 동사의 현재형」 형태의 직설법으로 바꿔 쓸 수 있다.

   I wish I **remembered** the answer. 내가 정답을 기억하면 좋을 텐데.
   = **I'm sorry (that)** I **don't remember** the answer. 내가 정답을 기억하지 못하는 것이 유감이다.

   (Tip) 「It's (about) time + 주어 + 동사의 과거형」은 '(이제) ~해야 할 때이다'의 의미로 하지 않은 일에 대한 유감이나 재촉을 나타낼 때 쓰며, 「It's (about) time + 주어 + should + 동사원형」으로 바꿔 쓸 수 있다.

   It's (about) time you **walked** the dog. 네가 개를 산책시켜야 할 때이다.
   = **It's (about) time** you **should walk** the dog.

2. 「I wish + 주어 + had p.p.」는 '~했다면 좋을 텐데'의 의미로 과거에 이루지 못한 일에 대한 아쉬움을 나타낼 때 쓴다.

   I wish you **had told** me your plan. 네가 너의 계획을 나에게 말했다면 좋을 텐데.
   I wish I **had found** my wallet. 내가 나의 지갑을 찾았다면 좋을 텐데.

   (Tip) 「I wish + 주어 + had p.p.」는 「I'm sorry (that) + 주어 + 동사의 과거형」 형태의 직설법으로 바꿔 쓸 수 있다.

   I wish he **had called** me. 그가 나에게 전화했다면 좋을 텐데.
   = **I'm sorry (that)** he **didn't call** me. 그가 나에게 전화하지 않았던 것이 유감이다.

연습문제 A 우리말과 같도록 괄호 안의 동사를 활용하여 문장을 완성하시오.

1 그 종업원이 우리에게 특별 메뉴를 제공했다면 좋을 텐데. (offer)

= I wish the server _____ us the special.

2 내가 그 수학 공식을 이해하면 좋을 텐데. (understand)

= I wish I _____ the math formula.

3 Charlie가 역사 대신 생물을 공부했다면 좋을 텐데. (study)

= I wish Charlie _____ biology instead of history.

4 네가 너의 여름방학을 더 즐겼다면 좋을 텐데. (enjoy)

= I wish you _____ your summer vacation more.

5 우리 아파트에 여분의 침실 하나가 더 있으면 좋을 텐데. (have)

= I wish we _____ an extra bedroom in our apartment.

6 우리 가족이 루브르 박물관에 있는 모나리자를 보기 위해 파리에 갔다면 좋을 텐데. (go)

= I wish my family _____ to Paris to see the *Mona Lisa* at the Louvre museum.

연습문제 B | 각 인물들의 말에 나온 표현을 활용하여 두 문장의 의미가 같도록 빈칸에 알맞은 말을 쓰시오.

1 Emma

> I wish you had been at the lecture with me.

= I'm sorry that you _____ at the lecture with me.

2 Sean

> I wish I could talk to the celebrity.

= I'm sorry that I _____ _____ to the celebrity.

3 Jinhee

> I'm sorry that he didn't come to the ceremony.

= I wish he _____ _____ to the ceremony.

4 Andy

> I wish I had read the manual before starting the machine.

= I'm sorry that I _____ _____ the manual before starting the machine.

5 Jane

> I wish my English got better faster.

= I'm sorry that my English _____ _____ better faster.

6 Daeho

> I'm sorry that my younger brother didn't learn the recipe.

= I wish my younger brother _____ _____ the recipe.

기출 적중문제

다음 대화의 빈칸에 들어갈 말이 순서대로 짝지어진 것은?

> *A*: I wish we _____ more time to play board games.
> *B*: Me too. That would be a lot of fun.
> *A*: It's too bad your mom won't let you stay over.
> *B*: I know. I wish she had _____ it was OK.

① have – say　② had – say　③ have – said
④ had – said　⑤ had – says

> 현재 실현 가능성이 매우 낮거나 없는 일을 소망할 때는 「I wish + 주어 + 동사의 과거형」의 형태를 써요.

as if[though] 가정법

정답 p.51

「as if[though] + 주어 + 동사의 과거형/had p.p.」는 '마치 ~한/했던/했었던 것처럼'의 의미이다.

주절	as if[though] 절	의미
주어 + 동사의 현재형	as if[though] + 주어 + 동사의 과거형	마치 ~한 것처럼 …한다 (주절과 동일한 현재 사실의 반대)
	as if[though] + 주어 + had p.p.	마치 ~했던 것처럼 …한다 (주절보다 이전인 과거 사실의 반대)
주어 + 동사의 과거형	as if[though] + 주어 + 동사의 과거형	마치 ~했던 것처럼 …했다 (주절과 동일한 과거 사실의 반대)
	as if[though] + 주어 + had p.p.	마치 ~했었던 것처럼 …했다 (주절보다 이전인 대과거 사실의 반대)

He talks **as if[though]** he **were** a billionaire.   그는 마치 (현재) 억만장자인 것처럼 말한다.
동사의 현재형   주어 + 동사의 과거형

He talks **as if[though]** he **had been** a billionaire.   그는 마치 (이전에) 억만장자였던 것처럼 말한다.
동사의 현재형   주어 + had p.p.

She talked **as if[though]** she **saw** a fairy.   그녀는 마치 (당시에) 요정을 봤던 것처럼 말했다.
동사의 과거형   주어 + 동사의 과거형

She talked **as if[though]** she **had seen** a fairy.   그녀는 마치 (이전에) 요정을 봤었던 것처럼 말했다.
동사의 과거형   주어 + had p.p.

연습문제 A 우리말과 같도록 괄호 안의 말을 활용하여 문장을 완성하시오.

1 진호와 수아는 마치 잘 지내는 척한다. (get along)
= Jinho and Sua pretend as if they _____ well.

2 그녀는 마치 화장을 어떻게 하는지 알았던 것처럼 행동했다. (know)
= She acted as if she _____ how to put on a makeup.

3 시장은 마치 그녀가 경제학을 공부했었던 것처럼 말했다. (study)
= The mayor spoke as though she _____ economics.

4 Jessica는 마치 좋은 소식을 받았었던 것처럼 보였다. (receive)
= Jessica looked as though she _____ good news.

5 나의 형은 마치 일주일 동안 잠을 못 잤었던 것처럼 느꼈다. (sleep)
= My older brother felt as if he _____ for a week.

6 그녀는 마치 이전에 오페라 노래를 불렀던 것처럼 말한다. (sing)

= She talks as if she _____ opera songs before.

7 그는 마치 화학을 잘 이해했던 것처럼 자랑했다. (understand)

= He bragged as if he _____ chemistry well.

연습문제 B 다음 두 문장을 한 문장으로 연결하시오.

1 The yellow house looks like it's not occupied. Actually, it is occupied.

→ The yellow house _____ as if it _____.

2 Minsoo was a patient. The nurse treated Minsoo like he was not a patient.

→ The nurse _____ Minsoo as though he _____ a patient.

3 He never saw a UFO. He talks like he saw a UFO before.

→ He _____ as if he _____ a UFO before.

4 The criminal behaved like an innocent person. However, he wasn't an innocent person.

→ The criminal _____ as if he _____ an innocent person.

5 Jacob has worries. He acts like his worries are gone.

→ Jacob _____ as if his worries _____.

6 They didn't participate in the group discussion. However, they talked like they had participated in the group discussion last week.

→ They _____ as if they _____ in the group discussion last week.

7 He never lived in Ulsan. He pretends like he lived in Ulsan before.

→ He _____ as if he _____ in Ulsan before.

8 John didn't get a lot of rest last night. However, he seemed like he had gotten a lot of rest last night.

→ John _____ as if he _____ a lot of rest last night.

기출 적중문제

<보기>와 같이 우리말과 같도록 괄호 안의 말을 활용하여 문장을 완성하시오.

> <보기> 그는 마치 왕자인 것처럼 말한다.
>
> = He talks as if _he were a prince_ .

> 그녀는 마치 복권에 당첨된 것처럼 행동한다. (win, the lottery)

= She acts as if _____ .

Ⓐ 우리말과 같도록 괄호 안의 말을 알맞게 배열하시오.

1 만약 내가 나의 학교 숙제를 끝낸다면, 내가 좋아하는 TV쇼를 볼 수 있을 텐데. (finished, could, if, watch, I, my school assignment, I, my favorite TV show)

= _____, _____.

2 만약 모차르트가 더 오래 살았다면, 더 많은 걸작들을 창작했을 텐데. (longer, have created, if, more masterpieces, Mozart, would, had lived, he)

= _____, _____.

3 만약 내가 네가 난처한 줄 알았다면, 너를 도왔을 텐데. (were, known, you, in trouble, would, you, had, I, that, have helped, I)

= _____, _____.

4 인터넷이 없었다면, 그는 그 소식을 듣지 못했을 텐데. (the Internet, have heard, without, he, the news, wouldn't)

= _____.

5 그 가수가 지난달에 그 새로운 앨범을 발표했다면 좋을 텐데. (the singer, I, had released, wish, last month, the new album)

= _____.

6 만약 그가 브라질에 있다면, 상파울루에 방문할 수 있을 텐데. (in Brazil, he, visit, Sao Paolo, were, could, he)

= _____.

7 그 고양이들은 마치 서로에게 이야기하고 있던 것처럼 보였다. (the cats, if, were talking, as, seemed, they, to each other)

= _____.

8 그 규제들이 없다면, 우리는 여기에 집을 지을 수 있을 텐데. (the restrictions, not, it, we, a house, could, here, were, build, for)

= _____, _____.

9 나의 친구는 마치 그녀가 나의 비밀들을 퍼뜨리지 않던 것처럼 행동했다. (acted, didn't, as though, my friend, spread, she, my secrets)

= _____.

10 만약 내가 어제 그 달걀을 깜박 잊어버리지 않았다면, 지금 쿠키를 만들 텐데. (I, the eggs, hadn't, if, yesterday, could, some cookies, make, forgotten, now, I)

= _____, _____.

B 괄호 안의 말을 활용하여 대화를 완성하시오.

1

Stella: I'm starving. Could you please give me something to eat?

Yunho: I only have bread. I wish I _____ more food to give you. (have)

2

Roy: This morning, my baby brother looked at a book as if he _____ how to read. (know)

Judy: Oh, my. He is so adorable.

3

Sumi: What would you do if you were a superhero?

Carl: Well, were I a superhero, I _____ people's lives. (save)

4

James: If you _____ the painting, we could hang it on the wall now. (buy)

Karen: I have another painting we can hang.

C 두 문장의 의미가 같도록 문장을 완성하시오.

1 I'm sorry that my dad has to go to hospital tomorrow.
= I wish _____.

2 I'm sorry that I didn't remember to call you this morning.
= I wish _____.

3 I wish I had taken a vacation in Bali last summer.
= I'm sorry _____.

4 But for their wings, birds would not be able to fly.
= If _____, birds would not be able to fly.

5 Without your help, I couldn't have solved the problem.
= If _____, I couldn't have solved the problem.

6 But for airplanes, people would find it hard to travel abroad.
= Were _____, people would find it hard to travel abroad.

1 다음 대화의 빈칸에 들어갈 말이 순서대로 짝지어진 것은?

> A: What _____ you do if you won the lottery, Robin?
> B: I would open a hospital for poor children.
> A: That is a good idea!
> B: Thanks. What about you?
> A: Well, if I _____ a lot of money, I would buy my parents a larger house.
> B: That would be such a nice thing to do.

① will – have
② would – have
③ would – had
④ will – had
⑤ would – didn't have

2 다음 중 어법상 어색한 것의 개수는?

> ⓐ If I hadn't slept late this morning, I wouldn't have had to get dressed quickly.
> ⓑ I would have been so angry if Peter had not finished his homework again.
> ⓒ If you were me, what will you do?
> ⓓ If Kate didn't start feeling ill, she wouldn't have gone home early.

① 0개
② 1개
③ 2개
④ 3개
⑤ 4개

[3-4] 다음 글을 읽고 주어진 질문에 답하시오.

> Few people visit the Children's Museum nowadays. The museum's curator said, (A) "The museum would be popular if it were closer to downtown." His friend agreed with his idea, and said, (B) "The museum doesn't get more customers because it isn't located near a busy area." Therefore, the curator has begun to look into moving the museum downtown near a busy area so more people will visit.

3 위 글의 밑줄 친 (A)를 직설법 문장으로 바꿔 쓰시오.

→ As _____

_____ .

4 위 글의 밑줄 친 (B)를 가정법 문장으로 바꿔 쓰시오.

→ If _____

_____ .

5 다음 우리말을 알맞게 영작한 것은?

> 네가 없었다면, 콘서트를 보는 것은 재미가 없었을 거야.

① Without you, watching the concert wouldn't have been fun.
② Without you, watching the concert wouldn't be fun.
③ Were it not for you, watching the concert wouldn't have been fun.
④ Had it not been for you, watching the concert wouldn't be fun.
⑤ If it had not been for you, watching the concert wouldn't be fun.

6 우리말과 같도록 괄호 안의 말을 활용하여 문장을 완성하시오.

> 내가 이곳에 더 일찍 도착했다면, 지금 앞자리에 앉을 수 있을 텐데. (arrive, here, sit, in the front row, earlier, now)

= If _____

_____ .

7 두 문장의 의미가 같도록 문장을 완성하시오.

> I wish I had gotten a better grade on the test.
> = I'm sorry that _____
>
> _____ .

8 밑줄 친 부분을 if를 사용하여 바꿔 쓰시오.

> <u>Without my dog's growling</u>, I would have gotten attacked by the wild cat.
> → _____
>
> _____, I would have gotten attacked by the wild cat.

9 다음 빈칸에 공통으로 들어갈 알맞은 것은?

> · I wish David _____ here with me right now.
> · She paints as if she _____ a professional painter.

① is   ② had been   ③ were
④ has been   ⑤ are

10 다음 빈칸에 들어갈 말이 순서대로 짝지어진 것은?

> · If we _____ a fan yesterday, we would not be so hot right now.
> · _____ rush hour, he would have gotten there on time.

① bought – Had it not been for
② had bought – Had it not been for
③ had bought – If it were not for
④ bought – Were it not for
⑤ have bought – If it were not for

11 다음 문장을 가정법 문장으로 바꿔 쓰시오.

> As I skipped the class, I am stuck here writing an apology letter to my teacher today.
>
> → If _____
>
> _____
>
> _____.

12 다음 문장을 가정법 문장으로 바르게 바꾼 것은?

> Since humans don't have gills like fish, they cannot breathe underwater.
>
> *gill 아가미

① If humans have gills like fish, they can breathe underwater.

② If humans have gills like fish, they breathe underwater.

③ If humans have gills like fish, they could breathe underwater.

④ If humans had gills like fish, they could breathe underwater.

⑤ If humans had gills like fish, they can breathe underwater.

13 다음 대화의 빈칸에 들어갈 알맞은 것은?

> A: I am planning to go camping over the holidays.
> B: Wow! That sounds very exciting. Who are you going with?
> A: No one. I'm going by myself.
> B: Really? _____. It's always better to travel with someone else.
> A: That's true. Why don't you join me?

① I won't go alone if I was you

② I wouldn't go alone if I am you

③ I wouldn't go alone if I were you

④ I won't go alone if I am you

⑤ I won't go alone if I were you

14 다음 중 어법상 바른 것은?

① If I were not exhausted, I can do the cleaning faster.

② If this hill is higher, I would not ride my bike up it.

③ If my cat weren't big, he can fit into the basket.

④ Had I gotten good grades, my parents would have given me a reward.

⑤ If Anna weren't tired, she will not have fallen down.

15 다음 대화를 읽고, 밑줄 친 우리말 (A)~(C)와 같도록 괄호 안의 말을 활용하여 영작하시오.

> *A*: (A) 내가 좀 더 나이 들어 보이면 좋을 텐데.
> (look a bit older, wish)
> *B*: Why is that?
> *A*: Well... (B) 만약 내가 더 나이 들어 보인다면, 대우를 더 잘 받을 텐데. (will, look older, if, be treated better)
> *B*: What do you mean?
> *A*: Everyone thinks I look like a kid, so they don't listen to me.
> *B*: Yeah. (C) 너는 나에게 마치 12살인 것처럼 보여. (look, to me, be twelve, as if)
> *A*: That's the problem! I'm 16!

(A) _____
(B) _____
(C) _____

16 주어진 문장과 의미가 같은 것은?

> If I had an extra ticket, I would take you to the magic show.

① I had an extra ticket.
② I have an extra ticket now.
③ I didn't take you to the magic show.
④ I don't have an extra ticket now.
⑤ I can take you to the magic show now.

17 다음 중 어법상 바른 것은?

① If I am there, I would buy that.
② If I didn't have to practice, I will take a nap.
③ Would you go to China if you have the chance?
④ If I were you, I would take some medicine.
⑤ If Steve paid attention in class, the teacher won't get angry.

[18-19] 다음 문장을 I wish 가정법 문장으로 바꿔 쓰시오.

18

> I'm sorry that the Wi-Fi doesn't work in this hotel.
> → _____
> _____

19

> I'm sorry that I didn't meet my cousin when she was in town.
> → _____
> _____

20

> Because I am not a wizard, I can't teleport anywhere.

① If I am a wizard, I could teleport anywhere.
② If I am a wizard, I could have teleported anywhere.
③ If I were a wizard, I could teleport anywhere.
④ If I were a wizard, I will teleport anywhere.
⑤ If I were a wizard, I could have teleported anywhere.

21

> The zebra didn't see the lion hiding in the grass, so it couldn't run away.

① If the zebra saw the lion hiding in the grass, it can run away.
② If the zebra saw the lion hiding in the grass, it could have run away.
③ If the zebra saw the lion hiding in the grass, it could run away.
④ If the zebra had seen the lion hiding in the grass, it could have run away.
⑤ If the zebra had seen the lion hiding in the grass, it can run away.

[22-23] 다음 문장을 as if 가정법 문장으로 바꿔 쓰시오.

22

> I am not a professional dancer. I can do a few dances well.
> → I can do a few dances well, _____
> _____.

23

> The book was not released yet. It is already being talked about by everyone.
> → The book is already being talked about by everyone, _____
> _____.

24 다음 대화를 읽고, 밑줄 친 우리말 (A), (B)와 같도록 괄호 안의 말을 활용하여 문장을 완성하시오.

> A: It's so hot and sticky today. (A) 만약 내가 수영장에 있다면 지금 기쁠 텐데. (happy, be, at the pool)
> B: Me too. I would love to swim today.
> A: (B) 만약 우리에게 자유시간이 있다면, 우리는 방과 후에 갈 수 있을 텐데. (have, go, free time)
> B: I know, but we have art lessons today. It's a shame.

(A) If _____
right now.
(B) If _____
after school.

25 우리말과 같도록 주어진 <조건>에 맞게 문장을 완성하시오.

> 만약 더 많은 사람들이 그 식당에 방문한다면, 그곳은 영업시간을 연장할 텐데.

> **<조건>**
> 1. 가정법을 사용하시오.
> 2. more people, its, will, visit, the restaurant, extend, it, opening hours를 활용하시오.

= If _____

_____.

26 다음 중 어법상 바른 것은?

① Were I free this weekend, I will go to the gym.
② Had he given up, he couldn't achieve his goal.
③ Were she taller, she could reach the top shelf.
④ Had you eaten too much junk food, you will gain weight.
⑤ Had I miss the bus, I would have taken the subway.

27 다음 중 짝지어진 두 문장의 의미가 <u>다른</u> 것은?

① As you aren't tall enough, you cannot ride the rollercoaster.
  = If you were tall enough, you could ride the rollercoaster.
② Since I didn't know you were coming, I didn't clean my room.
  = If I had known you were coming, I would have cleaned my room.
③ I wish I had a puppy at home.
  = I'm sorry that I have a puppy at home.
④ Were it not for a compass, we would not be able to sail.
  = But for a compass, we would not be able to sail.
⑤ Without the Internet, staying in touch with friends would be difficult.
  = Were it not for the Internet, staying in touch with friends would be difficult.

[28-29] 다음 문장을 가정법 문장으로 바꿔 쓰시오.

28

> As we didn't take a picture together, I don't have proof of our meeting now.
> → If _____
> _____.

29

> As the teacher explained the riddle, we could understand its answer.
> → If _____
> _____.
> *riddle 수수께끼

30 다음 글의 밑줄 친 우리말 (A)와 같도록 괄호 안의 말을 활용하여 영작하시오.

> My older sister is angry because I didn't help her move in to her new apartment. But she didn't tell me about it until yesterday, and I was busy all day. (A) 만약 그녀가 더 일찍 부탁했었더라면, 나는 그녀를 도와줬을 텐데. (ask, earlier, will, her, help)

= _____

_____

31 다음 빈칸에 들어갈 말이 순서대로 짝지어진 것은?

> · I'm sorry that I don't have more time to practice taekwondo.
> = I wish I _____ more time to practice taekwondo.
> · I'm sorry that we didn't visit Notre Dame Cathedral before the fire.
> = I wish we _____ Notre Dame Cathedral before the fire.
> *Notre Dame Cathedral 노트르담 성당

① had – visited
② have – had visited
③ had – had visited
④ have – visited
⑤ can have – visited

32 다음 두 문장의 의미가 같도록 빈칸에 알맞은 말을 쓰시오.

> William would have come if he had heard about the event.
> = William didn't come as he _____ about the event.

[33-34] 다음 우리말을 알맞게 영작한 것을 고르시오.

33

> 내가 그 보물의 위치를 기억할 수 있다면 좋을 텐데.

① I wish I remember the location of the treasure.
② I wish I remembered the location of the treasure.
③ I wish I can remember the location of the treasure.
④ I wish I could remember the location of the treasure.
⑤ I wish I had remembered the location of the treasure.

34

> 더 많은 사람들이 나의 공연에 참석했다면 좋을 텐데.

① I wish more people attend my performance.
② I wish more people attended my performance.
③ I wish more people had attended my performance.
④ I wish more people can attend my performance.
⑤ I wish more people could attend my performance.

35 다음 글의 밑줄 친 우리말과 같도록 괄호 안의 말을 알맞게 배열하시오.

I'm sorry I'm late. I had to stop and eat something. I skipped breakfast and got really hungry. 먹을 무언가가 없었다면, 나는 기절했을 텐데. (I, passed out, would have, something, to eat)

= Without _____

_____ .

36 다음 글의 빈칸에 들어갈 말이 순서대로 짝지어진 것은?

He likes ice skating, but he doesn't know how to play hockey. If he _____ the basic rules, he _____ to play hockey.

① has known – could try
② had known – can try
③ knows – could try
④ knew – can try
⑤ knew – could try

37 다음 우리말을 알맞게 영작한 것은?

나의 친구는 마치 그곳에 가봤었던 것처럼 사하라 사막을 묘사했다.

① My friend described the Sahara Desert as if he were there.
② My friend describes the Sahara Desert though he had been there.
③ My friend described the Sahara Desert as if he has been there.
④ My friend describes the Sahara Desert as if he had been there.
⑤ My friend described the Sahara Desert as if he had been there.

38 다음 중 어법상 바른 것은?

① If I am Michael, I would study hard to get a good grade.
② I wish I know how to play guitar.
③ It would be wonderful if I could change my name.
④ She wishes she is a singer.
⑤ If the weather will be better, I could wear a summer outfit.

39 다음 글의 밑줄 친 우리말 (A)와 같도록 <조건>에 맞게 영작하시오.

> I was so surprised when I saw Michelle in her school's play. She played the main character, Cinderella, in the play. (A) 그녀는 마치 진짜 공주였던 것처럼 보였다.

> <조건>
> 1. as if 가정법을 활용하시오.
> 2. 9단어로 쓰시오.
> 3. be, look, a real princess를 활용하시오.

= _____

40 다음 빈칸에 들어갈 말이 순서대로 짝지어진 것은?

> If Mario _____ his doctor's advice, he _____ better today.

① would take – would feel
② had taken – would feel
③ has taken – would have felt
④ has taken – would feel
⑤ taken – would have felt

41 다음 대화의 빈칸에 들어갈 말이 순서대로 짝지어진 것은?

> A: Thank God I made it. _____ the subway, I _____ here on time.
> B: Relax. The show has been delayed for 10 minutes.

① If I missed – wouldn't arrive
② Had I missed – wouldn't arrived
③ Had I missed – wouldn't have arrived
④ Were I missed – wouldn't have arrived
⑤ Were I missed – would have arrived

42 다음 중 어법상 어색한 것의 개수는?

> ⓐ They cook as if they have cooked for many years.
> ⓑ John plays the piano as if he were trained.
> ⓒ Jane looks as though she had a nightmare.
> ⓓ The cats meow as though they don't eat for weeks.
> ⓔ You sound as if you were unaware of the rules.

① 1개　　② 2개　　③ 3개
④ 4개　　⑤ 5개

[43-44] 다음 글을 읽고 주어진 질문에 답하시오.

> I have always wanted to go to Jamaica. It looks like a tropical paradise. It has beautiful beaches and lush jungles. (A) 만약 내가 작년에 약간의 돈을 모았다면, 나는 이번 여름에 그 곳에 갈 수 있었을 텐데. However, I'm not a very good saver, so I will have to wait until I have enough money to go there.
>
> *lush 무성한

43 위 글의 밑줄 친 우리말 (A)를 알맞게 영작한 것은?

① If I had saved some money last year, I could go there this summer.

② If I had saved some money last year, I can go there this summer.

③ If I saved some money last year, I can go there this summer.

④ If I saved some money last year, I could have gone there this summer.

⑤ If I had saved some money last year, I could have gone there this summer.

44 다음 빈칸에 들어갈 말이 순서대로 짝지어진 것은?

> [SUMMARY]
> My dream is to go to Jamaica. If I _____ a better saver, I could have gone there this summer. However, I will have to wait. I wish I _____ enough money to go now.

① had been – had had

② had been – had

③ were – had had

④ am – had

⑤ were – had

45 다음 중 짝지어진 두 문장의 의미가 <u>다른</u> 것은?

① If Jim had studied hard, he wouldn't have failed the test.
  = As Jim studied hard, he didn't fail the test.

② If I had not left my phone at home, I could have called you.
  = As I left my phone at home, I couldn't call you.

③ Rita paints wonderfully, as if she were an artist.
  = Rita is not an artist. She paints wonderfully.

④ If it had not been for one missed note, the song would have been absolutely perfect.
  = As there was one missed note, the song was not absolutely perfect.

⑤ Without the Internet, we would not have access to much information.
  = Were it not for the Internet, we would not have access to much information.

CHAPTER 15
일치와 화법

일치 **A sandwich is** on the table. 샌드위치가 식탁 위에 있다.

I thought that Mark **liked** sandwiches. 나는 Mark가 샌드위치를 좋아한다고 생각했다.

화법 Mark said, "I don't like sandwiches." Mark는 "나는 샌드위치를 좋아하지 않아."라고 말했다.

→ Mark said **that he didn't like** sandwiches.
Mark는 그가 샌드위치를 좋아하지 않는다고 말했다.

첫 번째 문장에서 주어진 단수명사 **A sandwich**에 맞춰 동사도 단수동사 **is**를 썼고, 두 번째 문장에서 주절의 과거시제 **thought**에 맞춰 종속절에도 과거시제 **liked**를 썼어요. 이렇게 문장 안에서 수나 시제를 맞추는 것을 **일치**라고 해요.

세 번째 문장처럼 Mark가 한 말을 따옴표(" ")를 사용하여 그가 말한 그대로 전달하는 것을 **직접 화법**이라고 하고, 네 번째 문장처럼 Mark가 한 말을 따옴표(" ") 없이 전달하는 사람 입장에서 바꿔 말하는 것을 **간접 화법**이라고 해요.

기출로 적중 POINT

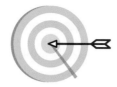

내신 100점 적중!
기출 출제율

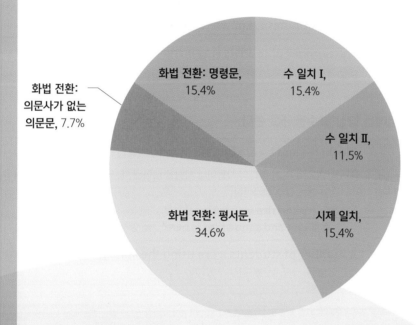

화법 전환: 명령문, 15.4%

수 일치 I, 15.4%

화법 전환: 의문사가 없는 의문문, 7.7%

수 일치 II, 11.5%

화법 전환: 평서문, 34.6%

시제 일치, 15.4%

TOP 1 화법 전환: 평서문 (34.6%)
평서문의 직접 화법을 간접 화법으로 바꿔 쓰는 문제가 자주 출제된다.

TOP 2 수 일치 I (15.4%)
시제 일치 (15.4%)
화법 전환: 명령문 (15.4%)
주어가 무엇인지에 따라 단수동사와 복수동사를 구별하는 문제가 자주 출제된다. 주절의 시제에 따라 종속절의 시제를 일치시키는 문제가 자주 출제된다. 명령문의 직접 화법을 간접 화법으로 바꿔 쓰는 문제가 자주 출제된다.

TOP 3 수 일치 II (11.5%)
상관접속사로 연결된 주어의 수 일치를 묻는 문제가 자주 출제된다.

수 일치 I

정답 p.54

1. 다음과 같은 주어에는 항상 단수동사를 쓴다.

구·절	**Making friends is** important. 친구들을 사귀는 것은 중요하다. **What I told my parents was** true. 내가 나의 부모님에게 말한 것은 사실이었다.
every, each가 포함된 주어	**Every picture** of the stars **was** amazing. 별들에 관한 모든 사진은 놀라웠다. **Each machine makes** different products. 각각의 기계는 다른 제품들을 만든다.
시간·거리·금액·무게	**Fifteen minutes is** enough time for a nap. 15분은 낮잠을 위한 충분한 시간이다.
학과명·국가명	**Economics is** a useful major. 경제학은 유용한 전공 과목이다. **The Philippines is** known for mangoes. 필리핀은 망고로 유명하다.
「the number of + 복수명사」	**The number of tourists was** increasing sharply. 관광객들의 수가 급격하게 증가하고 있었다.

2. 다음과 같은 주어에는 항상 복수동사를 쓴다.

(Both) A and B	**(Both) He and I were** born in March. 그와 나 둘 다 3월에 태어났다. (Tip) 「A and B」가 하나의 사물이나 사람을 나타낼 때, 또는 「A and 관사 없는 B」 일 때는 단수 취급한다. **Curry and rice was** my breakfast. 카레라이스는 나의 아침식사였다. **A singer and songwriter is** here. 가수 겸 작곡가인 사람이 여기 있다.
「a number of + 복수명사」	**A number of students were** using the library. 많은 학생들이 그 도서관을 이용하고 있었다.

연습문제 괄호 안에 들어갈 알맞은 말을 고르시오.

1 Every car (is / are) covered with snow today.

2 Two hours (is / are) how long I spent shopping today.

3 Both Sarah and Stephen (is / are) making the cake for the party.

4 Approximately 325 kilometers (is / are) the distance between Seoul and Busan.

5 The number of mistakes in the report (is / are) too high.

6 Being polite to others (is / are) the most important thing.

7 A number of our items (is / are) also available online.

8 Ham and cheese (is / are) my favorite sandwich.

기출로적중 POINT 1-2 수 일치 Ⅱ

정답 p.54

다음과 같은 주어에는 경우에 따라 단수동사 혹은 복수동사를 쓴다.

❶ 부분·전체를 나타내는 표현을 포함한 주어: of 뒤의 명사에 동사를 수일치시킨다.

| all, most, any, half, some, 분수 | + | of | + | 단수명사 | + | 단수동사 |
| | | | | 복수명사 | | 복수동사 |

All of the house was damaged in the flood. 그 집 전체가 홍수로 손상되었다.
Two-thirds of the members were satisfied with the result.
회원들의 3분의 2가 그 결과에 만족했다.

❷ 다음과 같은 상관접속사로 연결된 주어: B에 동사를 수일치시킨다.

| either A or B A나 B 둘 중 하나 | neither A nor B A도 B도 아닌 |
| not A but B A가 아니라 B | not only A but also B (= B as well as A) A뿐만 아니라 B도 |

Either you or Fred is responsible for the injury. 너나 Fred 둘 중 한 명이 그 부상에 책임이 있다.
Neither Tom nor I am studying hard now. Tom도 나도 지금 열심히 공부하고 있지 않다.
Not cheese but cookies are what I want. 치즈가 아니라 쿠키들이 내가 원하는 것이다.
Not only you but also Sam was right. 너뿐만 아니라 Sam도 옳았다.

연습문제 괄호 안의 말을 활용하여 빈칸에 알맞은 말을 쓰시오. (단, 현재형으로 쓰시오.)

1 Three-quarters of the milk in the bottle _____ gone. (be)

2 Most of my friends _____ in the same neighborhood. (live)

3 Either Carl or you _____ to speak in front of the class. (need)

4 Most of the sculptures in the exhibit _____ beautiful. (be)

5 The bed as well as some chairs _____ today. (arrive)

6 Half of the kids in my class _____ to be famous one day. (want)

7 Not only my older sister but also I _____ to the hockey team. (belong)

8 Not a high-level of education but skills _____ required for this job. (be)

9 Neither Olivia nor the mechanics _____ to know what's wrong with the car. (seem)

10 Only about half of the gallery visitors _____ this painting. (like)

11 Some of the people in my yoga class _____ to try harder positions. (want)

1. **주절이 현재시제인 경우 종속절에는 의미에 따라 모든 시제를 쓸 수 있다.**

현재시제	I **think** that the advice **is** helpful.	나는 그 조언이 도움이 된다고 생각한다.
현재완료시제	I **think** that the advice **has been** helpful.	나는 그 조언이 도움이 돼왔다고 생각한다.
과거시제	I **think** that the advice **was** helpful.	나는 그 조언이 도움이 됐다고 생각한다.
미래시제	I **think** that the advice **will be** helpful.	나는 그 조언이 도움이 될 것이라고 생각한다.

2. **주절이 과거시제인 경우 종속절에는 의미에 따라 과거시제나 과거완료시제를 쓴다.**

| 과거시제 | She **heard** (that) I **was** at home. | 그녀는 내가 집에 있다고 들었다. |
| 과거완료시제 | She **heard** (that) I **had been** at home. | 그녀는 내가 집에 있었다고 들었다. |

(Tip) 주절이 과거시제인 경우 종속절의 조동사도 과거형(would, could, might 등)을 쓴다.
They **knew** that they (~~will~~, **would**) meet again. 그들은 그들이 다시 만날 것을 알았다.

3. **다음의 경우 예외적으로 주절의 시제와 상관없이 종속절에 현재시제나 과거시제 중 한 가지를 쓴다.**

❶ 항상 현재시제를 쓰는 경우: 현재의 습관, 일반적·과학적 사실, 속담·격언을 말할 때

현재의 습관	Mary **said** (that) she **exercises** every morning.
	Mary는 그녀가 매일 아침에 운동한다고 말했다.
일반적 사실	I **learned** (that) Paris **is** the capital of France.
	나는 파리가 프랑스의 수도라고 배웠다.
과학적 사실	The teacher **will explain** (that) water **boils** at 100℃ in the next class. 선생님은 다음 수업에서 물이 섭씨 100도에서 끓는다는 것을 설명할 것이다.
속담·격언	Martin **said** (that) time **heals** all wounds. Martin은 시간이 약이라고 말했다.

❷ 항상 과거시제를 쓰는 경우: 역사적 사실을 말할 때

She **knows** (that) Mozart **died** in 1791. 그녀는 모차르트가 1791년에 사망했다는 것을 안다.

연습문제 A 다음 문장을 과거시제로 바꿀 때 빈칸에 알맞은 말을 써서 문장을 완성하시오.

1 The letter says I need to reply within a month.
→ The letter said I _____ to reply within a month.

2 I know that we will do well on our science exam.
→ I knew that we _____ well on our science exam.

3 I am surprised that you didn't notice my new hairstyle.
→ I was surprised that you _____ my new hairstyle.

4 Susan says that she has finished reading the book.

→ Susan said that she _____ reading the book.

5 I believe that I lost my phone on the bus.

→ I believed that I _____ my phone on the bus.

6 Jack tells me that he can find a good place for us to have dinner.

→ Jack told me that he _____ a good place for us to have dinner.

7 I promise that I won't tell your secret to anybody.

→ I promised that I _____ your secret to anybody.

연습문제 B 우리말과 같도록 괄호 안의 동사를 활용하여 빈칸에 쓰시오.

1 수미는 나에게 그녀가 하루에 세 번 그녀의 강아지를 산책시킨다고 말했다. (walk)

= Sumi told me she _____ her dog three times a day.

2 과학자들은 화성에 물이 있다는 것을 발견했다. (be)

= Scientists discovered that there _____ water on Mars.

3 Joseph은 구르는 돌에는 이끼가 끼지 않는다고 말했다. (gather)

= Joseph said that a rolling stone _____ no moss.

4 나는 달팽이들이 3년 동안 잘 수 있다는 것을 알게 되었다. (be)

= I found out that snails _____ able to sleep for three years.

5 Claire는 그녀가 주말마다 오전 10시에 아침을 먹는다고 말했다. (eat)

= Claire said that she _____ breakfast at 10 A.M. on weekends.

6 우리는 2차 세계대전이 1945년에 끝났다는 것을 배웠다. (end)

= We learned that the Second World War _____ in 1945.

7 나의 할아버지는 나에게 시간은 돈이라고 말씀하시곤 했다. (be)

= My grandfather used to tell me that time _____ money.

8 선생님은 타이타닉호가 1912년에 침몰했다고 설명했다. (sink)

= The teacher explained that the Titanic _____ in 1912.

기출 적중문제

우리말과 같도록 괄호 안의 말을 활용하여 문장을 완성하시오.

> 그녀는 Tom이 아팠다는 것을 들었다. (hear, be)

= She _____ that Tom _____ sick.

> 주절이 과거시제인 경우 종속절에는 의미에 따라 과거시제나 과거완료 시제를 쓸 수 있어요.

평서문의 직접 화법은 다음과 같이 간접 화법으로 바꿀 수 있다.

직접 화법   He said, "I can go home now." 그는 "나는 지금 집에 갈 수 있어."라고 말했다.

간접 화법   He said (that) he could go home then. 그는 그가 그때 집에 갈 수 있다고 말했다.
            ①   ② ④   ③   ④

① 주절의 전달동사가 say인 경우 그대로 쓰고, say to인 경우 tell로 바꾼다.
② 콤마(,)와 큰따옴표(" ")를 없애고, 접속사 that으로 두 절을 연결한다. 이때 that은 생략할 수 있다.
③ 주절의 전달동사가 현재시제인 경우 종속절의 시제를 그대로 쓰고, 과거시제인 경우 종속절의 현재시제를 과거시제로, 과거시제·현재완료시제를 과거완료시제로, 조동사를 과거형으로 바꾼다.
④ 인칭대명사, 지시대명사, 부사(구)를 전달하는 사람의 입장에 맞게 바꾼다.

this/these → that/those	here → there
now → then	ago → before
next → the following	last → the previous
today → that day	tonight → that night
yesterday → the previous day[the day before]	
tomorrow → the next[following] day	

She **said**, "**I am going to** buy **this** TV." 그녀는 "나는 이 TV를 살 거야." 라고 말했다.
→ She **said (that) she was going to** buy **that** TV. 그녀는 그녀가 저 TV를 살 거라고 말했다.

He **said to** me, "**I met** Eric **today**." 그는 나에게 "나는 오늘 Eric을 만났어."라고 말했다.
→ He **told** me (**that**) **he had met** Eric **that day**. 그는 나에게 그가 그날 Eric을 만났었다고 말했다.

연습문제 | 간접 화법은 직접 화법으로, 직접 화법은 간접 화법으로 바꿔 쓰시오.

1 My mom said, "I don't want to leave the restaurant."
→ My mom _____ that _____.

2 He said, "I can go to the movies tonight."
→ He _____ that _____.

3 She said to me, "I enjoyed running along the Hangang last week."
→ She _____ me that _____.

4 Subin said that her friend had arrived in Korea the previous day.
→ Subin _____, _____

5 The ice skater told me that she had won a gold medal the previous year.
→ The ice skater _____ me, _____

기출로적중 POINT 3-2 화법 전환: 의문사가 있는 의문문

정답 p.54

의문사가 있는 의문문의 직접 화법은 다음과 같이 간접 화법으로 바꿀 수 있다.

직접 화법　She said to me, "Where is my book?" 그녀는 나에게 "나의 책은 어디에 있니?"라고 말했다.

↓

간접 화법　She asked me where her book was. 그녀는 나에게 그녀의 책이 어디에 있는지 물었다.
　　　　　　　①　　　②　　　　③

① 주절의 전달동사 say나 say to를 ask로 바꾼다.
② 콤마(,), 큰따옴표(" "), 물음표(?)를 없애고, 의문사로 두 절을 연결한다.
③ 종속절의 시제, 대명사, 부사(구)를 평서문의 화법 전환과 같은 방법으로 바꾸고, 「의문사 + 주어 + 동사」의 어순으로 쓴다. 이때 의문사가 주어인 경우 「의문사 + 동사」의 어순을 그대로 쓴다.

Jisu **said**, "**What did you learn yesterday?**" 지수는 "너는 어제 무엇을 배웠니?"라고 말했다.
→ Jisu **asked what I had learned the day before**.
지수는 내가 그 전날에 무엇을 배웠었는지 물었다.

Tim **said to** me, "**Who is performing today?**" Tim은 나에게 "누가 오늘 공연하니?"라고 말했다.
→ Tim **asked** me **who was performing that day**. Tim은 나에게 누가 그날 공연했는지 물었다.

연습문제　간접 화법은 직접 화법으로, 직접 화법은 간접 화법으로 바꿔 쓰시오.

1 My homeroom teacher said, "Where is James?"
　→ My homeroom teacher _____.

2 My uncle said to me, "Why aren't you home now?"
　→ My uncle _____ me _____.

3 He said to me, "What did Alex tell you last night?"
　→ He _____ me _____.

4 Dad said, "Who is calling at this time?"
　→ Dad _____.

5 The coach asked his players what was going on there.
　→ The coach _____ his players, _____

6 She asked when I was going to fix her bicycle.
　→ She _____, _____

7 She asked me how I had made those pancakes.
　→ She _____ me, _____

화법 전환: 의문사가 없는 의문문

정답 p.54

의문사가 없는 의문문의 직접 화법은 다음과 같이 간접 화법으로 바꿀 수 있다.

직접 화법   He said to me, "Are you working now?"   그는 나에게 "너는 지금 일하는 중이니?"라고 말했다.

간접 화법   He <u>asked</u> me <u>if[whether]</u> <u>I was working then</u>.   그는 나에게 그때 일하고 있었는지 물었다.
                      ①   ②   ③

> ① 주절의 전달동사 say나 say to를 ask로 바꾼다.
> ② 콤마(,), 큰따옴표(" "), 물음표(?)를 없애고, if나 whether로 두 절을 연결한다.
> ③ 종속절의 시제, 대명사, 부사(구)를 평서문의 화법 전환과 같은 방법으로 바꾸고, 「if[whether] + 주어 + 동사」의 어순으로 쓴다.

She **said to** me, "**Will you study tonight?**"   그녀는 나에게 "너는 오늘 밤에 공부할 거니?"라고 말했다.

→ She **asked** me **if[whether]** **I would study that night**.
     그녀는 나에게 그날 밤에 공부할 것인지 물었다.

Ben **said to** Lisa, "**Did you eat** pizza **yesterday?**"
Ben은 Lisa에게 "너는 어제 피자를 먹었니?"라고 말했다.

→ Ben **asked** Lisa **if[whether]** **she had eaten** pizza **the day before**.
     Ben는 Lisa에게 그녀가 그 전날 피자를 먹었는지 물었다.

연습문제   간접 화법은 직접 화법으로, 직접 화법은 간접 화법으로 바꿔 쓰시오.

1   He said to me, "Are you good at remembering new vocabulary?"

    → He _____ me _____.

2   Jane said to me, "Will you stay at home tomorrow?"

    → Jane _____ me _____.

3   Yujin said, "Did they watch the drama last night?"

    → Yujin _____.

4   Steve said to me, "Have you ever been to Paris?"

    → Steve _____ me _____.

5   She asked me if I could play any musical instruments.

    → She _____ me, _____

6   They asked me if there was a nice gym in that neighborhood.

    → They _____ me, _____

7   He asked me whether I knew how to use that stove.

    → He _____ me, _____

화법 전환: 명령문

정답 p.54

명령문의 직접 화법은 다음과 같이 간접 화법으로 바꿀 수 있다.

직접 화법   Mom said to me, "Take your umbrella."   엄마는 나에게 "너의 우산을 가져가라."라고 말했다.

↓

간접 화법   Mom <u>told</u> me <u>to take</u> <u>my umbrella</u>.   엄마는 나에게 나의 우산을 가져가라고 말했다.
                             ①   ②   ③

① 주절의 전달동사를 명령문의 어조에 맞게 바꾼다.

명령	부탁·요청	충고·제안
tell, order, instruct	ask, beg	advise, suggest

② 콤마(,)와 큰따옴표(" ")를 없애고, 명령문의 동사원형을 to부정사로 바꾼다. 이때 부정 명령문은 Don't/Never를 없애고 「not + to부정사」를 쓴다.

③ 명령문의 대명사, 부사(구)를 평서문의 화법 전환과 같은 방법으로 바꾼다.

He **said to** me, "Please **hold** my bag."   그는 나에게 "제 가방을 들어주세요."라고 말했다.

→ He **asked** me **to hold** his bag.   그는 나에게 그의 가방을 들어달라고 부탁했다.

The doctor **said** to me, "**Don't forget** to take your medicine."

그 의사는 나에게 "당신의 약을 복용하는 것을 잊지 마세요."라고 말했다.

→ The doctor **advised** me **not to forget** to take my medicine.

그 의사는 나에게 나의 약을 복용할 것을 잊지 말라고 충고했다.

연습문제 괄호 안의 말을 활용하여 간접 화법은 직접 화법으로, 직접 화법은 간접 화법으로 바꿔 쓰시오.

1 She said to us, "Hand in your essays by Thursday."

   → She _____ us _____. (tell)

2 He said to me, "Don't throw your garbage on the street."

   → He _____ me _____. (instruct)

3 My mother said to me, "Get me some garlic from the supermarket, please."

   → My mother _____ me _____. (ask)

4 He said to me, "Please help me finish my homework on time."

   → He _____ me _____. (beg)

5 The guard said to people, "Never go onto the railroad tracks."

   → The guard _____ people _____. (instruct)

6 The teacher said to me, "Try to study harder for this test."

   → The teacher _____ me _____. (advise)

서술형 대비 문제

Ⓐ 주어진 우리말과 의미가 같도록 괄호 안의 말을 활용하여 문장을 완성하시오.

1 많은 사람들이 버스 정류장에서 기다리고 있다. (number, people, be waiting)

= _____ at the bus stop.

2 세 시간은 이 숙제를 끝내기에 충분한 시간이다. (three hours, be enough time)

= _____ to finish this homework.

3 패스트푸드를 먹는 것은 너의 건강에 매우 안 좋다. (eating fast food, be really bad)

= _____ for your health.

4 범죄의 수가 올해 상당히 줄었다. (number, crimes, have fallen)

= _____ significantly this year.

5 8킬로미터는 내가 매일 일하러 이동하는 거리이다. (eight kilometers, be the distance)

= _____ I travel to work each day.

6 Dave도 나도 오늘 밤 그 콘서트에 참석하지 않을 것이다. (neither, be attending)

= _____ the concert tonight.

7 고객들 중 절반이 가격 변동에 대해서 불만족스러워한다. (half, the customer, be unhappy)

= _____ about the price change.

Ⓑ 밑줄 친 부분이 어법상 맞으면 O를 쓰고, 틀리면 바르게 고쳐 쓰시오.

1 Amy knew that Max <u>was</u> older than her. → _____

2 The teacher said that water <u>was</u> made up of hydrogen and oxygen. → _____

3 He thought that his older brother <u>had taken</u> his bike. → _____

4 Dr. Lee believed that people <u>will live</u> up to 150 years someday. → _____

5 Jihyun claimed that I <u>had copied</u> her answers on the English exam. → _____

6 I thought that Sharon <u>is meeting</u> someone at the train station. → _____

7 I know that Willis Carrier <u>had invented</u> the air conditioner in 1902. → _____

8 She told me that she always <u>drinks</u> tea after lunch. → _____

9 My grandmother told me that good medicine <u>tasted</u> bitter. → _____

10 My customer said that he <u>would come</u> back to the store before 9 P.M. → _____

C 다음 문장을 간접 화법으로 바꿀 때 빈칸에 알맞은 말을 써서 문장을 완성하시오.

1 He said, "I am planning a trip to Europe next year."

→ He said _____.

2 Lena said to me, "When am I going to meet your friends?"

→ Lena asked me _____.

3 She said, "I took this writing class last year."

→ She said _____.

4 He said, "Can I borrow a pair of scissors?"

→ He asked _____.

5 The trainer said to him, "Stop throwing balls around the room."

→ The trainer ordered him _____.

6 I said, "Who left these eggs outside of the fridge?"

→ I asked _____.

7 Ann said to him, "Have you started your project for geography class yet?"

→ Ann asked him _____.

8 The building manager said to us, "Never leave your garbage outside your front door."

→ The building manager told us _____.

D 다음은 체스 동아리의 회의 기록이다. 학생들이 한 말을 직접 화법으로 바꿀 때 빈칸에 알맞은 말을 써서 문장을 완성하시오.

We discussed who should participate in the upcoming chess championship. (A) Kevin said that he wanted to participate in the championship. He was considered the best player in our club, so everyone seemed to agree. Suddenly, (B) Judy asked why she was not being considered. She thought she was clearly the best. Finally, (C) the president of the club told them to play a game between themselves to decide.

(A) Kevin said, _____

(B) Judy said, _____

(C) The president of the club said to them, _____

[1-2] 다음 빈칸에 들어갈 알맞은 말을 고르시오.

1

> The number of _____ 3,000.

① attendee at the concert is
② attendee at the concert are
③ attendees at the concert is
④ attendees at the concert are
⑤ attendees at the concert were

2

> Not only the table but also the chairs
> _____ damaged by the water
> yesterday.

① be   ② is   ③ are
④ was   ⑤ were

3 다음 빈칸에 들어갈 be동사를 알맞은 형태로 쓰시오.
(단, 현재형으로 쓰시오.)

> · Understanding different cultures
> ⓐ_____ difficult, but we need to
> have an open mind.
> · Both chopsticks and a spoon
> ⓑ_____ basic utensils in South
> Korea.

ⓐ: _____   ⓑ: _____

4 아래 대화의 밑줄 친 우리말을 영어로 바르게 옮긴 것은?

> *Jiwoo*: I had to walk all the way home
> because I forgot to bring my bus
> card.
> *Paula*: Oh, how far did you have to
> walk?
> *Jiwoo*: About five kilometers.
> *Paula*: Wow. 5킬로미터는 걷기에 먼 거리인데!

① Five kilometers are a long distance to
walk!
② Five kilometers is a long distance to walk!
③ Five kilometers were a long distance to
walk!
④ Five kilometers have been a long
distance to walk!
⑤ Five kilometers were being a long
distance to walk!

5 다음 문장을 직접 화법으로 바르게 바꾼 것은?

> She asked when I was coming home
> from soccer practice.

① She said, "When I am coming home from
soccer practice?"
② She said, "When are you coming home
from soccer practice?"
③ She said, "When am I coming home from
soccer practice?"
④ She said to me, "When were you coming
home from soccer practice?"
⑤ She said to me, "When you are coming
home from soccer practice?"

6 다음 중 어법상 바른 것은?

① Each item of clothing in this store have a different design.
② Physics are the subject which I find the most difficult.
③ A number of dessert options were provided for the banquet.
④ Swimming on weekends make me feel like a healthier person.
⑤ Twenty years are enough time to master a language.

7 다음 (A)~(C)에 들어갈 말이 바르게 짝지어진 것은?

- Politics ___(A)___ too complicated for me to understand.
- Catching whales ___(B)___ been banned by most countries.
- A number of motorcycles ___(C)___ parked illegally on the street.

	(A)	(B)	(C)
①	is	has	is
②	is	have	are
③	is	has	are
④	are	has	are
⑤	are	have	is

8 다음 중 어법상 바른 것끼리 묶인 것은?

ⓐ The number of car accidents goes up in the rainy season.
ⓑ Neither Irene nor her friends are able to join our club meeting today.
ⓒ Both animals and plants needs oxygen to survive.
ⓓ Eight dollars are a lot for a cup of coffee.
ⓔ Most of the buildings in the area are taller than ten stories.

① ⓐ, ⓑ, ⓒ   ② ⓐ, ⓑ, ⓔ   ③ ⓐ, ⓒ, ⓔ
④ ⓑ, ⓒ, ⓓ   ⑤ ⓑ, ⓓ, ⓔ

9 다음 빈칸에 들어갈 수 <u>없는</u> 것은?

He said that _____.

① Lucy was a responsible and kind person
② he had tried to learn Spanish before
③ there was nowhere to put the new sofa
④ he can pass the exam with an excellent score
⑤ I needed to read the e-mail from the principal

10 다음 문장에서 <u>어색한</u> 부분을 찾아 쓰고 바르게 고쳐 쓰시오.

Every car are supposed to have a license plate.

_____ → _____

11 다음 우리말을 알맞게 영작한 것은?

> 미나는 나에게 그녀가 북아메리카를 여행하고 있었다고 말했다.

① Mina tells me that she had been traveling in North America.
② Mina told me that she had been traveling in North America.
③ Mina tells me that she has been traveling in North America.
④ Mina told me that she has been traveling in North America.
⑤ Mina told me that she is traveling in North America.

[12-13] 다음 대화를 읽고 문장을 완성하시오.

12

> *Hana*: What did you do last night?
> *Paul* : I went to a baseball game with Woojin.

→ Hana asked Paul _____
_____. Paul told Hana _____
_____.

13

> *Mary*: Is there anything I can get for you?
> *Peter*: Please get me a cup of tea.

→ Mary asked Peter _____
_____. Peter asked Mary _____.

[14-15] 다음 문장을 과거시제로 바꿀 때 빈칸에 알맞은 말을 써서 문장을 완성하시오.

14

> I hear that Stella has gotten a new dress.
> → I heard that Stella _____ a new dress.

15

> I think that I can register online for this class.
> → I thought that I _____ online for this class.

16 다음 (A)~(C)에 들어갈 말이 바르게 짝지어진 것은?

> · The students learned that planets __(A)__ round because of gravity.
> · Tim told me he usually __(B)__ to school by bus.
> · My grandfather said that the Joseon dynasty __(C)__ in 1392.

	(A)	(B)	(C)
①	were	goes	had been founded
②	are	has gone	was founded
③	were	went	has been founded
④	are	goes	was founded
⑤	were	went	had been founded

17 다음 문장을 간접 화법으로 바꿀 때 빈칸에 들어갈 알맞은 것은?

He said to me, "I will repair the bike tonight."
→ He _____ me that he would repair the bike that night.

① says　　② said　　③ tells
④ told　　⑤ has told

18 다음 문장을 직접 화법으로 바꿀 때 빈칸에 알맞은 말을 써서 문장을 완성하시오.

Daeun said that she wouldn't be at the park the next day.
→ Daeun _____, "I _____ be at the park _____."

19 다음 문장을 간접 화법으로 바꿔 쓰시오.

My friend said, "Who brought a camera?"

→ _____

_____

20 다음 직접 화법을 간접 화법으로 바꾼 문장에서 어법상 어색한 부분을 찾아 쓰고 바르게 고쳐 쓰시오.

Ms. Kim said, "I saw a strange man coming out of the bank at 1 o'clock."
→ Ms. Kim said that she has seen a strange man coming out of the bank at 1 o'clock.

_____ → _____

21 빈칸에 들어갈 말을 모두 고르시오.

The tourist said, "Is the bathroom in the station?"
→ The tourist asked _____ the bathroom was in the station.

① whether　　② if　　③ when
④ that　　⑤ who

22 다음 문장을 직접 화법으로 바꿀 때 빈칸에 알맞은 말을 써서 문장을 완성하시오.

The shop owner told us that they had been closed the previous week.
→ The shop owner _____ us, "We _____ closed _____."

23 다음 중 어법상 어색한 것은?

① My mother said that practice made perfect.
② Jim thinks that his study plan will be successful.
③ He said that he gets his hair cut once a month.
④ The coach told me that I was the best player on the football team.
⑤ She believed that he had already completed all the assignments.

24 다음 문장을 간접 화법으로 바르게 바꾼 것은?

> Mike said to me, "I need a better computer to play this game."

① Mike told me I need a better computer to play this game.
② Mike told me I needed a better computer to play that game.
③ Mike said me that he needs a better computer to play this game.
④ Mike said me that he needed a better computer to play this game.
⑤ Mike told me he needed a better computer to play that game.

25 다음 중 간접 화법을 직접 화법으로 바르게 바꾼 것은?

① She told me that she knew a place we could go on the weekend.
   → She said to me, "She knows a place we can go on the weekend."
② He said he wanted to eat a pizza for dinner.
   → He said, "I wanted to eat a pizza for dinner."
③ He told us he had to prepare for his presentation then.
   → He said to us, "I have to prepare for my presentation now."
④ My teacher told me that I hadn't finished all of my homework.
   → My teacher said to me, "You didn't finish all of my homework."
⑤ She said that she had bought those pants the day before.
   → She said, "I bought these pants the following day.

26 다음 대화의 빈칸에 들어갈 말이 순서대로 짝지어진 것은?

> A: Do you want to see the new zombie movie on Friday?
> B: I thought you said you _____ no time on Friday.
> A: Well, my mom told me that I _____ to finish my homework, but I got it done early.
> B: Perfect! Let's go on Friday, then.

① had – need
② had – would need
③ had – will need
④ have – would need
⑤ have – will need

27 다음 문장을 간접 화법으로 바꿔 쓰시오.

> Susie said to me, "You arrived really late today."
> → _____
> _____

28 다음 직접 화법을 간접 화법으로 바꾼 문장에서 틀린 부분을 바르게 고쳐 완전한 문장을 쓰시오.

> My cousin said to me, "Don't change the channel on the TV."
> → My cousin told me to change the channel on the TV.

→ _____
_____

29 다음 직접 화법을 괄호 안의 말을 활용하여 간접 화법으로 바꿔 쓰시오.

> The police officer said to the thieves, "Raise your hands in the air."
>
> → _____
>
>   _____
>
> (order)

30 다음 중 직접 화법을 간접 화법으로 잘못 바꾼 것의 개수는?

> ⓐ I said to the driver, "Please turn the air conditioner on."
>   → I asked the driver to turn the air conditioner on.
> ⓑ My father said to me, "Call your brother, and tell him to buy some milk."
>   → My father ordered me call my brother, and tell him to buy some milk.
> ⓒ The actress said, "I'll be back tomorrow."
>   → The actress said that she would be back the following day.
> ⓓ The guide said to us, "Do you know the history of this building?"
>   → The guide asked us whether did we know the history of that building.
> ⓔ John said to me, "What time did your plane take off?"
>   → John asked me what time your plane had taken off.

① 1개 ② 2개 ③ 3개
④ 4개 ⑤ 5개

31 다음 중 직접 화법을 간접 화법으로 잘못 바꾼 것은?

① Tina said, "I want to thank everyone for coming."
  → Tina said she wanted to thank everyone for coming.
② They said to me, "Are you done with your food?"
  → They asked me I was done with my food.
③ He said, "You were so nice to my older brother at yesterday's graduation ceremony."
  → He said that I had been so nice to his older brother at the previous day's graduation ceremony.
④ She said to me, "When are you going to buy these earphones?"
  → She asked me when I was going to buy those earphones.
⑤ Minho said, "Where can we meet tomorrow?"
  → Minho asked where we could meet the next day.

32 다음 중 어법상 어색한 것은?

① He asked whether that was my book on the table.
② Lily told me that she was watering those flowers in the garden.
③ My little sister asked me what my favorite ice cream flavor was.
④ She told me don't cross the road when the light was red.
⑤ The teacher said that I should think carefully before answering the question.

CHAPTER 16
특수구문

I met James at the gym yesterday. 나는 어제 체육관에서 James를 만났다.
→ I **did meet** James at the gym yesterday. 나는 어제 체육관에서 James를 정말 만났다.
→ It was **James** that I met at the gym yesterday. 내가 어제 체육관에서 만난 사람은 바로 James였다.

두 번째 문장은 첫 번째 문장의 동사 met을 강조하고 있고, 세 번째 문장은 첫 번째 문장의 목적어 James를 강조하고 있어요. 이렇게 문장 요소 중 하나를 두드러지게 보이게 하는 **강조 구문**을 비롯하여, 문장 전체나 일부를 부정하는 **부정 구문**, 강조하려는 어구를 문장 맨 앞에 두고 주어와 동사의 순서를 바꾸는 **도치 구문**, 반복되는 어구 등을 생략하는 **생략 구문**, 문장 요소에 부연 설명을 덧붙이는 **동격 구문**, 같은 품사나 구조를 연결하는 **병치 구문** 등을 모두 일컬어 **특수구문**이라고 해요.

기출로 적중 POINT

내신 100점 적중!
기출 출제율

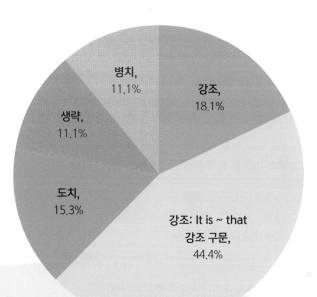

병치,
11.1%

강조,
18.1%

생략,
11.1%

도치,
15.3%

강조: It is ~ that
강조 구문,
44.4%

TOP 1 **강조: It is ~ that 강조 구문 (44.4%)**
「It is ~ that」 강조 구문을 활용하여 영작하는 문제가 자주 출제된다.

TOP 2 **강조 (18.1%)**
do를 활용하여 동사를 강조하는 법을 묻는 문제가 자주 출제된다.

TOP 3 **도치 (15.3%)**
장소를 나타내는 부사구를 강조하여 도치시켜 영작하는 문제가 자주 출제된다.

1. **일반동사를 강조할 때는 동사원형 앞에 do/does/did를 쓴다.**

   I **do want** to go home. 나는 집에 정말 가고 싶다.

   He **does like** snacks. 그는 과자를 정말 좋아한다.

   She **did look** beautiful yesterday. 어제 그녀는 정말 아름다워 보였다.

2. **비교급을 강조할 때는 비교급 앞에 much, even, still, far, a lot을 쓴다.**

   The weather today is **much better** than yesterday. 오늘 날씨는 어제보다 훨씬 더 좋다.

   Your bed is **even more** comfortable than mine. 너의 침대는 나의 것보다 훨씬 더 편안하다.

3. **명사를 강조할 때는 명사 앞에 the very를 쓴다.**

   This is **the very book** I read two days ago. 이것은 내가 이틀 전에 읽은 바로 그 책이다.

   Climate change threatens **the very survival** of humans.
   기후 변화는 인간의 생존 그 자체를 위협한다.

연습문제 <보기>의 말을 활용하여 밑줄 친 부분을 강조하는 문장을 완성하시오.

<보기> the very   do   a lot   does   did

1 These days, we are <u>busier</u> than ever before.

→ These days, we are _____ than ever before.

2 This is <u>the place</u> where the accident happened last month.

→ This is _____ where the accident happened last month.

3 We <u>appreciate</u> the favor you did for us.

→ We _____ the favor you did for us.

4 He <u>went</u> rock climbing with his friends three years ago.

→ He _____ rock climbing with his friends three years ago.

 기출 적중문제 ◎

do를 활용하여 밑줄 친 부분을 강조하는 문장을 쓰시오.

I <u>turned</u> in my homework on time.

→ _____

> 일반동사를 강조할 때는
> 동사의 시제나 주어의 인칭과
> 수에 따라 동사원형 앞에
> do/does/did를 써요.

강조: It is ~ that 강조 구문

정답 p.57

1. 「It is ~ that …」 강조 구문은 '…한 것은 바로 ~이다'의 의미로, 동사를 제외한 모든 문장 요소를 It is와 that 사이에 써서 강조할 수 있다. 이때 강조되는 말을 제외한 나머지 부분은 that 뒤에 쓴다.

I drink tea at noon. 나는 정오에 차를 마신다.
주어　목적어　부사구

주어 강조　　**It is I that** drink tea at noon. 정오에 차를 마시는 것은 바로 나다.
　　　　　　└→ 기존 문장의 시제에 일치시킨다.

목적어 강조　**It is tea that** I drink at noon. 내가 정오에 마시는 것은 바로 차다.

부사구 강조　**It is at noon that** I drink tea. 내가 차를 마시는 때는 바로 정오이다.

2. 강조하는 대상에 따라 that 대신 who/whom/which/where/when을 쓸 수 있다.

사람	who, whom	It was **he who** saw Lisa. Lisa를 본 사람은 바로 그였다. It was **Lisa whom[who]** he saw. 그가 본 사람은 바로 Lisa였다. 　　　　　　└→ 강조되는 말이 목적어인 경우 whom을 쓸 수 있다.
사물, 동물	which	It was **my cat which** scratched my face. 내 얼굴을 할퀸 것은 바로 나의 고양이였다.
장소	where	It was **in the park where** I took a walk. 내가 산책한 곳은 바로 공원 안이었다.
시간	when	It is **next Friday when** she is going to leave for Paris. 그녀가 파리로 떠날 예정인 날은 바로 다음 주 금요일이다.

연습문제 A 다음 문장을 괄호 안의 지시에 맞게 「It is ~ that …」 강조 구문으로 바꿔 쓰시오.

Amy bought the blue suit at this store last year.

1 (주어 강조)　　　It was ＿＿＿＿＿＿＿＿＿＿ that bought the blue suit at this store last year.

2 (목적어 강조)　　It was ＿＿＿＿＿＿＿＿＿＿ that Amy bought at this store last year.

3 (장소 부사구 강조)　It was ＿＿＿＿＿＿＿＿＿＿ that Amy bought the blue suit last year.

4 (시간 부사구 강조)　It was ＿＿＿＿＿＿＿＿＿＿ that Amy bought the blue suit at this store.

> My little brother ate a bagel at the café this morning.

5 (주어 강조)   It was _____ that ate a bagel at the café this morning.

6 (목적어 강조)   It was _____ that my little brother ate at the café this morning.

7 (장소 부사구 강조)   It was _____ that my little brother ate a bagel this morning.

8 (시간 부사구 강조)   It was _____ that my little brother ate a bagel at the café.

연습문제 B 괄호 안에서 알맞은 것을 고르시오.

1 It is at the fountain (when / where) the city tour begins.

2 It was in 1443 (which / when) King Sejong invented Hangeul.

3 It is the textbook (whom / which) makes my bag so heavy.

4 It was Johnny (who / which) won the Student of the Year Award.

5 It is tomorrow (where / when) we have our exams.

6 It was I (who / which) organized the graduation ceremony.

연습문제 C 다음 문장을 밑줄 친 부분을 강조하는 「It is ~ that …」 강조 구문으로 바꿔 쓰시오.

1 <u>Maggie</u> takes excellent photographs.

→ _____

2 I saw <u>my teacher</u> in the subway station.

→ _____

3 I promised to take my cousins <u>to the amusement park</u>.

→ _____

4 She found her scarf <u>behind the sofa</u>.

→ _____

5 Steve Jobs introduced the iPhone <u>in 2007</u>.

→ _____

🎯 **기출 적중문제**

우리말과 같도록 「It is ~ that …」 강조 구문과 괄호 안의 말을 활용하여 영작하시오.

> 내가 나의 여권을 잃어버린 것은 바로 그 공항 안에서였다. (in the airport, lose, my passport)

= _____

1. **Never/no/none/nothing/nobody/neither**는 '아무것도[아무도, 누구도] ~가 아니다'라는 의미로, 문장 전체를 부정할 때 쓴다.

   There will **never** be tickets to Hawaii available in July.
   7월에는 구할 수 있는 하와이행 티켓이 아무것도 없을 것이다.

   None of the stores had the shirt I wanted.
   그 가게들 중 아무 곳도 내가 원하는 셔츠를 가지고 있지 않았다.

2. 「**not + always/all/every/both**」는 '항상[모두, 둘 다] ~인 것은 아니다'라는 의미로, 문장 일부를 부정할 때 쓴다.

   We do **not always** make the best decisions. 우리가 항상 최상의 결정을 내리는 것은 아니다.
   Not every runner finishes the marathon. 모든 주자들이 마라톤을 완주하는 것은 아니다.

연습문제 │ 두 문장의 의미가 같도록 괄호 안에서 알맞은 것을 고르시오.

1 All of the computers in the lab are broken.

   = (None / Not all) of the computers in the lab are working.

2 Every seat is reserved for registered members.

   = There are (some / no) seats available for the guests.

3 A few of the paintings were sold at auction.

   = (Not all / None) of the paintings were sold at auction.

4 Some apples have not fallen from the tree.

   = (Every / Not every) apple has fallen from the tree.

5 Both of Jamie's parents are away from home.

   = (Neither / Not all) of Jamie's parents is at home.

6 Some people agreed with the new policy, but others were against it.

   = (Not every / Every) person agreed with the new policy.

7 Traveling is sometimes fun and relaxing, but sometimes it's not.

   = Traveling is (not always / neither) fun and relaxing.

8 Some of the paths lead to the top of the mountain, but others don't.

   = (Not all / None) of the paths lead to the top of the mountain.

9 There are two restaurants nearby, but only one is open.

   = There are two restaurants nearby, but (not both / neither) are open.

POINT 3 도치

부사(구)를 문장 맨 앞에 두고 문장의 주어와 동사의 순서를 서로 바꾸어 부사(구)의 의미를 강조할 수 있으며, 이와 같이 문장 안에서 어순이 바뀌는 것을 도치라고 한다.

❶ 방향/장소를 나타내는 부사(구)가 강조되어 문장 맨 앞으로 올 때: 「부사(구) + 동사 + 주어 ~」

The ball flew over the fence. 그 공이 울타리 너머로 날아갔다.

= Over the fence **flew the ball**. 울타리 너머로 그 공이 날아갔다.

Some rules you should follow are here. 네가 따라야 하는 몇 가지 규칙들이 여기에 있다.

= Here **are** some rules you should follow. 여기에 네가 따라야 하는 몇 가지 규칙들이 있다.

(Tip) 주어가 대명사일 때는 부사(구)나 there/here가 문장 맨 앞에 와도 주어와 동사가 도치되지 않는다.
Onto the roof it went. 지붕 위로 그것이 갔다.
There it sank in the ocean. 거기에서 그것이 바닷속으로 가라앉았다.

❷ 부정의 의미를 가진 부사(구)(never, hardly, seldom, rarely, not only 등)가 강조되어 문장 맨 앞으로 올 때: 「부사(구) + 조동사 + 주어 + 동사 ~」

I never **thought** of it.
= Never **did I think** of it. 나는 그것에 대해 생각해 본 적이 없다.

❸ '~도 그렇다/아니다'의 의미로 so/neither를 사용할 때: 「so/neither + 동사 + 주어 ~」

She is really exhausted today, and **so am I**. 그녀는 오늘 정말 지쳤고, 나도 그렇다.
He didn't agree with the plan, and **neither did I**.
그는 그 계획에 동의하지 않았고, 나도 그렇지 않았다.

[연습문제] 두 문장의 의미가 같도록 문장을 완성하시오.

1 He rarely played baseball in school.

= Rarely _____ baseball in school.

2 The keys you were looking for are there.

= There _____ you were looking for.

3 I'm fond of surfing in the ocean. – I'm fond of surfing in the ocean, too.

= I'm fond of surfing in the ocean. – So _____.

4 She is here with the daily newspaper.

= Here _____ with the daily newspaper.

5 I couldn't hear the thunder, and Roy couldn't hear the thunder, either.

= I couldn't hear the thunder, and neither _____.

POINT 4 생략

정답 p.57

1. **문장 내에서 반복되는 어구는 생략할 수 있다.**

   Jinsu took a shower and **(Jinsu)** dried his hair.   진수는 샤워를 하고 나서 그의 머리를 말렸다.

   You can take the test later if you want to **(take the test later)**.
   네가 원한다면 너는 그 시험을 나중에 치를 수 있다.

2. **부사절의 주어가 주절의 주어와 같을 때, 부사절의 「주어 + be동사」는 생략할 수 있다.**

   I met Sarah when **(I was)** in New York.   나는 뉴욕에 있을 때 Sarah를 만났다.

   Though **(it is)** old, the radio still works.   비록 낡았지만, 그 라디오는 여전히 작동한다.

3. **「주격 관계대명사 + be동사 + 분사」인 경우 「주격 관계대명사 + be동사」는 생략할 수 있다.**

   I bought a book **(that was)** written in English.   나는 영어로 쓰인 책을 샀다.

4. **목적격 관계대명사 who(m), which, that은 생략할 수 있다. 단, 「전치사 + 목적격 관계대명사」 형태인 경우에는 생략할 수 없다.**

   The repairperson **(whom)** he called is waiting.   그가 부른 수리공이 기다리고 있다.

   This was the event **for which** I prepared.   이것은 내가 준비했던 행사였다.

연습문제 | 다음 문장에서 생략할 수 있는 부분에 밑줄을 치시오.

1 I saw an old friend while I was at the museum.

2 The crowd yelled at the player who was sent off the field.

3 This belt is a lot cheaper than it was before the sale.

4 Don't turn on the air conditioner until I tell you to turn on the air conditioner.

5 Napoleon Bonaparte was born in 1769 and Napoleon Bonaparte died in 1821.

6 Josh won't swim in the lake, but I will swim in the lake.

7 Unless you are a member, you aren't allowed to use the gym.

8 The end of the movie was exciting though it was predictable.

9 This is the very painting that I like the most.

10 The man whom I introduced to you is my teacher.

11 She usually doesn't answer text messages if she is busy.

12 We saw some beautiful waterfalls when we were traveling in New Zealand.

문장의 주어·목적어·보어 뒤에 콤마(,), of, that을 써서 부연 설명을 덧붙일 수 있으며, 이를 동격이라고 한다.

「명사 + 콤마(,) + 명사」	**My friend**, **Betty**, will visit Seoul this month. 나의 친구인 Betty가 이번 달에 서울을 방문할 것이다. His favorite writer is **Emily Dickinson, the American author**. 그가 가장 좋아하는 작가는 미국 작가인 Emily Dickinson이다.
「명사 + of + 동명사구」	**The hope of recovering from illness** motivated her. 병에서 회복한다는 희망이 그녀에게 동기를 부여했다. The children love **the plan of going camping next week**. 아이들은 다음 주에 캠핑 가는 계획을 좋아한다.
「명사 + that절」	**The news that the king was sick** worried everyone. 왕이 아프다는 소식은 모두를 걱정시켰다. It was hard to accept **the fact that we lost the match**. 우리가 그 경기에서 졌다는 사실을 받아들이는 것은 힘들었다. (Tip) that 앞에는 news, fact, rumor, idea, thought, promise, hope, announcement, advice와 같은 명사가 주로 온다.

연습문제 | 다음 밑줄 친 부분과 동격인 부분에 밑줄을 치시오.

1 The thought of performing before an audience makes me nervous.

2 Beethoven, the German composer, started losing his hearing in his 20s.

3 Many students supported the idea that Sujin should be the class president.

4 Did you hear the announcement that the train has been delayed?

5 Not wearing proper gear increases the risk of getting injured.

6 Derek Lee, the actor, will appear in the new movie.

7 The thief couldn't sleep because his fear of getting caught was too great.

8 I appreciated your advice that I should go back to university.

9 Her dream of moving to Canada seems unlikely.

10 Mr. Lewis, my history teacher in middle school, was really good at cooking.

11 The rumor that he won the lottery made me jealous.

12 He made a promise that he would help Mary do her homework.

POINT 6 병치

정답 p.57

접속사로 연결된 말은 같은 품사나 구조로 연결해야 하며, 이를 병치라고 한다.

❶ 같은 품사(동사 – 동사, 형용사 – 형용사 등)끼리의 병치

He **lives** in the suburbs **but works** downtown. 그는 교외에 살지만 시내에서 일한다.
　　동사　　　　　　　　　　동사

She is **smart and kind**. 그녀는 똑똑하고 친절하다.
　　　　형용사　　형용사

❷ 같은 구조(동명사구 – 동명사구, 전치사구 – 전치사구 등)끼리의 병치

I enjoy **swimming** and **cycling** on weekends. 나는 주말마다 수영과 자전거 타기를 즐긴다.
　　　　동명사구　　　　동명사구

Class will start **either at noon or at 6 o'clock**. 수업은 정오 또는 6시에 시작할 것이다.
　　　　　　　　　　　전치사구　　　　전치사구

CHAPTER 16 특수구문　해커스 중학영문법 3학년

연습문제 괄호 안에서 알맞은 것을 고르시오.

1　I'm not really into hunting or (fishing / to fish).

2　The weather here is not only extremely cold but also (windy / wind).

3　During the discussion, he got angry and (walks / walked) out of the classroom.

4　We thought the speech was both inspiring and (interested / interesting).

5　Why don't you come and (see / saw) my brand new computer?

6　My grandmother likes to plant flowers and (decorating / to decorate) her garden.

7　Namho likes neither singing nor (listen / listening) to music.

8　The man is tall, (energy / energetic), and charismatic.

9　Please speak slowly and (clear / clearly) so that everyone can understand.

10　I believe that books should be either (helpful / help) or amusing.

11　We decided to stay home and (ordering / to order) pizza instead of going out.

기출 적중문제

다음 문장에서 어법상 어색한 부분을 찾아 쓰고 바르게 고쳐 쓰시오.

Mom took the laundry out of the washing machine and puts it in the dryer a while ago.

_____ → _____

접속사로 연결된 말은 같은 품사나 구조로 연결해야 해요.

Chapter 16 특수구문　**399**

서술형 대비 문제

(A) 다음 문장을 괄호 안의 지시대로 바꿔 쓰시오.

1 Jinho met Suji on the street yesterday.
→ It _____. (Jinho 강조)
→ Jinho _____. (met 강조)
→ It _____. (on the street 강조)

2 I want to have a hamburger for dinner tonight.
→ I _____. (want 강조)
→ It _____. (a hamburger 강조)
→ It _____. (I 강조)

3 Her watch is more expensive than the ring.
→ Her watch _____. (more expensive 강조)
→ It _____. (her watch강조)
→ It _____. (the ring 강조)

4 A storm destroyed the building in my hometown.
→ It _____. (in my hometown 강조)
→ A storm _____. (destroy 강조)
→ It _____. (a storm 강조)

(B) 다음 문장을 주어진 지시대로 바꿔 쓰시오.

1 All of the windows in the classroom are open. (none을 활용한 문장으로)
→ _____ in the classroom are closed.

2 The keys for the school gym are here. (here를 맨 앞으로)
→ _____ for the school gym.

3 Jane hardly expected to get the top score on the test. (hardly를 맨 앞으로)
→ _____ the top score on the test.

4 Some of the rooms in the hotel have beach views. (not all을 활용한 문장으로)
→ _____ in the hotel have beach views.

5 The house I grew up in is there. (there를 맨 앞으로)
→ _____ I grew up in.

6 She walked onto the stage to receive her award. (onto를 맨 앞으로)
→ _____ to receive her award.

ⓒ 다음 문장에서 생략된 부분을 넣어 완전한 문장을 쓰시오.

1 Unless invited by the host, you can't enter the venue.

→ _____

2 Send me the photos if you can.

→ _____

3 The book I fell in love with is going to be made into a movie.

→ _____

4 You may use my brush whenever you would like to.

→ _____

5 The children found some old coins while digging in the dirt.

→ _____

6 Though disappointed by the movie, we watched it until the end.

→ _____

7 The shoes I purchased were not very expensive.

→ _____

8 You can paint the walls whatever color you want to.

→ _____

9 Mike listened to the teacher and took some notes.

→ _____

ⓓ 다음은 민수가 자신이 가장 좋아하는 겨울 스포츠에 대해 쓴 글이다. 괄호 안의 말을 활용하여 문장을 완성하시오.

Every year, my family drives to Colorado or ⓐ_____(fly) to Canada to spend a week doing winter sports. We all love ⓑ_____(ski) and skating. However, my favorite is snowboarding. There's nothing I like more than hitting the slopes on a snowboard. When we are on vacation, I snowboard down the mountainside quickly and ⓒ_____(happy). I always head to the hills in the early morning or ⓓ_____(the afternoon) at the latest, and I don't come back to the lodge until dark.

중간·기말고사 실전 문제

1 다음 밑줄 친 부분이 어법상 어색한 것은?

① He <u>does know</u> the secret about me.
② <u>Do be</u> careful. The road is slippery.
③ She <u>does look</u> serious about her dream.
④ We <u>do sell</u> many of our products overseas.
⑤ The tires of your bicycle <u>did needed</u> to be changed.

2 우리말과 같도록 괄호 안의 말을 활용하여 문장을 완성하시오.

> 모두 산에 가는 것을 너만큼 즐기는 것은 아니다.
> (going, everybody, to, the mountain, enjoy)

= _____
as much as you do.

3 다음 중 밑줄 친 do의 쓰임이 같은 것끼리 묶인 것은?

> ⓐ Debra and Brian <u>do</u> hang out with me everyday.
> ⓑ They'll <u>do</u> their laundry after dinner.
> ⓒ You never forget anything, <u>do</u> you?
> ⓓ We <u>do</u> need to hurry to the airport.
> ⓔ What did you <u>do</u> with my computer?
> ⓕ I <u>do</u> want to help you and him if I can.

① ⓐ, ⓑ   ② ⓐ, ⓓ, ⓕ   ③ ⓐ, ⓒ, ⓓ
④ ⓑ, ⓔ, ⓕ   ⑤ ⓒ, ⓔ, ⓕ

4 괄호 안의 말을 활용하여 밑줄 친 부분을 강조하는 문장으로 바꿔 쓰시오.

> I lost <u>my umbrella</u> on the subway yesterday. (it, be, that)
> → _____
> _____

5 다음 빈칸에 들어갈 말로 어색한 것은?

> · My older brother Thomas is _____ taller than I am.
> · Judy is feeling _____ better this morning than last night.
> · The sun sets _____ earlier in the winter than in the summer.

① far   ② very   ③ much
④ even   ⑤ a lot

6 다음 중 「It is ~ that …」 강조 구문이 **아닌** 것은?

① It is my uncle who is coming to visit us next month.
② It was the store downtown that he purchased his piano from.
③ It was on Monday that Joseph caught a bad cold.
④ It was uncertain that Stella got back home from school right away.
⑤ It is global warming that threatens small islands.

7 다음 우리말을 영작한 것 중 어색한 것은?

① 내가 지난주 토요일에 나의 남동생을 데려간 곳은 바로 그 수족관이었다.
= It was to the aquarium that I took my little brother last Saturday.

② Lucy가 최근에 흥미 있는 것은 바로 춤추기이다.
= It is dancing that Lucy is interested in lately.

③ Tony가 그녀와 이야기했던 곳은 바로 그 공원이었다.
= It was at the park who Tony talked with her.

④ 나를 긴장하게 만든 것은 바로 너의 메시지였다.
= It was your message which made me nervous.

⑤ 그가 2년 전에 설계한 것은 바로 그 건물이었다.
= It was the building that he designed two years ago.

8 다음 중 어법상 어색한 것은?

① It was Jinho that heard someone snoring during the night.

② It is fresh vegetables which he visits the market to buy.

③ It was Jenny whom forgot to lock the front door.

④ It was in 1942 when Columbus discovered America.

⑤ It is at the bus stop where we're supposed to wait for her.

9 괄호 안의 말을 활용하여 밑줄 친 부분을 강조하는 문장으로 바꿔 쓰시오.

Mozart went on his first concert tour of Europe <u>at age seven</u>. (it, be, that)

→ _____

_____

[10-11] 다음은 Monica의 이번 주 일정표이다. 「It is ~ that …」 강조 구문을 사용하여 주어진 질문에 답하시오.

Monday	take a history test
Tuesday	take a math test
Wednesday	meet friends
Thursday	free
Friday	go to the National Art Museum

10

A: Does Monica take a math test on Monday?
B: No. _____
Monica has on Monday.

11

A: Does Monica go to the National Art Museum on Wednesday?
B: No. _____ she goes to the National Art Museum.

Chapter 16 특수구문 **403**

[12-13] 다음 문장을 밑줄 친 부분을 강조하는 문장으로 바꿔 쓰시오.

12

> I <u>wondered</u> what made my friend so angry.
>
> → _____
>
> _____

13

> This laptop is <u>lighter</u> than my old one.
>
> → _____
>
> _____

14 우리말과 같도록 괄호 안의 말을 알맞게 배열하시오.

> 그는 경찰이 수색하고 있는 바로 그 남자이다. (man, for, are, he, is, the, searching, very, the, police)

= _____

_____

15 다음 중 어법상 어색한 것은?

① From the clouds appeared the lightning.

② Never was it my intention to hurt you.

③ Down the hill slid the children.

④ In front of the school were many people.

⑤ There is she walking up the stairs.

16 다음 중 밑줄 친 부분을 <u>잘못</u> 강조한 것을 <u>모두</u> 고르시오.

① This is <u>the hat</u> I bought earlier today.

　→ This is the very hat I bought earlier today.

② <u>Michael</u> was accused of the robbery yesterday.

　→ It was Michael that was accused of the robbery yesterday.

③ His health is <u>worse</u> than it was last month.

　→ His health is very worse than it was last month.

④ Miyeon <u>forgot</u> to bring her science book today.

　→ Miyeon does forget to bring her science book today.

⑤ The band members liked <u>the song</u> a lot.

　→ It was the song which the band members liked a lot.

17 다음 대화의 밑줄 친 (A)를 괄호 안의 말로 시작하는 문장으로 바꿔 쓰시오.

> A: Brenda has helped me so much lately.
> B: I'm not surprised. She's one of the nicest people I know.
> A: I agree. (A) <u>I have never met such a caring person.</u> (never)

→ _____

18 다음 우리말을 영작할 때 빈칸에 들어갈 알맞은 것은?

> 이 종류의 식물은 좀처럼 1미터 높이 이상 자라지 않는다.
> = _____ more than one meter tall.

① Seldom did this type of plant grow
② Seldom does this type of plant grows
③ Seldom this type of plant grows
④ Seldom does this type of plant grow
⑤ Seldom did this type of plant grows

19 다음 밑줄 친 ⓐ~ⓔ 중 어법상 어색한 것을 찾아 기호를 쓰고 바르게 고쳐 쓰시오.

> · Into the microphone ⓐwhispered the speaker.
> · Hardly ⓑdo the town has any tourists.
> · Not only ⓒwas the movie long, but it was also boring.
> · ⓓThere are the new neighbors moving in today.
> · Along the river ⓔthe flock of birds flew.

(1) _____ → _____
(2) _____ → _____

[20-21] <보기>와 같이 밑줄 친 부분을 강조하는 문장으로 바꿔 쓰시오.

> **<보기>** The dogs ran across the road.
> → *Across the road ran the dogs.*

20

> She never thought she would write a novel.
> → _____
> _____

21

> The ships sailed into the sunset.
> → _____
> _____

22 다음 중 어법상 바른 것은?

① Washing your hands and brushing your teeth are important for good health.
② On our vacation, we might travel to the mountains or going on a cruise.
③ Working out three hours every day is hard not only physically but also mental.
④ When I get sleepy during the day, I either drink a cup of coffee or taking a quick nap.
⑤ Maria finds both raising her children and maintain a career difficult.

23 다음 중 부분 부정을 나타내는 문장이 <u>아닌</u> 것은?

① Nobody wants to help clean the classroom.

② Not all dogs are suitable for living in an apartment.

③ Not both of the dresses I bought last year fit me now.

④ I'm not always in the mood to talk.

⑤ Not every friend of Mina's went to her birthday party.

24 다음 대화의 빈칸에 들어갈 알맞은 것은?

> A: Calm down. We are just having a disagreement. You shouldn't shout.
>
> B: _____. It was you who yelled first. Don't you remember?

① So should you do

② So you should

③ Neither should you

④ Neither do you

⑤ Neither you should

25 다음 중 어법상 <u>어색한</u> 부분을 찾아 쓰고 바르게 고쳐 쓰시오.

> The speaker do sounds clearer after the repairs.

_____ → _____

26 다음 밑줄 친 ⓐ~ⓕ 중 생략할 수 있는 것끼리 묶인 것은?

> · The kids ⓐwho are running in the playground look happy.
> · The student ⓑwho studied all night got an A on the test.
> · Who is the woman to ⓒwhom Justin is talking?
> · We know a couple ⓓwho lives in a wooden house in the forest.
> · The foreign languages with ⓔwhich I'm familiar are French and English.
> · I made a list of things ⓕwhich I will do before I die.

① ⓐ, ⓑ, ⓕ

② ⓓ, ⓕ

③ ⓑ, ⓓ, ⓔ

④ ⓐ, ⓒ, ⓔ

⑤ ⓐ, ⓕ

27 다음 중 어법상 <u>어색한</u> 것을 <u>모두</u> 고르시오.

① Never had we attended such a fancy wedding.

② There are you. I've been looking for you all morning.

③ I'm not a very good driver, and neither is my brother.

④ On the top of the hill are standing some people.

⑤ He can play drums, and so I can.

28 다음 문장을 잘못 바꾼 것은?

① The actor looked into the camera.
   → Into the camera the actor looked.
② We rarely get a chance to travel these days.
   → Rarely do we get a chance to travel these days.
③ I have never eaten such a delicious cake.
   → Never have I eaten such a delicious cake.
④ He slipped on the wet floor.
   → On the wet floor he slipped.
⑤ All of the children jumped into the swimming pool.
   → Into the swimming pool jumped all of the children.

29 다음 문장의 밑줄 친 부분을 바르게 바꾼 것은?

Sally exercises every day, and her husband exercises every day, too.

① neither does her husband
② so is her husband
③ so her husband do
④ so does her husband
⑤ so her husband does

30 다음 밑줄 친 콤마(,)의 역할이 나머지 넷과 다른 것은?

① Our neighborhood, Green Estates, has tennis courts and a fitness center.
② The stadium, a popular tourist destination, is closed for renovations.
③ I went to watch my favorite football team, Manchester United.
④ In Venezuela we saw Angel Falls, the world's highest waterfall.
⑤ I'll introduce you to my new friend, and we can hang out together.

31 밑줄 친 that의 역할이 나머지 넷과 다른 것은?

① The rumor that the final exam is canceled is not true.
② I heard the news that my favorite singer is performing in Busan.
③ We are developing medicines that will cure many diseases.
④ I totally agree with your idea that schools need more funding.
⑤ I already know the fact that he cheated on the test.

[32-33] 다음 중 밑줄 친 부분을 생략할 수 <u>없는</u> 것을 고르시오.

32

① When <u>he was</u> in the hospital, he received a lot of flowers.
② I drank a glass of milk while <u>I was</u> checking my e-mail.
③ Electronic devices can be used for a long time if <u>they are</u> maintained well.
④ You should not miss class unless <u>you are</u> truly sick.
⑤ My mom entered my room when <u>I was</u> talking on the phone.

33

① The tall boy <u>that</u> you saw with me last night is my boyfriend.
② This is the very house <u>that</u> I wanted to move into.
③ I don't like sports <u>that</u> make me sweaty.
④ Olivia is the woman <u>that</u> I will get married to.
⑤ The flowers <u>that</u> my mother grew look beautiful.

[34-35] 다음 문장에서 생략할 수 있는 부분을 생략하여 완전한 문장을 쓰시오.

34

Your phone service will be cut off unless it is paid for in advance.

→ _____

_____

35

Jacob plans to enter the air force and his younger brother plans to enter the army.

→ _____

_____

36 다음 글에서 어법상 어색한 부분을 두 군데 찾아 쓰고 바르게 고쳐 쓰시오.

The new museum aims to feature local artists and introduced their artwork to the community. In addition, it will offer art classes to the public. Visitors to the museum can choose between either buying a single day pass or purchase a yearly pass at a discounted rate.

(1) _____ → _____
(2) _____ → _____

37 다음 중 어법상 바른 것은?

① He is interested in not only jogging but also hike.

② Becky not only donates money to charity but also volunteers on the weekends.

③ The pianist became very famous both domestically and international.

④ Fruit not only tastes good but also give you energy.

⑤ Sarah will either play the guitar or singing in the band.

38 다음 중 밑줄 친 부분이 어법상 어색한 것은?

If you ①do want to save money, it is important to follow a plan. First, decide how much money to save each month, and ②put that money in a savings account. Placing your money in a savings account not only makes it harder for you to spend it but also ③allow you to earn interest. ④Rarely do people save as much as they want to, but savings are helpful when things go wrong. ⑤It is sudden expenses like car repairs and hospital visits that you need savings for.

3학년 교과서 대표 문법 한 눈에 보기

1 동아 (윤정미)

LESSON		CH	POINT	PAGE
1	접속사 if와 whether	12	3-2	293
	to부정사의 형용사적 용법	5	3-1	117
2	5형식: 사역동사	1	4-3	26
	so that ~	12	4-5	302
3	관계대명사의 계속적 용법	13	7	330
	접속사 that: It ~ that	12	3-1	291
4	현재완료진행시제	2	4	45
	의문사 + to부정사	5	2-3	116
5	현재분사	7	2	157
	원급 비교: as + 원급 + as	10	1-1	234
6	과거완료시제	2	5	47
	관계대명사 what	13	4	326
7	분사구문	7	5-1, 5-2	162, 164
	접속사 as	12	5	304
8	to부정사의 의미상 주어	5	6	122
	가정법 과거	14	1	348

2 동아 (이병민)

LESSON		CH	POINT	PAGE
1	to부정사의 의미상 주어	5	6	122
	관계대명사 what	13	4	326
2	수 일치	15	1-2	375
	조동사가 있는 수동태	4	4	93
3	5형식: 사역동사	1	4-3	26
	It is ~ that 강조 구문	16	1-2	393
4	the + 비교급 ~, the + 비교급…	10	2-2	240
	접속사 since	12	4-2	297
5	가정법 과거	14	1	348
	의문사 + to부정사	5	2-3	116
6	so that ~	12	4-5	302
	enough to	5	5	121
7	소유격 관계대명사	13	2-3	323
	부사절을 이끄는 접속사: 시간	12	4-1	295
8	분사구문	7	5-1, 5-2	162, 164
	과거완료시제	2	5	47

3 천재 (이재영)

	LESSON	CH	POINT	PAGE
1	관계대명사 what	13	4	326
1	5형식: 지각동사	1	4-4	27
2	명사를 수식하는 분사	7	1, 2	156, 157
2	접속사 since와 though	12	4-2, 4-4	297, 300
3	현재완료진행시제	2	4	45
3	so ~ that …	12	4-6	302
4	관계부사	13	6	328
4	접속사 if와 whether	12	3-2	293
5	과거완료시제	2	5	47
5	It is ~ that 강조 구문	16	1-2	393
6	to부정사의 의미상 주어	5	6	122
6	가정법 과거	14	1	348
7	분사구문	7	5-1, 5-2	162, 164
7	조동사가 있는 수동태	4	4	93
8	조동사 + have + p.p.	3	5	71
8	관계대명사의 계속적 용법	13	7	330

4 천재 (정사열)

	LESSON	CH	POINT	PAGE
1	간접의문문	15	3-2, 3-3	379, 380
1	관계대명사의 계속적 용법	13	7	330
2	과거완료시제	2	5	47
2	비교급 강조	10	2-1	238
3	enough to	5	5	121
3	not only A but (also) B	12	2	289
4	분사구문	7	5-1, 5-2	162, 164
4	관계대명사 what	13	4	326
5	가정법 과거	14	1	348
5	소유격 관계대명사	13	2-3	323
6	the + 비교급 ~, the + 비교급…	10	2-2	240
6	It is ~ that 강조 구문	16	1-2	393
7	화법 전환: 평서문	15	3-1	378
7	접속사 if	12	3-2	293
8	부정대명사	8	6-1, 6-2, 6-3	194, 195, 196
8	5형식: to부정사	1	4-2	24

5 능률 (양현권)

	LESSON	CH	POINT	PAGE
1	to부정사의 의미상 주어	5	6	122
	관계대명사의 계속적 용법	13	7	330
2	It is ~ that 강조 구문	16	1-2	393
	5형식	1	4-1, 4-2	23, 24
3	관계대명사 what	13	4	326
	5형식: 사역동사	1	4-3	26
4	과거완료시제	2	5	47
	분사구문	7	5-1, 5-2	162, 164
5	의문사 + to부정사	5	2-3	116
	the + 비교급 ~, the + 비교급…	10	2-2	240
6	화법 전환: 평서문	15	3-1	378
	5형식: 지각동사	1	4-4	27
7	가정법 과거	14	1	348
	so ~ that …	12	4-6	302

6 능률 (김성곤)

	LESSON	CH	POINT	PAGE
1	현재완료진행시제	2	4	45
	관계대명사 what	13	4	326
2	관계대명사의 계속적 용법	13	7	330
	명사를 수식하는 분사	7	1, 2	156, 157
3	과거완료시제	2	5	47
	부사절을 이끄는 접속사	12	4-1, 4-2, 4-3, 4-4	295, 297, 298, 300
4	접속사 if와 whether	12	3-2	293
	조동사가 있는 수동태	4	4	93
5	to부정사의 의미상 주어	5	6	122
	관계부사	13	6	328
6	the + 비교급 ~, the + 비교급…	10	2-2	240
	분사구문	7	5-1, 5-2	162, 164
7	가정법 과거	14	1	348
	so that ~	12	4-5	302

11 지학사 (민찬규)

	LESSON	CH	POINT	PAGE
1	관계대명사 what	13	4	326
	5형식: 지각동사	1	4-4	27
2	to부정사의 의미상 주어	5	6	122
	명사를 수식하는 분사	7	1, 2	156, 157
3	not only A but (also) B	12	2	289
	간접의문문	15	3-2, 3-3	379, 380
4	과거완료시제	2	5	47
	to부정사의 부사적 용법	5	4	119
5	부정대명사: one	8	6-1	194
	분사구문	7	5-1, 5-2	162, 164
6	It is ~ that 강조 구문	16	1-2	393
	접속부사	12	6	306
7	가정법 과거	14	1	348
	5형식	1	4-1, 4-2	23, 24
8	too ~ to	5	5	121
	No one …	16	2	395

12 금성 (최인철)

	LESSON	CH	POINT	PAGE
1	5형식: 사역동사	1	4-3	26
	동명사 관용 표현	6	6	140
2	the + 비교급 ~, the + 비교급…	10	2-2	240
	to부정사의 의미상 주어	5	6	122
3	not only A but (also) B	12	2	289
	I wish 가정법	14	6	356
4	과거완료시제	2	5	47
	원급 비교: as + 원급 + as	10	1-1	234
5	so ~ that …	12	4-6	302
	5형식: 지각동사	1	4-4	27
6	It is ~ that 강조 구문	16	1-2	393
	분사구문	7	5-1, 5-2	162, 164
7	to부정사의 부사적 용법	5	4	119
	So + 동사 + 주어	16	3	396
8	접속사 whether	12	3-2	293
	It's time 가정법	14	6	356

MEMO

최신 개정 교과서 완벽 반영

기출로적중

해커스

중학영문법

3학년

초판 8쇄 발행 2024년 4월 1일
초판 1쇄 발행 2020년 11월 4일

지은이	해커스 어학연구소
펴낸곳	㈜해커스 어학연구소
펴낸이	해커스 어학연구소 출판팀

주소	서울특별시 서초구 강남대로61길 23 ㈜해커스 어학연구소
고객센터	02-537-5000
교재 관련 문의	publishing@hackers.com
	해커스북 사이트(HackersBook.com) 고객센터 Q&A 게시판
동영상강의	star.Hackers.com

ISBN	978-89-6542-408-6 (53740)
Serial Number	01-08-01

저작권자 ⓒ 2020, 해커스 어학연구소
이 책 및 음성파일의 모든 내용, 이미지, 디자인, 편집 형태에 대한 저작권은 저자에게 있습니다.
서면에 의한 저자와 출판사의 허락 없이 내용의 일부 혹은 전부를 인용, 발췌하거나 복제, 배포할 수 없습니다.

**중고등영어 1위,
해커스북 HackersBook.com**

해커스북 중·고등

· 핵심만 담았다! **문법 암기리스트+단어 암기장 및 단어 암기장 MP3**
· 교과서 문법 포인트 학습이 쉬워지는 **3학년 교과서 대표 문법 한 눈에 보기**
· 서술형 시험을 완벽하게 대비할 수 있는 **영작/해석 워크시트**

한경비즈니스 선정 2020 한국품질만족도 교육(온·오프라인 중·고등영어) 부문 1위 해커스

| 해커스 중고등 교재 MAP | 나에게 맞는 교재 선택!

	초5	초6	예비중	중1	중2
문법			Hackers Grammar Smart Starter	Hackers Grammar Smart Level 1	Hackers Grammar Smart Level 2
				기출로 적중 해커스 중학영문법 1학년	기출로 적중 해커스 중학영문법 2학년
				해커스 중학영문법 중간·기말 대비 문제집 Level 1	해커스 중학영문법 중간·기말 대비 문제집 Level 2
서술형				해커스 쓰기 자신감 Level 1	해커스 쓰기 자신감 Level 2
구문					
독해	Hackers Reading Smart Starter Level 1	Hackers Reading Smart Starter Level 2	Hackers Reading Smart Level 1	Hackers Reading Smart Level 2	Hackers Reading Smart Level 3
				Hackers Reading Ground Level 1	Hackers Reading Ground Level 2
				Hackers Reading Path Level 1	Hackers Reading Path Level 2
					해커스 첫수능 영어 기초독해
듣기				해커스 중학영어듣기 모의고사 24회 Level 1	해커스 중학영어듣기 모의고사 24회 Level 2
어휘			해커스 3연타 중학영단어		
				해커스 보카 중학 기초	해커스 보카 중학 필수
					해커스 보카 중학 숙어

	READING	LISTENING	VOCA
토플	HACKERS APEX READING for the TOEFL iBT — Basic/Intermediate/Advanced/Expert	HACKERS APEX LISTENING for the TOEFL iBT — Basic/Intermediate/Advanced/Expert	HACKERS APEX VOCA for the TOEFL iBT / HACKERS VOCABULARY

중3	예비고	고1	고2	고3
Hackers Grammar Smart Level 3				
기출로 적중 해커스 중학영문법 3학년		기출로 적중 해커스 고등영문법		
해커스 중학영문법 중간·기말 대비 문제집 Level 3		해커스 어법 제대로		
		해커스 수능 어법 불변의 패턴 필수편	해커스 수능 어법 불변의 패턴 실력편	
해커스 쓰기 자신감 Level 3				
	해커스 완전숙련 구문독해 입문	해커스 완전숙련 구문독해 기본	해커스 완전숙련 구문독해 심화	
Hackers Reading Smart Level 4	해커스 독해 제대로 기본독해	해커스 독해 제대로 구문독해		
Hackers Reading Ground Level 3				
Hackers Reading Path Level 3	Hackers Reading Path Level 4			
해커스 첫수능 영어 유형독해	해커스 수능 독해 불변의 패턴 유형편		해커스 수능 독해 불변의 패턴 실전편	
	해커스 수능영어독해 미니 모의고사 12+2회 기본	해커스 수능영어독해 미니 모의고사 12+2회 필수	해커스 수능영어독해 미니 모의고사 12+2회 완성 (* 출간 예정)	
해커스 중학영어듣기 모의고사 24회 Level 3		해커스 수능영어듣기 모의고사 20+4회 기본	해커스 수능영어듣기 모의고사 20+4회 실전	
		해커스 수능영어듣기 모의고사 30+5회 기본	해커스 수능영어듣기 모의고사 30+5회 실전	
	해커스 보카 고등 기본			
해커스 보카 중학 고난도		해커스 보카 수능 필수 2000+		
		해커스 보카 수능 완성 1800+		
			해커스 보카 수능 심화	
		해커스 보카 수능 숙어		
	해커스 보카 어원편			

해커스북[HackersBook.com]에서
교재에 대한 자세한 설명과 다양한 학습 자료를 확인하세요!

최신 개정 교과서 완벽 반영

기출로적중

해커스
중학영문법

3학년

해커스 중학영문법이 특별한 이유!

1. 실제 중학교 내신 **기출문제 빅데이터 및 최신 개정 교과서** 완벽 반영
2. **단계별 문제풀이**를 통해 내신 시험에 확실하게 대비 가능
3. 문법 포인트 이해에 **필수적인 기초 문법**으로 체계적인 학습 시작
4. 워크북의 **추가 문제**를 충분히 풀어보며 실력 완성
5. 내신 점수를 높여주는 **다양한 학습 자료** 제공

정가 **14,900** 원

53740

9 788965 424086

ISBN 978-89-6542-408-6

해커스북(HackersBook.com)에서
본 교재에 대한 다양한 추가 학습 자료를 이용하세요!

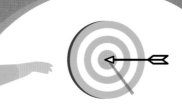

최신 개정 교과서 완벽 반영

기출로 적중
해커스
중학영문법

- 중학 내신 기출 빅데이터 반영
- 실전 · 서술형 문제로 내신 완벽 대비
- 예비고를 위한 영문법 기본 완성

워크북

3학년

해커스 교재는
다릅니다

펼쳐 보면 느껴집니다

단 한 줄도 배움의 공백이 생기지 않도록
문장 한 줄마다 20년이 넘는
해커스의 영어교육 노하우를 담았음을

덮고 나면 확신합니다

수많은 선생님의 목소리와
정확한 출제 데이터 분석으로 꽉 찬
교재 한 권이면 충분함을

해커스북 중·고등
HackersBook.com

기출로 적중 해커스 중학영문법 시리즈를 검토해주신 선생님들

경기
강상훈	평촌비상에듀학원
김원덕	올림피아드학원
박윤정	이지베스트학원
최승복	오른어학원
최지영	다른영어학원

서울
김가영	송정중학교
박유정	반포중학교
박은혜	송파중학교
박정은	대청중학교
양세희	양세희수능영어학원

이계윤	씨앤씨학원
이유빈	잉글리쉬&매쓰매니저학원
이혜원	대청중학교
정혜은	용곡중학교
최다빈	최강영어

해커스 어학연구소 자문위원단 3기

강원
박정선	잉글리쉬클럽
최현주	최샘영어

경기
강민정	김진성열정영어학원
강상훈	평촌RTS학원
강지인	강지인영어학원
권계미	A&T+ 영어
김미아	김쌤영어학원
김설화	업라이트잉글리쉬
김성재	스윗스터디학원
김세훈	모두의학원
김수아	더스터디(The STUDY)
김영아	백송고등학교
김유경	벨트학원
김유경	포시즌스어학원
김유동	이스턴영어학원
김지숙	위디벨럽학원
김지현	이지프레임영어학원
김해빈	해빛영어학원
김현지	지앤비영어학원
박가영	한민고등학교
박영서	스윗스터디학원
박은별	더킹영수학원
박재홍	록키어학원
성승민	SDH어학원 불당캠퍼스
신소연	Ashley English
오귀연	루나영어학원
유신애	에듀포커스학원
윤소정	ILP이화어학원
이동진	이룸학원
이상미	버밍엄영어교습소
이연경	명품M비온드수학영어학원
이은수	광주세종학원
이지혜	리케이온
이진희	이엠원영어학원
이충기	영어나무
이효명	갈매리드앤톡영어독서학원
임한글	Apsun앞선영어학원
장광명	엠케이영어학원
전상호	평촌이지학원
전성훈	훈선생영어교실
정선영	코어플러스영어학원
정준	고양외국어고등학교
조연아	카이트학원
채기림	고려대학교EIE영어학원
최지영	다른영어학원
최한나	석사영수전문
최희정	SJ클쌤영어학원
현지환	모두의학원
홍태경	공감국어영어전문학원

경남
강다위	더(the)오르다영어학원
라승희	아이작잉글리쉬
박주언	유니크학원
배송현	두잇영어교습소
안윤서	어썸영어학원
임진희	어썸영어학원

경북
권현민	삼성영어석적우방교실
김으뜸	EIE영어학원 옥계캠퍼스
배세왕	비케이영수전문고등관학원
유영선	아이비티어학원

광주
김유희	김유희영어학원
서희연	SDL영어수학학원
송수일	아이리드영어학원
오진우	SLT어학원수학원
정영철	정영철영어전문학원
최경옥	봉선중학교

대구
권익재	제이슨영어
김명일	독학인학원
김보곤	베스트영어
김연정	달서고등학교
김혜란	김혜란영어학원
문애주	프렌즈입시학원
박정근	공부의힘pnk학원
박희숙	열공열강영어수학학원
신동기	신통외국어학원
위영선	위영선영어학원
윤창원	공터영어학원 상인센터
이승현	학문당입시학원
이주현	이주현영어학원
이헌욱	이헌욱영어학원
장준현	장쌤독해종결영어학원
주현아	민샘영어학원
최윤정	최강영어학원

대전
곽선영	위드유학원
김지운	더포스둔산학원
박미현	라시움영어대동학원
박세리	EM101학원

부산
김건희	레지나잉글리쉬 영어학원
김미나	위드중고등영어학원
박수진	정모클영어국어학원
박수진	지니영어학원
박인숙	리더스영어전문학원
옥지윤	더센텀영어학원
윤진희	위니드영어전문교습소
이종혁	진수학원
정혜인	엠티엔영어학원
조정래	알파카의영어농장
주태양	솔라영어학원

서울
Erica Sull	하버드브레인영어학원
강고은	케이앤학원
강신아	교우학원
공현미	이은재어학원
권영진	경동고등학교
김나영	프라임클래스영어학원
김달수	대일외국어고등학교
김대니	채움학원
김문영	창문여자고등학교
김상백	강북세일학원
김정은	강북뉴스터디학원
김혜경	대동세무고등학교
남혜원	함영원입시전문학원
노시은	케이앤학원
박선정	강북세일학원
박수진	이은재어학원
박지수	이플러스영수학원
서승희	함영원입시전문학원
신지웅	강북세일학원
양세희	양세희수능영어학원
우정용	제임스영어앤드학원
이박원	이박원어학원
이승혜	스텔라영어
이정욱	이은재어학원
이지연	중계케이트영어학원
임예찬	학습컨설턴트
장지희	고려대학교사범대학부속고등학교
정미라	미라정영어학원
조민규	조민규영어
채가희	대성세그루영수학원

울산
김기태	그라티아어학원
이민주	로이아카데미
홍영민	더이안영어전문학원

인천
강재민	스터디위드제이쌤
고현순	정상학원
권효진	Genie's English
김솔	전문과외
김정아	밀턴영어학원
서상천	최정서학원
이윤주	트리플원
최예영	영웅아카데미

전남
강희진	강희진영어학원
김두환	해남맨체스터영수학원
송승연	송승연영수학원
윤세광	비상구영어학원

전북
김길자	맨투맨학원
김미영	링크영어학원
김효성	연세입시학원
노빈나	노빈나영어전문학원
라성남	하포드어학원
박재훈	위니드수학지앤비영어학원
박향숙	STA영어전문학원
서종원	서종원영어학원
이상훈	나는학원
장지원	링컨더글라스학원
지근영	한솔영어수학학원
최성령	연세입시학원
최혜영	이든영어수학학원

제주
김랑	KLS어학원
박자은	KLS어학원

충남
김예지	더배움프라임영수학원
김철홍	청경학원
노태겸	최상위학원

충북
라은경	이화윤스영어교습소
신유정	비타민영어클리닉학원

최신 개정 교과서 완벽 반영

기출로적중 해커스 중학영문법

3학년

이 책을 검토해주신 선생님들

강상훈 경기 평촌비상에듀학원 / **김가영** 서울 송정중학교 / **김원덕** 경기 올림피아드학원 / **박유정** 서울 반포중학교 / **박윤정** 경기 이지베스트학원

박은혜 서울 송파중학교 / **박정은** 서울 대청중학교 / **양세희** 서울 양세희수능영어학원 / **이계윤** 서울 씨앤씨학원 / **이유빈** 서울 잉글리쉬&매쓰매니저학원

이혜원 서울 대청중학교 / **정혜은** 서울 용곡중학교 / **최다빈** 서울 최강영어 / **최승복** 경기 오른어학원 / **최지영** 경기 다른영어학원

목차

목차

해커스북 중·고등

www.HackersBook.com

CHAPTER 1
문장의 형식

1형식과 2형식

정답 p.60

연습문제 밑줄 친 부분의 문장 성분을 <보기>에서 골라 차례대로 쓰고, 문장을 해석하시오.

<보기> 주격 보어   동사   수식어구   주어

1 <u>We</u> <u>stayed</u> at <u>their apartment</u> last weekend. [   ] [   ] [   ]
→ _____

2 <u>I</u> <u>fell</u> <u>asleep</u> after eating breakfast. [   ] [   ] [   ]
→ _____

3 <u>Some plants</u> <u>grow</u> <u>in water</u>. [   ] [   ] [   ]
→ _____

4 <u>We</u> usually <u>stay</u> <u>busy</u> during the holidays. [   ] [   ] [   ]
→ _____

5 <u>My uncle</u> recently <u>became</u> <u>famous</u>. [   ] [   ] [   ]
→ _____

6 <u>Mary</u> suddenly <u>appeared</u> <u>on the stage</u>. [   ] [   ] [   ]
→ _____

2형식: 감각동사

정답 p.60

연습문제 밑줄 친 부분이 어법상 맞으면 O를 쓰고, 틀리면 바르게 고쳐 쓰시오.

1 The children looked <u>excited</u> about their Christmas presents. → _____

2 All the people at the party <u>sounded like</u> very happy. → _____

3 Brad felt <u>anxious</u> about his performance in the school play. → _____

4 The apples at the market didn't taste <u>freshly</u>. → _____

5 I <u>felt</u> thankful for the support of my friends and family. → _____

6 That resort <u>looks</u> a great place to spend a weekend. → _____

7 This coffee <u>smells</u> chocolate and caramel. → _____

8 The bride and groom looked <u>amazingly</u> at their wedding. → _____

9 Your idea of going to the amusement park <u>sounds</u> a good plan. → _____

10 My mom's homemade pizza always tastes so <u>deliciously</u>. → _____

연습문제 A 밑줄 친 부분의 문장 성분을 <보기>에서 골라 차례대로 쓰고, 문장을 해석하시오.

<보기> 주어 동사 목적어

1 They <u>wrote</u> a good report. [　　　] → _____

2 I sold <u>my old bicycle</u>. [　　　] → _____

3 She <u>fed</u> the puppy. [　　　] → _____

4 <u>Brian</u> called his grandmother. [　　　] → _____

5 We bought <u>concert tickets</u>. [　　　] → _____

6 <u>He</u> ate a whole pie. [　　　] → _____

7 My dad <u>drove</u> the car. [　　　] → _____

8 That café makes <u>delicious bagels</u>. [　　　] → _____

9 <u>The singer</u> sang a beautiful song. [　　　] → _____

10 We <u>watched</u> the sunset on the beach. [　　　] → _____

연습문제 B 밑줄 친 부분이 어법상 맞으면 O를 쓰고, 틀리면 바르게 고쳐 쓰시오.

1 The coach <u>explained</u> the new rules of the tournament. → _____

2 Let's <u>discuss about</u> what we learned in class today. → _____

3 Kathy will <u>marry with</u> her boyfriend next month. → _____

4 Dad has to <u>attend</u> a meeting at 1 P.M. → _____

5 We must leave now to <u>reach to</u> the airport on time. → _____

6 My little brother's right sock does not <u>match</u> his left sock. → _____

7 Did Jihoon <u>enter to</u> the train station already? → _____

8 Nobody <u>mentioned about</u> the plan to us. → _____

9 We need to <u>contact</u> Kim about the upcoming event. → _____

10 He said that I <u>resemble with</u> a movie star. → _____

연습문제 A 우리말과 같도록 괄호 안의 말을 알맞게 배열하시오.

1 Kevin은 선생님에게 많은 질문을 했다. (the teacher, asked, many questions, Kevin)

= _____

2 나의 사촌은 나에게 웃긴 문자를 보냈다. (me, sent, a funny text message, my cousin)

= _____

3 그 가정교사는 주말마다 그 소녀에게 중국어를 가르친다. (the girl, teaches, Chinese, on weekends, the tutor)

= _____

4 Smith씨는 그 손님들에게 약간의 쿠키를 제공했다. (the guests, offered, some cookies, Ms. Smith)

= _____

5 탁자 위에 있는 저 펜을 나에게 건네주세요. (me, that pen, on the table, pass, please)

= _____

6 그는 어제 저녁에 우리에게 무서운 이야기를 말해주었다. (us, told, a scary story, last night, he)

= _____

7 엄마는 항상 우리 가족에게 건강한 식사를 요리해준다. (our family, cooks, healthy meals, always, mom)

= _____

8 나는 그에게 좋은 호텔 방을 찾아주었다. (him, found, a nice hotel room, I)

= _____

연습문제 B 다음 3형식 문장은 4형식 문장으로, 4형식 문장은 3형식 문장으로 바꿔 쓰시오.

1 The man made a picture frame for the artist. → _____

2 Mom used to read us fairy tales. → _____

3 She showed them her violin. → _____

4 We gave a bag of toys to the children. → _____

5 The police officer asked us some questions. → _____

6 They brought us some plants for our garden. → _____

연습문제 A 다음 문장의 목적어에는 동그라미를 치고, 목적격 보어에는 밑줄을 치시오.

1 They found the book interesting.

2 Bora helped her classmate study for the test.

3 We consider the neighbors nice people.

4 The farmer let us touch the animals.

5 I heard my brother and sister arguing in the other room.

6 The students considered the quiz difficult.

7 She calls her grandmother Mimi.

8 My dad had his car checked by the mechanic yesterday.

9 Carlos allowed Marie to use his computer.

10 The doctor asked the patient to sit on a chair.

11 I didn't find the joke funny, but some people laughed at it.

12 We got the heater repaired at the appliance shop.

연습문제 B 우리말과 같도록 괄호 안의 말을 알맞게 배열하시오.

1 우리는 이 웹사이트가 도움이 된다고 생각했다. (this website, we, helpful, found)

= _____

2 그 식당의 질 나쁜 서비스가 우리를 화나게 만들었다. (us, the restaurant's poor service, angry, made)

= _____

3 그 쥐가 그 고양이를 흥분하게 했다. (the cat, the mouse, excited, got)

= _____

4 그 관객들은 그 마술 공연을 재미있다고 여겼다. (the magic show, the audience, fun, considered)

= _____

5 우리는 Gina의 이야기를 사실이라고 믿었다. (Gina's story, we, true, believed)

= _____

6 그들은 방문자가 그들의 주차장에 주차하게 해준다. (in, let, they, their parking lot, park, a visitor)

= _____

연습문제 A 밑줄 친 부분이 어법상 맞으면 O를 쓰고, 틀리면 바르게 고쳐 쓰시오.

1 The children found the clown's behavior <u>funnily</u>. → _____

2 Nobody in the town believed the man <u>innocent</u>. → _____

3 The hot peppers made the soup <u>spicy</u>. → _____

4 Wendy called me <u>a liar</u>. → _____

5 This is the movie that made the actor <u>famously</u>. → _____

6 Because Sally is quiet, her classmates think her <u>shy</u>. → _____

7 I didn't consider Josh's Halloween costume <u>scarily</u>. → _____

8 My heavy coat and thick gloves kept me <u>warmly</u>. → _____

연습문제 B 우리말과 같도록 괄호 안의 말을 활용하여 문장을 완성하시오.

1 Paul은 나에게 밖에서 기다리라고 말했다. (me, wait, tell)
= Paul _____ outside.

2 나의 고모는 우리가 그녀의 집에 머무는 것을 허락했다. (allow, stay, us)
= My aunt _____ at her house.

3 Kyle은 그 밴드가 그가 가장 좋아하는 노래를 연주하기를 원했다. (perform, want, the band)
= Kyle _____ his favorite song.

4 그 주민들은 지역 정부가 불꽃놀이 공연을 취소하기를 기대한다. (cancel, expect, the local government)
= The community _____ the fireworks show.

5 나는 Michelle에게 그녀가 집에 오면 나에게 전화를 하라고 요청했다. (ask, call, Michelle)
= I _____ me when she got home.

6 나의 부모님은 내가 장학금을 신청하는 것을 격려했다. (encourage, apply, me)
= My parents _____ for a scholarship.

7 항공사들은 승객들이 병에 든 생수를 휴대하는 것을 허락하지 않는다. (permit, carry, passengers)
= Airlines do not _____ bottled water.

5형식: 사역동사

정답 p.61

연습문제 괄호 안에서 알맞은 것을 <u>모두</u> 고르시오.

1 This news website makes visitors (create / to create) an account.

2 The teacher let us (use / to use) a calculator during the test.

3 Jungmin got me (to mail / mail) a package for her at the post office.

4 This smartwatch can help you (stay / to stay) fit.

5 The K-pop star's success made me (follow / to follow) her on social media.

6 My older brother got me (to swim / swim) in the lake.

7 Steven had them (save / to save) him a seat.

8 He helped my younger sister (fix / to fix) her broken phone.

9 The neighbors had someone (to paint / paint) their garage.

10 I finally got her (to tell / tell) me the secret.

5형식: 지각동사

정답 p.61

연습문제 괄호 안에서 알맞은 것을 고르시오.

1 They heard the bell (ring / to ring) after the lecture.

2 We saw the people (leaving / left) the stadium.

3 Mom smelled something (to burn / burning) in the kitchen.

4 They watched the sun (rose / rising) above the sea.

5 Brandon listened to the music (to play / play) in his headphones.

6 She felt the spider (crawling / crawled) on her leg.

7 I saw them (holding / to hold) hands during the ceremony.

8 Kate listened to her friends (to argue / argue) in the other room.

9 She heard her baby (crying / cried) loudly.

10 The crowd watched the workers (repair / to repair) the sidewalk.

11 The children felt their feet (sliding / slid) across the ice.

1 다음 중 어법상 <u>어색한</u> 것은?

① I saw that Jaehoon painted a picture.

② The soup tasted delicious.

③ The feather fell slowly to the ground.

④ This soap smells fantastically.

⑤ Horses are running across the field.

2 우리말과 같도록 괄호 안의 말을 알맞게 배열하시오.

> 인터넷은 사람들이 정보에 빨리 접근할 수 있게 한다.
> (the Internet, people, lets, information, access, quickly)

= _____

_____

3 다음 밑줄 친 부분을 바르게 고치지 <u>못한</u> 것은?

① I don't let my sister <u>to use</u> my computer because she might break it. (→ use)

② She got the child <u>eat</u> all his vegetables. (→ to eat)

③ He watched a man <u>to take</u> pictures of flowers in the park. (→ taking)

④ We will go to watch my younger brother <u>performed</u> in a play tonight. (→ perform)

⑤ Shane saw his coat <u>to hang</u> on a hook by the door. (→ hang)

4 다음 빈칸에 들어갈 말이 순서대로 짝지어진 것은?

> · Amber gave a present _____ Mark.
> · My mother got some new clothes _____ me.

① of – for   ② to – for   ③ for – of

④ to – of   ⑤ of – to

[5-6] 우리말과 같도록 괄호 안의 말을 알맞게 배열하시오.

5

> Sandra는 그녀의 어머니가 저녁을 요리하는 것을 도왔다. (helped, dinner, her mother, cook, Sandra)

= _____

6

> 그녀는 그녀의 친구들이 설거지를 하게 할 것이다. (the dishes, get, her friends, wash, to, is going to, she)

= _____

_____

7 다음 (A)~(C)에 들어갈 말이 바르게 짝지어진 것은?

- To be honest, George considers the restaurant ____(A)____ .
- Ms. Lee tries to keep her house ____(B)____ .
- He found his sister's cat ____(C)____ .

	(A)	(B)	(C)
①	cost	tidily	annoyingly
②	costly	tidy	annoyingly
③	costly	tidily	annoying
④	costly	tidy	annoying
⑤	cost	tidily	annoying

8 다음 (A)~(C)에 들어갈 말이 바르게 짝지어진 것은?

- This application lets you ____(A)____ with your friends.
- My father's going to have our house ____(B)____ .
- Our teacher always makes us ____(C)____ our mobile phones in a box.

	(A)	(B)	(C)
①	chat	painted	to place
②	to chat	painted	to place
③	to chat	to paint	place
④	chat	painted	place
⑤	chat	to paint	place

9 다음 중 어법상 바른 것을 <u>모두</u> 고르시오.

① Did they have their television to repair yet?
② Let me putting my jacket on.
③ The director had the actors to practice the scene again.
④ I told her to have her answer checked by the teacher.
⑤ Ms. Bailey had me make a sign for the bake sale.

10 다음 문장에서 <u>틀린</u> 부분을 바르게 고쳐 완전한 문장을 쓰시오.

Kevin looks angrily because of the look on his face.

→ _____

_____

11 다음 우리말을 영작한 것 중 <u>어색한</u> 것은?

① 우리는 판사에게 증거를 설명했다.
   =We explained the evidence to the judge.
② 그는 내일 콘서트에 참석할 것이다.
   = He will attend to a concert tomorrow.
③ 나는 나의 계좌 비밀번호를 입력했다.
   = I entered my account password.
④ 그 소년은 그의 아버지와 닮았다.
   = The boy resembles his father.
⑤ Mindy는 그녀가 받은 상에 대해 언급했다.
   = Mindy mentioned the award she received.

[12-13] 다음 글을 읽고, 주어진 질문에 답하시오.

When I arrived home after school yesterday, I heard someone ⓐto scream in the apartment next door. I was surprised, because our neighbor is usually very ⓑquietly. I ⓒmentioned about this to my mother. She immediately went next door. She asked him ⓓstop making noise. He laughed and let her ⓔto enter his apartment. Pointing at the bird cage in the room, he said, "(A) 나는 나의 새 앵무새가 그 큰 소리를 냈다고 생각한다." (made, my, the loud noise, new parrot)

12 위 글의 밑줄 친 ⓐ~ⓔ를 바르게 고치지 <u>못한</u> 것은?

① ⓐ to scream → screaming

② ⓑ quietly → quiet

③ ⓒ mentioned about → mentioned

④ ⓓ stop → stopping

⑤ ⓔ to enter → enter

13 위 글의 밑줄 친 우리말 (A)와 같도록 괄호 안의 말을 알맞게 배열하시오.

= I think that _____

_____ .

14 다음 중 어법상 <u>어색한</u> 것은?

① He spoke poor in front of other people.

② I can stay awake until 10 P.M.

③ The shirt feels like silk.

④ As spring approaches, many new flowers appear.

⑤ The coffee stayed hot all morning.

15 다음 중 4형식 문장은 3형식으로, 3형식 문장은 4형식으로 바르게 바꾼 것은?

① Mike asked me a favor this morning.
  → Mike asked a favor to me this morning.

② They built a playground for the children.
  → They built to the children a playground.

③ I'm going to write a letter to my friend.
  → I'm going to write a letter my friend.

④ Our parents bought us a video game.
  → Our parents bought for us a video game.

⑤ My sister passed my brother the salt.
  → My sister passed the salt to my brother.

16 다음 중 어법상 바른 것의 개수는?

ⓐ Steve asked his mother to let him ride his bicycle.

ⓑ Am I the only one who felt terrible about the mistake?

ⓒ Roger's parents have him made his bed every morning.

ⓓ I saw a duck to land in the pond in the park.

① 0개　　　② 1개　　　③ 2개

④ 3개　　　⑤ 4개

17 다음 빈칸에 공통으로 들어갈 알맞은 전치사를 <보기>에서 골라 쓰시오.

> <보기> to   for   of

> · The city built a parking garage downtown _____ drivers.
> · Sam cooked pasta _____ our guests.

18 우리말과 같도록 괄호 안의 말을 활용하여 문장을 완성하시오.

> 나는 나의 사촌이 나를 쇼핑몰로 데려다주게 할 것이다. (bring, my cousin, get)

= I will _____ me to the shopping mall.

19 다음 밑줄 친 부분을 바르게 고치지 <u>못한</u> 것은?

① Jeff sent a letter <u>of</u> Minsu. (→ to)
② Our aunt cooked some meals <u>to</u> us. (→ for)
③ She gave the answers to the test <u>of</u> us. (→ for)
④ Do you mind if I offer some advice <u>of</u> you? (→ to)
⑤ Sarah asked a favor <u>to</u> her neighbor. (→ of)

20 다음 중 어법상 <u>어색한</u> 것은?

① I think these noodles tastes like great.
② The artist's new sculpture looks like his last one.
③ I don't think Minji looks happy today.
④ Your grandfather sounds like a very nice man.
⑤ The bread in the oven smelled amazing.

21 다음 중 어법상 바른 것은?

① The people entered to the elevator.
② That boy resembles with my cousin.
③ Laura is going to marry Jason.
④ All soccer players must attend to the practices.
⑤ They explained about the problem to us.

22 우리말과 같도록 괄호 안의 말을 알맞게 배열하시오.

> 나는 태호에게 그의 파티를 위해 내가 만든 과자를 가져다줄 것이다. (bring, the snacks, Taeho)

= I'm going to _____ I made for his party.

[23-24] 다음 대화를 읽고 괄호 안의 말을 활용하여 문장을 완성하시오. (단, 과거시제만 사용하시오.)

23

> Jane: Dad, can I go to the party tonight?
> Dad : What time does the party start?
> Jane: It starts at 6 P.M.
> Dad : OK, but come home as soon as
> the party is over.
> Jane: Thank you, Dad.

→ Jane's dad _____ to
the party tonight. (go, allow, her)
Also, he _____ home
right after the party. (come, tell, her)

24

> Alex : Mom, can I go to the park?
> Mom: Why do you want to go there?
> Alex : I want to meet my friends.
> Mom: Did you do your chores?
> Alex : Not yet. I'm going to do them after
> I play with my friends.
> Mom: You can go to the park after you
> finish your chores.

→ Alex's mom _____ to
the park. (go, permit, him)
However, She _____
his chores first. (do, want, him)

25 우리말과 같도록 괄호 안의 말을 활용하여 문장을 완성하시오.

> 나의 친구들은 나에게 동호회에 가입하라고 조언했다.
> (me, advise, join)

= My friends _____ a
club.

CHAPTER 2
시제

기출로 적중 POINT

연습문제 괄호 안의 말을 활용하여 빈칸에 알맞은 말을 쓰시오.

1 Tokyo _____ the capital of Japan. (be)

2 The Korean War _____ in 1950. (begin)

3 Light in a vacuum _____ at 299,792 kilometers per second. (travel)

4 People say that an empty vessel _____ much noise. (make)

5 I _____ not go to school yesterday. (do)

6 John still _____ Spanish for two hours every day. (study)

7 Abraham Lincoln _____ in 1865. (die)

8 China _____ the largest population in the world. (have)

9 I _____ my dad's computer monitor a couple of days ago. (break)

연습문제 우리말과 같도록 괄호 안의 말을 활용하여 문장을 완성하시오.

1 그 도시는 다음 달에 음악 페스티벌을 개최할 것이다. (be going to, a music festival, host, the city)
= _____ next month.

2 나는 수업이 끝나면 칠판을 닦을 것이다. (clean, will, I, the blackboard)
= _____ when the class is finished.

3 의사가 준비되면 간호사가 너의 이름을 부를 것이다. (your name, a nurse, call, will)
= _____ when the doctor is ready.

4 나의 여권은 1월에 막 만료되려는 참이다. (my passport, expire, be about to)
= _____ in January.

5 우리는 인도 식당에서 저녁을 먹을 것이다. (we, have, be going to, dinner)
= _____ at an Indian restaurant.

6 그 공연은 한 시간 후에 시작될 것이다. (start, the show, be going to)
= _____ in an hour.

연습문제 **A** | 우리말과 같도록 괄호 안의 말을 활용하여 현재완료시제 문장을 완성하시오. (단, 숫자는 영어로 쓰시오.)

1 Jana는 바이올린 수업을 5년 동안 받아왔다. (take, for)

= Jana _____ violin lessons _____.

2 Kevin은 전에 그의 할머니를 보기 위해 프랑스로 여행한 적이 있다. (travel, before)

= Kevin _____ to France to see his grandmother _____.

3 그 선생님은 얼마 동안 이 화학 수업을 가르쳐왔니? (teach, how long)

= _____ the teacher _____ this chemistry class for?

4 너는 고래 보기 투어를 가본 적이 있니? (go, ever)

= _____ you _____ on a whale watching tour?

5 그 배우는 지난 여름부터 두 편의 영화에 출연했다. (appear, since)

= The actor _____ in two movies _____ last summer.

연습문제 **B** | 현재완료시제를 이용하여 다음 두 문장을 한 문장으로 연결하시오.

1 My father wrote songs in the 1990s. He still writes songs.

→ My father _____ _____ songs since the 1990s.

2 She played soccer in high school. She still plays soccer.

→ She _____ _____ soccer.

3 She started taking taekwondo lessons in the second grade. She still takes them.

→ She _____ _____ taekwondo lessons since the second grade.

4 I was in a band a year ago. I am still in it.

→ I _____ _____ in a band.

5 Jim took pictures of his pets when he got them. He still takes them.

→ Jim _____ _____ pictures of his pets since he got them.

6 Kate went to Busan. She isn't at home now.

→ Kate _____ _____ to Busan.

7 He got some comic books when he was in school. He still reads them.

→ He _____ _____ comic books since he was in school.

8 Karla and Charles met in 2015. They still know each other.

→ Karla and Charles _____ _____ each other since 2015.

연습문제 괄호 안의 말을 활용하여 문장을 완성하시오. (단, 현재완료시제와 과거시제만 사용하시오.)

1 The baker _____ a beautiful cake in 2015. (make)

The baker _____ beautiful cakes since 2015. (make)

2 Cameron _____ TV yesterday afternoon. (watch)

Cameron _____ TV since yesterday afternoon. (watch)

3 Sally _____ to this summer camp in 2018. (go)

Sally _____ to this summer camp since 2018. (go)

4 Songmin _____ this morning. (cry)

Songmin _____ since this morning. (cry)

5 She _____ English last year. (study)

She _____ English since last year. (study)

6 Bella _____ a school uniform last month. (wear)

Bella _____ a school uniform since last month. (wear)

7 The weather service _____ hurricanes in 1900. (track)

The weather service _____ hurricanes since 1900. (track)

8 Davis _____ cooking classes last semester. (take)

Davis _____ cooking classes since last semester. (take)

9 The price of rice _____ a lot last September. (increase)

The price of rice _____ a lot over the last few months. (increase)

10 They _____ together on the soccer team last year. (play)

They _____ together on the soccer team since a couple of years ago. (play)

11 The actor _____ numerous awards in his debut year. (receive)

The actor _____ numerous awards since his debut. (receive)

12 It _____ a lot yesterday. (rain)

It _____ a lot in the past few days. (rain)

POINT 4

연습문제 | 우리말과 같도록 괄호 안의 말을 활용하여 현재완료진행시제 문장을 완성하시오.

1 Tyler는 오후 2시 30분부터 자고 있다. (sleep)

= Tyler _____ since 2:30 P.M.

2 나는 1시간 동안 운동하고 있다. (exercise)

= I _____ for an hour.

3 그 학생들은 오후 내내 공부하고 있다. (study)

= The students _____ all afternoon.

4 그 요리사는 오늘 아침부터 요리하고 있다. (cook)

= The chef _____ since this morning.

5 우리는 버스를 20분 동안 기다리고 있다. (wait)

= We _____ for the bus for 20 minutes.

6 그 마라톤 주자들은 거의 2시간 동안 달리고 있다. (run)

= The marathoners _____ for almost two hours.

7 Leila는 그녀가 집에 온 이후로 그녀의 숙제를 하고 있다. (do)

= Leila _____ her homework since she got home.

8 나는 몇 년 동안 그 밴드의 음악을 듣고 있다. (listen)

= I _____ to the band's music for years.

9 그는 정오부터 파티를 준비하고 있다. (prepare)

= He _____ the party since noon.

10 우리는 한 시간 넘게 그 영화에 대해 논의하고 있다. (discuss)

= We _____ the movie for over an hour.

11 그녀는 오전 10시부터 그녀의 컴퓨터를 고치고 있다. (fix)

= She _____ her computer since 10 A.M.

12 그 아이들은 50분 동안 풍경화를 그리고 있다. (draw)

= The children _____ a landscape picture for 50 minutes.

연습문제 A 밑줄 친 부분이 어법상 맞으면 O로 쓰고, 틀리면 바르게 고쳐 쓰시오.

1 The author had never <u>wrote</u> a romantic novel before.   → _____

2 We should have <u>went</u> to the farm last weekend.   → _____

3 Cathy's family <u>has donated</u> more than $10,000 to charity over the years.   → _____

4 Charles had <u>been</u> in the hospital for two weeks when he had surgery.   → _____

5 Dr. Barlett <u>work</u> at a pharmacy for 40 years before he retired.   → _____

6 I had just <u>got</u> in bed when the phone rang.   → _____

7 She had <u>visited</u> Manila many times before she moved there.   → _____

8 My test scores were a lot better than I had <u>expect</u>.   → _____

연습문제 B 과거완료시제를 이용하여 다음 두 문장을 한 문장으로 연결하시오.

1 The teacher was proud of his students. They all passed the test.
   → The teacher was proud of his students because they all _____ the test.

2 Minho went back to the check-in counter. He left his passport there.
   → Minho went back to the check-in counter because he _____ his passport there.

3 Walter fell off the ladder. He wasn't careful.
   → Walter fell off the ladder because he _____ careful.

4 We had to cut down the tree in our front yard. Lightning struck it.
   → We had to cut down the tree in our front yard because lightning _____ it.

5 We couldn't finish our baseball game this morning. It started to rain.
   → We couldn't finish our baseball game this morning because it _____ to rain.

6 The boys were excited to show the cake to their mother. They made it themselves.
   → The boys were excited to show the cake to their mother because they _____ it themselves.

7 The train did not arrive on time. It left the previous station late.
   → The train did not arrive on time because it _____ the previous station late.

8 Mina brought her computer to the repair shop. It stopped working.
   → Mina brought her computer to the repair shop because it _____ working.

9 Jake wrote a thank-you note to his grandmother. She sent him a birthday gift.
   → Jake wrote a thank-you note to his grandmother because she _____ him a birthday gift.

연습문제 A 우리말과 같도록 괄호 안의 말을 활용하여 과거완료진행시제 문장을 완성하시오.

1 우리 어머니가 집에 돌아왔을 때 우리는 비디오 게임을 3시간 동안 하고 있었다. (play)

= We _____ video games for three hours when our mother came home.

2 나는 나의 아버지가 나에게 자라고 말하기 전에 오랜 시간 동안 공부하고 있었다. (study)

= I _____ for a long time before my father told me to go to bed.

3 Lara는 그 개가 수영장에 뛰어들었을 때 10분 동안 수영을 하고 있었다. (swim)

= Lara _____ for ten minutes when the dog jumped in the pool.

4 Alex와 Jackson은 그들이 시간을 알아차리기 전에 몇 시간 동안 이야기하고 있었다. (talk)

= Alex and Jackson _____ for hours before they realized the time.

5 나의 알람이 울렸을 때 나는 몇 분 동안 낮잠을 자고 있었다. (nap)

= I _____ for a few minutes when my alarm went off.

6 Ken은 그의 목적지에 도착했을 때 네 시간 동안 운전하고 있었다. (drive)

= Ken _____ for four hours by the time he arrived at his destination.

7 Daniel의 가족은 그들이 이사하기 전에 댈러스에서 10년 동안 살고 있었다. (live)

= Daniel's family _____ in Dallas for ten years before they moved.

연습문제 B <보기>와 같이 괄호 안의 동사를 활용하여 대화를 완성하시오.

> <보기> A: Why didn't you come to the mall with us?
> B: I _was watching_ a movie last night. (watch)

1 A: Why didn't you answer the phone when I called?

B: I _____ a shower. (take)

2 A: Why were you late for class?

B: I _____ late this morning. (run)

3 A: Where was your dad during your party yesterday?

B: He _____ all day. (work)

4 A: Why didn't Lisa go to the party last night?

B: She _____ her mom decorate for Christmas. (help)

5 A: Why do you look so tired tonight?

B: I _____ furniture all afternoon. (move)

6 A: Why did Parker miss the graduation ceremony?

B: He broke his leg and _____ surgery to fix it this morning. (have)

1 다음 중 어법상 <u>어색한</u> 것은?

① I saw the TV show last weekend.
② Rosemary is going to meet her cousin at the airport last night.
③ Earth is the fifth largest planet in the solar system.
④ The First World War took place from 1914 to 1918.
⑤ Brazil is the most populated country in South America.

2 우리말과 같도록 괄호 안의 말을 활용하여 완료시제 문장을 완성하시오.

> Kelly는 이전에 골프를 치는 것을 시도해본 적이 있었지만, 그녀는 그것이 지루하다고 생각했다. (try)

= Kelly ＿＿＿＿＿＿＿＿＿ playing golf before, but she thought it was boring.

3 괄호 안의 말을 활용하여 대화를 완성하시오.

> A: ＿＿＿＿＿＿＿＿＿＿＿＿ from here before? (eat, ever, anything, have)
> B: Yes. It's my favorite restaurant. I recommend trying the chicken.

4 다음 빈칸에 들어갈 말이 순서대로 짝지어진 것은?

> Apollo ＿＿＿＿＿ the lead role in the play since last year, and his older brother ＿＿＿＿＿ it for a year before that.

① played – played
② played – had played
③ has played – played
④ has played – had played
⑤ had played – has played

5 다음 중 밑줄 친 부분의 용법이 나머지 넷과 <u>다른</u> 것은?

① He <u>has</u> just <u>returned</u> from his vacation.
② Chris <u>has</u> already <u>gotten</u> supplies for hiking trip.
③ <u>Has</u> the author <u>published</u> his latest book yet?
④ We <u>haven't decided</u> on which computer to purchase.
⑤ Sue <u>has been</u> to Miami many times.

6 다음 글을 아래와 같이 바꿔 쓸 때, 본문에 나온 단어를 활용하여 빈칸에 알맞은 말을 쓰시오.

> This morning, the bus arrived to pick me up as usual. However, I left for school before that. I had a meeting with my teacher when I got to school. Then, I went to my first class.

→ Today, I _____ _____ before the bus arrived to pick me up. At school, I _____ to my first class after I _____ _____ a meeting with my teacher.

7 다음 밑줄 친 부분을 바르게 고치지 <u>못한</u> 것은?

① Jisoo <u>has cooked</u> a delicious pasta dish for dinner last night. (→ cooked)

② Angela had been planning on buying new gloves until she <u>had found</u> her old ones. (→ has found)

③ Michelangelo <u>creates</u> paintings that are still admired today. (→ created)

④ He <u>graduates</u> from high school by the time he was 15. (→ had graduated)

⑤ Dr. Rand <u>had taught</u> a course on Chinese history since last semester. (→ has been teaching)

[8-9] 다음 표를 보고 표에 나온 표현을 활용하여 빈칸에 알맞은 말을 쓰시오.

8

12:00P.M.	Stuart began waiting for his sister Nikki at the restaurant.
12:45P.M.	Nikki finally arrived at the restaurant. Stuart was still waiting for her.

→ Stuart _____ _____ _____ for Nikki for 45 minutes when she _____ _____ the restaurant.

9

3:00 P.M.	I began to play video games with my older sister.
5:00 P.M.	My mother arrived at home. My older sister and I were still playing video games.

→ When my mother _____ at home, my older sister and I _____ _____ _____ _____ for two hours.

10 다음 빈칸에 들어갈 알맞은 것은?

> By the time we got to the campground, other campers _____ the best sites.

① take
② taking
③ have taken
④ have been taking
⑤ had taken

11 우리말과 같도록 괄호 안의 말을 활용하여 완료시제 문장을 완성하시오.

> 그녀는 그녀의 항공편을 놓쳤기 때문에 버스표를 예약했다. (book, miss)

= She ＿＿＿＿＿＿＿ a bus ticket because she ＿＿＿＿＿＿＿ her flight.

12 우리말과 같도록 주어진 <조건>에 맞게 문장을 완성하시오.

> Jordan은 8살 이후로 합창단에서 노래를 부르고 있다.

> <조건>
> 1. 현재완료진행시제를 사용하시오.
> 2. 6단어로 쓰시오.
> 3. sing, in the choir를 활용하시오.

= Jordan ＿＿＿＿＿＿＿＿＿＿＿＿
since she was eight years old.

13 다음 우리말을 영작할 때 빈칸에 들어갈 말이 순서대로 짝지어진 것은?

> 우리가 스키장에 이르렀을 때, 그 슬로프는 이미 문을 닫아버렸었다.
> = When we ＿＿＿＿＿＿＿ the ski resort, the slopes ＿＿＿＿＿＿＿.

① reached – has already closes
② reached – had already closed
③ reached – is already closing
④ had reached – has already closed
⑤ had reached – already closed

14 두 문장의 의미가 같도록 현재완료진행시제 문장을 완성하시오.

> The chef started making this dish when he opened his restaurant, and he is still making it.
> = The chef ＿＿＿＿＿＿＿＿＿ since ＿＿＿＿＿＿＿＿＿＿＿＿＿.

15 다음 중 어법상 바른 것의 개수는?

> ⓐ Hillary has been doing her homework for two hours.
> ⓑ They ate at the café that the owner have remodeled recently.
> ⓒ The concert has already started when I arrived at the arena.
> ⓓ Sumin was happy because she had won the tennis match.
> ⓔ My dog had eaten a whole bag of snacks before I noticed.

① 1개　　② 2개　　③ 3개
④ 4개　　⑤ 없음

16 괄호 안의 말을 활용하여 빈칸에 알맞은 말을 쓰시오.

> Benjamin joined a scuba diving club a few months ago. He ⓐ _____ _____ (meet) a lot of new friends since he joined the club. Over the last couple of months, he ⓑ _____ _____ (go) on many diving trips with them.

17 다음 중 어법상 어색한 것은?

① He got a new notebook because he had broken his last one.
② Alice and Maria have been classmates since they were in kindergarten.
③ She had never gotten perfect attendance until last year.
④ The ferry has already departed when I got to the dock.
⑤ Karen said that she had stayed at her grandmother's house for three weeks.

18 두 문장의 의미가 같도록 빈칸에 알맞은 말을 쓰시오.

> Joanne lived in Germany many years ago, and she still lives in Germany now.
> = Joanne _____ _____ in Germany for many years.

[19-20] 다음 글을 읽고 주어진 질문에 답하시오.

> I ①have been taking horseback riding lessons since I ②has been nine years old. Since starting middle school, I (A) have ridden my horse almost every weekday. Until recently, I ③loved going to my lessons. I didn't have much schoolwork to do, so there ④was never a problem getting everything done. But now, I'm very busy and ⑤have even missed some homework due to my riding lessons. I think I should take a break.

19 위 글의 밑줄 친 (A)와 용법이 같은 것은?

① Brian has never tried making dumplings.
② He has just ridden his bicycle in the parking lot.
③ How long has Hailey played the piano?
④ I have already replaced my old tablet.
⑤ Has your older brother gone to Colombia?

20 위 글의 밑줄 친 ①~⑤ 중, 어법상 어색한 것을 찾아 번호를 쓰고 바르게 고쳐 쓰시오.

_____ → _____

21 우리말과 같도록 괄호 안의 말을 활용하여 완료시제 문장을 완성하시오.

> Sarah는 학교에 그녀의 책들을 가져오지 않았다는 것을 깨달았다. (realize, bring)

= Sarah _____ that she _____ _____ her books to school.

22 두 문장의 의미가 같도록 빈칸에 알맞은 말을 쓰시오.

> My father owned a shoe store in 1995, and he still owns a shoe store now.
> = My father _____ _____ a shoe store since 1995.

23 다음 중 어법상 바른 것은?

① Have you been played with the puppy until now?
② I have been watch TV since 5 o'clock.
③ Christine has been gone to the same school second grade.
④ We have been looking for our lost cat.
⑤ Yujin has been slept on the sofa for two hours.

24 두 문장의 의미가 같도록 현재완료진행시제 문장을 완성하시오.

> Trey started working on his science project yesterday, and he is still working on it.
> = Trey _____ _____ since yesterday.

25 괄호 안의 말을 활용하여 질문에 대한 대답을 쓰시오.

> A: How long has David been taking painting classes?
> B: He _____ _____. (take, painting classes, ten years old, since)

CHAPTER 3
조동사

연습문제 A 다음 빈칸에 들어갈 알맞은 것을 <u>모두</u> 고르시오.

1 _____ you give Sally a message for me?
① Can ② May ③ Will

2 You _____ sit in this seat if you want.
① can't ② may ③ can

3 He _____ call me when his plane arrives at the airport.
① is going to ② will ③ going to

4 Cindy _____ do almost any yoga position.
① is able to ② is going ③ can

5 She _____ need some assistance with planning her trip.
① can ② may ③ might

6 You _____ borrow my laptop.
① can ② may ③ is able to

연습문제 B 괄호 안에서 밑줄 친 부분의 쓰임을 고르시오.

1 I <u>can</u> run a kilometer in six minutes.   (능력 / 추측 / 미래)

2 You <u>may</u> play video games for one hour.   (요청 / 허가 / 의지)

3 <u>Will</u> you hand me a towel?   (요청 / 추측 / 허가)

4 We <u>are going to</u> watch a play at the theater.   (추측 / 허가 / 미래)

5 <u>Can</u> we order pizza for dinner, please?   (추측 / 허가 / 미래)

6 The light is off in his room, so he <u>may</u> be asleep.   (요청 / 추측 / 미래)

7 <u>Can</u> you help me with my homework?   (허가 / 의지 / 요청)

8 The rumor about Ben <u>can't</u> be true.   (요청 / 추측 / 능력)

9 I <u>will</u> remember this day forever.   (의지 / 능력 / 요청)

10 The mall <u>might</u> be closed because of the holiday.   (허가 / 추측 / 요청)

11 He <u>will</u> send the e-mail later.   (능력 / 의지 / 요청)

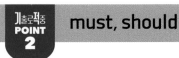

must, should

연습문제 A 괄호 안에서 알맞은 것을 고르시오.

1 According to the law, you (must / shouldn't) have a passport to travel abroad.

2 I already cleaned the kitchen, so you (should / don't have to) do it.

3 I hurt Laura's feelings, so I think I (don't have to / should) apologize to her.

4 It's OK to wear your shoes in this restaurant, so you (ought to / don't have to) take them off.

5 The baby's head feels hot. She (must / should) have a fever.

6 We (must not / should) visit Grandma in the hospital and take her some flowers.

7 You (must not / don't have to) make a lot of noise in the library.

8 My mom got a parking ticket, so she (shouldn't / must) pay a fine.

9 It's snowing. You (don't have to / shouldn't) drive too fast.

10 You (have to / shouldn't) fix the roof now, because it might fall apart.

연습문제 B 밑줄 친 부분이 강한 의무를 나타내는지 강한 추측을 나타내는지 쓰시오.

1 Citizens <u>must</u> pay taxes.   [   ]

2 Both parties <u>must</u> sign the contract.   [   ]

3 The neighbors <u>must</u> be on vacation.   [   ]

4 People in the army <u>must</u> keep their uniforms clean all the time.   [   ]

5 Paul <u>must</u> love comic books as he has so many.   [   ]

6 That café is always busy, so it <u>must</u> be popular.   [   ]

7 You <u>must</u> wear a life jacket on this boat.   [   ]

8 His severely sunburned skin <u>must</u> be painful.   [   ]

9 The patients <u>must</u> take the medicine twice a day.   [   ]

10 Her large diamond ring <u>must</u> be worth a lot of money.   [   ]

11 The patient <u>must</u> see her doctor now.   [   ]

12 The vending machine <u>must</u> be out of order.   [   ]

13 The milk in the fridge <u>must</u> be expired.   [   ]

14 The reporter <u>must</u> meet the deadline.   [   ]

15 She <u>must</u> be too busy to answer the phone.   [   ]

연습문제 우리말과 같도록 <보기>와 괄호 안의 말을 활용하여 빈칸에 쓰시오.

<보기>   suggest   recommend   insist   request   require   order

1 Mike는 우리가 우리의 안전벨트를 매야 한다고 주장했다. (put on)

→ Mike _____ that we _____ _____ our seat belts.

2 진호는 Rachel이 분홍색 드레스를 사야 한다고 제안했다. (buy)

→ Jinho _____ that Rachel _____ a pink dress.

3 그 버스 기사는 모두가 좌석에 머물러야 한다고 요구했다. (stay)

→ The bus driver _____ that everybody _____ in their seats.

4 그는 그 가게가 그에게 환불해 줄 것을 요청했다. (give)

→ He _____ that the store _____ him a refund.

5 그 여자는 우리가 Main Street에 있는 호텔 중 하나에 방을 잡을 것을 추천했다. (reserve)

→ The woman _____ that we _____ a room at one of the hotels on Main Street.

6 그 공원 경비원은 그들에게 모닥불을 끌 것을 명령했다. (put out)

→ The park ranger _____ that they _____ _____ the campfire.

7 이 레스토랑은 고객들이 현금으로 지불할 것을 요구한다. (pay)

→ This restaurant _____ that customers _____ with cash.

8 나의 고모는 내가 다음주에 그녀를 방문할 것을 요청했다. (visit)

→ My aunt _____ that I _____ her next weekend.

9 Hopkins씨는 그의 아이들이 어두워지기 전에 집에 있어야 한다고 주장했다. (be)

→ Mr. Hopkins _____ that his children _____ home before dark.

10 Monica는 Matt이 그녀와 함께 예술 박물관에 가야 한다고 제안했다. (go)

→ Monica _____ that Matt _____ to the art museum with her.

11 Lucy는 우리가 공항으로 일찍 떠나야 한다고 주장했다. (leave)

→ Lucy _____ that we _____ early for the airport.

연습문제 A 우리말과 같도록 used to와 괄호 안의 말을 활용하여 문장을 완성하시오.

1 그녀는 학교 밴드에서 트럼펫을 연주하곤 했다. (play)

= She _____ the trumpet in the school band.

2 Teresa는 매일 아침 일찍 일어나는 것에 익숙하다. (wake up)

= Teresa _____ early every morning.

3 그는 바다에서 수영하는 것에 익숙하다. (swim)

= He _____ in the sea.

4 Nicholas는 어렸을 때 독일에서 살았다. (live)

= Nicholas _____ in Germany when he was young.

5 이 카드는 많은 가게에서 할인을 받는데 사용된다. (get)

= This card _____ discounts at many stores.

6 Nancy는 매우 똑똑해서, 좋은 성적을 받는 것에 익숙하다. (receive)

= Nancy is very smart, so she _____ good grades.

7 이 혼합기는 빵 밀가루 반죽을 만드는 데 사용된다. (make)

= This mixer _____ bread dough.

연습문제 B 밑줄 친 부분이 어법상 맞으면 O를 쓰고, 틀리면 바르게 고쳐 쓰시오.

1 Jake has a pet cat that used to <u>living</u> on the street. → _____

2 I <u>would</u> hate onions, but I like them now. → _____

3 This machine is used to <u>generate</u> electricity. → _____

4 Air conditioners are used to <u>keep</u> us cool in the summer. → _____

5 She used to <u>take</u> yoga lessons on Fridays before she changed her schedule. → _____

6 We didn't use to <u>having</u> a public library, but now we have a very nice one. → _____

7 My mom used to <u>working</u> as a server in a restaurant. → _____

8 I wasn't used to <u>use</u> my new smartphone at first, but now I am. → _____

9 Sunmi just got her license, so she is not used to <u>drive</u> yet. → _____

10 As a child, I used to <u>believing</u> in Santa Claus. → _____

연습문제 A 우리말과 같도록 괄호 안의 말을 활용하여 문장을 완성하시오.

1 우리는 그가 그 건물에 들어오도록 허가하지 말았어야 했다. (permit)

= We _____ him to enter the building.

2 우리는 학교까지 버스를 탔어야 했다. (take)

= We _____ the bus to school.

3 그녀는 그 식물에게 물 주는 것을 잊었을 수도 있다. (forget)

= She _____ to water the plants.

4 나는 숙제를 끝냈을 수도 있었지만, 대신에 나는 야구 경기를 봤다. (do)

= I _____ my homework, but I watched a baseball game instead.

5 그 램프가 이제 작동하는 걸 보니 미나가 그 램프를 고쳤음이 틀림없다. (fix)

= Mina _____ the lamp, because it works now.

6 내가 그보다 먼저 떠났기 때문에, 그가 도착했을 리가 없다. (arrive)

= He _____ because I left before him.

연습문제 B 다음 두 문장의 의미가 같도록 「조동사 + have p.p.」를 활용하여 문장을 완성하시오.

1 It's not possible that she painted the house already.

= She _____ the house already.

2 I am sorry that I didn't offer him some help.

= I _____ him some help.

3 It's uncertain whether she convinced him to come.

= She _____ him to come.

4 It was not nice of you to lie to the teacher.

= You _____ to the teacher.

5 It's almost certain that the house was built in the 1980s.

= This house _____ built in the 1980s.

6 It was a bad idea for me to buy this expensive camera.

= I _____ this expensive camera.

POINT 6

연습문제 우리말과 같도록 괄호 안의 말을 배열하시오.

1 Tom이 거미를 무서워하는 것도 당연하다. (spiders, well, may, afraid of, Tom, be)

= _____

2 나는 휴식을 취하기보다 차라리 계속해서 일을 하겠다. (continue working, I, rather, take a break, than, would)

= _____

3 나는 나의 엄마가 이 그릇을 원한다고 생각한다. (this bowl, think, my mom, would, like, I)

= _____

4 그녀는 수리공에게 전화를 하는 편이 좋다. (may, as, a repair person, she, well, call)

= _____

5 그 경찰관은 너에게 몇 개의 질문을 하고 싶다. (you, would, some questions, to, like, the officer, ask)

= _____

6 너는 버스가 몇 시에 오는지 확인하는 것이 낫다. (what time, comes, better, check, had, you, the bus)

= _____

7 나는 여행 가방보다 차라리 배낭을 들겠다. (I, the suitcase, carry, rather, the backpack, than, would)

= _____

8 그녀가 말한 것이 사실인 것도 당연하다. (true, may, said, she, be, what, well)

= _____

9 나는 그에게 나의 책을 빌려주는 편이 좋다. (well, my book, may, as, him, lend, I)

= _____

10 나의 부모님은 프랑스로 여행하고 싶다. (to, would, parents, to, France, like, my, travel)

= _____

11 너는 네가 너의 여권을 가지고 있는지 확실히 하는 것이 낫다. (have, you, had, make sure, your passport, you, better)

= _____

기출로 적중 해카스 중학영문법 3학년 워크북

중간·기말고사 실전 문제

1 다음 중 자연스럽지 <u>않은</u> 대화를 <u>모두</u> 고르시오.

① A: Where is Sally? We were supposed to meet here at 1 P.M.
  B: She must have arrived a little earlier.

② A: That was a great game at the park last night.
  B: I didn't know you were there. You could have sat beside me.

③ A: I can't remember where I put my umbrella.
  B: You may have left it at the office.

④ A: Has mom left for the supermarket?
  B: She can't have gone yet. Her car keys are still here.

⑤ A: I'm sorry I missed your call. I didn't hear my phone ring.
  B: You should have turned off your phone.

3 우리말과 같도록 괄호 안의 말을 활용하여 문장을 완성하시오.

> Lesley는 우리가 교통 체증을 피하기 위해서 일찍 떠나야 한다고 제안했다. (suggest, early, we, that, leave)

= Lesley _____

_____ to avoid the heavy traffic.

4 다음 중 어법상 <u>어색한</u> 것은?

① She doesn't have to purchase the equipment now.
② Should we invite the new girl to join us for lunch?
③ He had not better go out while the storm is still strong.
④ Carol must pay for the plane ticket today.
⑤ You should tell the doctor about your chest pain.

2 다음 우리말과 같도록 빈칸에 알맞은 말을 고르시오.

> 오늘 저녁에 온도가 갑자기 떨어질지도 모른다.
> = Temperatures _____ drop suddenly this evening.

① may   ② used to   ③ will
④ must   ⑤ should

5 괄호 안의 말을 활용하여 대화를 완성하시오.

> A: Luis _____(must, be) here just a while ago.
> B: How can you tell?
> A: That's his coffee mug, and the coffee's still hot.

6 다음 밑줄 친 Can과 의미가 같은 것은?

> <u>Can</u> we order takeout for dinner this evening?

① You <u>can't</u> sit here as these seats are taken.
② <u>Could</u> you let me know when the item is restocked?
③ I <u>couldn't</u> get tickets for tomorrow's concert.
④ The entrance exam <u>can't</u> be that difficult.
⑤ We <u>could</u> tell how sad Sarah was by her crying.

7 우리말과 같도록 괄호 안의 말을 알맞게 배열하시오.

> 네가 세탁소에 가는 중이기 때문에, 네가 나의 코트를 가져오는 게 좋다. (as, you, may, my coat, bring, well)

= Since you are going to the cleaner's,

_____ .

8 다음 대화의 밑줄 친 우리말과 같도록 괄호 안의 말을 이용하여 빈칸에 알맞은 말을 쓰시오.

> A: Gerry is having second thoughts about going on the trip with us.
> B: Although we will miss him, <u>그는 갈 필요가 없어.</u> (go) Did he say why he can't go?
> A: He didn't say why. You should not ask him-it's probably a personal reason.

= he _____ _____ _____ _____

9 다음 밑줄 친 may와 의미가 같은 것은?

> The tour guide said we <u>may</u> go where we wish after we visit the museum.

① You <u>may</u> need to bring something to eat.
② You <u>may</u> bring a guest to the wedding.
③ I <u>may</u> have to leave a little earlier.
④ She <u>may</u> need to get a flu shot.
⑤ They <u>may</u> have to take the next flight.

10 두 문장의 의미가 같도록 빈칸에 알맞은 말을 쓰시오.

> Steve was once a top lawyer for a law firm, but he is now a chef at a seafood restaurant.

= Steve _____ _____ _____ a top lawyer.

11 다음 중 밑줄 친 부분의 의미가 나머지 넷과 <u>다른</u> 것은?

① You <u>must</u> be feeling dizzy after that blood test.
② He <u>must</u> be on time for his appointment.
③ <u>Must</u> we really buy that book today?
④ He <u>must</u> come earlier than he did yesterday.
⑤ She <u>must</u> submit that report by tomorrow.

12 다음 빈칸에 공통으로 들어갈 알맞은 것은?

> A: _____ I ask you for help?
> B: Yes. How may I help you?
> A: Would you put my bag on that luggage rack?
> B: Of course. I _____ do that for you.

① will   ② can   ③ should
④ would   ⑤ must

13 다음 빈칸에 들어갈 말이 순서대로 짝지어진 것은?

> • She _____ get an answer to her question.
> • You _____ eat too much at night.

① would like – should not
② would like to – should not
③ would like to – should
④ would like – should
⑤ would like to – need not

14 다음 글의 밑줄 친 ⓐ~ⓔ 중 어법상 어색한 것을 찾아 기호를 쓰고 바르게 고쳐 쓰시오.

> This year, I ⓐwill do something about my weight problem. I know I eat too much and exercise too little. I ⓑmay have to stop buying chips and colas, or ⓒmight even ask a doctor for help to control my appetite. I ⓓhave get some exercise by walking or jogging. I ⓔcould ask my family to help out, so I can eat healthy.

_____ → _____

15 <보기>의 말을 모두 사용하여 대화를 완성하시오.

> <보기> like   would   to   rather   would

> A: What would you like to do this weekend?
> B: I ⓐ_____ have a picnic at the park. How about you?
> A: I ⓑ_____ go see a movie.
> B: Sure. We can do that if that's what you want. We haven't seen a movie in a long time.

16 괄호 안의 말을 활용하여 문장을 완성하시오.

> Teenagers _____ (use, to) be on their phones all the time, but now it's normal.

17 다음 중 어법상 어색한 것은?

① Did Mary use to play with us when we were kids?
② This room is used to store old stuff.
③ Ella used to get some hot coffee every morning.
④ She didn't use to like working out at the gym.
⑤ We are used to eat dinner a little late in the evening.

18 다음 글의 빈칸에 들어갈 말이 순서대로 짝지어진 것은?

> There are important rules to follow for those taking the test today. We would like to just give you a reminder. First, you _____ talk to your seatmates or pass notes to them. Also, if you feel sick and you _____ complete the test, let me know immediately and I will inform the school authorities.

① must not – weren't able to
② don't have to – weren't able to
③ must not – might not
④ don't have to – might not
⑤ must not – aren't able to

19 다음 우리말을 알맞게 영작한 것은?

> 너는 도서관에 어떠한 종류의 음료도 가지고 오면 안 된다.

① You would not bring any kind of drink into the library.
② You might not bring any kind of drink into the library.
③ You don't have to bring any kind of drink into the library.
④ You must not bring any kind of drink into the library.
⑤ You could not bring any kind of drink into the library.

20 다음 글을 읽고 밑줄 친 우리말과 같도록 주어진 <조건>에 맞게 문장을 완성하시오.

> In some Middle Eastern countries, giving a compliment to someone for something they are wearing or something in their home is not always seen as praise. It is understood as a request to be given the object that you admire. So in these countries, 당신은 다른 사람의 물건에 대해 칭찬하지 않는 것이 낫다.

> **<조건>**
> 1. 7단어로 쓰시오.
> 2. had better, a compliment, give를 활용하시오.

= _____ about other's belongings.

21 다음 빈칸에 들어갈 말이 순서대로 짝지어진 것은?

> · You had _____ tell anyone what I just told you.
> · You may as well _____ a cab or else you'll be late.

① not better – take
② better not – take
③ better not – to take
④ not better – to take
⑤ better not – taking

22 <보기>의 말과 괄호 안의 말을 활용하여 문장을 완성하시오.

| <보기>   should   must |

(1) Bill fell asleep right after lunch. He
_____ (eat) too
much.

(2) Ron _____ (miss)
the test. He'll have to make up for it.

[24-25] 우리말과 같도록 괄호 안의 말을 활용하여 문장을 완성하시오.

24

너는 지금 우유를 냉장고에 넣는 것이 낫다. (better, now, in the fridge, the milk, put)

= _____

25

너는 이곳에 너의 차를 주차하면 안 된다. (must, your car, park, in this spot)

= _____

23 괄호 안의 말을 활용하여 대화를 완성하시오.

A: How did you prepare for important exams in school?

B: I ⓐ_____ (use, study) in a small booth at the library.

A: How often would you study there?

B: Well, I ⓑ_____ (would, go) there every day except when the library was closed.

A: That must have been very tiring

B: Sure, studying is hard work, but I ⓒ_____ (use, take) several breaks, so I never got too tired.

CHAPTER 4
수동태

연습문제 다음 문장을 괄호 안의 지시대로 바꿔 쓰시오.

1 A famous architect designed the airport. (수동태 문장으로)

→ _____ by a famous architect.

2 The hikers rode donkeys into the canyon. (수동태 문장으로)

→ _____ by the hikers into the canyon.

3 The fire chief confirmed the cause of the fire. (수동태 문장으로)

→ _____ by the fire chief.

4 The meteor was observed by NASA scientists. (의문문으로)

→ _____ by NASA scientists?

5 This shampoo is recommended for clients with dry hair. (의문문으로)

→ _____ with dry hair?

6 The main character in the book is married to a prince. (부정문으로)

→ _____ to a prince.

7 All the students are finished with the exam. (의문문으로)

→ _____ with the exam?

8 This dinosaur fossil was discovered by the English researcher. (when 의문문으로)

→ _____ by the English researcher?

9 The theory of relativity is understood by many people. (부정문으로)

→ _____ by many people.

10 Office supplies are purchased by the manager. (부정문으로)

→ _____ by the manager.

11 The residents were warned about the tropical storm. (의문문으로)

→ _____ about the tropical storm?

12 The champion boxer was challenged by a rookie. (when 의문문으로)

→ _____ by a rookie?

POINT 2 — 수동태로 쓸 수 없는 동사

정답 p.66

연습문제 밑줄 친 부분이 어법상 맞으면 O를 쓰고, 틀리면 바르게 고쳐 쓰시오.

1 My story <u>is resembled by</u> an old fairytale. → _____

2 Small miracles <u>are happened</u> every day. → _____

3 The hot air balloon <u>rose</u> quickly. → _____

4 A strange light <u>was appeared</u> in the sky. → _____

5 Pigs and chicken <u>are risen</u> on my uncle's farm. → _____

6 Emily <u>didn't arrive</u> at the picnic until 1 P.M. → _____

7 The stores <u>were remained</u> open on Christmas Day. → _____

8 Dinosaurs <u>disappeared</u> from the Earth millions of years ago. → _____

9 The tree <u>was fallen</u> to build a log cabin. → _____

10 The suit <u>was fitted</u> him well. → _____

POINT 3 — 수동태의 시제

정답 p.66

연습문제 괄호 안의 동사를 활용하여 빈칸에 쓰시오.

1 The car _____ _____ by Ms. Anderson yesterday. (buy)

2 Questions _____ _____ _____ at the end of the speech. (answer)

3 The cake _____ _____ by the customers yesterday. (eat)

4 The roller coaster _____ _____ _____ by over a million guests. (ride)

5 The actress's new movie _____ _____ _____ next month. (release)

6 The dog _____ _____ _____ by Susan at the moment. (wash)

7 Dinner _____ _____ _____ by my mother when I got home. (make)

8 The test _____ _____ _____ by all students tomorrow. (take)

9 Many cookies _____ _____ by the children yesterday for the bake sale. (bake)

10 Many good books _____ _____ _____ these days. (publish)

11 The problem _____ _____ _____ by tonight. (solve)

12 My computer _____ _____ _____ 14 times when I finally replaced it. (repair)

연습문제 우리말과 같도록 괄호 안의 말을 활용하여 문장을 완성하시오.

1 이 냉장고는 내일 아침까지 수리되어야 한다. (fix, should)

= This refrigerator _____ by tomorrow morning.

2 그 이야기는 Alex와 Maria에 의해 쓰여질 것이다. (write, will)

= The story _____ by Alex and Maria.

3 그 컴퓨터는 그 프로그램을 사용하기 위해 다시 시작되어야 한다. (restart, must)

= The computer _____ to use the program.

4 그 프로젝트는 다음 주 금요일까지 완료될 수 있다. (complete, can)

= The project _____ by next Friday.

5 이 울타리가 새 것으로 교체될 수 있나요? (replace, can)

= _____ this fence _____ with a new one?

연습문제 다음 능동태 문장을 수동태로 바꿔 쓰시오.

1 I gave Minji some snacks.

→ Some snacks _____.

→ Minji _____.

2 The woman showed him a picture.

→ He _____.

→ A picture _____.

3 He builds children doll houses.

→ Children _____.

→ Doll houses _____.

4 The students asked the teacher some questions.

→ The teacher _____.

→ Some questions _____.

연습문제 다음 능동태 문장은 수동태로, 수동태 문장은 능동태로 바꿔 쓰시오.

1 The coach expects Jason to become a legendary baseball player someday.

→ Jason _____ by the coach.

2 The painting is considered his best artwork by many people.

→ Many people _____.

3 She asked Robert to set the table.

→ Robert _____ by her.

4 We were encouraged to watch the educational TV series by Mr. Lee.

→ Mr. Lee _____.

5 The shepherd boy was called a liar by the villagers.

→ The villagers _____.

6 The heater will keep the building warm in winter.

→ The building _____ by the heater.

7 Motorists were made to exit the highway by police officers.

→ Police officers _____.

8 The government forced the criminal to return to his country.

→ The criminal _____ by the government.

9 Something was smelled burning by the cook when he entered the kitchen.

→ The cook _____ when he entered the kitchen.

10 Frank heard someone singing next door.

→ Someone _____ by Frank.

11 Melissa was helped to write an essay by her older sister.

→ Her older sister _____.

12 The principal didn't allow students to bring their phones to school.

→ Students _____ by the principal.

구동사의 수동태

POINT 7

정답 p.67

연습문제 우리말과 같도록 <보기>의 말을 활용하여 문장을 완성하시오.

| <보기>   set up   turn on   look down on   turn down   make use of |

1 그녀의 조언은 직원들에 의해 이용되었다.

= Her advice _____ by the employees.

2 그 콘서트홀은 Main Street에 세워졌다.

= The concert hall _____ on Main Street.

3 전기는 전기회사에 의해 켜졌다.

= The power _____ by the electric company.

4 그 장군의 제안은 모두에 의해 거절되었다.

= The general's offer _____ by everyone.

5 그 새로운 선수는 그녀의 경험 있는 팀 동료들에 의해 무시되었다.

= The new player _____ by her experienced teammates.

목적어가 that절인 문장의 수동태

POINT 8

정답 p.67

연습문제 다음 능동태 문장을 수동태로 바꿀 때 빈칸에 알맞은 말을 쓰시오.

1 Everyone knew that the law would be changed.

→ _____ _____ _____ _____ the law would be changed.

2 People said that Greg was the best painter at the school.

→ Greg _____ _____ _____ _____ _____ _____
_____ at the school.

3 We believe that money is not important.

→ _____ _____ _____ _____ money is not important.

4 People realized that the Earth goes around the Sun.

→ _____ _____ _____ that the Earth goes around the Sun.

5 They say that exercising increases your life span.

→ Exercising _____ _____ _____ _____ _____
_____ _____ .

연습문제 우리말과 같도록 괄호 안의 말을 활용하여 문장을 완성하시오.

1 그들은 그들의 시험 점수에 기뻐했다. (please, their test scores)
= They _____ .

2 그 소프트웨어는 게임을 만드는 데 사용된다. (use, create games)
= The software _____ .

3 그 박스들은 오래된 장난감으로 가득 차 있다. (fill, old toys)
= The boxes _____ .

4 우리는 우리의 지난 농구 시합에 실망했다. (disappoint, our last basketball match)
= We _____ .

5 그 식탁은 음식 부스러기로 덮여 있다. (cover, food crumbs)
= The table _____ .

6 이 주스는 포도로 만들어진다. (make, grapes)
= This juice _____ .

7 나의 아빠는 나를 차에 태우러 오기로 되어있었다. (suppose, pick me up)
= My dad _____ .

8 그녀는 수학 전문가로서 알려져 있다. (know, a math expert)
= She _____ .

9 나는 자전거를 타는데 흥미가 있다. (interest, ride a bicycle)
= I _____ .

10 그 회사의 야구 방망이들은 나무로 만들어진다. (make, wood)
= The company's baseball bats _____ .

11 그 나이 든 마술사는 그의 동전 마술들로 유명했다. (know, his coin tricks)
= The old magician _____ .

12 그 병사는 그의 영웅적인 행동들로 기억될 것이다. (remember, his heroic actions)
= The soldier _____ .

중간·기말고사 실전 문제

1 다음 중 수동태로 바꿀 수 <u>없는</u> 것을 <u>모두</u> 고르시오.

① Around 70 percent of people speak more than one language.

② I spent a lot of money to buy a computer.

③ The package arrived at my house on Saturday.

④ I resemble my mother more than my father.

⑤ The teacher told Jeremy to be quiet.

2 다음 중 수동태로 바르게 바꾼 것은?

① Street performers sing songs every weekend here.
  → Songs to be sung by street performers every weekend here.

② Beavers build dams to create a small pond.
  → Dams are built by beavers to create a small pond.

③ Erika arranged the mannequins in the display window.
  → The mannequins being arranged in the display window by Erika.

④ Most shops in airports offer duty-free products.
  → Duty-free products are offering at most shops in airports.

⑤ They thanked Mr. Kim for his donation.
  → Mr. Kim was thanking by them for his donation.

3 우리말과 같도록 괄호 안의 말을 활용하여 문장을 완성하시오.

> 그녀의 다리는 스키 사고 때문에 부러졌다. (break)

= Her leg _____ because of a skiing accident.

4 다음 문장을 수동태 문장으로 바꿔 쓰시오.

> Geologists explored the cave around ten years ago.
>
> → _____
>
> _____

[5-6] 두 문장의 의미가 같도록 빈칸에 알맞은 말을 쓰시오.

5

> My friend takes care of my cats when I go on a trip.
> = My cats _____ _____
> _____ _____ by my friend
>   when I go on a trip.

6

> The baseball player turned down the new contract.
> = The new contract _____
> _____ _____ _____
> _____ _____ _____ .

7 다음 중 어법상 어색한 것은?

① Baking ingredients should be measured carefully.
② All of my things were packed by the movers.
③ The wallet was returned to the owner.
④ Social issues are talked about in debate class.
⑤ The rabbit was disappeared in the magician's hat.

9 다음 중 어법상 어색한 것은?

① The singer was surrounded by reporters and fans.
② Clothes have to be returned within three days for a refund.
③ Your science project should be finished by next week.
④ Files should organized by subject not date.
⑤ The restroom must not be used until the toilet is fixed.

10 괄호 안의 말을 알맞게 배열하여 문장을 완성하시오.

The children _____
_____.
(entertained, by, the clowns, were)

8 다음 글의 빈칸에 공통으로 들어갈 알맞은 것은?

Kyle loves to cook and experiment with different recipes. He is known _____ some people as the Inventor Chef because of his creative dishes. For instance, waffles are supposed _____ be a breakfast food. Kyle makes pizzas with them! Chocolate is typically used _____ make desserts, but not for Kyle. He makes chocolate-covered bacon sandwiches.

① at   ② in   ③ by
④ with   ⑤ to

11 다음 문장을 수동태로 바르게 바꾼 것을 모두 고르시오.

The guide showed the visitors the new exhibit in the museum.

① The new exhibit in the museum was shown to the visitors by the guide.
② The new exhibit in the museum were shown to the visitors by the guide.
③ The new exhibit in the museum was show to the visitors by the guide.
④ The visitors were showing the new exhibit in the museum by the guide.
⑤ The visitors were shown the new exhibit in the museum by the guide.

12 다음 빈칸에 들어갈 말이 순서대로 짝지어진 것은?

· I saw the man climbing up the mountain.
→ The man was seen _____ up the mountain by me.
· Everyone knew that she dresses in fashionable outfits.
→ She was known _____ in fashionable outfits by everyone.

① climbing – to dress
② climbing – dress
③ to climb – dress
④ to climb – dressed
⑤ to climb – to dress

13 다음 문장을 수동태로 바꿔 쓰시오.

The farmer does not grow tropical fruits.
→ _____

14 다음 우리말을 알맞게 영작한 것은?

UFO는 세계 곳곳에서 고대부터 발견되어왔다.

① UFOs have been spot around the world since ancient times.
② UFOs have being spot around the world since ancient times.
③ UFOs have been spotted around the world since ancient times.
④ UFOs have been spotting around the world since ancient times.
⑤ UFOs have being spotted around the world since ancient times.

[15-17] 우리말과 같도록 괄호 안의 말을 활용하여 빈칸에 쓰시오.

15

그 책은 20개가 넘는 언어로 프린트될 것이다.
(print)

= The book _____ _____ _____ in more than 20 languages.

16

나의 강아지는 보호소에서 입양되었다. (adopt)

= My puppy _____ _____ from a shelter.

17

올해 열 개의 새로운 단어가 사전에 추가되었다.
(add)

= Ten new words _____ _____ _____ to the dictionary this year.

18 다음 중 문장의 태를 <u>잘못</u> 바꾼 것은?

① The gallery displayed his paintings.

→ His paintings were displayed by the gallery.

② The government didn't build this monument.

→ This monument wasn't built by the government.

③ Did the committee approve the plans?

→ Were the plans be approved by the committee?

④ When did they show the documentary on TV?

→ When was the documentary shown on TV?

⑤ Tamara has knitted a scarf for her niece.

→ A scarf has been knitted for her niece by Tamara.

19 우리말과 같도록 괄호 안의 말을 활용하여 문장을 완성하시오.

> 낙엽은 길 위에서 치워져야 한다. (have to, clean)

= Fallen leaves _____ from the streets.

20 다음 문장을 수동태로 바꿔 쓰시오.

> Some people don't believe in ghosts.
>
> → _____

21 다음 빈칸에 들어갈 알맞은 것은?

> William _____ for the football team this time.

① might chose

② might being chosen

③ might be choosing

④ might be chosen

⑤ might been chosen

22 다음 밑줄 친 부분을 바르게 고친 것끼리 묶인 것은?

> ⓐ Outside food <u>does not</u> allowed inside the movie theater. (→ is not)
>
> ⓑ The patient <u>has</u> examined by the doctor. (→ been)
>
> ⓒ A new railroad is <u>been built</u>. (→ being build)
>
> ⓓ The winner of the lottery will <u>being</u> announced on the news. (→ be)

① ⓐ, ⓑ   ② ⓐ, ⓓ   ③ ⓑ, ⓓ

④ ⓑ, ⓒ   ⑤ ⓒ, ⓓ

23 우리말과 같도록 괄호 안의 말을 활용하여 빈칸에 쓰시오.

> 이탈리아인들은 음식에 대한 그들의 사랑으로 유명하다. (know)

= Italians _____ _____
_____ their love of food.

25 다음 중 문장의 태를 바르게 바꾼 것은?

① Mr. Lee told me to review the intern applications.
  → I was told review the intern applications by Mr. Lee.
② My dog chased after the birds in the backyard.
  → The birds in the backyard chased after were by my dog.
③ He gave his girlfriend a box of chocolates.
  → A box of chocolates was given his girlfriend by him.
④ Several people saw the man drive through a red light.
  → The man was seeing by several people to drive through a red light.
⑤ The archeologist didn't find the lost treasure.
  → The lost treasure wasn't found by the archeologist.

24 다음 빈칸에 들어갈 말이 순서대로 짝지어진 것은?

> · A letter was written _____ the president of the company.
> · The app is made _____ smartphones and smart watches.

① for – to   ② of – to   ③ for – of
④ of – for   ⑤ to – for

CHAPTER 5
부정사

기출로 적중 POINT

연습문제 A 밑줄 친 부분이 어법상 맞으면 O를 쓰고, 틀리면 바르게 고쳐 완전한 문장을 쓰시오.

1 The teacher instructed the class to prepare for a test.

→ _____

2 My plan is to stays home on Sunday.

→ _____

3 George asked me to meet him at the mall.

→ _____

4 Mr. Miller told me rewriting the essay.

→ _____

5 The team's goal is to making it to the championship.

→ _____

연습문제 B 밑줄 친 to부정사의 용법과 같은 것을 <보기>에서 골라 그 기호를 쓰시오.

<보기>	ⓐ I want to have some Indian food.
	ⓑ Dave owns a lot of tools to fix cars.
	ⓒ I bought a tablet to read electronic books.

1 We got up early to see the sun rise.   [   ]

2 You can use the stairs to reach the second floor.   [   ]

3 Tracy studied hard to pass the exam.   [   ]

4 The builder's plan is to finish the mansion this year. [   ]

5 To vote in national elections is a duty.   [   ]

6 He is looking for someone to speak with about the problem. [   ]

7 Minsu left because he couldn't find a place to sit.   [   ]

8 Take care not to damage the items on the shelves.   [   ]

9 They decided to park at the garage down the street.   [   ]

연습문제 │ 밑줄 친 to부정사의 용법과 같은 것을 <보기>에서 골라 그 기호를 쓰시오.

> <보기> ⓐ To make pizzas is Harold's job.
>   ⓑ The repair person's advice was to buy a new laptop.
>   ⓒ I asked my dad to pay for the tickets.

1 Jenna doesn't want some friends to come to her party. [　]

2 Eric's ambition is to become a professional surfer. [　]

3 The server's suggestion was to try the daily special. [　]

4 The manager's idea was to hire some temporary workers. [　]

5 His parents only allow him to play video games on the weekend. [　]

6 It is easy to obtain information on the website. [　]

7 It is tiring to climb the stairs when the elevator is broken. [　]

8 Her decision was to stay with a friend in New York. [　]

9 The customer wanted the store to replace his item. [　]

10 It is impossible not to laugh at Jeremy's jokes. [　]

11 To win the championship will make our coach proud. [　]

12 The company is reminding staff to sign up for the seminar. [　]

13 To bake bread is a new hobby of mine. [　]

14 Everyone's recommendation is to watch the movie when it comes out. [　]

15 A crew member instructed the passenger to return to his seat. [　]

16 I asked my roommate to clean up his side of the room. [　]

17 The doctor's recommendation was to eat less junk food. [　]

18 To win the sports match would be wonderful. [　]

19 I reminded my brother to pick up mom at the clinic. [　]

20 To hear from him would make her happy. [　]

연습문제 우리말과 같도록 괄호 안의 말을 활용하여 문장을 완성하시오.

1 그 풀은 햇빛이 부족했기 때문에 자라지 못했다. (grow, fail)

= The grass _____ because it lacked sunlight.

2 네가 약속을 지킬 수 없게 되면 나에게 알릴 필요가 있다. (need, inform)

= You _____ me if you cannot make the appointment.

3 Veronica는 그녀가 더 어렸을 때 노래 부르는 것을 좋아했다. (sing, like)

= Veronica _____ when she was younger.

4 배관공은 부서진 파이프를 용케 고쳤다. (manage, repair)

= A plumber _____ the broken pipe.

5 우리는 다음 주말에 산에 오르는 것에 동의했다. (hike up, agree)

= We _____ in the mountains next weekend.

6 Thomas는 더 큰 아파트로 이사하기로 결심했다. (move, decide)

= Thomas _____ into a larger apartment.

7 나는 라스베이거스로 비행하는 대신 차를 운전해서 가기로 결정했다. (drive, choose)

= I _____ to Las Vegas instead of flying.

8 그 은행은 도시 전역에 더 많은 현금 인출기를 추가하는 것을 목표로 한다. (aim, add)

= The bank _____ more ATMs throughout the city.

9 그 고객은 개인용 테이블을 예약하기를 바란다. (wish, book)

= The customer _____ a private table.

10 Paula는 오늘 오후에 그녀의 시험 결과를 받기를 기대한다. (expect, receive)

= Paula _____ her test results this afternoon.

11 그녀는 도서관에서 나를 만나기로 약속했다. (meet, promise)

= She _____ me at the library.

POINT 2-3

연습문제 A 우리말과 같도록 괄호 안의 말을 활용하여 문장을 완성하시오.

1 그는 나에게 그 스피커 장치를 어떻게 설치하는지 말해주었다. (install)

= He told me _____ the speaker system.

2 그들은 그들의 결혼식에 누구를 초대할지 이야기하고 있다. (invite)

= They're talking about _____ to their wedding.

3 너는 오래된 기록을 어디에서 찾아야 할지 알고 있니? (find)

= Do you know _____ old records?

4 그 설명서는 건전지를 어떻게 교체할지 설명한다. (replace)

= The manual explains _____ the batteries.

5 Mila는 공항으로 언제 출발할지 결정하지 못했다. (leave)

= Mila hasn't decided _____ for the airport.

6 너는 나에게 나의 걱정에 대해 누구에게 이야기할지 조언해 줄 수 있니? (talk)

= Can you advise me on _____ about my concern?

7 좋은 TV 프로그램들이 많지만, 나는 어느 것을 시청할지 잘 모르겠다. (watch)

= There are a lot of good TV shows, but I'm not sure _____.

연습문제 B 다음 두 문장의 의미가 같도록 to부정사를 이용하여 문장을 완성하시오.

1 The letter doesn't say whom I should call for questions.

= The letter doesn't say _____.

2 She always forgets when she should take her medicine.

= She always forgets _____.

3 I don't know which task I should finish first.

= I don't know _____.

4 The attendant told us where we should park.

= The attendant told us _____.

5 The website tells you how you should place an order.

= The website tells you _____.

연습문제 <보기>와 같이 to부정사를 이용하여 다음 두 문장을 한 문장으로 연결하시오.

<보기> Sandra has a doll. She plays with the doll.
→ Sandra _has a doll to play with_ .

1 Let me have a sheet of paper. I need to write on the sheet of paper.
→ Let me _____ .

2 Dennis has many pens. He writes with the pens.
→ Dennis _____ .

3 Mr. and Ms. Hill purchased a house. They are going to live in the house.
→ Mr. and Ms. Hill _____ .

4 Kate called a friend. She will talk to her friend.
→ Kate _____ .

5 There isn't a single chair left. I'd like to sit on a chair.
→ There _____ .

연습문제 우리말과 같도록 괄호 안의 말을 활용하여 문장을 완성하시오.

1 만약 네가 팀에 머무르려고 한다면, 너는 연습하러 와야 한다. (stay)
= If you _____ on the team, you must come to practice.

2 몇몇 장비들은 창고 밖에서 찾을 수 있었다. (found)
= Some equipment _____ outside the storage room.

3 모든 사람들은 정오까지 과제를 마쳐야 한다. (finish)
= Everyone _____ the assignment by noon.

4 Robinson씨의 비행기는 오후 11시에 도착할 것이다. (arrive)
= Ms. Robinson's flight _____ at 11 P.M.

5 해리 포터는 마지막에 볼드모트를 물리칠 운명이었다. (defeat)
= Harry Potter _____ Lord Voldemort in the end.

연습문제 A 밑줄 친 부분의 의미를 <보기>에서 골라 그 기호를 쓰시오.

<보기> ⓐ 목적   ⓑ 감정의 원인   ⓒ 판단의 근거   ⓓ 결과   ⓔ 형용사 수식

1 Many trees live <u>to be</u> hundreds of years old.   [   ]

2 We were annoyed <u>to learn</u> that the concert was canceled.   [   ]

3 We were disappointed <u>to hear</u> that he had gone.   [   ]

4 The food will be ready <u>to eat</u> in five minutes.   [   ]

5 Tommy must be ambitious <u>to work</u> two different jobs.   [   ]

6 Everyone must buy a ticket <u>to enter</u> the amusement park.   [   ]

7 <u>To do</u> the art project, I should buy some brushes and paint. [   ]

연습문제 B 우리말과 같도록 괄호 안의 말을 활용하여 빈칸에 쓰시오.

1 그들은 휴일이 거의 다 끝나간다는 것을 깨닫게 되어 슬프다. (sad, realize)

= They're _____ _____ _____ that the holidays are almost over.

2 그녀는 자라서 아동용 도서의 유명한 작가가 되었다. (live, become)

= She _____ _____ _____ a famous writer of children's books.

3 아주 많은 손님이 있다니 그 식당은 형편없을 리가 없다. (so, have, customers, many)

= The restaurant can't be bad _____ _____ _____ _____

_____.

4 Jamie는 프로그램을 시청하기 위해 늦게까지 깨어 있었다. (watch, a program)

= Jamie stayed up late _____ _____ _____ _____.

5 이 과는 배우기에 쉽지 않다. (easy, learn)

= This lesson isn't _____ _____ _____.

6 그 기기는 작동하기에 어렵다. (hard, operate)

= The appliance is _____ _____ _____.

연습문제 | 다음 두 문장의 의미가 같도록 문장을 완성하시오.

1 A dog's nose is so sensitive that it can smell distant objects.

= A dog's nose is _____ distant objects.

2 The celebrity is so famous that she can sell products using her name.

= The celebrity is _____ products using her name.

3 She lives too far away to come and visit.

= She lives _____ .

4 The van is big enough to accommodate twelve people.

= The van is _____ twelve people.

5 I was too tired to do my homework.

= I was _____ my homework.

6 It is so hot that you can't play outside.

= It is _____ outside.

7 Her food is so good that it can be served at a restaurant.

= Her food is _____ at a restaurant.

8 The fire was big enough to be seen from far away.

= The fire was _____ from far away.

9 The dance is so difficult that it can't be learned in one day.

= The dance is _____ in one day.

10 He is so young that he can't drive a car.

= He is _____ a car.

11 Steve's coat is too tight for me to wear.

= Steve's coat is _____ it.

12 The man is so rich that he can fly first class.

= The man is _____ first class.

to부정사의 의미상의 주어

연습문제 A 괄호 안에서 가장 알맞은 것을 고르시오.

1 Wasn't that careless (to / for / of) William to leave his wallet lying around?

2 There was nothing interesting (to / for / of) see at the museum.

3 It was selfish (to / for / of) Nayeon to leave a mess in the living room.

4 It was thoughtful (to / for / of) you to remember my birthday.

5 It is too late (to / for / of) us to go to the shopping center today.

6 There was no food (to / for / of) eat by the time we arrived.

7 It is important (to / for / of) you to pay your bills on time.

8 It is difficult (to / for / of) me to wake up early in the morning.

연습문제 B 우리말과 같도록 괄호 안의 말을 활용하여 문장을 완성하시오.

1 그의 돈 전부를 만화책에 쓰다니 Carl은 어리석었다. (foolish, Carl, spend)

= It was _____ all his money on comic books.

2 나는 우리가 지금 우리의 표를 바꾸는 것은 불가능할 것이라고 생각한다. (impossible, us, change)

= I think it will be _____ our tickets now.

3 우리는 훌륭한 시민으로 행동하는 것이 중요하다는 것에 모두 동의한다. (important, behave)

= We all agree that it's _____ as good citizens.

4 너의 돈을 돌려주다니 그는 매우 정직했다. (return, him, honest)

= It was very _____ your money.

5 그녀는 그들이 보수가 좋은 직업을 가진 것이 행운이었다고 말했다. (them, lucky, have)

= She said that it was _____ jobs that pay well.

6 그가 꼭대기 선반에 손이 닿는 것은 어렵다. (hard, reach, him)

= It is _____ the top shelf.

7 다른 사람들을 친절하게 대하는 것은 중요하다. (necessary, treat)

= It is _____ others with kindness.

8 너에게 고함치다니 그녀는 무례했다. (rude, yell, her)

= It was _____ at you.

1 다음 빈칸에 들어갈 알맞은 것은?

> The students agreed _____ in the hallway.

① not run
② run not
③ run to not
④ not to run
⑤ run not to

2 다음 빈칸에 들어갈 말이 순서대로 짝지어진 것은?

> · Please find me a chair to sit _____.
> · The customer needs someone to talk _____.

① on – to
② on – on
③ on – for
④ at – for
⑤ for – to

3 다음 빈칸에 들어갈 말로 <u>어색한</u> 것은?

> It is _____ for the plant to be watered daily.

① good
② necessary
③ crucial
④ careful
⑤ helpful

[4-5] 다음 문장에서 어법상 <u>어색한</u> 부분을 찾아 쓰고 바르게 고쳐 쓰시오.

4

> Alex promised sending pictures to me of his trip.

_____ → _____

5

> Lisa's parents gave her a kitten to take care.

_____ → _____

6 다음 우리말을 알맞게 영작한 것을 <u>모두</u> 고르시오.

> 나는 너무 졸려서 책을 읽을 수가 없다.

① I am too sleepy read a book.
② I am too sleepy not to read a book.
③ I am too sleepy to read a book.
④ I am so sleepy that I can't read a book.
⑤ I am so sleepy that I can read a book.

7 우리말과 같도록 괄호 안의 말을 활용하여 문장을 완성하시오.

> 농산물 직판장에는 시도해볼 매우 많은 종류의 야채들이 있다. (try, vegetables)

= There are so many kinds of _____ _____ at the farmers' market.

8 다음 대화의 (A)~(C)에 들어갈 말이 바르게 짝지어진 것은?

> A: What present did you get for your mom's birthday?
> B: I've decided ___(A)___ a dish for her.
> A: Oh, isn't that too difficult? You'll need ___(B)___ the right ingredients.
> B: I've already planned ___(C)___.

	(A)	(B)	(C)
①	to cook	to have	where to buy
②	cooking	to have	what to buy
③	to cook	to have	what to buy
④	cooking	having	where to buy
⑤	to cook	having	what to buy

9 우리말과 같도록 괄호 안의 말을 배열할 때 다섯 번째에 오는 것은?

> 그 물은 수영하기에 너무 차갑다. (to, is, too, the, water, cold, in, swim)

① to   ② too   ③ cold
④ in   ⑤ swim

[10-11] 다음 글을 읽고 질문에 답하시오.

> My dad says he is happy ⓐto know his neighbors. (A) To have neighbors as friends is never a bad idea. One time, my dad failed ⓑto park his car on the right side of the street. His neighbor managed ⓒtelling him before he got a ticket. He also informed my dad when ⓓto place the trash outside on the street. I thought it was kind ⓔfor the neighbor to help him.

10 위 글의 밑줄 친 ⓐ~ⓔ 중 어법상 어색한 것을 찾아 기호를 쓰고 바르게 고쳐 쓰시오.

(1) _____ ➡ _____

(2) _____ ➡ _____

11 위 글의 밑줄 친 (A)와 의미가 같도록 주어진 <조건>에 맞게 문장을 완성하시오.

> **<조건>**
> 1. 가주어 it을 사용하시오.
> 2. have, a good idea를 활용하시오.

= _____ neighbors as friends.

12 주어진 문장과 의미가 같은 것은?

> To understand math is hard for me.

① It was hard for me to understand math.
② It is hard for me to understand math.
③ It is hard of me to understand math.
④ It will be hard of me to understand math.
⑤ It will be hard for me to understand math.

13 다음 빈칸에 들어갈 말이 순서대로 짝지어진 것은?

> · My dad wants me _____ the grass
>   in the yard tomorrow.
> · Do you aim _____ to university next
>   year?

① cut – go   ② cut – to go
③ to cut – go   ④ to cut – going
⑤ to cut – to go

14 우리말과 같도록 괄호 안의 말을 활용하여 문장
을 완성하시오.

> 그들은 이번 주에 이사하기를 기대한다. (move,
> expect, this week)

= They _____.

15 다음 중 어법상 어색한 것을 모두 고르시오.

① The couch is too expensive for me to
   buy.
② It was rude for Shawn not to say thank
   you.
③ It was generous for him to pay for the
   meal.
④ It is not hard for me to lose weight.
⑤ It is impossible for us to drive in this
   weather.

16 우리말과 같도록 괄호 안의 말을 알맞게 배열하
시오.

> 새로운 상품들은 다음 달에 출시될 예정이다.
> (released, new products, be, next
> month, to, are)

= _____

17 다음 우리말을 알맞게 영작한 것을 모두 고르시오.

> Linda는 나에게 토마토를 어떻게 기르는지 가르쳐
> 주었다.

① Linda taught me what to grow tomatoes.
② Linda taught me what I should grow
   tomatoes.
③ Linda taught me how growing tomatoes.
④ Linda taught me how to grow tomatoes.
⑤ Linda taught me how I should grow
   tomatoes.

[18-19] 다음 글을 읽고 주어진 질문에 답하시오.

> The dhole is a type of wild dog that lives in parts of India, China, and Russia. It is small, has red fur, and often travels in a group. (A) 그 무리는 다른 동물들을 사냥하기 위해 협력한다. (together, hunt, works, other animals). A long time ago, there used to be many dholes around the world. Today, only a small number of them remain. Several countries hope ⓐto save the dhole from extinction. They have introduced laws that protect the animal.
>
> *dhole: 승냥이

18 위 글의 밑줄 친 ⓐ의 용법과 같은 것은?

① Is there a place for me to sit?

② Now is a good time to go to sleep.

③ They waited four hours to board the plane.

④ Most people want to succeed at their jobs.

⑤ Simon figured out a way to save some money.

19 위 글의 밑줄 친 우리말 (A)와 같도록 괄호 안의 말을 활용하여 문장을 완성하시오.

= The group _____

_____ .

20 다음 밑줄 친 to부정사의 용법이 같은 것끼리 묶인 것은?

> ⓐ Could you hand me some string to tie this box?
> ⓑ I plan to rent a car for the trip.
> ⓒ I turned off the air conditioner to save on electricity.
> ⓓ There are many options to choose from.
> ⓔ Avery wishes to visit Korea one day.

① ⓐ, ⓑ   ② ⓐ, ⓓ   ③ ⓑ, ⓒ
④ ⓒ, ⓔ   ⑤ ⓓ, ⓔ

[21-22] 두 문장의 의미가 같도록 문장을 완성하시오.

21

> To eat too many sweets is bad for your health.
> = It _____
> too many sweets.

22

> I paid extra to get a comfortable seat on the plane.
> = I paid extra _____
> get a comfortable seat on the plane.

23 우리말과 같도록 괄호 안의 말을 활용하여 문장을 완성하시오.

> 나는 카드를 보내기 위해 우체국에 들렀다. (stop by, mail, the post office)

= I _____ a card.

24 우리말과 같도록 괄호 안의 말을 배열할 때 세 번째에 오는 것을 쓰시오.

> 모든 방문객들은 안내 데스크에서 서명해야 한다.
> (are, the front desk, visitors, to, all, at, sign in)

→ _____

25 두 문장의 의미가 같도록 문장을 완성하시오.

> The hotel clerk told us where we should change our money.
> = The hotel clerk told us _____
> _____.

CHAPTER 6
동명사

연습문제 A 밑줄 친 부분이 어법상 맞으면 O를 쓰고, 틀리면 바르게 고쳐 완전한 문장을 쓰시오.

1 How about to fix the bicycle after school?

→ _____

2 Interviewing celebrities are what the reporter does.

→ _____

3 Thank you for talking not during the movie.

→ _____

4 What I really miss is seeing my grandparents on the weekend.

→ _____

5 I enjoy to jog every morning.

→ _____

6 Bob's hobby is taking pictures of flowers.

→ _____

연습문제 B 밑줄 친 동명사의 쓰임과 같은 것을 <보기>에서 골라 그 기호를 쓰시오.

> <보기>
> ⓐ Learning to ride a skateboard is not easy for everyone.
> ⓑ It started snowing lightly in the morning.
> ⓒ We're talking about going to the theater later.
> ⓓ Alexa's hobby is listening to classical music.

1 Jason's goal is learning to speak three languages.   [   ]

2 Matthew's parents recommended getting a used laptop.   [   ]

3 She is excited about buying new summer clothes.   [   ]

4 Always helping others is a good way to make friends.   [   ]

5 We delayed doing our homework because we wanted to watch TV.   [   ]

6 Nate quit eating at restaurants because he wanted to save money.   [   ]

7 Swimming in the ocean is my favorite summer activity.   [   ]

8 I look forward to meeting you tomorrow evening.   [   ]

연습문제 | <보기>와 같이 두 문장의 의미가 같도록 문장을 완성하시오.

> <보기> I was unaware that Tom traveled during summer vacation.
> = I was unaware of *Tom's traveling during summer vacation* .

1 We usually don't mind that he comes late to class.

= We usually don't mind _____.

2 I am aware that Daniel forgets to bring his textbook to class.

= I am aware of _____.

3 I remember that my mom will act in the play.

= I remember _____.

4 Susan is thankful that her dad drives her to school.

= Susan is thankful for _____.

5 I can't stand that my little sister sings at home.

= I can't stand _____.

6 We are sure that David met the project deadline.

= We are sure of _____.

7 Joohoon doesn't like that his older brother uses his computer.

= Joohoon doesn't like _____.

8 Mr. Carter was disappointed that his son returned home not on time.

= Mr. Carter was disappointed at _____.

9 She was excited that Billy completed the project.

= She was excited about _____.

10 I appreciate that the waiter brought us some free food.

= I appreciate _____.

11 She is certain that her friend received the present.

= She is certain of _____.

12 I felt sorry that Brian failed the test.

= I felt sorry for _____.

연습문제 다음 <보기>와 같이 동명사를 이용하여 두 문장의 의미가 같도록 문장을 완성하시오.

<보기> His mother is angry that she lost her wallet.
= His mother is angry about *having lost her wallet* .

1 His younger brother eventually admitted that he had taken his candy.
= His younger brother eventually admitted _____.

2 The bus passengers complained that they had not arrived on time.
= The bus passengers complained about _____.

3 She regrets that she tore the cover of her book.
= She regrets _____.

4 My older sister hates that she takes the subway to work in the morning.
= My older sister hates _____.

5 He is proud that he was given an award at school.
= He is proud of _____.

6 Martin is worried that he will be late for the dinner party.
= Martin is worried about _____.

7 She acknowledged that she had cheated on the exam.
= She acknowledged _____.

8 He mentioned that he had participated in the summer camp.
= He mentioned _____.

9 Chris was surprised that he was not invited to the party.
= Chris was surprised about _____.

10 She misses that she had been able to see her friends.
= She misses _____.

11 They reported that the airline had damaged their luggage.
= They reported the airline _____.

12 Everyone was excited that they met the singer in person.
= Everyone was excited _____.

동명사를 목적어로 쓰는 동사

POINT **4**

정답 p.71

연습문제 | 우리말과 같도록 괄호 안의 말을 활용하여 문장을 완성하시오.

1 그의 의사는 하루에 두 번 약을 복용할 것을 추천한다. (recommend, take)

= His doctor _____ the medicine twice a day.

2 Alice는 공항에 가기 위해 버스를 탈 것을 제안했다. (suggest, ride)

= Alice _____ the bus to get to the airport.

3 그들은 Daniel의 과학 교과서를 훔친 것을 부인했다. (deny, steal)

= They _____ Daniel's science textbook.

4 Robert는 주말까지 시험공부를 하는 것을 미룰 것이다. (postpone, study)

= Robert will _____ for the test until the weekend.

5 그녀는 토요일에 그녀의 친구들과 도보 여행을 즐겼다. (enjoy, hike)

= She _____ with her friends on Saturday.

6 그는 언젠가 과학자가 되는 것을 상상했다. (imagine, become)

= He _____ a scientist someday.

7 그녀는 스페인으로의 그녀의 여행에 대해 계속해서 이야기한다. (keep, talk)

= She _____ about her trip to Spain.

8 그들은 방과 후에 매일 기타 연주하는 것을 연습한다. (practice, play)

= They _____ the guitar each day after school.

9 그들은 그들의 아들을 위해 강아지를 갖는 것을 고려했다. (consider, get)

= They _____ a dog for their son.

10 Isabella는 그녀가 할 수 있는 한 매운 음식 먹는 것을 피한다. (avoid, eat)

= Isabella _____ spicy foods as much as she can.

11 그는 그 체육관에서 운동하는 것을 그만뒀다. (stop, exercise)

= He _____ at the gym.

12 그녀는 부정적인 의견들을 듣는 것을 싫어한다. (dislike, hear)

= She _____ negative comments.

연습문제 A 괄호 안에서 알맞은 것을 <u>모두</u> 고르시오.

1 Bella resisted (apologizing / to apologize) for her mistake.

2 The band continued (playing / to play) until just after midnight.

3 My younger sister likes (taking / to take) our dog for a walk at night.

4 A ballerina must practice (dancing / to dance) for several hours each day.

5 Warren loves (baking / to bake) cookies with his mother.

6 She quit (working / to work) to enroll in school full-time.

7 He started (running / to run) as soon as he stepped out of the house.

8 We began (cleaning / to clean) the yard of the fallen leaves.

9 She intended (watching / to watch) the game on TV but went to bed instead.

10 I prefer (buying / to buy) juice from a shop when I go to the park.

연습문제 B 우리말과 같도록 괄호 안의 말을 활용하여 문장을 완성하시오.

1 그 소년은 나무에 오르려고 노력했으나, 그것은 매우 높았다. (try, climb)
= The boy _____ the tree, but it was too high.

2 Carlos는 그의 아파트 현관문을 잠글 것을 기억했다. (remember, lock)
= Carlos _____ the front door of his apartment.

3 그 팀은 농구 선수권 대회에서 이긴 것을 절대 잊지 못할 것이다. (forget, win)
= The team will never _____ the basketball championship.

4 그 아기는 그녀에게 병이 주어지자 우는 것을 멈췄다. (stop, cry)
= The baby _____ once she was given a bottle.

5 David는 그 파티에서 Sandy를 만난 것을 기억하지 못한다. (remember, meet)
= David doesn't _____ Sandy at the party.

6 나의 친구는 나에게 생일 선물을 줄 것을 잊었다. (forget, give)
= My friend _____ me a birthday gift.

7 Lisa는 과학 시험을 위해 공부를 더 하지 않은 것을 후회한다. (regret, study)
= Lisa _____ more for the science test.

POINT
6

연습문제 A   밑줄 친 부분이 어법상 맞으면 O를 쓰고, 틀리면 바르게 고쳐 완전한 문장을 쓰시오.

1   The workers <u>are busy building</u> a new office building.

→ _____

2   Mark prefers comedies <u>when it comes to watched</u> movies.

→ _____

3   My father <u>is good in playing</u> sports like soccer and baseball.

→ _____

4   The politician <u>dreams of become</u> the country's president.

→ _____

5   The taxi driver <u>is tired of working</u> on holidays.

→ _____

연습문제 B   우리말과 같도록 <보기>와 괄호 안의 동사를 활용하여 문장을 완성하시오.

<보기> be interested in + V-ing be afraid of + V-ing It is no use + V-ing	
be worth + V-ing have difficulty + V-ing look forward to + V-ing by + V-ing	

1   Mindy는 밤에 혼자 집에 걸어가는 것을 두려워한다. (go)

= Mindy _____ home by herself at night.

2   그 학생들은 지역 역사에 대해 배우는 것에 흥미가 있다. (learn)

= The students _____ about local history.

3   이 빵 굽는 기구는 그것의 많은 기능들 때문에 살만한 가치가 있다. (buy)

= This toaster _____ because of its many features.

4   나의 할아버지는 계단을 오르는 것에 어려움이 있다. (walk)

= My grandfather _____ up the stairs.

5   너는 모바일 애플리케이션을 이용해서 음식을 주문할 수 있다. (use)

= You can order food _____ this mobile application.

6   Simmons씨는 그 소설을 읽는 것을 기대한다. (read)

= Mr. Simmons _____ the novel.

7   네가 얼마나 많은 숙제가 있는지에 대해 불평해도 소용 없다. (complain)

= _____ about how much homework you have.

중간·기말고사 실전 문제

1 다음 대화의 밑줄 친 우리말과 같도록 괄호 안의 말을 활용하여 영작하시오.

> *A:* 토요일에 야영 가는 게 어때?
> (on Saturday, camp)
> *B:* Sorry. I have to work this weekend.

= _____

2 우리말과 같도록 괄호 안의 말을 활용하여 문장을 완성하시오.

> 요리하는 것에 관한 한 Andre보다 잘하는 사람은 없다. (cook, when it comes to)

= _____, no one is better than Andre.

3 다음 글의 밑줄 친 ⓐ~ⓔ를 바르게 고친 것은?

> I love ⓐplay baseball. When I was little, I even dreamed of ⓑto become a professional player. My teacher suggested ⓒjoin a youth baseball team. I wasn't sure because I dislike ⓓto meeting new people. However, everyone was very nice and welcomed me warmly. From then on, I was able to enjoy ⓔto competing with my new friends.

① ⓐ play → to playing
② ⓑ to become → become
③ ⓒ join → to join
④ ⓓ to meeting → meeting
⑤ ⓔ to competing → compete

4 다음 빈칸에 들어갈 말이 순서대로 짝지어진 것은?

> · His job is _____ a city bus.
> · Visiting museums _____ my favorite thing to do on a trip.

① driving – is
② drove – is
③ driving – are
④ driven– is
⑤ drove – are

5 우리말과 같도록 괄호 안의 말을 활용하여 영작하시오.

> 나는 시험 삼아 일주일 동안 음료수를 마시지 않아 보았다. (try, drink, soda, for a week)

= _____

6 다음 글의 밑줄 친 ⓐ~ⓔ 중 어법상 어색한 부분을 세 군데 찾아 기호를 쓰고 바르게 고쳐 쓰시오.

> Scientists have introduced various way of ⓐreduce global warming. Lowering global temperatures ⓑare only a partial solution. While many nations have been taking steps ⓒto reduce air pollution, experts say we must do more. ⓓNot act quickly enough may lead to us ⓔdestroying the planet.

(1) _____ → _____
(2) _____ → _____
(3) _____ → _____

7 다음 (A)~(C)에 들어갈 말이 바르게 짝지어진 것은?

> · The plant will continue ___(A)___ as long as you water it.
> · Please stop ___(B)___ some peaches at the market on your way home today.
> · Do you mind ___(C)___ the windows for a little bit?

	(A)	(B)	(C)
①	to grow	to buy	opening
②	growing	to buy	open
③	to grow	buying	to open
④	growing	buying	to open
⑤	to grow	buying	opening

8 다음 중 밑줄 친 부분이 어법상 어색한 것을 모두 고르시오.

> Do you remember ①to get up on the first day of school? You couldn't wait for class. Then, at some point, you may have started ②hated to go. The work became too hard and you quit ③trying to learn new things. But imagine ④not attend school at all. You would never learn valuable life skills or make new friends. If you begin ⑤to doubt whether school is valuable, take a moment to think about what you'd be giving up.

9 다음 우리말을 영작한 것 중 어법상 어색한 것은?

① Darren은 자전거에 그의 돈을 다 써버렸다.
= Darren spent all his money on a bicycle.

② 그녀는 새로운 언어를 배우는 데 어려움이 있다.
= She has difficulty learning new languages.

③ 나는 내일 나의 할아버지와 함께 낚시하러 갈 것이다.
= I will go to fishing with my grandfather tomorrow.

④ 한국 역사에 대한 이 다큐멘터리는 볼 가치가 있다.
= This documentary on Korean history is worth watching.

⑤ 나는 전화가 울렸을 때 빨래를 하느라 바빴다.
= I was busy doing the laundry when the phone rang.

10 다음 (A)~(C)에 들어갈 말이 바르게 짝지어진 것은?

> · They postponed ___(A)___ until next month.
> · I like ___(B)___ to classical music while I work.
> · These days, Paul is trying ___(C)___ healthier meals.

	(A)	(B)	(C)
①	moving	listening	cooks
②	to move	listening	to cook
③	moving	to listen	cooks
④	moving	to listen	to cook
⑤	to move	listening	cooking

11 다음 중 어법상 어색한 것은?

① Stephen is not interested in to study overseas.
② I am looking forward to joining a biking club.
③ Improve your piano skills by practicing every day.
④ I am so sorry for arriving late to the meeting.
⑤ She is tired of walking up the stairs to her apartment.

12 다음 대화를 읽고 괄호 안의 말을 활용하여 빈칸에 알맞은 말을 쓰시오.

> Yunsu: Do you think I could borrow your notes from yesterday's class?
> Minji : I don't have them with me now, but you can borrow them from Adam.

→ Minji suggested _____ _____
_____. (borrow, Adam's notes)

13 다음 문장에서 어법상 어색한 부분을 찾아 쓰고 바르게 고쳐 쓰시오.

> I couldn't sleep last night because my neighbor's dog kept to bark.

_____ → _____

14 두 문장의 의미가 같도록 빈칸에 알맞은 말을 쓰시오.

> I am sorry that I broke your glasses.
> = I _____ you that I broke your glasses.

15 다음 대화의 빈칸에 들어갈 알맞은 것은?

> A: Why did you miss the train?
> B: On _____ at the station, I remembered I had left my wallet at home.

① enter   ② entered
③ has entered   ④ to enter
⑤ entering

16 다음 빈칸에 들어갈 알맞은 것은?

> Naeun feels thankful that she passed the test.
> = Naeun feels thankful for _____ the test.

① pass   ② passed
③ have passed   ④ having passed
⑤ being passed

17 괄호 안의 말을 활용하여 빈칸에 알맞은 말을 쓰시오.

A: I regret ⓐ _____(tell) you that we don't have any of the shoes you're looking for in stock.
B: Oh, could I get them at a different branch of your store, then?
A: I'm not sure, but I can find out for you.
B: Thanks. Just remember ⓑ _____(mention) both shoe styles that I want.

18 다음 우리말과 같도록 빈칸에 알맞은 말을 고르시오.

Riley는 사진과 영상을 편집하는 것을 잘한다.
= Riley is good at _____ photos and videos.

① edit   ② editing   ③ edited
④ be edit   ⑤ being edited

19 다음 중 어법상 바른 것의 개수는?

ⓐ Andrew prefers exercising outside rather than in a gym.
ⓑ Michelle couldn't resist to take a bite of the cake.
ⓒ I love looking at the stars with my telescope.
ⓓ It stopped snowing right before noon.
ⓔ The principal intends to give a speech on the first day of school.

① 1개   ② 2개   ③ 3개
④ 4개   ⑤ 5개

20 다음 중 어법상 <u>어색한</u> 것은?

① Going to law school is her dream.
② Gina's parents were aware of her studying late at night.
③ Do you mind helping me complete the research?
④ Kenny will practice him singing for the competition.
⑤ Most people who live in the city are used to taking public transportation.

21 다음 우리말을 알맞게 영작한 것은?

그녀는 많은 양의 식사를 하는 것을 끝마치지 못했다.

① She couldn't finish to eat the heavy meal.
② She couldn't finish eating the heavy meal.
③ She couldn't finish eat the heavy meal.
④ She couldn't finish to be eaten the heavy meal.
⑤ She couldn't finish being eaten the heavy meal.

22 다음 중 어법상 어색한 것은?

① A: It's so hot today. Why are you wearing long sleeves?
   B: I'm afraid of getting a sunburn.

② A: You lost your phone more than a week ago?
   B: Yes, so it's no use to look for it anymore.

③ A: Did Stephanie finally decide where she would go for her vacation?
   B: She ended up staying at home.

④ A: Shouldn't you be saving some money?
   B: Yes, but I cannot help buying new clothes.

⑤ A: I don't feel like eating anything.
   B: Why don't you go see a doctor?

24 <보기>의 말을 활용하여 빈칸에 알맞은 말을 쓰시오.

| <보기>   feel get keep |

Pets Paradise is my favorite TV show. It has taught me many things about having a pet. For instance, people who work all day should avoid ⓐ＿＿＿＿＿ a dog. Dogs need lots of attention, and they will begin ⓑ＿＿＿＿＿ ＿＿＿＿＿ depressed if they are alone for too long. Instead, the program recommends ⓒ＿＿＿＿＿ a fish or hamster.

23 우리말과 같도록 괄호 안의 말을 활용하여 영작하시오.

| 나는 잠에 들기 전에 알람을 켤 것을 잊었다.
(turn on, my alarm, forget, I, before, went to bed) |

= ＿＿＿＿＿＿＿＿＿＿＿＿＿＿＿＿＿＿＿

＿＿＿＿＿＿＿＿＿＿＿＿＿＿＿＿＿＿＿

25 다음 중 어법상 어색한 것은?

① Most children enjoy to play outside with their friends.

② We will start rehearsing the play next week.

③ I postponed mowing the lawn because of the thunderstorm.

④ I don't mind looking after my mother's dog when she goes on vacation.

⑤ The students continued talking even though the teacher asked them to stop.

CHAPTER 7
분사

기출로 적중 POINT

보기 **연습문제 A** 다음 문장의 분사에는 동그라미를 치고, 분사가 수식하거나 보충 설명하는 부분에는 밑줄을 치시오.

1 There are some people walking along the beach.

2 I got embarrassed because of my mistake.

3 The soup made with broccoli was delicious.

4 The doctor treated the patient injured in the car accident.

5 We saw a kid drinking apple juice.

6 The play's plot was surprising.

7 The man found the painting painted by Vincent van Gogh.

8 I heard my mom calling my name in the kitchen.

9 My test score was disappointing.

10 The finding made the researchers confused.

11 There are some baseball players practicing in the field.

12 Let's fix the broken window.

보기 **연습문제 B** 우리말과 같도록 괄호 안의 말을 알맞게 배열하시오.

1 Mike는 눈으로 뒤덮인 산을 봤다. (saw, with, covered, snow, Mike, the mountain)

= _____

2 그 매니저는 좌절한 것처럼 들린다. (sounds, the manager, frustrated)

= _____

3 Amy는 흥미로운 영화를 봤다. (watched, an, interesting, Amy, movie)

= _____

4 그 소설은 흥미진진한 시작 부분을 가지고 있다. (has, an, opening, exciting, the novel)

= _____

5 그는 마라톤 이후에 피곤해 보였다. (looked, after, tired, he, the marathon)

= _____

POINT 2

연습문제 A   괄호 안의 말을 활용하여 빈칸에 알맞은 말을 쓰시오.

1   A: Did you see the _____ _____? (dog, bark)

     B: No, I didn't see it.

2   A: I heard that you are planning to purchase a car.

     B: Yes, I'm going to purchase a _____ _____. (car, use)

3   A: Who is that _____ _____ next to him? (girl, sit)

     B: Oh, that's my older sister.

4   A: Can I help you?

     B: Yes. Can you fix my _____ _____, please? (laptop, break)

5   A: Did you go to the library yesterday?

     B: Yes. There were many _____ _____ books there. (students, read)

연습문제 B   우리말과 같도록 <보기>의 말을 활용하여 빈칸에 쓰시오.

<보기>   sing   burn   excite   talk   wait

1   그 소년은 큰 소리로 얘기하고 있는 선생님을 들었다.

     = The boy heard the teacher _____ in a loud voice.

2   나는 점심으로 탄 소시지를 먹었다.

     = I ate the _____ sausage for lunch.

3   그 농구 게임은 사람들을 흥분되게 했다.

     = The basketball game made the people _____.

4   그 남자는 유명한 가수에 의해 불러진 노래를 들었다.

     = The man listened to a song _____ by a popular singer.

5   나는 나의 집 앞에서 친구를 기다리게 했다.

     = I kept my friend _____ in front of my house.

연습문제 A 괄호 안의 동사를 알맞은 형태로 바꿔 빈칸에 쓰시오.

1 (bore) ① The author's new novel was _____ to Julie.

② Julie felt _____ when she read the author's new novel.

2 (excite) ① The soccer game made the crowd _____.

② The soccer game was _____ to the crowd.

3 (move) ① I was _____ when I heard the story about my grandmother.

② The story about my grandmother was _____ to me.

4 (amuse) ① The kids think that the folk tales are _____.

② The kids are _____ by the folk tales.

5 (fascinate) ① Most people feel _____ when seeing Niagara Falls.

② Seeing Niagara Falls is _____ for most people.

6 (please) ① The concert was _____ to the audience.

② The audience felt _____ by the concert.

연습문제 B 밑줄 친 부분이 어법상 맞으면 O를 쓰고, 틀리면 바르게 고쳐 완전한 문장을 쓰시오.

1 The gloomy weather made many people <u>depressed</u>.

→ _____

2 Going on a trip was a <u>thrilled</u> experience for me.

→ _____

3 The student was <u>interesting</u> in history.

→ _____

4 Rachel was <u>worried</u> when her son didn't come home.

→ _____

5 My older brother read a <u>surprised</u> article in the paper.

→ _____

연습문제 A 밑줄 친 부분의 쓰임이 나머지 둘과 다른 것을 고르시오.

1 ① They looked at the <u>smiling</u> baby.
   ② David likes <u>reading</u> books about world history.
   ③ I heard the <u>pleasing</u> news about the summer vacation.

2 ① He is not good at <u>speaking</u> Spanish.
   ② <u>Watching</u> television for a long time can make your eyes hurt.
   ③ The film director's new movie is <u>shocking</u>.

3 ① My younger sister is <u>talking</u> to her friend on the phone.
   ② <u>Waiting</u> for a bus, I met my classmate.
   ③ My parents had a meal in the <u>dining</u> room.

4 ① <u>Taking</u> pictures in the museum is not allowed.
   ② Do you know the girl <u>waving</u> her hand at us?
   ③ The volunteers enjoy <u>helping</u> people in need.

5 ① <u>Skating</u> is one of the most popular winter sports.
   ② The team should get a <u>satisfying</u> result from this match.
   ③ Judy and Michelle are <u>screaming</u> at each other.

연습문제 B 다음 밑줄 친 부분이 현재분사인지 동명사인지 쓴 후, 해석하시오.

1 Please wait for your turn in the <u>waiting</u> room.
  [   ], _____

2 It was the most <u>exciting</u> trip I have ever taken.
  [   ], _____
  _____

3 My mom is really good at <u>baking</u> cookies.
  [   ], _____
  _____

4 Every kid knows the fairy tale <u>called</u> *Sleeping Beauty*.
  [   ], _____
  _____

5 The director wanted to make that <u>touching</u> story into a film.
  [   ], _____
  _____

6 I saw a man <u>standing</u> by the entrance door.
  [   ], _____

7 She finished <u>studying</u> for the quiz tomorrow.
  [   ], _____
  _____

8 <u>Taking</u> a nap can make you feel better.
  [   ], _____
  _____

연습문제 A 우리말과 같도록 괄호 안의 말을 활용하여 빈칸에 쓰시오.

1 Sally는 버스를 봤을 때, 버스 정류장으로 뛰기 시작했다. (see, the bus)

= When Sally ＿＿＿＿＿ ＿＿＿＿＿ ＿＿＿＿＿, she began running to the bus stop.

= ＿＿＿＿＿ ＿＿＿＿＿ ＿＿＿＿＿, Sally began running to the bus stop.

2 그는 목이 마르지 않았기 때문에, 그는 생수가 필요하지 않았다. (be, thirsty)

= Because he ＿＿＿＿＿ ＿＿＿＿＿, he didn't need a bottle of water.

= ＿＿＿＿＿ ＿＿＿＿＿ ＿＿＿＿＿, he didn't need a bottle of water.

3 Jay는 컴퓨터 게임을 하면서, 사과 주스를 마셨다. (play, a computer game)

= While Jay ＿＿＿＿＿ ＿＿＿＿＿ ＿＿＿＿＿ ＿＿＿＿＿, he drank apple juice.

= ＿＿＿＿＿ ＿＿＿＿＿ ＿＿＿＿＿ ＿＿＿＿＿, Jay drank apple juice.

4 기차가 지연되었기 때문에, 나는 야구 연습에 늦었다. (delay, be)

= Since the train ＿＿＿＿＿ ＿＿＿＿＿, I was late for baseball practice.

= ＿＿＿＿＿ ＿＿＿＿＿ ＿＿＿＿＿ ＿＿＿＿＿, I was late for baseball practice.

5 그가 택시를 탄다면, 그 경기장에 한 시간 안에 도착할 텐데. (take, a taxi)

= If he ＿＿＿＿＿ ＿＿＿＿＿ ＿＿＿＿＿, he would arrive at the stadium within an hour.

= ＿＿＿＿＿ ＿＿＿＿＿ ＿＿＿＿＿, he would arrive at the stadium within an hour.

연습문제 B 두 문장의 의미가 같도록 괄호 안의 접속사를 활용하여 문장을 완성하시오.

1 Being tired, I couldn't run fast in the race. (as)

= ＿＿＿＿＿＿＿＿＿＿＿＿＿＿＿＿＿, I couldn't run fast in the race.

2 Being sleepy, the boy decided to take a nap. (because)

= ＿＿＿＿＿＿＿＿＿＿＿＿＿＿＿＿＿, he decided to take a nap.

3 Climbing the mountain, the hiker sprained his ankle. (while)

= ＿＿＿＿＿＿＿＿＿＿＿＿＿＿＿＿＿, he sprained his ankle.

4 Drinking my tea, I began to slowly relax. (while)

= ＿＿＿＿＿＿＿＿＿＿＿＿＿＿＿＿＿, I began to slowly relax.

5 Not being old enough, I can't drive a car. (since)

= ＿＿＿＿＿＿＿＿＿＿＿＿＿＿＿＿＿, I can't drive a car.

6 Being designed by a famous architect, the building looked amazing. (as)

= ＿＿＿＿＿＿＿＿＿＿＿＿＿＿＿＿＿, it looked amazing.

정답 p.73

연습문제 A 다음 문장의 밑줄 친 부분을 분사구문으로 바꿔 쓰시오.

1 Because <u>we come from another country</u>, we know little about this place.

→ _____, we know little about this place.

2 Laura forgot the pot on the stove, <u>and she burned the food.</u>

→ Laura forgot the pot on the stove, _____.

3 <u>While Dongho did his homework,</u> he listened to music.

→ _____, Dongho listened to music.

4 <u>As I lived in a dormitory,</u> I couldn't see my family often.

→ _____, I couldn't see my family often.

5 <u>While the customers waited in line,</u> they looked at the menu.

→ _____, the customers looked at the menu.

6 <u>When Larry tripped on the sidewalk,</u> he grabbed his friend's arm.

→ _____, Larry grabbed his friend's arm.

연습문제 B 우리말과 같도록 괄호 안의 말을 활용하여 분사구문 문장을 완성하시오.

1 Mary는 얼음 위에서 미끄러져서, 그녀의 발목을 삐었다. (her ankle, sprain)

= Mary slipped on the ice, _____.

2 나에게 기회가 주어진다면, 나는 유럽으로 여행을 갈 것이다. (the chance, give)

= _____ I would travel to Europe.

3 그들이 모바일 어플리케이션을 개발했기 때문에, 많은 돈을 벌었다. (the mobile application, develop)

= _____, they made a lot of money.

4 연주자들은 무대에 올라가면서, 매우 긴장했다. (on stage, go up)

= _____, the performers felt very nervous.

5 그녀는 배가 고파졌기 때문에, 요리를 하기 위해 주방에 갔다. (hungry, feel)

= _____, she went to the kitchen to cook.

6 나는 그 영화를 보면서, 나의 고등학교 시절을 기억했다. (the movie, watch)

= _____, I remembered my high school days.

7 Shawn은 기타를 연주하는 동안, 노래도 불렀다. (the guitar, play)

= _____, Shawn also sang a song.

연습문제 A 두 문장의 의미가 같도록 분사구문을 이용하여 문장을 완성하시오. (단, 부사절의 접속사를 생략하시오.)

1 After Christina arrived at the hotel, she went to the front desk.

= _____, Christina went to the front desk.

2 Because she felt exhausted, she lay down on the sofa.

= _____, she lay down on the sofa.

3 While I drew a picture, I listened to the music.

= _____, I listened to the music.

4 As I had learned how to speak French, I could help Sarah with her French homework.

= _____, I could help Sarah with her French homework.

5 When I meet someone, I usually get nervous.

= _____, I usually get nervous.

6 Since Tony finished his homework, he has nothing to do now.

= _____, Tony has nothing to do now.

7 If it were made of cotton, the shirt would be more comfortable to wear.

= _____, the shirt would be more comfortable to wear.

연습문제 B 다음 분사구문은 부사절로, 부사절은 분사구문으로 바꿔 쓰시오.

1 Having played for the team for 15 years, Joshua became the captain.

→ After _____, Joshua became the captain.

2 Because they were not interested in art, they didn't go to the art gallery.

→ _____, they didn't go to the art gallery.

3 Jogging in the park, they picked up some trash.

→ When _____, they picked up some trash.

4 As Peter was good at biology, he decided to become a biologist.

→ _____, Peter decided to become a biologist.

5 Doing your best in everything, you will be a successful person.

→ If _____, you will be a successful person.

6 Being decorated with colorful lights, the Christmas tree looked beautiful.

→ Since _____, it looked beautiful.

with + 명사 + 분사

정답 p.73

연습문제 우리말과 같도록 괄호 안의 말을 활용하여 문장을 완성하시오.

1 그는 그의 엄마가 그의 손을 잡은 채로 진료를 받으러 갔다. (hold, his mom, his hand)

= He went to see a doctor _____.

2 Suzy는 TV를 켜놓은 채로 잠이 들었다. (turn on, the TV)

= Suzy fell asleep _____.

3 나는 나의 남동생이 나를 도와주는 채로 그 그림을 그렸다. (help, my little brother, me)

= I painted the picture _____.

4 나는 나의 다리를 꼰 채로 신문을 읽고 있었다. (cross, my legs)

= I was reading a newspaper _____.

5 그 소녀는 문이 닫힌 채로 플루트를 연주했다. (close, the door)

= The girl played the flute _____.

분사구문 관용 표현

정답 p.73

연습문제 우리말과 같도록 분사구문 관용 표현을 이용하여 문장을 완성하시오.

1 솔직히 말하면, 나는 어떤 스포츠에도 관심이 없다.

= _____, I am not interested in any sport.

2 엄밀히 말하면, 마법과 같은 것은 없다.

= _____, there is no such thing as magic.

3 일반적으로 말하면, 대부분의 청소년들은 랩 음악을 좋아한다.

= _____, most teenagers are into rap music.

4 시계의 질을 고려하면, 그것은 매우 비싸다.

= _____ the quality of the watch, it is too expensive.

5 취미에 관해서 말한다면, 나는 보드 게임을 하는 것을 좋아한다.

= _____ hobbies, I love playing board games.

6 그의 겉모습으로 판단하건대, 그는 나보다 나이가 많음에 틀림없다.

= _____ his appearance, he must be older than me.

중간 · 기말고사 실전 문제

1 다음 중 어법상 바른 것은?

① There were pieces of the falling vase on the floor.

② Do you know that man stood by the elevator?

③ The woman cleaned the house is my aunt.

④ Look at the ducks swimming in the pond.

⑤ The last song singing at the concert was my favorite.

2 다음 글의 밑줄 친 ⓐ~ⓔ를 바르게 고친 것은?

The girl ⓐstand on the stage is my older sister. ⓑDance in the contest earlier, she did a great job. The audience was ⓒamazing by her skill. She won first place, and the trophy ⓓholding in her hands is her prize. Seeing her ⓔsmiled face makes me happy.

① ⓐ stand → stood

② ⓑ Dance → Danced

③ ⓒ amazing → amazed

④ ⓓ holding → holds

⑤ ⓔ smiled → smile

3 다음 문장을 주어진 <조건>에 맞게 바꿔 쓰시오.

<조건>
1. 접속사 if를 포함하시오.
2. 밑줄 친 부분을 부사절로 바꿔 쓰시오.

Looking out the window, you will see the beautiful sunset.

→ _____, you will see the beautiful sunset.

4 다음 빈칸에 들어갈 알맞은 것은?

There is an old man _____ flowers on the street.

① sell ② sold ③ is selling

④ is sold ⑤ selling

5 다음 (A)~(C)에 들어갈 말이 바르게 짝지어진 것은?

· The ___(A)___ dog woke me up last night.

· Can you help me pick up the ___(B)___ glass?

· We should return the ___(C)___ product and get a refund.

	(A)	(B)	(C)
①	barking	broken	damaging
②	barked	broken	damaging
③	barking	breaking	damaged
④	barking	broken	damaged
⑤	barked	broken	damaged

6 다음 문장을 주어진 <조건>에 맞게 바꿔 쓰시오.

> Having completed the race, the runners drank water.

> <조건>
> 1. 부사절이 있는 완전한 문장으로 바꿔 쓰시오.
> 2. 접속사 when을 활용하시오.

→ _____

_____

7 다음 괄호 안의 단어를 알맞은 형태로 바꿔 빈칸에 쓰시오.

> My friends and I went to see a sci-fi movie last night. It had _____ (amaze) special effects. Overall, we were very _____ (impress) by the film.

8 두 문장의 의미가 같도록 밑줄 친 부분을 분사구문으로 바꿔 쓰시오.

> <u>After we had finished our meal</u>, we went into the living room.

= _____, we went into the living room.

9 다음 중 어법상 <u>어색한</u> 것의 개수는?

> ⓐ The picture painted by your cousin is lovely.
> ⓑ We saw a dolphin jumped out of the water.
> ⓒ The police caught the man stolen money.
> ⓓ Mary had her hair styled for her wedding.
> ⓔ I was embarrassing about my big mistake.

① 1개   ② 2개   ③ 3개
④ 4개   ⑤ 5개

10 다음 빈칸에 들어갈 말이 순서대로 짝지어진 것은?

> The new baseball stadium opens today. _____ in the center of downtown, it will be more convenient than the old one. Whether _____ the bus or subway, people can now easily get to the stadium to watch a game.

① Locating – taken
② Locating – taking
③ Located – taking
④ Located – taken
⑤ Located – take

[11-13] 다음 대화를 읽고 주어진 질문에 답하시오.

> *Will* : I'm so ⓐ_____(worry) about the book report. I don't like reading fiction books.
> *Carol*: Really? You might enjoy this story. I already read it, and it is ⓑ_____(fascinate).
> *Will* : Hmm... The teacher did say that the author is ⓒ_____(admire) around the world.
> *Carol*: I can understand why. (A) 솔직히 말해서, 이것은 내가 지금껏 읽은 최고의 책들 중 한 권이다. (B) 많은 흥미로운 캐릭터들을 포함하면서, (interesting, feature, characters, many) the story is very enjoyable.

11 괄호 안의 말을 활용하여 빈칸 ⓐ~ⓒ에 알맞은 말을 쓰시오.

ⓐ _____

ⓑ _____

ⓒ _____

12 위 대화의 밑줄 친 우리말 (A)와 의미가 같도록 괄호 안의 말을 알맞게 배열하시오.

> (speaking, one of the best books, read, ever, frankly, have, it, is, I)

= _____

_____

13 위 대화의 밑줄 친 우리말 (B)와 같도록 괄호 안의 말을 활용하여 문장을 완성하시오.

= _____

14 다음 대화의 밑줄 친 문장을 분사구문을 포함한 문장으로 바꿔 쓰시오.

> *A*: Can I ask you a favor?
> *B*: Sure. What is it?
> *A*: Because my younger sister is sick, I can't attend class today. Could I borrow your notes later?
> *B*: No problem. I hope she feels better soon!

→ _____

_____

15 다음 문장에서 어법상 어색한 부분을 찾아 쓰고 바르게 고쳐 쓰시오.

> Our fitness program can be exhausted, but it is great for your health.

_____ → _____

16 다음 우리말을 알맞게 영작한 것은?

> 그 고양이는 눈을 감은 채로 소파에서 잠을 잤다.

① The cat slept on the sofa with its eyes closing.

② The cat slept on the sofa with its eyes close.

③ The cat slept on the sofa with its eyes being close.

④ The cat slept on the sofa with its eyes having closed.

⑤ The cat slept on the sofa with its eyes closed.

[17-18] 다음 글을 읽고 주어진 질문에 답하시오.

My friend and I had a (A) <u>무서운 경험</u> (frighten, experience) yesterday. (B) <u>강한 바람을 일으키는 폭풍</u> (a storm, cause, strong winds) appeared suddenly. (C) <u>우리의 안전이 위협받는 채로</u> (with, our safety, threaten), we ran toward the house. ⓐ<u>Running as fast as we could</u>, we were able to reach the house safely.

17 위 글의 밑줄 친 우리말 (A)~(C)와 같도록 괄호 안의 말을 활용하여 문장을 완성하시오.

(A) _____

(B) _____

(C) _____

18 위 글의 밑줄 친 ⓐ와 바꿔 쓸 수 있는 것은?

① If we had run as fast as we could

② But we ran as fast as we could

③ While we ran as fast as we could

④ Though we ran as fast as we could

⑤ Because we ran as fast as we could

19 다음 빈칸에 들어갈 알맞은 것은?

When I picked up the phone, I found the screen _____.

① break   ② to break   ③ breaking
④ broken   ⑤ breaks

20 다음 대화를 읽고, 괄호 안의 말을 활용하여 대화를 완성하시오.

A: Who are those ⓐ_____ pictures? (people, take)

B: They're professional photographers.

A: Oh, really? Who is that ⓑ_____? (woman, sit near them) She has ⓒ_____. (her legs, cross)

B: She's a ⓓ_____. (pay, model) They're making an advertisement for a yoga studio.

21 다음 문장과 바꿔 쓸 수 있는 것을 <u>모두</u> 고르시오.

Hoping to surprise my brother, I'm planning a graduation party for him.

① As I hope to surprise my brother, I'm planning a graduation party for him.

② While I hope to surprise my brother, I'm planning a graduation party for him.

③ Although I hope to surprise my brother, I'm planning a graduation party for him.

④ As I hoped to surprise my brother, I'm planning a graduation party for him.

⑤ Because I hope to surprise my brother, I'm planning a graduation party for him.

22 다음 중 밑줄 친 부분이 어법상 바른 것은?

I had an ①excited vacation in Paris. While I was there, I got to see many ②interested sites. In particular, seeing the Eiffel Tower was ③thrilled. I was ④moving by how beautiful the city was. It was so great that I didn't want to leave. In fact, getting on the plane to return home was ⑤depressing.

23 다음 중 분사구문으로 잘못 바꾼 것은?

① Since Paul didn't clean his room, he can't play outside with his friends.
　→ Not having cleaned his room, Paul can't play outside with his friends.
② After I had argued with my older brother, I apologized to him.
　→ Arguing with my older brother, I apologized to him.
③ Because Todd didn't know the other guests, he introduced himself.
　→ Not knowing the other guests, Todd introduced himself.
④ As he was scolded by his mother, he felt sorry for what he said.
　→ Scolded by his mother, he felt sorry for what he said.
⑤ If you turn left at the next corner, you'll see the bank.
　→ Turning left at the next corner, you'll see the bank.

24 다음 문장의 밑줄 친 부분과 쓰임이 다른 것은?

The girl holding the doll is my younger sister.

① The magazine looks interesting.
② I saw Bennie running in the park.
③ The lizard climbing up the tree is green.
④ My puppy is playing with his new toy.
⑤ Katie's favorite hobby is drawing pictures.

25 다음 중 어법상 어색한 것은?

① Damaged by the fire, the museum lost many works of art.
② Wrapping in a blanket, the baby slept peacefully.
③ With the children listening, the librarian read the story.
④ Lifting the heavy box, Mr. Miller hurt his back.
⑤ Becky cleaned the whole house, pleasing her parents.

CHAPTER 8
명사와 대명사

기출로 적중 POINT

연습문제 | 밑줄 친 부분이 어법상 맞으면 O를 쓰고, 틀리면 바르게 고쳐 완전한 문장을 쓰시오.

1 Plastic <u>bags</u> are harmful to the environment.

→ _____

2 There are many <u>pianos</u> in the music room.

→ _____

3 Park visitors often feed the <u>gooses</u> in the pond.

→ _____

4 Those <u>shelfs</u> are easy to assemble.

→ _____

5 The athletes were doing a <u>ten-minutes</u> run.

→ _____

6 Irene will take many science <u>classes</u> the next term.

→ _____

7 My grandmother used to tell me many <u>storys</u>.

→ _____

8 You have to brush your <u>tooths</u> before going to bed.

→ _____

9 We bought some <u>pencils</u> and erasers to sketch with.

→ _____

10 <u>Volcanos</u> are about to explode.

→ _____

11 I met many interesting <u>peoples</u> at the party.

→ _____

12 The farmer raises <u>sheeps</u> for their wool.

→ _____

연습문제 우리말과 같도록 괄호 안의 말을 활용하여 문장을 완성하시오. (단, 숫자는 영어로 쓰시오.)

1 Henry는 그의 차에 설탕 한 숟가락을 넣었다. (sugar)

= Henry put _____ in his tea.

2 제가 가구 한 점을 저의 방으로 옮기는 것을 도와주세요. (furniture)

= Please help me with moving _____ to my room.

3 나는 당신이 문구점에서 잉크 한 병을 나에게 가져다 주기를 원한다. (ink)

= I want you to get me _____ from the stationery store.

4 나의 언니는 점심식사 후에 케이크 두 조각을 후식으로 먹었다. (cake)

= My older sister ate _____ for dessert after lunch.

5 김 선생님이 나에게 종이 한 장을 건네주셨다. (paper)

= Ms. Kim handed me _____.

6 그들은 그들의 딸들을 위해 비누 세 개를 샀다. (soap)

= They bought _____ for their daughters.

7 소금 한 숟가락을 추가하는 것은 수프를 더 맛있게 만들 것이다. (salt)

= Adding _____ would make the soup taste better.

8 Jacob의 엄마는 아침으로 그에게 시리얼 한 그릇을 주었다. (cereal)

= Jacob's mom gave him _____ for breakfast.

9 선생님은 그의 학생들에게 내일 현장 학습을 위해 물 두 병을 가져오라고 말했다. (water)

= The teacher told his students to bring _____ for tomorrow's field trip.

10 Joshua는 그 큰 유리 컵을 한 장의 신문지로 포장했다. (newspaper)

= Joshua wrapped the big glass cup with _____.

11 금괴 하나는 훨씬 더 쌌었다. (gold)

= _____ used to cost a lot less.

12 와인 잔 옆에 치즈 세 장이 있다. (cheese)

= There are _____ next to a glass of wine.

연습문제 A 우리말과 같도록 괄호 안의 말을 활용하여 빈칸에 알맞은 말을 쓰시오.

1 한국의 대통령이 최근 인도네시아를 방문했다. (Korea, the president)

= _____ _____ _____ _____ visited Indonesia recently.

2 나의 아빠의 트럭은 그 집 앞에 주차되어 있다. (truck, my dad)

= _____ _____ _____ is parked in front of the house.

3 곧 있을 설문은 한국사에 대한 학생들의 지식을 시험할 것이다. (knowledge, students)

= The upcoming survey will test _____ _____ of Korean history.

4 그 게임의 규칙들은 아주 간단하다. (the rules, the game)

= _____ _____ _____ _____ _____ are very simple.

5 Jane의 새 집은 언덕 위에 있다. (Jane, new house)

= _____ _____ _____ is on the hill.

6 Jake는 그의 부모님의 TV를 낯선 사람에게 팔았다. (his parents, TV)

= Jake sold _____ _____ _____ to a stranger.

연습문제 B 다음 밑줄 친 부분이 어법상 맞으면 O, 틀리면 바르게 고쳐 완전한 문장을 쓰시오.

1 A friend of mine will be visiting this evening.

→ _____

2 A classmate of your called to borrow your history notes.

→ _____

3 I'm going to Kate's dorm to return a coat of her.

→ _____

4 These Daniel's essays are among the best I have ever read.

→ _____

5 She wants to see those kids of his to tell them they are too noisy.

→ _____

6 I washed the mug of yours that was on the counter.

→ _____

POINT 4 재귀대명사

정답 p.76

연습문제 A 다음 빈칸에 알맞은 재귀대명사를 쓰고, 생략할 수 있으면 O, 생략할 수 없으면 X를 쓰시오.

1 I _____ was a naughty boy when I was little. [   ]

2 You must reflect on _____ more often. [   ]

3 Taeho introduced _____ to his new classmates. [   ]

4 The kids cleaned the dining room _____. [   ]

5 The man _____ asked for help with the project. [   ]

6 Minju deserved to be proud of _____. [   ]

7 She is a runner _____ and competes in many races. [   ]

8 Many people make promises to _____ to become a better person. [   ]

9 I consider _____ a passionate person. [   ]

10 The problem is that the computer _____ is too old. [   ]

연습문제 B 우리말과 같도록 <보기>의 말을 활용하여 문장을 완성하시오.

<보기>   help oneself   by oneself   for oneself   talk to oneself   in itself   between ourselves

1 나는 나 혼자서 이 일을 끝낼 수 있다고 생각하지 않는다.
= I don't think I can finish this work _____.

2 몇몇 아이들은 지루할 때 혼잣말을 한다.
= Some children _____ when feeling bored.

3 그 오류 그 자체는 현재로는 별일이 아니다.
= The error _____ is not a big deal for now.

4 우리는 부모님이 집에 없을 때 스스로 저녁 식사를 준비하려고 노력했다.
= We tried to cook dinner _____ when our parents were not home.

5 이 대화는 우리끼리의 이야기로 하자.
= Let's keep this conversation _____.

6 식탁 위에 있는 쿠키들을 마음껏 드세요.
= Please _____ to the cookies on the table.

기출로 작중 해커스 중학영문법 3학년 워크북

Chapter 8 명사와 대명사 **99**

it의 다양한 쓰임 I

정답 p.76

연습문제 | 밑줄 친 it의 쓰임과 같은 것을 <보기>에서 골라 그 기호를 쓰시오.

<보기>
ⓐ I don't think I can finish it by next week.
ⓑ It is getting warm out here.
ⓒ It is important to save energy.
ⓓ Daisy found it relaxing to drink chamomile tea.

1 Oliver found it difficult to master the English grammar. → _____

2 It is dark outside, so you should just stay home. → _____

3 Don't forget to bring it to class tomorrow. → _____

4 It is impossible for them to arrive in Japan tonight. → _____

5 The doctor made it clear that the patient should take the medicine on time. → _____

6 It is 12 in the morning, so you need to go to bed right away. → _____

7 It is surprising that she won second place in the competition. → _____

it의 다양한 쓰임 II

정답 p.76

연습문제 | 두 문장의 의미가 같도록 문장을 완성하시오.

1 The bridge in London seems to be old.
= It _____ is old.

2 It seems that you two have so many things in common.
= You two _____ so many things in common.

3 She seemed to be disappointed in her friend.
= It _____ in her friend.

4 It seems that Jessica is really excited about the trip.
= Jessica _____ really excited about the trip.

5 It seemed that the pottery was not made by the artisan.
= The pottery _____ made by the artisan.

부정대명사: one

정답 p.76

연습문제 밑줄 친 부분이 어법상 맞으면 O를 쓰고, 틀리면 바르게 고쳐 쓰시오.

1 If you want to read my comic book, you can borrow <u>it</u>. → _____

2 This T-shirt is too big. Can I try a smaller <u>one</u>? → _____

3 Jacob has two younger sisters, and <u>ones</u> are nice and polite. → _____

4 Minsu really liked your soccer ball. Why don't you buy him <u>one</u>? → _____

5 These apples look fresher than those <u>one</u> over there. → _____

6 You can use my pencil if you don't have <u>it</u>. → _____

7 I'm going to bring some pictures and decorate the wall with <u>one</u>. → _____

8 Can I have these cookies? – Yes, you can have <u>them</u> all. → _____

9 I wanted to buy red pens, but the store only had black <u>one</u>. → _____

부정대명사: some, any

POINT 6-2

정답 p.76

연습문제 우리말과 같도록 문장을 완성하시오.

1 나의 안경을 본 어떤 사람이라도 있니?
= Has _____ seen my glasses?

2 나는 그 사고에 대해 어떤 것도 알지 못한다.
= I don't know _____ about the incident.

3 나의 옷들 중 어떤 것들은 학교에 입고 가기에 너무 화려하다.
= _____ of my clothes are too fancy to wear to school.

4 내가 다음 기차를 탈 수 있는 어떤 방법이 있니?
= Is there _____ way I can take the next train?

5 주방 바닥에 무엇인가 끈적이는 것이 있었다.
= There was _____ sticky on the kitchen floor.

6 우리는 영어를 잘하는 누군가를 찾아야 한다.
= We need to find _____ who is good at English.

연습문제 A 다음 빈칸에 알맞은 말을 <보기>에서 골라 쓰시오.

<보기> one   another   other   others   the other   the others

1 There are four sandwiches. _____ is ham, _____ is egg, and _____ are chicken.

2 Many students are wearing headphones. Some are listening to rap music, and _____ are listening to classical music.

3 I have two quizzes tomorrow. _____ is on chemistry, and _____ is on history.

4 When you finish eating that muffin, I can give you _____ .

5 Five kids are playing on the playground. _____ is on the swing, and _____ are on the see-saws.

6 I'm worried about what _____ might think of me.

7 The boy has three balls. _____ is for soccer, _____ is for golf, and _____ is for tennis.

8 Using chopsticks is also common in _____ countries.

9 Of the three laptops on the table, two are out of date, while _____ is new.

10 Jaewoo speaks in a soft tone when communicating with _____ .

연습문제 B 밑줄 친 부분이 어법상 맞으면 O를 쓰고, 틀리면 바르게 고쳐 쓰시오.

1 After climbing a mountain yesterday, he climbed <u>other</u> today. → _____

2 Angela cares about <u>the other</u>, but doesn't care about herself. → _____

3 There are two customers in the hair salon. <u>One</u> is getting her hair dyed, and the other is having her hair cut. → _____

4 Many people are gathered in front of the French embassy. Some are French, and <u>other</u> are Korean. I don't know about the others. → _____

5 Would you like to have <u>another</u> cup of coffee? → _____

6 Some people are more optimistic than <u>others</u>. → _____

7 You should try to get along well with <u>other</u> on your team. → _____

8 Chloe has two watches. One is metal, and <u>others</u> is leather. → _____

부정대명사: all, each, every

POINT 6-4

정답 p.76

연습문제 | 우리말과 같도록 괄호 안의 말을 활용하여 빈칸에 쓰시오.

1 모든 사람들은 오늘 점심으로 볶음밥을 먹기를 원한다. (want)

= Everyone _____ to have fried rice for lunch today.

2 도시의 모든 도로가 눈 때문에 막혀 있다. (road, be)

= Every _____ in the city _____ blocked due to the snow.

3 각각의 요리사들은 자신만의 특별한 요리법이 있다. (chef, have)

= Each _____ _____ his or her own special recipe.

4 모든 선생님들은 재미있는 방법으로 가르쳐야 한다. (teacher, have)

= All the _____ _____ to teach in a fun way.

5 각각의 환자들은 치료 시간을 기다린다. (patient, wait)

= Each of the _____ _____ for a therapy session.

6 모든 식당들은 손님들로 가득 차 있다. (restaurant, be)

= All of the _____ _____ full of customers.

 부정대명사: both, either, neither

POINT 6-5

정답 p.76

연습문제 | 밑줄 친 부분이 어법상 맞으면 O를 쓰고, 틀리면 바르게 고쳐 완전한 문장을 쓰시오.

1 Neither hotdog <u>were</u> delicious to him.

→ _____

2 Both of my sisters <u>have</u> been to Europe before.

→ _____

3 You can choose between an ocean view and a city view. Either view <u>is</u> fine to me.

→ _____

4 There are two T-shirts, but the customer doesn't like <u>neither</u> of them.

→ _____

5 Both the students <u>seems</u> to be happy with the solution to the problem.

→ _____

기출로 작중 해커스 중학영문법 3학년 워크북

중간·기말고사 실전 문제

1 다음 중 어법상 어색한 것을 <u>모두</u> 고르시오.

① The town has two beach resorts, and either of them would be nice.

② There wasn't fun anything on TV last night.

③ Are any of the paintings in the gallery famous?

④ There are two vending machines, but either machine are working.

⑤ Is there any juice in the fridge?

2 다음 (A)~(C)에 들어갈 말이 바르게 짝지어진 것은?

· Mr. and Mrs. Williams have ___(A)___ twins.
· Two ___(B)___ were working in the field.
· London is one of my favorite ___(C)___ in Europe.

	(A)	(B)	(C)
①	three-years-old	oxes	cities
②	three-year-old	oxes	cities
③	three-year-old	oxen	cities
④	three-year-old	oxen	citys
⑤	three-years-old	oxen	citys

3 우리말과 같도록 괄호 안의 말을 활용하여 문장을 완성하시오.

우리는 점심으로 수프 두 그릇과 후식으로 케이크 두 조각을 주문했다. (soup, cake)

= We ordered _____ for lunch and _____ for dessert.

4 다음 중 밑줄 친 부분이 어법상 어색한 것은?

Last weekend, ①everyone in my family went on a camping trip. On Saturday, we enjoyed a hike together. Then we ate dinner and told stories to each ②other around the campfire. Afterward, all of us ③was tired and fell asleep. On Sunday morning, I decided to go fishing by myself, while ④the others went on a boat ride. Unfortunately, I didn't catch ⑤anything, but it was very peaceful. Overall, we had a good time, and we plan to go camping again soon.

5 우리말과 같도록 <보기>의 말을 활용하여 빈칸에 쓰시오.

<보기> either   neither

(1) 나는 상점에서 드레스 두 벌을 입어봤는데, 둘 중 어느 것도 나에게 어울리지 않았다.

= I tried on two dresses at the store, but _____ _____ _____ looked good on me.

(2) 하나의 액션 영화와 하나의 공포 영화가 있다. 둘 중 어느 것이든 재미있어 보인다.

= There is an action movie and a horror movie. _____ _____ _____ seems exciting.

6 다음 빈칸에 공통으로 들어갈 알맞은 것은?

> · He eats two eggs and a _____ of bread every morning.
> · Natalie wrote my phone number on a _____ of paper.
> · I would like to share a _____ of information with you.

① spoonful ② piece ③ sheet
④ loaf ⑤ slice

7 우리말과 같도록 <보기>의 말을 활용하여 문장을 완성하시오.

> <보기> next year, tournament
>   the building, the lobby

(1) 내년의 대회는 매우 치열할 것이다.
= _____ will be very competitive.

(2) 나는 Rachel을 그 건물의 로비에서 만났다.
= I met Rachel _____ .

8 다음 중 어법상 바른 것은?

① After the lesson, each of the students was allowed to ask a question.
② None of the furniture in the shop are on sale.
③ Every fan were trying to get the star's autograph.
④ My grandfather recently had surgery on both of his eye.
⑤ All the zoo animals is treated with care.

9 다음 빈칸에 공통으로 들어갈 알맞은 대명사를 쓰시오.

> · Nick traded in his old smartphone for the latest _____ .
> · _____ should be as kind as possible at all times.

10 다음 중 밑줄 친 부분을 생략할 수 있는 것은?

① We couldn't finish the project by <u>ourselves</u>.
② I <u>myself</u> have played in many tennis tournaments.
③ Sometimes Caroline talks to <u>herself</u>.
④ Please come in and make <u>yourself</u> at home.
⑤ Taemin poured a cup of coffee for <u>himself</u>.

11 주어진 문장의 밑줄 친 one과 쓰임이 같은 것은?

> <u>One</u> must always obey the law.

① Her new hairstyle is much cuter than her last <u>one</u>.
② I don't like sad movies, so let's watch a funny <u>one</u>.
③ There is a dog inside the fence and <u>one</u> outside the fence.
④ <u>One</u> should sometimes try new things.
⑤ Do you like the silver necklace or the gold <u>one</u>?

12 다음 중 어느 빈칸에도 들어갈 수 없는 것은?

ⓐ_____ believe in aliens, and ⓑ_____ don't. The people who believe in ⓒ_____ are convinced that they are real. How about you? Do you believe in aliens, and have you ever seen ⓓ_____?

① other ② one ③ some
④ them ⑤ others

13 다음 밑줄 친 부분의 쓰임이 같은 것끼리 묶인 것은?

ⓐ According to the weather report, it's going to snow tonight.
ⓑ I find it surprising that John did not win the award.
ⓒ It is a lot of fun to meet new people.
ⓓ It's almost 8 o'clock, so we should leave soon.
ⓔ Do you know what day it is?

① ⓐ, ⓑ, ⓓ ② ⓑ, ⓓ, ⓔ ③ ⓐ, ⓒ, ⓓ
④ ⓑ, ⓒ, ⓔ ⑤ ⓐ, ⓓ, ⓔ

14 우리말과 같도록 주어진 <조건>에 맞게 영작하시오.

Mary가 그 손님들에게 편히 쉬라고 말했다.

<조건>
1. Mary, tell, the guests, to, make를 활용하시오.
2. 9단어로 쓰시오.

= _____

_____

15 우리말과 같도록 괄호 안의 말을 알맞게 배열하시오.

Greg는 그가 외로움을 느낄 때 항상 혼잣말을 한다. (he, feels, always, lonely, himself, to, when, talks)

= Greg _____

_____.

16 우리말과 같도록 괄호 안의 말을 배열할 때 네 번째에 오는 것을 쓰시오.

그의 이 발명품은 정말로 놀랍다.
(amazing, this, is, truly, of, his, invention)

→ _____

17 다음 대화의 빈칸에 알맞은 말을 쓰시오.

A: Have you been to the art museum lately?
B: No, I haven't. Have you?
A: Yes. There are two new exhibits. You should go and check them out.
B: Really? What kind of exhibits are they?
A: Well, ⓐ_____ includes ancient Greek sculptures, and ⓑ_____ features abstract paintings from France.

18 두 문장의 의미가 같도록 문장을 완성하시오.

It seems that Junho is not going to the gym much these days.
= Junho _____
   to the gym much these days.

19 우리말과 같도록 괄호 안의 말을 알맞게 배열하시오.

많은 젊은이들은 다른 행성에서 생명이 발견될 것이 가능하다고 생각한다. (life, it, many young adults, possible, that, will be found, on other planets, think)

= _____
  _____
  _____

20 다음 글을 아래와 같이 요약할 때 <보기>의 말을 활용하여 빈칸에 알맞은 말을 쓰시오.

Plants have many defensive strategies that help them survive. For example, there are plants that have a chemical defense, such as poison. The poison makes them taste bad, and this prevents animals from eating them. There are also plants that have a physical defense. One is the cactus. Cactuses have sharp thorns, which are painful to any animal that tries to eat these plants.

<보기> one   some   other   others

_____ plants use a chemical defense to survive, and _____ use a physical defense.

21 다음 대화의 빈칸에 알맞은 말을 <보기>에서 한 번씩 골라 쓰시오.

<보기> the other   either
        anything   other

A: Is there ⓐ_____ I can help you with?
B: I'm trying to decide between the lobster and the steak.
A: I'd recommend the lobster, but you won't be disappointed by ⓑ_____ of them.

22 다음 중 짝지어진 두 문장의 의미가 <u>다른</u> 것은?

① It seemed that the castle was not occupied.

= The castle seemed to be occupied.

② It seemed that he was stronger than anyone else on the team.

= He seemed to be stronger than anyone else on the team.

③ It seemed that the speech pleased the audience.

= The speech seemed to please the audience.

④ It seems that those people need help.

= Those people seem to need help.

⑤ It seemed that Amy was not sleeping when we arrived.

= Amy seemed not to be sleeping when we arrived.

23 다음 밑줄 친 부분 중 어법상 <u>어색한</u> 것을 찾아 기호를 쓰고 바르게 고쳐 쓰시오.

- Nate runs in the park often. He @<u>seems enjoy to</u> jogging in the park.
- Kim was sick yesterday. However, she ⓑ<u>seemed to be feeling</u> better today.
- Steve likes Korean food. He ⓒ<u>seem to think</u> it's delicious.
- We saw Tim at the library. He ⓓ<u>seemed to be studying</u> for an exam.
- Jinho and Jinhee were talking. They ⓔ<u>seemed to be having</u> a great conversation.

(1) _____ → _____

(2) _____ → _____

24 다음 중 어법상 <u>어색한</u> 것은?

① There are some flies on the picnic table.

② I brush my teeths three times every day.

③ I have some coins in my pocket.

④ The shelves are too high to reach.

⑤ Our classes are difficult this year.

25 주어진 문장의 밑줄 친 it과 쓰임이 같은 것은?

<u>It</u> is almost noon. We should decide what we will eat for lunch.

① <u>It</u> is always fun to explore new places while on vacation.

② I find <u>it</u> helpful to have basic knowledge of Korean history.

③ The company made <u>it</u> impossible to access the database without permission.

④ <u>It</u> is the first day of spring.

⑤ <u>It</u> is difficult to solve the question.

CHAPTER 9
형용사와 부사

연습문제 A 괄호 안에서 알맞은 것을 고르시오.

1 Jeremy is a (student diligent / diligent student) in that class.

2 Many people like him because he is a (glad / joyful) man.

3 I wish to be friends with (someone cheerful / cheerful someone).

4 The girl wanted to be (alone / sole) in her room.

5 The teacher complimented the (creative kid / kid creative).

6 I watched an (video interesting / interesting video) last night.

7 There is (loud nobody / nobody loud) in the theater.

8 Which shirt should I wear for the (presentation important / important presentation)?

9 Did the thief steal (anything valuable / valuable anything)?

10 We'd like to move to (somewhere warm / warm somewhere).

11 I was (shame / ashamed) of my terrible mistakes.

연습문제 B 우리말과 같도록 괄호 안의 말을 알맞게 배열하시오.

1 그 소파는 눕기에 편하다. (comfortable, lie on, is, to, the sofa)
= _____

2 나는 연설하는 것이 두려웠다. (a speech, was, I, afraid of, giving)
= _____

3 너는 저 배우처럼 매력적인 누군가를 만난 적 있니? (charming, have, that actor, anybody, met, like, you)
= _____

4 그는 그의 개를 혼자 남겨두는 것을 원하지 않았다. (his dog, didn't, leave, he, want, alone, to)
= _____

5 그 팀은 많은 국제적인 선수들을 가지고 있다. (has, the team, international, players, many)
= _____

6 그녀는 오전 3시에 깨어있었다. (in the morning, was, she, at, awake, 3)
= _____

연습문제 A 괄호 안에서 알맞은 것을 모두 고르시오.

1 (A few / A little / Some) paintings were painted by the same artist.

2 There are (many / much / a lot of) luxurious rooms in the new hotel.

3 There are (some / many / a little) teachers checking the attendance.

4 I didn't save (a number of / much / any) money this month.

5 (A little / Few / A few) students wanted to take the physics class.

6 The boy ate (a great deal of / much / many) food and had a stomachache.

7 Cathy saw (a lot of / much / lots of) stars in the sky last night.

8 The journalist wrote (a little / a number of / plenty of) articles in the magazine.

9 He gave the plant (a little / a few / little) water.

10 (Plenty of / Some / Much) Chinese restaurants are in my neighborhood.

연습문제 B 우리말과 같도록 <보기1>과 <보기2>의 말을 하나씩 골라 문장을 완성하시오.

> <보기1>　 little　a little　much　a few　many

> <보기2>　 information　homework　books　sugar　days

1 Thomson씨는 항상 그의 커피에 약간의 설탕을 넣는다.
= Mr. Thomson always puts ＿＿＿＿＿＿＿＿＿＿＿ in his coffee.

2 우리 가족은 며칠 전에 뉴욕으로 이사했다.
= My family moved to New York ＿＿＿＿＿＿＿＿＿＿＿ ago.

3 Tina는 새로운 학생들에 대한 정보가 거의 없다.
= Tina has ＿＿＿＿＿＿＿＿＿＿＿ about the new students.

4 많은 책이 있기 때문에 그는 종종 도서관에 간다.
= He often goes to the library because ＿＿＿＿＿＿＿＿＿＿＿ are there.

5 우리에게 매일 너무 많은 숙제가 있는 것은 슬프다.
= It's sad that we have so ＿＿＿＿＿＿＿＿＿＿＿ every day.

연습문제 | 괄호 안의 말을 활용하여 빈칸에 알맞은 말을 쓰시오.

1 The pill is not an _____ treatment for headaches. (effective)

2 The weather is _____ cold today. (incredible)

3 The gallery is _____ accessible by public transportation. (easy)

4 _____, her advice was not helpful to me. (unfortunate)

5 The scientist's hypothesis is _____ wrong. (complete)

6 The novel was _____ written in French. (original)

7 My grandfather has been _____ ill for a week. (serious)

8 The reporter gave me a _____ question to answer. (tough)

9 _____, Josh didn't come home yesterday. (actual)

POINT 4 형용사와 형태가 같은 부사

정답 p.78

연습문제 | 밑줄 친 부분의 의미를 <보기>에서 골라 쓰고, 괄호 안에서 알맞은 품사를 고르시오.

| <보기> | 어려운 | 늦은 | 충분한 | 빠른 | 빠르게 | 이른 | 늦게 | 열심히 | 충분히 | 일찍 |

1 I stayed up late watching the soccer game last night. → _____ (형용사 / 부사)

2 This express bus is fast, so I think I won't be late. → _____ (형용사 / 부사)

3 Make sure you get enough sleep before the test day. → _____ (형용사 / 부사)

4 Mr. Davidson had a hard day at work. → _____ (형용사 / 부사)

5 Sammy left home early to get to the airport by noon. → _____ (형용사 / 부사)

6 My friend and I studied hard to pass the math exam. → _____ (형용사 / 부사)

7 The student was late for the class again. → _____ (형용사 / 부사)

8 He can type very fast without looking. → _____ (형용사 / 부사)

9 Ashley was brave enough to try bungee jumping. → _____ (형용사 / 부사)

10 Her favorite time of the day is the early morning. → _____ (형용사 / 부사)

POINT 5 -ly가 붙으면 의미가 달라지는 부사

정답 p.78

연습문제 | 우리말과 같도록 괄호 안의 말을 활용하여 문장을 완성하시오.

1 그 두 사건들은 밀접하게 관련되었다. (related, close)

= The two incidents were _____.

2 만약 네가 정답을 안다면 손을 높게 들어라. (high, raise)

= _____ your hand _____ if you know the answer.

3 그 관람객은 공연 도중에 거의 잠들었다. (fall asleep, near)

= The audience member _____ in the middle of the performance.

4 교통 체증 때문에 상호는 춤 연습에 늦었다. (late, be)

= Due to the traffic jam, Sangho _____ for the dance practice.

5 내 친구가 말한 것은 대부분 사실이었다. (true, most)

= What my friend said was _____.

6 그의 강한 억양 때문에 나는 그를 거의 이해할 수 없었다. (hard, understand)

= I could _____ him because of his strong accent.

7 나의 조부모님은 근처에 사셨었다. (live, close)

= My grandparents used to _____ by.

8 최근에 많은 이상한 일들이 일어나고 있다. (happen, late)

= Many strange things have been _____.

9 다른 사람들이 너를 들을 수 있도록 가까이 와라. (near, come)

= _____ so that the others can hear you.

10 그녀는 완벽한 친구가 되기 위해 너무 열심히 노력하고 있다. (hard, too)

= She's trying _____ to be a perfect friend.

11 그 작가는 매우 성공적인 사람들의 공통적인 습관들을 찾았다고 말한다. (high, successful)

= The author says he has identified the habits of _____ people.

12 그 밴드의 가장 최근 앨범이 언제 출시되었니? (recent, most)

= When was the band's _____ album released?

연습문제 다음 문장을 괄호 안의 의미를 가진 빈도부사를 포함한 문장으로 바꿔 쓰시오.

1 Michael is polite and considerate towards others. (항상)

→ _____

2 You can buy things cheaper online. (보통)

→ _____

3 Ms. Smith takes a nap on the couch. (때때로)

→ _____

4 Stephanie allows her brother to come into her room. (결코 ~않다)

→ _____

5 They have time to check their e-mails. (거의 ~않다)

→ _____

6 The interview takes two hours. (보통)

→ _____

7 The United States is called a melting pot. (종종)

→ _____

8 You can find useful information on the website. (항상)

→ _____

9 Kate does the dishes for her mom. (가끔)

→ _____

10 I watch TV on weekdays. (결코 ~않다)

→ _____

연습문제 우리말과 같도록 <보기>와 괄호 안의 명사를 활용하여 문장을 완성하시오.

<보기> put on   turn on   take off   throw away   turn down   turn in
try on   fill in   make up   wake up   look up

1 너는 그것을 버리고 새로운 것을 사야 한다. (it)

= You should _____ and get a new one.

2 너의 재킷을 벗어서 옷장 안에 걸어라. (your jacket)

= _____ , and hang it in the closet.

3 이 셔츠를 입어보는 게 어때? (this shirt)

= Why don't you _____ ?

4 정답을 찾고 그것을 답안지에 작성해라. (it)

= Find the answer and _____ on the answer sheet.

5 Dennis는 지각한 것에 대해서 변명을 만들어냈다. (an excuse)

= Dennis _____ about being late.

6 Lucy는 바빴기 때문에 그 초대를 거절했다. (the invitation)

= Lucy _____ because she was busy.

7 우리 엄마는 라디오를 듣고 싶어했다, 그래서 나는 그것을 켰다. (it)

= My mom wanted to listen to the radio, so I _____ .

8 그들은 제시간에 그들의 첫 번째 원고를 제출하는데 실패했다. (their first draft)

= They failed to _____ on time.

9 그 소년은 그의 양말을 뒤집어 입었다. (his socks)

= The boy _____ inside out.

10 나의 강아지가 아침 5시에 우리를 깨웠다. (us)

= My dog _____ at 5 in the morning.

11 만약 네가 그 장치를 어떻게 사용하는지 모른다면, 그것을 설명서에서 찾아봐라. (it)

= If you don't know how to use the device, _____ in the manual.

1 다음 중 어법상 어색한 것은?

① She opened the door slowly.

② He enjoys loud music.

③ Dogs are funny animals.

④ I'd like fresh fruit.

⑤ They can easy afford the items.

2 다음 ⓐ~ⓔ 중 어법상 어색한 것을 찾아 기호를 쓰고 바르게 고쳐 쓰시오.

> · ⓐSomebody nice sent you some flowers.
> · I read ⓑinteresting something earlier.
> · Do you want to visit ⓒspecific anywhere?
> · The experiment produced ⓓsomething unintended.
> · She said ⓔthings wonderful about you.

(1) _____ → _____

(2) _____ → _____

(3) _____ → _____

3 다음 중 어법상 어색한 것은?

① My uncle is sleep on the couch.

② Denise drove alone, and got lost along the way.

③ Everyone was glad to learn Monday was a holiday.

④ Gary and his brother sound alike on the phone.

⑤ I'm ashamed of my poor performance during the game.

4 우리말과 같도록 괄호 안의 단어를 알맞게 배열하시오.

> A: Why does that man look familiar?
> B: 나는 그가 유명한 누군가라고 생각해.
> (somebody, is, he, I, famous, think)

= _____

5 다음 중 어법상 어색한 것은?

① Sue always is first to arrive at the office.

② I have never eaten sushi until today.

③ She usually gets up late on Sunday mornings.

④ They often treat friends to a meal.

⑤ I will sometimes order food online.

6 다음 중 어법상 바른 것끼리 묶인 것은?

> ⓐ The insect is common seen in tropical countries.
> ⓑ Harold is reading quietly in his room.
> ⓒ We studied hard for the test.
> ⓓ The train from London will be arriving late.
> ⓔ They have to raise a certainly amount of money.
> ⓕ Every article is careful checked for mistakes.

① ⓐ, ⓑ, ⓕ   ② ⓑ, ⓒ, ⓓ   ③ ⓐ, ⓒ, ⓔ

④ ⓑ, ⓓ, ⓔ   ⑤ ⓑ, ⓓ, ⓕ

7 다음 ⓐ~ⓔ 중 어법상 어색한 것을 찾아 기호를 쓰고 바르게 고쳐 쓰시오.

I went to my friend Maya's birthday party last Saturday. I planned to buy her ⓐunique something from a store in the city. I was busy all week, though, and had ⓑlittle time to go shopping. ⓒLucky, my friend Kevin asked me to contribute ⓓsome money for a gift he found.
So, I just gave him some cash. In the end, I didn't go ⓔspecial anywhere to find Maya's gift.

(1) _____ → _____
(2) _____ → _____
(3) _____ → _____

8 다음 (A)~(C)에 들어갈 말이 바르게 짝지어진 것은?

· ___(A)___ children asked about the book.
· There is ___(B)___ water left in the cup.
· We sold ___(C)___ products at the event.

	(A)	(B)	(C)
①	Lots of	little	a great deal of
②	Much	little	a number of
③	Lots of	little	a number of
④	Much	few	a number of
⑤	Lots of	few	a great deal of

[9-10] 다음 글을 읽고 주어진 질문에 답하시오.

Around the world, people are producing too much trash. The problem with this is that ___(A)___ trash is not actually being recycled. There are ___(B)___ reasons for this. ⓐOne is that recycling can be incredible expensive to do. Recycling demands ___(C)___ commitment in terms of time, money, equipment, and materials. This is why the world needs to find other solutions to the trash crisis.

9 위 글의 (A)~(C)에 들어갈 말이 바르게 짝지어진 것을 고르시오.

	(A)	(B)	(C)
①	a lot of	many	a number of
②	many	a little	a great deal of
③	a lot of	many	a great deal of
④	many	many	a great deal of
⑤	a lot of	a little	a number of

10 위 글의 밑줄 친 ⓐ에서 틀린 부분을 바르게 고쳐 완전한 문장을 쓰시오.

→ _____

_____

11 다음 대화의 밑줄 친 우리말 (A)와 같도록 괄호 안의 말을 활용하여 문장을 완성하시오.

A: Is there a discount on these items?
B: (A) 내가 너를 위해 그것을 알아볼게. (out, find, I, that)

= _____ for you.

12 다음 중 어법상 바른 것의 개수는?

> ⓐ They've been to Mexico many times before.
> ⓑ We fed a large amount of ducks at the pond.
> ⓒ I have few experience in sales.
> ⓓ There is a few food left on the table over there.
> ⓔ She has little interest in becoming a doctor.

① 1개   ② 2개   ③ 3개
④ 4개   ⑤ 5개

13 다음 빈칸에 공통으로 들어갈 알맞은 것은?

> · My parents brought _____ stuff back from their trip.
> · My dog needs _____ attention.
> · We played _____ games when we were kids.
> · The book has _____ difficult words.

① a few   ② much   ③ a little
④ lots of   ⑤ a number of

14 다음 중 어법상 <u>어색한</u> 것은?

① He broke a lamp in the store accidental.
② She never really thought about going to Africa before.
③ Generally, Koreans are friendly to others.
④ I found a mysterious box in the basement.
⑤ Jessica has already heard the news.

15 우리말과 같도록 주어진 <조건>에 맞게 빈칸에 쓰시오.

> 나는 그들의 음식에 대해 특별한 어떤 것도 결코 발견하지 못했다.

> **<조건>**
> 1. 현재완료시제를 사용하시오.
> 2. 알맞은 빈도부사를 사용하시오.
> 3. find, special, anything을 활용하시오.

= I _____ _____ _____ _____ _____ about their food.

16 다음 중 밑줄 친 부분이 어법상 바른 것은?

> The Ohio Dental Association's ①<u>biannual</u> conference has been moved to a different date. Although it ②<u>is usual scheduled</u> for October, it will now take place in November. ③<u>Unfortunate</u>, the hotel we selected for this year's event made an error. Just as when similar changes have occurred at ④<u>events past</u>, we will refund any member who is unable to attend. If you are one of these, please contact us ⑤<u>prompt</u>. We apologize for the inconvenience and thank you for your understanding.

17 다음 중 밑줄 친 enough의 쓰임이 나머지 넷과 다른 것은?

① Jessie is strong enough to carry the heavy box.
② It seems we don't have enough food for everyone.
③ The hall was spacious enough for 100 people.
④ Her French is fluent enough.
⑤ The knife is sharp enough to cut a pineapple.

18 다음 중 어법상 어색한 것은?

① We can never agree on what color to paint the walls.
② She locks always the door before going to bed.
③ I rarely eat out these days to save money.
④ Now that he works full time, he seldom exercises.
⑤ Do you sometimes wish you had more money?

19 <보기>의 말을 활용하여 빈칸에 알맞은 말을 쓰시오.

<보기> high most close

(A) City people _____ take the bus or train to get to work.
(B) You must look _____ at the painting to see the detail.
(C) Mr. Barnes is _____ respected by everyone in the community.

20 다음 대화의 밑줄 친 ⓐ~ⓔ 중 어법상 어색한 것을 찾아 기호를 쓰고 바르게 고쳐 쓰시오.

A: Do you ⓐalways go to big supermarkets to buy food?
B: I've been going ⓑlate for things that small stores don't have.
A: The stuff there is ⓒreally expensive, though.
B: Some items are too ⓓcost, but you'll find bargains.
A: Sure, but that's ⓔrarely.

(1) _____ → _____
(2) _____ → _____
(3) _____ → _____

21 다음 중 어법상 어색한 것을 모두 고르시오.

① Let's find secure somewhere to put his expensive necklace.
② Don't leave anything valuable in your hotel room.
③ We need someone entertaining to host the program.
④ I don't know anyone excited about that movie.
⑤ You can discuss personally things with your doctor.

22 다음 중 어법상 바른 것끼리 묶인 것은?

ⓐ She eats always the same thing for lunch.
ⓑ It's cold outside, so get your hat and put on it.
ⓒ I'll look up his phone number and call him myself.
ⓓ You should never take a nap right after eating.
ⓔ People walk often in the park in the evenings.

① ⓐ, ⓒ   ② ⓐ, ⓑ   ③ ⓑ, ⓒ
④ ⓒ, ⓓ   ⑤ ⓓ, ⓔ

24 다음 중 어법상 바른 것의 개수는?

ⓐ He turned down the job offer because it didn't pay enough.
ⓑ There's a deadline for this assignment, so please hand in it on time.
ⓒ That's not junk mail, so please don't throw away it.
ⓓ I'll pick up the coats at the dry cleaner's on my way home.
ⓔ You should try the dress on to see if you like it.

① 1개   ② 2개   ③ 3개
④ 4개   ⑤ 5개

23 다음 중 밑줄 친 부분이 어법상 어색한 것은?

① The author's new novel was just released, so go <u>check it out</u>.
② Do you mind if I <u>turn off it</u>?
③ The students <u>wrote down what the teacher said</u>.
④ The police officers tried to <u>find out the cause</u> of the accident.
⑤ My dad <u>wakes my sister up</u> every morning.

25 다음 글의 밑줄 친 ⓐ~ⓔ 중 어법상 어색한 것을 찾아 기호를 쓰고 바르게 고쳐 쓰시오.

Every March, there is ⓐ<u>high</u> anticipation for an ⓑ<u>annual</u> event that is held around the world. It is called Earth Hour, and during that hour, ⓒ<u>nearly</u> all communities and businesses turn off non-essential lights to raise awareness about energy conservation. The event was ⓓ<u>original</u> held only in Australia. It was started by the World Wide Fund for Nature in 2004. It became a ⓔ<u>globally</u> event in 2008.

(1) _____ → _____
(2) _____ → _____

CHAPTER 10
비교구문

연습문제 A 우리말과 같도록 괄호 안의 말을 알맞게 배열하시오.

1 나의 엄마는 나만큼 여행을 좋아한다. (likes, do, as, traveling, my mom, as, I, much)

= _____

2 회전목마는 롤러코스터만큼 흥분되지 않는다. (is, thrilling, the merry-go-round, as, the roller coaster, not, as)

= _____

3 피아노를 연주하는 것은 바이올린을 연주하는 것만큼 어렵다. (hard, the piano, is, as, playing, the violin, as, playing)

= _____

4 장미 정원은 코스모스 밭만큼 예쁘다. (as, is, a garden of roses, pretty, as, a field of cosmos)

= _____

5 새 소파는 이전 것만큼 편하지 않다. (not, the new sofa, is, comfortable, as, the old one, as)

= _____

6 나의 남동생은 나만큼 비디오 게임을 하는 것을 즐긴다. (enjoys, do, as, playing, my younger brother, as, I, much, video games)

= _____

7 나의 역사 수업은 나의 과학 수업만큼 신나지 않는다. (is, exciting, my history class, as, my science class, not, as)

= _____

8 나의 방을 청소하는 것은 설거지를 하는 것만큼 지루하다. (boring, my room, is, as, cleaning, the dishes, as, washing)

= _____

9 우리의 새로운 집은 이전 집만큼 크지 않다. (not, our new home, is, large, as, the old one, as)

= _____

10 나의 머리카락은 나의 엄마의 머리카락만큼 검다. (is, dark, as, my mother's hair, as, my hair)

= _____

1 Jayden's height is 180 centimeters. My height is 180 centimeters, too. (tall)

→ I'm _____ Jayden.

2 There are 20 desks in my classroom. There are also 20 desks in his classroom, too. (many, desks)

→ His classroom has _____ mine.

3 This chili soup was delicious. That broccoli soup was not delicious. (delicious)

→ That broccoli soup was _____ this chili soup.

4 The street in this area is clean. The street in that area is not that clean. (clean)

→ The street in that area is _____ the one in this area.

5 Sunmi knows me well. Jihye knows me well, too. (well)

→ Jihye knows me _____ Sunmi does.

6 My dog is three years old. Her dog is three years old, too. (old)

→ Her dog is _____ my dog.

7 There are 500 people in this theater. There are 500 people in that theater, too. (many, people)

→ This theater has _____ that one.

8 The doughnuts were sweet. Those cookies were not as sweet. (sweet)

→ Those cookies were _____ those doughnuts.

9 The office in this building is neat. The office in that building is not that neat. (neat)

→ The office in that building is _____ the one in this building.

10 Linda speaks loud. Ginny speaks loud, too. (loud)

→ Linda speaks _____ Ginny does.

11 Ivy reads a lot of books. Lucy reads a lot of books, too. (many, book)

→ Ivy reads _____ Lucy does.

12 The musical is interesting. The concert is interesting, too. (interesting)

→ The musical is _____ the concert.

13 My thick sweater is warm. My jacket is warm, too. (warm)

→ My thick sweater is _____ my jacket.

14 Jenna's Halloween costume was strange. Brad's costume was strange, too. (strange)

→ Jenna's Halloween costume was _____ Brad's costume.

연습문제 A 다음 문장을 원급 관련 표현과 괄호 안의 말을 활용하여 바꿔 쓰시오. (단, 숫자는 영어로 쓰시오.)

1 This store has six kinds of fruit, and that market has three kinds of fruit. (many)
→ This store has _____ that market.

2 Bianca took a taxi to get there as early as possible. (can)
→ Bianca took a taxi to get there _____ .

3 The gorilla weighs 50 kg, and the koala weighs 10 kg. (heavy)
→ The gorilla is _____ the koala.

4 I play soccer once a week, and she plays soccer four times a week. (often)
→ She plays soccer _____ I do.

5 The historical movie has to show history as accurately as it can. (possible)
→ The historical movie has to show history _____ .

6 The basketball court is 500 square meters, and the hockey field is 5,000 square meters. (big)
→ The hockey field is _____ the basketball court.

7 Jason exercised every day to become as strong as possible. (can)
→ Jason exercised every day to become _____ .

8 The red desk costs $150, and the blue one costs $50. (expensive)
→ The red desk is _____ the blue one.

연습문제 B 우리말과 같도록 <보기>에서 알맞은 말을 골라 쓰시오.

<보기> as far as   as good as   as long as   as often as

1 Emma는 할 수 있을 때마다 그녀의 할머니를 방문한다.
= Emma visits her grandmother _____ she can.

2 그 신문 기자는 이 테니스 경기가 진 것이나 다름없다고 말했다.
= The news reporter said that this tennis match is _____ lost.

3 나는 네가 다치지 않는 한 네가 오토바이를 타는 것을 신경 쓰지 않는다.
= I don't mind you riding a motorcycle _____ you don't get hurt.

4 그의 사유지는 그 강까지 이어진다.
= His private land extends _____ the river.

연습문제 우리말과 같도록 괄호 안의 말을 활용하여 문장을 완성하시오.

1 그 학생의 목소리는 선생님의 목소리보다 더 크다. (loud)

= The student's voice is _____ the teacher's.

2 그녀의 주장은 그의 주장보다 훨씬 더 타당하게 들린다. (reasonable)

= Her argument sounds _____ his argument.

3 내일 날씨는 오늘보다 훨씬 더 나쁠 것이다. (bad)

= The weather tomorrow will be _____ today.

4 이 라떼는 이 아메리카노보다 덜 뜨겁다. (hot)

= This latte is _____ this Americano.

5 역사책을 읽는 것은 패션 잡지를 읽는 것보다 덜 재미있다. (entertaining)

= Reading a history book is _____ reading a fashion magazine.

6 Jessie는 방 안의 모든 다른 사람들보다 더 조용하게 말했다. (quietly)

= Jessie spoke _____ all the others in the room.

7 그 왕복 티켓은 편도 티켓보다 훨씬 더 싸다. (cheap)

= The round-trip ticket is _____ the one-way ticket.

8 이 장치는 저것보다 덜 효과적이다. (effective)

= This device is _____ than that one.

9 내가 아이였을 때, 지금보다 훨씬 더 귀여웠다. (cute)

= When I was a kid, I was _____ I am now.

10 Usain Bolt는 다른 주자들보다 더 빠르다. (fast)

= Usain Bolt is _____ other runners.

11 그 콘서트는 내가 예상했던 것보다 더 굉장했다. (fantastic)

= The concert was _____ I had expected.

12 Hannah의 드레스는 내 것보다 훨씬 더 예쁘게 보인다. (pretty)

= Hannah's dress looks _____ mine.

연습문제 A <보기>와 같이 다음 문장을 「the + 비교급, the + 비교급」 형태로 바꿔 쓰시오.

> <보기> When the beach is cleaner, the view becomes more beautiful.
>
> → *The cleaner the beach is, the more beautiful the view becomes* .

1 When I buy things cheaper than usual, I feel happier.

→ _____

2 As the movie got more popular, the main actor became more popular, too.

→ _____

3 When you work harder at something, you will do it better.

→ _____

4 When you get to know her more, you will want to become friends with her more.

→ _____

5 If the coat gets more expensive, it will be less affordable.

→ _____

6 If you speak English more frequently, you will be more fluent in it.

→ _____

연습문제 B 우리말과 같도록 괄호 안의 말을 활용하여 문장을 완성하시오. (단, 숫자는 영어로 쓰시오.)

1 그 하이킹 코스는 끝으로 가면서 점점 더 넓어진다. (wide)

= The hiking trail becomes _____ toward the end.

2 한라산은 저 산보다 다섯 배 더 높다. (high, than)

= Hallasan is _____ that mountain.

3 그 드라마 시리즈는 매 시즌 점점 더 흥미로워진다. (interesting)

= The drama series gets _____ each season.

4 이 소재는 플라스틱보다 열 배 더 강하다. (strong, than)

= This material is _____ plastic.

5 은미는 요즘 점점 더 피로를 느끼고 있다. (tired)

= Eunmi is feeling _____ these days.

연습문제 A 우리말과 같도록 괄호 안의 말을 활용하여 문장을 완성하시오.

1 그 작곡가의 새 노래는 그녀가 써 온 모든 노래들 중 가장 훌륭한 작품이다. (great, piece)

= The composer's new song is _____ among all the songs she has written.

2 수미는 그 반에서 가장 우수한 학생들 중 한 명이다. (brilliant, student)

= Sumi is _____ in the class.

3 신문을 읽는 것은 내가 들은 가장 덜 흥미로운 취미이다. (exciting, hobby)

= Reading newspapers is _____ I've ever heard of.

4 식기 세척기는 집에서 가장 유용한 가전 제품이다. (appliance, useful)

= A dishwasher is _____ in a house.

5 Liam은 나의 형의 가장 가까운 친구이다. (friend, close)

= Liam is _____ of my older brother.

연습문제 B 다음 문장들의 의미가 같도록 문장을 완성하시오.

1 Cameron is the most attractive movie star in America.

= _____ in America is _____ Cameron.

= _____ in America is _____ Cameron.

= Cameron is _____ in America.

= Cameron is _____ in America.

2 That watch is the cheapest item in the shop.

= _____ in the shop is _____ that watch.

= _____ in the shop is _____ that watch.

= That watch is _____ in the shop.

= That watch is _____ in the shop.

3 David is the most talented player on our baseball team.

= _____ on our baseball team is _____ David.

= _____ on our baseball team is _____ David.

= David is _____ on our baseball team.

= David is _____ on our baseball team.

중간·기말고사 실전 문제

1 다음 빈칸에 들어갈 말이 순서대로 짝지어진 것은?

> The mall is less busy on Monday than on Saturday.
> = The mall is _____ busy on Monday _____ it is on Saturday.

① so – than
② not much – as
③ not less – than
④ not so – as
⑤ as – as not

2 주어진 문장과 의미가 같은 것은?

> This piano is more expensive than all the other instruments I own.

① This piano is more expensive than any other instrument I own.
② This piano is as expensive as all the other instruments I own.
③ All the instruments I own are more expensive than this piano.
④ All the other instruments I own are as expensive as this piano.
⑤ No instrument is more expensive than the instruments I own.

3 다음 우리말을 알맞게 영작한 것은?

> 너는 토끼가 말만큼 빠르게 달릴 수 있는 것을 알았니?

① Did you know that a horse can run as fast as a rabbit?
② Did you know that a rabbit can run as fast as a horse?
③ Did you know that a rabbit can run not so fast as a horse?
④ Did you know that a rabbit can run as faster as a horse?
⑤ Did you know that a rabbit can run not as fast as a horse?

4 다음 중 어법상 바른 것의 개수는?

> ⓐ Do you have as more toys as Tom?
> ⓑ We've sold less furniture than we did last year.
> ⓒ Catching a fish is not as easier as it looks.
> ⓓ Traveling alone is not as fun as traveling with friends.
> ⓔ Alex is so shy as his sister.

① 1개
② 2개
③ 3개
④ 4개
⑤ 5개

5 다음 빈칸에 들어갈 수 있는 것을 <u>모두</u> 고르시오.

> The speaker was not _____ I believed he would be.

① as more nervous as

② as nervous so

③ so nervous as

④ as nervous as

⑤ nervous than

8 다음 중 어법상 바른 것끼리 묶인 것은?

> ⓐ Only strongest men can join this competition.
> ⓑ She is one of the most clever people I've met.
> ⓒ This is the most scary book that I own.
> ⓓ He is one of the most talented player on the team.
> ⓔ This is one of the funniest movies of the year.

① ⓐ, ⓑ   ② ⓐ, ⓔ   ③ ⓒ, ⓔ

④ ⓑ, ⓒ   ⑤ ⓑ, ⓔ

[6-7] 다음은 한 가게의 물품 가격을 나타낸 표이다. 괄호 안의 단어를 활용하여 문장을 완성하시오. (단, 원급을 사용하시오.)

Item	Hat	Jacket	Shoes
Price	$30	$90	$30

6

> The hat is _____ the shoes. (cheap)

7

> The jacket is _____ the hat. (expensive)

9 우리말과 같도록 괄호 안의 말을 활용하여 영작하시오.

> 고래는 지구 상의 모든 동물들 중 가장 크다.
> (large, all animals on Earth, whales, of)

= _____

10 우리말과 같도록 괄호 안의 말을 배열할 때 다섯 번째에 오는 것을 쓰시오.

> 달리기는 걷기보다 두 배 더 빠르다.
> (fast, as, walking, twice, running, is, as)

→ _____

11 다음 우리말을 알맞게 영작한 것을 <u>모두</u> 고르시오.

이 시험은 지난번 것 보다 세 배 더 어려웠다.

① This test was three times as harder as the last one.
② This test was three times as hard as the last one.
③ This test was three times hardest than the last one.
④ This test was three times as hardest as the last one.
⑤ This test was three times harder than the last one.

12 우리말과 같도록 괄호 안의 말을 알맞게 배열하시오.

그녀가 더 오래 제주도에 머물수록, 그녀는 서울에서 살던 것을 더 그리워했다.
(living, in Seoul, she, the, stayed, longer, in Jejudo, missed, the, more, she)

= _____

_____

13 다음 중 어법상 바른 것은?

① Which bed do you think is more comfortabler to sleep on?
② Some words are least commonly used than others.
③ Taking a taxi is more faster than taking a bus.
④ Jaewon dances more beautiful than he used to.
⑤ This puzzle is more complicated than the one we did yesterday.

14 다음 (A)~(C)에 들어갈 말이 바르게 짝지어진 것은?

· The manager was as ____(A)____ as everyone else about the announcement.
· Bill Gates used to be the ____(B)____ person in the world.
· The weather today is ____(C)____ than it has been all week.

	(A)	(B)	(C)
①	more shocked	richest	pleasant
②	more shocked	richer	more pleasant
③	shocked	richest	more pleasant
④	shocked	richer	more pleasant
⑤	shocked	richest	pleasant

15 우리말과 같도록 주어진 <조건>에 맞게 영작하시오.

이것은 내가 받은 것 중 가장 예쁜 선물이다.

<조건>
1. 최상급을 활용하시오.
2. pretty, gift, receive, this, have, that을 활용하시오.

= _____

[16-17] 다음 글을 읽고 주어진 질문에 답하시오.

> People think electric cars are a new invention. But actually, electric cars are @as older as gasoline cars. These days, electric cars are becoming ⓑvery more popular, even though they are ⓒmuch more expensive. Additionally, they can't travel ⓓas far as gasoline cars can in one trip. However, an electric car could save you money over time. (A) Owning a gasoline car is twice more costly than owning an electric car per year. This is because electric cars operate ⓔa lot most efficiently than gasoline cars.

16 @~ⓔ 중 어법상 어색한 것을 찾아 기호를 쓰고 바르게 고쳐 쓰시오.

(1) _____ → _____

(2) _____ → _____

(3) _____ → _____

17 밑줄 친 (A)와 의미가 같도록 문장을 완성하시오.

= Owning a gasoline car is _____

_____ .

18 다음 밑줄 친 부분과 바꿔 쓸 수 <u>없는</u> 것은?

> Children are <u>far</u> more likely to get hurt playing basketball than playing baseball.

① a lot　　② very　　③ still

④ much　　⑤ even

[19-20] 다음 대화를 읽고 주어진 질문에 답하시오.

> *Jack* : Who do you think will win tomorrow's soccer match, David?
>
> *David*: Probably the Bats. <u>That team is more competitive than any other team in the league.</u>
>
> *Jack* : That's true. Their players have been improving, too.
>
> *David*: Yes. (A) 나는 그들이 매 경기 점점 더 나아지고 있다고 생각해. (good)
>
> *Jack* : Their coach must be training them really well.
>
> *David*: I think you're right. I hope they win.

19 위 글의 밑줄 친 문장을 <조건>에 맞게 바꿔 쓰시오.

<조건>

1. No other로 문장을 시작하시오

2. 비교급을 사용하시오.

= _____

_____

20 위 글의 밑줄 친 (A)와 같도록 괄호 안의 단어를 활용하여 문장을 완성하시오.

= I think they have been getting

_____ each game.

21 다음 글의 밑줄 친 ⓐ~ⓔ 중 어법상 어색한 것은?

Most people know that Mount Everest is ⓐtaller than any other mountain in the world. But they probably don't know that it's also ⓑone of the dirtiest mountains. Mount Everest attracts thousands of climbers each year. They leave equipment and trash, making it ⓒdirtier and dirtier. People are encouraging climbers to leave ⓓas less trash as possible. Some organizations are collecting trash to give to artists, who use it to make art that they sell to help clean up the mountain. The ⓔmore money they raise, the cleaner Mount Everest will become.

① ⓐ   ② ⓑ   ③ ⓒ
④ ⓓ   ⑤ ⓔ

22 다음 빈칸에 들어갈 가장 알맞은 것은?

Ever since he started his new job he's been getting _____.

① busier and more busy
② more and more busier
③ busier and busy
④ more and more busy
⑤ busier and busier

23 주어진 문장과 의미가 같은 것은?

Some people say that money is not as important as happiness.

① Some people say that money shouldn't be as important as happiness.
② Some people say that money is less important than happiness.
③ Some people say that money is more important than happiness.
④ Some people say that money is as important as happiness.
⑤ Some people say that money is not the most important.

24 우리말과 같도록 괄호 안의 말을 활용하여 문장을 완성하시오.

커피 없이 나는 하루 내내 점점 더 졸리게 된다.
(sleepy)

= Without coffee, I become

_____ throughout the day.

25 다음 빈칸에 들어갈 가장 알맞은 것은?

The museum is _____ today than it usually is.

① very less crowded
② very most crowded
③ the most crowded
④ much less crowded
⑤ least crowded

CHAPTER 11
전치사

기출로 적중 POINT

연습문제 다음 빈칸에 at, on, in 중 알맞은 것을 쓰고, 필요하지 않는 곳에는 X표를 하시오.

1   The new clothing store will open _____ September 10.

2   Many people like to go swimming, especially _____ the summer.

3   My older brother graduated from high school _____ many years ago.

4   Mr. Jefferson usually leaves home for work _____ 7:30.

5   All of them go to church _____ Sundays.

6   I usually eat cereal for breakfast _____ the morning.

7   I make a study plan _____ the beginning of each day.

8   I'm planning to go camping _____ next Saturday.

9   We always have a meeting _____ Wednesday morning.

10 A friend of mine went to the gym from time to time _____ the past.

11 Fred always has dinner after completing his chores _____ 7:00.

12 Most stores are closed _____ Thanksgiving, as it's the biggest holiday.

13 Chris goes to piano practice _____ the afternoon every day.

14 _____ Monday, my dad and I are going to a baseball game.

15 _____ January, the weather becomes incredibly cold across the north.

16 I returned those library books _____ Thursday of last week.

17 Mrs. Grant asks the class questions _____ the end of the lecture.

18 Julie was prepared to get on the bus _____ 6 in the morning.

19 I go to the beach with my friends every day _____ the summer.

20 My favorite movie released _____ 1971, when my dad was a kid.

기출로적중 POINT 1-2 | 시간을 나타내는 전치사 II

정답 p.83

연습문제 A | 괄호 안에서 알맞은 전치사를 고르시오.

1 The community center will be closed for renovation (from / since) October 15.

2 Minsu waited for his friend (by / until) 5 P.M.

3 I have had the same English tutor (from / since) elementary school.

4 The package is supposed to be delivered (by / until) next Wednesday.

5 Charlotte has been living in Seoul (from / since) last winter.

6 Jaeho needs to hand in his book report (by / until) tomorrow.

7 The flea market is held (from / since) July 2 to July 10.

8 The organization will accept applications (by / until) December 20.

9 (After / Since) getting home from school, the student usually takes a short nap.

10 I went down a mountain (before / from) it got too dark.

연습문제 B | 우리말과 같도록 <보기>에서 알맞은 말을 골라 쓰시오.

<보기>   after   since   before   by   until   from

1 너는 아이스크림을 먹기 전에 식사를 끝내야 한다.
= You have to finish your meal _____ having ice cream.

2 나는 며칠 전 이후로 약간의 열이 있어 왔다.
= I've had a slight fever _____ a few days ago.

3 그 아이는 비행기가 시야에서 사라질 때까지 그것을 보았다.
= The kid looked at the airplane _____ it disappeared from sight.

4 Murphy의 아빠는 다음 달까지 돌아오겠다고 약속했다.
= Murphy's dad promised to come back _____ next month.

5 그 축구 대회는 5월 31일부터 6월 30일 까지 열렸다.
= The soccer tournament was held _____ May 31 to June 30.

6 Sophia는 설거지를 한 후에 빨래를 했다.
= Sophia did the laundry _____ doing the dishes.

기출로 적중 해카스 중학영문법 3학년 워크북

시간을 나타내는 전치사 III

정답 p.83

연습문제 for와 during 중 다음 빈칸에 들어갈 전치사가 나머지 둘과 <u>다른</u> 것을 고르시오.

1 ① It can be harmful to eat too much sugar _____ pregnancy.
② It has been snowing _____ almost a week now.
③ She only slept _____ three hours last night, so she feels tired.

2 ① The girl hasn't seen her grandparents _____ almost five years.
② The flu is more common _____ the colder months.
③ The electricity was out _____ a few hours yesterday.

3 ① Students should not sleep _____ class hours.
② I went hiking almost every day _____ the summer.
③ I have been on a diet _____ three weeks now.

4 ① Remember that this bus pass is valid _____ a month.
② The store is open only _____ the daytime hours.
③ Students are not allowed to talk _____ the exam.

5 ① The movie runs _____ two and a half hours.
② Many innocent people died _____ the war.
③ The boy studied English in Canada _____ a year.

장소를 나타내는 전치사 I

정답 p.83

연습문제 우리말과 같도록 괄호 안에서 알맞은 전치사를 고르시오.

1 탁자 위에 물 한 잔이 있다.
= There is a glass of water (at / on / in) the table.

2 그는 횡단보도를 건너고 있다.
= He is crossing (at / on / in) the crosswalk.

3 정원에 다채로운 꽃들이 있다.
= There are colorful flowers (at / on / in) the garden.

4 트럭들이 도로에 있다.
= The trucks are (at / on / in) the road.

연습문제 A 다음 빈칸에 at, on, in 중 알맞은 것을 쓰시오.

1 This stop is Gangnam Station. The door is _____ your right.

2 I had to come back because I left my book _____ home.

3 She knows a few words _____ Chinese.

4 Don't chat with your friend too long _____ the phone.

5 The report stated that fossil fuels are _____ danger of running out.

6 The girl is the captain of the cheerleading team _____ school.

7 _____ my way home, I stopped by the market to get some eggs.

8 You should look up the words you don't know _____ a dictionary.

9 The rock band spoke to news reporters _____ the press conference.

10 Dave woke up _____ the middle of the night due to a nightmare.

11 There is a big window _____ the left of the hallway.

12 Mr. John's car is _____ need of repair.

연습문제 B 밑줄 친 부분이 어법상 맞으면 O를 쓰고, 틀리면 바르게 고쳐 쓰시오.

1 We bumped into our teacher <u>on</u> the street this morning. → _____

2 Our clothing shop is <u>at</u> the third floor, so come take a look. → _____

3 I think a storm is coming because there are dark clouds <u>in</u> the sky. → _____

4 That marine species lives deep <u>on</u> the ocean. → _____

5 There were hundreds of people screaming <u>in</u> the concert. → _____

6 We just had a big fight <u>in</u> a taxi on our way here. → _____

7 My older brother is looking for job postings <u>at</u> the Internet. → _____

8 I wrote down my name and phone number <u>at</u> the bottom of the page. → _____

9 Canada is the second largest country <u>on</u> the world. → _____

10 The patient spent almost six months <u>in</u> the hospital room. → _____

11 People should wear seatbelts when they ride <u>on</u> a car. → _____

12 Go down three blocks, turn left, and you'll see the bank <u>in</u> your right. → _____

연습문제 우리말과 같도록 괄호 안에서 알맞은 전치사를 고르시오.

1 그 새들이 집 위에서 날고 있다.

= The birds are flying (under / above) the house.

2 그 우체부가 소포를 입구 앞에 놓고 갔다.

= The mailperson left the package (in front of / behind) the entrance.

3 그 소년은 그의 엄마와 아빠 사이에 앉았다.

= The boy sat (between / among) his mom and dad.

4 크리스마스트리 아래에 많은 선물들이 있다.

= There are many presents (under / above) the Christmas tree.

5 그 미술관은 그 조각상 뒤에 있다.

= The gallery is (behind / below) the statue.

6 Tony는 사람들 사이에서 그의 친구를 찾았다.

= Tony found his friend (among / above) the crowd.

7 그 벤치는 그 자판기 옆에 있다.

= The bench is (beside / among) the vending machine.

POINT 4 방향을 나타내는 전치사

정답 p.83

연습문제 괄호 안에서 알맞은 전치사를 고르시오.

1 They built a wall (around / across) the house for their security.

2 The runner ran (towards / into) the finish line.

3 My sister suddenly walked (up / out of) the room.

4 The subway station is just (across / around) from his home.

5 The firefighter is climbing (into / up) the ladder.

6 The treasure hunters went (down / into) the woods.

7 The passengers are boarding (around / through) the gate.

8 There are many cars parked (along / for) the street.

POINT 5 기타 전치사

정답 p.83

정답 p.83

연습문제 괄호 안에서 알맞은 전치사를 고르시오.

1 Thomas went to the beach (with / by) his family during summer break.

2 It is (without / against) the law to leave a child alone at home.

3 The price of rice has decreased (like / by) 15 percent.

4 My flight has been delayed (due to / instead of) the hurricane.

5 The smell (of / by) the food made him hungry.

6 The journalist wrote an article (like / about) air pollution.

7 The national museum is open (as / throughout) the year.

8 All the other players (from / except) Felix came to practice on time.

9 The doctor told me to drink water (instead of / such as) soda from now on.

10 The singer decided to make a song (for / as) his longtime fans.

11 The building is now being used (except / as) a warehouse.

POINT 6-1 전치사 관용 표현: 형용사 + 전치사

정답 p.83

연습문제 다음 빈칸에 알맞은 전치사를 쓰시오.

1 The Lakers are likely _____ win the game tonight.

2 Hyemin is good _____ painting with watercolors.

3 Many countries are short _____ food.

4 Her new sweater is similar _____ the other ones in her closet.

5 All the streets are crowded _____ protesters.

6 They don't feel like they are ready _____ the final exam.

7 The history museum is full _____ tourists from Italy.

8 We will give you a refund if you are not satisfied _____ our product.

9 Mr. Gordon was jealous _____ his friend's success in business.

10 I am tired _____ my friend complaining all the time.

연습문제 다음 빈칸에 알맞은 전치사를 쓰시오.

1 This workbook consists _____ 16 chapters.

2 You should always believe _____ yourself.

3 The customer finished his coffee and asked _____ a refill.

4 Wendy tried to concentrate _____ writing her essay.

5 Undoubtedly, that island belongs _____ Korea.

6 I'd like to apply _____ a visa for the United States.

7 She has to look _____ her baby sister when her parents are away.

8 The value of an autograph depends _____ the popularity of the celebrity.

9 AI stands _____ artificial intelligence.

10 Alchemists tried to turn metals _____ gold.

11 Creative people often come up _____ brilliant ideas.

12 Those priests live _____ a strict set of rules.

13 Billy rarely laughs _____ others' jokes.

14 Still in shock, the earthquake survivor couldn't focus _____ anything.

15 Mr. Miller divided his students _____ two groups to have a discussion.

16 The politician apologized _____ his inappropriate comment.

17 The recent advertisements resulted _____ an increase in sales.

18 The comedian succeeded _____ making the audience laugh.

19 Carter spent hundreds of dollars _____ his new bike.

20 I ran _____ my childhood friend Jimmy at the park yesterday.

POINT 6-3

연습문제 우리말과 같도록 문장을 완성하시오.

1 보고서를 작성할 때는 적절한 언어를 이용하는 것이 중요하다.

= It is important to _____ proper language when writing the report.

2 나의 할머니는 내가 아이였을 때 나를 돌봐주셨다.

= My grandmother used to _____ me when I was a kid.

3 너는 어떻게 흙을 제거하는 지 알고 있니?

= Do you know how to _____ the dirt?

4 그 커플은 그 고아를 불쌍히 여겨서 그녀를 입양하기로 결정했다.

= The couple _____ the orphan and chose to adopt her.

5 그 시장은 모든 시민들이 선거에 참여해야 한다고 말했다.

= The mayor said that all citizens should _____ the election.

6 그들은 그들의 선생님이 말하는 것에 관심을 갖지 않았다.

= They didn't _____ what their teacher was saying.

7 Doris는 어젯밤 콘서트에서 그녀의 친구들과 즐거운 시간을 보냈다.

= Doris _____ her friends at the concert last night.

8 나의 누나는 내가 하지 말라고 해도 항상 나를 바보 취급한다.

= My older sister always _____ me even if I tell her not to.

9 세균을 제거하기 위해서 너의 손을 자주 씻어라.

= Wash your hands frequently in order to _____ germs.

10 부모들은 항상 그들의 아이들에게 관심을 가져야 한다.

= Parents have to _____ their children all the time.

1 다음 빈칸에 들어갈 알맞은 것은?

> I haven't seen the house so clean in a long time. It feels _____ a brand new home.

① as   ② about   ③ like
④ with   ⑤ by

2 다음 중 밑줄 친 부분이 어법상 어색한 것은?

① The Statue of Liberty was completed <u>in</u> 1886.
② I never stay out late <u>at</u> night.
③ I wish I was <u>on</u> vacation right now.
④ We have lunch together <u>at</u> Sundays.
⑤ The leaves turn red and yellow <u>in</u> fall.

3 다음 (A)~(C)에 들어갈 말이 바르게 짝지어진 것은?

> Recently, I changed my study habits. I always studied at night ___(A)___ the past. However, I often got tired ___(B)___ I was studying. Now, I do my studies in the morning from 6 o'clock ___(C)___ around 7:30.

	(A)	(B)	(C)
①	at	while	by
②	in	while	until
③	in	during	until
④	at	during	by
⑤	in	while	by

4 다음 빈칸에 들어갈 알맞은 것은?

> Michelle had fun _____ her younger sister at the shopping mall.

① about   ② for   ③ to
④ with   ⑤ on

5 다음 문장에서 어법상 어색한 부분을 찾아 밑줄 치고 바르게 고쳐 쓰시오.

> (A) The café is not open on present.
> (B) She walks in her neighborhood at the morning.
> (C) I usually prepare cards for my friends in Valentine's Day.

(A) → _____ (B) → _____ (C) → _____

6 <보기>의 전치사를 활용하여 빈칸에 알맞은 말을 쓰시오.

> <보기>   for   during   from   since

> · The store was closed ⓐ_____ Tuesday to Friday for renovations.
> · It was ⓑ_____ the winter of 2014 that it snowed the most.
> · My family has lived in this apartment ⓒ_____ 2015.
> · This morning, I exercised ⓓ_____ 45 minutes.

7 다음 중 밑줄 친 부분이 어법상 바른 것은?

① Maggie is ready of her bath now.

② Dan was crazy at soccer as a teenager.

③ I was absent to class yesterday because of a cold.

④ Karen has been married to John for a year.

⑤ Those buckets are filled of water.

8 다음 빈칸에 들어갈 알맞은 것은?

She is capable _____ planning the book fair by herself.

① for   ② by   ③ of
④ about   ⑤ in

9 다음 대화의 빈칸에 들어갈 말이 같은 것끼리 묶인 것은?

A: Hi, Mrs. Jones. Is Sandy home? B: Yes, she is. She's ⓐ_____ her bedroom. I think she's ⓑ_____ the phone. A: Great. I want to talk ⓒ_____ her about something we discussed ⓓ_____ class. B: OK. You can wait ⓔ_____ her in the living room. I'll tell her you're here.

① ⓐ, ⓑ   ② ⓐ, ⓓ   ③ ⓑ, ⓒ
④ ⓒ, ⓔ   ⑤ ⓓ, ⓔ

10 다음 빈칸에 들어갈 말이 나머지 넷과 다른 것은?

① The location of the wedding will depend _____ the weather.

② The documentary is based _____ the life of Picasso.

③ You spend too much money _____ video games.

④ Sometimes it's hard to focus _____ the lesson after lunch.

⑤ These toys belong _____ my little brother.

11 다음 (A)~(C)에 들어갈 말이 바르게 짝지어진 것은?

· Margaret was ___(A)___ a hurry when we saw her. · A shipwreck was discovered ___(B)___ the bottom of the ocean. · The wildfire in the forest put the animals ___(C)___ danger.

	(A)	(B)	(C)
①	on	at	at
②	on	at	in
③	in	at	at
④	in	at	in
⑤	in	in	in

12 다음 빈칸에 들어갈 말이 순서대로 짝지어진 것은?

> · Firefighters pulled the man _____ the burning vehicle.
> · Steven will leave _____ Paris on Sunday.

① out of – for ② into – for
③ to – for ④ out of – around
⑤ into – to

13 다음 대화의 빈칸에 들어갈 말이 순서대로 짝지어진 것은?

> A: What are you doing _____ Saturday?
> B: I don't have plans yet. Why?
> A: Some friends and I are going to Mario's Restaurant. Would you like to join us?
> B: Sure! I know the place. It's the best Italian restaurant _____ the city.

① for - on ② in - on ③ on - in
④ on - for ⑤ in - for

14 다음 문장의 밑줄 친 for와 의미가 같은 것은?

> Are you for the new rule?

① My cousin attends a camp for athletes.
② Most people are for creating more holidays.
③ This medicine is used for treating fevers.
④ I bought a new toy for my puppy.
⑤ The website has a radar map for following the weather.

15 다음 빈칸에 공통으로 들어갈 알맞은 것은?

> · The children will attend a puppet show _____ Sunday.
> · Mozart was born _____ January 27, 1756.

① in ② at ③ on
④ for ⑤ by

16 다음 빈칸에 알맞은 전치사를 <보기>에서 골라 쓰시오.

> <보기> after along down from

> · There are so many signs (A) _____ the highway.
> · Dan drove (B) _____ Canada to Mexico.
> · Billy slid (C) _____ the slide over and over.
> · Katie took some time off work (D) _____ the birth of her child.

17 다음 빈칸에 공통으로 들어갈 알맞은 것은?

> · Butter consists _____ cream and salt.
> · The soccer stadium was full _____ screaming fans.
> · His grandfather died _____ heart disease.

18 다음 밑줄 친 ⓐ~ⓔ 중 어법상 어색한 것을 찾아 기호를 쓰고 바르게 고쳐 쓰시오.

My family and I stayed at a hotel ⓐat Busan. Our hotel was right ⓑby the beach. Unfortunately, the weather was stormy the whole time, so we spent most of our vacation ⓒin our hotel room. We watched a lot of movies ⓓin TV. We were unhappy ⓔabout the weather, but at least we got to spend time together.

(1) _____ → _____
(2) _____ → _____

19 다음 빈칸에 들어갈 알맞은 것은?

Mark looks _____ a popular actor. Many people think he is famous.

① by   ② for   ③ about
④ as   ⑤ like

20 다음 중 어느 빈칸에도 들어갈 수 <u>없는</u> 것은?

· A helicopter was flying _____ the building's roof.
· Sue moved _____ her sick aunt's house to take care of her.
· The girl sitting in the seat _____ Alice and Nancy is my older sister.
· There were many people _____ the swimming pool.

① above   ② between   ③ in
④ among   ⑤ into

[21-22] 다음 글을 읽고 주어진 질문에 답하시오.

Last week, my class went to an assembly ⓐ_____ the rest of the school. It was about working ⓑ_____ part of a team to succeed. We sat ⓒ_____ the stage, so I thought we would have good seats to listen to the speakers. However, we didn't spend a lot of time in our seats. We were quickly put into groups to take part ⓓ_____ team-building exercises. (A) 그 목표는 학생 개개인을 유능한 팀 구성원으로 바꾸기 위함이었다.

21 다음 빈칸에 알맞은 말을 <보기>에서 골라 쓰시오.

<보기>   near   as   in   with

ⓐ_____   ⓑ_____
ⓒ_____   ⓓ_____

22 밑줄 친 우리말 (A)와 같도록 괄호 안의 말을 활용하여 문장을 완성하시오.

= The goal was to _____

_____.

(the individual students, turn, effective team members, into)

23 다음 빈칸에 공통으로 들어갈 알맞은 것은?

> · Tonight, I'm going out to dinner
> _____ my family and some friends.
> · I bought a new bag _____ my
> allowance money.
> · Ken's neighborhood has problems
> _____ people making too much
> noise.

① with   ② like   ③ by
④ of   ⑤ about

24 다음 문장의 밑줄 친 like와 쓰임이 다른 것은?

> Howard wanted to buy a new sweater
> <u>like</u> the one he saw in a magazine.

① Jerry wants to visit somewhere with a
different culture, <u>like</u> Brazil, this summer.
② The nurse who treated me seemed <u>like</u> a
good person.
③ No one can inspire me <u>like</u> my teachers.
④ These days, companies <u>like</u> Samsung
are introducing new products constantly.
⑤ Joohoon <u>likes</u> to experiment with new
styles of cooking.

25 다음 빈칸에 들어갈 가장 알맞은 것은?

> I will be flying to another city to visit my
> grandparents next month. I'm a little
> nervous because it's my first time flying
> by myself, _____ my parents.

① by   ② for   ③ as
④ of   ⑤ without

CHAPTER 12
접속사

기출로 적중 POINT

연습문제 │ <보기>에서 가장 알맞은 접속사를 골라 다음 두 문장을 한 문장으로 연결하시오.

<보기>   and   but   or   so

1 I won a doll at the fair. + I lost it on the way home.
→ I won a doll at the fair, _____ I lost it on the way home.

2 I called my mother. + I told her I would be late for dinner.
→ I called my mother _____ told her I would be late for dinner.

3 Sally's cousin only speaks Spanish. + She can't talk to him.
→ Sally's cousin only speaks Spanish, _____ she can't talk to him.

4 Do you want an apple? + Do you want a plum?
→ Do you want an apple _____ a plum?

5 Boris needs to buy some school supplies. + He doesn't have any money.
→ Boris needs to buy some school supplies, _____ he doesn't have any money.

6 Lower your voice. + Your parents will wake up.
→ Lower your voice, _____ your parents will wake up.

7 The boy is nice and funny. + All his classmates like him.
→ The boy is nice and funny, _____ all his classmates like him.

8 Whale sharks are very big. + They are not dangerous.
→ Whale sharks are very big, _____ they are not dangerous.

9 Michael enjoys watching TV. + He likes playing video games.
→ Michael enjoys watching TV, _____ he likes playing video games.

10 Nancy woke up late this morning. + She was late for school.
→ Nancy woke up late this morning, _____ she was late for school.

연습문제 A 밑줄 친 부분이 어법상 맞으면 O를 쓰고, 틀리면 바르게 고쳐 쓰시오.

1 Either Robert or I <u>have</u> to clean the classroom after school. → _____

2 Both Ms. Kim and Ms. Cho always <u>gets</u> up at 7 A.M. for work. → _____

3 Neither the comic books nor the mystery novel <u>are</u> on the shelf. → _____

4 The cups as well as a set of dishes <u>is</u> on the dining table. → _____

5 Not only this room but also that room <u>has</u> two windows. → _____

6 Both Isaac and Dylan <u>likes</u> to jog in the early morning. → _____

7 The door as well as the window <u>needs</u> to be opened for now. → _____

8 Either Stella or you <u>has</u> to feed the pet today. → _____

9 Not only Anna but also her friends <u>is</u> working out on the treadmill. → _____

10 Neither my younger sister nor I <u>am</u> good at playing the cello. → _____

연습문제 B 우리말과 같도록 괄호 안의 말을 활용하여 문장을 완성하시오.

1 파스타와 쌀은 둘 다 좋은 에너지원이다. (pasta, be, rice)
= _____ good sources of energy.

2 영어뿐만 아니라 중국어도 배우기에 어렵다. (be, English, Chinese)
= _____ difficult to learn.

3 나는 캐나다가 아니라 미국에 방문했다. (Canada, the United States)
= I visited _____.

4 그나 그녀 둘 중 한 명이 그 여행 기사를 쓸 것이다. (she, write, will, he)
= _____ the travel article.

5 Chloe도 Jacob도 요리 하는 것을 좋아하지 않는다. (like, Chloe, Jacob)
= _____ to cook.

6 그녀는 말하는 것이 아니라 듣는 것을 좋아한다. (to talk, to listen)
= She likes _____.

연습문제 A 밑줄 친 that절의 역할을 <보기>에서 골라 그 기호를 쓰시오.

<보기> ⓐ 주어   ⓑ 목적어   ⓒ 보어

1 Luna heard that her best friend will move to Canada in October.   [   ]

2 It is important that we support and help each other.   [   ]

3 The fact is that Russia is the largest country in the world.   [   ]

4 It is necessary that you attend the meeting after lunch.   [   ]

5 The teacher noticed that the students were not interested in his lecture.   [   ]

6 It is terrible that the boy fell down the stairs and sprained his ankle.   [   ]

7 The worst part was that the police couldn't find any evidence.   [   ]

8 They knew that they had to try harder to win.   [   ]

연습문제 B 우리말과 같도록 <보기>와 괄호 안의 말을 알맞게 배열하시오.

<보기> the thought   the idea   the news   the suggestion   the fact

1 그는 그가 가장 좋아하는 밴드가 5월에 앨범을 발매할 것이라는 소식을 들었다. (that, favorite, band, his, will, an, release, album, May, in)

= He heard _____.

2 그는 아이들이 많은 다양한 것들을 경험해야 한다는 생각에 강력히 동의한다. (that, kids, experience, should, many, different, things)

= He strongly agrees with _____.

3 내가 시험을 떨어질 수도 있다는 생각이 나를 불안하게 만들었다. (that, might, fail, I, the exam)

= _____ made me nervous.

4 학생들이 더 긴 방학을 가져야 한다는 의견은 받아들여지지 않았다. (the students, longer, vacations, that, take)

= _____ was not accepted.

5 경쟁팀이 그 경기를 이겼다는 사실은 실망스러웠다. (that, won, the match, the rival team)

= _____ was disappointing.

POINT 3-2 명사절을 이끄는 접속사: if/whether

정답 p.86

연습문제 밑줄 친 부분이 어법상 맞으면 O, 틀리면 바르게 고쳐 쓰시오.

1 No one knows <u>whether</u> the book is based on a true story. → _____

2 It doesn't matter <u>if</u> or not you are talented. → _____

3 My sisters are taking bets on <u>if</u> I will keep my long hair. → _____

4 I wasn't sure <u>if</u> I would wear that costume for Halloween. → _____

5 Their major concern is <u>if</u> the victims are alive or not. → _____

6 You can find online <u>whether</u> or not the book is available. → _____

7 <u>If</u> the player will participate in the game is uncertain. → _____

8 He was wondering <u>whether</u> his friends were willing to help him. → _____

POINT 3-3 명사절을 이끄는 접속사: 의문사

정답 p.86

연습문제 우리말과 같도록 괄호 안의 말을 활용하여 문장을 완성하시오.

1 찬미는 어떻게 그녀가 그 초콜릿을 만들었는지에 대한 세부사항을 공유할 것이다. (make)
= Chanmi is going to share details on _____ that chocolate.

2 나는 조만간 너에게 내가 언제 호주에 방문할지를 말해줄 것이다. (visit, will)
= I will tell you soon _____ Australia.

3 Andrew는 왜 그가 지난주 수업에 오지 않았는지 설명하려고 노력했다. (come)
= Andrew tried to explain _____ to class last week.

4 내가 이 정보를 어떻게 얻었는지는 비밀이다. (get)
= _____ this information is secret.

5 누가 경주에서 우승할지 아무도 확실히 알 수 없다. (would, win)
= No one could be sure _____ the race.

6 혹시 너는 그들이 어제 어디에 있었는지 아니? (be)
= Do you happen to know _____ yesterday?

연습문제 A 괄호 안에서 가장 알맞은 것을 고르시오.

1 Joshua took a nap (after / while) he finished eating lunch.

2 He promised to finish the project (as soon as / until) he could.

3 My older sister has cooked for us (till / since) she was twelve.

4 The students became excited (as / as soon as) it got closer to break time.

5 The restaurant is open (since / till) 11 P.M. on weekends.

6 They went shopping for her birthday present (before / as soon as) the birthday party.

7 What do you usually do (before / when) you have free time?

8 Isabel didn't talk to him (until / since) he came to apologize.

9 Don't forget to turn off the light (since / as) you leave the room.

10 I've been living in this city (after / since) I was a kid.

11 Can I call you back (when / until) I am done with my assignment?

12 He unpacked his bags (since / as soon as) he arrived here.

연습문제 B 밑줄 친 부분이 어법상 맞으면 O를 쓰고, 틀리면 바르게 고쳐 쓰시오.

1 He ran back home as soon as he got that phone call. → _____

2 The patient shouldn't eat anything until the doctor will tell him to do so. → _____

3 I didn't know much about history before I watched that documentary. → _____

4 The class will start as soon as the school bell rang. → _____

5 Please mop the floor while I will dust the furniture. → _____

6 She ran around the park until she felt exhausted. → _____

7 He will travel around the world after he will graduate from school. → _____

8 They have had a serious conversation since they entered the classroom. → _____

9 When I will become a film director, I want to make many different kinds of movies. → _____

10 Grace discovered her talent as time passed. → _____

연습문제 A 괄호 안에서 가장 알맞은 것을 고르시오.

1 I was humming to myself (now that / while) I was taking a shower.

2 I decided to read a book (as / till) I had nothing else to do.

3 The girl ate a whole pizza by herself (since / before) she was starving.

4 We can't predict (because / when) the rain will stop.

5 We arrived there early (because / till) we took the express bus.

6 Calvin had physical therapy (till / as) he had severe back pain.

7 He goes snowboarding every weekend (before / now that) it's winter.

8 Many audience members were disappointed (since / because of) the show was not entertaining.

9 All the kids have to stay home (now that / until) it is too dark outside.

10 (Because / Until) an earthquake happened, they went under the table.

11 Soyeon fell asleep on the sofa (since / after) it was so comfortable and soft.

12 My older sister can drive a car (till / now that) she is old enough to do so.

연습문제 B 다음 빈칸에 because나 because of 중 알맞은 것을 쓰시오.

1 The soccer match was canceled ＿＿＿＿＿＿＿ bad weather.

2 The painter couldn't finish his painting ＿＿＿＿＿＿＿ he ran out of paint.

3 His food is delicious ＿＿＿＿＿＿＿ he is a great cook.

4 Eddie was surprised ＿＿＿＿＿＿＿ the thunderstorm.

5 We couldn't get home ＿＿＿＿＿＿＿ there was an accident on the road.

6 The band became famous ＿＿＿＿＿＿＿ their latest album.

7 They tried their best ＿＿＿＿＿＿＿ they were desperate to win.

8 Everyone had to leave the school ＿＿＿＿＿＿＿ the fire.

9 The beach was crowded ＿＿＿＿＿＿＿ the national holiday.

10 I couldn't walk to school ＿＿＿＿＿＿＿ it snowed heavily.

연습문제 A 밑줄 친 부분이 어법상 맞으면 O를 쓰고, 틀리면 바르게 고쳐 쓰시오.

1 Try to do your best <u>if</u> you want to achieve your goal.

→ _____

2 You shouldn't make an appointment <u>if</u> you can keep it.

→ _____

3 Unless Brandon <u>will get</u> to the airport on time, he will miss the flight.

→ _____

4 You will realize she is actually nice <u>unless</u> you become friends with her.

→ _____

5 <u>Once</u> we find the solution, we will contact you.

→ _____

6 We won't make it to the movie on time <u>once</u> we don't leave now.

→ _____

7 Once the building construction <u>is</u> done, the noise will stop bothering us.

→ _____

연습문제 B <보기>와 같이 우리말과 같도록 괄호 안의 말을 활용하여 문장을 완성하시오.

> **<보기>** 만약 네가 창문을 닫지 않는다면, 너무 추울 것이다. (close the window)
> = *If you don't close the window*, it will be too cold.
> = *Unless you close the window*, it will be too told.

1 만약 네가 제대로 먹지 않는다면, 너는 건강을 유지할 수 없을 것이다. (eat properly)

= _____, you won't be able to stay healthy.

= _____, you won't be able to stay healthy.

2 만약 네가 너의 약속을 지키지 않는다면, 너의 부모님은 기쁘지 않을 것이다. (keep your promise)

= _____, your parents won't be happy.

= _____, your parents won't be happy.

3 만약 네가 너의 지원서를 내일까지 제출하지 않는다면, 너는 기회를 잃을 것이다. (submit your application)

= _____ by tomorrow, you will lose the opportunity.

= _____ by tomorrow, you will lose the opportunity.

4 만약 네가 무책임하다면, 너는 좋은 평판을 가질 수 없을 것이다. (be responsible)

= _____, you won't have a good reputation.

= _____, you won't have a good reputation.

연습문제 A 밑줄 친 부분이 어법상 맞으면 O를 쓰고, 틀리면 바르게 고쳐 쓰시오.

1 Many of my classmates are funny, <u>while</u> I'm not. → _____

2 The weather is still cold, <u>even if</u> it's already May. → _____

3 Ben enjoys watching horror films, <u>whereas</u> I enjoy watching romance films. → _____

4 Jiwon likes spicy food, <u>despite</u> she is not good at eating it. → _____

5 Everything went as planned, <u>although</u> their worries. → _____

6 We have to obey the law, <u>even if</u> it seems wrong. → _____

7 Josh agreed to the proposal, <u>whereas</u> Benny disagreed with it. → _____

8 He is not famous, <u>whereas</u> he is a creative artist. → _____

9 <u>Despite</u> the language barrier, she communicated well with the locals. → _____

10 <u>In spite of</u> the hot weather, he went jogging. → _____

11 <u>Despite</u> my grandfather is old, he is quite strong. → _____

12 <u>Even if</u> you don't speak French, you'll still be able to understand the show. → _____

연습문제 B 우리말과 같도록 괄호 안의 말을 알맞게 배열하시오.

1 비록 우리는 그것을 예상했었지만, 실제로 우리가 그 경기를 졌을 때 우리는 실망했다. (had expected, although, it, we)

= _____, we were disappointed when we actually lost the match.

2 그 소년은 포도 주스를 마신 반면 그의 아빠는 뜨거운 커피를 마셨다. (drank, whereas, hot coffee, his dad)

= The boy drank grape juice, _____.

3 비록 Taylor는 길을 잘 못 찾지만, 그는 길을 잃진 않았다. (is, even though, bad at directions, he)

= Taylor didn't get lost, _____.

4 비록 Kate는 공부하기 위해 밤을 지새웠지만, 그녀는 시험을 통과하지 못했다. (stayed up, though, all night, to study, she)

= Kate didn't pass the exam, _____.

연습문제 | <보기>와 같이 다음 문장을 괄호 안의 말을 활용하여 바꿔 쓰시오.

<보기> I went to sleep at 9:00 to wake up early. (so that)
→ I went to sleep at 9:00 _so that I could wake up early_ .

1 She put her cell phone on silent so as to concentrate on her studying. (so that)
→ She put her cell phone on silent _____.

2 Speak clearly for people to understand what you are saying. (so that)
→ Speak clearly _____.

3 Megan saved money so that she could buy a gold necklace for her mom. (so as to)
→ Megan saved money _____.

4 Do your best in everything to not have any regrets afterwards. (so that)
→ Do your best in everything _____.

5 I went grocery shopping to cook dinner. (so that)
→ I went grocery shopping _____.

6 William practiced playing the trumpet so that he could join the school band. (so as to)
→ William practiced playing the trumpet _____.

7 The monkey climbed the tree so that it could get some fruit. (in order to)
→ The monkey climbed the tree _____.

8 We went to the park to play hide-and-seek. (so that)
→ We went to the park _____.

연습문제 우리말과 같도록 괄호 안의 말을 알맞게 배열하시오.

1 귀신의 집은 너무 무서워서 아무도 그곳에 들어갈 수 없었다. (could, no one, so, it, that, scary, go in)
= The haunted house was _____ .

2 그는 너무 지쳐서 움직일 수 없었다. (couldn't, he, so, that, exhausted, move)
= He was _____ .

3 저 기사는 너무 어려워서 충분히 이해할 수 없다. (to, fully understand, too, difficult)
= That article is _____ .

4 그 소설은 너무 길어서 그가 하루에 끝낼 수가 없다. (to, finish, it, too, long, in one day, for him)
= The novel is _____ .

5 Nicole은 스키를 너무 잘 타서 그녀는 항상 국제적으로 경쟁한다. (competes, she, so, internationally, that, good at, skiing, always)
=Nicole is _____ .

6 그 남자아이는 너무 작아서 롤러코스터를 탈 수 없다. (to, too, the roller coaster, ride, short)
= The boy is _____ .

7 그 방은 너무 시끄러워서 그들은 서로 들을 수 없었다. (hear, so, that, couldn't, they, each other, noisy)
= The room was _____ .

8 그는 너무 바빠서 오늘 밤 영화를 볼 수 없다. (busy, the movie, can't, that, so, tonight, watch, he)
= He is _____ .

9 그는 너무 빨리 걸어서 나는 그를 따라갈 수 없었다. (I, catch up with, fast, so, couldn't, that, him)
= He walked _____ .

10 그녀는 너무 게걸스럽게 먹어서 음식의 맛을 즐기지 못했다. (enjoy, greedily, the taste of, too, to, the food)
= She ate _____ .

11 그 책 한 박스는 너무 무거워서 내가 그것을 들 수가 없다. (to, lift, it, too, heavy, for me)
= The box of books was _____ .

12 Brad는 너무 배가 고파서 그는 피자 전부를 다 먹었다. (ate, hungry, an entire pizza, so, he, that)
= Brad was _____ .

연습문제 A 다음 중 밑줄 친 as의 의미가 나머지 둘과 다른 것을 고르시오.

1 ① As Somi was doing her homework, her little brother kept bothering her.
   ② The boy nearly fell as he was getting off the bus.
   ③ The result didn't turn out well as we expected.

2 ① As he was too tired, he went to bed early at 8 P.M.
   ② My grandfather used to work as an engineer.
   ③ As it was very sunny yesterday, many people went on a picnic.

3 ① My sister and I sat at our desks as we were told.
   ② As the days passed, the rumor about the celebrity was forgotten.
   ③ As the year passed, she grew wiser.

4 ① As I got back home, my dog started barking.
   ② She tried to encourage other members as the team leader.
   ③ As he was taking a bath, he listened to music.

연습문제 B 우리말과 같도록 since 또는 while과 괄호 안의 말을 활용하여 문장을 완성하시오.

1 나는 역에서 기차를 기다리는 동안 Cindy와 마주쳤다. (be waiting)
   = I ran into Cindy _____ for a train at the station.

2 나의 가족은 내가 태어난 이후로 이 지역에 살고 있다. (be born)
   = My family has been living in this area _____.

3 그녀는 그 사고 이후로 종종 우울한 상태이다. (the accident)
   = She has been often depressed _____.

4 그는 그 공연이 시작되는 동안 극장에 도착했다. (be going on)
   = He got to the theater _____.

5 그 여자아이가 매우 어렸기 때문에, 그녀는 뉴스보도를 이해할 수 없었다. (be)
   = _____ too young, she couldn't understand the news report.

6 그 초인종이 내가 아침을 만드는 동안 울렸다. (be making)
   = The doorbell rang _____.

POINT 6

연습문제 A   빈칸에 알맞은 말을 <보기>에서 골라 쓰시오.

<보기>   for example   however   in fact   instead   moreover

1   I slept for almost ten hours last night. _____, I still feel sleepy now.

2   My friend and I have many things in common. _____, we both like to go hiking.

3   She did really well on the test. _____, she scored the highest score in class.

4   Ryan is a talented singer. _____, he is also a popular songwriter.

5   They couldn't play soccer outside because of the rain. _____, they went to an indoor soccer field.

<보기>   for instance   on the other hand   indeed   in addition   thus

6   I didn't meet the deadline for the assignment. _____, I got an F on it.

7   There are many ways to relieve stress. _____, you can listen to relaxing music.

8   All the food in the restaurant was quite delicious. _____, the servers were polite and kind.

9   John dropped the ball many times. _____, his mistakes made us lose the game.

10   She enjoys spending her time with others. _____, he enjoys spending his time alone.

연습문제 B   우리말과 같도록 빈칸에 알맞은 접속부사를 쓰시오.

1   나는 우리가 환경을 보호하기 위해 노력해야 한다고 생각한다. 그러므로, 나는 플라스틱 컵 대신에 도자기 컵을 사용하기 시작했다.

= I think we should try to protect the environment. _____, I started using a ceramic mug instead of a plastic cup.

2   아시아 사람들은 보통 아침으로 밥을 먹는다. 그에 반해서, 미국 사람들은 보통 아침으로 시리얼을 먹는다.

= People in Asia usually eat rice for breakfast. _____, people in America usually eat cereal for breakfast.

3   항상 다른 사람들에게 정직해라. 그렇지 않으면, 사람들은 너를 믿을 수 없다고 여길 것이다.

= Always be honest with others. _____, people will consider you not trustworthy.

1 우리말과 같도록 괄호 안의 말을 활용하여 문장을 완성하시오.

> 나는 내가 샌드위치를 먹어야 할지 또는 샐러드를 먹어야 할지 결정할 수 없다. (if, a sandwich, should have, a salad)

= I can't decide _____

_____.

2 다음 중 어느 빈칸에도 들어갈 수 <u>없는</u> 것은?

> · Jisu visited the hospital _____ a headache.
> · I cut my finger _____ I was preparing lunch.
> · David read over his report again _____ he noticed an error in it.
> · Due to safety concerns, we couldn't leave the class _____ the rain stopped.

① until ② because of
③ unless ④ since
⑤ while

3 우리말과 같도록 괄호 안의 말을 활용하여 문장을 완성하시오.

> 은비는 그녀가 그 노래를 암기할 수 있도록 여러 번 연습했다. (memorize it)

= Eunbi practiced the song many times,

_____.

4 다음 문장에 대한 설명이 바른 것끼리 묶인 것은?

> (A) You should be quiet while the teacher is speaking. : while이 '~인 반면에'라는 의미로 사용되었다.
> (B) John has been studying French since he was in the first grade. : since가 '~이기 때문에'라는 의미로 사용되었다.
> (C) I'm going to stay in Dallas until the tournament ends. : 시간을 나타내는 부사절에서 현재시제 ends를 사용하여 미래를 나타냈다.

① (A) ② (B) ③ (C)
④ (A), (B) ⑤ (B), (C)

5 다음 빈칸에 공통으로 들어갈 알맞은 것은?

> · _____ the dog was scared was clear.
> · The trouble is _____ we wasted too much money.

① because ② if ③ but
④ that ⑤ whether

6 다음 중 밑줄 친 that을 생략할 수 있는 것을 <u>모두</u> 고르시오.

① <u>That</u> Carl was coming home for Christmas was a surprise.

② The problem is <u>that</u> many of the lights were not working.

③ Minju learned <u>that</u> her family would be moving to Daegu.

④ I wish <u>that</u> we could go to Greece together this summer.

⑤ It is clear <u>that</u> he is the best player on the team.

7 두 문장의 의미가 같도록 문장을 완성할 때, 빈칸에 알맞은 말을 쓰시오. (단, as를 반드시 활용하시오.)

> Not only my wallet but also my passport was lost.
>
> = _____ _____ _____
> _____ _____ _____
> _____ was lost.

8 우리말과 같도록 주어진 말을 알맞게 배열하시오.

> 너는 무엇이 그 실험을 실패하게 했는지 이해해야 한다.
> (what, to fail, the experiment, caused)

= You should understand _____
_____ .

9 다음 빈칸에 들어갈 말이 나머지 넷과 <u>다른</u> 것은?

① Paul had to go home early _____ his illness.

② The girl screamed _____ she saw a snake.

③ She wasn't hungry _____ she had just eaten.

④ The car was spotless _____ my older sister and I washed it.

⑤ The house got very cold _____ the heater broke.

10 다음 문장을 주어진 <조건>에 맞게 바꿔 쓰시오.

> If you wear a seatbelt, you will reduce your risk of injuries.

> <조건>
> 1. 명령문으로 쓰시오.
> 2. 11단어로 쓰시오.

= _____
_____

11 다음 중 밑줄 친 as의 쓰임이 나머지 넷과 다른 것은?

① I should study tonight <u>as</u> I have a test in the morning.
② My younger brother is excited <u>as</u> he won the science competition.
③ Mr. Parker is known <u>as</u> a kind teacher.
④ He needs a new computer <u>as</u> his old one stopped working.
⑤ Bailey can't go on the roller coaster <u>as</u> he is too short.

12 <보기>와 같이 두 문장의 의미가 같도록 문장을 완성하시오.

<보기>
Because the fog was so thick, we couldn't see the road.
= *The fog was so thick that we couldn't see the road* .

(1) Because the singer is famous, he cannot go out in public alone.
= _____

(2) Because the fence was damaged badly, it had to be replaced.
= _____

13 다음 글의 빈칸에 들어갈 말이 순서대로 짝지어진 것은?

Alligators and crocodiles look similar, but they have major differences. Alligators have a wide, round snout. _____, crocodile snouts are thinner and V-shaped. _____, crocodiles are generally much larger than alligators.

*snout (돼지 같은 동물의) 주둥이, 코

① However – For example
② Therefore – However
③ In contrast – However
④ Therefore – Moreover
⑤ In contrast – Moreover

14 다음 문장을 주어진 <조건>에 맞게 바꿔 쓰시오.

If you don't follow school rules, you'll get in trouble.

<조건> unless를 사용하시오.

→ You'll _____
_____ .

15 다음 중 어법상 어색한 것은?

① Jessica is so upset that she won't talk to me.

② The band played so loudly that it hurt our ears.

③ The water was so hot that we couldn't swim in it.

④ The new jet is so big plane that it can't land at many airports.

⑤ My father is too sick to go to work today.

16 우리말과 같도록 빈칸에 알맞을 말을 쓰시오.

> 그 영화는 시간 낭비였을 뿐 아니라 돈 낭비이기도 했다.

= The movie was _____ _____ a waste of time _____ _____ a waste of money.

17 다음 중 밑줄 친 if의 쓰임이 나머지 넷과 다른 것은?

① You should talk to the teacher if you have questions.

② I don't know if I need to bring anything to the party.

③ If you want advice, give me a call.

④ Don't forget your bathing suit if you go to the beach.

⑤ I won't make it to the concert on time if I take the subway.

18 다음 문장의 밑줄 친 as와 같은 의미로 쓰인 것은?

> We couldn't go to the bank, as it was closed for the holidays.

① Karen called me as I was getting in bed.

② Give yourself a quiz as you study for the test.

③ Minji doesn't eat crabs, as she is allergic to seafood.

④ Walter was named "Student of the Month" again, as we expected.

⑤ It was cold last night as the weather forecast had predicted.

19 다음 우리말과 같도록 알맞은 접속사를 고르시오.

> 당신이 이곳에 있기 때문에 우리는 우리의 밴드 연습을 시작할 수 있다.
>
> = _____ you are here, we can start our band practice.

① Now that ② If ③ Whether
④ Unless ⑤ After

20 다음 중 밑줄 친 부분이 어법상 어색한 것은?

> ①Before I joined the soccer team, I couldn't play very well. ②Since I joined, I've done various exercises and drills to get better. ③For instance, I now jog 5 kilometers every day to stay fit. ④In addition, I practice kicking balls with my friends every day. ⑤Besides, I am getting a lot better at soccer now.

21 다음 문장에서 어법상 어색한 부분을 찾아 쓰고 바르게 고쳐 쓰시오.

> The room was hot despite the air
> conditioner was on.

_____ → _____

22 다음 밑줄 친 as와 의미가 같은 것을 <보기>에서 골라 쓰시오.

> <보기> before because once when

(1) We got the day off of school, <u>as</u> the
snow caused streets to close.

→ _____

(2) The barber talked a lot <u>as</u> he was cutting
my hair.

→ _____

23 우리말과 같도록 괄호 안의 말을 활용하여 문장을 완성하시오.

> 나는 초콜릿 한 개를 샀고, 그녀는 빵 두 조각을 샀다.
> (piece, bread)

= I bought a bar of chocolate, _____

_____ .

24 다음 빈칸에 공통으로 들어갈 알맞은 것은?

> · Do your laundry quickly, _____ you
> will miss your favorite TV show.
> · Rachel either sets the table _____
> washes the dishes after dinner.

① so   ② that   ③ and
④ but   ⑤ or

25 다음 빈칸에 들어갈 수 있는 것을 <u>모두</u> 고르시오.

> _____ Ivan was friendly, he was
> nervous around strange people.

① Despite   ② Although
③ As soon as   ④ If
⑤ Though

CHAPTER 13
관계사

연습문제 다음 빈칸에 알맞은 관계대명사를 쓰고, 괄호 안에서 알맞은 역할을 고르시오.

1 This is the watch _____ was imported from Italy. (주격 / 목적격 / 소유격)

2 She is the girl _____ I had dinner with a few days ago. (주격 / 목적격 / 소유격)

3 There were two men _____ names were unknown. (주격 / 목적격 / 소유격)

4 He found the wallet _____ he had lost last week. (주격 / 목적격 / 소유격)

5 We walked along the street _____ was covered with snow. (주격 / 목적격 /소유격)

6 Those are the kids _____ parents couldn't pick them up. (주격 / 목적격 / 소유격)

7 I haven't seen the boy _____ lives upstairs. (주격 / 목적격 / 소유격)

8 They read the story _____ main characters are rabbits. (주격 / 목적격 / 소유격)

9 I told my mom about the stranger _____ I met. (주격 / 목적격 / 소유격)

10 That girl _____ has red hair and brown eyes is Jimin. (주격 / 목적격 / 소유격)

연습문제 관계대명사를 이용하여 다음 두 문장을 한 문장으로 연결하시오. (단, that은 쓰지 마시오.)

1 My dad got a new pair of glasses. They are scratch proof.

→ My dad _____.

2 There is the vase. The vase is my mom's favorite.

→ There _____.

3 I heard the surprising news. It was about the famous movie star.

→ I _____.

4 She went to an art exhibition with her friend. Her friend is interested in modern art.

→ She _____.

5 The singer composed a song for his son. His son died in a car accident.

→ The singer _____.

목적격 관계대명사

정답 p.88

연습문제 관계대명사를 이용하여 다음 두 문장을 한 문장으로 연결하시오. (단, that은 쓰지 마시오.)

1 We want to apologize for our mistake. We made the mistake yesterday.

→ We _____.

2 I made small talk with my old friend. I ran into him on the street.

→ I _____.

3 I have a lot of comic books. My younger brother wants to borrow them.

→ I _____.

4 The school bus will be here in a minute. The student needs to take it.

→ The school bus _____.

5 The singer is now on TV. My friend used to be a fan of the singer.

→ The singer _____.

소유격 관계대명사

정답 p.88

연습문제 우리말과 같도록 관계대명사 whose와 괄호 안의 말을 알맞게 배열하시오.

1 너는 꼭대기가 눈으로 덮인 그 산을 볼 수 있니? (snow, the mountain, you, covered with, can, top, is, see)

→ _____

2 크기와 모양이 다른 이 동전들을 봐라. (these coins, sizes, shapes, different, look at, are, and)

→ _____

3 딸이 입원해 있는 그 여자 분은 매우 슬퍼 보인다. (daughter, looks, very sad, in the hospital, is, the lady)

→ _____

4 우리는 모래가 하얗던 해변에서 수영했다. (was, white, sand, at the beach, swam, we)

→ _____

5 선수들이 가장 열심히 연습해 온 팀이 승리할 것이다. (the hardest, players, the team, will, win, have practiced)

→ _____

연습문제 A 관계대명사 that을 이용하여 다음 두 문장을 한 문장으로 연결하고, that과 바꿔 쓸 수 있는 말을 <u>모두</u> 쓰시오.

1 Tommy is a student. Jaemin found Tommy hard working.

→ Tommy _____ . → _____

2 Do you want to go to the park? It has many pine trees.

→ Do _____ ? → _____

3 I respect the nurse. She always helps people in need.

→ I _____ . → _____

4 That is the restaurant. The locals recommend the restaurant.

→ That _____ . → _____

5 Do you still talk to the woman? We used to work with her.

→ Do _____ ? → _____

연습문제 B that이 들어갈 수 있는 곳을 찾고, that의 역할을 <보기>에서 골라 쓰시오.

<보기>	명사절 접속사	관계대명사	지시대명사	지시형용사

1 ⓐ The fact ⓑ the world ⓒ is round ⓓ is common ⓔ knowledge. → _____

2 ⓐ They ⓑ went to ⓒ a shopping center ⓓ had ⓔ many popular stores. → _____

3 ⓐ Is ⓑ woman who is giving ⓒ a speech ⓓ our new mayor ⓔ? → _____

4 ⓐ Appearance is ⓑ more important ⓒ than ⓓ personality ⓔ is false. → _____

5 ⓐ The laptop ⓑ I recently bought ⓒ is broken ⓓ already ⓔ. → _____

6 ⓐ The coach ⓑ had to open ⓒ window for ⓓ fresh air ⓔ. → _____

7 ⓐ It seemed ⓑ the drummer ⓒ was the leader of ⓓ the band ⓔ. → _____

8 ⓐ I climbed ⓑ mountain ⓒ with ⓓ John last weekend ⓔ. → _____

9 ⓐ She ⓑ tried to write ⓒ an article ⓓ kids ⓔ would want to read. → _____

10 ⓐ What is this? – ⓑ is a ⓒ robot vacuum ⓓ cleaner ⓔ. → _____

11 ⓐ The man ⓑ said ⓒ there was no such ⓓ thing as ⓔ Santa Claus. → _____

연습문제 우리말과 같도록 관계대명사 what과 괄호 안의 말을 활용하여 문장을 완성하시오.

1 너는 내가 방금 말한 것을 이해했니? (say, just)

= Did you understand _____ ?

2 대부분의 사람들이 믿는 것이 항상 사실은 아니다. (believe, most people)

= _____ is not always true.

3 네가 되고 싶은 것은 너의 부모님의 기대보다 더 중요하다. (want, be)

= _____ is more important than your parent's expectations.

4 John은 그가 잘할 수 있는 것을 찾을 필요가 있다. (do, well)

= John needs to find out _____ .

5 그 경찰관은 그 용의자가 그의 주머니에 가지고 있던 것을 확인했다. (have, the suspect)

= The police officer checked _____ in his pocket.

6 나는 Cathy가 그에게 말했던 것을 알아야 한다. (say to)

= I need to know _____ .

7 네가 지금 당장 할 수 있는 것을 빨리 끝내라. (do, right now)

= Finish quickly _____ .

8 가장 좋은 구매는 그녀가 제안한 것이다. (offer)

= The best deal is _____ .

9 Kathy는 그녀가 해야 하는 것에 대한 조언을 부탁했다. (should, do)

= Kathy asked for advice on _____ .

10 Kyle은 그의 친구들이 그에 대해 말한 것에 감사했다. (his friends, say)

= Kyle appreciated _____ about him.

연습문제 <보기>와 같이 관계대명사를 이용하여 다음 두 문장을 한 문장으로 연결하시오.

<보기> The painter has a set of brushes. She is painting the portrait with them.
→ The painter has a set of brushes *which[that] she is painting the portrait with* .
→ The painter has a set of brushes *with which she is painting the portrait* .

1 The office chair is comfortable. Mr. Woods can sit on it for a long time.
→ The office chair _____ is comfortable.
→ The office chair _____ is comfortable.

2 Do you know the girl? My uncle is waving at her.
→ Do you know the girl _____ ?
→ Do you know the girl _____ ?

3 The movie was finally released. Many people were waiting for it.
→ The movie _____ was finally released.
→ The movie _____ was finally released.

4 The candidate lost the election. I voted for her.
→ The candidate _____ lost the election.
→ The candidate _____ lost the election.

5 Her manager is a man. I went to school with him.
→ Her manager is a man _____ .
→ Her manager is a man _____ .

6 The town is the most beautiful place in the world. I live in the town.
→ The town _____ is the most beautiful place in the world.
→ The town _____ is the most beautiful place in the world.

7 There is the tree. I left my bike under it.
→ There is the tree _____ .
→ There is the tree _____ .

연습문제 A 관계부사를 이용하여 두 문장을 한 문장으로 연결하시오.

1 The day was the happiest day of my life. I became a doctor on that day.
→ The day _____.

2 That is the park. We run around in that park every morning.
→ That _____.

3 Can you tell me the reason? You made this decision for that reason.
→ Can _____?

4 The broken window was the way. The thief could come into the room.
→ The broken window _____.

5 The café is a block away. They can have some coffee there.
→ The café _____.

연습문제 B 다음 문장의 밑줄 친 부분을 알맞은 관계부사로 고쳐 쓰시오.

1 This is the library at which most students borrow books.   → _____

2 She wanted to learn the way to relax her muscles.   → _____

3 Can you recall the time at which we were kids?   → _____

4 I tried to explain to them the reason for which I arrived late.   → _____

5 That is the house in which my best friend lived before moving to Canada.   → _____

6 My mom doesn't like the way in which my older sister talks.   → _____

7 The hotel at which many national events are held is near here.   → _____

8 September 11 is the day on which my little brother was born.   → _____

9 I like the way in which she forms relationships with others.   → _____

10 Daniel didn't show up at the time at which we were supposed to meet.   → _____

11 I was going to tell you the reason I couldn't attend the meeting yesterday.   → _____

12 Can you show the tourists the way to hold chopsticks?   → _____

13 Christmas is the day on which the whole family gathers together.   → _____

연습문제 A 우리말과 같도록 관계사와 괄호 안의 말을 활용하여 문장을 완성하시오.

1 그 선생님은 그녀의 개를 데려왔는데, 그것은 하루 종일 짖었다. (her dog, bark)

= The teacher brought _____ all day.

2 Gina는 노래를 불렀는데, 그것은 내가 더 창의적이 되도록 영감을 주었다. (a song, me, inspire)

= Gina sang _____ to be more creative.

3 나는 우리가 공원에서 만났던 그 여자아이의 이름을 안다. (the girl, meet, we)

= I know the name of _____ at the park.

4 나는 형이 한 명 있는데, 나는 종종 그와 싸운다. (an older brother, fight, I, often)

= I have _____ with.

5 그는 내가 어릴 때부터 항상 좋아해온 배우이다. (the actor, have, like, I, always)

= He is _____ since childhood.

6 나는 매일 아침 버스를 타는데, 그것은 7분마다 온다. (the bus, come, every morning)

= I take _____ every seven minutes.

7 몇몇 규칙들이 있는데, 너는 그것들을 따라야 한다. (several rules, you, follow, have to)

= There are _____ .

연습문제 B 다음 두 문장의 의미가 같도록 알맞은 관계사를 이용하여 문장을 완성하시오.

1 We visited the Colosseum, and it was built around 70 A.D.

= We _____ 70 A.D.

2 The girl loves her dog, and it follows her everywhere.

= The girl _____ everywhere.

3 They will travel to New York next year, and there they can see the Statue of Liberty.

= They _____ .

4 Oliver went to the restaurant, and there all customers had to dress up.

= Oliver _____ .

POINT
8

연습문제 두 문장의 의미가 같도록 복합관계사를 이용하여 문장을 완성하시오.

1 No matter which you buy, you'll be satisfied.

= _____

2 I will support no matter what you decide to do in the future.

= _____

3 Jackson watches action movies at any time he has nothing to do.

= _____

4 His parents don't care for anyone whom he hangs out with.

= _____

5 No matter how tired Kenneth is, he needs to get his essay done by tonight.

= _____

6 No matter what she wants, I will buy it for her.

= _____

7 No matter how rich you are, you shouldn't waste your money on useless things.

= _____

8 Anyone who wants to participate, raise your hand.

= _____

9 No matter where he lives, we can go visit him.

= _____

10 No matter how busy you are, you shouldn't skip meals.

= _____

11 No matter what you are saying, they won't be interested.

= _____

12 Becky always tries her best at anything that she does.

= _____

13 No matter where she goes, her fans gather around her.

= _____

1 다음 빈칸에 들어갈 말이 순서대로 짝지어진 것은?

> · He should buy a phone _____ has all the new features.
> · Is there someone _____ speaks English at the tax office?

① who – that
② that - which
③ which – who
④ which - which
⑤ whose - who

2 다음 중 어법상 바른 것끼리 묶인 것은?

> ⓐ His best school year was last year when he got the highest marks in all his classes.
> ⓑ That's the room in that you can hang your coats.
> ⓒ Do you want to eat at that place where we had some great food?
> ⓓ This is where we plan to meet for the next group study.
> ⓔ We want to know the reason how the gym was closed.

① ⓐ, ⓒ, ⓓ
② ⓐ, ⓑ, ⓓ
③ ⓑ, ⓒ, ⓓ
④ ⓑ, ⓒ, ⓔ
⑤ ⓑ, ⓓ, ⓔ

3 관계대명사를 이용하여 다음 두 문장을 한 문장으로 연결하시오.

> The movie is about children. They discover a hidden cave.
>
> → _____
> _____

4 다음 (A)~(C)에 들어갈 말이 바르게 짝지어진 것은?

> · That is the place ___(A)___ I go for peace and quiet.
> · That was the month ___(B)___ I had a bicycle accident.
> · Does anyone know the reason ___(C)___ they didn't meet the deadline?

	(A)	(B)	(C)
①	when	why	where
②	when	where	why
③	where	why	when
④	where	when	how
⑤	where	when	why

5 다음 빈칸에 들어갈 말이 순서대로 짝지어진 것은?

> · The passengers boarded the train, _____ was a few minutes late.
> · I saw my teacher, _____ does her shopping at the same supermarket.

① which – that
② which – whom
③ which – which
④ which – who
⑤ that – that

[6-7] 다음 글을 읽고 주어진 질문에 답하시오.

> Johannes Gutenberg was the person
> ⓐ_____ invented the printing press.
> He created a new technique ⓑ_____
> people could use to print books more
> quickly and cheaply. (A) There were
> many advantages of Gutenberg's
> technique. (B) The technique made it
> possible for everyone to buy books.
> The number of people who learned to
> read increased after the invention of this
> machine.

6 위 글의 빈칸 ⓐ와 ⓑ에 들어갈 말이 순서대로 짝지어진 것은?

① who – that　　② who – whose
③ whom – that　　④ which – that
⑤ that – who

7 관계대명사를 이용하여 밑줄 친 (A)와 (B)를 한 문장으로 연결하시오. (단, that은 쓰지 마시오.)

→ _____
_____, _____
_____

8 다음 빈칸에 공통으로 들어갈 알맞은 것은?

> · Kimberly is my friend _____ hair is
>   brown.
> · We can contact the passenger
>   _____ bag was left on the bus.

① that　　② who　　③ which
④ whom　　⑤ whose

9 다음 두 문장을 한 문장으로 바르게 연결한 것은?

> He repaired an appliance for the woman.
> Her microwave oven wasn't working.

① He repaired an appliance for the woman
　 which microwave oven wasn't working.
② He repaired an appliance for the woman
　 whose microwave oven wasn't working.
③ He repaired an appliance for the woman
　 whom microwave oven wasn't working.
④ He repaired an appliance for the woman
　 who microwave oven wasn't working.
⑤ He repaired an appliance for the woman
　 that microwave oven wasn't working.

10 다음은 *Flight to Nowhere*를 보고 친구들이 나눈 대화이다. 대화를 보고 관계대명사를 이용하여 문장을 완성하시오. (단, that은 쓰지 마시오.)

> *Hoon*: I heard the movie won an award.
> *Jiye* : Yes, that's true. The movie was
> 　　　　based on a children's book.
> *Sua* : Really? I have never read the
> 　　　　book. The plot of the movie was
> 　　　　exciting.

Movie Review: *Flight to Nowhere*

(1) Hoon: *Flight to Nowhere* is a movie
_____ .

(2) Jiye: *Flight to Nowhere* is a movie
_____ .

(3) Sua: It is a movie _____
_____ .

11 다음 빈칸에 공통으로 들어갈 알맞은 관계대명사를 <보기>에서 골라 쓰시오.

<보기> who that whom which

(A) Did you get the box _____ I left on the desk?
(B) Those are the sports shoes _____ I want to buy.
(C) The shuttle bus is for people _____ need to get to the subway station.

12 다음 각 빈칸에 알맞은 말을 쓰시오. (단, that은 쓰지 마시오.)

· She worked at a factory ⓐ_____ the owner closed last week.
· I bumped into my dentist ⓑ_____ I see at the clinic every six months.

13 다음 밑줄 친 that과 쓰임이 같은 것은?

I finished reading the book that I borrowed at the school library.

① Please give me that red book on the top shelf.
② It is so reassuring that my phone was in my bag all along.
③ She's singing the song that she heard on the radio.
④ That is the earring I lost a few days ago!
⑤ That she quit her high-paying job is truly shocking.

14 다음 빈칸에 들어갈 복합관계사가 같은 것끼리 묶인 것은?

ⓐ _____ we hear the alarm, we need to get in line and leave.
ⓑ _____ finishes the race first will be the winner.
ⓒ _____ strong you are, there's always someone stronger.
ⓓ _____ you see someone in trouble, call 1-1-9.
ⓔ _____ you'd like to leave, just let me know.

① ⓐ, ⓑ, ⓔ   ② ⓐ, ⓓ, ⓔ   ③ ⓑ, ⓒ, ⓔ
④ ⓑ, ⓓ, ⓔ   ⑤ ⓒ, ⓓ, ⓔ

15 우리말과 같도록 괄호 안의 말을 알맞게 배열하시오.

네가 한 것은 다른 학생들에게 도움이 되었다. (did, you, helpful, students, other, what, was, to)

→ _____

16 다음 빈칸에 공통으로 들어갈 알맞은 말을 쓰시오.

· I don't know _____ you're talking about.
· Sarah asked her dad _____ she could do to help.

17 다음 글의 밑줄 친 ⓐ~ⓔ 중 어법상 어색한 것을 찾아 기호를 쓰고 바르게 고쳐 쓰시오.

Today, a friend and I went to the aquarium, ⓐwhere we saw an octopus, a giant turtle, dolphins, and three sharks. My friend John got in trouble with an employee, ⓑwho told us not to get too close to the exhibits. John didn't listen to ⓒthat the employee said. He got really close to an exhibit to look at some dolphins. I couldn't believe ⓓwhat happened next. A dolphin pulled him into the tank, ⓔwhich was hilarious. I used to think the aquarium wasn't much fun, but now I can't wait to go back.

_____ → _____

18 다음 ⓐ~ⓒ 중 어법상 어색한 것을 찾아 기호를 쓰고 바르게 고쳐 쓰시오.

ⓐ I picked up the author's new book, which was an exciting read.
ⓑ Jacob read about da Vinci, that painted the *Mona Lisa*.
ⓒ My mom bought a new car, which is really fast and pretty.

_____ → _____
_____

19 다음 대화의 빈칸 ⓐ와 ⓑ에 알맞은 말을 쓰시오.

Q: Are great white sharks the most dangerous animals?
A: No. Great white sharks are probably the most dangerous animals ⓐ_____ live in water. They're responsible for the most attacks on humans. But ⓑ_____ may surprise you is that the most dangerous animals to humans are mosquitoes, which spread a lot of diseases. Because of this, many people die every year from mosquito bites.

20 (A), (B) 문장에서 생략된 말이 들어갈 위치와 생략된 말이 순서대로 짝지어진 것을 고르시오.

(A) This is the ⓐ very book ⓑ I recommend you ⓒ read.
(B) He was happy to visit ⓓ the cathedral ⓔ designed ⓕ by Antoni Gaudi.

	(A)	(B)
①	ⓐ that	ⓓ which was
②	ⓑ that are	ⓓ that
③	ⓑ that	ⓔ which was
④	ⓒ who are	ⓔ that
⑤	ⓒ whom	ⓕ that was

21 다음 ⓐ~ⓒ 중 어법상 어색한 것을 찾아 기호를 쓰고 주어진 <조건>에 맞게 바르게 고쳐 쓰시오.

> ⓐ The chess player plans most effectively will win.
> ⓑ The old lady was thankful to the man helping her carry groceries.
> ⓒ The train leaving soon is boarding on platform three.

> <조건> 관계대명사를 활용하여 쓰시오.

_____ → _____

_____

22 주어진 <조건>에 맞게 다음 두 문장을 한 문장으로 연결하시오.

> He studied the vocabulary words. They were included on the test.

> <조건> 9단어로 이루어진 문장을 완성하시오.

→ _____

_____

23 다음 빈칸 (A)와 (B)에 들어갈 알맞은 말을 <보기>에서 골라 쓰시오.

> <보기> that   who   whom   which

> · I am meeting a person with (A) _____ I used to go to the same school.
> · San Diego is a city in (B) _____ you can rest and relax easily.

24 다음 두 문장을 한 문장으로 연결할 때, 빈칸 ⓑ에 올 수 있는 것은?

> Jason is the man. The package was delivered to him.
> → Jason is the man ⓐ ⓑ ⓒ ⓓ ⓔ delivered.

① was   ② to   ③ package
④ the   ⑤ whom

25 다음 두 문장을 한 문장으로 바르게 연결하지 못한 것을 모두 고르시오.

> This is the field. I played soccer on the field yesterday.

① This is the field on that I played soccer yesterday.
② This is the field that I played soccer on yesterday.
③ This is the field which I played soccer on yesterday.
④ This is the field on which I played soccer yesterday.
⑤ This is the field where I played soccer on yesterday.

CHAPTER 14
가정법

연습문제 A | 다음 문장의 밑줄 친 부분을 바르게 고쳐 쓰시오.

1 If you got enough sleep, you <u>wouldn't have felt</u> tired during the day. → _____

2 If you come here to visit me, I <u>would pick</u> you up at the airport. → _____

3 If I had left home early, I <u>wouldn't be</u> late for school yesterday. → _____

4 If I were good at chess, I <u>could have entered</u> the chess tournament. → _____

5 If Jongwon <u>had been</u> older, he would try to get a driver's license. → _____

6 If we could speak Spanish, we <u>would have talked</u> to the new student. → _____

7 If she <u>received</u> my letter, she will be very happy and excited. → _____

8 If she played the drums well, she <u>could have joined</u> the band. → _____

9 If I <u>read</u> the textbook, I might have passed the test. → _____

10 If I <u>was</u> you, I would help him with the report. → _____

11 If the author <u>were</u> more creative, she could have written a better story. → _____

12 If he <u>didn't make</u> that mistake, we could have won the game. → _____

연습문제 B | 우리말과 같도록 괄호 안의 말을 알맞게 배열하시오.

1 만약 내가 아프지 않다면, 나의 친구들과 수영하러 갈 수 있을 텐데. (swimming, sick, were, with, go, my friends, could, I, not, I)

= If _____ , _____ .

2 만약 그녀가 사실을 알아냈다면, 충격을 받았을 텐데. (found out, she, been, had, the truth, would, shocked, she, have)

= If _____ , _____ .

3 만약 나의 전화기가 고장나지 않았다면, 나는 너에게 전화를 걸 수 있었을 텐데. (broken, you, could, my phone, called, had, not, I, have)

= If _____ , _____ .

4 만약 네가 전에 거짓말을 하지 않았다면, 그들은 너를 믿었을 텐데. (would, have, not, you, trusted, they, before, had, told, you, lies)

= If _____ , _____ .

기출로적중 POINT 2 혼합 가정법

정답 p.91

연습문제 우리말과 같도록 괄호 안의 말을 활용하여 문장을 완성하시오.

1 만약 그가 버스를 놓치지 않았다면, 지금쯤 여기에 있을 텐데. (miss, be)

= If _____ the bus, he _____ here by now.

2 만약 Laura가 서둘렀다면, 지금 서울로 가는 기차를 잡아탈 수 있을 텐데. (hurry, catch)

= If _____ , she _____ the train to Seoul now.

3 만약 그녀가 그 오류를 정정했다면, 그 책들은 지금 재인쇄될 필요가 없을 텐데. (correct, need)

= If _____ the error, the books _____ to be reprinted now.

4 만약 그 소년이 수업을 빠지지 않았다면, 그의 엄마는 지금 화나지 않을 텐데. (skip, be)

= If the boy _____ his class, his mom _____ angry now.

기출로적중 POINT 3 가정법을 직설법으로 바꾸는 법

정답 p.91

연습문제 다음 가정법 문장은 직설법 문장으로, 직설법 문장은 가정법 문장으로 바꿔 쓰시오.

1 If I had known how to snowboard, I could have joined the snowboarding club.

→ Because _____.

2 As the movie was boring, everyone in the theater fell asleep.

→ If _____.

3 If Ann played the violin well, she could participate in the contest.

→ Since _____.

4 As you didn't ask me earlier, I can't come shopping with you now.

→ If _____.

5 If the supermarket weren't still open, I couldn't go grocery shopping.

→ Because _____.

6 Somin doesn't wear her watch, so she can't know the time.

→ If _____.

7 Since the novel is sold out, I can't buy it from the bookstore.

→ If _____.

연습문제 다음 가정법 문장은 if를 생략한 가정법 문장으로, if를 생략한 가정법 문장은 가정법 문장으로 바꿔 쓰시오.

1 If I were you, I would book the table right away.

→ _____, I would book the table right away.

2 If he were a wise team leader, the members would look up to him.

→ _____, the members would look up to him.

3 If you were good at cooking, you could try to become a chef.

→ _____, you could try to become a chef.

4 If Ian had eaten breakfast, he would feel more energetic now.

→ _____, he would feel more energetic now.

5 Had Hyeju been here, I wouldn't have watched the show alone.

→ _____, I wouldn't have watched the show alone.

6 Were I as smart as Einstein, I could be a great physicist.

→ _____, I could be a great physicist.

7 Had the players practiced harder, they could have won the game.

→ _____, they could have won the game.

8 Had Mr. Kim been qualified, he would have participated in the national judo championship.

→ _____, he would have participated in the national judo championship.

9 If you were interested in Egyptian art, you could go to that art exhibit.

→ _____, you could go to that art exhibit.

10 Had you brushed your teeth every day, you would have healthier teeth.

→ _____, you would have healthier teeth.

11 If Jonathan had not moved to Australia, I would hang out with him often.

→ _____, I would hang out with him often.

12 Had Sandra told me she was upset, I would have apologized to her.

→ _____, I would have apologized to her.

Without 가정법

정답 p.92

연습문제 A 우리말과 같도록 빈칸에 알맞은 말을 쓰시오.

1 Jamie가 없었다면, 그 프로젝트는 연기되었을 텐데.

= _____ _____ Jamie, the project would have been delayed.

= If _____ _____ _____ _____ _____ Jamie, the project would have been delayed.

= Had _____ _____ _____ _____ Jamie, the project would have been delayed.

2 물이 없다면, 인간은 살 수 없을 텐데.

= _____ water, humans couldn't live.

= If _____ _____ _____ _____ water, humans couldn't live.

= Were _____ _____ _____ water, humans couldn't live.

3 너의 도움이 없었다면, 나는 아마 곤경에 처했을 텐데.

= _____ your help, I might have been in trouble.

= Had _____ _____ _____ _____ your help, I might have been in trouble.

= If _____ _____ _____ _____ _____ your help, I might have been in trouble.

연습문제 B 다음 두 문장의 의미가 같도록 괄호 안의 말로 시작하는 가정법 문장을 완성하시오.

1 Without glasses, people with poor eyesight couldn't see things clearly. (if)

= _____, people with poor eyesight couldn't see things clearly.

2 Were it not for electricity, these machines wouldn't run. (if)

= _____, these machines wouldn't run.

3 If it had not been for this workbook, I would have failed the grammar quiz. (had)

= _____, I would have failed the grammar quiz.

4 If it hadn't been for the flowers, my room wouldn't have been beautifully decorated. (but)

= _____, my room wouldn't have been beautifully decorated.

5 If it hadn't been for the spices, this curry wouldn't have been so tasty. (without)

= _____, this curry wouldn't have been so tasty.

6 But for regular customers, the store would have shut down. (had)

= _____, the store would have shut down.

연습문제 A   우리말과 같도록 괄호 안의 말을 활용하여 I wish 가정법 문장을 영작하시오.

1 나의 아빠가 내 컴퓨터를 고쳤다면 좋을 텐데. (fix, my computer, my dad)

= _____

2 내가 저 문제를 어떻게 푸는지 알면 좋을 텐데. (answer, know, that question, how to)

= _____

3 그 환자가 약을 시간에 맞춰 먹었다면 좋을 텐데. (the pill, take, the patient, on time)

= _____

4 네가 더 자주 체육관에 갔다면 좋을 텐데. (go, more often, to the gym)

= _____

5 우리가 차를 운전하도록 허락된다면 좋을 텐데. (a car, allow, to drive, be)

= _____

6 내가 저 드레스를 살 충분한 돈이 있으면 좋을 텐데. (have, that dress, to buy, enough money)

= _____

연습문제 B   두 문장의 의미가 같도록 문장을 완성하시오.

1 I wish you had received my e-mail.

= I'm sorry that _____.

2 I'm sorry that I can't visit my uncle in New York.

= I wish _____.

3 I wish we had another day to finish this project.

= I'm sorry that _____.

4 I wish she had invited you to her birthday party.

= I'm sorry that _____.

5 I'm sorry that I didn't prepare for the presentation better.

= I wish _____.

6 I'm sorry that my favorite singer isn't more popular.

= I wish _____.

연습문제 A 우리말과 같도록 괄호 안의 말을 활용하여 문장을 완성하시오.

1 그녀는 마치 내가 전혀 모르는 사람인 것처럼 나를 대했다. (be, as if, treat, a complete stranger)

= She _____ .

2 그는 마치 그가 대학생인 것처럼 말했다. (speak, as though, be, a college student)

= He _____ .

3 그 남자는 마치 그가 오랫동안 나의 엄마를 알았던 것처럼 말한다. (as if, my mom, talk, for a long time, know)

= The man _____ .

4 그 소녀는 마치 그녀가 저 초상화를 그렸던 것처럼 행동했다. (paint, that portrait, as though, act)

= The girl _____ .

5 오늘의 날씨는 마치 그것이 이미 봄인 것처럼 느껴진다. (be, spring, already, as if, feel)

= The weather today _____ .

6 그 낡은 건물은 마치 그것이 최근에 지어진 것처럼 보인다. (be, recently, build, as if, look)

= The old building _____ .

연습문제 B 다음 두 문장을 as if 가정법 문장으로 바꿔 쓰시오.

1 Nothing had been found. However, the police officer talked like he had found something.

→ The police officer _____ as if he _____ .

2 The politician had heard the news. However, she acted like she hadn't heard the news.

→ The politician _____ as if she _____ .

3 The boy looks like he is five years old. Actually, he is not five years old.

→ The boy _____ as if he _____ .

4 The chef speaks like his restaurant is popular. However, it's not popular.

→ The chef _____ as if his restaurant _____ .

5 Nadia has never been to Atlanta. She talks like she has been there.

→ Nadia _____ as if she _____ .

6 He was not in a good mood. He acted like he was in a good mood.

→ He _____ as if he _____ .

1 다음 대화의 빈칸에 들어갈 말이 순서대로 짝지어진 것은?

> A: What _____ you do if someone gave you a million dollars?
> B: I would travel around the world.
> A: I'm sure that would be fun!
> B: I think so. How about you?
> A: Well, if I _____ a million dollars, I would use it to save the environment.
> B: Wow! That's really kind of you!

① will – got
② will – get
③ would – didn't get
④ would – get
⑤ would – got

2 우리말과 같도록 괄호 안의 말을 활용하여 문장을 완성하시오.

> 우리가 표를 샀다면, 그 콘서트에 참석할 수 있을 텐데. (buy, the concert, tickets, attend)

= If _____
_____.

3 두 문장의 의미가 같도록 문장을 완성하시오.

> I wish I had apologized to Amy sooner.

= I'm sorry that _____
_____.

[4-5] 다음 글을 읽고 주어진 질문에 답하시오.

> Many young people do not use the public library these days. I think that (A) the public library would be attractive to them if it had youth programs. In my opinion, (B) the public library doesn't attract more young people because it doesn't have interesting activities for them.

4 다음 글의 밑줄 친 (A)를 직설법 문장으로 바꿔 쓰시오.

→ As _____
_____.

5 다음 글의 밑줄 친 (B)를 가정법 문장으로 바꿔 쓰시오.

→ If _____
_____.

6 다음 중 어법상 바른 것은?

① If I am at the beach, I would put on sunscreen.
② If Dad didn't have to work, he will play with us.
③ Would you go to the dance with Rob if he asks you?
④ If Nicole took the subway, she won't get stuck in traffic every day.
⑤ If I were in Paris, I would visit the Louvre.

7 다음 대화의 빈칸에 들어갈 말이 순서대로 짝지어진 것은?

> A: I'm sorry that I wasn't at your party.
> _____ about it, I _____ it.
> B: Don't worry about it. I understand.

① Were I heard – would have missed
② Had I heard – wouldn't have missed
③ If I heard – wouldn't miss
④ Were I heard – wouldn't have missed
⑤ Had I heard – wouldn't miss

8 다음 빈칸에 공통으로 들어갈 알맞은 것은?

> · I wish we _____ on vacation right now.
> · He acts as if he _____ the school president.

① is   ② are   ③ has been
④ had been   ⑤ were

9 다음 빈칸에 들어갈 말이 순서대로 짝지어진 것은?

> · If we _____ a lighter, we could start a campfire.
> · _____ my alarm clock, I would have overslept.

① brought - Were it not for
② had brought - It had not been for
③ had brought - It had not been for
④ brought - Were it not for
⑤ had brought - Had it not been for

10 다음 중 짝지어진 두 문장의 의미가 <u>다른</u> 것은?

① I wish you felt better.
  = I'm sorry that you feel better.
② Without your help, finishing the project on time would have been impossible.
  = Had it not been for your help, finishing the project on time would have been impossible.
③ If you were old enough, you could vote in the election.
  = As you aren't old enough, you can't vote in the election.
④ Were it not for this flashlight, we would not be able to see.
  = But for this flashlight, we would not be able to see.
⑤ If Jane had been at the café, we could have had coffee together.
  = Since Jane wasn't at the café, we couldn't have coffee together.

11 다음 중 어법상 바른 것은?

① If he were not so tired, he can go to the gym.
② If the test is not so easy, I would not pass it.
③ If the instructions weren't so complicated, everyone can understand them.
④ Had we asked for directions, we would be there by now.
⑤ If Peter weren't busy, he will not cancel the trip.

12 다음 문장을 가정법 문장으로 바르게 바꾼 것은?

> As that restaurant doesn't have good food, it cannot have more customers.

① If that restaurant had good food, it can have more customers.
② If that restaurant had good food, it could have more customers.
③ If that restaurant has good food, it could have more customers.
④ If that restaurant had good food, it has more customers.
⑤ If that restaurant has good food, it can have more customers.

13 다음 대화의 빈칸에 들어갈 알맞은 것은?

> A: I might sell my coin collection.
> B: Really? I didn't know you collected coins.
> A: Actually, my grandfather gave it to me.
> B: Oh. _____. It might be really valuable one day.
> A: Maybe you're right.

① I wouldn't sell it if I were you
② I won't sell it if I were you
③ I won't sell it if I was you
④ I won't sell it if I am you
⑤ I wouldn't sell it if I am you

[14-15] 다음 문장을 I wish 가정법 문장으로 바꿔 쓰시오.

14

> I'm sorry that we don't have more space for the guests.
> → _____
> _____

15

> I'm sorry that I didn't take swimming lessons.
> → _____
> _____

16 다음 우리말을 알맞게 영작한 것은?

> 나의 코치님이 없었다면, 축구를 배우는 것은 쉽지 않았을 텐데.

① Were it not for my coach, learning soccer wouldn't have been easy.
② Had it not been for my coach, learning soccer wouldn't be easy.
③ Without my coach, learning soccer wouldn't have been easy.
④ Without my coach, learning soccer wouldn't be easy.
⑤ If it had not been for my coach, learning soccer wouldn't be easy.

17 다음 대화를 읽고, 밑줄 친 우리말 (A)~(C)와 같도록 괄호 안의 말을 활용하여 영작하시오.

> A: (A) <u>내가 프랑스어를 말하면 좋을 텐데.</u>
>   (French, wish, speak)
> B: Really? Are you interested in France?
> A: It's not that. (B) <u>내가 프랑스어를 이해하면, 나는 미래에 더 많은 기회를 가질 텐데.</u> (more opportunities, understand, in the future, French, have)
> B: Why is that?
> A: Well, to many people, (C) <u>영어는 마치 가장 중요한 언어인 것처럼 보여.</u> (seem, English, be the most important language, as if)
> B: Isn't that true?
> A: Actually, French is one of the fastest-growing languages in the world.

(A) _____

(B) _____

_____

(C) _____

_____

18 주어진 문장과 의미가 같은 것은?

> If I had an extra pen, I would let you borrow it.

① I don't have an extra pen now.
② I didn't let you borrow a pen.
③ I have an extra pen now.
④ I had an extra pen.
⑤ I can let you borrow a pen now.

[19-20] 다음 문장을 가정법 문장으로 바르게 바꾼 것은?

19

> Because I don't have a house in the mountains, I can't go hiking whenever I want.

① If I have a house in the mountains, I could go hiking whenever I want.
② If I have a house in the mountains, I could have go hiking whenever I want.
③ If I had a house in the mountains, I could go hiking whenever I want.
④ If I had a house in the mountains, I can go hiking whenever I want.
⑤ If I had a house in the mountains, I could have gone hiking whenever I want.

20

> We didn't notice the other car, so we couldn't avoid the accident.

① If we noticed the other car, we can avoid the accident.
② If we had noticed the other car, we could have avoided the accident.
③ If we noticed the other car, we could have avoided the accident.
④ If we noticed the other car, we could avoid the accident.
⑤ If we had noticed the other car, we can avoid the accident.

[21-22] 다음 문장을 as if 가정법 문장으로 바꿔 쓰시오.

21

It was not raining. He opened his umbrella.

→ He opened his umbrella _____

_____ .

22

The bird hasn't been injured. It drags its wing anyway.

→ The bird drags its wing _____

_____ .

24 우리말과 같도록 주어진 <조건>에 맞게 문장을 완성하시오.

만약 모두가 자선 단체에 돈을 기부한다면, 자선 단체는 더 많은 사람들을 도울 수 있을 텐데.

<조건>
1. 가정법을 사용하시오.
2. can, more people, money, it, everyone, give, help, to the charity를 활용하시오.

→ If _____ ,

_____ .

23 다음 대화를 읽고, 밑줄 친 우리말 (A), (B)와 같도록 괄호 안의 말을 활용하여 문장을 완성하시오.

A: (A) 만약 날씨가 더 나았다면 좋을 텐데. (nice, better, the weather)
B: I know. It's so rainy today.
A: (B) 만일 비가 멈추면, 우리는 밖에서 놀 수 있을 텐데. (the rain, play, stop)
B: Maybe it will clear up later.

(A) _____ if _____

_____ .

(B) If _____ , _____

outside.

25 다음 중 어법상 어색한 것의 개수는?

ⓐ If Kate hadn't reminded me, I would have forgotten about my appointment.
ⓑ Mary would have missed the train if she didn't run to the station.
ⓒ If you were me, what would you do about the problem?
ⓓ If the firefighters hadn't arrived, the building might not be here today.

① 0개 ② 1개 ③ 2개
④ 3개 ⑤ 4개

CHAPTER 15
일치와 화법

수 일치 I

연습문제 밑줄 친 부분이 어법상 맞으면 O를 쓰고, 틀리면 바르게 고쳐 쓰시오.

1 Three days <u>are</u> too short to complete this assignment. → _____

2 Heejin and her friend <u>likes</u> to have a sweet dessert after a meal. → _____

3 A number of studies <u>shows</u> that the report is reliable. → _____

4 Every product <u>are</u> tested before being sold. → _____

5 Collecting coins <u>is</u> my grandfather's hobby. → _____

6 Two kilometers <u>are</u> not that far to walk. → _____

7 The number of homeless people <u>has</u> increased greatly. → _____

8 Both bulgogi and japchae <u>are</u> popular Korean foods. → _____

수 일치 II

연습문제 괄호 안에서 알맞은 것을 고르시오.

1 Both my uncle and aunt (has / have) been living in London for 15 years.

2 Two-thirds of Earth's surface (is / are) ocean.

3 All of the students (needs / need) to pass the final exam to graduate.

4 Either Jinsu or Minhee (has / have) to do the house chores.

5 Half of the articles in the newspaper (is / are) about that accident.

6 Most of the buildings (needs / need) to be renovated.

7 Jack as well as his brothers (likes / like) playing video games.

8 Some of Ms. White's colleagues (do / does) not agree with her proposal.

9 Not only my mother but also my sisters (enjoy / enjoys) reading adventure novels.

10 Each chapter of this workbook (focuses / focus) on a different grammar point.

11 Neither Sally nor her classmates (is / are) ready for the pop quiz.

POINT 2

연습문제 A 밑줄 친 부분이 어법상 맞으면 O를 쓰고, 틀리면 바르게 고쳐 쓰시오.

1 The reporter said that the mayor <u>was</u> responsible for that issue. → _____

2 I thought that James <u>will</u> help us correct the sentences. → _____

3 My mom was mad that I <u>hadn't passed</u> my math test. → _____

4 Hosung told me that he <u>has</u> been to England. → _____

5 The teacher said that the students <u>had</u> to be quiet. → _____

6 Jaeho knew that Sumi <u>has</u> been sick yesterday. → _____

7 Wendy thinks that Mark <u>will</u> leave early tonight. → _____

8 I told him that I <u>had baked</u> the cake. → _____

9 The fish was so slippery that I <u>can't</u> hold it. → _____

연습문제 B 다음 문장의 밑줄 친 부분을 과거시제로 바꿔 완전한 문장을 쓰시오.

1 My grandmother <u>says</u> that good health is more important than wealth.

→ _____

2 The teacher <u>teaches</u> the students that the Korean War began on June 25, 1950.

→ _____

3 Josh <u>says</u> that he goes hiking with his parents every weekend.

→ _____

4 Galileo <u>believes</u> that Earth goes around the Sun.

→ _____

5 Owen <u>tells</u> me that he usually gets up at 11 A.M. on Saturdays.

→ _____

6 This book <u>states</u> that the Parthenon was completed in 432 BC.

→ _____

7 Elle <u>says</u> that empty vessels make the most noise.

→ _____

8 We just <u>learn</u> that snakes sleep in winter.

→ _____

화법 전환: 평서문

POINT 3-1

정답 p.94

연습문제 간접 화법은 직접 화법으로, 직접 화법은 간접 화법으로 바꿔 쓰시오.

1 She said that she would visit her grandparents in Vancouver the following day.
→ She _____

2 Mr. Green told his friend that he had studied hard the previous year.
→ Mr. Green _____

3 David said, "I am very busy at this moment."
→ David _____

4 Suhee said to me, "I received the package last Friday."
→ Suhee _____

5 My little sister said, "I want to go to the playground."
→ My little sister _____

화법 전환: 의문사가 있는 의문문

POINT 3-2

정답 p.94

연습문제 간접 화법은 직접 화법으로, 직접 화법은 간접 화법으로 바꿔 쓰시오.

1 Kevin asked me how I had solved those questions.
→ Kevin _____

2 The man said, "Where is the nearest bank?"
→ The man _____

3 The teacher said, "Why didn't you come to class yesterday?"
→ The teacher _____

4 My mom said to me, "When are you going to go to bed?"
→ My mom _____

5 He asked why I was in such a hurry.
→ He _____

6 She said to me, "What TV program did you watch last weekend?"
→ She _____

7 The detective asked the witness what she had seen on the street.
→ The detective _____

화법 전환: 의문사가 없는 의문문

정답 p.94

연습문제 | 간접 화법은 직접 화법으로, 직접 화법은 간접 화법으로 바꿔 쓰시오.

1 He asked me whether I wanted to play badminton with him.

→ He _____

2 Nick said to me, "Do you like watching horror movies?"

→ Nick _____

3 Vanessa said to me, "Have you met Tom before?"

→ Vanessa _____

4 They asked me if there had been many people at the concert the previous night.

→ They _____

5 The chef said, "Are you happy with the food here?"

→ The chef _____

화법 전환: 명령문

정답 p.94

연습문제 | 괄호 안의 말을 활용하여 다음 문장을 간접 화법으로 바꿔 쓰시오.

1 The teacher said to us, "Don't use your cell phones in class." (order)

→ The teacher _____ us _____ .

2 The doctor said to him, "Try to get enough sleep every night." (advise)

→ The doctor _____ him _____ .

3 The manager said to Mr. Choi, "Report the progress of the project." (instruct)

→ The manager _____ Mr. Choi _____ .

4 Naeun said to me, "Say sorry to your friend first." (suggest)

→ Naeun _____ me _____ .

5 My dad said to me, "Come back home before 9 o'clock." (tell)

→ My dad _____ me _____ .

6 She said to me, "Please watch my bag while I'm gone." (ask)

→ She _____ me _____ .

중간 · 기말고사 실전 문제

1 다음 중 직접 화법을 간접 화법으로 **잘못** 바꾼 것의 개수는?

ⓐ I said to the speaker, "Please talk a little louder."
  → I asked the speaker to talk a little louder.
ⓑ My mother said to me, "Wash the dishes and clean the kitchen after dinner."
  → My mother ordered me wash the dishes and clean the kitchen after dinner."
ⓒ The teacher said, "We'll finish the lesson next week."
  → The teacher said that we would finish the lesson the following week."
ⓓ The security guard said to us, "Do you have an identification card?"
  → The security guard asked us whether we did have an identification card.
ⓔ Youngbin said to me, "What do you want to eat for lunch?"
  → Youngbin asked me what you wanted to eat for lunch.

① 1개   ② 2개   ③ 3개
④ 4개   ⑤ 5개

2 빈칸에 들어갈 말을 <u>모두</u> 고르시오.

The doctor said, "Are there any more patients in the waiting room?"
→ The doctor asked _____ there were any more patients in the waiting room.

① when   ② if   ③ who
④ that   ⑤ whether

3 아래 대화의 밑줄 친 우리말을 영어로 바르게 옮긴 것을 고르시오.

Sumin: I'm so upset. I don't have any money, because I lost my wallet.
Tom : How much money did you lose?
Sumin: About fifty dollars.
Tom : Oh, my... <u>50달러는 잃기엔 많은 돈인데!</u>

① Fifty dollars are a lot of money to lose!
② Fifty dollars were a lot of money to lose!
③ Fifty dollars is a lot of money to lose!
④ Fifty dollars have a lot of money to lose!
⑤ Fifty dollars do be a lot of money to lose!

4 다음 문장을 간접 화법으로 바꿔 쓰시오.

My younger sister said, "Who took the television's remote control?"
→ _____
_____

5 다음 중 어법상 <u>어색한</u> 것은?

① Katie asked whether those were my boots by the door.

② My grandmother told me that she was going to Mexico.

③ She asked me what song I was listening to.

④ He said that we should clean the classroom before we leave.

⑤ Chris told me don't leave my bike on the sidewalk.

6 다음 문장을 직접 화법으로 바꿀 때 빈칸에 알맞은 말을 써서 문장을 완성하시오.

Peter said that he wouldn't be coming to school the next day.

→ Peter _____, "I _____ be coming to school _____."

7 괄호 안에 들어갈 말이 순서대로 짝지어진 것은?

· Russia ___(A)___ too large to drive across in a week.

· Collecting stamps ___(B)___ been a popular hobby for many years.

· A number of singers ___(C)___ performing at the concert.

	(A)	(B)	(C)
①	is	has	is
②	is	has	are
③	is	have	are
④	are	has	are
⑤	are	have	is

8 다음 중 어법상 옳은 것을 고르시오.

① Each singer in this band have a different microphone.

② Economics are my favorite subject.

③ A number of movies were shown at the film festival.

④ Going to the beach help me relax on the weekend.

⑤ Ten kilograms are a lot of weight to lose.

9 다음 문장을 간접 화법으로 바르게 바꾼 것은?

Chef Lemonis said, "I need more ingredients to make this dish."

① Chef Lemonis said I need more ingredients to make this dish.

② Chef Lemonis said that he needs more ingredients to make this dish.

③ Chef Lemonis said I needed more ingredients to make that dish.

④ Chef Lemonis said that he needed more ingredients to make this dish.

⑤ Chef Lemonis said he needed more ingredients to make that dish.

10 어법상 옳은 것끼리 짝지어진 보기를 고르시오.

ⓐ Both cherries and strawberries grows well here.
ⓑ Neither Donald nor his friends are coming to the party.
ⓒ The number of insects increases during the summer.
ⓓ Most of the windows in my bedroom are shaking because of the wind.
ⓔ Fifteen dollars are too much for a sandwich.

① ⓐ, ⓑ, ⓒ   ② ⓐ, ⓑ, ⓔ   ③ ⓐ, ⓒ, ⓔ
④ ⓑ, ⓒ, ⓓ   ⑤ ⓑ, ⓓ, ⓔ

11 다음 직접 화법을 간접 화법으로 바꾼 문장에서 틀린 부분을 바르게 고쳐 완전한 문장을 쓰시오.

The bus driver said to me, "Don't put your feet on the seat."
→ The bus driver told me to put my feet on the seat.

→ _____
_____

12 다음 빈칸에 들어갈 알맞은 것은?

The number of _____ 240.

① car in the parking lot is
② car in the parking lot are
③ cars in the parking lot is
④ cars in the parking lot are
⑤ cars in the parking lot were

13 다음 문장을 간접 화법으로 바꿀 때 빈칸에 들어갈 알맞은 것은?

Cindy said to Jacob, "I will ride my bike tonight."
→ Cindy _____ Jacob that she would ride her bike that night.

① says   ② said   ③ tells
④ told   ⑤ was telling

14 다음 문장에서 어색한 부분을 찾아 올바르게 고치시오.

Every radio are playing the same song.

_____ → _____

15 다음 우리말을 알맞게 영작한 것은?

Susan은 Anne에게 그녀가 온두라스에서 일하고 있었다고 말했다.

① Susan tells Anne that she had been working in Honduras.
② Susan tells Anne that she has been working in Honduras.
③ Susan told Anne that she had been working in Honduras.
④ Susan told Anne that she has been working in Honduras.
⑤ Susan told Anne that she is working in Honduras.

16 다음 대화의 빈칸에 들어갈 말이 순서대로 짝지어진 것은?

> A: Do you want to go to the water park this weekend?
> B: What? I thought you said you _____ to work with your dad all weekend.
> A: Well, he said he _____ my uncle to help him instead, so I'm free now.
> B: That's great! Let's go on Saturday morning.

① has – would ask
② has – will ask
③ would have – will ask
④ had – will ask
⑤ had – would ask

17 다음 빈칸에 들어갈 수 <u>없는</u> 것은?

> She said that _____.

① Carl was a trustworthy and honest boy
② she had visited Spain once before
③ she finishes the project by herself
④ there was nowhere to sit in the auditorium
⑤ I had to be at restaurant by 6 o'clock

18 다음 문장을 직접 화법으로 바꿀 때 빈칸에 알맞은 말을 써서 문장을 완성하시오.

> The football player told me that he had been injured in a game two days before.
> → The football player _____ me, "I _____ in a game _____."

19 다음 중 직접 화법을 간접 화법으로 <u>잘못</u> 바꾼 것은?

① Claire said, "I need to go to the doctor after school."
　→ Claire said she needed to go to the doctor after school.
② I said to them, "Are you enjoying your meals?"
　→ I asked them they were enjoying their meals.
③ Mary said, "Everything looked great at yesterday's fashion show."
　→ Mary said that everything had looked great at the previous day's fashion show.
④ Melvin said to Lisa, "What are you going to do over summer break?"
　→ Melvin asked Lisa what she was going to do over summer break.
⑤ Sora said, "Where can we go skiing tomorrow?"
　→ Sora asked where we could go skiing the next day.

20 괄호 안에 들어갈 be동사를 알맞은 형태로 쓰시오. (단, 현재형으로 쓰시오.)

> · Both credit cards and cash ⓐ_____ acceptable forms of payment.
> · Speaking foreign languages ⓑ_____ fun, but it takes a lot of practice.

ⓐ: _____　　ⓑ: _____

[21-22] 다음 대화를 읽고 문장을 완성하시오.

21

> *Julie* : Where did you go last weekend?
> *David*: I visited my cousin's house in the countryside.

→ Julie asked David _____
_____. David told Julie
_____
_____.

22

> *Chris*: Is there anything I can do for you?
> *Betty*: Please check my essay for errors.

→ Chris asked Betty _____
_____. Betty
asked Chris _____.

23 다음 (A)~(C)에 들어갈 말이 바르게 짝지어진 것은?

> · We learned that light ___(A)___ faster than sound.
> · Eric told me that he usually ___(B)___ games on his phone.
> · The teacher told us that President Lincoln ___(C)___ in 1860.

	(A)	(B)	(C)
①	was	plays	had been elected
②	is	has played	was elected
③	was	play	had been elected
④	is	plays	was elected
⑤	was	played	had been elected

[24-25] 다음 문장을 과거시제로 바꿀 때 빈칸에 알맞은 말을 써서 문장을 완성하시오.

24

> I see that Bob has bought a new computer.
> → I saw that Bob _____ a new computer.

25

> I believe that our team can win the baseball tournament.
> → I believed that our team _____ the baseball tournament.

CHAPTER 16
특수구문

기출로 적중 POINT

POINT 1-1

연습문제 | 우리말과 같도록 do, much, the very와 괄호 안의 말을 활용하여 문장을 완성하시오.

1 주희는 오늘이 어제보다 훨씬 더 춥다고 생각한다. (cold)

= Juhee thinks it is ＿＿＿＿＿＿＿＿ today than yesterday.

2 저것은 내가 수개월 동안 보기 원해 온 바로 그 영화이다. (movie)

= That is ＿＿＿＿＿＿＿＿ I have been wanting to watch for months.

3 그들은 어젯밤 라이벌 팀과의 경기를 정말 이겼다. (win)

= They ＿＿＿＿＿＿＿＿ the match against their rival team last night.

4 Jessica는 동물을 정말 사랑해서 정기적으로 동물 보호소에서 자원 봉사한다. (love)

= Jessica ＿＿＿＿＿＿＿＿ animals, so she volunteers at animal shelters regularly.

5 이것은 내가 지난 번에 이곳에서 먹었을 때 주문했던 바로 그 요리이다. (dish)

= This is ＿＿＿＿＿＿＿＿ that I ordered the last time I ate here.

6 그 현지 강의 물은 지난해보다 훨씬 더 더럽다. (dirty)

= The water of the local river is ＿＿＿＿＿＿＿＿ than last year.

7 Robert는 그의 형 Edward와 정말 많이 닮았다. (look)

= Robert ＿＿＿＿＿＿＿＿ a lot like his older brother, Edward.

8 그 도시는 겨울보다 여름에 훨씬 더 좋다. (nice)

= The city is ＿＿＿＿＿＿＿＿ in the summer than it is in the winter.

9 나는 너의 이메일을 정말 받았지만, 답장할 시간이 없었다. (receive)

= I ＿＿＿＿＿＿＿＿ your e-mail, but I didn't have time to respond.

10 그녀는 내가 예술가가 될 수 있도록 격려해준 바로 그 사람이다. (person)

= She is ＿＿＿＿＿＿＿＿ who inspired me to become an artist.

11 그 시험은 내가 생각했던 것보다 훨씬 더 어려웠다. (hard)

= The test was ＿＿＿＿＿＿＿＿ than I thought.

12 이것이 내가 어릴 때 살았던 바로 그 집이다. (house)

= This is ＿＿＿＿＿＿＿＿ that I lived in as a child.

정답 p.96

연습문제 다음 문장을 괄호 안의 지시에 맞게 「It is ~ that …」 강조 구문으로 바꿔 쓰고, that과 바꿔 쓸 수 있는 말을 모두 쓰시오.

Tina played basketball on the court.

1 (주어 강조) _____ → _____

2 (목적어 강조) _____ → _____

3 (장소 부사구 강조) _____ → _____

Jim goes traveling to Europe next month.

4 (주어 강조) _____ → _____

5 (시간 부사구 강조) _____ → _____

The thief stole the diamond ring from the jewelry shop.

6 (목적어 강조) _____ → _____

7 (장소 부사구 강조) _____ → _____

I watched a play at the theater this afternoon.

8 (목적어) _____ → _____

9 (장소 부사구 강조) _____ → _____

10 (시간 부사구 강조) _____ → _____

He saw Nancy on the street an hour ago.

11 (주어 강조) _____ → _____

12 (목적어 강조) _____ → _____

13 (장소 부사구 강조) _____ → _____

We ate dumplings in Chinatown.

14 (주어 강조) _____ → _____

15 (목적어 강조) _____ → _____

16 (장소 부사구 강조) _____ → _____

연습문제 우리말과 같도록 <보기>와 괄호 안의 말을 활용하여 문장을 완성하시오.

<보기>   neither of   not always   not all of   never   none of

1 선생님이 물어본 모든 질문들이 대답하기에 쉬운 것은 아니었다. (the questions)

= _____ the teacher asked were easy to answer.

2 그들 중 아무도 무엇이 문제인지 알지 못했다. (they)

= _____ knew what the problem was.

3 그 요리사의 특별 요리는 항상 이용할 수 있는 것이 아니다. (available)

= The chef's special is _____.

4 그들은 영어와 스페인어로 서비스를 제공하지만, 그는 그것들 둘 중 아무것도 말하지 못한다. (they)

= They offer service in English and Spanish, but he speaks _____.

5 그는 자기 사업을 개업하는 것에 절대로 관심이 없었다. (interest)

= He was _____ in opening his own business.

6 나의 도시의 모든 놀이공원들이 재미있는 것은 아니다. (the amusement park)

= _____ in my city are fun.

7 그 차량들 둘 중 아무것도 그 사고에서 손상되지 않았다. (the car)

= _____ was damaged in the accident.

8 그 식당은 일요일에 항상 여는 것은 아니다. (open)

=That restaurant is _____ on Sundays.

9 상어는 물 속에서 움직이는 것을 절대로 멈추지 않는다. (stop)

= A shark _____ moving in the water.

10 영화관에서 상영하는 영화들 중 아무것도 흥미진진해 보이지 않았다. (the movies)

= _____ playing at the theater looked exciting.

11 슈퍼마켓의 모든 채소들이 신선한 것은 아니었다. (the vegetables)

= _____ in the supermarket were fresh.

12 나의 아파트의 모든 불들이 항상 켜져 있는 것은 아니다. (on)

= The lights in my apartment are _____.

연습문제 두 문장의 의미가 같도록 문장을 완성하시오.

1 I couldn't come to your birthday party yesterday, and Julie couldn't come, either.
= I couldn't come to your birthday party yesterday,
and neither _____.

2 He hardly had any time to take a nap.
= Hardly _____.

3 The books you wanted to borrow are here.
= Here _____.

4 Mr. Smith rarely buys flowers for his wife.
= Rarely _____.

5 Jason likes walking along the beach. – I like walking along the beach, too.
= Jason likes walking along the beach. – So _____.

6 The magician has never failed to please an audience.
= Never _____.

7 You will rarely make use of the new features of the device.
= Rarely _____.

8 The refrigerator is not only cheap, but it looks nice.
= Not only _____, but it looks nice.

9 The children slid down the hill.
= Down the hill _____.

10 My father never complained about doing yard work.
= Never _____.

11 Chris didn't make a hotel reservation, and Kara didn't make one, either.
= Chris didn't make a hotel reservation, and neither _____.

12 The deer ran through the forest.
= Through the forest _____.

연습문제 다음 문장에서 생략된 부분을 넣어 완전한 문장을 쓰시오.

1 I listened to music with headphones while on the subway.

= _____

2 Though most people remained seated during the performance, some people didn't.

= _____

_____

3 Let's go to the dessert place you told me about yesterday.

= _____

4 She drank a cup of coffee while reading the newspaper.

= _____

5 Jamie was looking at her younger sister sleeping on the couch.

= _____

기출로픽중 **POINT 5** 동격 정답 p.97

연습문제 콤마(,)나 of, 또는 that을 활용하여 다음 두 문장을 한 문장으로 바꿔 쓰시오. (단, 관계대명사는 쓰지 마시오.)

1 The idea sounds wonderful. The idea is traveling around the world.

→ _____

2 Claude Monet is called the Father of Impressionism. He is one of the most popular painters.

→ _____

3 The news surprised many fans. The news was that David and Victoria got married.

→ _____

4 Minji is the one I tell everything to. She is my best friend since childhood.

→ _____

5 His dream was realized. His dream was opening his own café.

→ _____

연습문제 | 괄호 안의 말을 활용하여 빈칸에 알맞은 말을 쓰시오.

1 You can either listen to the radio or _____ a book while waiting for your turn. (read)

2 I enjoy listening to music and _____ stories when I have time. (write)

3 We can go to a Korean restaurant or _____ _____ _____ _____ for dinner tonight. (an Italian restaurant)

4 After receiving the acceptance letter, she got excited and _____ around the room. (jump)

5 The facility is not only for people with disabilities but also _____ _____ _____ _____. (the general public)

6 Why don't you come and _____ us for dinner tonight? (join)

7 My brother went out and _____ soccer with his friends. (play)

8 The documentary was not only informative but also _____ to watch. (enjoy)

9 He seemed neither worried nor _____. (surprise)

10 It is going to be rainy and _____ all day tomorrow. (cloud)

11 Remember to close the window and _____ _____ off the light when you leave the room. (turn)

12 Her baby is adorable, cute, and _____. (gentle)

13 Customers can either buy the product in stores or _____ it online. (order)

14 Danny asked me to stop at the store and _____ _____ up some juice. (pick)

15 The water isn't just safe to swim in but also _____. (warm)

16 Some news articles are neither useful nor _____ to read. (interest)

17 The car ride was long, bumpy, and _____. (uncomfortable)

1 다음 밑줄 친 부분이 어법상 어색한 것은?

① She <u>does have</u> a social media account.

② The batteries <u>did needed</u> to be replaced.

③ He <u>does appear</u> worried about the exam.

④ They <u>do welcome</u> visits during the weekend.

⑤ <u>Do tell</u> me. I will wait for your reply.

2 다음 중 어법상 어색한 부분을 찾아 쓰고 바르게 고쳐 쓰시오.

Playing an instrument do gets better with a lot of practice.

_____ → _____

3 다음 중 밑줄 친 do의 쓰임이 같은 것끼리 묶인 것은?

ⓐ You don't like reptiles, <u>do</u> you?

ⓑ He'll <u>do</u> his homework later tonight.

ⓒ Lucy and Carl <u>do</u> exercise at least twice a week.

ⓓ What did the dry cleaner <u>do</u> to my coat?

ⓔ They <u>do</u> require us to bring extra socks.

ⓕ I <u>do</u> think we should take a cab to the airport.

① ⓒ, ⓔ　　② ⓐ, ⓓ, ⓕ　　③ ⓐ, ⓒ, ⓓ

④ ⓑ, ⓔ, ⓕ　　⑤ ⓒ, ⓔ, ⓕ

4 다음 중 부분 부정을 나타내는 문장이 <u>아닌</u> 것은?

① Not all universities offer that course.

② I didn't eat both of the cookies on the table.

③ Nobody listened to the speech.

④ She's not always easy to talk to.

⑤ Not every student in Ms. Park's class passed the test.

5 다음 빈칸에 들어갈 말로 어색한 것은?

· My mother walks _____ faster than I do.

· The street is _____ quieter tonight than last night.

· The air is _____ cooler at dawn than in the morning.

① very　　② far　　③ much

④ even　　⑤ a lot

6 다음 중 「It is ~ that …」 강조 구문이 <u>아닌</u> 것은?

① It is my sister who will prepare the food for this year's celebration.

② It was the nearby supermarket that delivered these watermelons.

③ It is unsure that the museum will open again.

④ It was this morning that Jinsu found our cat.

⑤ It was the powerful winds that blew the trees down.

7 다음 우리말을 영작한 것 중 어색한 것은?

① 내가 넘어지고 발목을 다친 것은 바로 그 보도 위에서였다.

= It was on the sidewalk that I tripped and hurt my ankle.

② Bill이 요즘 읽고 있는 것은 바로 추리 소설이다.

= It is a mystery novel that Bill is reading nowadays.

③ Ryan이 간 곳은 바로 그 기차역이었다.

= It was the train station that Ryan went to.

④ 나를 신나게 한 것은 바로 그 통화이다.

= It was the phone call which got me excited.

⑤ 우리가 그 정원의 사진을 찍은 것은 바로 작년 봄이다.

= It was last spring where we took a picture of the garden.

8 다음 문장에서 생략할 수 있는 부분을 생략하여 완전한 문장을 쓰시오.

> Your application will not be accepted unless it is accompanied by the required documents.
>
> → _____
>
> _____
>
> _____

9 괄호 안의 말을 활용하여 밑줄 친 부분을 강조하는 문장으로 바꿔 쓰시오.

> World War II broke out in 1939. (it, be, that)
>
> → _____

[10-11] 다음은 한 학교의 이번 학기 일정표이다. 「It is ~ that …」 강조 구문을 사용하여 주어진 질문에 답하시오.

March	visit city hall
April	plant trees at the national park
May	have a French cooking class
June	hold a sports competition
July	have a seminar on video games

10

> A: Does the school have a Spanish cooking class in May?
>
> B: No. _____
>
> the school has in May.

11

> A: Does the school plant trees at the national park in July?
>
> B: No. _____ the school plants trees at the national park.

[12-13] 다음 문장을 밑줄 친 부분을 강조하는 문장으로 바꿔 쓰시오.

12

> I <u>asked</u> why Alice changed her mind about the gift.
>
> → _____
>
> _____

13

> California is <u>larger</u> than Florida.
>
> → _____
>
> _____

14 우리말과 같도록 괄호 안의 말을 알맞게 배열하시오.

> 이것은 나의 할아버지가 나의 할머니에게 준 바로 그 반지이다.
> (my grandfather, ring, very, this, that, my grandmother, gave, is, to, the)

= _____

_____

15 다음 중 어법상 바른 것은?

① Brad not only runs but also lifts weights every day.
② She not only travels abroad but also speak many languages.
③ People escaped the burning building both quickly and safe.
④ You can either calling me or send me an e-mail.
⑤ We were impressed by not only his dancing but also his sing.

16 다음 중 어법상 어색한 것은?

① At the train station we waited.
② There is he riding a merry-go-round.
③ Across the river flew the eagle.
④ Into the cave went the scientists.
⑤ Rarely do we talk to foreigners.

17 다음 우리말을 영작할 때 빈칸에 들어갈 알맞은 것은?

> 이 호텔은 좀처럼 많은 손님이 있지 않다.
> = _____ many guests.

① Seldom this hotel has
② Seldom does this hotel has
③ Seldom did this hotel have
④ Seldom did this hotel has
⑤ Seldom does this hotel have

18 다음 밑줄 친 ⓐ~ⓔ 중 어법상 <u>어색한</u> 것을 찾아 기호를 쓰고 바르게 고쳐 쓰시오.

> · Hardly ⓐ<u>do the zoo keeps</u> any wildlife around here.
> · Into the sky ⓑ<u>flew the rocket</u>.
> · Not only ⓒ<u>was the speech</u> educational, but it was also entertaining.
> · Over the fence ⓓ<u>the kangaroo jumped</u>.
> · ⓔ<u>There is the mailperson</u> walking on the sidewalk.

(1) _____ → _____
(2) _____ → _____

20 <보기>와 같이 밑줄 친 부분을 강조한 문장으로 바꿔 쓰시오.

> <보기>   The children slid <u>down the slide</u>.
> → *Down the slide slid the children* .

> The thieves disappeared <u>into the darkness</u>.
> → _____

21 다음 대화의 밑줄 친 (A)를 괄호 안의 말로 시작하는 문장으로 바꿔 쓰시오.

> *A*: Marsha is an excellent cook.
> *B*: I know. (A) <u>I have seldom tasted such delicious food.</u> (seldom)
> *A*: She should open a restaurant.

→ _____

19 다음 밑줄 친 콤마(,)의 역할이 나머지와 넷과 <u>다른</u> 것은?

① Our town had a festival on June 20<u>,</u> the longest day of the year.
② A new resort<u>,</u> Ocean Breeze, was built near the beach.
③ We visited our favorite city<u>,</u> Paris, last winter.
④ I'll come to your party<u>,</u> but I can't stay long.
⑤ The statue<u>,</u> a famous monument, is being examined.

22 다음 중 어법상 바른 것은?

① I either make coffee at home or going to a café every morning.
② Eating vegetables and to exercise regularly will keep you healthy.
③ The hockey teams competed not only intense but also respectfully.
④ Sally enjoys both writing short stories and read fiction books.
⑤ You can pay with a credit card or use our payment application.

23 다음 대화의 빈칸에 들어갈 알맞은 것은?

> *A*: That movie wasn't very good. I didn't enjoy it.
> *B*: _____ . We should have watched another movie.

① Neither do I
② So did I
③ Neither I did
④ So do I
⑤ Neither did I

25 다음 문장의 밑줄 친 부분을 바르게 바꾼 것은?

> Mr. Riley voted, and <u>Ms. Riley voted, too</u>.

① so did Ms. Riley
② so is Ms. Riley
③ so Ms. Riley did
④ so does Ms. Riley
⑤ neither did Ms. Riley

24 다음 밑줄 친 ⓐ~ⓕ 중 생략할 수 있는 것끼리 묶인 것은?

> · We went to the house in ⓐ<u>which</u> I used to live.
> · This is the sport ⓑ<u>that</u> I enjoyed the most.
> · The man ⓒ<u>who</u> this bag belongs to is over there.
> · The general ⓓ<u>who</u> had served for 30 years retired.
> · The workers ⓔ<u>who are</u> resting on the benches look tired.
> · She wants to find the lady to ⓕ<u>whom</u> Justin was talking.

① ⓐ, ⓑ, ⓒ
② ⓑ, ⓒ, ⓓ
③ ⓑ, ⓒ, ⓔ
④ ⓑ, ⓓ, ⓔ
⑤ ⓑ, ⓔ, ⓕ

중·고등영어 **1위*** 해커스
* 한경비즈니스 선정 2020 한국품질만족도 교육(온·오프라인 중·고등영어) 부문 1위

선생님 수업자료부터 교재 추천&문제은행까지!

원하는 건 **다~** 있는

해커스북
바로가기

" 해커스**북** ^{중·고등}

선생님을 위한 **특별 자료실** "

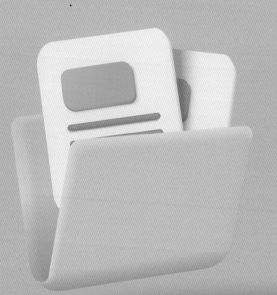

수업자료

문제은행

단어시험지
제작 프로그램

교재 선택
가이드

해커스북 HackersBook.com

| 해커스 중고등 교재 MAP | 나에게 맞는 교재 선택!

	초5	초6	예비중	중1	중2
문법			Hackers Grammar Smart Starter	Hackers Grammar Smart Level 1	Hackers Grammar Smart Level 2
				기출로 적중 해커스 중학영문법 1학년	기출로 적중 해커스 중학영문법 2학년
				해커스 중학영문법 중간·기말 대비 문제집 Level 1	해커스 중학영문법 중간·기말 대비 문제집 Level 2
서술형				해커스 쓰기 자신감 Level 1	해커스 쓰기 자신감 Level 2
구문					
독해	Hackers Reading Smart Starter Level 1	Hackers Reading Smart Starter Level 2	Hackers Reading Smart Level 1	Hackers Reading Smart Level 2	Hackers Reading Smart Level 3
				Hackers Reading Ground Level 1	Hackers Reading Ground Level 2
				Hackers Reading Path Level 1	Hackers Reading Path Level 2
					해커스 첫수능 영어 기초독해
듣기				해커스 중학영어듣기 모의고사 24회 Level 1	해커스 중학영어듣기 모의고사 24회 Level 2
어휘				해커스 3연타 중학영단어	
				해커스 보카 중학 기초	해커스 보카 중학 필수
					해커스 보카 중학 숙어

READING
HACKERS APEX READING for the TOEFL iBT
Basic/Intermediate/Advanced/Expert

LISTENING
HACKERS APEX LISTENING for the TOEFL iBT
Basic/Intermediate/Advanced/Expert

VOCA
HACKERS APEX VOCA for the TOEFL iBT

HACKERS VOCABULARY

토플

중3	예비고	고1	고2	고3
Hackers Grammar Smart Level 3				
기출로 적중 해커스 중학영문법 3학년		기출로 적중 해커스 고등영문법		
해커스 중학영문법 중간·기말 대비 문제집 Level 3		해커스 어법 제대로		
		해커스 수능 어법 불변의 패턴 필수편	해커스 수능 어법 불변의 패턴 실력편	
해커스 쓰기 자신감 Level 3				
	해커스 완전숙련 구문독해 입문	해커스 완전숙련 구문독해 기본	해커스 완전숙련 구문독해 심화	
Hackers Reading Smart Level 4	해커스 독해 제대로 기본독해	해커스 독해 제대로 구문독해		
Hackers Reading Ground Level 3				
Hackers Reading Path Level 3	Hackers Reading Path Level 4			
해커스 첫수능 영어 유형독해		해커스 수능 독해 불변의 패턴 유형편		해커스 수능 독해 불변의 패턴 실전편
	해커스 수능영어독해 미니 모의고사 12+2회 기본	해커스 수능영어독해 미니 모의고사 12+2회 필수	해커스 수능영어독해 미니 모의고사 12+2회 완성 (* 출간 예정)	
해커스 중학영어듣기 모의고사 24회 Level 3		해커스 수능영어듣기 모의고사 20+4회 기본	해커스 수능영어듣기 모의고사 20+4회 실전	
		해커스 수능영어듣기 모의고사 30+5회 기본		해커스 수능영어듣기 모의고사 30+5회 실전
	해커스 보카 고등 기본			
해커스 보카 중학 고난도		해커스 보카 수능 필수 2000+		
			해커스 보카 수능 완성 1800+	
			해커스 보카 수능 심화	
		해커스 보카 수능 숙어		
	해커스 보카 어원편			

해커스북[HackersBook.com]에서
교재에 대한 자세한 설명과 다양한 학습 자료를 확인하세요!

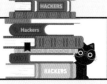

최신 개정 교과서 완벽 반영

기출로 적중

해커스
중학영문법

3학년

워크북

최신 개정 교과서 완벽 반영

기출로적중

해커스

중학영문법

3학년

해설집

최신 개정 교과서 완벽 반영

기출로적중 해커스 중학영문법

중학영문법

3학년

해설집

이 책을 검토해주신 선생님들

강상훈 경기 평촌비상에듀학원 / **김가영** 서울 송정중학교 / **김원덕** 경기 올림피아드학원 / **박유정** 서울 반포중학교 / **박윤정** 경기 이지베스트학원

박은혜 서울 송파중학교 / **박정은** 서울 대청중학교 / **양세희** 서울 양세희수능영어학원 / **이계윤** 서울 씨앤씨학원 / **이유빈** 서울 잉글리쉬&매쓰매니저학원

이혜원 서울 대청중학교 / **정혜은** 서울 용곡중학교 / **최다빈** 서울 최강영어 / **최승복** 경기 오른어학원 / **최지영** 경기 다른영어학원

CHAPTER 1
문장의 형식

p.18

POINT 1-1 1형식과 2형식

연습 문제		
	1	동사: became / 주격 보어: parents / 2형식
	2	동사: matters / 1형식
	3	동사: appeared / 1형식
	4	동사: grows / 1형식
	5	동사: didn't fall / 주격 보어: asleep / 2형식
	6	동사: stayed / 1형식
	7	동사: doesn't stay / 주격 보어: angry / 2형식
	8	동사: appear / 주격 보어: ripe / 2형식

POINT 1-2 2형식: 감각동사

연습 문제				
	1	unhappy	**2**	sound
	3	comfortable	**4**	fresh
	5	awful	**6**	looks like
	7	tastes	**8**	wonderful
	9	sounds like	**10**	delicious
	11	felt	**12**	smells like
	13	sounds like		

POINT 2 3형식

연습 문제						
	1	O	**2**	enter	**3**	O
	4	resembles	**5**	mention	**6**	attend
	7	O	**8**	O	**9**	contact
	10	O				

POINT 3 4형식

연습 문제 A								
	1	ⓐ	**2**	ⓑ	**3**	ⓑ	**4**	ⓐ
	5	ⓑ	**6**	ⓐ				

연습 문제 B								
	1	for	**2**	to	**3**	for	**4**	for
	5	to	**6**	of	**7**	to		

연습 문제 C		
	1	the man a table

---

2 fairy tales to me
3 his new guitar to her
4 me a bunch of flowers
5 a favor of me
6 some books about history to him

 기출 적중문제

정답 ⑤

해설 She showed the beautiful palace the visitors.
→ She showed the visitors the beautiful palace.
[She showed the beautiful palace to the visitors.]

POINT 4-1 5형식

연습 문제		
	1	목적어: the movie / 목적격 보어: boring
	2	목적어: our minds / 목적격 보어: stay
	3	목적어: Maggie / 목적격 보어: a good student
	4	목적어: his daughter / 목적격 보어: ride
	5	목적어: my little sister / 목적격 보어: talking
	6	목적어: my cat / 목적격 보어: cute
	7	목적어: their first dog / 목적격 보어: Milo
	8	목적어: her ears / 목적격 보어: checked
	9	목적어: me / 목적격 보어: to play
	10	목적어: me / 목적격 보어: to do
	11	목적어: that video game / 목적격 보어: fun
	12	목적어: my headphones / 목적격 보어: repaired
	13	목적어: me / 목적격 보어: to close
	14	목적어: us / 목적격 보어: late

POINT 4-2 5형식: 명사·형용사·to부정사를 목적격
보어로 쓰는 동사

연습 문제 A						
	1	wonderful	**2**	O	**3**	O
	4	clean	**5**	sad	**6**	gentle
	7	O				

연습 문제 B				
	1	energetic	**2**	to stay
	3	her dog Hector	**4**	warm
	5	to kick		

연습 문제 C		
	1	told him to take
	2	advised me to exercise
	3	wanted more people to come
	4	expected our dad to play

5 asked Susan to remind

기출 적중문제

정답 She allowed me to borrow her skateboard.
해설 5형식 문장에서 동사 allow의 목적격 보어 자리에는 to부정
사를 쓴다.

POINT 4-3 5형식: 사역동사

연습
문제
1	go	**2**	travel
3	to practice	**4**	stay[to stay]
5	become	**6**	to write
7	wave	**8**	pass[to pass]
9	share	**10**	to lower

POINT 4-4 5형식: 지각동사

연습
문제
1	standing	**2**	practicing	**3**	fall
4	running	**5**	blow	**6**	burning
7	perform	**8**	shouting	**9**	sing
10	studying	**11**	beating	**12**	play
13	dance				

기출 적중문제

정답 heard my dad knock[knocking] on the door.
해설 5형식 문장에서 동사 hear의 목적격 보어 자리에는 동사원
형이나 V-ing형이 올 수 있다.

서술형 대비 문제

(A)
1	calm	**2**	look like	**3**	attend
4	for	**5**	of	**6**	come
7	O				

(B)
1 entered the museum
2 explained the menu
3 contacted my teacher
4 looked like a cat
5 smelled like a fresh apple
6 discussed the new book

(C)
1 I gave my new home address to Sora.
2 Mr. Smith bought a used car for his
daughter.
3 We brought Claire some books.
4 I showed my new baseball bat to him.
5 I found the children some new toys.

6 The man sent the police the video.

(D)
1 Please let me know how many students will
come to volunteer.
2 Dr. Lee wanted to help people remember[to
remember] things better.
3 She heard the boys fight[fighting] each
other in the playground.
4 I saw a child chase[chasing] after a
butterfly.
5 He had his dog trained by a specialist a few
years ago.
6 The firefighters are respected because they
keep people safe.
7 The museum didn't permit visitors to take
photographs.

중간·기말고사 실전 문제

1 ⑤ **2** looked like an old castle **3** ⑤
4 ④ **5** Mark helped his friends move boxes.
6 She is going to get her dogs to learn new tricks.
7 ④ **8** bring Eunbi the cookies **9** ②
10 ② **11** ④ **12** ④ **13** he can make our
band popular **14** ③, ⑤ **15** ③ **16** ③, ⑤
17 ⑤ **18** The teacher gave us the answers for
the test. **19** ③ **20** forced us to memorize a
poem **21** advised him to stop
22 permitted her to go / told her to remember
23 allowed him to use / expected him to finish
24 ③ **25** The whole audience fell silent once the
play started. **26** My voice sounds strange
today because I'm sick. **27** ③ **28** Social
media helps people contact each other easily.
29 ②, ⑤ **30** for **31** ④ **32** to look for
33 to participate **34** ③ **35** ②
36 (1) had him write in a diary before bed (2) told
him to clean his room every Saturday **37** ⑤
38 ② **39** got my ticket canceled **40** ②
41 ① **42** ⑤ **43** ③ **44** ⑤ **45** ③
46 ⓓ → encouraged me to begin

1 ⑤ impressively → impressive

2 감각동사 뒤에 명사가 오는 경우 「감각동사 + like + 명사」의 형
태로 쓴다.

3 ⑤ make → made

4 (A): 5형식 문장에서 동사 consider의 목적격 보어 자리에는 명
사나 형용사가 온다. '솔직히 말하자면 나는 Sally를 사랑스

럽다고 여긴다.'는 의미이므로 형용사 lovely가 온다.

(B): 5형식 문장에서 동사 keep의 목적격 보어 자리에는 형용사가 올 수 있으므로 neat가 온다.

(C): 5형식 문장에서 동사 find의 목적격 보어 자리에는 형용사가 올 수 있으므로 interesting이 온다.

5 준사역동사 help의 목적격 보어 자리에는 동사원형이 올 수 있다.

6 준사역동사 get은 목적격 보어 자리에 to부정사가 온다.

7 ④ attend to → attend

8 4형식 문장은 「주어 + 동사(bring) + 간접 목적어(Eunbi) + 직접 목적어 (the cookies)」의 형태로 쓴다.

9 첫 번째 빈칸: 3형식 문장에서 동사 give는 전치사 to를 간접 목적어 앞에 쓴다.

두 번째 빈칸: 3형식 문장에서 동사 get은 전치사 for를 간접 목적어 앞에 쓴다.

10 ② attractively → attractive

11 (A): 5형식 문장에서 사역동사 let의 목적격 보어 자리에는 동사원형(check)이 온다.

(B): 5형식 문장에서 사역동사 have의 목적어와 목적격 보어의 관계가 수동이므로 목적격 보어 자리에 과거분사(dyed)가 온다.

(C): 5형식 문장에서 사역동사 make의 목적격 보어 자리에는 동사원형(do)이 온다.

12 ④ ⓓ joining → to join

13 5형식 문장에서 동사 make의 목적격 보어 자리에는 형용사가 올 수 있으므로 popular를 쓴다.

14 ① to cut → cut
② finishing → finish
④ to go → go

15 ⓐ washed → wash
ⓑ to ring → ring[ringing]

16 ③ 4형식 문장은 「주어 + 동사(show) + 간접 목적어(you) + 직접 목적어(the path)」의 형태로 쓴다.

⑤ 4형식 문장을 3형식으로 바꿀 때, 동사 show는 전치사 to를 간접 목적어 앞에 쓴다.

17 ⑤ for → to

18 4형식 문장은 「주어 + 동사(gave) + 간접 목적어(us) + 직접 목적어(the answers for the test)」의 형태로 쓴다.

19 (A): 2형식 문장의 주격 보어 자리에는 형용사가 올 수 있으므로 quiet가 온다.

(B): 5형식 문장에서 동사 consider의 목적격 보어 자리에는 형용사가 올 수 있으므로 rude가 온다.

(C): 2형식 문장의 주격 보어 자리에는 형용사가 올 수 있으므로 strong가 온다.

20 5형식 문장에서 동사 force의 목적격 보어 자리에는 to부정사가 온다.

21 5형식 문장에서 동사 advise의 목적격 보어 자리에는 to부정사가 온다.

22 5형식 문장에서 동사 permit의 목적격 보어 자리에는 to부정사가 온다.

5형식 문장에서 동사 tell의 목적격 보어 자리에는 to부정사가 온다.

23 5형식 문장에서 동사 allow의 목적격 보어 자리에는 to부정사가 온다.

5형식 문장에서 동사 expect의 목적격 보어 자리에는 to부정사가 온다.

24 ① to → of
② a new house our dog → our dog a new house
④ to → for
⑤ an e-mail my cousin → my cousin an e-mail

25 2형식 문장에서 동사 fall의 주격 보어 자리에는 형용사가 올 수 있으므로 silent가 온다.

26 2형식 문장에서 동사 sound의 주격 보어 자리에는 형용사가 올 수 있으므로 strange가 온다.

27 ③ tastes like → tastes

28 5형식 문장은 「주어 + 동사 + 목적어 + 목적격 보어」의 형태이며, 5형식 문장에서 준사역동사 help의 목적격 보어 자리에는 동사원형이 올 수 있다.

29 ② experiencing → to experience
⑤ delayed → delay

30 · 4형식 문장을 3형식으로 바꿔 쓸 때 동사 cook은 간접 목적어 앞에 전치사 for를 쓴다.

· 4형식 문장을 3형식으로 바꿔 쓸 때 동사 build는 간접 목적어 앞에 전치사 for를 쓴다.

31 ① entered to → entered
② resemble with → resemble
③ attend to → attend
⑤ explained about → explained

32 5형식 문장에서 동사 permit의 목적격 보어 자리에는 to부정사가 온다.

33 5형식 문장에서 동사 expect의 목적격 보어 자리에는 to부정사가 온다.

34 (A) 4형식 문장을 3형식으로 바꿔 쓸 때 동사 show는 간접 목적어 앞에 전치사 to를 쓴다.

(B) 4형식 문장을 3형식으로 바꿔 쓸 때 동사 get은 간접 목적어 앞에 전치사 for를 쓴다.

(C) 4형식 문장을 3형식으로 바꿔 쓸 때 동사 ask는 간접 목적어 앞에 전치사 of를 쓴다.

35 ⓑ mentioned about → mentioned
ⓔ reaches to → reaches

36 (1) 사역동사 have의 목적격 보어 자리에는 동사원형(write)이 온다.

(2) 5형식 문장에서 동사 tell의 목적격 보어 자리에는 to부정사가 온다.

37 주어진 문장과 ⑤: 5형식
① 1형식　　② 2형식　　③④ 4형식

38 ① of → to
③ snacks everyone → everyone snacks
④ to → for
⑤ of → to

39 5형식 문장에서 준사역동사 get의 목적어와 목적격 보어의 관계가 수동이면 목적격 보어 자리에는 과거분사(canceled)가 온다.

40 5형식 문장은 「주어 + 동사 + 목적어 + 목적격 보어」의 형태이며, 5형식 문장에서 동사 keep의 목적격 보어 자리에는 형용사가 올 수 있으므로 clean이 온다.

41 5형식 문장은 「주어 + 동사 + 목적어 + 목적격 보어」의 형태이며, 5형식 문장에서 동사 see의 목적격 보어 자리에는 V-ing형이 올 수 있다. '축구를 하는 것을 보았다'고 했으므로 과거동사(saw)를 쓴다.

42 ⑤ raised → raise[raising]

43 ③ to do → do

44 ① lazily → lazy
② to be the team leader → the team leader
③ to Fluffy → Fluffy
④ amusingly → amusing

45 (A): 5형식 문장에서 사역동사 have의 목적어와 목적격 보어의 관계가 수동이므로 목적격 보어 자리에 과거분사(fixed)가 온다.
(B): 5형식 문장에서 사역동사 make의 목적어와 목적격 보어의 관계가 능동이므로 목적격 보어 자리에 동사원형(check out)이 온다.
(C): 5형식 문장에서 사역동사 let의 목적어와 목적격 보어의 관계가 능동이므로 목적격 보어 자리에 동사원형(jump up)이 온다.

46 ⓓ 5형식 문장에서 동사 encourage의 목적격 보어 자리에는 to부정사가 온다.

CHAPTER 2
시제
p.40

POINT 1　현재시제와 과거시제

 연습문제

1 share	**2** grow	**3** painted
4 used	**5** gets	**6** works
7 was	**8** play	**9** twisted
10 lost	**11** took	**12** enjoys

POINT 2　미래시제

연습문제

1 The boxer is going to fight again
2 She will do volunteer work in the city
3 Thomas isn't going to pick us up
4 I won't send Minsu another message
5 He is about to buy his mother's birthday present

POINT 3-1　현재완료시제

 연습문제 A

1 have bought	**2** has built
3 have / studied	**4** Have / been
5 has made	**6** has gone
7 have / ridden	**8** Has / received
9 has lost	**10** hasn't started
11 have been	**12** has sold
13 has climbed	**14** have tried

연습문제 B

1 경험	**2** 결과	**3** 계속	**4** 완료
5 결과	**6** 경험	**7** 완료	**8** 계속
9 경험	**10** 계속		

기출 적중문제

정답　I have exercised every day since last month.
해설　과거에 발생하여 현재까지 영향을 미치는 일을 나타내므로 「have/has + p.p.」 형태인 현재완료시제를 쓴다.

POINT 3-2　현재완료시제 vs. 과거시제

 연습문제

1 hasn't tried	**2** launched
3 have traveled	**4** didn't look
5 haven't studied	**6** Did you see
7 has taught	**8** Has Jane done

9	didn't watch	**10**	hasn't eaten
11	Did Lewis meet	**12**	haven't heard
13	won	**14**	hasn't been

9 didn't watch　**10** hasn't eaten
11 Did Lewis meet　**12** haven't heard
13 won　**14** hasn't been

POINT 4　현재완료진행시제

연습문제 A

1 has been walking　**2** has been talking
3 has been drawing　**4** have been growing
5 have been discussing
6 has been carving

연습문제 B

1 have been playing the drum
2 has been fixing his computer
3 has been recording a new movie
4 has been learning to dance
5 have been chatting on the phone
6 have been preparing for the exam
7 have been searching for the treasure
8 has been writing a romance novel

연습문제 C

1 has been studying　**2** have been making
3 O　**4** have been trying
5 has been chatting　**6** have been watching
7 O　**8** has been standing
9 O　**10** have been waiting
11 O

기출 적중문제

정답　②, ⑤
해설　① is working → has worked[has been working]
　　③ has singing → has sung[has been singing]
　　④ is wearing → has been wearing

POINT 5　과거완료시제

연습문제 A

1 had　**2** couldn't　**3** hadn't
4 had　**5** entered　**6** was
7 had　**8** became　**9** returned
10 went　**11** had

연습문제 B

1 had drawn　**2** had left
3 had come　**4** had made

기출 적중문제

정답　⑤
해설　'나는 자러가기 전에 양치를 하는 것을 잊어버렸었다.'는 의미
　　이므로 「had+ p.p.」 형태의 결과를 의미하는 과거완료시제
　　를 쓴다.

POINT 6　과거완료진행시제

연습문제

1 has been painting　**2** had been living
3 had been playing　**4** have been taking
5 had been running　**6** had been staying
7 had been trying　**8** hasn't been focusing
9 had been discussing

서술형 대비 문제

Ⓐ **1** had been
2 have been studying
3 played
4 have exercised[have been exercising]

Ⓑ **1** We have watched the documentary film
2 She had never traveled abroad
3 Andrew has lost his umbrella
4 The students had been at school
5 My younger brother hadn't written a poem
6 He has researched global warming
7 I have won awards
8 my friends had already gone home
9 They hadn't taken a cruise
10 He has gained weight
11 Sumi hasn't answered my calls

Ⓒ **1** has been using the scanner
2 has been crying
3 hadn't been talking to each other
4 has been learning the piano
5 had been sleeping
6 hasn't been swimming
7 had been practicing
8 have been drinking a glass of milk

중간·기말고사 실전 문제

1 ④　**2** ④　**3** ③　**4** ⓒ → We went to
a soccer practice last Thursday. **5**　am about to
catch the bus to school　**6** ④　**7** ③
8 ⑤　**9** ②　**10** ③　**11** ⓐ heard ⓑ has
done　**12** has been painting this picture / he
moved into his new studio　**13** had been waiting
/ arrived　**14** came / had been making jam
15 ④　**16** ⓑ → haven't　**17** has worked

18 has made
learned / has lost   **19** ④   **20** ③   **21** has
    22 ③   **23** ② → was
24 ④   **25** ⑤   **26** has been teaching English
at our school   **27** had gotten up / took / had
had   **28** have been talking about our exam
29 has been working on her science homework
30 has been taking swimming lessons for 5 years
31 ④   **32** ②, ⑤   **33** hasn't studied
cooking / have worked in restaurants   **34** ③
35 realized / hadn't brought   **36** seemed / hadn't
slept   **37** booked / had missed   **38** ate /
had bought   **39** ④   **40** Have you ever
bought clothes   **41** ④   **42** had hurt → hurt
43 ⓐ began   ⓑ have been dancing   **44** ②
45 hasn't played   **46** had tried   **47** had
been practicing

1 ④ visits → visited

2 ⓐ was bringing → bring
ⓔ was → is

3 ③ won't participate → didn't participate

4 last Thursday는 과거시제와 주로 함께 쓰이는 부사(구)이다.

5 '막 ~하려는 참이다'는 의미이므로 「be about to + 동사원형」을 쓴다.

6 ④ went → will go

7 ⓐ has wrote → has written[has been writing]
ⓒ have bought → bought
ⓓ has fixed → fixed

8 ⑤: 경험
①②③④: 완료

9 밑줄 친 부분과 ②: 경험
①③⑤: 계속   ④: 결과

10 ① have been → went
② Has → Had
④ has → had
⑤ has completed → completed

11 ⓐ 과거의 특정한 시점을 나타내는 부사 yesterday가 쓰였으므로 과거시제를 쓴다.
ⓑ '그가 정치인이 된 이후로 사람들을 돕기 위해 많은 멋진 일들을 해왔다.'는 의미이므로 현재완료시제를 쓴다.

12 첫 번째 빈칸: 과거에 발생한 일이 현재도 계속 진행 중임을 강조하고 있으므로 현재완료진행시제를 쓴다.
두 번째 빈칸: 과거의 특정한 시점을 나타내므로 과거시제를 쓴다.

13 Sophia가 우체국에 도착했을 때, 민주는 Sophia를 한 시간 동안 기다리고 있었음을 알 수 있다. Sophia가 우체국에 도착한 일은 과거의 특정 시점을 나타내는 과거시제를 쓰고, 민주가 계속 기다리고 있었던 일은 과거완료진행시제를 쓴다.

14 내가 집에 왔을 때, 나의 아버지와 남동생은 30분 동안 잼을 만드는 중이었음을 알 수 있다. 내가 집에 온 일은 과거의 특정 시점을 나타내는 과거시제를 쓰고, 나의 아버지와 남동생이 잼을 만들고 있었던 일은 과거완료진행시제를 쓴다.

15 ④ has fallen → had fallen

16 '너는 저 새로운 액션 영화 *Star Heroes*를 본 적이 있니?'라는 현재완료시제의 의문문에 대한 부정의 대답은 「No, 주어 + have/has + not」의 형태이다.

17 '그녀가 2013년에 사서로 일하기 시작했고, 지금도 계속 사서로 일을 하고 있다.'는 의미이므로 계속을 의미하는 현재완료시제를 쓴다.

18 '그가 수년 전에 옷을 만드는 것을 시작했고, 지금도 계속 옷을 만들고 있다.'는 의미이므로 계속을 의미하는 현재완료시제를 쓴다.

19 '오늘 아침부터 같은 곡을 흥얼거리기 시작해서 지금까지 하고 있다.'는 의미이므로, 과거에 발생한 일이 현재도 계속 진행 중임을 강조하는 현재완료진행시제를 쓴다.

20 ⓑ has worked on → had worked on
ⓒ has already begun → had already begun

21 ⓐ: '그녀는 그 이후로 요가하는 법을 배워왔다.'는 의미이므로 계속을 의미하는 현재완료시제를 쓴다.
ⓑ: '지난 몇 주 동안, 그녀는 살이 조금씩 빠져왔다.'는 의미이므로 계속을 의미하는 현재완료시제를 쓴다.

22 밑줄 친 (A)와 ③: 계속
①: 경험   ②④: 완료   ⑤: 결과

23 ② 과거의 특정한 시점을 나타내므로 과거시제를 쓴다.

24 ① been eaten → been eating
② have been study → have been studying
③ been wear → been wearing
⑤ has been written → has been writing

25 '나의 친구들과 내가 그곳에 도착했을 때, 많은 사람들은 그 축제를 떠나버렸었다.'는 의미이므로 결과를 의미하는 과거완료시제를 쓴다.

26 현재완료진행시제는 「have/has + been + V-ing」 형태로 쓴다.

27 첫 번째 문장: '오늘, 나의 엄마가 나를 깨우러 나의 방에 들어오기 전에 내가 일어났었다.'는 의미이다. 내가 일어난 일이 나의 엄마가 내 방에 들어온 일보다 먼저 일어난 일이므로 「had + p.p.」 형태의 대과거를 쓴다.
두 번째 문장: '학교에서, 나는 점심을 먹은 이후에 수학 시험을 보았다.'는 의미이다. 내가 점심을 먹은 일이 수학 시험을 본 일보다 먼저 일어난 일이므로 「had + p.p.」 형태의 대과거를 쓴다.

28 '우리는 휴식 시간 이후로 우리의 시험에 관해 이야기하고 있다.'는 의미이므로 과거에 발생한 일이 현재도 계속 진행 중임을 강조하는 현재완료진행시제를 쓴다.

29 'Claire는 수요일 이후로 그녀의 과학 숙제를 하고 있다.'는 의미이므로, 과거에 발생한 일이 현재도 계속 진행 중임을 강조하는 현

재완료진행시제를 쓴다.

30 '그녀는 5년 동안 수영 강습을 받아오고 있다.'는 의미이므로, 과거에 발생한 일이 현재도 계속 진행 중임을 강조하는 현재완료진행시제를 쓴다.

31 첫 번째 빈칸: 과거의 특정한 시점을 나타내므로 과거시제를 쓴다.
두 번째 빈칸: '그 비행기는 이미 이륙해버렸었다.'는 의미이므로 결과를 의미하는 과거완료시제를 쓴다.

32 has waited는 현재완료시제이므로 과거의 특정한 시점을 나타내는 부사구와 함께 쓸 수 없다.

33 첫 번째 빈칸: Iris는 요리 공부를 해본 경험이 없으므로 현재완료시제의 부정형을 쓴다.
두 번째 빈칸: Alex와 Iris 둘 다 식당에서 일해본 경험이 있으므로 현재완료시제를 쓴다.

34 (A): '그는 어린 소년이었을 때부터 현재인 지금까지 축구를 해왔다.'는 의미이므로 현재완료시제를 쓴다.
(B): '그는 그의 감독이 한 경기에서 공격수로 뛸 기회를 제안하기 전에 오랫동안 수비수였었다.'는 의미이므로 계속을 의미하는 과거완료시제를 쓴다.
(C): 과거의 특정한 시점을 나타내므로 과거시제를 쓴다.

35 첫 번째 빈칸: Austin이 깨달았던 것은 그가 도시락을 가져오지 않았었던 일보다 나중에 일어난 일이므로 과거시제를 쓴다.
두 번째 빈칸: Austin이 도시락을 가져오지 않았던 것은 그가 깨달았던 일보다 먼저 일어난 일이므로 「had + p.p.」 형태의 대과거를 쓴다.

36 첫 번째 빈칸: 그 소방관들이 피곤해 보였던 것은 그들이 잠을 못 잤었던 일보다 나중에 일어난 일이므로 과거시제를 쓴다.
두 번째 빈칸: 그 소방관들이 잠을 못 잤었던 일은 그들이 피곤해 보였던 것보다 먼저 일어난 일이므로 「had + p.p.」 형태의 대과거를 쓴다.

37 첫 번째 빈칸: 그가 다른 티켓을 예약했던 것은 그가 그 기차를 놓쳤었던 일보다 나중에 일어난 일이므로 과거시제를 쓴다.
두 번째 빈칸: 그가 그 기차를 놓쳤었던 일은 그가 다른 티켓을 예약했던 것보다 먼저 일어난 일이므로 「had + p.p.」 형태의 대과거를 쓴다.

38 '나의 남동생과 나는 내가 가장 좋아하는 케이크 가게에서 나의 어머니가 사 오셨었던 딸기 케이크를 먹었다.'는 의미이다. 나의 남동생과 내가 딸기 케이크를 먹었던 것은 나의 어머니가 케이크를 사 오셨었던 일보다 나중에 일어난 일이므로 과거시제를 쓰고, 어머니가 케이크를 사 오셨었던 일은 「had + p.p.」 형태의 대과거를 쓴다.

39 ① have been studying → had studied[had been studying]
② hasn't finished → hadn't finished
③ have lived → had lived
⑤ have been working → had been working

40 현재완료시제의 경험의 의미이므로 「Have/Has + 주어 + p.p. ~?」로 쓴다.

41 첫 번째 빈칸: 'Mary는 작년부터 연극 동아리의 연극에서 현재인 지금까지 연기를 해왔다.'는 의미이므로 계속을 의미하는 현재완료시제를 쓴다.
두 번째 빈칸: '그녀의 오빠는 그가 18세가 될 때까지 연극 동아리의 연극에서 연기를 해왔었다.'는 의미이므로 계속을 의미하는 과거완료시제를 쓴다.

42 과거의 특정한 시점을 나타내므로 과거시제 hurt를 쓴다.

43 ⓐ '그 공연자들은 30분 전에 무대 위에서 춤추는 것을 시작했다.'는 의미로 과거의 특정한 시점을 나타내므로 과거시제를 쓴다.
ⓑ 그 공연자들은 30분 동안 지금까지 무대 위에서 춤을 추고 있으므로 현재완료진행시제를 쓴다.

44 ② has heard → heard
Lily가 누군가가 첼로를 연주하는 소리를 들었던 것은 그녀가 기타를 배우는 것을 생각하고 있었던 일보다 나중에 일어난 일이므로 과거시제를 쓴다.

45 과거부터 현재까지의 경험을 나타내고 있으므로 현재완료시제를 쓴다.

46 진호가 이전에 하키를 하는 것을 시도했던 일은 그가 그것이 매우 흥미롭다고 알게 되었던 일보다 먼저 일어난 일이므로 「had + p.p.」 형태의 대과거를 쓴다.

47 그 오케스트라는 그가 합류했을 때 세 시간 동안 계속해서 함께 연습하고 있었음을 의미하므로, 특정 과거 시점을 기준으로 그 이전에 발생한 일이 그 시점에도 계속 진행 중임을 강조하는 과거완료진행시제를 쓴다.

CHAPTER 3
조동사

p.64

POINT 1 can, may, will

1 Can / Will	**2** can / may	
3 can't	**4** could / might	
5 Can	**6** can / is able to	

1 Can[Could/Will/Would] you send
2 may[might/can/could] go
3 will[is going to] let
4 can't be
5 can cause
6 can[may] turn in
7 can[is able to] solve
8 will[is going to] go

기출 적중문제

정답 She can't be overseas.
해설 '해외에 있을 리가 없다'고 하였으므로 추측을 나타내는
can't를 쓴다.

POINT 2 must, should

1 ⓐ	**2** ⓑ	**3** ⓒ	**4** ⓑ
5 ⓑ	**6** ⓒ	**7** ⓐ	

1 must / have to	**2** must
3 don't have to	**4** must not
5 must	**6** must / have to
7 must not	**8** doesn't have to
9 can't	**10** must not / should not

1 should wash	**2** shouldn't talk
3 should make	**4** should study

기출 적중문제

정답 ②
해설 ②: 강한 추측
밑줄 친 부분과 ①③④⑤: 강한 의무

POINT 3 should의 생략

연습문제

1 demanded / dress up **2** suggested / try
3 requires / wear **4** requested / return

---

5 insists / protect **6** ordered / leave

기출 적중문제

정답 ②, ⑤
해설 ① wore → wear
③ cleaning → clean
④ to eat → eat

POINT 4 used to, would

1 used	**2** used	**3** carry
4 used to	**5** is used	**6** used to
7 pump	**8** used	**9** go
10 jogging		

1 guide	**2** O	**3** spending
4 keep	**5** taking	**6** used to
7 O	**8** used to	**9** O
10 watching		

1 used to make	**2** is used to riding
3 didn't use to play	**4** used to be
5 are used to filter	

기출 적중문제

정답 used to live
해설 '나의 가족은 수영장이 있는 집에서 살곤 했다.'는 의미이므로
과거의 상태를 나타내는 used to를 쓴다.

POINT 5 조동사 + have + p.p

1 could	**2** might	**3** should
4 could	**5** may	**6** must
7 might	**8** should	**9** can't
10 shouldn't	**11** must	**12** could
13 can't		

1 shouldn't have been
2 should have drunk
3 may[might] have recorded
4 could have swum
5 must have turned off
6 can't have gotten

1 can't have eaten	**2** should have painted
3 must have arrived	**4** must have walked
5 must have received	**6** can't have gone

정답   should have apologized
해설   '~했어야 했다'고 했으므로 should have p.p.를 쓴다.

POINT 6   조동사 관용 표현

연습
문제
1 would like to have	**2** had better lower
3 may well be	**4** would rather buy
5 may as well ask	**6** would like a manual

서술형 대비 문제

(A)
1 O   **2** O
3 used to be   **4** avoid
5 may as well take   **6** ought to put
7 O   **8** had better drink
9 O
10 could have visited [should have visited]
11 O

(B)
1 must not run   **2** must wear
3 must have been

(C)
1 can't have completed
2 should have brought
3 may[might] have watched
4 shouldn't have spoken
5 must have been delivered
6 shouldn't have skipped
7 must have paid

(D)
1 Jenny may well be scared by the movie.
2 I would rather go skating than skiing.
3 I think my younger brother would like this show.
4 He may as well give up his reelection campaign.
5 The customer would like to make a reservation.
6 You had better offer your seat to the elderly man.

중간·기말고사 실전 문제

1 ②   **2** you may as well visit Switzerland
3 ③   **4** ①   **5** ④   **6** ⑤   **7** ②
8 don't have to buy   **9** ①   **10** used
to be   **11** ③   **12** ③   **13** ④   **14** ⓔ →
ought to   **15** ⓐ would like to ⓑ would rather
16 ④   **17** ③   **18** ①   **19** didn't use to
20 you had better say happy birthday on the right
day.   **21** (1) must have gotten (2) shouldn't
have yelled   **22** ③   **23** You had better
use this coupon by Wednesday.
24 We shouldn't leave our bicycles here.
25 ⓐ used to live ⓑ would go ⓒ used to fly
26 (1) had to (2) used to (3) might   **27** ④
28 suggested that we (should) get up early
29 insisted that they (should) stay in the classroom
30 must have been late   **31** ⑤   **32** ④
33 shouldn't have left   **34** ④
35 shouldn't have stayed   **36** must have
missed   **37** used to go to the market   **38** used
to be afraid   **39** ③   **40** (1) ⓐ → used to
having (2) ⓔ → be used to get   **41** ①, ③   **42** used
to be my neighbor   **43** ③   **44** may[might] have
dropped   **45** should have kept
46 (A) ought to log in (B) should ask   **47** ⑤
48 ⓐ might have missed ⓑ must have forgotten

1   ② '나는 영어와 세 개의 다른 언어를 할 수 있다.'라는 능력의 의미로 am able to와 의미가 같다.

2   '~하는 편이 좋다'는 의미의 조동사 관용 표현 may as well 뒤에는 동사원형을 쓴다.

3   ③ '눈이 많이 올지도 모른다'고 하였으므로 약한 추측을 나타내는 may를 쓴다.

4   ① '나의 이메일을 확인하기 위해 너의 컴퓨터를 사용해도 되니?'라는 허가의 의미로 May와 의미가 같다.

5   ④ ought read → ought to read

6   ⑤ 과거의 습관과 정중한 요청을 나타내므로 would를 쓴다.

7   밑줄 친 부분과 ②: 허가
①⑤: 능력   ③: 추측   ④: 요청

8   '너는 나에게 그것을 사 줄 필요가 없다.'는 의미이므로 don't have to를 쓴다.

9   ① '꽃들을 꺾으면 안 된다'고 하였으므로 강한 금지를 나타내는 must not을 쓴다.

10   'Brown씨는 유명한 음악가였다.'는 의미이므로 과거의 상태를 나타내는 「used to + 동사원형」을 쓴다.

11 ③: 강한 추측
①②④⑤: 강한 의무

12 ③ 허가, 능력을 나타내는 can이 빈칸에 공통으로 올 수 있다.

13 · '나는 읽을 만한 좋은 소설을 찾고 싶다.'는 의미이므로 would like to를 쓴다.
· '너는 영화 중에 전화로 이야기해서는 안 된다.'는 의미이므로 should not을 쓴다.

14 ⓔ '~해야 한다'는 의미로 ought to를 쓴다.

15 ⓐ '나는 오늘 저녁 식사로 피자를 먹고 싶다.'는 의미이므로 would like to를 쓴다.
ⓑ '나는 차라리 초밥을 먹겠다.'는 의미이므로 would rather를 쓴다.

16 ④ am used to get → used to get[am used to getting]

17 첫 번째 빈칸: '너는 줄을 서면서 시간을 낭비하지 않기 위해 다른 놀이기구를 찾는 편이 좋다.'는 의미이므로 may as well을 쓴다.
두 번째 빈칸: '너는 너의 간식과 음료를 가져와야 한다.'는 의미이므로 should를 쓴다.

18 ①: 약한 추측
밑줄 친 부분과 ②③④⑤: 허가

19 과거에는 '해외 여행을 많이 하지 않았지만 지금은 매우 일반적이다.'는 의미이므로 과거의 상태를 나타내는 didn't use to를 쓴다.

20 '~하는 것이 낫다'고 했으므로 「had better + 동사원형」을 쓴다.

21 (1) '그는 길을 잃었음이 틀림없다.'는 의미이므로 must have p.p.를 쓴다.
(2) 'Jake는 우리에게 소리를 지르지 말았어야 했다.'는 의미이므로 shouldn't have p.p.를 쓴다.

22 · '그의 시험이 끝날 때까지 Jack을 부르지 않는 것이 낫다.'는 의미이므로 had better not을 쓴다.
· '~하는 편이 좋다'는 의미의 may as well 뒤에는 동사원형을 쓴다.

23 '~하는 것이 낫다'고 했으므로 「had better + 동사원형」을 쓴다.

24 약한 의무를 나타내므로 「shouldn't + 동사원형」을 쓴다.

25 ⓐ '나는 서울에 있는 한강 공원 근처의 아파트에 살곤 했다.'는 의미이므로 used to live를 쓴다.
ⓑ '나는 주말마다 한강에 가곤 했다.'는 의미로 과거의 습관을 나타내므로 would go를 쓴다.
ⓒ '우리는 그곳에서 연을 날리곤 했다.'는 의미이므로 used to fly를 쓴다.

26 (1): '우리는 어제 저녁에 강당에서 조용히 해야 했다.'는 의미이므로 had to를 쓴다.
(2): '내가 어렸을 때, 가지고 놀만한 것들이 많이 있었다.'는 의미이므로 과거의 상태를 나타내는 used to를 쓴다.
(3): 'Laura는 바쁘지 않다면 그녀의 부모님께 이메일을 쓸지도 모른다.'는 의미이므로 약한 추측을 나타내는 might를 쓴다.

27 (A): '그 새로운 영화는 영화관에 이미 나왔을 수도 있다.'는 의미이므로 may have p.p.를 쓴다.
(B): 'James는 내가 아는 가장 똑똑한 사람이기 때문에 그 시험에서 떨어졌을 리가 없다.'는 의미이므로 can't have p.p.를 쓴다.
(C): '그녀의 가방이 그녀의 방에 없기 때문에 그녀는 밖에 나갔음이 틀림없다.'는 의미이므로 must have p.p.를 쓴다.

28 제안의 동사인 suggest 뒤의 that 절에는 「(should) + 동사원형」을 쓴다.

29 주장의 동사인 insist 뒤의 that 절에는 「(should) + 동사원형」을 쓴다.

30 'Katie는 어제 그녀의 약속에 늦었음이 틀림없다.'는 의미이므로 must have p.p.를 쓴다.

31 ⑤ should not leave → can't have left

32 ④ 그는 지금 시카고에 있기 때문에 여기에 있을 리가 없다. (추측)
≠ 그는 지금 시카고에 있기 때문에 여기에 있을 수 없다. (능력)

33 '너는 쪽지를 쓰지 않고 떠나지 말았어야 했다.'는 의미이므로 shouldn't have p.p를 쓴다.

34 '그는 돈이 없기 때문에 그가 새 휴대폰을 샀다는 것은 불가능하다.'라는 의미이므로 '④ 그는 새 휴대폰을 샀을 리가 없다.'와 의미가 같다.

35 '~하지 말았어야 했다'고 했으므로 shouldn't have p.p.를 쓴다.

36 '~했음이 틀림없다'고 했으므로 must have p.p.를 쓴다.

37 '나의 할머니와 나는 매주 토요일에 과일을 사기 위해 시장에 가곤 했다.'는 의미이므로 과거의 습관을 나타내는 「used to + 동사원형」을 쓴다.

38 '나는 사람들과 말하는 것을 두려워하곤 했다.'는 의미이므로 과거의 습관을 나타내는 「used to + 동사원형」을 쓴다.

39 (A): 제안의 동사 suggest 뒤의 that 절에는 동사원형을 쓴다.
(B): 주장의 동사 insist 뒤의 that 절에는 동사원형을 쓴다.
(C): 요구의 동사 demand 뒤의 that 절에는 동사원형을 쓴다.

40 (1) ⓐ '우리가 그곳에 있을 때, 나는 자유시간이 많은 것에 익숙했다.'는 의미이므로 「be used to + V-ing」를 쓴다.
(2) ⓔ '나는 다시 건강해지는 데 사용할 수 있는 운동기구 몇 개를 살까 생각 중이다.'는 의미이므로 「be used to + 동사원형」를 쓴다.

41 ① should have slept → shouldn't have slept
③ can't have practiced → must have practiced

42 '그녀는 나의 이웃이었다'는 의미이므로 과거의 상태를 나타내는 「used to + 동사원형」을 쓴다.

43 · '그녀는 땅콩 아이스크림을 먹었을 리가 없다.'는 의미이므로 can't have p.p.를 쓴다.
· '그는 그의 이어폰을 사용하고 있었음이 틀림없다.'는 의미이므로 must have p.p.를 쓴다.

44 '나는 집에 오는 길에 나의 반지를 떨어뜨렸을 수도 있다.'는 의미이므로 may[might] have p.p.를 쓴다.

45 '우리는 비상 훈련을 하는 동안 차분하게 있었어야 했다.'는 의미이므로 should have p.p.를 쓴다.

46 (A) '~해야 한다'고 했으므로 「ought to + 동사원형」을 쓴다.
(B) '~해야 한다'고 했으므로 「should + 동사원형」을 쓴다.

47 ⑤ would → used to

48 ⓐ '나는 그녀를 놓쳤을 수도 있어서 걱정했다.'는 의미이므로 might have p.p.를 쓴다.
ⓑ '그녀는 우리의 회의에 대해 잊었음이 틀림없다.'는 의미이므로 must have p.p.를 쓴다.

CHAPTER 4
수동태
p.88

POINT 1 수동태 문장 만드는 법

연습문제 A

1 Ginger tea is made
2 This court is used
3 These trees were planted
4 A lighthouse on the coast was operated
5 the cows are fed
6 The convention center will be rented

연습문제 B

1 The living room wasn't cleaned
2 Are pork dishes served
3 The movie isn't liked
4 Were all the windows closed
5 The wall of the church wasn't painted
6 When was her old computer donated

▎기출 적중문제
정답 ③
해설 ① were catch → were caught
② didn't reviewed → wasn't reviewed
④ to → by
⑤ was building → was built

POINT 2 수동태로 쓸 수 없는 동사

연습문제

1 costs   **2** happened
3 rose   **4** appeared
5 was raised   **6** lacked
7 arrived   **8** remained
9 was laid   **10** disappeared

POINT 3 수동태의 시제

연습문제 A

1 is brought   **2** have been grown
3 will be provided
4 are not being accepted
5 was loved   **6** had been locked
7 is being played   **8** will be estimated
9 has been struck   **10** were being sorted
11 have been watered

연습문제 B

1 will be served   **2** has been developed
3 had been broken   **4** was held

5 is being installed

기출 적중문제

정답 More than ten songs have been composed by Carl.

해설 현재완료의 수동태는 「have/has + been + p.p.」의 형태를 쓰므로 have been composed를 쓴다.

POINT 4 조동사가 있는 수동태

 연습 문제

1 should be taken		**2** will be conducted	
3 must be entered		**4** should be put	
5 can be solved		**6** should be left	
7 can be finished		**8** may be used	

POINT 5 4형식 문장의 수동태

 연습 문제 A

1 to	**2** for	**3** to	**4** of
5 to	**6** for	**7** of	**8** for
9 to	**10** for		

연습 문제 B

1 was given some flowers / were given to my grandmother

2 was shown a diamond ring / was shown to the woman

3 were taught math / was taught to the students

4 was asked the direction of the train station / was asked of me

기출 적중문제

정답 ①, ⑤

해설 ② of → to
③ to → for
④ of → for

POINT 6 5형식 문장의 수동태

연습 문제

1 was painted yellow

2 was asked to do the dishes

3 was considered a good friend

4 was seen to jump across the stream

5 was made to pay a fine

6 was heard to sing on the stage

POINT 7 구동사의 수동태

 연습 문제

1 was turned on		**2** are put off	
3 was laughed at		**4** was picked up	
5 was set up		**6** are made use of	

POINT 8 목적어가 that절인 문장의 수동태

연습 문제

1 was thought that the test would be difficult (by them)

2 was said to be outdated (by everyone)

3 is believed that spirits live in natural objects (by people)

4 are reported to be suffering

5 is known that Neil Armstrong walked on the moon (by people)

6 is said to raise blood pressure (by people)

7 was expected that the coach would praise us

8 was thought to be destroyed

POINT 9 수동태 관용 표현

 연습 문제

1 to	**2** with	**3** in	**4** as
5 with	**6** to	**7** for	**8** at
9 from	**10** with	**11** for	

서술형 대비 문제

Ⓐ
1 O	**2** O
3 is being repaired	
4 has been delivered	
5 was raised	**6** O
7 O	**8** be given
9 were laid	

Ⓑ
1 is prepared by the chefs

2 hasn't been revised by Charles

3 was developed by the scientists

4 is being organized by Jiho

5 will be played by the pianist

6 have been uploaded to the school's Web page

7 were made by her

8 may be shocked by his many talents

Ⓒ ⓐ known for ⓑ made of

ⓒ filled with ⓓ pleased with

Ⓓ **1** The opportunity to study abroad was turned down by Harry.
2 Luck is said to come to those who look after it (by people).
3 Fruits are known to be helpful for our bodies (by us).
4 It was thought that Mount Everest was impossible to climb (by them).
5 The Earth was believed to be flat (by people).
6 The elderly neighbor is taken care of by Calvin.
7 The Statue of Liberty was given to America by France.
8 I was helped to move the heavy boxes by Jordan.
9 A gift was sent to me on my birthday by Daniel.

중간·기말고사 실전 문제

1 ①, ⑤ **2** ⑤ **3** was delayed
4 Many insect species were found in the Amazon rainforest. **5** is spoken to (by someone)
6 is made use of by the citizens **7** ④
8 The musical is being played **9** ⑤
10 is held by the neighbors **11** ①, ⑤ **12** ⑤
13 will be built **14** was caught **15** have been shown **16** That type of wallet isn't offered by the store. **17** I was told to stay calm by my friends. **18** ③
19 have to be worn **20** Dangerous goods aren't delivered by the postal service. **21** ③ **22** ①
23 Justin is interested in **24** ① **25** ⑤
26 ⑤ **27** was thought that the choir was magnificent (by everyone) **28** ③ **29** was made to memorize at least 30 vocabulary words a day by the teacher **30** ④ **31** He is considered an expert **32** ② **33** (1) ⓒ → fell (2) ⓓ → was used to **34** was laughed at **35** was turned on by **36** ④ **37** ③ **38** ① **39** ① **40** ②
41 is known for **42** ①, ③ **43** is known as Bobby to **44** ②, ④ **45** (1) The class was divided into two sections by the teacher. (2) The class wasn't divided into two sections by the teacher. (3) Was the class divided into two sections by the teacher?

1 ① 상태를 나타내는 동사(have)는 수동태로 쓸 수 없다.
⑤ 목적어를 가지지 않는 동사(appear)는 수동태로 쓸 수 없다.

2 ① to have been → to be
② are saying to → are said to
③ expected to → expected that
④ to get → to be getting

3 '기차가 지연되었다'는 의미이므로 수동태를 쓴다. 과거시제의 수동태는 「was/were + p.p.」의 형태를 쓰므로 was delayed를 쓴다.

4 과거시제의 수동태는 「was/were + p.p.(+ by + 행위자)」의 형태를 쓰므로 were found를 쓴다.

5 구동사 speak to를 수동태로 쓰는 경우 be spoken to를 쓴다.

6 구동사 make use of를 수동태로 쓰는 경우 be made use of를 쓴다. 행위자는 「by + 목적격」의 형태이므로 by the citizens를 쓴다.

7 ④ was remained → remained

8 현재진행시제의 수동태는 「am/is/are + being + p.p.」의 형태를 쓰므로 is being played를 쓴다.

9 ⑤ should organize → should be organized

10 현재시제의 수동태는 「am/is/are + p.p.(+ by + 행위자)」의 형태를 쓰므로 is held by the neighbors를 쓴다.

11 ① 4형식 문장은 목적어가 두 개이므로 간접 목적어가 주어인 수동태 문장을 만들 수 있다.
⑤ 4형식 문장은 목적어가 두 개이므로 직접 목적어가 주어인 수동태 문장을 만들 수 있다. 이때 give는 간접 목적어 앞에 전치사 to를 쓰는 동사이다.

12 과거시제의 수동태는 「was/were + p.p.(+ by + 행위자)」의 형태를 쓰므로 were recovered by a technician을 쓴다.

13 미래시제의 수동태는 「will + be + p.p.」의 형태를 쓰므로 will be built를 쓴다.

14 과거시제의 수동태는 「was/were + p.p.」의 형태를 쓰므로 was caught를 쓴다.

15 현재완료의 수동태는 「have/has + been + p.p.」의 형태를 쓰므로 have been shown을 쓴다.

16 수동태의 동사는 「be동사 + p.p.」의 형태이고, 주어 That type of wallet은 단수이므로 isn't offered를 쓴다. 행위자는 「by + 목적격」의 형태이므로 by the store를 쓴다.

17 목적격 보어가 to부정사인 5형식 문장을 수동태 문장으로 만들 때는 to부정사를 「be동사 + p.p.」 뒤에 그대로 쓴다. 행위자는 「by + 목적격」의 형태이므로 by my friends를 쓴다.

18 ③ for → to

19 조동사가 있는 수동태는 「조동사 + be + p.p.」의 형태를 쓰므로 have to be worn을 쓴다.

20 수동태의 동사는 「be동사 + p.p.」의 형태이고, 주어 Dangerous goods는 복수이므로 aren't delivered를 쓴다. 행위자는 「by + 목적격」의 형태이므로 by the postal service

를 쓴다.

21 ③ 현재완료의 수동태는 「have/has + been + p.p.」의 형태를 쓰므로 have been driven을 쓴다.

22 ⓒ being melt → being melted
ⓓ be risen → be raised

23 '~에 흥미가 있다'는 의미의 수동태 관용 표현인 be interested in을 쓴다.

24 · 직접 목적어가 주어인 수동태 문장에서 buy는 간접 목적어 앞에 for를 쓴다.
· 직접 목적어가 주어인 수동태 문장에서 give는 간접 목적어 앞에 to를 쓴다.

25 ① lent me → lent to me
② was hearing → was heard
③ told take → told to take
④ was put off the members → was put off by the members

26 ⑤ of → to

27 목적어가 that절인 문장에서 that절 전체를 수동태 문장의 주어로 쓰는 경우 가주어 it을 쓰고 that절은 수동태 동사 뒤에 쓴다. 행위자가 일반 사람이거나 언급할 만큼 중요하지 않은 경우 「by+목적격」은 생략할 수 있다.

28 ③ is satisfied for → is satisfied with

29 목적격 보어가 동사원형인 5형식 문장을 수동태 문장으로 만들 때는 동사원형을 to부정사로 바꿔서 「be동사 + p.p.」 뒤에 쓴다.
행위자는 「by + 목적격」의 형태이므로 by the teacher를 쓴다.

30 ④ was helped preparing → was helped to prepare

31 목적격 보어가 명사인 5형식 문장을 수동태 문장으로 만들 때는 명사를 「be동사 + p.p.」 뒤에 그대로 쓴다.

32 · 목적격 보어가 동사원형인 5형식 문장을 수동태 문장으로 만들 때는 동사원형을 to부정사로 바꿔 「be동사 + p.p.」 뒤에 쓴다.
· 목적격 보어가 분사인 5형식 문장을 수동태 문장으로 만들 때는 「be동사 + p.p.」 뒤에 분사를 그대로 쓴다.

33 (1) ⓒ '그것이 거센 바람에 의해 떨어졌을 때, 그녀는 죽을 것이다.'라는 의미이다. 이때, fall은 목적어를 가지지 않는 동사이므로 수동태로 쓸 수 없다.
(2) ⓓ '그녀는 그 나뭇잎을 보는 데 그녀의 날을 보내는 것에 익숙했다.'는 의미이므로, '~에 익숙하다'는 의미의 수동태 관용 표현인 be used to -ing를 쓴다.

34 구동사 laugh at을 수동태로 쓰는 경우 be laughed at을 쓴다.

35 구동사 turn on을 수동태로 쓰는 경우 be turned on을 쓴다.

36 ④ is got → was gotten

37 ③ has been broken → was broken

38 조동사가 있는 수동태는 「조동사 + be + p.p.(+ by + 행위자)」의 형태를 쓰므로 could be completed를 쓴다.

39 첫 번째 빈칸: '~으로 덮여 있다'는 의미의 be covered with를 쓴다.
두 번째 빈칸: '~으로 가득 차 있다'는 의미의 be filled with를 쓴다.
세 번째 빈칸: '~에 기뻐하다'는 의미의 be pleased with를 쓴다.
따라서 빈칸에는 공통으로 with를 쓴다.

40 · '~을 하기로 되어 있다'는 의미의 be supposed to를 쓴다.
· '~에 흥미가 있다'는 의미의 be interested in을 쓴다.
· '~으로 만들어지다(재료 성질이 변하지 않음)'는 의미의 be made of를 쓴다.
· '~에 실망하다'는 의미의 be disappointed at을 쓴다.

41 '~으로 유명하다'는 의미의 be known for를 쓴다.

42 ① 목적어가 that절인 문장을 수동태 문장으로 만들 때 that절의 주어를 수동태 문장의 주어 자리에 쓰고 that절의 동사를 to부정사로 바꾼다.
③ 목적어가 that절인 문장을 수동태 문장의 주어로 쓰는 경우 가주어 it을 쓰고 that절은 수동태 동사 뒤에 쓴다.

43 '~으로서 알려져 있다'는 의미의 be known as를 쓴다.

44 ② to us → for us
④ turned down → was turned down

45 (1) 과거시제의 수동태는 「was/were + p.p.(+ by + 행위자)」의 형태를 쓴다.
(2) 과거시제의 수동태는 「was/were + p.p.(+ by + 행위자)」의 형태를 쓰고 부정문은 be동사 뒤에 not을 쓴다.
(3) 수동태의 의문문은 「be동사 + 주어 + p.p. ~?」의 형태로 쓴다.

CHAPTER 5
부정사

p.112

POINT 1 to부정사의 형태와 용법

연습 문제	1 ⓐ	2 ⓒ	3 ⓑ	4 ⓐ
	5 ⓒ	6 ⓑ	7 ⓐ	8 ⓒ
	9 ⓑ			

POINT 2-1 명사적 용법: 주어와 보어로 쓰이는 to부정사

연습 문제	1 ⓐ	2 ⓒ	3 ⓑ	4 ⓐ
	5 ⓑ	6 ⓒ	7 ⓑ	8 ⓐ
	9 ⓒ	10 ⓒ	11 ⓐ	12 ⓑ
	13 ⓒ	14 ⓐ	15 ⓒ	

POINT 2-2 명사적 용법: 목적어로 쓰이는 to부정사

연습 문제 A	1 expect to learn	2 decided to sell
	3 chose to visit	4 aims to help
	5 agreed to meet	6 need to tell
	7 wants to visit	8 promise to return
	9 hopes to become	10 planned to have

연습 문제 B	1 managed to arrive	2 learned to swim
	3 wished to win	4 failed to pass
	5 refused to lend	6 chose to order

기출 적중문제

정답 ②
해설 ① reading → to read
③ building → build
④ reduce → to reduce
⑤ performing → perform

POINT 2-3 명사적 용법: 의문사 + to부정사

연습 문제	1 What to eat	2 when to go
	3 how to assemble	4 whom to call

기출 적중문제

정답 ②, ④
해설 ② 「what + to부정사」는 '무엇을 ~할지'라는 의미를 나타낸다.
④ 「의문사 + to부정사」는 「의문사 + 주어 + should + 동사원형」으로 바꿔 쓸 수 있다.

POINT 3-1 형용사적 용법: 명사·대명사 수식

연습 문제	1 room to paint	2 someone to talk to
	3 a pen to write with	4 the plan to take
	5 a house to live in	6 somewhere to visit

POINT 3-2 형용사적 용법: be동사 + to부정사

연습 문제	1 were to die	2 are to beat
	3 is to see	4 was to be found
	5 are to finish	6 are to stay
	7 is to take	

POINT 4 부사적 용법

연습 문제 A	1 to learn Spanish
	2 to eat some spicy food for dinner
	3 to see his grandchildren graduate from high school
	4 to think of such creative solutions
	5 to constantly argue with his friends
	6 to begin the soccer game
	7 to win the first prize in the competition

연습 문제 B	1 ⓒ	2 ⓓ	3 ⓐ	4 ⓒ
	5 ⓑ	6 ⓓ	7 ⓒ	8 ⓑ
	9 ⓐ			

기출 적중문제

정답 ④
해설 밑줄 친 부분과 ④: 판단의 근거
①②⑤: 목적
③: 형용사 수식

POINT 5 too ~ to, enough to

연습 문제	1 too tired to work
	2 so hot that it can burn
	3 so busy that she can't help

4 popular enough to win
5 so long that it can't fit
6 so strong that he could lift
7 ripe enough to be sold
8 too young to drive
9 fast enough to catch

2 what he should show Amy
3 so mild that it can be used on a baby's skin
4 so hungry that she couldn't continue working
5 loudly enough to wake me up in the morning
6 too lazy to answer her messages
7 how he should spend money wisely
8 in order to[so as to] make our family album

POINT 6 to부정사의 의미상의 주어

1	for	2	of	3	of	4	of
5	for	6	for	7	of	8	of
9	for	10	for				

1 hard for Kevin to see
2 foolish of them to dive
3 important for Sumi to take
4 impossible for him to get
5 rude of you to act
6 honest of you to inform
7 lucky for him to get
8 desirable for kids to talk
9 easy for children to understand
10 necessary (for people[us]) to follow
11 important (for people[us]) to vote

기출 적중문제

정답 ⑤
해설 · to부정사의 의미상의 주어는 「for + 목적격」의 형태로 to부정사 앞에 쓴다.
· 사람의 성격·태도를 나타내는 형용사와 쓰인 경우 의미상의 주어는 「of + 목적격」의 형태로 to부정사 앞에 쓴다.

서술형 대비 문제

(A)
1	O	2	what to do
3	important for me	4	O
5	a spoon to eat with	6	O
7	O	8	O
9	kind of you	10	takes

(B)
1	how to ride a bike	2	promised to come
3	a house to live in	4	are to provide
5	exercise to minimize	6	are to watch
7	where to sign your name		

(C)
1 nice of him to help his friend
2 dangerous for the boy to run
3 clever of the monkey to unlock

(D)
1 fast enough to set a world record

중간·기말고사 실전 문제

1 decided to feed the cat   2 ④   3 ①, ④
4 ①, ⑤   5 is important to prevent
6 in order to[so as to]   7 winning → to win
8 ③   9 where to go   10 ③   11 ④
12 large bodies to protect the nest   13 ④
14 to   15 ④, ⑤   16 ③   17 managed to reach the North Pole   18 ③   19 new mysteries to solve   20 ⓒ → to tell, ⓔ → of
21 It is easy (for people[us]) to become   22 ②
23 ③   24 apologizing → to apologize   25 write → write on   26 ①   27 ①, ② 28 ②
29 (1) ⓑ → to order (2) ⓒ → to touch   30 too small to be identified   31 ④   32 ⑤
33 ⑤   34 It was foolish of me to lend him money.
35 tall enough to reach   36 ④   37 went outside to watch

1 decide는 to부정사를 목적어로 쓰는 동사이므로 to feed를 쓴다.

2 · to부정사는 명사처럼 목적어를 보충 설명하는 목적격 보어로 쓰일 수 있다.
· to부정사는 명사처럼 목적어를 보충 설명하는 목적격 보어로 쓰일 수 있다.

3 ① 「too + 형용사/부사 + to부정사」는 '…하기에 너무 ~한/~하게'라는 뜻으로 쓰인다.
④ 「too + 형용사/부사 + to부정사」는 「so + 형용사/부사 + that + 주어 + can't + 동사원형」으로 바꿔 쓸 수 있다.

4 ① of → for
⑤ for → of

5 to부정사구가 주어 자리에 와서 주어가 길어진 경우, 주어 자리에 가주어 it을 쓰고 to부정사구를 문장 맨 뒤로 보낼 수 있다.

6 to부정사가 부사처럼 쓰일 때, 목적의 의미를 나타내는 경우 to부정사 대신 in order to나 so as to를 쓸 수 있다.

7 expect는 to부정사를 목적어로 쓰는 동사이므로 to win을 쓴다.

8 to부정사는 명사처럼 목적어를 보충 설명하는 목적격 보어로 쓰일 수 있다. to부정사의 부정형은 to 앞에 not을 붙인 「not to + 동사원형」의 형태로 not to use를 쓴다.

9 「의문사 + 주어 + should + 동사원형」은 「의문사 + to부정사」로 바꿔 쓸 수 있다.

10 (A): plan은 to부정사를 목적어로 쓰는 동사이므로 to start를 쓴다.
(B): '하지만, 무엇을 심을지 결정하지 못했다.'는 의미이므로 what to plant를 쓴다.
(C): want는 to부정사를 목적어로 쓰는 동사이므로 to get을 쓴다.

11 밑줄 친 ⓐ와 ④: 부사적 용법
①③⑤: 형용사적 용법   ②: 명사적 용법

12 to부정사는 형용사처럼 명사를 수식하는 데 쓰이며, '~할'의 의미이다.

13 ④: 명사적 용법
①②③⑤: 부사적 용법

14 「be동사 + to부정사」는 예정의 의미를 나타내는 데 쓰인다. 'We are to leave at noon.'이므로 세 번째에 오는 것은 to이다.

15 ④ 「how + to부정사」는 '어떻게 ~할지'라는 의미를 나타낸다.
⑤ 「의문사 + to부정사」는 「의문사 + 주어 + should + 동사원형」으로 바꿔 쓸 수 있다.

16 · '(안에) 살 집'이라는 표현으로 a house to live in이라고 쓴다.
· '(가지고) 놀 장난감'이라는 표현으로 a toy to play with라고 쓴다.

17 manage는 to부정사를 목적어로 쓰는 동사이므로 to reach를 쓴다.

18 ③의 빈칸: too
①②④⑤의 빈칸: to

19 to부정사는 형용사처럼 명사를 수식할 수 있고, '~할'의 의미이다.

20 (1) ⓒ: to부정사는 부사처럼 쓰여 목적의 의미를 나타낼 수 있으므로 to tell을 쓴다.
(2) ⓔ: 사람의 성격·태도를 나타내는 형용사 nice와 쓰인 경우 의미상의 주어를 「of + 목적격」의 형태로 to부정사 앞에 쓴다.

21 to부정사구가 주어 자리에 와서 주어가 길어진 경우, 주어 자리에 가주어 it을 쓰고 to부정사구를 문장 맨 뒤로 보낼 수 있다.

22 ② 사람의 성격·태도를 나타내는 형용사 wise와 쓰인 경우 의미상의 주어를 「of + 목적격」의 형태로 to부정사 앞에 쓴다.

23 ⓑⓒ: 형용사적 용법
ⓐⓔ: 명사적 용법   ⓓ: 부사적 용법

24 refuse는 to부정사를 목적어로 쓰는 동사이므로 to apologize를 쓴다.

25 '(위에) 쓸 종이'라는 표현으로 paper to write on이라고 쓴다.

26 ② me → for me
③ be → to be
④ too strongly → strongly
⑤ for → of

27 밑줄 친 부분과 ①②: 형용사적 용법
③④⑤: 명사적 용법

28 ② buying → to buy

29 (1) ⓑ: to부정사는 부사처럼 쓰여 목적의 의미를 나타내므로 to order를 쓴다.
(2) ⓒ: '…하기에 너무 ~한/~하게'라는 의미로 「too + 형용사/부사 + to부정사」를 쓴다.

30 '…하기에 너무 ~한/~하게'라는 의미로 「too + 형용사/부사 + to부정사」를 쓴다.

31 '…하기에 너무 ~한/~하게'라는 의미로 「too + 형용사/부사 + to부정사」를 쓴다. 'The swimming pool was too crowded to swim in.'이므로 다섯 번째에 오는 것은 ④ too이다.

32 ⑤ to부정사구가 주어 자리에 와서 주어가 길어진 경우, 주어 자리에 가주어 it을 쓰고 to부정사구를 문장 맨 뒤로 보낼 수 있다.

33 밑줄 친 부분과 ⑤: 부사적 용법
①③: 명사적 용법   ②④: 형용사적 용법

34 주어 자리에 가주어 it을 쓰고 to부정사구를 문장 맨 뒤로 보내서 쓴다. 사람의 성격·태도를 나타내는 형용사 foolish와 쓰인 경우 의미상의 주어를 「of + 목적격」의 형태로 to부정사 앞에 쓴다.

35 「so + 형용사/부사 + that + 주어 + can/could + 동사원형」은 「형용사/부사 + enough + to부정사」의 형태로 바꿔 쓸 수 있다.

36 · to부정사의 의미상의 주어는 「for + 목적격」의 형태로 to부정사 앞에 쓴다.
· 사람의 성격·태도를 나타내는 형용사 polite와 쓰인 경우 의미상의 주어를 「of + 목적격」의 형태로 to부정사 앞에 쓴다.

37 to부정사는 부사처럼 쓰여 목적의 의미를 나타내므로 to watch를 쓴다.

CHAPTER 6
동명사

p.134

POINT 1 동명사의 형태와 쓰임

1 not[never] wearing your shoes
2 Reading books is
3 going for lunch
4 Not[Never] getting enough sleep is
5 meeting new people
6 persuading his parents

POINT 2 동명사의 의미상의 주어

1 his cooking dinner for me
2 my mom's losing her bag at the store
3 Billy's winning a trophy at the science contest
4 Daniel's playing the piano well
5 a child's making a noise
6 his older sister's eating her food loudly
7 his son's failing his math exam
8 her friend's helping her study

POINT 3 동명사의 시제와 태

1	having waited	2	being chosen
3	being asked	4	having broken
5	wearing	6	talking
7	having been defeated		

POINT 4 동명사를 목적어로 쓰는 동사

1 quit drinking
2 suggested going
3 can't imagine performing
4 decided to give
5 will postpone meeting
6 hope to live

기출 적중문제

정답 (1) to visit → visiting (2) throw → throwing
해설 (1) 동사 recommend는 동명사를 목적어로 쓴다.
　　(2) 동사 enjoy는 동명사를 목적어로 쓴다.

POINT 5 동명사와 to부정사를 모두 목적어로 쓰는 동사

1	visiting / to vsit	2	opening
3	spending	4	growing / to grow
5	diving	6	singing / to sing

1	forgot to bring	2	remember putting
3	tried to fix	4	forget taking
5	regrets going	6	remembered to take
7	stopped playing		

기출 적중문제

정답 ⑤
해설 첫 번째 빈칸: '~할 것을 잊다'는 의미로 「forget + to부정사」를 쓴다.
　　두 번째 빈칸: '~할 것을 기억하다'는 의미로 「remember + to부정사」를 쓴다.

POINT 6 동명사 관용 표현

1 can't help eating
2 is afraid of speaking
3 looks forward to visiting
4 It is no use worrying
5 by pressing
6 has difficulty hearing
7 On arriving
8 when it comes to swimming

1	How about having	2	is busy watering
3	is tired of listening	4	is good at designing
5	went camping	6	is not used to riding

기출 적중문제

정답 ⑤
해설 interested at → interested in

서술형 대비 문제

1	is	2	O
3	O	4	Eating
5	is not having		
6	like being treated[like to be treated]		
7	O	8	at being invited
9	Writing songs is		

Ⓑ 1 enjoys going to the movies

2 begin taking[to take] yoga lessons
3 disliked eating garlic
4 tried listening to jazz music
5 forgot to charge my cell phone
6 continue studying[to study] French
7 postponed going to Hawaii

(C)
1 is good at solving math problems
2 goes fishing during weekends
3 Thank you for coming
4 is interested in joining the school's debate team
5 looks forward to meeting you
6 are busy decorating the wedding cake
7 is sorry for missing his birthday party
8 dreamed of traveling to Spain one day

(D)
ⓐ Playing[To play]   ⓑ is
ⓒ her   ⓓ having started
ⓔ On arriving   ⓕ forgot to bring
ⓖ considered asking   ⓗ sharing

중간·기말고사 실전 문제

1 ②   **2** ①, ⑤   **3** I admitted having asked Yeji   **4** ②   **5** ④   **6** ⑤
7 (1) ⓐ → preventing[to prevent] (2) ⓒ → means
(3) ⓔ → not limting   **8** ③   **9** how about going skiing next weekend?   **10** I'm not used to eating spicy food.   **11** ④   **12** ③   **13** using Minji's computer   **14** Nick tried not eating meat for a week.   **15** ③   **16** ⓐ watching ⓑ cooking ⓒ providing[to provide]   **17** to write → writing   **18** ③   **19** ⓐ to say ⓑ to ask   **20** ③   **21** ②   **22** ④
23 (1) ⓑ → walking (2) ⓓ → takes   **24** How about trying to take a break   **25** ⑤   **26** ④
27 denied knowing   **28** ⑤   **29** ②   **30** regret to tell   **31** (1) ⓐ → watching (2) ⓒ → being
32 ②   **33** ⑤   **34** ②   **35** ④   **36** ⑤
37 ⑤   **38** ④   **39** (A) working (B) picking (C) shopping (D) asking   **40** I suggest your going to Keller's Bakery   **41** ④   **42** (1) ⓑ → saying (2) ⓒ → trying (3) ⓔ → not changing
43 ④   **44** ④   **45** On arriving home
46 am not used to living   **47** worth reading

1 · 동명사는 문장 안에서 보어로 쓰일 수 있다.
· 동명사가 쓰인 주어는 항상 단수 취급한다.

2 ① Listen → Listening

---

⑤ make → makes

3 admit은 동명사를 목적어로 쓴다. 동명사의 시제가 문장의 시제보다 이전인 경우 완료형인 「having + p.p.」를 쓴다.

4 avoid는 동명사를 목적어로 쓴다. 동명사의 의미가 수동이므로 수동형인 「being + p.p」를 쓴다

5 (A) 동사 resist는 동명사를 목적어로 쓴다.
(B) 동사 continue는 동명사와 to부정사를 모두 목적어로 쓴다.
(C) '~할 것을 잊다'는 의미로 「forget + to부정사」를 쓴다.

6 ⑤ regret to try → regret trying

7 (1) 동명사와 to부정사는 문장 안에서 보어로 쓰일 수 있다.
(2) 동명사가 쓰인 주어는 항상 단수 취급한다.
(3) 동명사는 문장 안에서 주어로 쓰일 수 있다.

8 ③ '~하는 것을 멈추다'는 의미로 「stop + V-ing」를 쓴다.

9 '~하는 게 어때?'의 의미로 「how about + V-ing」를 쓴다. '~하러 가다'의 의미로 「go + V-ing」를 쓴다.

10 '~하는 것에 익숙하다'는 의미로 「be used to + V-ing」를 쓴다.

11 ④ she winning → her winning

12 ③ to brush → brushing

13 동사 deny는 동명사를 목적어로 쓴다.

14 '(시험 삼아) ~해보다'라는 의미로 「try + V-ing」를 쓴다. 동명사의 부정형은 동명사 앞에 not[never]을 쓴다.

15 (A) 동사 intend는 동명사와 to부정사를 모두 목적어로 쓴다.
(B) '~하는 것을 멈추다'는 의미로 「stop + V-ing」를 쓴다.
(C) 동사 finish는 동명사를 목적어로 쓴다.

16 ⓐ 동사 enjoy는 동명사를 목적어로 쓴다.
ⓑ 동사 practice는 동명사를 목적어로 쓴다.
ⓒ 동사 begin은 동명사와 to부정사를 모두 목적어로 쓴다.

17 동사 postpone은 동명사를 목적어로 쓴다.

18 ⓐ to leave → leaving
ⓒ arriving → to arrive

19 ⓐ '~할 것을 잊다'는 의미로 「forget + to부정사」를 쓴다.
ⓑ '~할 것을 기억하다'는 의미로 「remember + to부정사」를 쓴다.

20 ③ edit → editing

21 ② help fall → help falling

22 ④ 동명사의 시제가 문장의 시제보다 이전인 경우 「having + p.p.」를 쓴다.

23 (1) '~하는 데 시간을 쓰다'는 의미로 「spend + 시간 + V-ing」를 쓴다.
(2) 동명사가 쓰인 주어는 항상 단수 취급한다.

24 '~하는 게 어때?'의 의미로 「How about + V-ing?」를 쓴다.
'~하려고 노력하다'는 의미로 「try + to부정사」를 쓴다.

25 ⑤ to recycle → recycling

26 ① to practicing → practicing[to practice]
    ② going → to going
    ③ to play → playing
    ⑤ to tell → telling

27 동사 deny는 동명사를 목적어로 쓴다.

28 · 동사 imagine은 동명사를 목적어로 쓴다.
    · '~하느라 바쁘다'는 의미로 「be busy + V-ing」를 쓴다.

29 ⓑ to go → going
    ⓒ sing → singing
    ⓓ to win → winning

30 '~하게 되어 유감이다'는 의미로 「regret + to부정사」를 쓴다.

31 (1) '~하는 것을 기대하다'는 의미로 「look forward to + V-ing」를 쓴다.
    (2) '~한 것을 기억하다'는 의미로 「remember + V-ing」를 쓴다.

32 ② she → her

33 ⑤ '~하는 것을 무서워하다'는 의미로 「be afraid of + V-ing」를 쓴다. 동명사의 의미가 수동이면 수동형인 「being + p.p」를 쓴다

34 ⓑ make → makes
    ⓒ see → seeing
    ⓔ cost → costs

35 ④ '문을 열자마자, 그녀는 누군가가 그녀의 집에 침입했었다는 것을 깨달았다.'는 의미로, '~하자마자'는 뜻을 가진 「on + V-ing」를 쓴다.

36 ⑤ '~한 것을 기억하다'는 의미로 「remember + V-ing」를 쓴다.

37 ⑤ to have → having

38 ④ '~하는 데 시간을 쓰다'는 의미로 「spend + 시간 + V-ing」를 쓴다.

39 (A) '~하느라 바쁘다'는 의미로 「be busy + V-ing」를 쓴다.
    (B) 동사 mind는 동명사를 목적어로 쓴다.
    (C) 동사 dislike는 동명사를 목적어로 쓴다.
    (D) '~하는 것에 대해 유감이다'는 의미로 「sorry for + V-ing」를 쓴다.

40 동사 suggest는 동명사를 목적어로 쓴다. 보통 동명사 앞에 「소유격 + V-ing」 형태로 의미상의 주어를 나타낸다.

41 ④ to eat → eating

42 (1) 동사 suggest는 동명사를 목적어로 쓴다.
    (2) 동사 quit는 동명사를 목적어로 쓴다.
    (3) '~한 것을 후회하다'는 의미로 「regret + V-ing」를 쓴다.

43 ④ '~할 것을 잊다'는 의미로 「forget + to부정사」를 쓴다.

44 ④ to spend → spending

45 '~하자마자'는 의미로 「on + V-ing」를 쓴다.

46 '~하는 것에 익숙하다'는 의미로 「be used to + V-ing」를 쓴다. 동명사의 부정형은 동명사 앞에 not[never]을 쓴다.

47 '~할 가치가 있다'는 의미로 「worth + V-ing」를 쓴다.

CHAPTER 7
분사

p.156

POINT 1 분사의 형태와 쓰임

1 ⓐ, daughter		**2** ⓑ, I	
3 ⓐ, The pineapple		**4** ⓑ, her house	
5 ⓑ, a bear			
6 ⓑ, The new action movie			
7 ⓐ, the gift		**8** ⓑ, someone	
9 ⓐ, a novel		**10** ⓑ, My dad	
11 ⓐ, a few children		**12** ⓐ, student	

POINT 2 현재분사 vs. 과거분사

1 cooked		**2** skiing	
3 amazing		**4** embarrassing	
5 watered		**6** broken	
7 satisfying		**8** caught	
9 ticking		**10** waiting	
11 sleeping		**12** shouting	
13 damaged		**14** carved	

1 surprising news		**2** frozen lake
3 man waving at us		**4** folded paper
5 people waiting in line		

1 screaming boy
2 sketches painted by Michelangelo
3 guy standing next to the door
4 flying airplanes
5 The novel published last month

기출 적중문제

정답 ②
해설 ① 명사 This house와 수동의 관계이므로 과거분사 built
　　 를 쓴다.
　　 ③ '그들은 3년 전에 나무로 된 오두막을 지었다.'는 의미이므
　　 로 build의 과거동사 built를 쓴다.
　　 ④ 명사 The nest와 수동의 관계이므로 과거분사 built를
　　 쓴다.
　　 ⑤ 명사 many churches와 수동의 관계이므로 과거분사
　　 built를 쓴다.

POINT 3 감정을 나타내는 분사

1 ① relaxing	② relaxed		
2 ① embarrassed	② embarrassing		
3 ① exciting	② excited		
4 ① disappointed	② disappointing		

1 confused	**2** shocking	**3** exhausted	
4 impressed	**5** satisfying		

기출 적중문제

정답 (1) ⓒ → moving (2) ⓓ → fascinated
해설 (1) ⓒ speech가 감정을 일으키는 주체이므로 현재분사
　　 moving을 쓴다.
　　 (2) ⓓ The audience가 감정을 느끼는 대상이므로 과거분
　　 사 fascinated를 쓴다.

POINT 4 현재분사 vs. 동명사

1 ⓐ	**2** ⓑ	**3** ⓐ	**4** ⓐ
5 ⓑ	**6** ⓐ	**7** ⓑ	**8** ⓑ
9 ⓑ			

POINT 5-1 분사구문 만드는 법

1 Listening to the music
2 Not[Never] forgetting her birthday
3 (Being) Injured in training last week
4 Boarding the train
5 Living in France
6 (Being) Put in prison
7 My older sister cooking dinner

1 Looking		**2** Causing
3 Not[Never] having		**4** (Being) Created
5 Leaving		**6** Chris coming back

기출 적중문제

정답 ③
해설 ③ Satisfying → Satisfied

POINT 5-2 분사구문의 다양한 의미

1 Arriving at the café
2 breaking his arm
3 (Being) Confused by the question
4 Listening to the storyteller

5 (Being) Given the prize

6 Having enough money

7 Digging up the site

8 Not[Never] worrying about the score

연습
문제
B

1 When he left Korea

2 and they stopped traffic for several hours

3 If you study hard

4 Because he is exhausted from work

기출 적중문제

정답 Drinking milk

해설 '~하면서'의 의미의 접속사 while/as와 주어 Brad를 생략
하고 동사 drink를 Drinking으로 바꾼다.

POINT 5-3 분사구문의 시제와 태

연습
문제
A

1 Having taken Spanish in high school

2 Waiting for my mother

3 (Having been) Offered the chance

4 Not[Never] having any free time

5 Having finished his painting

6 Having gotten lost

7 Not[Never] having seen her

8 Studying by myself

연습
문제
B

1 (Being) Treated like a child

2 Having fallen down

3 (Being) Covered with butter

4 (Having been) Stored in the refrigerator

5 Staying in London

6 (Being) Known to everyone

7 Having stood in line

8 Turning right

기출 적중문제

정답 ⑤

해설 ⑤ Surprising → (Being) Surprised

POINT 6 with + 명사 + 분사

연습
문제

1 with his hand raised

2 with my head covered

3 with his coach cheering

4 with his computer turned on

5 with her leg bandaged

6 with my dog following

7 with the windows closed

8 with her arms swinging

9 with the crowd watching

10 with her hair tied back

POINT 7 분사구문 관용 표현

연습
문제

1 Frankly speaking   2 Generally speaking

3 Speaking of   4 Judging from

5 Considering   6 Strictly speaking

7 Frankly speaking   8 Judging from

서술형 대비 문제

(A)

1 sliced cheese   2 team planning

3 stolen sculptures   4 students playing

5 shivering girl   6 meal cooked

7 man standing   8 broken glass

(B) ⓐ excited   ⓑ found

ⓒ amazing   ⓓ Reassembling

ⓔ discovered   ⓕ growing

ⓖ Researching   ⓗ fascinated

ⓘ dwelling

(C)

1 I studied for an exam with my little sister
   sitting beside me.

2 Judging from her reaction, she liked the gift.

3 The boy sat on the floor with his legs bent.

4 Speaking of music, we should go to a
   concert.

(D)

1 Climbing up the mountain

2 (Being) Proven innocent

3 Hoping to get there before the train
   departed

4 Having finished our work

5 (Being) Praised by the teacher

6 Cleaning his room

7 Mixing yellow paint and blue paint

중간·기말고사 실전 문제

1 ⑤   2 ④   3 ③   4 ④

5 (A) a cabin owned by his grandfather (B) the
animals hiding in the forest   6 ⑤   7 ②

8 ⓐ protected ⓑ interested ⓒ used   9 ③

10 boiling water   11 A man riding a bike

12 ④   13 The girl sitting at the table   14 ④

15 (A) frightening experience (B) Two men wearing masks (C) With his face exposed **16** ⑤
17 ④ **18** ⑤ **19** ⑤ **20** ③ **21** ⓐ the girl sitting over there ⓑ her face covered ⓒ lost dog
22 amazing / impressed **23** Opening my mouth to sing the song **24** (After) Having quit my piano lessons **25** satisfying → satisfied **26** ⑤ **27** with her baby hanging on her back **28** ②, ④
29 Knowing how to solve the math problem, he got the correct answer. **30** When she had finished the painting, she put it in a gold frame. **31** with his eyes closed **32** The concert being over
33 ④ **34** (A) known (B) produced (C) pleased
35 Living in Vienna in the late 1700s **36** ②
37 As she approached[was approaching] the reception desk **38** If you look up **39** ②
40 ②, ⑤ **41** ② **42** with his shoe laces untied
43 ⓐ seen ⓑ fascinating ⓒ researching
44 Frankly speaking, I think many car accidents can be avoided. **45** making the car much safer
46 ② **47** ③ **48** ① **49** My bike being stolen, I had no way to get there.

1　① breaking → broken
　② stealing → stolen
　③ sat → sitting
　④ creating → created

2　① ⓐ waited → waiting
　② ⓑ Played → Playing
　③ ⓒ surprise → surprised
　⑤ ⓔ treated → treating

3　③ writing → written

4　(A) 명사 stars와 능동의 관계이므로 현재분사 shining을 쓴다.
　(B) 명사 the man과 능동의 관계이므로 현재분사 standing을 쓴다.
　(C) 명사 the money와 수동의 관계이므로 과거분사 raised를 쓴다.

5　(A) 명사 a cabin과 수동의 관계이므로 과거분사 owned를 쓴다.
　(B) 명사 the animals와 능동의 관계이므로 현재분사 hiding을 쓴다.

6　'나는 이탈리아 음식을 제공하는 식당을 찾고 있다.'는 의미로 명사 a restaurant와 능동의 관계이므로 현재분사인 serving을 쓴다.

7　②: 동명사
　①③④⑤: 현재분사

8　ⓐ 목적어 the environment를 보충 설명하고 목적어와 수동의 관계이므로 과거분사 protected를 쓴다.

ⓑ People이 감정을 느끼는 대상이므로 과거분사 interested를 쓴다.
ⓒ 명사 products와 수동의 관계이므로 과거분사 used를 쓴다.

9　ⓐ designing → designed
　ⓒ embarrassing → embarrassed
　ⓓ cheated → cheating

10　명사 water와 능동의 관계이므로 현재분사 boiling을 쓴다.

11　명사 a man과 능동의 관계이므로 현재분사 riding을 쓴다.

12　(A) 'Michael의 연설은 매우 충격을 줬다.'는 의미로 speech가 감정을 일으키는 주체이므로 현재분사 shocking을 쓴다.
　(B) '나는 만화책을 보고 즐거웠다.'는 의미로 I가 감정을 느끼는 대상이므로 과거분사 amused를 쓴다.
　(C) '나는 지난 몇 주 동안 우울함을 느껴왔다.'는 의미로 I가 감정을 느끼는 대상이므로 과거분사 depressed를 쓴다.

13　명사 The girl과 능동의 관계이므로 현재분사 sitting을 쓴다.

14　④ Missed → Missing

15　(A) experience가 감정을 일으키는 주체이므로 현재분사 frightening을 쓴다.
　(B) 명사 Two men과 능동의 관계이므로 현재분사 wearing을 쓴다.
　(C) '~가 -한 채로/하면서'는 「with + 명사 + 분사」의 형태로 쓴다. 명사 his face와 수동의 관계이므로 과거분사 exposed를 쓴다.

16　⑤ '그가 보안 카메라를 설치했기 때문에'의 의미이므로 이유를 나타내는 접속사 Because를 쓴다. 분사구문을 접속사가 있는 문장으로 바꿀 때, 분사구문의 시제가 주절의 시제보다 이전이므로 과거완료시제로 쓴다.

17　④ Trapping → (Being) Trapped

18　⑤: 동명사
　밑줄 친 부분과 ①②③④: 현재분사

19　① exciting → excited
　② disappointing → disappointed
　③ confused → confusing
　④ boring → bored

20　③ Being taken → Having taken

21　ⓐ 명사 the girl과 능동의 관계이므로 현재분사 sitting을 쓴다.
　ⓑ 명사 her face와 수동의 관계이므로 과거분사 covered를 쓴다.
　ⓒ 명사 dog와 수동의 관계이므로 과거분사 lost를 쓴다.

22　첫 번째 빈칸: '선수들은 마지막 순간에 놀라운 승리를 거두었다.'는 의미로 명사 win과 능동의 관계이므로 현재분사 amazing을 쓴다.
　두 번째 빈칸: I가 감정을 느끼는 대상이므로 과거분사 impressed를 쓴다.

23　접속사 As와 주어 I를 생략하고 동사 opened를 Opening으로 바꾼다.

24 접속사 After와 주어 I를 생략하고 분사구문의 시제가 주절의 시제보다 이전이므로 동사 had quit을 Having quit으로 바꾼다. 이때, 분사구문의 의미를 분명하게 하기 위해 부사절 접속사 After를 생략하지 않을 수 있다.

25 Patients가 감정을 느끼는 대상이므로 과거분사 satisfied를 쓴다.

26 첫 번째 빈칸: 주절의 주어 it(Greek restaurant)과 분사구문의 관계가 능동이므로 Using을 쓴다.
두 번째 빈칸: 명사 the restaurant와 능동의 관계이므로 현재분사 earning을 쓴다.

27 '~가 −한 채로/하면서'는 「with + 명사 + 분사」의 형태로 쓴다. 명사 her baby와 능동의 관계이므로 현재분사 hanging을 쓴다.

28 ② 이유를 나타내는 분사구문이므로 접속사 As를 쓸 수 있다. 분사구문의 시제와 주절의 시제가 같으므로 현재시제로 쓴다.
④ 이유를 나타내는 분사구문이므로 접속사 Because를 쓸 수 있다. 분사구문의 시제와 주절의 시제가 같으므로 현재시제로 쓴다.

29 접속사 Since와 주어 he를 생략하고 동사 knew를 Knowing으로 바꾼다.

30 분사구문을 접속사가 있는 문장으로 바꿀 때, 분사구문의 시제가 주절의 시제보다 이전이므로 과거완료시제로 쓴다. 생략된 주어인 she를 이용해서 완전한 문장으로 쓴다.

31 '~가 −한 채로/하면서'는 「with + 명사 + 분사」의 형태로 쓴다. 명사 his eyes와 수동의 관계이므로 과거분사 closed를 쓴다.

32 부사절의 주어와 주절의 주어가 다르기 때문에 부사절의 주어를 생략하지 않고 분사구문 맨 앞에 쓴다.

33 ⓐ barked → barking
ⓓ won → winning
ⓕ moved → moving

34 (A) 주절의 주어 베토벤과 분사구문의 관계가 수동이므로 known을 쓴다.
(B) 명사 some songs와 수동의 관계이므로 과거분사 produced를 쓴다.
(C) 베토벤이 감정을 느끼는 대상이므로 과거분사 pleased를 쓴다.

35 분사구문의 시제와 주절의 시제가 같으므로 동사 live를 Living으로 바꾸고, 부사절의 주어와 주절의 주어가 같으므로 부사절의 주어를 생략해서 쓴다.

36 ② 분사구문의 시제가 주절의 시제보다 이전이므로 동사 had been given을 Having been given으로 바꾼다.

37 분사구문의 시제와 주절의 시제가 같으므로 과거시제나, 과거진행시제를 쓴다. 생략된 주어인 she를 이용해서 쓰고, '~하면서'의 의미이므로 접속사 As를 쓴다.

38 분사구문의 시제와 주절의 시제가 같으므로 현재시제를 쓴다. 생략된 주어인 you를 이용해서 쓰고, '~라면'의 조건의 의미이므로 접속사 If를 쓴다.

39 ① ⓐ sell → selling
③ ⓒ displaying → displayed
④ ⓓ amaze → amazing
⑤ ⓔ Thought → Thinking

40 ② '그것을 읽고 난 후, 나는 정말 배고파졌다.'는 의미의 분사구문이므로 Reading을 쓴다.
⑤ '~한 후에'라는 의미의 접속사 After와 주어 I를 쓰고, 과거 동사 read를 쓴다.

41 ② 접속사 As와 주어 I를 생략하고 분사구문의 시제가 주절의 시제보다 이전이므로 동사 had arrived를 Having arrived로 바꾼다.

42 '~가 −한 채로/하면서'는 「with + 명사 + 분사」의 형태로 쓴다. 명사 his shoe laces와 수동의 관계이므로 과거분사 untied를 쓴다.

43 ⓐ 명사 a program과 수동의 관계이므로 과거분사 seen을 쓴다.
ⓑ Your system이 감정을 일으키는 주체이므로 fascinating을 쓴다.
ⓒ be동사(been)와 함께 진행시제를 만드는 현재분사 researching을 쓴다.

44 분사구문 관용 표현으로 '솔직히 말하면'은 Frankly speaking을 쓴다.

45 '자동차를 훨씬 더 안전하게 만들면서'의 의미인 분사구문이므로 주어 I를 생략하고 동사 make를 making으로 바꾼다.

46 목적어 the door를 보충 설명하고 목적어와 수동의 관계이므로 과거분사 unlocked를 쓴다.

47 ③ '~가 −한 채로/하면서'는 「with + 명사 + 분사」의 형태로 쓴다. 명사 her legs와 수동의 관계이므로 과거분사 crossed를 쓴다.

48 (A) '시계를 가지고 있지 않았기 때문에, Jacob은 시험 시간이 얼마나 남았는지 불확실했다.'는 의미의 분사구문이므로 Having을 쓴다.
(B) 명사 the clock과 수동의 관계이므로 과거분사 located를 쓴다.
(C) 주절의 주어 he가 감정을 느끼는 대상이므로 과거분사 exhausted를 쓴다.

49 접속사 Because를 생략하고 동사 was stolen을 being stolen으로 바꾼다. 부사절의 주어와 주절의 주어가 다르기 때문에 부사절의 주어를 생략하지 않고 분사구문 맨 앞에 쓴다.

CHAPTER 8
명사와 대명사

p.184

POINT 1 셀 수 있는 명사

1 orange	**2** get	**3** chairs
4 were	**5** families	**6** snakes
7 were	**8** teams	**9** Lions
10 are		

1 boxes	**2** photos	**3** shoes
4 babies	**5** Tomatoes	**6** oxen
7 teeth	**8** year	**9** wolves
10 roofs	**11** dishes	**12** women

기출 적중문제

정답 ①, ②
해설 ③ sheeps → sheep
④ deers → deer
⑤ mouses → mice

POINT 2 셀 수 없는 명사

1 ②	**2** ③	**3** ②	**4** ①
5 ②	**6** ①	**7** ③	

1 cup	**2** bowl	**3** slices
4 glasses	**5** cans	**6** loaves
7 spoonfuls	**8** piece	**9** bottle
10 pieces	**11** bar	**12** slices
13 sheet	**14** can	

기출 적중문제

정답 a bowl of salad, two loaves of bread
해설 셀 수 없는 명사의 수량을 표현할 때 '그릇'의 의미는 bowl로, '빵 두 덩어리'의 의미는 two loaves of bread를 쓴다.

POINT 3 명사의 소유격

1 children's room
2 Tom's family
3 patients' chart
4 people's pictures
5 grandparents' house
6 men's bathroom
7 the title of the movie

---

8 the lobby of the building
9 two hours' work
10 those pants of his
11 a dog's tail
12 the legs of the desk
13 the computer of Jack's

1 O	**2** O
3 that shirt of yours[your shirt]	
4 O	
5 a relative of hers[her relative]	
6 O	**7** Mr. Smith's house
8 O	
9 this cell phone of my mom's[my mom's cell phone]	
10 ten miles' distance	**11** O
12 O	
13 this story of yours[your story]	
14 These songs of John's[John's songs]	

기출 적중문제

정답 the desk of yours
해설 명사 앞에 관사가 쓰였을 때는 소유격을 명사 뒤에 「of + 소유대명사」의 형태로 나타낸다.

POINT 4 재귀대명사

1 myself	**2** us	**3** herself
4 ourselves	**5** me	**6** him
7 themselves		

1 X	**2** O	**3** O	**4** O
5 X			

연습문제 C

1 helped himself
2 make yourself[yourselves] at home
3 between ourselves
4 in itself

기출 적중문제

정답 ④
해설 밑줄 친 재귀대명사와 ④: 재귀 용법
①②③⑤: 강조 용법

POINT 5-1 it의 다양한 쓰임 I

1 ⓑ	**2** ⓒ	**3** ⓐ	**4** ⓓ
5 ⓒ	**6** ⓐ	**7** ⓒ	**8** ⓑ
9 ⓐ	**10** ⓓ		

POINT 5-2 it의 다양한 쓰임 Ⅱ

1 seem to be
2 seemed to be
3 seems that the computer monitor is
4 seemed to be
5 seems to be working
6 seems to know
7 seems that the weather is getting
8 seemed not to have[didn't seem to have]
9 seems to be based
10 seemed not to be affected[didn't seem to be affected]

POINT 6-1 부정대명사: one

A
1 one   2 them   3 O
4 O   5 ones   6 one

B
1 them   2 one   3 it
4 ones   5 ones   6 One

POINT 6-2 부정대명사: some, any

1 Some   2 something   3 anyone
4 Some   5 anyone   6 someone
7 any   8 anything

POINT 6-3 부정대명사: another, other

A
1 others   2 others   3 another
4 others   5 another 6 other

B
1 One / another / the others
2 One / the other   3 One / the others
4 some / the others

기출 적중문제

정답 (1) Others (2) another
해설 (1) '다른 학생들은 동의하지 않는다.'는 의미로 Others를 쓴다.
     (2) '만약 네가 저 한 잔의 물을 마시고도 여전히 목이 마르다면, 너는 하나 더 마실 수 있다.'는 의미이므로 another를 쓴다.

POINT 6-4 부정대명사: all, each, every

A
1 plant   2 was   3 Each
4 teacher   5 All

B
1 seats / are   2 living things / need
3 wants   4 person / has

POINT 6-5 부정대명사: both, either, neither

1 neither / fits[fit]   2 both / paintings
3 Either / helps[help] 4 Either / is
5 neither / is[are]   6 Both teachers
7 Neither / was   8 both students

서술형 대비 문제

(A)
1 mice   2 spoonfuls
3 ourselves   4 loaves
5 O   6 shelves
7 O   8 at home
9 O

(B)
1 It was dark at the campsite
2 You seem not to understand
3 It is difficult to find a soccer player
4 It seemed that they were looking
5 Some people believed it impossible
6 It is unusual that
7 It seems that she had
8 The noise made it difficult

(C)
ⓐ any   ⓑ some
ⓒ One   ⓓ another
ⓔ the other

(D)
1 Each of the rooms has
2 All (of) the products have
3 Both (of) my little brothers like
4 Either of the books is[are]
5 All (of) the money is
6 Neither of the countries wants[want]
7 All (of) the kids are
8 Each of the machines has
9 Every student needs
10 Neither of the men knows[know]

1 ③ **2** ③ **3** two bowls of cereal / three bars of chocolate **4** ③ **5** (1) neither of them (2) Either of them **6** My father told our guests to make themselves at home **7** ②
8 ⑤ **9** one **10** ⑤ **11** (1) ⓐ It ⓑ one (2) ⓒ ones **12** ③ **13** ③ **14** ②
15 ③ **16** a dream of his **17** the top floor of the building **18** talks to herself when she feels a lot of stress **19** seems that / is frozen
20 ⑤ **21** ③ **22** it impossible that a large earthquake will happen soon **23** other → the other
24 neither of them has[have] cucumber **25** ④
26 (1) ⓐ → seems to like (2) ⓒ → seems to think
27 ④ **28** Neither of the documentary films is about the Amazon River. **29** ③ **30** ③, ④
31 some / the others **32** ⓐ anything ⓑ either **33** ④ **34** ④ **35** seems not to be studying[doesn't seem to be studying] **36** ③
37 ②, ⑤ **38** ② **39** ⓑ → All of them look
40 All the passengers / seem to try **41** some / others **42** ⓐ One ⓑ the other

1 ③ is → are

2 (A) 「숫자 + 하이픈(-) + 단위표현」이 형용사처럼 쓰여 명사 앞에서 명사를 꾸밀 때는 숫자 뒤의 단위 표현을 단수형으로 쓴다.
(B) goose의 복수형은 geese로 쓴다.
(C) story의 복수형은 stories로 쓴다.

3 셀 수 없는 명사의 수량 표현을 할 때 '그릇'의 의미는 bowl로, '바'의 의미는 bar를 쓴다.

4 ⓒ slices → slice
ⓔ photoes → photos

5 (1) '둘 중 어느 것도'라는 의미로 「neither of + 복수명사」를 쓴다.
(2) '둘 중 어느 것이든'이라는 의미로 「either of + 복수명사」를 쓴다.

6 '(집에서처럼) 편히 쉬다'는 의미로 make oneself at home을 쓴다.

7 · '한 조각의 치즈'라는 의미로 piece를 쓴다.
· '한 점의 가구'라는 의미로 piece를 쓴다.
· '한 건의 뉴스'라는 의미로 piece를 쓴다.

8 ⑤ it → one

9 · 앞에서 언급된 명사인 job과 같은 종류지만 다른 대상이므로 one을 쓴다.
· 일반적인 사람을 나타내는 말로 one을 쓴다.

10 ⑤ 재귀대명사의 강조 용법이므로 생략할 수 있다.

11 (1) ⓐ 앞에서 언급된 특정한 대상(new apartment)을 가리키고 있으므로 it을 쓴다.
ⓑ 앞에서 언급된 명사(apartment)와 같은 종류의 불특정한 대상을 가리키고 있으므로 부정대명사 one을 쓴다.
(2) ⓒ 앞에서 언급된 복수명사(flowers)와 같은 종류의 불특정한 대상을 가리키고 있으므로 부정대명사 ones를 쓴다.

12 ⓐ '몇몇은'이라는 의미로 Some을 쓴다.
ⓑ '다른 사람들'이라는 의미로 others를 쓴다.
ⓒ 명사 mottos를 가리키는 them을 쓴다.
ⓓ 앞에서 언급된 명사(motto)와 같은 종류의 불특정한 대상을 가리키고 있으므로 부정대명사 one을 쓴다.
따라서 ③ other는 어느 빈칸에도 들어갈 수 없다.

13 ③ in myself → by myself

14 ⓐⓒⓔ: 비인칭 주어 it
ⓑ 가주어 it ⓓ 가목적어 it

15 밑줄 친 부분과 ③: 비인칭 주어 it
①⑤ 가주어 it ②④ 가목적어 it

16 명사(dream) 앞에 관사(a)가 쓰였으므로, 「of + 소유대명사」로 나타낼 수 있다.

17 무생물을 나타내는 명사의 소유격은 「of + 명사」로 나타낼 수 있다.

18 '혼잣말을 하다'는 의미로 talk to oneself를 쓴다.

19 「It seems that ~」은 that절의 주어를 문장의 주어 자리에 쓰고 that절의 동사를 to부정사로 바꿔 쓸 수 있다.

20 ⑤ was → were

21 (A) 주어인 the bus가 단수형이고 문장이 현재시제이므로 is를 쓴다.
(B) 「It seems that ~」은 that절의 주어를 문장의 주어 자리에 쓰고 that절의 동사를 to부정사로 바꿔 쓸 수 있다.
(C) 주어인 the kittens가 복수형이고 문장이 과거시제이므로 were를 쓴다.

22 문장의 목적어가 긴 경우 목적어 자리에 가목적어 it을 쓰고 진목적어인 that절을 뒤로 보내서 쓴다.

23 '나머지 하나'라는 의미로 other를 the other로 고친다.

24 '둘 중 어느 것도'라는 의미로 「neither of + 복수명사」를 쓴다.

25 ④ The mufflers seemed to be hers. → The mufflers seemed not to be hers.[The mufflers didn't seem to be hers.]

26 (1) ⓐ 「It seems that ~」은 that절의 주어를 문장의 주어 자리에 쓰고 that절의 동사를 to부정사로 바꿔 쓸 수 있다.
(2) ⓒ 주어가 3인칭(she)이므로 seems로 쓴다.

27 ① other → another / the others / others
② another → the others
③ other → the other / another

⑤ others → the others

28 '둘 중 어느 것도'라는 의미로 「neither of + 복수명사」를 쓴다.

29 (A) '혼자서'라는 의미로 by oneself를 쓴다.
(B) 명사(My cousins and I)를 강조하기 위해 강조 용범의 재귀대명사를 쓰고, 나(I)를 포함한 we의 재귀대명사로 ourselves를 쓴다.
(C) 문장의 주어와 목적어가 같을 때 목적어 자리에 재귀대명사를 쓴다.

30 ③ everything → anything
④ students were → student was

31 첫 번째 빈칸: '작품 몇몇'이라는 의미로 some을 쓴다.
두 번째 빈칸: '나머지 작품들 전부'라는 의미로 the others를 쓴다.

32 ⓐ '어떤 것'이라는 의미로 부정문과 의문문에서 anything을 쓴다.
ⓑ '둘 중 어느 것이든'이라는 의미로 「either of + 복수명사」를 쓴다.

33 (A) '나머지 하나'라는 의미로 the other를 쓴다.
(B) '(셋 중) 다른 하나'라는 의미로 Another를 쓴다.
(C) '(셋 중) 나머지 하나'라는 의미로 The other를 쓴다.

34 ⓐ themselves → them
ⓓ himself → him

35 「It seems that ~」은 that절의 주어를 문장의 주어 자리에 쓰고 that절의 동사를 to부정사로 바꿔 쓸 수 있다. 부정형은 not을 to부정사 앞에 쓰거나, do 동사의 부정형을 seem 앞에 쓴다.

36 밑줄 친 부분과 ③: 일반적인 사람
①②④⑤ 앞에서 언급된 명사와 같은 종류이지만 다른 대상을 가리킨다.

37 ② '~인 것 같다'는 의미인 「It seems that ~」을 쓸 수 있다.
⑤ 「It seems that ~」은 that절의 주어를 문장의 주어 자리에 쓰고 that절의 동사를 to부정사로 바꿔 쓸 수 있다.

38 ① work → works
③ people were → person was
④ friend → friends
⑤ has → have

39 ⓑ 「all (of) + 복수명사 + 복수동사」이므로 복수동사를 쓴다.

40 「It seems that ~」은 that절의 주어를 문장의 주어 자리에 쓰고 that절의 동사를 to부정사로 바꿔 쓸 수 있다.

41 첫 번째 빈칸: '몇몇 동물들에게 북극은 너무 춥다'는 의미이므로 some을 쓴다.
두 번째 빈칸: '북극여우와 같은 다른 동물들은 그곳에서 쉽게 살아남을 수 있다.'는 의미이므로 others를 쓴다.

42 ⓐ '(둘 중) 하나의 눈은 파란색이고'라는 의미이므로 One을 쓴다.
ⓑ '나머지 하나의 눈은 초록색이다.'라는 의미이므로 the other를 쓴다.

CHAPTER 9
형용사와 부사

p.212

POINT 1 형용사의 용법

연습문제 A
1 popular brand　　2 anything special
3 challenging puzzles　4 someone fun
5 somewhere relaxing　6 physical health
7 anybody strange

연습문제 B
1 were useful　　　2 made me excited
3 someone tall　　　4 looks soft
5 delicious things　　6 keep you safe

연습문제 C
1 alike　　　2 sleepy　　　3 alive
4 scared　　5 lonely

기출 적중문제

정답 ①

해설 첫 번째 빈칸: '신문에는 흥미 있는 어떤 것도 없다.'라는 의미로 -thing으로 끝나는 대명사(anything)는 형용사(interesting)가 명사 뒤에 온다.
두 번째 빈칸: '내게 입을 만한 따뜻한 무언가를 달라.'는 의미로 -thing으로 끝나는 대명사(something)는 형용사(warm)가 명사 뒤에 온다.

POINT 2 수량형용사

연습문제 A
1 A few　　　　2 many
3 some　　　　4 much
5 A few　　　　6 many
7 a lot of　　　8 a number of
9 a little　　　10 Plenty of
11 little　　　12 a large amount of
13 The number of

연습문제 B
1 few stores　　　2 little time
3 a few books
4 a little whipped cream
5 many friends　　6 much difference

기출 적중문제

정답 ①, ③

해설 ①, ③ '많은 상들이 그 대회의 우승자에게 주어질 것이다.'라는 의미이고 prizes는 셀 수 있는 명사의 복수형이므로 Many, Lots of를 쓸 수 있다.

POINT 3 부사의 역할

 연습문제

1 O		**2** happily	
3 truly		**4** O	
5 O		**6** O	
7 genuine		**8** O	
9 certainly		**10** Hopefully	

기출 적중문제

정답 complete → completely

해설 형용사(different)를 꾸미는 부사(completely)를 쓴다.

POINT 4 형용사와 형태가 같은 부사

연습문제

1 ⓑ	**2** ⓐ	**3** ⓑ	**4** ⓐ
5 ⓐ	**6** ⓑ	**7** ⓑ	**8** ⓐ
9 ⓐ	**10** ⓑ		

POINT 5 -ly가 붙으면 의미가 달라지는 부사

연습문제

1 closely	**2** hardly	**3** nearly
4 late	**5** mostly	**6** lately
7 high	**8** close	**9** near

기출 적중문제

정답 hardly → hard

해설 '많은 사람들이 그 공연을 성공시키기 위해 열심히 일했다.'라는 의미이므로 '열심히'라는 의미의 부사 hard를 쓴다.

POINT 6 빈도부사

연습문제

1 always listens to
2 can usually find
3 rarely[hardly/seldom] visit
4 often plays
5 was sometimes
6 often adds
7 never forgets
8 rarely[hardly/seldom] see

POINT 7 타동사 + 부사

 연습문제 A

1 throw it away
2 take off your shoes / take your shoes off
3 try those coats on / try on those coats

4 bring it up
5 made the entire story up / made up the entire story
6 turned him down
7 turn on the heater / turn the heater on
8 check it out
9 find it out
10 turn in our report / turn our report in
11 call it off

연습문제 B

1 put on my boots[put my boots on]
2 pick him up
3 turn off the lights[turn the lights off]
4 woke me up
5 handed in their tests[handed their tests in]
6 write down your name[write your name down]
7 look it up
8 put off the trip[put the trip off]
9 called it off

기출 적중문제

정답 ②

해설 ② picks up me → picks me up

서술형 대비 문제

 A
1 Nancy finished her homework early, so she is glad.
2 These shoes are comfortable enough to wear.
3 We found somewhere fun to go for a vacation.
4 Matthew has never been to Europe.
5 Football players often get injured while playing.

B
1 a little milk		**2** much food	
3 little free time		**4** Many parents	
5 the number of black rhinos			
6 a few days		**7** few apples	

 C
1 near	**2** closely	**3** high
4 mostly	**5** hardly	**6** late
7 hard		

D
1 handed it in
2 call off the field trip[call the field trip off]
3 turn down your invitation[turn your invitation down]
4 wrote down her recipe[wrote her recipe down]

5 put off the game[put the game off]
6 pick them up
7 put it on

중간·기말고사 실전 문제

1 ④　**2** (1) ⓑ → anything sweet (2) ⓓ → something astonishing (3) ⓔ → positive thing
3 ④　**4** I expected somebody older **5** ③
6 ⑤　**7** (1) ⓐ → something fun (2) ⓒ → Surprisingly (3) ⓔ → somewhere boring　**8** ①
9 ④　**10** This is because most of our buildings are inefficiently designed.　**11** nothing
12 ②　**13** ⑤　**14** (A) nearly (B) close (C) highly **15** ④　**16** ③　**17** ⑤　**18** ①
19 ⑤　**20** (1) ⓑ → closely (2) ⓓ → busy (3) ⓔ → completely　**21** ④　**22** ①　**23** ③
24 ⑤　**25** (1) ⓒ → shortly (2) ⓔ → warm
26 ⑤　**27** I gave it up　**28** ①
29 (1) always (2) sometimes (3) usually **30** ③, ⑤
31 ③　**32** ①　**33** ⑤　**34** ③　**35** ⑤
36 ④　**37** (1) ⓑ → frequently (2) ⓓ → recently (3) ⓔ → bring it up　**38** have had much[a great deal of/a large amount of/a lot of/lots of/plenty of] homework **39** I want to buy something memorable for my mom's birthday present.　**40** ③　**41** have never found anything harder than diamond

1 ④ comfortable → comfortably

2 (1) ⓑ -thing으로 끝나는 대명사(anything)는 형용사(sweet) 가 대명사 뒤에 온다.
(2) ⓓ -thing으로 끝나는 대명사(something)는 형용사 (astonishing)가 대명사 뒤에 온다.
(3) ⓔ '것, 물건'이라는 의미의 명사 thing을 수식할 때는 형용사 (positive)가 명사 앞에 온다.

3 ④ alive → live

4 -body로 끝나는 대명사(somebody)는 형용사(older)가 대명 사 뒤에 온다.

5 ③: 목적격 보어로, 서술적 용법으로 쓰였다.
①②④⑤: 한정적 용법으로 쓰였다.

6 ⓐ interestingly → interesting
ⓒ hardly → hard
ⓔ natural → naturally

7 (1) ⓐ -thing으로 끝나는 대명사(something)는 형용사(fun) 가 대명사 뒤에 온다.
(2) ⓒ 문장 전체를 꾸미는 부사(Surprisingly)를 쓴다.

8 (A) '그 기사는 새로운 법에 대한 의견들을 거의 제공하지 않았다.' 라는 의미이고 opinions는 셀 수 있는 명사의 복수형이므로 few를 쓴다.
(B) '웹사이트에는 그 수업에 대한 정보가 거의 없다.'라는 의미 이고 information은 셀 수 없는 명사이므로 little을 쓴다.
(C) '많은 수하물이 비행기에 남아 있었다.'는 의미이고 baggage는 셀 수 없는 명사이므로 Plenty of나 A lot of 를 쓴다.

9 (A) '많은 에너지가 매일 에어컨에 낭비된다.'라는 의미이고 energy는 셀 수 없는 명사이므로 A lot of를 쓴다.
(B) '약간의 변화가 에어컨에 대한 우리의 필요성을 낮출 수 있을 것이다.'라는 의미이고 changes는 셀 수 있는 명사의 복수 형이므로 A few를 쓴다.
(C) '높은 천장을 짓는 것과 같은 약간의 조치'라는 의미이고 steps는 셀 수 있는 명사의 복수형이므로 some을 쓴다.

10 동사(are designed)를 꾸미는 부사(inefficiently)를 쓴다.

11 -thing으로 끝나는 대명사(nothing)는 형용사(remarkable) 가 대명사 뒤에 온다. 'Junho thought his childhood was nothing remarkable.'이므로 여섯 번째에는 nothing이 온다.

12 ⓑ A number of → A lot of/ Lots of/ Plenty of
ⓒ A little → A few/ Few
ⓔ The number of → A number of

13 ⑤: 형용사
①②③④: 부사

14 (A) 'Jane은 거의 2,000달러의 비용이 드는 새 노트북을 샀다.' 는 의미이므로 '거의'라는 의미의 부사(nearly)를 쓴다.
(B) '그 회의는 점심시간 가까이에 끝났다.'는 의미이므로 '가까이' 라는 의미의 부사(close)를 쓴다.
(C) '우리는 매우 자격이 있는 직원을 찾는 중이다.'는 의미이므로 '매우'라는 의미의 부사(highly)를 쓴다.

15 ④ topics는 셀 수 있는 명사의 복수형이므로 셀 수 없는 명사와 쓰는 much는 쓸 수 없다.

16 ① annually → annual
② Previous → Previously
④ eager → eagerly
⑤ is considered usually → is usually considered

17 · beef는 셀 수 없는 명사이므로 much, a lot of를 쓸 수 있다.
· books는 셀 수 있는 명사의 복수형이므로 a few, many, a number of, a lot of를 쓸 수 있다.
· photographs는 셀 수 있는 명사의 복수형이므로 a few, many, a number of, a lot of를 쓸 수 있다.
· deer는 셀 수 있는 명사의 복수형이므로 a few, many, a number of, a lot of를 쓸 수 있다.
따라서 빈칸에 공통으로 들어갈 말은 a lot of이다.

18 ① always can → can always

19 ⑤ easy → easily

20 (1) ⓑ '나는 요즘 스포츠를 열심히 지켜보지않아.'라는 의미이므로 '열심히'라는 의미의 부사(closely)를 쓴다.
(2) ⓓ '하지만 나는 나의 숙제를 하느라 너무 바빠.'라는 의미이므로 형용사(busy)를 쓴다.
(3) ⓔ '나는 완전히 이해해.'라는 의미이므로 동사(understand)를 수식하는 부사(completely)를 쓴다.

21 ④ throw away them → throw them away

22 ⓑ use rarely → rarely use
ⓓ performs always → always performs
ⓔ turn off it → turn it off

23 (A) '너는 그것을 거의 빠지지 않잖아.'라는 의미이므로 '거의 ~않다'라는 의미의 부사(hardly)를 쓴다.
(B) '나는 모든 학교 활동들 때문에 최근에 자유시간이 없었어.'는 의미이므로 '최근에'라는 의미의 부사(lately)를 쓴다.
(C) '가끔은 지속하는 것이 어려울 수도 있다.'는 의미이므로 형용사(hard)를 쓴다.

24 ⑤ made her happily → made her happy

25 (1) ⓒ '하지만, 그렇지 않다면, 추운 날씨는 곧 끝날 것이다.'는 의미이므로 동사(end)를 꾸미는 부사(shortly)를 쓴다.
(2) ⓔ '사람들은 따뜻한 봄이 오고 있다는 징조를 찾는다.'는 의미이므로 형용사(warm)를 쓴다.

26 '사람들은 종종 그의 예측에 대해 불평한다.'는 의미이다. 다음 문장에서 frequent errors가 나왔으므로 빈도부사 ⑤ often을 쓴다.

27 '~을 포기하다'는 의미의 give up을 쓴다. 「타동사 + 부사」의 목적어가 대명사인 경우 「타동사 + 대명사 + 부사」의 어순으로 쓰므로 gave it up으로 쓴다.

28 ① ⓐ a great deal of → many/a number of/a large number of/a lot of/lots of/plenty of

29 (1) Emily는 매일 강아지에게 밥을 주므로 always를 쓴다.
(2) Emily는 주말에 사촌들을 찾아 가므로 sometimes를 쓴다.
(3) Emily는 평일에 오전 6시에 일어나므로 usually를 쓴다.

30 ③ dangerous anywhere → anywhere dangerous
⑤ incorrectly → incorrect

31 ⓒ make up it → make it up
ⓔ pick up you → pick you up

32 · -thing으로 끝나는 대명사(anything)는 형용사(healthier)가 대명사 뒤에 온다.
· '~을 확인하다'의 의미의 check out을 쓴다. 「타동사 + 부사」의 목적어가 대명사인 경우 「타동사 + 대명사 + 부사」의 어순으로 쓰므로 checked it out으로 쓴다.

33 ⑤ will help sometimes → will sometimes help

34 '~을 찾아보다'의 의미의 look up을 쓴다. 「타동사 + 부사」의 목적어가 대명사인 경우 「타동사 + 대명사 + 부사」의 어순으로 쓰므로 look it(the address of a local restaurant) up으로 쓴다.

35 · '~을 거절하다'는 의미의 turn down을 쓴다. 「타동사 + 부사」의 목적어가 대명사인 경우 「타동사 + 대명사 + 부사」의 어순으로 쓰므로 turn it down으로 쓴다. offer는 셀 수 있는 명사의 단수형이므로 it을 쓴다.
· '~을 버리다'의 의미의 throw away를 쓴다. 「타동사 + 부사」의 목적어가 대명사인 경우 「타동사 + 대명사 + 부사」의 어순으로 쓰므로 throw it away로 쓴다. cup은 셀 수 있는 명사의 단수형이므로 it을 쓴다.

36 ④: 형용사
①②③⑤: 부사

37 (1) ⓑ '나는 자주 아팠다.'는 의미이므로 동사(have been getting sick)를 꾸미는 부사(frequently)를 쓴다.
(2) ⓓ '나는 최근에 뒤처져있다.'는 의미이므로 문장 전체를 꾸미는 부사(recently)를 쓴다.
(3) ⓔ '나는 선생님에게 말을 꺼내봐야겠다.'는 의미이므로 bring up을 쓴다. 「타동사 + 부사」의 목적어가 대명사인 경우 「타동사 + 대명사 + 부사」의 어순으로 쓰므로 bring it up으로 쓴다.

38 homework은 셀 수 없는 명사이므로, '많은'의 의미이고 셀 수 없는 명사와 쓸 수 있는 much/a great deal of/a large amount of/a lot of/lots of/plenty of를 쓸 수 있다.

39 -thing으로 끝나는 대명사(something)는 형용사(memorable)가 대명사 뒤에 온다.

40 ⓑ entirely → entire
ⓒ actual → actually
ⓔ tropically → tropical

41 -thing으로 끝나는 대명사(anything)는 형용사(harder)가 대명사 뒤에 온다.

CHAPTER 10
비교구문
p.234

POINT 1-1 원급비교: as + 원급 + as

연습
문제
A

1	as hot as	**2**	as[so] skillfully as
3	as cold as	**4**	not as[so] heavy as
5	as fluently as	**6**	not as[so] difficult as
7	as flat as	**8**	as tired as
9	not as[so] interesting as		

연습
문제
B

1 am as strong as
2 was as entertaining as
3 can dance for as long as
4 isn't as[so] expensive as
5 can't jump as[so] high as
6 exercises as often as
7 didn't wake up as[so] early as
8 isn't as[so] close as
9 isn't as[so] long as
10 am not as[so] tall as
11 isn't as crowded as
12 doesn't have as many ideas as

기출 적중문제

정답 ①
해설 ② so not → not so
　　 ③ as not → not as
　　 ④ as honest so → as honest as
　　 ⑤ as loudly so → as loudly as

POINT 1-2 원급 관련 표현

연습
문제
A

1 ten times as fast as
2 five times as often as
3 four times as many pieces of pizza as
4 twice as busy as
5 half as loud as

연습
문제
B

1 as regularly as I could
2 as kindly as she could
3 as hot as you can
4 as frequently as they can
5 as high as they could

연습
문제
C

1	as far as	**2**	as long as
3	as good as	**4**	as often as

기출 적중문제

정답 ①
해설 ①「배수사 + as + 원급 + as」는 '…보다 –배 더 ~한/하게' 라는 의미이다.

POINT 2-1 비교급 비교: 비교급 + than

연습
문제
A

1	smaller than	**2**	cleaner than
3	more colorful than	**4**	heavier than
5	lonelier than	**6**	less beautiful than

연습
문제
B

1	saltier	**2**	O
3	O	**4**	cheaper
5	much[even, still, far, a lot]		
6	more cheerful		
7	O	**8**	more active
9	O	**10**	loudly

연습
문제
C

1	braver than	**2**	much curlier than
3	older than	**4**	a lot stronger than
5	even better than		

기출 적중문제

정답 far advanced → far more advanced
해설 「비교급 + than」은 '…보다 더 ~한/하게'라는 의미로, 비교급 앞에 far를 써서 '훨씬'이라는 의미로 비교급을 강조할 수 있다.

POINT 2-2 비교급 관련 표현

연습
문제
A

1 The harder I exercise, the hungrier[more hungry] I feel.
2 The older we get, the more we rely on our friends.
3 The warmer the earth gets, the more the ice in Antarctica will melt.
4 The more you practice bowling, the easier it becomes.
5 The more you eat junk food, the unhealthier [more unhealthy] your body gets.
6 The earlier you buy a train ticket, the cheaper the tickets are.

연습
문제
B

1	sadder and sadder	**2**	safer and safer
3	faster and faster	**4**	happier and happier
5	more and more angrily		
6	more and more often		
7	less and less		

C
1 more and more interesting
2 The smaller / the easier
3 three times softer than[three times as soft as]
4 The brighter / the more pleasant
5 eight times spicier than[eight times as spicy as]
6 five times colder
7 The closer / the more convenient

기출 적중문제

정답 the longer / the more
해설 「the + 비교급 ~, the + 비교급 …」은 '~할수록 더 …하다'라는 의미이다.

POINT 3 최상급 비교와 관련된 표현

A
1 the most precious item
2 one of the tallest buildings
3 the least interesting way
4 the most fantastic dress
5 the dirtiest shoes

B
1 No (other) man / as[so] diligent as
No (other) man / more diligent than
more diligent than any other man
more diligent than all the other men
2 No (other) scientist / as[so] brilliant as
No (other) scientist / more brilliant than
more brilliant than any other scientist
more brilliant than all the other scientists
3 No (other) country / as[so] big as
No (other) country / bigger than
bigger than any other country
bigger than all the other countries
4 No (other) person / as[so] successful as
No (other) person / more successful than
more successful than any other person
more successful than all the other people

기출 적중문제

정답 one of the greatest writers
해설 '가장 ~한 것들 중 하나'라는 의미로 「one of the + 최상급 + 복수명사」를 쓴다.

서술형 대비 문제

A
1 longer than
2 the deepest
3 not as[so] deep as
4 narrower than
5 the widest

B
1 four times more complicated than
2 three times safer than
3 ten times more passionately than
4 as spicy as possible
5 as tightly as he could
6 as neatly as she could
7 less nervous than

C
1 The more frequently you repeat an action, the better you will perform it.
2 The scarier the book got, the more anxious I felt.
3 The more interesting a zoo is, the more popular it will be.
4 As the argument continued, she became angrier and angrier.
5 Because of their lifestyle changes, they became healthier and healthier.
6 The snow fell more and more heavily over the weekend.

D
1 (other) person / as[so] dramatic as Carter
(other) person / more dramatic than Carter
more dramatic / any other person
more dramatic / all the other people
2 (other) empire / as[so] large as the British Empire
(other) empire / larger than the British Empire
larger / any other empire
larger / all the other empires
3 (other) planet / as[so] far as Neptune
(other) planet / further than Neptune
further / any other planet
further / all the other planets

중간·기말고사 실전 문제

1 ② 　2 ④ 　3 ③, ⑤ 　　　4 ④
5 ④ 　6 as frequently as 　7 four times more often than[four times as often as] 　　8 ③
9 as lazy as possible[as lazy as I can]
10 calories 　　11 ①, ④ 　12 heavy → heavier
13 ④ 　14 ① 　15 ② 　16 (1) ⓒ → much[even, still, far, a lot] (2) ⓓ → as long as (3) ⓔ → even more frequently 　　17 four times as popular as the Taj Mahal 　18 ④ 　19 ⑤
20 ④ 　21 ④ 　22 ③ 　23 more and more convenient 　　24 ⑤ 　25 ② 　26 ⑤
27 ③, ⑤ 28 The more people we have, the more

fun the party becomes! **29** ③ **30** the warmest of my winter clothes **31** ④ **32** ④ **33** ③ **34** ③ **35** is the spiciest food William has ever eaten **36** projects → project **37** The more positive words you hear, the happier you will be. **38** The more excited my older brother was, the louder he laughed. **39** ① **40** one of the busiest celebrities **41** ②, ⑤ **42** ⑤ **43** ④ **44** ⑤ **45** The more food they eat, the bigger they grow. **46** (1) ⓐ → larger (2) ⓑ → heavy (3) ⓓ → colder **47** No other person I know is brighter than my grandfather. **48** wiser and wiser **49** ③ **50** ④ **51** ③ **52** less complicated than

1 첫 번째 빈칸: 「less + 원급 + than」은 '···보다 덜 ~한/하게'라는 의미로, 「not + as[so] + 원급 + as」로 바꿔 쓸 수 있다. 따라서 첫 번째 빈칸에는 not so를 쓴다.
두 번째 빈칸: 두 번째 빈칸에는 as를 쓴다.

2 ④ as quiet as → as quietly as

3 ③ 「not + as + 원급 + as」는 '···만큼 ~하지 않은/않게'라는 의미이다.
⑤ 「not + so + 원급 + as」는 '···만큼 ~하지 않은/않게'라는 의미이다.

4 ⓐ as more food as → as much food as
ⓓ not as more embarrassing as → not as embarrassing as
ⓔ important as → as important as

5 「less + 원급 + than」은 '···보다 덜 ~한/하게'라는 의미이다.

6 「as + 원급 + as」는 '···만큼 ~한/하게'라는 의미로, 비교하는 두 대상의 정도가 비슷하거나 같음을 나타낸다.

7 「배수사 + 비교급 + than」은 '···보다 -배 더 ~한/하게'라는 의미로, 「배수사 + as + 원급 + as」로 바꿔 쓸 수 있다.

8 ③ 「as + 원급 + as + possible」은 '가능한 한 ~한/하게'라는 의미이다.

9 「as + 원급 + as + possible」은 '가능한 한 ~한/하게'라는 의미이며, 「as + 원급 + as + 주어 + can[could]」으로 바꿔 쓸 수 있다.

10 Running burns three times as many calories as swimming. 이므로 일곱 번째 오는 단어는 calories이다.

11 ① 「배수사 + as + 원급 + as」는 '···보다 -배 더 ~한/하게'라는 의미이다.
④ 「배수사 + 비교급 + than」은 '···보다 -배 더 ~한/하게'라는 의미이다.

12 「배수사 + 비교급 + than」은 '···보다 -배 더 ~한/하게'라는 의미이므로 비교급인 heavier를 쓴다.

13 ① slow → slower

14 (A) '그 실험은 이전 것들만큼 성공적이었다.'는 의미로, 「as + 원급 + as」를 쓰고 빈칸에 원급인 successful을 쓴다.
(B) '비행기의 발명은 지난 세기의 가장 큰 발전이었다.'는 의미이므로 최상급인 biggest를 쓴다.
(C) '내가 그것을 세탁했음에도 불구하고, 이 셔츠는 나의 다른 셔츠보다 더럽다.'는 의미이므로 비교급인 dirtier를 쓴다.

15 · 'Claire가 Emma보다 키가 작니?'라는 의미로, 「비교급 + than」을 쓰고 빈칸에 비교급인 shorter를 쓴다.
· '영화를 보는 것은 책을 읽는 것보다 덜 흥미로웠다.'는 의미로, 「less + 원급 + than」을 쓰고 빈칸에 원급인 interesting을 쓴다.

16 (1) ⓒ 비교급 앞에 much, even, still, far, a lot을 써서 '훨씬'이라는 의미로 비교급을 강조할 수 있다.
(2) ⓓ 「as + 원급 + as」는 '···만큼 ~한/하게'라는 의미로, 비교하는 두 대상의 정도가 비슷하거나 같음을 나타낸다.
(3) ⓔ 「비교급 + than」은 '···보다 더 ~한/하게'라는 의미로, 비교급 앞에 even을 써서 '훨씬'이라는 의미로 비교급을 강조할 수 있다.

17 「배수사 + 비교급 + than」은 '···보다 -배 더 ~한/하게'라는 의미로, 「배수사 + as + 원급 + as」로 바꿔 쓸 수 있다.

18 ⓐ more and more hard → harder and harder
ⓑ the more higher → the higher
ⓓ the most → the more

19 ⑤ more popular → less popular

20 ④ 비교급 앞에 far를 써서 '훨씬'이라는 의미로 비교급을 강조할 수 있다.

21 「the + 비교급 ~, the + 비교급 ···」은 '~할수록 더 ···하다'라는 의미이다.

22 ③ 「less + 원급 + than」은 '···보다 덜 ~한/하게'라는 의미이다. 비교급 앞에 much를 써서 '훨씬'이라는 의미로 비교급을 강조할 수 있다.

23 「비교급 + and + 비교급」은 '점점 더 ~한/하게'라는 의미이다.

24 ⑤ ⓔ The lesser → The less

25 ② 「비교급 + and + 비교급」은 '점점 더 ~한/하게'라는 의미이다.

26 ① the most → the more
② more weight → the more weight
③ the loud → the louder
④ more impressed am I → the more impressed I am

27 ① more than I can → as much as I can
② not as durable as → more durable than
④ as rare as → is rarer than

28 「the + 비교급 ~, the + 비교급 ···」은 '~할수록 더 ···하다'라는

의미이다.

29 ⓒ as more creative as → more creative than[as creative as]

ⓓ not as luckier as → not as lucky as

30 「the + 최상급 + (명사)」는 '가장 ~한/하게'라는 의미이므로 최상급인 the warmest를 쓴다.

31 ⓐ bravest → the bravest

ⓑ the most easy → the easiest

ⓒ the most dense → the densest

32 비교급 앞에 much, even, still, far, a lot을 써서 '훨씬'이라는 의미로 비교급을 강조할 수 있다. ④ very는 비교급을 강조할 수 없다.

33 「the + 비교급 ~, the + 비교급 …」은 '~할수록 더 …하다'라는 의미이다.
The more goals the team scored, the more cheerful the crowd became.이므로 전체 문장에서 아홉 번째에 오는 것은 ③ cheerful이다.

34 ① the more accurate → the most accurate

② a small → a smaller

④ the most largest → the largest

⑤ cheapest → the cheapest

35 「the + 최상급 + (명사)」는 '가장 ~한/하게'라는 의미이므로 최상급인 the spiciest를 쓴다.

36 '다른 어떤 …보다 더 ~한'이라는 의미로 「비교급 + than any other + 단수명사」를 쓴다.

37 「the + 비교급 ~, the + 비교급 …」은 '~할수록 더 …하다'라는 의미이다.

38 「the + 비교급 ~, the + 비교급 …」은 '~할수록 더 …하다'라는 의미이다.

39 ② most amazing → the most amazing

③ the most prettier → the prettiest

④ item → items

⑤ least expensive → the least expensive

40 '가장 ~한 것들 중 하나'라는 의미로 「one of the + 최상급 + 복수명사」를 쓴다.

41 ② 마이클 펠프스는 올림픽 역사상 다른 어떤 수영선수만큼이나 뛰어나다.

⑤ 마이클 펠프스는 올림픽 역사상 다른 수영선수들보다 뛰어나지 않다.

①③④: 마이클 펠프스는 올림픽 역사상 가장 뛰어난 수영선수이다.

42 ① more often than → less often than

② more frequently than → less frequently than

③ the least frequently → the most frequently

④ Michael → Emma, Emma → Michael

43 ④ 「not + as[so] + 원급 + as」는 '…보다 덜 ~한/하게'라는 의

미로, 「less + 원급 + than」으로 바꿔 쓸 수 있다.

44 ① the more skillful → the most skillful

② all the other one → all the other ones

③ most generous → the most generous

④ thoughtful as → as[so] thoughtful as

45 「the + 비교급 ~, the + 비교급 …」은 '~할수록 더 …하다'라는 의미이다.

46 (1) ⓐ 「비교급 + than all the other + 복수명사」는 '다른 모든 …보다 더 ~한'이라는 의미이다.

(2) ⓑ 「배수사 + as + 원급 + as」는 '…보다 -배 더 ~한/하게'라는 의미이다.

(3) ⓓ '그러므로, 그들은 다른 어느 곳보다 더 추운 곳을 좋아한다.'는 의미이므로 비교급 colder를 쓴다.

47 「비교급 + than any other + 단수명사」는 「No (other) + 단수명사 ~ 비교급 + than」으로 바꿔 쓸 수 있다.

48 「비교급 + and + 비교급」은 '점점 더 ~한/하게'라는 의미이다.

49 ③ 「비교급 + than all the other + 복수명사」는 「비교급 + than any other + 단수명사」로 바꿔 쓸 수 있다.

50 (A) '그 가수의 최신 앨범은 긍정적인 평가를 받았다.'라는 의미이므로 최상급인 the latest를 쓴다.

(B) '나는 숲에서 더 많은 시간을 보낼수록 더 차분해진다.'는 의미로, 「the + 비교급 ~, the + 비교급 …」을 쓰고 빈칸에 the calmer를 쓴다.

(C) '가능한 한 그 밧줄을 세게 잡도록 노력해라.'는 의미로, 「as + 원급 + as + 주어 + can[could]」를 쓰고, 빈칸에 원급인 tightly를 쓴다.

51 ③ as long as는 원급 관련 관용 표현으로 '~하기만 하면'이라는 의미이다.

52 「not + as[so] + 원급 + as」는 '보다 덜 ~한/하게'라는 의미로, 「less + 원급 + than」으로 바꿔 쓸 수 있다.

CHAPTER 11
전치사

p.258

POINT 1-1 시간을 나타내는 전치사 I

연습문제
1 in	**2** in	**3** on	**4** on
5 on	**6** at	**7** in	**8** at
9 on			

POINT 1-2 시간을 나타내는 전치사 II

연습문제 A
1 ① After	② before
2 ① before	② After
3 ① after	② Before
4 ① after	② before
5 ① before	② After

연습문제 B
1 by	**2** since	**3** until
4 since	**5** from	**6** by
7 Since	**8** from	**9** until
10 by	**11** from	

기출 적중문제

정답 ④

해설 첫 번째 빈칸: '19세기 중반에, 사람들은 기차로 여행하기 시작했다.'는 의미이므로 전치사 In(~에)을 쓴다.
두 번째 빈칸: '예를 들어, 비행기 여행은 20세기 중반 이후로 흔해져왔다.'는 의미이므로 전치사 since(~ 이후로)를 쓴다.

POINT 1-3 시간을 나타내는 전치사 III

연습문제
1 for	**2** during	**3** for
4 while	**5** during	

기출 적중문제

정답 ③

해설 첫 번째 빈칸: '~ 동안'이라는 의미로 뒤에 숫자를 포함한 시간 표현(150 years)이 오므로 전치사 for를 쓴다.
두 번째 빈칸: '~ 동안'이라는 의미로 뒤에 명사(the past year)가 오므로 전치사 during을 쓴다.

POINT 2-1 장소를 나타내는 전치사 I

연습문제
1 on	**2** at	**3** on	**4** in
5 at	**6** in	**7** on	**8** on

기출 적중문제

정답 on / in / at

해설 첫 번째 빈칸: '도로 위에 두 대의 차가 있다.'는 의미이므로 표면에 접촉한 상태를 나타내는 전치사 on(~ 위에)을 쓴다.
두 번째 빈칸: 공간의 내부(a blue car) 앞에는 전치사 in을 쓴다.
세 번째 빈칸: 하나의 지점(the crosswalk) 앞에는 전치사 at을 쓴다.

POINT 2-2 장소를 나타내는 전치사 II

연습문제 A
1 in	**2** in	**3** in	**4** at
5 in	**6** on	**7** in	**8** On
9 at	**10** in	**11** on	**12** at
13 on	**14** at	**15** in	

연습문제 B
1 on the street	**2** in the ocean
3 on the phone	**4** in prison
5 on the sixth floor	**6** in the world
7 at school	**8** in a car
9 at a concert	**10** in danger

기출 적중문제

정답 ④

해설 ④: on   ①②③⑤: in

POINT 3 위치를 나타내는 전치사

연습문제
1 over	**2** above	**3** below
4 under	**5** near	**6** beside
7 among	**8** in front of	**9** between
10 above	**11** under	**12** behind

기출 적중문제

정답 among

해설 '~ (셋 이상) 사이에'라는 의미의 전치사 among을 쓴다.

POINT 4 방향을 나타내는 전치사

연습문제
1 down	**2** into	**3** out of
4 through	**5** toward	**6** up
7 across	**8** along	**9** around

정답 ②
해설 return과 함께 쓰여 도착 지점을 나타내고 있으므로 전치사 to(~으로)를 쓴다.

POINT 5 기타 전치사

1	with	2	by
3	about	4	like
5	without	6	as
7	of	8	throughout
9	for	10	due to
11	except	12	instead of
13	against	14	by
15	such as	16	according to

POINT 6-1 전치사 관용 표현: 형용사 + 전치사

1	with	2	of	3	for
4	from	5	of	6	for
7	on	8	to	9	to
10	of	11	to	12	to
13	about	14	at	15	for
16	with				

POINT 6-2 전치사 관용 표현: 동사 + 전치사

1	on	2	with	3	in	4	for
5	to	6	at	7	by	8	into

기출 적중문제

정답 ③
해설 '~에 속하다'라는 의미이므로 belong to를 쓴다.

POINT 6-3 전치사 관용 표현: 동사 + 명사 + 전치사

1	takes care of	2	took pity on
3	took part in	4	get rid of
5	pay attention to	6	had fun with
7	make use of	8	made a fool of
9	take care of	10	pay attention to
11	taking part in		

서술형 대비 문제

(A)
1	in	2	until
3	at	4	near
5	through	6	with
7	for	8	according to
9	Due to	10	of

(B)
1	from	2	on	3	with
4	O	5	for	6	O
7	with	8	on	9	O

(C) ⓐ to ⓑ over ⓒ on ⓓ next to ⓔ at

(D) ⓐ at ⓑ on ⓒ across ⓓ down ⓔ with ⓕ to ⓖ between

중간·기말고사 실전 문제

1 ③ **2** ① **3** ② **4** (A) at → in (B) on → at (C) in → on **5** ③
6 ⓐ during ⓑ for ⓒ since ⓓ from **7** ③
8 ② **9** ② **10** ③ **11** ①
12 (1) ⓐ → in (2) ⓔ → on **13** ④ **14** ③
15 ② **16** behind **17** ③ **18** (A) from (B) after (C) down (D) along **19** ⓐ as ⓑ with ⓒ near ⓓ in **20** turned a rabbit into a dove
21 ③ **22** ② **23** ⑤ **24** ④ **25** ⑤
26 ② **27** ④ **28** ① **29** ⑤
30 ⓐ about ⓑ against ⓒ at ⓓ like **31** for letting younger people vote **32** of **33** in
34 ② **35** ④ **36** (1) ⓑ → to (2) ⓒ → of (3) ⓔ → for **37** ⑤ **38** ③ **39** ②
40 ③ **41** ② **42** ⑤ **43** ③ **44** ④
45 ② **46** ⑤ **47** ⓐ on ⓑ with ⓒ to ⓓ for ⓔ without **48** they are frightened at[by] them

1 ③ at → on

2 (A) '과거에'라는 의미로 in the past를 쓴다.
(B) '~ 동안'이라는 의미의 while은 접속사로 뒤에 완전한 문장이 온다.
(C) 특정 시점까지 어떤 행동이나 상황이 계속되는 것을 나타낼 때는 전치사 until을 쓴다.

3 · 요일(Saturday and Sunday) 앞에는 전치사 on을 쓴다.
· 날짜(March 26, 2003) 앞에는 전치사 on을 쓴다.

4 (A) 아침(the morning) 앞에는 전치사 in을 쓴다.
(B) '현재에'라는 의미의 at present를 쓴다.
(C) 금요일 저녁(Friday evening)을 나타낼 때는 on을 쓴다.

5 · '~ 동안'이라는 의미로 뒤에 명사(my vacation)가 오므로 전치사 during을 쓴다.
· 정해진 시점까지 어떤 행동이나 상황이 완료되는 것을 나타낼 때는 전치사 by를 쓴다.

6 ⓐ '~ 동안'이라는 의미로 뒤에 명사(the earthquake)가 오므로 전치사 during을 쓴다.
ⓑ '~ 동안'이라는 의미로 뒤에 숫자를 포함한 시간 표현(30 minutes)이 오므로 전치사 for를 쓴다.
ⓒ '~ 이후로'라는 의미의 전치사 since를 쓴다.
ⓓ '우리의 전기가 월요일부터 수요일까지 나갔었다.'라는 의미이므로 전치사 from(~부터)을 쓴다.

7 ⓑ until → by
ⓓ during → for

8 · '앉을만한 몇몇 개의 의자가 있다.'라는 의미로 표면에 접촉한 상태를 나타내는 전치사 on을 쓴다.
· '내가 넘어졌을 때 나는 도서관에 가는 길이었다.'라는 의미로 전치사 on을 쓴다.
· '누군가가 화장실 벽 위에 글자를 썼다.'라는 의미로 표면에 접촉한 상태를 나타내는 전치사 on을 쓴다.

9 ⓐⓓ: on ⓑ: with[to] ⓒ: about ⓔ: in[after]

10 ③: in
①②④⑤: on

11 (A) '반으로'라는 의미이므로 in half를 쓴다.
(B) '위험에 빠진'이라는 의미이므로 in danger를 쓴다.
(C) '~의 아래에'라는 의미이므로 at the bottom of를 쓴다.

12 (1) ⓐ '나는 지난 주말을 춘천에서 보냈다.'는 의미이므로 비교적 넓은 장소(Chuncheon) 앞에는 전치사 in을 쓴다.
(2) ⓔ '다음에는, 나는 가기 전에 인터넷에서 일기 예보를 확인할 것이다.'는 의미이므로 통신수단을 나타내는 전치사 on을 쓴다.

13 · '박쥐들은 소리로 사물의 위치를 찾아낸다.'는 의미이므로 전치사 by(~로)를 쓴다.
· '나는 나의 영웅에 의해 사인된 야구 카드를 가지고 있다.'는 의미이므로 전치사 by(~에 의해)를 쓴다.
· '그 박물관에 가는 가장 빠른 방법은 버스를 타고 가는 것이다.'라는 의미이므로 전치사 by(~을 타고)를 쓴다.

14 · leave와 함께 쓰여 가고자 하는 방향을 나타내고 있으므로 전치사 for(~으로)를 쓴다.
· '그 여자는 커피를 사기 위해 그녀의 지갑을 가방 밖으로 꺼냈다.'는 의미이므로 전치사 out of(~ 밖으로)를 쓴다.

15 · '너는 이 길을 따라가면 공원에 갈 수 있다.'라는 의미이므로 전치사 to(~에)를 쓴다.
· '30분 후에, 너는 오븐 밖으로 쿠키들을 꺼내야 할 것이다.'는 의미이므로 전치사 out of(~밖으로)를 쓴다.
· '한국 식료품점에서 팔리는 많은 과일은 필리핀으로부터 수입된다.'는 의미이므로 전치사 from(~으로부터)을 쓴다.
· 'A를 B에 쓰다'라는 의미이므로 spend A on B를 쓴다.
· '다음 여름에 휴가를 위해 미시간 호수에 돌아가기로 결정했다.'

는 의미이므로 전치사 to(~에)를 쓴다.
따라서 전치사 to는 2개이다.

16 '~ 뒤에'라는 의미의 전치사 behind를 쓴다.

17 첫 번째 빈칸: '그는 헬멧과 하키 스틱과 같은 몇몇 장비를 사야 했다.'는 의미이므로 전치사 such as(~와 같은)를 쓴다.
두 번째 빈칸: '그 팀은 일요일을 제외하고는 매일 연습한다.'는 의미이므로 전치사 except(~을 제외하고는)를 쓴다.
세 번째 빈칸: '그는 바쁜 일정 때문에 매우 피곤하다'는 의미이므로 전치사 because of(~ 때문에)를 쓴다.
네 번째 빈칸: '다른 팀에 맞서는 그의 첫 경기는 다음 주 토요일이다.'는 의미이므로 전치사 against(~에 맞서는)를 쓴다.
따라서 instead of는 들어갈 수 없다.

18 (A) '우리는 지난 주말에 시애틀부터 포틀랜드까지 기차를 탔다.'는 의미이므로 전치사 from(~부터)을 쓴다.
(B) '그 경비원은 큰 소음을 들은 후에 주차장을 수색했다.'는 의미이므로 전치사 after(~ 후에)를 쓴다.
(C) 'Kevin은 소방서를 방문했을 때 기둥을 타고 아래로 미끄러져 내려갔다.'는 의미이므로 전치사 down(~ 아래로)을 쓴다.
(D) '그 정원사는 울타리를 따라서 꽃을 심었다.'는 의미이므로 전치사 along(~을 따라서)을 쓴다.

19 ⓐ '그것은 나의 가장 친한 친구의 전문 마술사로서 첫 번째 공연이었다.'는 의미이므로 전치사 as(~로)를 쓴다.
ⓑ '~으로 붐비다'라는 의미이므로 be crowded with를 쓴다.
ⓒ '나는 무대 가까이에 앉았다'는 의미이므로 전치사 near(~ 가까이에)를 쓴다.
ⓓ '~에 참가하다'라는 의미이므로 take part in을 쓴다.

20 'A를 B로 바꾸다'라는 의미이므로 turn A into B를 쓴다.

21 밑줄 친 부분과 ③: '~에 찬성하는'
①: ~으로, ~을 향해 ②④⑤: '~을 위해'

22 '나의 친구 재민이는 딱 그녀의 여동생처럼 생겼다.'는 의미이므로 전치사 like(~처럼)를 쓴다.

23 · 'Emily는 Jessica와 함께 해변에 갔다.'는 의미이므로 전치사 with(~와 함께)를 쓴다.
· '나는 항상 나의 피자를 여분의 치즈와 함께 주문한다.'는 의미이므로 전치사 with(~와 함께)를 쓴다.
· '그 도시는 폭풍 이후로 전기에 대해 많은 문제가 있어왔다.'는 의미이므로 전치사 with(~에 대해)를 쓴다.

24 · '그 볼링 선수는 1점 정도로 시합에서 졌을 때 실망했다.'는 의미이므로 전치사 by(~(정도)로)를 쓴다.
· '그 학생은 루이지애나의 생태계에 대한 질문을 했다.'는 의미이므로 전치사 about(~에 대한)을 쓴다.
· 'Brown씨는 여행 중일 때 그녀의 아이들을 위한 작은 선물들을 샀다.'는 의미이므로 전치사 for(~을 위해)를 쓴다.
· '나는 어젯밤 멋진 일몰의 사진을 찍을 수 있을 만큼 충분히 운이 좋았다.'는 의미이므로 전치사 of(~의)를 쓴다.
· 'David는 전 세계에 있는 그의 친구들과 이야기하기 위해 그의 컴퓨터를 사용한다.'는 의미이므로 전치사 for(~을 위해)를 쓴다.
따라서 like는 어느 빈칸에도 들어갈 수 없다.

25 '나는 나의 친구들 없이 학교 가는 것을 싫어할까 봐 무섭다.'는 의미이므로 전치사 without(~없이)을 쓴다.

26 ② '~을 제외하고는'이라는 의미의 전치사 except를 쓴다.

27 ④ '~ 때문에'라는 의미의 전치사 due to를 쓴다.

28 (A) '우리는 오후 동안 마을을 걸어서 답사하였다.'는 의미이므로 on foot(걸어서)을 쓴다.
(B) '예진이는 많은 유명한 별들을 발견한 천문학자와 함께 이야기했다.'는 의미이므로 전치사 with(~와 함께)를 쓴다.
(C) '그는 나에게 그를 위해 사진을 찍어달라고 부탁했다.'는 의미이므로 전치사 for(~을 위해)를 쓴다.

29 · '우리 가족은 새로운 아파트 안으로 이사했다.'는 의미이므로 전치사 into(~ 안으로)를 쓴다.
· '간식 수납장 안에 다양한 종류의 쿠키들이 있다.'는 의미이므로 전치사 in(~ 안에)을 쓴다.
· '두 병원 사이에 있는 약국은 항상 매우 붐빈다.'는 의미이므로 전치사 between(~ (둘) 사이에)을 쓴다.
· '주연 배우의 이름은 포스터의 제목 위에 있었다.'는 의미이므로 전치사 above(~ 위에)를 쓴다.
따라서 among은 어느 빈칸에도 들어갈 수 없다.

30 ⓐ '그것에 대한 생각은 어떠니?'라는 의미이므로 전치사 about(~에 대한)을 쓴다.
ⓑ '나는 투표 연령을 낮추는 것에 반대한다.'는 의미이므로 전치사 against(~에 반대하는)를 쓴다.
ⓒ '그들은 오로지 집에서 부모님으로부터 들은 것만 알고 있다.'는 의미이므로 전치사 at(~에서)을 쓴다.
ⓓ '이것은 그들의 부모에게 추가로 표를 주는 것과 같을 것이다.'는 의미이므로 전치사 like(~같이)를 쓴다.

31 '~에 찬성하는'이라는 의미의 전치사 for를 쓴다.

32 · '~으로 이루어지다'는 의미이므로 consist of를 쓴다.
· '~으로 가득 차 있다'는 의미이므로 be full of를 쓴다.
· '~으로 죽다'는 의미이므로 die of를 쓴다.

33 · 아침(the morning) 앞에는 전치사 in을 쓴다.
· '어려움에 처한'이라는 의미이므로 in need를 쓴다.
· '취침 중인'이라는 의미이므로 in bed를 쓴다.

34 · '그는 그의 태블릿을 주로 게임기로 사용했다.'는 의미이므로 전치사 as(~로)를 쓴다.
· '그녀는 학교 연극에서 백설 공주로 캐스팅되었다.'는 의미이므로 전치사 as(~로)를 쓴다.
· '그 리조트의 모든 손님들은 왕과 왕비로 대접 받는다.'는 의미이므로 전치사 as(~로)를 쓴다.

35 ④ 동사(좋아하다)
밑줄 친 부분과 ①②③⑤: 전치사(~처럼)

36 (1) ⓑ '~에 익숙하다'는 의미이므로 be accustomed to를 쓴다.
(2) ⓒ '~이 부족하다'는 의미이므로 be short of를 쓴다.
(3) ⓔ '~으로 알려져 있다'는 의미이므로 be known for를 쓴다.

37 ⑤ '~을 할 수 있다'는 의미이므로 be capable of를 쓴다.

38 ③ '~에 책임이 있다'는 의미이므로 be responsible for를 쓴다.

39 ① off → at
③ to → from
④ at → about
⑤ with → of

40 '처음처럼 느껴진다.'는 의미이므로 전치사 like(~처럼)를 쓴다.

41 'Greg는 생일파티에서 그의 친구들과 함께 즐거운 시간을 보냈다.'는 의미이므로 전치사 with(~와 함께)를 쓴다.

42 (A) '~을 제안하다, 생각해내다'라는 의미이므로 come up with를 쓴다.
(B) '~을 믿다'라는 의미이므로 believe in을 쓴다.
(C) '~에 대해 사과하다'라는 의미이므로 apologize for를 쓴다.

43 ① divide the cake on → divide the cake into
② resulted with → resulted in
④ is likely of → is likely to
⑤ is good to → is good at

44 ④: to
①②③⑤: on

45 첫 번째 빈칸: 요일(Thursday) 앞에는 전치사 on을 쓴다.
두 번째 빈칸: 비교적 넓은 장소(the city) 앞에는 전치사 in을 쓴다.

46 ⑤: on
①②③④: of

47 ⓐ 'A를 B에 쓰다'라는 의미이므로 spend A on B를 쓴다.
ⓑ '만약 특정한 사람들이 일정하지 않은 모양의 구멍을 가진 사물들의 사진을 보면'이라는 의미이므로 전치사 with(~을 가진)를 쓴다.
ⓒ '~에 따르면'이라는 의미로 according to를 쓴다.
ⓓ '~에 책임이 있다'는 의미로 be responsible for를 쓴다.
ⓔ '그리고 사람들은 온라인에서 이 공포증에 대해 읽는 것 없이는 이것에 대해 알지 못할 것이다.'라는 의미이므로 전치사 without(~ 없이)을 쓴다.

48 '~에 겁먹다'는 의미로 be frightened at[by]을 쓴다.

CHAPTER 12
접속사

p.288

POINT 1 등위접속사: and, but, or, so

1 and	**2** but	**3** or
4 and	**5** or	**6** but
7 and	**8** so	**9** but
10 or	**11** and	

POINT 2 상관접속사

 A

1 Both / and	**2** as well as
3 neither / nor	**4** either / or
5 not / but	**6** not only / but also
7 either / or	**8** Both / and
9 Neither / nor	

연습문제 **B**

1 have	**2** are	**3** is
4 are	**5** has	**6** is
7 take	**8** have	**9** are
10 needs	**11** like	**12** costs
13 are	**14** were	

기출 적중문제

정답 ④

해설 ① is → are
　　② playing → plays
　　③ needs → need
　　⑤ were → was

POINT 3-1 명사절을 이끄는 접속사: that

 A

1 ⓐ	**2** ⓑ	**3** ⓑ	**4** ⓐ
5 ⓒ	**6** ⓐ	**7** ⓑ	**8** ⓐ
9 ⓑ	**10** ⓒ	**11** ⓐ	**12** ⓑ
13 ⓒ	**14** ⓑ		

연습문제 **B**

1 The fact[truth] that celebrities make a lot of money
2 the promise that she would wake up early
3 the fact[truth] that their dog was lost
4 The idea[thought] that a dangerous criminal was in the town
5 the news that our plane had been delayed
6 The evidence that the man stole the painting
7 The idea[thought] that we might lose the game
8 The suggestion that Dylan started the rumor

기출 적중문제

정답 ②, ⑤

해설 밑줄 친 부분과 ②⑤: 주어 역할
　　①, ④ 목적어 역할　③ 보어 역할

POINT 3-2 명사절을 이끄는 접속사: if/whether

1 Whether	**2** O
3 O	**4** Whether
5 whether	**6** O
7 Whether	**8** whether

기출 적중문제

정답 ③

해설 ③ If → Whether

POINT 3-3 명사절을 이끄는 접속사: 의문사

연습문제

1 when we will meet	**2** Who gave
3 where they will go	**4** why he was
5 who would be	**6** How I get
7 who will replace	**8** how she could fix

POINT 4-1 부사절을 이끄는 접속사: 시간

연습문제 **A**

1 when	**2** after
3 since	**4** as soon as
5 until	**6** as
7 since	**8** while
9 before	**10** after
11 before	**12** when
13 till	**14** before
15 as soon as	

연습문제 **B**

1 examine	**2** O
3 O	**4** fixes
5 O	**6** has been
7 arrives	**8** O
9 get	**10** O
11 O	**12** enters

기출 적중문제

정답 (1) Since (2) While (3) Until

해설 (1) '그가 다섯 살이었을 때 이래로 그는 싱가포르에서 살고
있다.'의 의미이므로 Since(~한 이래로)를 쓴다.

(2) '나는 그 자동차에서 내리는 동안 나의 머리를 부딪혔다.'
는 의미이므로 While(~하는 동안)을 쓴다.

(3) '날씨가 다시 맑아질 때까지, 그 경기는 연기되어야 한다.'
는 의미이므로 Until(~할 때까지)을 쓴다.

POINT 4-2 부사절을 이끄는 접속사: 이유

1	because	**2**	now that
3	while	**4**	as
5	since	**6**	because
7	when	**8**	now that
9	because of	**10**	because
11	since	**12**	since
13	now that	**14**	as

POINT 4-3 부사절을 이끄는 접속사: 조건

A

1	once / taste	**2**	unless
3	if	**4**	Once / opens
5	if	**6**	Once
7	Unless / stop		

B

1	or	**2**	or	**3**	and
4	Unless	**5**	If	**6**	Unless
7	or				

기출 적중문제

정답 ④

해설 ④ '~인지'의 의미의 명사절을 이끄는 접속사로 쓰였다.
①②③⑤ '만약 ~한다면'의 의미의 부사절을 이끄는 접속사
로 쓰였다.

POINT 4-4 부사절을 이끄는 접속사: 양보

A

1	though[although/even though]
2	O
3	O
4	O
5	despite[in spite of]
6	though[although/even though]
7	while[whereas]
8	O
9	though[although/even though]
10	O
11	O
12	though[although/even though]

B

1	while my older brother will buy a laptop
2	although he had stayed up all night
3	even if it snows tomorrow
4	even though he ate only one piece of pizza
5	Although I took a pill
6	whereas the front door is for customers
7	even if I receive an invitation
8	while my younger sister prefers best-selling novels
9	Though Karen was quite famous

기출 적중문제

정답 even though they look cute

해설 '비록 곰은 귀여워 보이지만 아주 위험한 동물이다.'는 의미이
므로 '비록 ~이지만'이라는 의미인 even though를 쓴다.

POINT 4-5 부사절을 이끄는 접속사: so that ~

1	so that everyone could take photos
2	so that I can lend it to you
3	so that people can share
4	so that I can have a conversation with you
5	in order to fix the chair
6	so that I could prevent mosquitoes from coming inside
7	so as to easily find what she needed
8	so that it can attract more customers

POINT 4-6 부사절을 이끄는 접속사: so ~ that …

1	so curious that she read her daughter's diary
2	so fast that the cat couldn't catch it
3	too large to fit in his closet
4	so slowly that I take the stairs
5	too huge to find the exhibit
6	so quickly that she got a headache
7	so boring that half of the audience left before it ended

POINT 5 다양한 의미의 부사절을 이끄는 접속사

A

1	ⓐ	**2**	ⓓ	**3**	ⓒ	**4**	ⓑ
5	ⓔ	**6**	ⓑ	**7**	ⓐ	**8**	ⓒ
9	ⓓ	**10**	ⓔ				

연습문제 **B**
1 since I moved
2 while it takes
3 while we were having
4 since the beginning of summer
5 since I graduated
6 while I was taking
7 Since Tommy was

기출 적중문제
정답 ④
해설 ④ '~인 반면에'라는 의미로 사용되었다.
①②③⑤ '~동안'이라는 의미로 사용되었다.

POINT 6 접속부사

연습문제 **A**
1	However	2	Thus
3	In contrast	4	Therefore
5	Moreover	6	In addition
7	Otherwise	8	On the other hand
9	Besides	10	Anyway
11	For example		

연습문제 **B**
1	As a result	2	In contrast
3	In fact	4	Instead
5	Therefore[Thus]	6	However
7	For example[For instance]		
8	Otherwise		

기출 적중문제
정답 ④
해설 첫 번째 빈칸: '사람들이 해외 여행하는 것을 좋아한다. 그러나, 어느 나라가 가장 많은 관광객들을 끌어들이는지 아는 사람은 많지 않다.'는 의미이므로 However(그러나)를 쓴다.
두 번째 빈칸: 'UN에 따르면, 8940만 명의 관광객들이 2018년에 프랑스에 방문했다. 게다가, 관광객들의 수가 매년 증가하고 있다.'는 의미이므로 Moreover(게다가)를 쓴다.

서술형 대비 문제

(A)
1	O	2	is	3	O
4	clean	5	O	6	nor

(B)
1 is interesting that humans aren't the only animals that dream
2 should remind yourself that planning your schedule is important
3 are told that they should eat healthy food
4 don't know whether I should laugh or cry

5 wonder if there is life on Mars
6 wonders if the product is safe for babies
7 you decided whether you will order some more dessert
8 you guess what this picture means
9 have no idea when this broken door will be fixed

(C)
1 When the wave hit the boat
2 Until I finally succeed
3 While we practiced[were practicing] soccer
4 If you want to help people
5 Though I own a hanbok
6 As Betty can type fast
7 so that no one could find it
8 so tall that he can touch the ceiling
9 Even if we catch a plane

(D) Therefore / For example / In addition / However

중간·기말고사 실전 문제

1 and she bought two boxes of cookies 2 ⑤
3 ⑤ 4 ② 5 ② 6 ④ 7 ②
8 ② 9 (1) The shopping mall is so popular that it is always crowded. (2) Paul was injured so badly that he had to cancel all his appointments.
10 ④ 11 Confidence as well as courage
12 Try to keep your promises, and people will start to trust you. 13 ② 14 ①, ④ 15 ①
16 because he wanted good luck 17 Since time is limited 18 ⑤ 19 not only / but also
20 ④ 21 feel guilty unless you apologize to your parents 22 the fact that her group lost the competition 23 ③ 24 ③ 25 ⑤
26 (1) when (2) because 27 ②, ⑤ 28 what made your parents upset yesterday 29 when this store opens 30 ①, ④ 31 so that I don't make a mistake 32 ⑤ 33 ④ 34 while
35 ① 36 If you are nice to people, you will present a good image to them. 37 ② 38 if I should buy a skirt or a dress 39 ① 40 ③
41 ⑤ 42 while 43 If you keep practicing
44 despite → though[although/even though]
45 in order[so as] to 46 so hot that it melted the metal 47 As a result 48 ②

1 '그리고'라는 의미의 and를 쓴다.

2 · 접속사 that은 문장 안에서 주어 역할을 하는 명사절을 이끌 수 있다.

- 접속사 that은 문장 안에서 보어 역할을 하는 명사절을 이끌 수 있다.

3
- '이순신 장군은 거북선 때문에 많은 전투에서 이겼다.'는 의미이므로 because of(~ 때문에)를 쓴다.
- '네가 누군가와 이야기하는 동안 너는 문자 메시지를 보내서는 안 된다.'는 의미이므로 while(~하는 동안)을 쓴다.
- 'Jenny는 갑각류에 알레르기가 있기 때문에 조개 먹는 것을 멈췄다.'는 의미이므로 since(~이기 때문에)를 쓴다.
- '교통체증 때문에, 나는 오전 9시까지 수업에 갈 수 없었다.'는 의미이므로 until(~할 때까지)을 쓴다.
따라서 ⑤ unless는 빈칸에 들어갈 수 없다.

4 ② '새로운 형제자매가 태어날 때'라고 했으므로 when(~할 때)을 쓴다. 시간을 나타내는 부사절에서는 미래를 표현할 때 현재시제를 쓴다.

5 (A) while이 '~하는 동안'이라는 의미로 사용되었다.
(C) since가 '~한 이래로'라는 의미로 사용되었다.

6
- '나는 지도를 확인했지만 출구를 찾을 수 없었다.'는 의미이므로 but(하지만)을 쓴다.
- '이 병은 심각하지만, 우리는 치료제를 가지고 있다.'는 의미이므로 but(하지만)을 쓴다.

7
- '너의 과제를 내일까지 제출해라, 그렇지 않으면 너는 곤경에 빠지게 될 것이다.'라는 의미이므로 or를 쓴다. 「명령문 + or ~」는 '…해라, 그렇지 않으면 ~'의 의미이다.
- 'Jason은 주말마다 체육관에 가거나 한강을 따라서 조깅을 한다.'는 의미이므로 either A or B를 쓴다.

8 ② because of 뒤에는 명사(구)가 온다.

9 (1) 「so + 형용사/부사 + that …」 '너무 ~해서/~하게 …한'의 의미이며, 결과를 나타내는 부사절을 이끈다.
(2) 「so + 형용사/부사 + that …」 '너무 ~해서/~하게 …한'의 의미이며, 결과를 나타내는 부사절을 이끈다.

10 ④ taking → took

11 'A뿐만 아니라 B도'라는 의미의 not only A but (also) B 구문은 B as well as A로 바꿔 쓸 수 있다.

12 '만약 네가 너의 약속을 지키기 위해 노력한다면, 사람들은 너를 신뢰하기 시작할 것이다.'는 의미이다. 따라서 '…해라, 그러면 ~'의 의미로 「명령문 + and ~」로 바꿔 쓸 수 있다.

13 첫 번째 빈칸: 앞 문장과 반대의 의미이므로 In contrast(그에 반해서)를 쓴다.
두 번째 빈칸: 앞 문장의 추가 설명을 하고 있으므로 Moreover(게다가)를 쓴다.

14 '비록 다른 팀이 경험이 더 풍부했지만, 그의 팀이 그 경기에서 이겼다.'는 의미이므로 ① Although(비록 ~이지만)와 ④ Though(비록 ~이지만)를 쓸 수 있다.

15 ① '~로서'라는 의미의 전치사 as가 쓰였다.
②③④⑤ '~이기 때문에'라는 의미의 접속사 as가 쓰였다.

16 'Peter는 행운을 원했기 때문에 네 잎 클로버를 찾았다.'는 의미이

므로 because(~이기 때문에)를 쓴다.

17 '시간이 제한되어 있기 때문에, 너는 너의 연설을 10분 내에 끝내야 한다.'는 의미이므로 since(~때문에)를 쓴다.

18 ⑤ so busy person that → so busy that

19 'A뿐만 아니라 B도'라는 의미의 not only A but (also) B를 쓴다.

20 ④ '~한 이래로'라는 시간의 의미로 쓰였다.
①②③⑤ '~때문에'라는 이유의 의미로 쓰였다.

21 '만약 네가 너의 부모님께 사과하지 않으면, 너는 죄책감을 느낄 것이다.'는 의미이고, If ~ not은 unless(만약 ~하지 않으면)로 바꿔 쓸 수 있다.

22 that은 '사실'을 의미하는 명사 fact를 설명하는 명사절을 이끌 수 있으며, 이때 that은 생략할 수 없다.

23 ③ if와 whether는 명사절을 이끄는 접속사로, '~인지'의 의미이다.

24 ③ Though → Because[Since/As]

25 (A) am → were[are](both A and B 뒤에는 항상 복수동사를 쓴다)

26 (1) 밑줄 친 as가 '~할 때'의 의미로 쓰였으므로 when(~할 때)을 쓴다.
(2) 밑줄 친 as가 '~이기 때문에'의 의미로 쓰였으므로 because(~이기 때문에)를 쓴다.

27 ②, ⑤ that절이 목적어로 쓰였을 때 that은 생략할 수 있다.

28 의문사가 이끄는 명사절 안에서 의문사가 주어 역할을 하는 경우, 의문사 뒤에 동사를 바로 쓴다.

29 의문사가 이끄는 명사절은 「의문사 + 주어 + 동사」의 형태로 쓴다.

30 '나쁜 자세는 해로울 수 있기 때문에 사람들은 똑바로 앉아야 한다.'는 의미이므로 ① because(~이기 때문에)와 ④ since(~이기 때문에)를 쓸 수 있다.

31 so that은 '~하기 위해'의 의미로, 목적을 나타내는 부사절을 이끈다.

32 ⑤ Besides → Therefore[Thus/As a result]

33 ④ '~인지'의 의미의 명사절 접속사로 쓰였다.
①②③⑤ '만약 ~한다면'의 의미의 부사절 접속사로 쓰였다.

34
- '나는 버스를 기다리는 동안 기사들을 몇 개 읽었다.'는 의미이므로 while(~하는 동안)을 쓴다.
- '나의 언니는 요리에 뛰어난 반면 나는 아니다.'는 의미이므로 while(~인 반면에)을 쓴다.

35 앞의 문장인 '런던은 흥미로운 관광명소들로 가득하다.'의 예시를 보여주는 문장이므로 ① For example(예를 들어)을 쓴다.

36 '사람들에게 친절하게 대해라, 그러면 너는 그들에게 좋은 인상을 줄 것이다.'는 의미이고, 접속사 if를 쓰라고 했으므로 '만약 네가

사람들에게 친절하게 대한다면, 너는 그들에게 좋은 인상을 줄 것이다.'는 의미로 쓴다.

37 밑줄 친 부분과 ②: 주어 역할
①③④ 목적어 역할 　⑤ 보어 역할

38 명사절을 이끄는 접속사 if는 '~인지'의 의미이다. '치마를 사야 할지 또는 드레스를 사야 할지'라고 했으므로 '또는'을 의미하는 or을 쓴다.

39 첫 번째 빈칸: '스포츠에서 가장 중요한 것은 이기는 것이 아니라 정직하게 승부하는 것임을 명심해라.'라는 의미이므로 첫 번째 빈칸에는 not을 쓴다.
두 번째 빈칸: not A but B는 'A가 아니라 B'라는 의미이므로 두 번째 빈칸에는 but을 쓴다.

40 ③ or not은 if와는 쓸 수 없으므로 whether를 쓴다.

41 ⑤ Now that은 '~이기 때문에'라는 의미이다.

42 '~하는 동안'이라는 의미로 while을 쓴다.

43 '만약 ~한다면'이라는 의미로 if를 쓴다.

44 despite는 전치사이므로 뒤에 절이 아닌 명사(구)를 쓴다. '나는 비록 그녀에게 동의하지 않지만 그녀의 의견을 존중한다.'는 의미이며, 절을 이끄는 접속사가 필요하므로 '비록 ~이지만'이라는 의미인 though/although/even though를 쓴다.

45 「so that ~」은 「in order[so as] + to부정사」로 바꿔 쓸 수 있다.

46 '그 용암은 너무 뜨거워서 그 금속을 녹였다.'는 의미이므로 '너무 ~해서 …한'의 의미인 「so + 형용사 + that …」을 쓴다.

47 '결과적으로'라는 의미인 As a result를 쓴다.

48 밑줄 친 부분과 ②: '~이기 때문에'의 의미로 쓰였다.
① '~로서'의 의미로 쓰였다.
③ '~하면서'의 의미로 쓰였다.
④⑤ '~처럼, ~듯이'의 의미로 쓰였다.

CHAPTER 13
관계사

p.320

POINT 1　관계대명사의 역할과 종류

연습문제

1 ⓐ	**2** ⓑ	**3** ⓒ	**4** ⓑ
5 ⓐ	**6** ⓒ	**7** ⓐ	**8** ⓒ
9 ⓑ	**10** ⓐ		

POINT 2-1　주격 관계대명사

연습문제 A

1 the green bin which[that] is for recycling
2 a lot of children who[that] live in Mark's neighborhood
3 a picture which[that] showed my mother as a child
4 a new TV model which[that] has many special features
5 the woman who[that] answered the door

연습문제 B

| **1** O | **2** O |
| **3** X | **4** O |

POINT 2-2　목적격 관계대명사

연습문제

1 who[whom/that] I met last month
2 which[that] Ms. Johnson wrote a few days ago
3 which[that] we can take to Paris
4 who[whom/that] my mother used to babysit
5 which[that] we explored on our vacation
6 who[whom/that] I play with every weekend
7 who[whom/that] I missed the most while studying abroad

POINT 2-3　소유격 관계대명사

연습문제

1 whose location suits you best[the location of which suits you best]
2 whose order was late
3 whose walls had been painted blue[the walls of which had been painted blue]
4 whose invention won the competition
5 whose face had turned red in the sun

기출 적중문제

정답 ③

해설 · 선행사(the author)가 소유하는 대상이 되는 명사(book)가 있으므로 소유격 관계대명사 whose를 쓴다.

· 선행사(The children)가 소유하는 대상이 되는 명사(names)가 있으므로 소유격 관계대명사 whose를 쓴다.

POINT 3 관계대명사 that

연습문제 A

1 who, whom		**2** which	
3 who		**4** which	
5 who		**6** which	
7 who, whom		**8** which	

연습문제 B

1 whose	**2** O	**3** O			
4 that	**5** whose	**6** O			
7 O					

연습문제 C

1 ⓐ	**2** ⓑ	**3** ⓒ	**4** ⓔ				
5 ⓐ	**6** ⓑ	**7** ⓓ	**8** ⓓ				
9 ⓒ							

기출 적중문제

정답 ①

해설 ①: 명사절 접속사
②③④⑤: 관계대명사

POINT 4 관계대명사 what

연습문제

1 What he discovered
2 what I said to you
3 What we did yesterday
4 what he explained

기출 적중문제

정답 ⑤

해설 ⑤: that
①②③④: what

POINT 5 전치사 + 관계대명사

연습문제

1 which[that] he cuts fish with / with which he cuts fish
2 which[that] we spent our vacation at / at which we spent our vacation
3 who[whom/that] the nurse gave some medicine to / to whom the nurse gave some medicine

4 which[that] we were invited to / to which we were invited

POINT 6 관계부사의 역할과 종류

연습문제 A

1 when your kids graduated from middle school
2 where I met my wife for the first time
3 why I gained weight lately
4 how John beat the video game
5 where you can buy paints
6 when I went to the park
7 how she makes her bread
8 why temperatures are unstable
9 where he makes his paintings

연습문제 B

1 where	**2** which	**3** which			
4 why	**5** which	**6** in which			
7 why					

기출 적중문제

정답 ②, ⑤

해설 ① the way which → the way/how/the way in which
③ what → where/when/why/how
④ the reason for why → the reason for which/the reason why

POINT 7 관계사의 계속적 용법

연습문제 A

1 who[whom]		**2** when	
3 which		**4** where	
5 who		**6** which	
7 who[whom]		**8** where	

연습문제 B

1 who is a great baker
2 which was built 100 years ago
3 where we visited many historic sites
4 when we purchased skateboards
5 which caused great damage
6 who will move to America
7 where I bought a bottle of juice
8 which saved some time
9 who founded the company
10 who makes me laugh

기출 적중문제

정답 She tried to open the door, which was locked.

해설 관계사의 계속적 용법으로 선행사(the door)가 사물이므로 사물을 선행사로 하는 주격 관계대명사 which를 쓸 수 있다. (that은 콤마 뒤에 쓸 수 없다.)

POINT 8 복합관계사

연습문제 A
1 Whichever you wear
2 However hungry you are
3 whatever you require for the event
4 whenever he has no work to do
5 whomever we wish to invite
6 Whatever he chooses
7 Wherever you shop

연습문제 B
1	whatever	2	However	3	Whenever
4	Whoever	5	However	6	Wherever
7	Whatever				

기출 적중문제

정답 ③

해설 ① Whatever → Whenever
② whomever → whenever/whatever
④ Whoever → Whatever
⑤ Wherever → However

서술형 대비 문제

(A)
1 ⓐ which[that] ⓑ where ⓒ whom
ⓓ who[that]
2 ⓐ which[that] ⓑ what ⓒ who[that] ⓓ why

(B)
1 I forgot the name of that country which[that] is next to Thailand.
2 Lily is my neighbor who[whom/that] everybody likes very much.
3 Mr. Hwang is a writer whose book became a best seller.
4 Let me show you how my grandmother bakes scones.
5 This is the street where Jason said he would meet us.
6 I can still remember the day when I won the dance contest.

(C)
1 The soccer players practiced on the field, which was still wet due to the rain.
2 This is the restaurant's chef, who has worked here for years.
3 I saw my cousin in June, when I went to Texas.
4 She went to the store, where she bought some potatoes.
5 I sent him a birthday card, which he didn't receive.

(D)
1 Whatever he says
2 Whoever needs a new textbook
3 However upset you feel
4 Wherever you travel
5 Whoever visits this museum
6 Whenever I have an exam
7 However famous the singer is

중간·기말고사 실전 문제

1 ① 2 ⑤ 3 This novel is about a girl who[that] becomes a brave soldier. 4 ③
5 ① 6 ⓐ who[whom] ⓑ which 7 ③
8 ② 9 There are many benefits of this electrical technology which makes our lives more convenient. 10 ④ 11 (1) which became a best seller (2) which was written by a young woman (3) whose main character reminded me of myself[the main character of which reminded me of myself] 12 that 13 ① 14 ① 15 What we need is to respect foreign cultures. 16 what
17 ⓓ → what 18 ② 19 (A) that (B) what
20 ③ 21 ⓒ → We listened to a speaker who[that] gives motivational speeches. 22 He showed us sample tools made of wood.
23 (A) which (B) whom 24 ② 25 ③, ④
26 ③ 27 (A) who (B) which (C) that 28 ⓒ → I visited China with my parents, who had never been there before. 29 which made me too exhausted 30 in that → where[in which]
31 (1) a person who travels a lot (2) a horror movie which many people watched 32 ③ 33 ②
34 ⓐ where ⓑ how 35 where 36 ④, ⑤ 37 ③
38 (1) what Jacob wants to do (2) where my husband proposed 39 ① 40 (1) Whatever you want to do today (2) Whenever you get angry
41 ② 42 ③ 43 ③ 44 ⑤ 45 What / whose 46 which[that] / where

1 · 선행사(anyone)가 사람이므로 관계대명사 who, that을 쓸 수 있다.
· 선행사(oven)가 사물이므로 관계대명사 which, that을 쓸 수 있다.

2 (A) 선행사(a person)가 단수명사이므로 단수동사 works를 쓴다.
(B) 선행사(people)가 복수명사이므로 복수동사 love를 쓴다.
(C) 선행사(a vending machine)가 단수명사이므로 단수동사 sells를 쓴다.

3 두 번째 문장은 첫 번째 문장의 a girl에 대해 보충 설명하고 있고, 선행사(a girl)가 사람을 나타내므로 사람을 선행사로 하는 주격 관계대명사 who[that]를 쓴다.

4 ③ 소유격(Her)이 쓰였으므로 소유격 관계대명사 whose를 쓴다.

5 ① who is → who are

6 ⓐ 선행사(the roommate)가 사람이므로 사람을 선행사로 하는 목적격 관계대명사 who[whom]를 쓴다.
ⓑ 선행사(the new camera)가 사물이므로 사물을 선행사로 하는 목적격 관계대명사 which를 쓴다.

7 · 선행사(a friend of mine)가 소유하는 대상이 되는 명사 (hobby)가 있으므로 소유격 관계대명사 whose를 쓴다.
· 선행사(the person)가 소유하는 대상이 되는 명사 (computer)가 있으므로 소유격 관계대명사 whose를 쓴다.

8 ⓐ 선행사(the person)가 사람이므로 사람을 선행사로 하는 주격 관계대명사 who를 쓴다.
ⓑ 선행사(a kind of electric current)가 사물이므로 사물을 선행사로 하는 목적격 관계대명사 which를 쓴다.

9 두 번째 문장은 첫 번째 문장의 this electrical technology에 대해 보충 설명하고 있고, 선행사(this electrical technology)가 사물을 나타내므로 사물을 선행사로 하는 주격 관계대명사 which를 쓴다.

10 ⓐ (A)는 주격 관계대명사 that과 바꿔 쓸 수 있다.
ⓑ (A)와 (C)는 주격 관계대명사로 생략할 수 없다.
ⓔ (D)는 선행사가 Animals이므로 have가 맞다.

11 (1) 선행사(a book)가 사물이므로 사물을 선행사로 하는 주격 관계대명사 which를 쓴다.
(2) 선행사(a novel)가 사물이므로 사물을 선행사로 하는 주격 관계대명사 which를 쓴다.
(3) 선행사(a book)가 소유하는 대상이 되는 명사(main character)가 있으므로 소유격 관계대명사 whose를 쓴다. 이때, 선행사가 사물이므로 「whose + 명사」는 「명사 + of which」로 바꿔 쓸 수 있다.

12 (A) 선행사(people)가 사람이므로 사람을 선행사로 하는 주격 관계대명사 who나 that을 쓴다.
(B) 선행사(the flowers)가 사물이므로 사물을 선행사로 하는 목적격 관계대명사 which나 that을 쓴다.
(C) 선행사(the cutest dog)가 사물이고 선행사에 최상급이 포함되므로 목적격 관계대명사 that을 쓴다.

13 밑줄 친 부분과 ①: 관계대명사 that
②: 지시형용사   ③: 지시대명사   ④⑤: 명사절 접속사

14 ①: 관계대명사
②③④⑤: 명사절 접속사

15 관계대명사 what은 선행사를 포함하고 있으며, '~한 것'을 의미한다.

16 · '그 결과는 내가 기대했던 것이 아니었다.'는 의미이므로 관계대명사 what을 쓴다.
· '오렌지 주스와 우유는 우리가 냉장고에 가지고 있는 것이다.'는 의미이므로 관계대명사 what을 쓴다.

17 ⓓ '그는 우리가 찾았던 것을 재확인했다'는 의미이므로 관계대명사 what을 쓴다.

18 ②: 의문사
①③④⑤: 관계대명사

19 (A) 선행사(the most famous animals)가 사물이고 선행사에 최상급이 포함되므로 관계대명사 that을 쓴다.
(B) '이것은 세계의 몇몇 다른 나라에서 벌어졌던 것과 유사하다.' 는 의미이므로 관계대명사 what을 쓴다.

20 (A) '내가 너에게 보기를 추천하는 공연'이라는 의미이므로 shows 뒤에 관계대명사가 필요하다. 선행사(the shows)가 동사 see의 목적어이므로 목적격 관계대명사 that을 쓴다. (목적격 관계대명사는 생략할 수 있다.)
(B) '지난밤 그 피아니스트에 의해 연주된 노래'라는 의미이므로 the song 뒤에 관계대명사가 필요하다. 선행사(the song)가 동사 played의 주어이므로 주격 관계대명사와 함께 수동태 동사 「be + p.p.」의 형태를 만드는 which was를 쓴다. (「주격 관계대명사 + be동사」는 생략할 수 있다.)

21 ⓒ 주격 관계대명사는 생략할 수 없다.

22 두 번째 문장은 첫 번째 문장의 sample tools에 대해 보충 설명하고 있고, 선행사(sample tools)가 사물을 나타내므로 사물을 선행사로 하는 주격 관계대명사 which[that]를 쓴다. 'He showed us sample tools which[that] were made of wood.'의 문장에서 「주격 관계대명사 + be 동사」는 생략할 수 있다.

23 (A) 관계대명사가 전치사의 목적어일 때, 전치사를 관계대명사 바로 앞에 쓸 수 있다. 선행사(a subject)가 사물이므로 사물을 선행사로 하는 목적격 관계대명사 which를 쓴다. 전치사 뒤에는 관계대명사 that을 쓸 수 없다.
(B) 관계대명사가 전치사의 목적어일 때, 전치사를 관계대명사 바로 앞에 쓸 수 있다. 선행사(Amy)가 사람이므로 사물을 선행사로 하는 목적격 관계대명사 whom을 쓴다. 전치사 뒤에는 관계대명사 who나 that을 쓸 수 없다.

24 빈칸은 to whom my uncle is이므로 ⓑ에는 whom이 들어간다.

25 ③ 전치사 뒤에는 관계대명사 that을 쓸 수 없다.
④ 관계부사 where는 「전치사 + 관계대명사」이므로 in을 중복으로 쓸 수 없다.

26 · 관계대명사의 계속적 용법으로 선행사(my friend)가 사람이므로 사람을 선행사로 하는 주격 관계대명사인 who를 쓸 수 있다. (that은 콤마 뒤에 쓸 수 없다.)
· 관계대명사의 계속적 용법으로 선행사(the math test)가 사물이므로 사물을 선행사로 하는 목적격 관계대명사인 which를 쓸 수 있다. (that은 콤마 뒤에 쓸 수 없다.)

27 (A) '어제 나는 나의 형과 이야기를 했는데, 그는 수의사이다.'라는

의미이므로 사람을 선행사로 하는 주격 관계대명사인 who를
쓸 수 있다. (that은 콤마 뒤에 쓸 수 없다.)

(B) '그는 병원에서 일하는데, 그곳은 집에서 가깝다.'는 의미이므
로 사물을 선행사로 하는 주격 관계대명사인 which를 쓸 수
있다. (that은 콤마 뒤에 쓸 수 없다.)

(C) '그는 아프거나 다친 많은 동물들을 도와준다.'는 의미이므로
주격 관계대명사 that을 쓴다.

28 ⓒ 계속적 용법에서 관계대명사 that은 쓸 수 없다.

29 '나는 빙상 스케이트를 온종일 연습했는데, 그것이 나를 매우 지치
게 했다.'는 의미이므로 관계대명사의 계속적 용법이다. 이때 관계
대명사는 which를 쓸 수 있다.

30 전치사 뒤에는 관계대명사 that을 쓸 수 없으므로 in which를 쓰
거나, in which 대신 장소를 나타내는 관계부사 where를 쓴다.

31 (1) 선행사(a person)가 사람이므로 사람을 선행사로 하는 주격
관계대명사 who를 쓴다.

(2) 선행사(a horror movie)가 사물이므로 사물을 선행사로 하
는 목적격 관계대명사 which를 쓴다.

32 (A) '그때는 내가 서울에서 런던으로 이사했던 그 해다.'라는 의미
이므로 시간을 나타내는 관계부사 when을 쓴다.

(B) '이곳은 나의 팀이 축구를 연습하곤 했던 축구장이다.'라는 의
미이므로 장소를 나타내는 관계부사 where를 쓴다.

(C) '너는 그들이 역사를 그렇게 많이 좋아하는 이유를 아니?'라
는 의미이므로 이유를 나타내는 관계부사 why를 쓴다.

33 ⓒ the reason how → the reason why
ⓔ where → which

34 ⓐ '나는 많은 물고기가 내 주변에서 헤엄치고 있던 장소에 있었
다.'라는 의미이므로 장소를 나타내는 관계부사 where를 쓴
다.

ⓑ '나중에, 나의 선생님은 내가 물속에서 자연스럽게 숨 쉴 수 있
는 방법을 알려주셨다.'라는 의미이므로 방법을 나타내는 관계
부사 how를 쓴다.

35 두 번째 문장은 첫 번째 문장의 the museum에 대해 보충 설명
하고 있고, 선행사(the museum)가 장소를 나타내므로 관계부
사 where를 쓴다.

36 ④ for which → the thing which[that]
⑤ at which → for which

37 ⓐⓓⓔ: which
ⓑⓒ: where

38 (1) '너는 주말에 Jacob이 하고 싶어 하는 것에 대해 생각해 보았
니?'라는 의미이므로 관계대명사 what을 쓴다.

(2) '이곳은 나의 남편이 나에게 프러포즈한 장소이다.'라는 의미
이므로 장소를 나타내는 관계부사 where를 쓴다.

39 (A) '이곳은 학생들이 디자인에 대해 배우는 교실이다.'는 의미이
다. 전치사 in이 있으므로 관계대명사 which를 쓴다.

(B) '2월은 내가 항상 따뜻한 나라로 가고 싶어 하는 달이다.'는 의
미이므로 시간을 나타내는 관계부사 when을 쓴다.

(C) '내가 대학 시절 동안 일했던 서점을 너에게 보여줄게.'라는 의

미이므로 장소를 나타내는 관계부사 where를 쓴다.

40 (1) '네가 오늘 하고 싶어 하는 무엇이든지 나는 괜찮다.'라는 의미
이므로 Anything that은 Whatever로 바꿔 쓸 수 있다.

(2) '네가 화날 때마다 말하기 전에 심호흡을 하려고 노력해라.'라
는 의미로 At any time when은 Whenever로 쓸 수 있다.

41 ⓐⓒⓓ: whenever
ⓑ: whoever   ⓔ: However

42 ③ 「전치사 + 관계대명사」에서 관계대명사는 생략할 수 없다.

43 밑줄 친 부분과 ③: 관계대명사
①②④⑤: 의문사

44 ⑤ wherever → whatever

45 첫 번째 빈칸: 관계대명사 what은 선행사를 포함하고 있으며,
'~한 것'을 의미한다.
두 번째 빈칸: 관계대명사 앞에 선행사(a cream doughnut)가
소유하는 대상이 되는 명사(taste)가 있으므로 소유격 관계대명
사 whose를 쓴다.

46 첫 번째 빈칸: 선행사(The hospital)가 사물이므로 사물을 선행
사로 하는 주격 관계대명사 which[that]를 쓴다.
두 번째 빈칸: 선행사(the site)가 장소이므로 장소를 나타내는
관계부사 where를 쓴다.

CHAPTER 14
가정법

p.348

POINT 1 가정법 과거와 가정법 과거완료

1	moved	2	could walk
3	had practiced	4	would have given
5	returned	6	will view
7	had paid	8	wouldn't have been
9	get		

1 had / would buy
2 had received / would have replied
3 weren't / could fall
4 had been / could have helped
5 were given / would study
6 hadn't fallen / wouldn't have occurred
7 were / would go
8 had used / wouldn't have gotten
9 finishes / will come

기출 적중문제

정답 ②
해설 ② 가정법 과거는 '만약 ~한다면 …할 텐데'의 의미로,「If + 주어 + 동사의 과거형, 주어 + 조동사의 과거형 + 동사원형」으로 쓴다.

POINT 2 혼합 가정법

1 hadn't broken / could play
2 had been / wouldn't need
3 hadn't helped / would be tired
4 hadn't caught / couldn't feel
5 had packed / would be
6 had brought / could play

POINT 3 가정법을 직설법으로 바꾸는 법

1 I don't remember Christine's e-mail address, I can't send her a note
2 I didn't know the deadline, I made other plans
3 Angela doesn't know how to sew, she can't make herself a dress
4 you didn't come at 3 P.M., you didn't see my parents
5 she didn't study for today's quiz, she failed it

6 Tom didn't exercise regularly, he is out of shape now

1 Minsu were good at soccer
2 I can't go to the concert
3 the book weren't so interesting
4 Clara doesn't have a bus card
5 I wasn't invited
6 it hadn't started to snow
7 you didn't tell Mina about the contest
8 you didn't wash your shirt in cold water
9 wouldn't feel uncomfortable now

기출 적중문제

정답 I spent all of my money on snacks / I'm broke now
해설 밑줄 친 부분은 혼합 가정법이므로 혼합 가정법을 직설법으로 바꾸려면 if절의 과거완료시제를 과거시제로, 주절의 과거시제를 현재시제로 바꾸고 if절과 주절의 긍정·부정을 뒤바꾼다.

POINT 4 if를 생략한 가정법

1 Were I an architect
2 Had you not been at the party
3 Were he here
4 Had Adam spent more time on the painting
5 Had she not followed the rules
6 Were I as fast as a cheetah
7 Had she not known how to use this oven
8 Had you bought a good quality speaker

POINT 5 Without 가정법

1 could have been
2 would get lost
3 wouldn't know
4 wouldn't have laughed
5 wouldn't have woken up
6 wouldn't be able to
7 couldn't have passed
8 would have been

1 If it were not for water
2 If it were not for my mother's rules
3 If it were not for the dark curtains
4 If it were not for the air conditioner
5 If it had not been for Josh
6 If it had not been for Derek's help
7 If it had not been for your warning

8 If it had not been for the lifeguard

정답 Elizabeth, the play wouldn't have been touching

해설 「If it had not been for ~」에서 if를 생략한 「Had it not been for ~」는 「Without + 명사, 가정법 과거완료」로 바꿔 쓸 수 있다.

POINT 6 I wish 가정법

1	had offered	**2**	understood
3	had studied	**4**	had enjoyed
5	had	**6**	had gone

1	weren't	**2**	can't talk
3	had come	**4**	didn't read
5	doesn't get	**6**	had learned

정답 ④

해설 첫 번째 빈칸: 「I wish + 주어 + 동사의 과거형」은 '~하면 좋을 텐데'의 의미로 현재 실현 가능성이 매우 낮거나 없는 일을 소망할 때 쓴다.
두 번째 빈칸: 「I wish + 주어 + had p.p.」는 '~했다면 좋을 텐데'의 의미로 과거에 이루지 못한 일에 대한 아쉬움을 나타낼 때 쓴다.

POINT 7 as if[though] 가정법

1	got along	**2**	knew
3	had studied	**4**	had received
5	hadn't slept	**6**	had sung
7	understood		

1	looks / weren't occupied
2	treated / weren't
3	talks / had seen
4	behaved / were
5	acts / were gone
6	talked / had participated
7	pretends / had lived
8	seemed / had gotten

정답 she won the lottery

해설 「주어 + 동사의 현재형 + as if + 주어 + 동사의 과거형」은 '마치 ~한 것처럼 …한다'의 의미이다.

서술형 대비 문제

A
1. If I finished my school assignment / I could watch my favorite TV show
2. If Mozart had lived longer / he would have created more masterpieces
3. Had I known that you were in trouble / I would have helped you
4. Without the Internet, he wouldn't have heard the news
5. I wish the singer had released the new album last month
6. Were he in Brazil, he could visit Sao Paolo
7. The cats seemed as if they were talking to each other
8. Were it not for the restrictions / we could build a house here
9. My friend acted as though she didn't spread my secrets
10. If I hadn't forgotten the eggs yesterday / I could make some cookies now

B

1	had	**2**	knew
3	would save	**4**	had bought

C
1. my dad didn't have to go to hospital tomorrow
2. I had remembered to call you this morning
3. (that) I didn't take a vacation in Bali last summer
4. it were not for their wings
5. it had not been for your help
6. it not for airplanes

중간·기말고사 실전 문제

1 ③   **2** ③   **3** the museum isn't closer to downtown, it isn't popular   **4** the museum were located near a busy area, it would get more customers   **5** ①   **6** I had arrived here earlier, I could sit in the front row now   **7** I didn't get a better grade on the test   **8** If it had not been for my dog's growling   **9** ③   **10** ②
11 I hadn't skipped the class, I wouldn't be stuck here writing an apology letter to my teacher today
12 ④   **13** ③   **14** ④   **15** (A) I wish I looked a bit older. (B) If I looked older, I would be treated better. (C) You look as if you were twelve to

me.　**16** ④　**17** ④　**18** I wish the Wi-Fi worked in this hotel.　**19** I wish I had met my cousin when she was in town.　**20** ③　**21** ④ **22** as if I were a professional dancer　**23** as if it had been released　**24** (1) I were at the pool, I would be happy (2) we had free time, we could go　**25** more people visited the restaurant, it would extend its opening hours　**26** ③ **27** ③　**28** we had taken a picture together, I would have proof of our meeting now　**29** the teacher had not explained the riddle, we couldn't have understood its answer　**30** If she had asked earlier, I would have helped her.**31** ③　**32** didn't hear　**33** ④　**34** ③　**35** something to eat, I would have passed out　**36** ⑤　**37** ⑤ **38** ③　**39** She looked as if she were a real princess.　**40** ②　**41** ③　**42** ② **43** ⑤　**44** ②　**45** ①

1 첫 번째 빈칸: 가정법 과거의 주절에는 「주어 + 조동사의 과거형 + 동사원형」을 쓰므로 would를 쓴다.
두 번째 빈칸: 가정법 과거의 if절에는 「If + 주어 + 동사의 과거형」을 쓰므로 had를 쓴다.

2 ⓒ will → would
ⓓ didn't start → hadn't started

3 밑줄 친 (A)는 가정법 과거이므로 가정법 과거를 직설법으로 바꾸려면 if절과 주절의 과거 시제를 현재 시제로 바꾸고, 긍정·부정을 뒤바꾼다.

4 밑줄 친 (B)는 현재의 사실을 이야기하는 직설법 문장이므로 가정법으로 바꾸려면 「If + 주어 + 동사의 과거형, 주어 + 조동사의 과거형 + 동사원형」의 형태인 가정법 과거를 쓴다.

5 「Without + 명사, 가정법 과거완료」는 '~가 없었다면 …했을 텐데'의 의미이다.

6 혼합 가정법은 과거의 사실과 반대되는 일이 현재까지 영향을 미치는 상황을 가정할 때 쓰며 「If + 주어 + had p.p., 주어 + 조동사의 과거형 + 동사원형」을 쓴다.

7 「I wish + 주어 + had p.p.」는 「I'm sorry (that) + 주어 + 동사의 과거형」 형태의 직설법으로 바꿔 쓸 수 있다.

8 주절이 「조동사의 과거형 + have + p.p.」이므로 가정법 과거완료 형태이고, 「Without + 명사」는 「If it had not been for + 명사」로 바꿔 쓸 수 있다.

9 ·「I wish + 주어 + 동사의 과거형」은 '~하면 좋을 텐데'의 의미로 현재 실현 가능성이 매우 낮거나 없는 일을 소망할 때 쓴다.
·「주어 + 동사의 현재형 + as if[though] + 주어 + 동사의 과거형」은 '마치 ~한 것처럼 …한다'의 의미이다.

10 첫 번째 빈칸: '만약 우리가 어제 선풍기를 샀다면, 우리는 지금 너무 덥지 않을 텐데.'의 의미이므로 혼합 가정법을 쓴다. 혼합 가정법의 if절에는 「If + 주어 + had p.p.」를 쓴다.

두 번째 빈칸: 주절이 「조동사의 과거형 + have + p.p.」이므로 가정법 과거완료 형태이며, 가정법에서 if절의 동사가 조동사 had를 포함한 경우 if를 생략할 수 있다. 이때 if절의 주어와 had의 위치를 바꿔 「Had + 주어」의 형태로 쓴다.

11 혼합 가정법은 과거의 사실과 반대되는 일이 현재까지 영향을 미치는 상황을 가정할 때 쓰며 「If + 주어 + had p.p., 주어 + 조동사의 과거형 + 동사원형」을 쓴다.

12 ④ 현재의 사실과 반대되는 일을 가정하고 있으므로 가정법 과거 「If + 주어 + 동사의 과거형, 주어 + 조동사의 과거형 + 동사원형」을 쓴다.

13 ③ 현재의 사실과 반대되는 일을 가정하고 있으므로 가정법 과거 「If + 주어 + 동사의 과거형, 주어 + 조동사의 과거형 + 동사원형」을 쓴다.

14 ① can → could
② is → were
③ can → could
⑤ will not have fallen → would not have fallen

15 (A) 「I wish + 주어 + 동사의 과거형」은 '~하면 좋을 텐데'의 의미이다.
(B) 가정법 과거는 「If + 주어 + 동사의 과거형, 주어 + 조동사의 과거형 + 동사원형」을 쓴다.
(C) 「주어 + 동사의 현재형 + as if[though] + 주어 + 동사의 과거형」은 '마치 ~한 것처럼 …한다'의 의미이다.

16 ④ 가정법 과거는 「If + 주어 + 동사의 과거형, 주어 + 조동사의 과거형 + 동사원형」을 쓰고, 주어진 문장은 현재의 사실과 반대되는 일을 가정하고 있으므로 지금 여분의 표를 가지고 있지 않다는 것을 나타낸다.

17 ① am → were
② will → would
③ have → had
⑤ won't → wouldn't

18 「I'm sorry (that) + 주어 + 동사의 현재형」은 「I wish + 주어 + 동사의 과거형」으로 바꿔 쓸 수 있다.

19 「I'm sorry (that) + 주어 + 동사의 과거형」은 「I wish + 주어 + had p.p.」로 바꿔 쓸 수 있다.

20 ③ 현재의 사실과 반대되는 일을 가정하는 가정법 과거 「If + 주어 + 동사의 과거형, 주어 + 조동사의 과거형 + 동사원형」으로 바꿔 쓸 수 있다.

21 ④ 과거의 사실과 반대되는 일을 가정하는 가정법 과거완료 「If + 주어 + had + p.p., 주어 + 조동사의 과거형 + have + p.p.」로 바꿔 쓸 수 있다.

22 주절의 시제(현재시제)와 같은 시점의 사실과 반대되는 일을 가정하는 「as if[though] + 주어 + 동사의 과거형」를 쓴다.

23 주절의 시제(현재시제)보다 이전 시점의 사실과 반대되는 일을 가정하는 「as if[though] + 주어 + had + p.p.」를 쓴다.

24 (A) 가정법 과거는 「If + 주어 + 동사의 과거형, 주어 + 조동사의

과거형 +동사원형」의 형태로 쓴다.

(B) 가정법 과거는 「If + 주어 + 동사의 과거형, 주어 + 조동사의 과거형 +동사원형」의 형태로 쓴다.

25 현재의 사실과 반대되는 일을 가정하고 있으므로 가정법 과거 「If + 주어 + 동사의 과거형, 주어 + 조동사의 과거형 + 동사원형」을 쓴다.

26 ① will → would
② couldn't achieve → couldn't have achieved
④ will gain → would have gained
⑤ miss → missed

27 ③ I'm sorry that I don't have a puppy at home.으로 써야 두 문장의 의미가 같다.

28 직설법 문장을 혼합 가정법 문장으로 바꾸기 위해서는 as절의 과거시제를 과거완료시제로, 주절의 현재시제를 과거시제로 바꾸고, as절과 주절의 긍정·부정을 뒤바꾼다.

29 직설법 문장을 가정법 과거완료로 바꾸기 위해서는 as절과 주절의 과거시제를 과거완료시제로 바꾸고 긍정·부정을 바꾼다.

30 과거의 사실과 반대되는 일을 가정하고 있으므로 가정법 과거완료 「If + 주어 + had + p.p., 주어 + 조동사의 과거형 + have + p.p.」를 쓴다.

31 · 「I'm sorry (that) + 주어 + 동사의 현재형」은 「I wish + 주어 + 동사의 과거형」으로 바꿔 쓸 수 있다.
· 「I'm sorry (that) + 주어 + 동사의 과거형」은 「I wish + 주어 + had p.p.」로 바꿔 쓸 수 있다.

32 가정법 과거완료 문장을 직설법 문장으로 바꾸기 위해서는 if절과 주절의 과거완료시제를 과거시제로 바꾸고 긍정·부정을 뒤바꾼다.

33 「I wish + 주어 + 동사의 과거형」은 '~하면 좋을 텐데'의 의미로 현재 실현 가능성이 매우 낮거나 없는 일을 소망할 때 쓴다.

34 「I wish + 주어 + had p.p.」는 '~했다면 좋을 텐데'의 의미로 과거에 이루지 못한 일에 대한 아쉬움을 나타낼 때 쓴다.

35 「Without + 명사, 가정법 과거완료」는 '~가 없었다면 …했을 텐데'의 의미이다.

36 첫 번째 빈칸: 현재의 사실과 반대되는 일을 가정하는 가정법 과거 「If + 주어 + 동사의 과거형, 주어 + 조동사의 과거형 + 동사원형」을 써야 하므로 knew를 쓴다.
두 번째 빈칸: 현재의 사실과 반대되는 일을 가정하는 가정법 과거 「If + 주어 + 동사의 과거형, 주어 + 조동사의 과거형 + 동사원형」을 써야 하므로 could try를 쓴다.

37 '마치 ~했었던 것처럼 …했다'는 의미이므로 「주어 + 동사의 과거형 + as if[though] + 주어 + had p.p.」를 쓴다.

38 ① am → were
② know → knew
④ is → were
⑤ will be → were

39 '마치 ~했던 것처럼 …했다'의 의미이므로 「주어 + 동사의 과거형

+ as if + 주어 + 동사의 과거형」를 쓴다.

40 첫 번째 빈칸: '만약 Mario가 그의 의사의 조언을 들었다면, 그는 오늘 나아졌을 텐데.'라는 의미이므로 혼합 가정법을 쓴다. 혼합 가정법의 if절에는 「If + 주어 + had p.p.」를 쓴다.
두 번째 빈칸: 혼합 가정법의 주절에는 「주어 + 조동사의 과거형 + 동사원형」을 쓴다.

41 첫 번째 빈칸: 과거의 사실과 반대되는 일을 가정하는 가정법 과거완료를 쓴다. 가정법 과거완료에서 if절에는 「If + 주어 + had p.p.」를 쓴다. 가정법에서 if절의 동사가 조동사 had를 포함하므로 if를 생략할 수 있다. 이때 if절의 주어와 had의 위치를 바꿔 「Had + 주어」의 형태로 쓴다.
두 번째 빈칸: 가정법 과거완료에서 주절에는 「주어 + 조동사의 과거형 + have p.p.」를 쓴다.

42 ⓐ have cooked → had cooked
ⓓ don't eat → didn't eat[hadn't eaten]

43 과거의 사실과 반대되는 일을 가정하고 있으므로 가정법 과거완료 「If + 주어 + had + p.p., 주어 + 조동사의 과거형 + have + p.p.」를 쓴다.

44 첫 번째 빈칸: '만약 내가 더 나은 절약가였다면 이번 여름에 그곳에 갈 수 있었을 텐데.'라는 의미의 가정법 과거완료를 쓴다. 가정법 과거완료의 if절에는 「If + 주어 + had + p.p.」를 쓴다.
두 번째 빈칸: 현재 실현 가능성이 매우 낮거나 없는 일을 소망하는 「I wish + 주어 + 동사의 과거형」을 써야 하므로 had를 쓴다.

45 ① As Jim didn't study hard, he failed the test.로 써야 두 문장의 의미가 같다.

CHAPTER 15
일치와 화법

p.374

POINT 1-1 수 일치 Ⅰ

1 is	**2** is	**3** are	**4** is				
5 is	**6** is	**7** are	**8** is				

POINT 1-2 수 일치 Ⅱ

1 is	**2** live	**3** need
4 are	**5** arrives	**6** want
7 belong	**8** are	**9** seem
10 like	**11** want	

POINT 2 시제 일치

A
1 needed	**2** would do
3 hadn't noticed	**4** had finished
5 had lost	**6** could find
7 wouldn't tell	

B
1 walks	**2** is	**3** gathers
4 are	**5** eats	**6** ended
7 is	**8** sank	

기출 적중문제

정답 heard / had been

해설 첫 번째 빈칸: 주절에는 과거시제를 쓴다.
두 번째 빈칸: 주절이 과거시제이고 종속절은 그 이전 시점의 일을 말하므로 과거완료시제를 쓴다.

POINT 3-1 화법 전환: 평서문

1 said / she didn't want to leave the restaurant
2 said / he could go to the movies that night
3 told / she had enjoyed running along the Hangang the previous week
4 said / "My friend arrived in Korea yesterday."
5 said to / "I won a gold medal last year."

POINT 3-2 화법 전환: 의문사가 있는 의문문

1 asked where James was
2 asked / why I wasn't home then
3 asked / what Alex had told me the previous night
4 asked who was calling at that time
5 said to / "What is going on here?"
6 said / "When are you going to fix my bicycle?"
7 said to / "How did you make these pancakes?"

POINT 3-3 화법 전환: 의문사가 없는 의문문

1 asked / if[whether] I was good at remembering new vocabulary
2 asked / if[whether] I would stay at home the next[following] day
3 asked if[whether] they had watched the drama the previous night
4 asked / if[whether] I had ever been to Paris
5 said to / "Can you play any musical instruments?"
6 said to / "Is there a nice gym in this neighborhood?"
7 said to / "Do you know how to use this stove?"

POINT 3-4 화법 전환: 명령문

1 told / to hand in our essays by Thursday
2 instructed / not to throw my garbage on the street
3 asked / to get her some garlic from the supermarket
4 begged / to help him finish his homework on time
5 instructed / not to go onto the railroad tracks
6 advised / to try to study harder for that test

서술형 대비 문제

A
1 A number of people are waiting
2 Three hours is enough time
3 Eating fast food is really bad
4 The number of crimes has fallen
5 Eight kilometers is the distance

6 Neither Dave nor I am attending

7 Half of the customers are unhappy

(B)
1 O		**2** is	
3 O		**4** would live	
5 O		**6** was meeting	
7 invented		**8** O	
9 tastes		**10** O	

(C)

1 (that) he was planning a trip to Europe the following year

2 when she was going to meet my friends

3 (that) she had taken that writing class the previous year

4 if[whether] he could borrow a pair of scissors

5 to stop throwing balls around the room

6 who had left those eggs outside of the fridge

7 if[whether] he had started his project for geography class yet

8 not to leave our garbage outside our front door

(D)
(A) "I want to participate in the championship."
(B) "Why am I not being considered?"
(C) "Play a game between yourselves to decide."

중간·기말고사 실전 문제

1 ③　**2** ⑤　**3** ⓐ is ⓑ are　**4** ②
5 ②　**6** ③　**7** ③　**8** ②　**9** ④
10 are → is　**11** ②　**12** what he had done the previous night / (that) he had gone to a baseball game with Woojin　**13** if[whether] there was anything she could get for him / to get him a cup of tea　**14** had gotten　**15** could register
16 ④　**17** ④　**18** said / won't / tomorrow
19 My friend asked who had brought a camera
20 has seen → had seen　**21** ①, ②　**22** said to / were / last week　**23** ①　**24** ⑤　**25** ③
26 ②　**27** Susie told me (that) I had arrived really late that day.　**28** My cousin told me not to change the channel on the TV.　**29** The police officer ordered the thieves to raise their hands in the air.
30 ③　**31** ②　**32** ④

1　③「the number of + 복수명사」에는 항상 단수동사를 쓴다.

2　⑤ not only A but also B는 B에 동사를 수일치시키므로 were

를 쓴다.

3　ⓐ is: 주어가 구면 항상 단수동사를 쓴다.
　　ⓑ are: Both A and B는 항상 복수동사를 쓴다.

4　② 주어가 거리면 항상 단수동사를 쓴다. 우리말의 시제에 맞추어 현재시제를 쓴다.

5　② 간접 화법을 직접 화법으로 바꿀 때, 주절의 전달동사 asked 를 said로 바꾸고, 「의문사 + 동사 + 주어」의 어순으로 쓴다. 간접 화법의 주절과 종속절의 시제가 같으므로 직접 화법은 현재시제를 쓴다.

6　① have → has
　　② are → is
　　④ make → makes
　　⑤ are → is

7　(A) 주어가 학과명이면 항상 단수동사를 쓴다.
　　(B) 주어가 구면 항상 단수동사를 쓴다.
　　(C)「a number of + 복수명사」는 항상 복수동사를 쓴다.

8　ⓒ needs → need
　　ⓓ are → is

9　④ 주절이 과거시제이므로 종속절에는 현재시제를 쓸 수 없다.

10　every가 포함된 주어에는 항상 단수동사를 쓴다.

11　주절이 과거시제이고 종속절은 그 이전부터 지속된 일을 말하므로, 주절에는 과거시제 told를 쓰고 종속절에는 과거완료진행시제 had been traveling을 쓴다.

12　첫 번째 빈칸: 의문사가 있는 의문문의 간접 화법은 의문사(what)로 주절과 종속절을 연결하고, 종속절을 「의문사 + 주어 + 동사」의 어순으로 쓴다. 전달동사가 과거시제이므로 종속절의 과거시제 did ~ do를 과거완료 시제 had done으로 바꾼다. 인칭대명사를 전달하는 사람의 입장에 맞게 바꿔야 하므로 you를 he로 바꾸고, 부사(구)를 전달하는 사람의 입장에 맞게 바꿔야 하므로 last night를 the previous night으로 바꿔 쓴다.
　　두 번째 빈칸: 전달동사가 과거시제이므로 종속절의 과거시제 went를 과거완료 시제 had gone으로 바꾸고, 인칭대명사를 전달하는 사람의 입장에 맞게 바꿔야 하므로 I를 he로 바꿔 쓴다.

13　첫 번째 빈칸: 의문사가 없는 의문문의 간접 화법은 if나 whether로 주절과 종속절을 연결하고, 전달동사가 과거시제이므로 종속절의 현재시제 Is ~ can get을 과거시제 was ~ could get으로 바꾼다. 인칭대명사를 전달하는 사람의 입장에 맞게 바꿔야 하므로 I를 she로 바꾸고 you를 him으로 바꿔 쓴다.
　　두 번째 빈칸: 명령문의 간접 화법은 동사원형을 to부정사로 바꾸고, 인칭대명사를 전달하는 사람의 입장에 맞게 바꿔야 하므로 me를 him으로 바꿔 쓴다.

14　주절이 과거시제이므로 종속절을 과거완료시제 had gotten으로 바꿔 쓴다.

15　주절이 과거시제이므로 종속절을 과거시제 could register로 바꿔 쓴다.

16　(A) 일반적 사실을 말하는 것이므로 주절의 시제와 상관없이 종속

절에는 항상 현재시제를 쓴다.
(B) 현재의 습관을 말하는 것이므로 주절의 시제와 상관없이 종속절에는 항상 현재시제를 쓴다.
(C) 역사적 사실을 말하는 것이므로 종속절에는 항상 과거시제를 쓴다.

17 전달동사 said to는 간접 화법으로 바꿀 때 시제를 일치시켜 told로 바꾼다.

18 첫 번째 빈칸: 간접 화법의 주절이 과거시제이므로 직접 화법의 주절도 과거시제 said를 쓴다.
두 번째 빈칸: 간접 화법의 종속절에 과거형 wouldn't가 쓰였으므로 직접 화법에는 현재형 won't를 쓴다.
세 번째 빈칸: 간접 화법의 the next day는 직접 화법에서 tomorrow로 바꿔 쓴다.

19 전달동사가 과거시제이므로 said를 asked로 바꾸고, 의문사가 의문의 주어이므로 「의문사 + 동사」의 어순을 그대로 쓴다. 전달동사가 과거시제이고 종속절의 동사가 과거시제 brought이므로 간접 화법의 종속절의 동사를 과거완료시제 had brought로 바꾼다.

20 전달동사가 과거시제이고 종속절의 동사가 과거시제 saw이므로 간접 화법의 종속절의 동사를 과거완료시제 had seen으로 바꾼다.

21 '그 관광객은 역 안에 화장실이 있는지를 물었다.'는 의미이다. 의문사가 없는 의문문은 if나 whether로 두 절을 연결한다.

22 첫 번째 빈칸: 간접 화법을 직접 화법으로 바꿀 때, 전달동사 told를 said to로 바꾼다.
두 번째 빈칸: 간접 화법의 종속절의 동사가 과거완료시제 had been closed이므로 직접 화법에는 과거시제 were closed를 쓴다.
세 번째 빈칸: 간접 화법의 the previous week은 직접 화법에서 last week으로 바꿔 쓴다.

23 ① made → makes

24 평서문을 간접 화법으로 바꿀 때, 주절의 전달동사가 said to인 경우 told로 바꿔 쓰고, 주절이 과거시제인 경우 종속절에는 현재시제 need를 과거시제 needed로 바꿔 쓴다.

25 ① She knows → I know
② wanted → want
④ my → your
⑤ the following day → yesterday

26 첫 번째 빈칸: 주절이 과거시제이므로 종속절에는 과거시제인 had를 쓴다.
두 번째 빈칸: 주절이 과거시제이므로 종속절에는 「조동사의 과거형 + 동사원형」인 would need를 쓴다.

27 직접 화법을 간접 화법으로 바꿀 때, 주절의 전달동사 said to를 told로 바꾼다. 직접 화법의 주절과 종속절이 모두 과거시제이므로 간접 화법의 종속절의 동사는 과거완료시제 had arrived를 쓴다. 직접 화법의 today는 간접 화법에서 that day로 바꿔 쓴다.

28 부정 명령문의 간접 화법은 명령문의 Don't를 「not + to부정사」의 형태로 바꾸므로 not to change를 쓴다.

29 전달동사 said to를 명령문의 어조에 따라 ordered로 바꿔 쓴다. 명령문의 동사원형을 to부정사로 바꾸므로 to raise를 쓰고, 인칭대명사를 전달하는 사람의 입장에 맞게 바꿔야 하므로 your를 their로 바꿔 쓴다.

30 ⓑ me call → me to call
ⓓ did we know → we knew
ⓔ your plane → my plane

31 ② I was done → if[whether] I was done

32 ④ don't cross → not to cross

CHAPTER 16
특수구문

p.392

POINT 1-1 강조

연습문제

1 a lot busier	**2** the very place
3 do appreciate	**4** did go

기출 적중문제

정답 I did turn in my homework on time.

해설 동사를 강조할 때는 동사원형 앞에 do를 주어의 인칭과 수, 시제에 맞춰 쓴다

POINT 1-2 강조: It is ~ that 강조 구문

연습문제 A

1 Amy	**2** the blue suit
3 at this store	**4** last year
5 my little brother	**6** a bagel
7 at the café	**8** this morning

연습문제 B

1 where	**2** when	**3** which
4 who	**5** when	**6** who

연습문제 C

1. It is Maggie that[who] takes excellent photographs.
2. It was my teacher that[who/whom] I saw in the subway station.
3. It was to the amusement park that[where] I promised to take my cousins.
4. It was behind the sofa that[where] she found her scarf.
5. It was in 2007 that[when] Steve Jobs introduced the iPhone.

기출 적중문제

정답 It was in the airport that[where] I lost my passport.

해설 「It is ~ that …」 강조 구문은 '…한 것은 바로 ~이다'의 의미로, 동사를 제외한 모든 문장 요소를 It is와 that 사이에 써서 강조할 수 있다. 이때 강조되는 말을 제외한 나머지 부분은 that 뒤에 쓰며, 기존 문장의 시제에 일치시킨다.

POINT 2 부정

연습문제

1 None	**2** no
3 Not all	**4** Not every
5 Neither	**6** Not every
7 not always	**8** Not all
9 not both	

POINT 3 도치

연습문제

1 did he play	**2** are the keys
3 am I	**4** she is
5 could Roy	

POINT 4 생략

연습문제

1 I was	**2** who was
3 it was	
4 turn on the air conditioner	
5 Napoleon Bonaparte	
6 swim in the lake	
7 you are	**8** it was
9 that	**10** whom
11 she is	**12** we were

POINT 5 동격

연습문제

1. performing before an audience
2. the German composer
3. Sujin should be the class president
4. the train has been delayed
5. getting injured
6. the actor
7. getting caught
8. I should go back to university
9. moving to Canada
10. my history teacher in middle school
11. he won the lottery
12. he would help Mary do her homework

POINT 6 병치

연습문제

1 fishing	**2** windy
3 walked	**4** interesting
5 see	**6** to decorate
7 listening	**8** energetic
9 clearly	**10** helpful
11 to order	

정답 puts → put
해설 took과 병치를 이루어야 하므로 put을 써야 한다.

서술형 대비 문제

Ⓐ **1** was Jinho that[who] met Suji on the street yesterday
   did meet Suji on the street yesterday
   was on the street that[where] Jinho met Suji yesterday

2 do want to have a hamburger for dinner tonight
   is a hamburger that[which] I want to have for dinner tonight
   is I that[who] want to have a hamburger for dinner tonight

3 is much[even/still/far/a lot] more expensive than the ring
   is her watch that[which] is more expensive than the ring
   is the ring that[which] her watch is more expensive than

4 was in my hometown that[where] a storm destroyed the building
   did destroy the building in my hometown
   was a storm that[which] destroyed the building in my hometown

Ⓑ **1** None of the windows
2 Here are the keys
3 Hardly did Jane expect to get
4 Not all (of) the rooms
5 There is the house
6 Onto the stage she walked

Ⓒ **1** Unless you are[were] invited by the host, you can't enter the venue.
2 Send me the photos if you can send me the photos.
3 The book that[which] I fell in love with is going to be made into a movie.
4 You may use my brush whenever you would like to use my brush.
5 The children found some old coins while they were digging in the dirt.
6 Though we were disappointed by the movie, we watched it until the end.
7 The shoes that[which] I purchased were not very expensive.

8 You can paint the walls whatever color you want to paint the walls.
9 Mike listened to the teacher and Mike[he] took some notes.

Ⓓ ⓐ flies   ⓑ skiing
   ⓒ happily   ⓓ in the afternoon

중간·기말고사 실전 문제

1 ⑤   **2** Not everybody enjoys going to the mountain **3** ②   **4** It was my umbrella that I lost on the subway yesterday. **5** ②   **6** ④   **7** ③   **8** ③   **9** It was at age seven that Mozart went on his first concert tour of Europe.   **10** It is a history test that[which]   **11** It is on Friday that[when]   **12** I did wonder what made my friend so angry.   **13** This laptop is much[even, still, far, a lot] lighter than my old one.   **14** He is the very man the police are searching for.   **15** ⑤   **16** ③, ④   **17** Never have I met such a caring person.   **18** ④   **19** (1) ⓑ → does the town have (2) ⓔ → flew the flock of birds   **20** Never did she think she would write a novel.   **21** Into the sunset sailed the ships.   **22** ①   **23** ①   **24** ③   **25** do sounds → does sound   **26** ⑤   **27** ②, ⑤   **28** ①   **29** ④   **30** ⑤   **31** ③   **32** ⑤   **33** ③   **34** Your phone service will be cut off unless paid for in advance.   **35** Jacob plans to enter the air force and his younger brother the army.   **36** (1) introduced → introduce (2) purchase → purchasing   **37** ②   **38** ③

1 ⑤ did needed → did need

2 '모두 ~인 것은 아니다'라는 의미로 문장 일부를 부정할 때는 「not + every」를 쓴다.

3 ⓐⓓⓕ: 동사를 강조
   ⓑⓔ: 동사   ⓒ: 부가 의문문

4 「It is ~ that …」 강조 구문은 '…한 것은 바로 ~이다'의 의미로, 동사를 제외한 모든 문장 요소를 It was와 that 사이에 써서 강조할 수 있다. 이때 강조되는 말을 제외한 나머지 부분은 that 뒤에 쓰며, 기존 문장의 시제에 일치시킨다.

5 비교급을 강조할 때는 비교급 앞에 much, even, still, far, a lot을 쓴다.

6 ④ 가주어 It
   ①②③⑤ 「It is ~ that …」 강조구문의 It

7 ③ who → that[where]

8 ③ whom → that[who]

9 「It is ~ that …」 강조 구문은 '…한 것은 바로 ~이다'의 의미로, 동사를 제외한 모든 문장 요소를 It was와 that 사이에 써서 강조할 수 있다. 이때 강조되는 말을 제외한 나머지 부분은 that 뒤에 쓰며, 기존 문장의 시제에 일치시킨다.

10 대답의 목적어인 a history test를 강조하는 문장을 쓴다. 강조하는 대상이 사물이므로 that이나 which를 쓸 수 있다.

11 대답의 부사구인 on Friday를 강조하는 문장을 쓴다. 강조하는 대상이 시간이므로 that이나 when을 쓸 수 있다.

12 동사 wondered를 강조할 때는 동사원형 wonder 앞에 did를 쓴다.

13 비교급을 강조할 때는 비교급 앞에 much, even, still, far, a lot 을 쓴다.

14 명사 man을 강조할 때는 명사 앞에 the very를 쓴다.

15 ⑤ There is she → There she is

16 ③ very worse → much[even/still/far/a lot] worse
④ does → did

17 부정의 의미를 가진 부사 never가 강조되어 문장의 맨 앞으로 올 때, 주어와 동사를 도치시켜 「부사(구) + 조동사 + 주어 + 동사 ~」를 쓴다.

18 ④ 부정의 의미를 가진 부사 seldom이 문장의 맨 앞으로 올 때, 주어와 동사를 도치시켜 「부사(구) + 조동사 + 주어 + 동사 ~」를 쓴다.

19 (1) ⓑ has는 단수동사이므로 도치시킬 때는 동사 앞에 does를 쓰고 주어 뒤에 동사원형인 have를 쓴다.
(2) ⓔ 방향을 나타내는 부사구 Along the river가 문장의 맨 앞으로 올 때, 주어와 동사를 도치시켜 「부사(구) + 동사 + 주어 ~」를 쓴다.

20 부정의 의미를 가진 부사 never가 강조되어 문장의 맨 앞으로 올 때, 주어와 동사를 도치시켜 「부사(구) + 조동사 + 주어 + 동사 ~」를 쓴다.

21 방향을 나타내는 부사구 into the sunset이 강조되어 문장의 맨 앞으로 올 때, 주어와 동사를 도치시켜 「부사(구) + 동사 + 주어 ~」를 쓴다.

22 ② going → go
③ mental → mentally
④ taking → take
⑤ maintain → maintaining

23 ① nobody는 '아무도 ~가 아니다'라는 의미로, 문장 전체를 부정할 때 쓴다.

24 '~도 아니다'는 의미로 neither를 사용할 때 주어와 동사를 도치시켜 「neither + 동사 + 주어 ~」를 쓴다.

25 동사를 강조할 때는 동사원형 앞에 do를 주어의 인칭과 수, 시제에 맞춰 쓴다.

26 ⓐ 「주격 관계대명사 + be동사」는 생략할 수 있다.
ⓕ 목적격 관계대명사 which는 생략할 수 있다.

27 ② There are you → There you are
⑤ so I can → so can I

28 ① the actor looked → looked the actor

29 '~도 그렇다'는 의미로 so를 사용할 때 주어와 동사를 도치시켜 「so + 동사 + 주어 ~」를 쓴다.

30 ⑤ 주절과 종속절을 연결하는 콤마(,)이다.
①②③④ 동격을 나타내는 콤마(,)이다.

31 ③ 관계대명사 that이다.
①②④⑤ 동격의 that이다.

32 ⑤ 주절과 부사절의 주어가 다르기 때문에 생략할 수 없다.

33 ③ 주격 관계대명사 that이므로 생략할 수 없다.

34 부사절의 주어가 주절의 주어와 같을 때 부사절의 「주어 + be동사」는 생략할 수 있다.

35 문장 내에서 반복되는 어구인 plans to enter는 생략할 수 있다.

36 (1) feature와 병치를 이루어야 하므로 introduce를 써야 한다.
(2) buying과 병치를 이루어야 하므로 purchasing을 써야 한다.

37 ① hike → hiking
③ international → internationally
④ give → gives
⑤ singing → sing

38 ③ allow → allows

CHAPTER 1
문장의 형식

p.8

POINT 1-1 1형식과 2형식

 연습문제

1 주어 / 동사 / 수식어구 / 우리는 지난 주말에 그들의 아파트에 머물렀다.
2 주어 / 동사 / 주격 보어 / 나는 아침을 먹은 후 잠이 들었다.
3 주어 / 동사 / 수식어구 / 몇몇 식물들은 물에서 자란다.
4 주어 / 동사 / 주격 보어 / 우리는 보통 휴일 동안 바쁘게 지낸다.
5 주어 / 동사 / 주격 보어 / 나의 삼촌은 최근에 유명해졌다.
6 주어 / 동사 / 수식어구 / Mary가 갑자기 그 무대 위에 나타났다.

POINT 1-2 2형식: 감각동사

연습문제

1	O	2	sounded
3	O	4	fresh
5	O	6	looks like
7	smells like	8	amazing
9	sounds like	10	delicious

POINT 2 3형식

 연습문제 A

1 동사 / 그들은 좋은 보고서를 썼다.
2 목적어 / 나는 나의 오래된 자전거를 팔았다.
3 동사 / 그녀는 그 강아지를 먹였다.
4 주어 / Brian은 그의 할머니를 불렀다.
5 목적어 / 우리는 콘서트 티켓들을 샀다.
6 주어 / 그는 파이 하나를 전부 먹었다.
7 동사 / 나의 아빠가 그 차를 운전했다.
8 목적어 / 그 카페는 맛있는 베이글을 만든다.
9 주어 / 그 가수는 아름다운 노래를 불렀다.
10 동사 / 우리는 해변에서 일몰을 봤다.

연습문제 B

1	O	2	discuss
3	marry	4	O
5	reach	6	O

7	enter	8	mentioned
9	O	10	resemble

POINT 3 4형식

 연습문제 A

1 Kevin asked the teacher many questions.
2 My cousin sent me a funny text message.
3 The tutor teaches the girl Chinese on weekends.
4 Ms. Smith offered the guests some cookies.
5 Please pass me that pen on the table.
6 He told us a scary story last night.
7 Mom always cooks our family healthy meals.
8 I found him a nice hotel room.

 연습문제 B

1 The man made the artist a picture frame.
2 Mom used to read fairy tales to us.
3 She showed her violin to them.
4 We gave the children a bag of toys.
5 The police officer asked some questions of us.
6 They brought some plants to us for our garden.

POINT 4-1 5형식

 연습문제 A

1 목적어: the book / 목적격 보어: interesting
2 목적어: her classmate / 목적격 보어: study
3 목적어: the neighbors / 목적격 보어: nice people
4 목적어: us / 목적격 보어: touch
5 목적어: my brother and sister / 목적격 보어: arguing
6 목적어: the quiz / 목적격 보어: difficult
7 목적어: her grandmother / 목적격 보어: Mimi
8 목적어: his car / 목적격 보어: checked
9 목적어: Marie / 목적격 보어: to use
10 목적어: the patient / 목적격 보어: to sit
11 목적어: the joke / 목적격 보어: funny
12 목적어: the heater / 목적격 보어: repaired

 연습문제 B

1 We found this website helpful.
2 The restaurant's poor service made us angry.
3 The mouse got the cat excited.
4 The audience considered the magic show fun.
5 We believed Gina's story true.
6 They let a visitor park in their parking lot.

POINT 4-2 5형식: 명사·형용사·to부정사를 목적격 보어로 쓰는 동사

연습문제 A

1 funny	2 O
3 O	4 O
5 famous	6 O
7 scary	8 warm

연습문제 B

1 told me to wait
2 allowed us to stay
3 wanted the band to perform
4 expects the local government to cancel
5 asked Michelle to call
6 encouraged me to apply
7 permit passengers to carry

POINT 4-3 5형식: 사역동사

연습문제

1 create	2 use
3 to mail	4 stay / to stay
5 follow	6 to swim
7 save	8 fix / to fix
9 paint	10 to tell

POINT 4-4 5형식: 지각동사

연습문제

1 ring	2 leaving
3 burning	4 rising
5 play	6 crawling
7 holding	8 argue
9 crying	10 repair
11 sliding	

중간·기말고사 실전 문제

1 ④ 2 The Internet lets people access information quickly. 3 ⑤ 4 ②
5 Sandra helped her mother cook dinner.
6 She is going to get her friends to wash the dishes. 7 ④ 8 ④ 9 ④, ⑤
10 Kevin looks angry because of the look on his face. 11 ② 12 ④ 13 my new parrot made the loud noise 14 ① 15 ⑤ 16 ③
17 for 18 get my cousin to bring 19 ③
20 ① 21 ③ 22 bring Taeho the snacks
23 allowed her to go / told her to come

24 permitted him to go / wanted him to do
25 advised me to join

1 ④ fantastically → fantastic

2 5형식 문장은 「주어 + 동사 + 목적어 + 목적격 보어」의 형태이며, 5형식 문장에서 사역동사 let의 목적격 보어 자리에는 동사원형이 올 수 있다.

3 ⑤ hang → hung

4 첫 번째 빈칸: 3형식 문장에서 동사 give는 전치사 to를 간접 목적어 앞에 쓴다.
두 번째 빈칸: 3형식 문장에서 동사 get은 전치사 for를 간접 목적어 앞에 쓴다.

5 준사역동사 help의 목적격 보어 자리에는 동사원형이 올 수 있다.

6 준사역동사 get은 목적격 보어 자리에 to부정사가 온다.

7 (A): 5형식 문장에서 동사 consider의 목적격 보어 자리에는 형용사(costly)가 온다.
(B): 5형식 문장에서 동사 keep의 목적격 보어 자리에는 형용사(tidy)가 온다.
(C): 5형식 문장에서 동사 find의 목적격 보어 자리에는 형용사(annoying)가 온다.

8 (A): 5형식 문장에서 사역동사 let의 목적격 보어 자리에는 동사원형(chat)이 온다.
(B): 5형식 문장에서 사역동사 have의 목적어와 목적격 보어의 관계가 수동이므로 목적격 보어 자리에는 과거분사(painted)가 온다.
(C): 5형식 문장에서 사역동사 make의 목적격 보어 자리에는 동사원형(place)이 온다.

9 ① to repair → repaired
② putting → put
③ to practice → practice

10 2형식 문장에서 동사 look의 주격 보어 자리에는 형용사(angry)가 온다.

11 ② attend to → attend

12 ④ ⓓ stopping → to stop

13 3형식 문장에서 동사 make의 목적어 자리에는 명사(the loud noise)가 올 수 있다.

14 ① poor → poorly

15 ① to me → of me
② to the children a playground → the children a playground
③ a letter my friend → my friend a letter
④ for us a video game → a video game for us

16 ⓒ made → make
ⓓ to land → land[landing]

17 · 4형식 문장을 3형식으로 바꿔 쓸 때 동사 build는 간접 목적어

앞에 전치사 for를 쓴다.
- 4형식 문장을 3형식으로 바꿔 쓸 때 동사 cook은 간접 목적어 앞에 전치사 for를 쓴다.

18 5형식 문장에서 준사역동사 get의 목적격 보어 자리에는 to부정사가 온다.

19 ③ for → to

20 ① tastes like → taste

21 ① entered to → entered
② resembles with → resembles
④ attend to → attend
⑤ explained about → explained

22 4형식 문장은 「주어 + 동사 + 간접목적어(Taeho) + 직접 목적어 (the snacks)」의 형태로 쓴다.

23 5형식 문장에서 동사 allow의 목적격 보어 자리에는 to부정사가 온다.
5형식 문장에서 동사 tell의 목적격 보어 자리에는 to부정사가 온다.

24 5형식 문장에서 동사 permit의 목적격 보어 자리에는 to부정사가 온다.
5형식 문장에서 동사 want의 목적격 보어 자리에는 to부정사가 온다.

25 5형식 문장에서 동사 advise의 목적격 보어 자리에는 to부정사가 온다.

CHAPTER 2
시제
p.20

POINT 1 현재시제와 과거시제

1 is	**2** began
3 travels	**4** makes
5 did	**6** studies
7 died	**8** has
9 broke	

POINT 2 미래시제

1 The city is going to host a music festival
2 I will clean the blackboard
3 A nurse will call your name
4 My passport is about to expire
5 We are going to have dinner
6 The show is going to start

POINT 3-1 현재완료시제

연습문제 **A**
1 has taken / for five years
2 has traveled / before
3 How long has / taught
4 Have / ever gone
5 has appeared / since

연습문제 **B**
1 has written	**2** has played
3 has taken	**4** have been
5 has taken	**6** has gone
7 has read	**8** have known

POINT 3-2 현재완료시제 vs. 과거시제

1 made / has made			
2 watched / has watched			
3 went / has gone		**4** cried / has cried	
5 studied / has studied		**6** wore / has worn	
7 tracked / has tracked		**8** took / has taken	
9 increased / has increased			
10 played / have played			
11 received / has received			
12 rained / has rained			

POINT 4 현재완료진행시제

연습문제

1 has been sleeping
2 have been exercising
3 have been studying 4 has been cooking
5 have been waiting 6 have been running
7 has been doing 8 have been listening
9 has been preparing
10 have been discussing
11 has been fixing 12 have been drawing

POINT 5 과거완료시제

연습문제 A

1 written 2 gone
3 O 4 O
5 had worked 6 O
7 O 8 expected

연습문제 B

1 had passed 2 had left
3 hadn't been 4 had struck
5 had started 6 had made
7 had left 8 had stopped
9 had sent

POINT 6 과거완료진행시제

연습문제 A

1 had been playing 2 had been studying
3 had been swimming 4 had been talking
5 had been napping 6 had been driving
7 had been living

연습문제 B

1 was taking 2 was running
3 was working 4 was helping
5 was moving 6 was having

중간·기말고사 실전 문제

1 ② 2 had tried 3 Have you ever
eaten anything 4 ④ 5 ⑤ 6 had
left / went / had had 7 ② 8 had
been waiting / arrived at
been playing video games 9 arrived / had
10 ⑤
11 booked / had missed 12 has been singing
in the choir 13 ② 14 has been making
this dish / he opened his restaurant 15 ③
16 has met / has gone 17 ④ 18 has
lived 19 ③ 20 ② → was
21 realized / hadn't brought 22 has owned
23 ④ 24 has been working on his science
project 25 has been taking painting classes since
he was ten years old

1 ② is going to meet → met

2 Kelly가 골프를 치는 것을 시도했던 일은 그녀가 그것이 지루하
다고 생각했던 일보다 먼저 일어난 일이므로 「had + p.p.」 형
태의 경험을 의미하는 과거완료시제를 쓴다.

3 현재완료시제의 경험의 의미이므로 「Have/Has + 주어 + p.p.
~?」로 쓴다.

4 첫 번째 빈칸: 'Apollo는 작년부터 그 연극의 주연으로 연기를 해
왔다.'는 의미이므로 현재완료시제를 쓴다.
두 번째 빈칸: '그리고 그의 형은 그 전에 일 년 동안 연기를 해왔었
다.'는 의미이므로 과거완료시제를 쓴다.

5 ⑤: 경험
①②③④: 완료

6 첫 번째 문장: '오늘, 버스가 나를 데리러 오기 전에 내가 떠났었
다.'는 의미이다. 내가 떠난 일이 버스가 나를 데리러 온 일보다 먼
저 일어난 일이므로 과거완료시제를 쓴다.
두 번째 문장: '내가 나의 선생님과 회의를 한 후에 나는 나의 첫 번
째 수업에 갔다.'는 의미이다. 내가 나의 선생님과 회의를 한 일은
나의 첫 번째 수업에 간 일보다 먼저 일어난 일이므로 과거완료시
제를 쓴다.

7 ② has found → found

8 'Nikki가 식당에 도착했을 때, Stuart는 그녀를 45분 동안 기다리
고 있었다.'는 의미이다. Stuart가 계속 기다리고 있었던 일은 과
거완료진행시제를 쓰고, Nikki가 식당에 도착한 일은 과거의 특정
시점을 나타내는 과거시제를 쓴다.

9 '나의 어머니가 집에 도착했을 때, 나의 누나와 나는 비디오 게임
을 두 시간 동안 하는 중이었다.'는 의미이다. 어머니가 집에 도착
한 일은 과거의 특정 시점을 나타내는 과거시제를 쓰고, 누나와 내
가 게임을 하고 있었던 일은 과거완료진행시제를 쓴다.

10 '우리가 야영지에 도착했을 때, 다른 야영객들은 가장 좋은 자리를
차지했었다.'는 의미이므로 「had + p.p.」 형태의 대과거를 쓴다.

11 첫 번째 빈칸: 그녀가 버스표를 예약했던 것은 그녀가 그녀의 항공
편을 놓쳤던 일보다 나중에 일어난 일이므로 과거시제를 쓴다.
두 번째 빈칸: 그녀가 그녀의 항공편을 놓쳤던 일은 그녀가 버스
표를 예약했던 것보다 먼저 일어난 일이므로 「had + p.p.」 형태
의 대과거를 쓴다.

12 현재완료진행시제는 「have/has + been + V-ing」 형태로 쓴
다.

13 첫 번째 빈칸: 과거의 특정한 시점을 나타내므로 과거시제를 쓴다.

두 번째 빈칸: '그 슬로프는 이미 문을 닫아버렸었다'는 의미이므로 과거완료시제를 쓴다.

14 첫 번째 빈칸: 과거에 발생한 일이 현재도 계속 진행 중임을 강조하고 있으므로 현재완료진행시제를 쓴다.
두 번째 빈칸: 과거의 특정한 시점을 나타내므로 과거시제를 쓴다.

15 ⓑ have remodeled → had remodeled
ⓒ has already started → had already started

16 ⓐ: '그는 그가 동아리에 가입한 이후로 새로운 친구들을 많이 만났다.'는 의미이므로 현재완료시제를 쓴다.
ⓑ: '지난 몇 달 동안, 그는 그들과 많은 다이빙 여행을 갔다.'는 의미이므로 현재완료시제를 쓴다.

17 ④ has already departed → had already departed

18 'Joanne이 몇 년 전에도 독일에 살았고, 지금도 계속 살고 있다.'는 의미이므로 현재완료시제를 쓴다.

19 밑줄 친 (A)와 ③: 계속
①: 경험   ②④: 완료   ⑤: 결과

20 ② 과거의 특정한 시점을 나타내므로 과거시제를 쓴다.

21 첫 번째 빈칸: Sarah가 깨달았던 것은 그녀가 학교에 그녀의 책들을 가져오지 않았던 일보다 나중에 일어난 일이므로 과거시제를 쓴다.
두 번째 빈칸: Sarah가 학교에 그녀의 책들을 가져오지 않았었던 것은 그녀가 깨달았던 일보다 먼저 일어난 일이므로 「had + p.p.」 형태의 대과거를 쓴다.

22 '나의 아버지가 1995년에 신발 가게를 소유했고, 지금도 계속 신발 가게를 소유하고 있다'는 의미이므로 현재완료시제를 쓴다.

23 ① been played → played/been playing
② have been watch → have been watching/have watched
③ has been gone → has been going/has gone
⑤ has been slept → has been sleeping/has slept

24 현재완료진행시제는 「have/has + been + V-ing」 형태로 쓴다.

25 '그는 10살 이후로 그림 수업을 들어오고 있다.'는 의미이므로 현재완료진행시제를 쓴다.

CHAPTER 3
조동사

p.32

POINT 1   can, may, will

 연습문제 A

1 ①, ③		**2** ②, ③		**3** ①, ②	
4 ①, ③		**5** ②, ③		**6** ①, ②	

 연습문제 B

1 능력		**2** 허가		**3** 요청	
4 미래		**5** 허가		**6** 추측	
7 요청		**8** 추측		**9** 의지	
10 추측		**11** 의지			

POINT 2   must, should

연습문제 A

1 must		**2** don't have to
3 should		**4** don't have to
5 must		**6** should
7 must not		**8** must
9 shouldn't		**10** have to

연습문제 B

1 강한 의무		**2** 강한 의무
3 강한 추측		**4** 강한 의무
5 강한 추측		**6** 강한 추측
7 강한 의무		**8** 강한 추측
9 강한 의무		**10** 강한 추측
11 강한 의무		**12** 강한 추측
13 강한 추측		**14** 강한 의무
15 강한 추측		

POINT 3   should의 생략

 연습문제

1 insisted / put on
2 suggested / buy
3 required[requested] / stay
4 requested / give
5 recommended / reserve
6 ordered / put out
7 requires[requests] / pay
8 requested / visit
9 insisted / be
10 suggested / go
11 insisted / leave

POINT 4 used to, would

1 used to play	2 is used to waking up
3 is used to swimming	4 used to live
5 is used to get	6 is used to receiving
7 is used to make	

1 live	2 used to
3 O	4 O
5 O	6 have
7 work	8 using
9 driving	10 believe

POINT 5 조동사 + have + p.p.

1 shouldn't have permitted
2 should have taken
3 may[might] have forgotten
4 could have done
5 must have fixed
6 can't have arrived

1 can't have painted
2 should have offered
3 may[might] have convinced
4 shouldn't have lied
5 must have been
6 shouldn't have bought

POINT 6 조동사 관용 표현

1 Tom may well be afraid of spiders.
2 I would rather continue working than take a break.
3 I think my mom would like this bowl.
4 She may as well call a repair person.
5 The officer would like to ask you some questions.
6 You had better check what time the bus comes.
7 I would rather carry the backpack than the suitcase.
8 What she said may well be true.
9 I may as well lend him my book.
10 My parents would like to travel to France.
11 You had better make sure you have your passport.

중간·기말고사 실전 문제

1 ①, ⑤   2 ①   3 suggested that we (should) leave early   4 ③   5 must have been
6 ①   7 you may as well bring my coat
8 doesn't have to go   9 ②   10 used to be   11 ①   12 ②   13 ②   14 ⓓ → have to   15 ⓐ would like to ⓑ would rather
16 didn't use to   17 ⑤   18 ⑤   19 ④
20 you had better not give a compliment   21 ②
22 (1) must have eaten (2) shouldn't have missed
23 ⓐ used to study ⓑ would go ⓒ used to take
24 You had better put the milk in the fridge now.
25 You must not park your car in this spot.

1 ① must have arrived → should have arrived
⑤ should have turned off → shouldn't have turned off

2 ① '온도가 갑자기 떨어질지도 모른다'고 하였으므로 약한 추측을 나타내는 may를 쓴다.

3 제안의 동사인 suggest 뒤의 that절에는 「(should) + 동사원형」을 쓴다.

4 ③ had not better → had better not

5 'Luis는 조금 전에 여기 있었음이 틀림없다.'는 의미이므로 must have p.p.를 쓴다.

6 밑줄 친 부분과 ①: 허가
②: 요청   ③⑤: 능력   ④: 추측

7 '~하는 편이 좋다'는 의미의 조동사 관용 표현 may as well 뒤에는 동사원형을 쓴다.

8 '그는 갈 필요가 없어.'라는 의미이므로 doesn't have to를 쓴다.

9 밑줄 친 부분과 ②: 허가
①③④⑤: 약한 추측

10 'Steve는 최고의 변호사였다.'는 의미이므로 과거의 상태를 나타내는 「used to + 동사원형」을 쓴다.

11 ①: 강한 추측
②③④⑤: 강한 의무

12 ② 허가, 능력을 나타내는 can이 빈칸에 공통으로 올 수 있다.

13 · '그녀는 그녀의 질문에 대한 대답을 얻고 싶다.'는 의미이므로 would like to를 쓴다.
· '너는 밤에 너무 많이 먹으면 안 된다.'는 의미이므로 should not을 쓴다.

14 ⓓ '~해야 한다'는 의미로 have to를 쓴다.

15 ⓐ '나는 공원에서 소풍을 하고 싶다.'는 의미이므로 would like to를 쓴다.
ⓑ '나는 차라리 영화를 보러 가겠다.'는 의미이므로 would rather를 쓴다.

16 '십대들은 그들의 휴대폰을 항상 사용하지 않았지만, 현재는 매우 흔하다.'는 의미이므로 과거의 상태를 나타내는 didn't use to를 쓴다.

17 ⑤ are used to eat → used to eat[are used to eating]

18 첫 번째 빈칸: '첫 번째로, 너는 옆사람과 이야기를 하거나 그들에게 쪽지를 전달하면 안 된다.'는 강한 금지를 나타내므로 must not을 쓴다.
두 번째 빈칸: '또한, 네가 아프고 시험을 완료할 수 없으면, 즉시 나에게 알려주고 내가 학교 당국에 알리겠다.'는 의미이므로 aren't able to를 쓴다.

19 ④ '어떠한 종류의 음료도 가지고 오면 안된다'고 하였으므로 강한 금지를 나타내는 must not을 쓴다.

20 '~하지 않는 것이 낫다'고 했으므로 「had better not + 동사원형」을 쓴다.

21 · '너는 내가 방금 말한 것을 누구에게도 말하지 않는 것이 낫다.'는 의미이므로 had better not을 쓴다.
· '~하는 편이 좋다'는 의미의 조동사 관용 표현 may as well 뒤에는 동사원형을 쓴다.

22 (1) '그는 너무 많이 먹었음이 틀림없다.'는 의미이므로 must have p.p.를 쓴다.
(2) 'Ron은 그 시험을 놓치지 않았어야 했다.'는 의미이므로 shouldn't have p.p.를 쓴다.

23 ⓐ '나는 도서관의 작은 공간에서 공부하곤 했다.'는 의미이므로 used to study를 쓴다.
ⓑ '음, 나는 도서관이 닫았을 때를 제외하고 매일 그곳에 가곤 했다.'는 의미로 과거의 습관을 나타내므로 would go를 쓴다.
ⓒ '물론이지, 공부하는 것은 어려운 일이지만, 나는 여러 번 휴식을 취하곤 해서, 나는 너무 피곤한 적이 없었다.'는 의미이므로 used to take를 쓴다.

24 '~넣는 것이 낫다'고 했으므로 「had better + 동사원형」을 쓴다.

25 강한 금지를 나타내므로 must not을 쓴다.

POINT 1   수동태 문장 만드는 법

1 The airport was designed
2 Donkeys were ridden
3 The cause of the fire was confirmed
4 Was the meteor observed
5 Is this shampoo recommended for clients
6 The main character in the book isn't married
7 Are all the students finished
8 When was this dinosaur fossil discovered
9 The theory of relativity isn't understood
10 Office supplies aren't purchased
11 Were the residents warned
12 When was the champion boxer challenged

POINT 2   수동태로 쓸 수 없는 동사

1	resembles	2	happen
3	O	4	appeared
5	are raised	6	O
7	remained	8	O
9	was felled	10	fit

POINT 3   수동태의 시제

1	was bought	2	will be answered
3	was eaten	4	has been ridden
5	will be released	6	is being washed
7	was being made	8	will be taken
9	were baked		
10	are being published		
11	will be solved	12	had been repaired

POINT 4   조동사가 있는 수동태

1	should be fixed	2	will be written
3	must be restarted	4	can be completed
5	Can / be replaced		

POINT 5 　4형식 문장의 수동태

연습문제

1　were given to Minji by me / was given some snacks by me
2　was shown a picture by the woman / was shown to him by the woman
3　are built doll houses by him / are built for children by him
4　was asked some questions by the students / were asked of the teacher by the students

POINT 6 　5형식 문장의 수동태

연습문제

1　is expected to become a legendary baseball player someday
2　consider the painting his best artwork
3　was asked to set the table
4　encouraged us to watch the educational TV series
5　called the shepherd boy a liar
6　will be kept warm in winter
7　made motorists exit the highway
8　was forced to return to his country
9　smelled something burning
10　was heard singing next door
11　helped Melissa (to) write an essay
12　weren't allowed to bring their phones to school

POINT 7 　구동사의 수동태

연습문제

1　was made use of　　2　was set up
3　was turned on　　4　was turned down
5　was looked down on

POINT 8 　목적어가 that절인 문장의 수동태

연습문제

1　It was known that
2　was said to be the best painter
3　It is believed that
4　It was realized
5　is said to increase your life span

POINT 9 　수동태 관용 표현

연습문제

1　were pleased with their test scores

2　is used to create games
3　are filled with old toys
4　were disappointed at our last basketball match
5　is covered with food crumbs
6　is made from grapes
7　was supposed to pick me up
8　is known as a math expert
9　am interested in riding a bicycle
10　are made of wood
11　was known for his coin tricks
12　will be remembered for his heroic actions

중간·기말고사 실전 문제

1　③, ④　2　②　3　was broken　4　The cave was explored by geologists around ten years ago.　5　are taken care of　6　was turned down by the baseball player　7　⑤　8　⑤　9　④　10　were entertained by the clowns　11　①, ⑤　12　①　13　Tropical fruits aren't grown by the farmer.　14　③　15　will be printed　16　was adopted　17　have been added　18　③　19　have to be cleaned　20　Ghosts aren't believed in by some people.　21　④　22　②　23　are known for　24　⑤　25　⑤

1　③ 목적어를 가지지 않는 동사(arrive)는 수동태로 쓸 수 없다.
　④ 상태를 나타내는 동사(resemble)는 수동태로 쓸 수 없다.

2　① to be sung → are sung
　③ being arranged → were arranged
　④ are offering → are offered
　⑤ was thanking → was thanked

3　'다리가 부러졌다'는 의미이므로 수동태를 쓴다. 과거시제의 수동태는 「was/were + p.p.」의 형태를 쓰므로 was broken을 쓴다.

4　과거시제의 수동태는 「was/were + p.p.(+ by + 행위자)」의 형태를 쓰므로 was explored를 쓴다.

5　구동사 take care of를 수동태로 쓰는 경우 be taken care of를 쓴다.

6　구동사 turn down을 수동태로 쓰는 경우 be turned down을 쓴다. 행위자는 「by + 목적격」의 형태이므로 by the baseball player를 쓴다.

7　⑤ was disappeared → disappeared

8　첫 번째 빈칸: '~에게 알려져 있다'는 의미의 be known to를 쓴다.
　두 번째 빈칸: '~을 하기로 되어 있다'는 의미의 be supposed to를 쓴다.
　세 번째 빈칸: '~을 하는 데 사용되다'는 의미의 be used to를 쓴다.

따라서 빈칸에는 공통으로 to를 쓴다.

9 ④ should organized → should be organized

10 과거시제의 수동태는 「was/were + p.p.(+ by + 행위자)」의 형태를 쓰므로 were entertained by the clowns를 쓴다.

11 ① 4형식 문장은 목적어가 두 개이므로 직접 목적어가 주어인 수동태 문장을 만들 수 있다. 이때 show는 간접 목적어 앞에 전치사 to를 쓰는 동사이다.
⑤ 4형식 문장은 목적어가 두 개이므로 간접 목적어가 주어인 수동태 문장을 만들 수 있다.

12 · 목적격 보어가 분사인 5형식 문장을 수동태 문장으로 만들 때는 「be동사 + p.p.」 뒤에 분사를 그대로 쓴다.
· 목적어가 that절인 문장을 수동태 문장으로 만들 때 that절의 주어를 수동태 문장의 주어 자리에 쓰고 that절의 동사를 to부정사로 바꾼다.

13 수동태의 동사는 「be동사 + p.p.」의 형태이고, 주어 Tropical fruits는 복수이므로 aren't grown을 쓴다. 행위자는 「by + 목적격」의 형태이므로 by the farmer를 쓴다.

14 ③ 현재완료시제의 수동태는 「have/has + been + p.p.」의 형태를 쓰므로 have been spotted를 쓴다.

15 미래시제의 수동태는 「will + be + p.p.」의 형태를 쓰므로 will be printed를 쓴다.

16 과거시제의 수동태는 「was/were + p.p.」의 형태를 쓰므로 was adopted를 쓴다.

17 현재완료시제의 수동태는 「have/has + been + p.p.」의 형태를 쓰므로 have been added를 쓴다.

18 ③ Were the plans be approved by the committee?
→ Were the plans approved by the committee?

19 조동사 have to를 이용한 수동태는 「조동사 + be + p.p.」의 형태를 쓰므로 have to be cleaned를 쓴다.

20 수동태의 동사는 「be동사 + p.p.」의 형태이고, 주어 Ghosts는 복수이므로 aren't believed를 쓴다. 행위자는 「by + 목적격」의 형태이므로 by some people을 쓴다.

21 조동사가 있는 수동태는 「조동사 + be + p.p.」의 형태를 쓰므로 might be chosen을 쓴다.

22 ⑤ been → has been
ⓒ being build → being built

23 '~으로 유명하다'는 의미의 be known for를 쓴다.

24 · 직접 목적어가 주어인 수동태 문장에서 write는 간접 목적어 앞에 to를 쓴다.
· 직접 목적어가 주어인 수동태 문장에서 make는 간접 목적어 앞에 for를 쓴다.

25 ① told review → told to review
② chased after were → were chased after
③ was given → was given to
④ was seeing → was seen

POINT 1 to부정사의 형태와 용법

연습문제 A
1 O
2 My plan is to stay home on Sunday.
3 O
4 Mr. Miller told me to rewrite the essay.
5 The team's goal is to make it to the championship.

연습문제 B
1 ⓒ	**2** ⓒ	**3** ⓒ
4 ⓐ	**5** ⓐ	**6** ⓑ
7 ⓑ	**8** ⓒ	**9** ⓐ

POINT 2-1 명사적 용법: 주어와 보어로 쓰이는 to부정사

연습문제
1 ⓒ	**2** ⓑ	**3** ⓑ
4 ⓑ	**5** ⓒ	**6** ⓐ
7 ⓐ	**8** ⓑ	**9** ⓒ
10 ⓐ	**11** ⓐ	**12** ⓒ
13 ⓐ	**14** ⓑ	**15** ⓒ
16 ⓒ	**17** ⓑ	**18** ⓐ
19 ⓒ	**20** ⓐ	

POINT 2-2 명사적 용법: 목적어로 쓰이는 to부정사

연습문제
1 failed to grow	**2** need to inform
3 liked to sing	**4** managed to repair
5 agreed to hike up	**6** decided to move
7 chose to drive	**8** aims to add
9 wishes to book	**10** expects to receive
11 promised to meet	

POINT 2-3 명사적 용법: 의문사 + to부정사

연습문제 A
1 how to install	**2** whom[who] to invite
3 where to find	**4** how to replace
5 when to leave	**6** whom[who] to talk to
7 which to watch	

연습문제 B
1 whom[who] to call for questions
2 when to take her medicine

3 which task to finish first

4 where to park

5 how to place an order

POINT 3-1 형용사적 용법: 명사·대명사 수식

1 have a sheet of paper to write on

2 has many pens to write with

3 purchased a house to live in

4 called a friend to talk to

5 isn't a single chair left to sit on

POINT 3-2 형용사적 용법: be동사 + to부정사

1 are to stay   **2** was to be found

3 is to finish   **4** is to arrive

5 was to defeat

POINT 4 부사적 용법

A

1 ⓓ   **2** ⓑ   **3** ⓑ

4 ⓔ   **5** ⓒ   **6** ⓐ

7 ⓐ

B

1 sad to realize

2 lived to become

3 to have so many customers

4 to watch a program

5 easy to learn

6 hard to operate

POINT 5 too ~ to, enough to

1 sensitive enough to smell

2 famous enough to sell

3 so far away that she can't come and visit

4 so big that it can accommodate

5 so tired that I couldn't do

6 too hot for you to play

7 good enough to be served

8 so big that it could be seen

9 too difficult to be learned

10 too young to drive

11 so tight that I can't wear

12 rich enough to fly

POINT 6 to부정사의 의미상의 주어

A

1 of   **2** to

3 of   **4** of

5 for   **6** to

7 for   **8** for

B

1 foolish of Carl to spend

2 impossible for us to change

3 important (for us) to behave

4 honest of him to return

5 lucky for them to have

6 hard for him to reach

7 necessary (for people) to treat

8 rude of her to yell

중간·기말고사 실전 문제

1 ④   **2** ①   **3** ④   **4** sending → to send   **5** take care → take care of   **6** ③, ④ **7** vegetables to try **8** ③   **9** ③   **10** (1) ⓒ → to tell (2) ⓔ → of **11** It is a good idea to have **12** ②   **13** ⑤   **14** expect to move this week **15** ②, ③ **16** New products are to be released next month. **17** ④, ⑤ **18** ④   **19** works together to hunt other animals **20** ②   **21** is bad for your health to eat   **22** in order to[so as to] **23** stopped by the post office to mail **24** are   **25** where to change our money

1 agree는 to부정사를 목적어로 쓰는 동사이다. to부정사의 부정형은 to 앞에 not을 붙인 「not to + 동사원형」의 형태이므로 not to run을 쓴다.

2 ·'(위에) 앉을 의자'라는 표현으로 a chair to sit on이라고 쓴다.
·'말할 누군가'라는 표현으로 someone to talk to라고 쓴다.

3 ④ 성격·태도를 나타내는 형용사 careful과 쓰인 경우 의미상의 주어를 「of + 목적격」의 형태로 to부정사 앞에 쓴다.

4 promise는 to부정사를 목적어로 쓰는 동사이므로 to send를 쓴다.

5 '돌볼 새끼 고양이'라는 표현으로 a kitten to take care of라고 쓴다.

6 ③ 「too + 형용사/부사 + to부정사」는 '…하기에 너무 ~한/하게'라는 뜻으로 쓰인다.
④ 「too + 형용사/부사 + to부정사」는 「so + 형용사/부사 + that + 주어 + can't + 동사원형」으로 바꿔 쓸 수 있다.

7 to부정사는 형용사처럼 명사를 수식할 수 있고, '~할'의 의미이다.

8 (A): decide는 to부정사를 목적어로 쓰는 동사이므로 to cook 를 쓴다.
   (B): need는 to부정사를 목적어로 쓰는 동사이므로 to have를 쓴다.
   (C): '나는 이미 무엇을 살지 계획했다.'는 의미이므로 what to buy를 쓴다.

9 '…하기에 너무 ~한/하게'라는 의미로 「too + 형용사/부사 + to 부정사」를 쓴다. 'The water is too cold to swim in.'이므로 다섯 번째에 오는 것은 ③ cold이다.

10 (1) ⓒ: manage는 to부정사를 목적어로 쓰는 동사이므로 to tell을 쓴다.
   (2) ⓔ: 성격·태도를 나타내는 형용사 kind와 쓰인 경우 의미상의 주어를 「of + 목적격」의 형태로 to부정사 앞에 쓴다.

11 to부정사구가 주어 자리에 와서 주어가 길어진 경우, 주어 자리에 가주어 it을 쓰고 to부정사구를 문장 맨 뒤로 보낼 수 있다.

12 ② to부정사구가 주어 자리에 와서 주어가 길어진 경우, 주어 자리에 가주어 it을 쓰고 to부정사구를 문장 맨 뒤로 보낼 수 있다.

13 ·to부정사는 명사처럼 목적어를 보충 설명하는 목적격 보어로 쓰일 수 있다.
   ·aim은 to부정사를 목적어로 쓰는 동사이므로 to go를 쓴다.

14 expect는 to부정사를 목적어로 쓰는 동사이므로 to move를 쓴다.

15 ② for Shawn → of Shawn
   ③ for him → of him

16 「be동사 + to부정사」는 예정의 의미를 나타내는 데 쓰인다.

17 ④ 「how + to부정사」는 '어떻게 ~할지'라는 의미를 나타낸다.
   ⑤ 「의문사 + to부정사」는 「의문사 + 주어 + should + 동사원형」으로 바꿔 쓸 수 있다.

18 밑줄 친 ⓐ와 ④: 명사적 용법
   ①②⑤: 형용사적 용법   ③: 부사 용법

19 to부정사는 부사처럼 쓰여 목적의 의미를 나타내므로 to hunt를 쓴다.

20 ⓐⓓ: 형용사적 용법
   ⓑⓔ: 명사적 용법   ⓒ: 부사적 용법

21 to부정사구가 주어 자리에 와서 주어가 길어진 경우, 주어 자리에 가주어 it을 쓰고 to부정사구를 문장 맨 뒤로 보낼 수 있다.

22 to부정사가 부사처럼 쓰일 때, 목적의 의미를 나타내는 경우 to부정사 대신 in order to나 so as to를 쓸 수 있다.

23 to부정사는 부사처럼 쓰여 목적의 의미를 나타내므로 to mail을 쓴다.

24 「be동사 + to부정사」는 의무의 의미를 나타내는 데 쓰인다. 'All visitors are to sign in at the front desk.'이므로 세 번째에 오는 것은 are이다.

25 「의문사 + 주어 + should + 동사원형」은 「의문사 + to부정사」로 바꿔 쓸 수 있다.

CHAPTER 6
동명사
p.70

POINT 1 동명사의 형태와 쓰임

1 How about fixing the bicycle after school?
2 Interviewing celebrities is what the reporter does.
3 Thank you for not talking during the movie.
4 O
5 I enjoy jogging every morning.
6 O

1 ⓓ	**2** ⓑ	**3** ⓒ
4 ⓐ	**5** ⓑ	**6** ⓑ
7 ⓐ	**8** ⓒ	

POINT 2 동명사의 의미상의 주어

1 his coming late to class
2 Daniel's forgetting to bring his textbook to class
3 my mom's acting in the play
4 her dad's driving her to school
5 my little sister's singing at home
6 David's meeting the project deadline
7 his older brother's using his computer
8 his son's returning home not on time
9 Billy's completing the project
10 the waiter's bringing us some free food
11 her friend's receiving the present
12 Brian's failing the test

POINT 3 동명사의 시제와 태

1 having taken his candy
2 not having arrived on time
3 having torn the cover of her book
4 taking the subway to work in the morning
5 having been given an award at school
6 being late for the dinner party
7 having cheated on the exam
8 having participated in the summer camp
9 not being invited to the party
10 having been able to see her friends
11 having damaged their luggage

12 meeting the singer in person

POINT 4 동명사를 목적어로 쓰는 동사

1 recommends taking   **2** suggested riding
3 denied stealing   **4** postpone studying
5 enjoyed hiking   **6** imagined becoming
7 keeps talking   **8** practice playing
9 considered getting   **10** avoids eating
11 stopped exercising   **12** dislikes hearing

POINT 5 동명사와 to부정사를 모두 목적어로 쓰는 동사

1 apologizing   **2** playing / to play
3 taking / to take   **4** dancing
5 baking / to bake   **6** working
7 running / to run   **8** cleaning / to clean
9 watching / to watch   **10** buying / to buy

1 tried to climb   **2** remembered to lock
3 forget winning   **4** stopped crying
5 remember meeting   **6** forgot to give
7 regrets not studying

POINT 6 동명사 관용 표현

1 O
2 Mark prefers comedies when it comes to watching movies.
3 My father is good at playing sports like soccer and baseball.
4 The politician dreams of becoming the country's president.
5 O

1 is afraid of going
2 are interested in learning
3 is worth buying
4 has difficulty walking
5 by using
6 looks forward to reading
7 It is no use complaining

중간·기말고사 실전 문제

1 How[What] about going camping on Saturday?
2 When it comes to cooking   **3** ④   **4** ①
5 I tried not[never] drinking soda for a week. **6**
(1) ⓐ → reducing   (2) ⓑ → is   (3) ⓓ → Not acting
7 ①   **8** ①, ②, ④   **9** ③   **10** ④
11 ①   **12** borrowing Adam's notes   **13** to bark
→ barking **14** regret to tell   **15** ⑤   **16** ④
17 ⓐ to tell ⓑ to mention   **18** ②   **19** ④
20 ④   **21** ②   **22** ②   **23** I forgot to turn on
my alarm before I went to bed. **24** ⓐ getting
ⓑ feeling[to feel] ⓒ keeping   **25** ①

1 '~하는 게 어때?'의 의미로 「How[What] about + V-ing?」를 쓴다.

2 '~하는 것에 관한 한'의 의미로 「When it comes to + V-ing」를 쓴다.

3 ① to playing → playing[to play]
② become → becoming
③ to join → joining
⑤ compete → competing

4 · 동명사는 문장 안에서 보어로 쓰인다.
· 동명사가 쓰인 주어는 항상 단수 취급한다.

5 '(시험 삼아) ~해보다'라는 의미로 「try + V-ing」를 쓴다. 동명사의 부정형은 동명사 앞에 not[never]을 쓴다.

6 (1) 동명사는 문장 안에서 전치사의 목적어로 쓰일 수 있다.
(2) 동명사가 쓰인 주어는 항상 단수 취급한다.
(3) 동명사는 문장에서 주어로 쓰일 수 있다.

7 (A) 동사 continue는 동명사와 to부정사를 모두 목적어로 쓴다.
(B) '~하기 위해 멈추다'는 의미로 「stop + to부정사」를 쓴다.
(C) 동사 mind는 동명사를 목적어로 쓴다.

8 ① to get → getting
② hated → hating[to hate]
④ not attend → not attending

9 ③ go to fishing → go fishing

10 (A) 동사 postpone은 동명사를 목적어로 쓴다.
(B) 동사 like는 동명사와 to부정사를 모두 목적어로 쓴다.
(C) '~하려고 노력하다'는 의미로 「try + to부정사」를 쓴다.

11 ① to study → studying

12 동사 suggest는 동명사를 목적어로 쓴다.

13 동사 keep은 동명사를 목적어로 쓴다.

14 '~하게 되어 유감이다'는 의미로 「regret + to부정사」를 쓴다.

15 ⑤ '역에 들어가자마자, 나는 나의 지갑을 집에 두고 왔다는 것을 기억했다.'는 의미로 「on + V-ing」를 쓴다.

16 ④ 동명사의 시제가 문장의 시제보다 이전인 경우 「having + p.p.」를 쓴다.

17 ⓐ '~하게 되어 유감이다'는 의미로 「regret + to부정사」를 쓴다.
ⓑ '~할 것을 기억하다'는 의미로 「remember + to부정사」를 쓴다.

18 ② '~을 잘하다'는 의미로 「be good at + V-ing」를 쓴다.

19 ⓑ to take → taking

20 ④ him → his

21 동사 finish는 동명사를 목적어로 쓴다.

22 ② to look → looking

23 '~할 것을 잊다'는 의미로 「forget + to부정사」를 쓴다.

24 ⓐ 동사 avoid는 동명사를 목적어로 쓴다.
ⓑ 동사 begin은 동명사와 to부정사를 모두 목적어로 쓴다.
ⓒ 동사 recommend는 동명사를 목적어로 쓴다.

25 ① to play → playing

POINT 1 분사의 형태와 쓰임

 연습문제 A
1 분사: walking / 수식: some people
2 분사: embarrassed / 수식: I
3 분사: made / 수식: The soup
4 분사: injured / 수식: the patient
5 분사: drinking / 수식: a kid
6 분사: surprising / 수식: The play's plot
7 분사: painted / 수식: the painting
8 분사: calling / 수식: my mom
9 분사: disappointing / 수식: My test score
10 분사: confused / 수식: the researchers
11 분사: practicing / 수식: some baseball players
12 분사: broken / 수식: window

 연습문제 B
1 Mike saw the mountain covered with snow.
2 The manager sounds frustrated.
3 Amy watched an interesting movie.
4 The novel has an exciting opening.
5 He looked tired after the marathon.

POINT 2 현재분사 vs. 과거분사

 연습문제 A
1 barking dog   2 used car
3 girl sitting   4 broken laptop
5 students reading

 연습문제 B
1 talking   2 burned
3 excited   4 sung
5 waiting

POINT 3 감정을 나타내는 분사

 연습문제 A
1 ① boring   ② bored
2 ① excited   ② exciting
3 ① moved   ② moving
4 ① amusing   ② amused
5 ① fascinated   ② fascinating
6 ① pleasing   ② pleased

 연습문제 B
1 O
2 Going on a trip was a thrilling experience for me.
3 The student was interested in history.

4　O

5　My older brother read a surprising article in the paper.

POINT 4　현재분사 vs. 동명사

연습문제 A

1 ②	2 ③	3 ③
4 ②	5 ①	

연습문제 B

1　동명사 / 대기실에서 당신의 차례를 기다리세요.
2　현재분사 / 그것은 내가 갔던 여행 중에 가장 신나는 여행이었다.
3　동명사 / 나의 엄마는 쿠키 굽는 것을 아주 잘하신다.
4　현재분사 / 모든 아이들은 "잠자는 숲 속의 공주"라고 불리는 동화를 안다.
5　현재분사 / 그 감독은 그 감동적인 이야기를 영화로 만들고 싶어했다.
6　현재분사 / 나는 출입문 옆에 서있는 남자를 보았다.
7　동명사 / 그녀는 내일 퀴즈를 위해 공부하는 것을 끝냈다.
8　동명사 / 낮잠을 자는 것은 너의 기분을 나아지게 할 수 있다.

POINT 5-1　분사구문 만드는 법

연습문제 A

1　saw the bus / Seeing the bus
2　wasn't thirsty / Not being thirsty
3　played a computer game / Playing a computer game
4　was delayed / The train being delayed
5　took a taxi / Taking a taxi

연습문제 B

1　As I was tired
2　Because the boy was sleepy
3　While the hiker climbed the mountain
4　While I drank my tea
5　Since I'm not old enough
6　As the building was designed by a famous architect

POINT 5-2　분사구문의 다양한 의미

연습문제 A

1　Coming from another country
2　burning the food
3　Doing his homework
4　Living in a dormitory
5　Waiting in line
6　Tripping on the sidewalk

연습문제 B

1　spraining her ankle
2　(Being) Given the chance
3　Developing the mobile application
4　Going up on stage
5　Feeling hungry
6　Watching the movie
7　Playing the guitar

POINT 5-3　분사구문의 시제와 태

연습문제 A

1　Arriving at the hotel
2　Feeling exhausted
3　Drawing a picture
4　Having learned how to speak French
5　Meeting someone
6　Having finished his homework
7　(Being) Made of cotton

연습문제 B

1　Joshua had played for the team for 15 years
2　Not (being) interested in art
3　they jogged in the park
4　(Being) Good at biology
5　you do your best in everything
6　the Christmas tree was decorated with colorful lights

POINT 6　with + 명사 + 분사

연습문제

1　with his mom holding his hand
2　with the TV turned on
3　with my little brother helping me
4　with my legs crossed
5　with the door closed

POINT 7　분사구문 관용 표현

연습문제

1 Frankly speaking	2 Strictly speaking
3 Generally speaking	4 Considering
5 Speaking of	6 Judging from

중간·기말고사 실전 문제

1 ④	2 ③	3 If you look out the window
4 ⑤	5 ④	6 When the runners had completed the race, they drank water.

7 amazing / impressed　　**8** (After) Having finished our meal　　**9** ③　　**10** ③
11 ⓐ worried ⓑ fascinating ⓒ admired
12 Frankly speaking, it is one of the best books I have ever read.　　**13** Featuring many interesting characters　　**14** My younger sister being sick, I can't attend class today.　　**15** exhausted → exhausting　　**16** ⑤　　**17** (A) frightening experience　(B) A storm causing strong winds　(C) With our safety threatened　　**18** ⑤　　**19** ④
20 ⓐ people taking ⓑ woman sitting near them ⓒ her legs crossed ⓓ paid model　　**21** ①, ⑤
22 ⑤　　**23** ②　　**24** ⑤　　**25** ②

1 ① falling → fallen
② stood → standing
③ cleaned → cleaning
⑤ singing → sung

2 ③ ⓒ 명사 audience가 감정을 느끼는 대상이므로 과거분사 amazed를 쓴다.
① ⓐ stood → standing
② ⓑ Danced → Dancing
④ ⓓ holds → held
⑤ ⓔ smile → smiling

3 분사구문의 시제와 주절의 시제가 같으므로 현재시제를 쓴다. 생략된 주어인 you를 이용해서 쓴다.

4 '길에서 꽃을 파는 늙은 남자가 있다.'는 의미로 명사 an old man과 능동의 관계이므로 현재분사인 ⑤ selling을 쓴다.

5 (A) 명사 dog와 능동의 관계이므로 현재분사 barking을 쓴다.
(B) 명사 glass와 수동의 관계이므로 과거분사 broken을 쓴다.
(C) 명사 product와 수동의 관계이므로 과거분사 damaged를 쓴다.

6 분사구문을 접속사가 있는 문장으로 바꿀 때, 분사구문의 시제가 주절의 시제보다 이전이므로 과거완료시제로 쓴다. 생략된 주어인 the runners를 이용해서 완전한 문장으로 쓴다.

7 첫 번째 빈칸: '그것은 놀라운 특수 효과들을 가지고 있었다.'는 의미로 명사 special effects가 감정을 일으키는 주체이므로 현재분사 amazing을 쓴다.
두 번째 빈칸: we가 감정을 느끼는 대상이므로 과거분사 impressed를 쓴다.

8 접속사 After와 주어 we를 생략하고 분사구문의 시제가 주절의 시제보다 이전이므로 동사 had finished를 Having finished로 바꾼다. 이때, 분사구문의 의미를 분명하게 하기 위해 부사절 접속사 After를 생략하지 않을 수 있다.

9 ⓑ jumped → jumping
ⓒ stolen → stealing
ⓔ embarrassing → embarrassed

10 첫 번째 빈칸: '시내 중심에 위치해 있기 때문에, 그것은 이전의 것

보다 더 편리할 것이다.'라는 의미의 분사구문이므로 Located를 쓴다.
두 번째 빈칸: 명사 people과 능동의 관계이므로 현재분사 taking을 쓴다.

11 ⓐ I가 감정을 느끼는 대상이므로 과거분사 worried를 쓴다.
ⓑ 명사 it이 감정을 일으키는 주체이므로 fascinating을 쓴다.
ⓒ 명사 author와 수동의 관계이므로 과거분사 admired를 쓴다.

12 분사구문 관용 표현으로 '솔직히 말하면'은 Frankly speaking을 쓴다.

13 '많은 흥미로운 캐릭터들을 포함하면서'의 의미인 분사구문이므로 주어 the story를 생략하고 동사 feature를 Featuring으로 바꾼다.

14 접속사 Because를 생략하고 동사 is sick을 being sick으로 바꾼다. 부사절의 주어와 주절의 주어가 다르기 때문에 부사절의 주어를 생략하지 않고 분사구문 맨 앞에 쓴다.

15 명사 Our fitness program이 감정을 일으키는 주체이므로 현재분사 exhausting을 쓴다.

16 ⑤ '~가 -한 채로/하면서'는 「with + 명사 + 분사」의 형태로 쓴다. 명사 its eyes와 수동의 관계이므로 과거분사 closed를 쓴다.

17 (A) experience가 감정을 일으키는 주체이므로 현재분사 frightening을 쓴다.
(B) 명사 A storm과 능동의 관계이므로 현재분사 causing을 쓴다.
(C) '~가 -한 채로/하면서'는 「with + 명사 + 분사」의 형태로 쓴다. 명사 our safety와 수동의 관계이므로 과거분사 threatened를 쓴다.

18 ⑤ '우리가 할 수 있는 한 빠르게 달렸기 때문에'의 의미이므로 이유를 나타내는 접속사 Because를 쓴다.

19 목적어 the screen을 보충 설명하고 목적어와 수동의 관계이므로 과거분사 broken을 쓴다.

20 ⓐ 명사 people과 능동의 관계이므로 현재분사 taking을 쓴다.
ⓑ 명사 woman과 능동의 관계이므로 현재분사 sitting을 쓴다.
ⓒ 명사 her legs와 수동의 관계이므로 과거분사 crossed를 쓴다.
ⓓ 명사 model과 수동의 관계이므로 과거분사 paid를 쓴다.

21 ① 이유를 나타내는 분사구문이므로 접속사 As를 쓸 수 있다. 분사구문의 시제와 주절의 시제가 같으므로 현재시제로 쓴다.
⑤ 이유를 나타내는 분사구문이므로 접속사 Because를 쓸 수 있다. 분사구문의 시제와 주절의 시제가 같으므로 현재시제로 쓴다.

22 ① excited → exciting
② interested → interesting
③ thrilled → thrilling
④ moving → moved

23 ② Arguing → Having argued

24 ⑤: 동명사
밑줄 친 부분과 ①②③④: 현재분사

25 ② Wrapping → (Being) Wrapped

CHAPTER 8
명사와 대명사

p.96

POINT 1 셀 수 있는 명사

1 O
2 O
3 Park visitors often feed the geese in the pond.
4 Those shelves are easy to assemble.
5 The athletes were doing a ten-minute run.
6 O
7 My grandmother used to tell me many stories.
8 You have to brush your teeth before going to bed.
9 O
10 Volcanoes are about to explode.
11 I met many interesting people at the party.
12 The farmer raises sheep for their wool.

POINT 2 셀 수 없는 명사

1 a spoonful of sugar   **2** a piece of furniture
3 a bottle of ink   **4** two pieces of cake
5 a sheet of paper   **6** three bars of soap
7 a spoonful of salt   **8** a bowl of cereal
9 two bottles of water
10 a sheet of newspaper
11 A bar of gold
12 three slices of cheese

POINT 3 명사의 소유격

1 The president of Korea
2 My dad's truck
3 students' knowledge
4 The rules of the game
5 Jane's new house
6 his parents' TV

1 O
2 A classmate of yours[Your classmate] called to borrow your history notes.
3 I'm going to Kate's dorm to return a coat of hers[her coat].
4 These essays of Daniel's[Daniel's essays] are among the best I have ever read.

5 O
6 O

POINT 4 재귀대명사

연습문제 A

1 myself / O	2 yourself / X
3 himself / X	4 themselves / O
5 himself / O	6 herself / X
7 herself / O	8 themselves / X
9 myself / X	10 itself / O

연습문제 B

1 by myself	2 talk to themselves
3 in itself	4 for ourselves
5 between ourselves	
6 help yourself[yourselves]	

POINT 5-1 it의 다양한 쓰임 I

연습문제

1 ⓓ	2 ⓑ	3 ⓐ
4 ⓒ	5 ⓓ	6 ⓑ
7 ⓒ		

POINT 5-2 it의 다양한 쓰임 II

연습문제

1 seems that the bridge in London
2 seem to have
3 seemed that she was disappointed
4 seems to be
5 seemed not to be[didn't seem to be]

POINT 6-1 부정대명사: one

연습문제

1 O	2 O
3 they	4 O
5 ones	6 one
7 them	8 O
9 ones	

POINT 6-2 부정대명사: some, any

연습문제

1 anyone	2 anything
3 Some	4 any
5 something	6 someone

POINT 6-3 부정대명사: another, other

연습문제 A

1 One / another / the others	
2 others[the others]	3 One / the other
4 another	5 One / the others
6 others	
7 One / another / the other	
8 other	9 the other
10 others	

연습문제 B

1 another	2 others
3 O	4 others
5 O	6 O
7 others	8 the other

POINT 6-4 부정대명사: all, each, every

연습문제

1 wants	2 road / is
3 chef has	4 teachers have
5 patients waits	6 restaurants are

POINT 6-5 부정대명사: both, either, neither

연습문제

1 Neither hotdog was delicious to him.
2 O   3 O
4 There are two T-shirts, but the customer doesn't like either of them.
5 Both the students seem to be happy with the solution to the problem.

중간·기말고사 실전 문제

1 ②, ④ **2** ③ **3** two bowls of soup / two pieces of cake **4** ③ **5** (1) neither of them (2) Either of them **6** ②
7 (1) Next year's tournament (2) in the lobby of the building **8** ① **9** one **10** ② **11** ④
12 ① **13** ⑤ **14** Mary told the guests to make themselves at home. **15** always talks to himself when he feels lonely **16** his **17** ⓐ one ⓑ the other **18** seems not to be going[doesn't seem to be going] **19** Many young adults think it possible that life will be found on other planets. **20** Some / others **21** ⓐ anything ⓑ either **22** ① **23** (1) ⓐ → seems to enjoy (2) ⓒ → seems to think **24** ② **25** ④

1 ② fun anything → anything fun
④ either machine are → neither machine is

2 (A) 「숫자 + 하이픈(-) + 단위표현」이 형용사처럼 쓰여 명사 앞에서 명사를 꾸밀 때는 숫자 뒤의 단위 표현을 단수형으로 쓴다.
(B) ox의 복수형은 oxen으로 쓴다.
(C) city의 복수형은 cities로 쓴다.

3 셀 수 없는 명사의 수량 표현을 할 때 '그릇'의 의미는 bowl로, '조각'의 의미는 piece를 쓴다.

4 ③ was → were

5 (1) '둘 중 어느 것도'라는 의미로 「neither of + 복수명사」를 쓴다.
(2) '둘 중 어느 것이든'이라는 의미로 「either of + 복수명사」를 쓴다.

6 · '한 조각의 빵'이라는 의미로 piece를 쓴다.
· '한 장의 종이'라는 의미로 piece를 쓴다.
· '한 가지 정보'라는 의미로 piece를 쓴다.

7 (1) 시간을 나타내는 명사의 소유격은 명사에 -'(s)를 붙여 쓴다.
(2) 무생물을 나타내는 명사의 소유격은 주로 「of + 명사」로 쓴다.

8 ② are → is
③ were → was
④ eye → eyes
⑤ is → are

9 · 앞에서 언급된 명사인 smartphone과 같은 종류지만 다른 대상이므로 one을 쓴다.
· 일반적인 사람을 나타내는 말로 One을 쓴다.

10 ② 재귀대명사의 강조 용법이므로 생략할 수 있다.

11 밑줄 친 부분과 ④: 일반적인 사람
①②③⑤: 앞에서 언급된 명사와 같은 종류이지만 다른 대상을 가리킨다.

12 ⓐ '몇몇은'이라는 의미로 Some을 쓴다.
ⓑ '다른 사람들' 라는 의미로 others를 쓴다.
ⓒ 명사 aliens를 가리키는 them을 쓴다.
ⓓ 앞에서 언급된 명사(alien)와 같은 종류의 불특정한 대상을 가리키고 있으므로 부정대명사 one을 쓴다.
따라서 ① other는 어느 빈칸에도 들어갈 수 없다.

13 ⓐⓓⓔ: 비인칭 주어 it
ⓑ: 가목적어 it   ⓒ: 가주어 it

14 '(집에서처럼) 편히 쉬다'는 의미로 make oneself at home을 쓴다.

15 '혼잣말을 하다'는 의미로 talk to oneself를 쓴다.

16 명사 앞에 지시대명사가 쓰였을 때는 소유격을 명사 뒤에 「of + 소유대명사」의 형태로 나타낸다. 'This invention of his is truly amazing.'이므로 네 번째에 오는 것은 his이다.

17 ⓐ '(둘 중) 하나의 전시는 고대 그리스 조각품을 포함하고'라는 의미이므로 one을 쓴다.
ⓑ '나머지 하나의 전시는 프랑스에서 온 추상화를 특별히 포함한다.'라는 의미이므로 the other를 쓴다.

18 「It seems that ~」은 that절의 주어를 문장의 주어 자리에 쓰고 that절의 동사를 to부정사로 바꿔 쓸 수 있다. 부정형은 not을 to부정사 앞에 쓴다.

19 문장의 목적어가 긴 경우 목적어 자리에 가목적어 it을 쓰고 진목적어는 that절을 뒤로 보내서 쓴다.

20 첫 번째 빈칸: '몇몇 식물들은 살아남기 위해 화학적 방어를 사용한다'는 의미이므로 Some을 쓴다.
두 번째 빈칸: '다른 식물들은 물리적인 방어를 사용한다'는 의미이므로 others를 쓴다.

21 ⓐ '어떤 것'이라는 의미로 부정문과 의문문에서 anything을 쓴다.
ⓑ '둘 중 어느 것이든'이라는 의미로 「either of + 복수명사」를 쓴다.

22 ① The castle seemed to be occupied. → The castle seemed not to be occupied.[The castle didn't seem to be occupied.]

23 (1) ⓐ 「It seems that ~」은 that절의 주어를 문장의 주어 자리에 쓰고 that절의 동사를 to부정사로 바꿔 쓸 수 있다.
(2) ⓒ 주어가 3인칭(He)이므로 seems를 쓴다.

24 ② teeths → teeth

25 밑줄 친 부분과 ④: 비인칭 주어 it
①⑤: 가주어 it   ②③: 가목적어 it

CHAPTER 9
형용사와 부사

p.110

POINT 1 형용사의 용법

1 diligent student
2 joyful
3 someone cheerful
4 alone
5 creative kid
6 interesting video
7 nobody loud
8 important presentation
9 anything valuable
10 somewhere warm
11 ashamed

1 The sofa is comfortable to lie on.
2 I was afraid of giving a speech.
3 Have you met anybody charming like that actor?
4 He didn't want to leave his dog alone.
5 The team has many international players.
6 She was awake at 3 in the morning.

POINT 2 수량형용사

1 A few, Some
2 many, a lot of
3 some, many
4 much, any
5 Few, A few
6 a great deal of, much
7 a lot of, lots of
8 a number of, plenty of
9 a little, little
10 Plenty of, Some

1 a little sugar
2 a few days
3 little information
4 many books
5 much homework

POINT 3 부사의 역할

1 effective
2 incredibly
3 easily
4 Unfortunately
5 completely
6 originally
7 seriously
8 tough
9 Actually

POINT 4 형용사와 형태가 같은 부사

1 늦게 / 부사
2 빠른 / 형용사
3 충분한 / 형용사
4 어려운 / 형용사
5 일찍 / 부사
6 열심히 / 부사
7 늦은 / 형용사
8 빠르게 / 부사
9 충분히 / 부사
10 이른 / 형용사

POINT 5 −ly가 붙으면 의미가 달라지는 부사

1 closely related
2 Raise / high
3 nearly fell asleep
4 was late
5 mostly true
6 hardly understand
7 live close
8 happening lately
9 Come near
10 too hard
11 highly successful
12 most recent

POINT 6 빈도부사

1 Michael is always polite and considerate towards others.
2 You can usually buy things cheaper online.
3 Ms. Smith sometimes takes a nap on the couch.
4 Stephanie never allows her brother to come into her room.
5 They rarely[hardly/seldom] have time to check their e-mails.
6 The interview usually takes two hours.
7 The United States is often called a melting pot.
8 You can always find useful information on the website.
9 Kate sometimes does the dishes for her mom.
10 I never watch TV on weekdays.

POINT 7 타동사 + 부사

1 throw it away
2 Take off your jacket[Take your jacket off]
3 try on this shirt[try this shirt on]
4 fill it in
5 made up an excuse[made an excuse up]
6 turned down the invitation[turned the invitation down]
7 turned it on
8 turn in their first draft[turn their first draft in]
9 put on his socks[put his socks on]

10 woke us up

11 look it up

중간·기말고사 실전 문제

1 ⑤　**2** (1) ⓑ → something interesting　(2) ⓒ → anywhere specific　(3) ⓔ → wonderful things
3 ①　**4** I think he is somebody famous.
5 ①　**6** ②　**7** (1) ⓐ → something unique
(2) ⓒ → Luckily　(3) ⓔ → anywhere special
8 ③　**9** ③　**10** One is that recycling can be incredibly expensive to do.　**11** I will find that out
12 ②　**13** ④　**14** ①　**15** have never found anything special　**16** ①　**17** ②　**18** ②
19 (A) mostly　(B) closely　(C) highly　**20** (1) ⓑ → lately　(2) ⓓ → costly　(3) ⓔ → rare　**21** ①, ⑤
22 ④　**23** ②　**24** ③　**25** (1) ⓓ → originally
(2) ⓔ → global

1 ⑤ easy → easily

2 (1) ⓑ -thing으로 끝나는 대명사(something)는 형용사
(interesting)가 대명사 뒤에 온다.
(2) ⓒ -where로 끝나는 대명사(anywhere)는 형용사
(specific)가 대명사 뒤에 온다.
(3) ⓔ '것, 물건'이라는 의미의 명사 thing을 수식할 때는 형용사
(wonderful)가 명사 앞에 온다.

3 ① is sleep → is asleep

4 -body로 끝나는 대명사(somebody)는 형용사(famous)가 대
명사 뒤에 온다.

5 ① always is first → is always first

6 ⓐ common seen → commonly seen
ⓔ a certainly amount of money → a certain amount of
money
ⓕ careful checked → carefully checked

7 (1) ⓐ -thing으로 끝나는 대명사(something)는 형용사
(unique)가 대명사 뒤에 온다.
(2) ⓒ 문장 전체를 꾸미는 부사(Luckily)를 쓴다.
(3) ⓔ -where로 끝나는 대명사(anywhere)는 형용사
(special)가 대명사 뒤에 온다.

8 (A) '많은 아이들이 그 책에 대해 물었다.'라는 의미이고 children
은 셀 수 있는 명사의 복수형이므로 Lots of를 쓴다.
(B) '컵 안에 남은 물이 거의 없다.'라는 의미이고 water는 셀 수
없는 명사이므로 little을 쓴다.
(C) '그 행사에서 우리는 많은 제품들을 팔았다.'라는 의미이고
products는 셀 수 있는 명사의 복수형이므로 a number
of를 쓴다.

9 (A) '이것의 문제는 많은 쓰레기가 실제로 재활용되지 않고 있다

는 것이다'라는 의미이고 trash는 셀 수 없는 명사이므로 a
lot of를 쓴다.
(B) '이것에는 많은 이유들이 있다.'라는 의미이고 reasons는 셀
수 있는 명사의 복수형이므로 many를 쓴다.
(C) '재활용은 시간, 돈, 장비, 재료 면에서 큰 노력을 요구한다.'
라는 의미이고 commitment는 셀 수 없는 명사이므로 a
great deal of를 쓴다.

10 형용사(expensive)를 꾸미는 부사(incredibly)를 쓴다.

11 '~을 알아내다'는 의미의 find out을 쓴다. 「타동사 + 부사」의 목
적어가 대명사인 경우 「타동사 + 대명사 + 부사」의 어순으로 쓰
므로 find that out으로 쓴다.

12 ⓑ a large amount of → many[a number of/a large
number of/a lot of/lots of/plenty of]
ⓒ few → little
ⓓ a few → a little[some]

13 · stuff는 셀 수 없는 명사이므로 much, a little, lots of를 쓸 수
있다.
· attention은 셀 수 없는 명사이므로 much, a little, lots of를
쓸 수 있다.
· games는 셀 수 있는 명사의 복수형이므로 a few, lots of, a
number of를 쓸 수 있다.
· words는 셀 수 있는 명사의 복수형이므로 a few, lots of, a
number of를 쓸 수 있다.
따라서 빈칸에 공통으로 들어갈 말은 ④ lots of이다.

14 ① accidental → accidentally

15 -thing으로 끝나는 대명사(anything)는 형용사(special)가 대
명사 뒤에 온다.

16 ② is usual scheduled → is usually scheduled
③ Unfortunate → Unfortunately
④ events past → past events
⑤ prompt → promptly

17 ②: 형용사
①③④⑤: 부사

18 ② locks always → always locks

19 (A) '도시 사람들은 대부분 버스나 기차를 타고 일을 하러 간다.'는
의미이므로 '대부분'이라는 의미의 부사(mostly)를 쓴다.
(B) '너는 세부 사항을 보기 위해 그림을 면밀히 보아야 한다.'는
의미이므로 '면밀히'라는 의미의 부사(closely)를 쓴다.
(C) 'Barnes씨는 그 지역 사회 내의 모두에 의해 매우 존경 받는
다.'는 의미이므로 '매우'라는 의미의 부사(highly)를 쓴다.

20 (1) ⓑ '나는 최근에 작은 가게에는 없는 것들 때문에 가고 있어.'
라는 의미이므로 '최근에'라는 의미의 부사(lately)를 쓴다.
(2) ⓓ '몇몇 물품들은 너무 비싸지만, 너는 싸게 살 수 있는 물건
들을 찾을 수 있을 거야.'라는 의미이므로 형용사(costly)를
쓴다.
(3) ⓔ '물론이지, 하지만 그것은 드문 일이야.'라는 의미이므로
형용사(rare)를 쓴다.

21 ① secure somewhere → somewhere secure
⑤ personally things → personal things

22 ⓐ eats always → always eats
ⓑ put on it → put it on
ⓔ walk often → often walk

23 ② turn off it → turn it off

24 ⓑ hand in it → hand it in
ⓒ throw away it → throw it away

25 (1) ⓓ '이 행사는 원래 호주에서만 개최되었다.'는 의미이므로 동사(held)를 꾸미는 부사(originally)를 쓴다.
(2) ⓔ '이것은 2008년에 세계적인 행사가 되었다.'는 의미이므로 형용사(global)를 쓴다.

CHAPTER 10
비교구문

p.122

POINT 1-1 원급 비교: as + 원급 + as

1 My mom likes traveling as much as I do.
2 The merry-go-round is not as thrilling as the roller coaster.
3 Playing the piano is as hard as playing the violin.
4 A garden of roses is as pretty as a field of cosmos.
5 The new sofa is not as comfortable as the old one.
6 My younger brother enjoys playing video games as much as I do.
7 My history class is not as exciting as my science class.
8 Cleaning my room is as boring as washing the dishes.
9 Our new home is not as large as the old one.
10 My hair is as dark as my mother's hair.

1 as tall as   **2** as many desks as
3 not as[so] delicious as
4 not as[so] clean as
5 as well as   **6** as old as
7 as many people as **8** not as[so] sweet as
9 not as[so] neat as **10** as loud as
11 as many books as   **12** as interesting as
13 as warm as   **14** as strange as

POINT 1-2 원급 관련 표현

1 twice as many kinds of fruit as
2 as early as she could
3 five times as heavy as
4 four times as often as
5 as accurately as possible
6 ten times as big as
7 as strong as he could
8 three times as expensive as

1 as often as   **2** as good as
3 as long as   **4** as far as

POINT 2-1 비교급 비교: 비교급 + than

연습문제

1 louder than
2 much[even, still, far, a lot] more reasonable than
3 much[even, still, far, a lot] worse than
4 less hot than
5 less entertaining than
6 more quietly than
7 much[even, still, far, a lot] cheaper than
8 less effective
9 much[even, still, far, a lot] cuter than
10 faster than
11 more fantastic than
12 much[even, still, far, a lot] prettier than

POINT 2-2 비교급 관련 표현

연습문제 A

1 The cheaper I buy things than usual, the happier I feel.
2 The more popular the movie got, the more popular the main actor became, too.
3 The harder you work at something, the better you will do it.
4 The more you get to know her, the more you will want to become friends with her.
5 The more expensive the coat gets, the less affordable it will be.
6 The more frequently you speak English, the more fluent you will be in it.

연습문제 B

1 wider and wider
2 five times higher than
3 more and more interesting
4 ten times stronger than
5 more and more tired

POINT 3 최상급 비교와 관련된 표현

연습문제 A

1 the greatest piece
2 one of the most brilliant students
3 the least exciting hobby
4 the most useful appliance
5 the closest friend

연습문제 B

1 No (other) movie star / as[so] attractive as
No (other) movie star / more attractive than
more attractive than any other movie star
more attractive than all the other movie stars

2 No (other) item / as[so] cheap as
No (other) item / cheaper than
cheaper than any other item
cheaper than all the other items
3 No (other) player / as[so] talented as
No (other) player / more talented than
more talented than any other player
more talented than all the other players

중간·기말고사 실전 문제

1 ④ 2 ① 3 ② 4 ② 5 ③, ④
6 as cheap as 7 three times as expensive as [three times more expensive than] 8 ⑤
9 Whales are the largest of all animals on Earth.
10 fast 11 ②, ⑤ 12 The longer she stayed in Jejudo, the more she missed living in Seoul.
13 ⑤ 14 ③ 15 This is the prettiest gift that I have received. 16 (1) ⓐ → as old as (2) ⓑ → much[even, still, far, a lot] (3) ⓔ → a lot more efficiently 17 twice as costly as owning an electric car per year 18 ② 19 No other team in the league is more competitive than that team.
20 better and better 21 ④ 22 ⑤ 23 ②
24 sleepier and sleepier 25 ④

1 첫 번째 빈칸: 「less + 원급 + than」은 '…보다 덜 ~한/하게'라는 의미로, 「not + as[so] + 원급 + as」로 바꿔 쓸 수 있다. 따라서 첫 번째 빈칸에는 not so를 쓴다.
두 번째 빈칸: 두 번째 빈칸에는 as를 쓴다.

2 ① 「비교급 + than all the other + 복수명사」는 「비교급 + than any other + 단수명사」로 바꿔 쓸 수 있다.

3 「as + 원급 + as」는 '…만큼 ~한/하게'라는 의미로, 비교하는 두 대상의 정도가 비슷하거나 같음을 나타낸다.

4 ⓐ as more toys as → as many toys as
ⓒ not as easier as → not as easy as
ⓔ so shy as → as shy as

5 ③ 「not + so + 원급 + as」는 '…만큼 ~하지 않은/않게'라는 의미이다.
④ 「not + as + 원급 + as」는 '…만큼 ~하지 않은/않게'라는 의미이다.

6 「as + 원급 + as」는 '…만큼 ~한/하게'라는 의미로, 비교하는 두 대상의 정도가 비슷하거나 같음을 나타낸다.

7 「배수사 + as + 원급 + as」는 '…보다 -배 더 ~한/하게'라는 의미로, 「배수사 + 비교급 + than」으로 바꿔 쓸 수 있다.

8 ⓐ Only strongest → Only the strongest
ⓒ the most scary → the scariest

ⓓ player → players

9 「the + 최상급 + (명사)」는 '가장 ~한/하게'라는 의미이므로 최상급인 the largest를 쓴다.

10 Running is twice as fast as walking.이므로 다섯 번째에 오는 단어는 fast이다.

11 ② 「배수사 + as + 원급 + as 」는 '…보다 -배 더 ~한/하게'라는 의미이다.
⑤ 「배수사 + 비교급 + than」은 '…보다 -배 더 ~한/하게'라는 의미이다.

12 「the + 비교급 ~, the + 비교급 …」은 '~할수록 더 …하다'라는 의미이다.

13 ① comfortabler → comfortable
② least commonly → less commonly
③ more faster → faster
④ more beautiful → more beautifully

14 (A) '그 관리자는 그 소식에 대해 다른 사람들만큼이나 충격을 받았다.'는 의미이므로 원급인 shocked를 쓴다.
(B) '빌 게이츠는 세상에서 가장 부유한 사람이었다.'는 의미이므로 최상급인 richest를 쓴다.
(C) '오늘의 날씨는 일주일 내내 날씨보다 더욱 쾌적했다.'는 의미이므로 비교급인 more pleasant를 쓴다.

15 「the + 최상급 + (명사)」는 '가장 ~한/하게'라는 의미이므로 최상급인 the prettiest를 쓴다.

16 (1) ⓐ 「as + 원급 + as」는 '…만큼 ~한/하게'라는 의미로, 비교하는 두 대상의 정도가 비슷하거나 같음을 나타낸다.
(2) ⓑ 비교급 앞에 much, even, still, far, a lot을 써서 '훨씬'이라는 의미로 비교급을 강조할 수 있다.
(3) ⓔ 「비교급 + than」은 '…보다 더 ~한/하게'라는 의미로, 비교급 앞에 a lot을 써서 '훨씬'이라는 의미로 비교급을 강조할 수 있다.

17 「배수사 + as + 원급 + as」는 '…보다 -배 더 ~한/하게'라는 의미이다.

18 비교급 앞에 much, even, still, far, a lot을 써서 '훨씬'이라는 의미로 비교급을 강조할 수 있다. ② very는 비교급을 강조할 수 없다.

19 「비교급 + than any other + 단수명사」는 「No (other) + 단수명사 ~ 비교급 + than」으로 바꿔 쓸 수 있다.

20 「비교급 + and + 비교급」은 '점점 더 ~한/하게'라는 의미이다.

21 ④ ⓓ as less trash as possible → as little trash as possible

22 ⑤ 「비교급 + and + 비교급」은 '점점 더 ~한/하게'라는 의미이다.

23 ② 「not + as[so] + 원급 + as」는 '…보다 덜 ~한/하게'라는 의미로, 「less + 원급 + than」으로 바꿔 쓸 수 있다.

24 「비교급 + and + 비교급」은 '점점 더 ~한/하게'라는 의미이다.

25 ④ 「less + 원급 + than」은 '…보다 덜 ~한/하게'라는 의미이다. 비교급 앞에 much를 써서 '훨씬'이라는 의미로 비교급을 강조할 수 있다.

CHAPTER 11
전치사

POINT 1-1 시간을 나타내는 전치사 I

연습문제

1 on		**2** in		**3** X	
4 at		**5** on		**6** in	
7 at		**8** X		**9** on	
10 in		**11** at		**12** on	
13 in		**14** On		**15** In	
16 on		**17** at		**18** at	
19 in		**20** in			

POINT 1-2 시간을 나타내는 전치사 II

연습문제 A

1 from		**2** until	
3 since		**4** by	
5 since		**6** by	
7 from		**8** until	
9 After		**10** before	

연습문제 B

1 before		**2** since	
3 until		**4** by	
5 from		**6** after	

POINT 1-3 시간을 나타내는 전치사 III

연습문제

1 ①		**2** ②		**3** ③	
4 ①		**5** ②			

POINT 2-1 장소를 나타내는 전치사 I

연습문제

1 on		**2** at		**3** in	
4 on					

POINT 2-2 장소를 나타내는 전치사 II

연습문제 A

1 on		**2** at		**3** in	
4 on		**5** in		**6** at	
7 On		**8** in		**9** at	
10 in		**11** on		**12** in	

POINT 3 위치를 나타내는 전치사

연습문제

1 above		**2** in front of	
3 between		**4** under	
5 behind		**6** among	
7 beside			

POINT 4 방향을 나타내는 전치사

연습문제

1 around		**2** towards	
3 out of		**4** across	
5 up		**6** into	
7 through		**8** along	

POINT 5 기타 전치사

연습문제

1 with		**2** against	
3 by		**4** due to	
5 of		**6** about	
7 throughout		**8** except	
9 instead of		**10** for	
11 as			

POINT 6-1 전치사 관용 표현: 형용사 + 전치사

연습문제

1 to		**2** at	
3 of		**4** to	
5 with		**6** for	
7 of		**8** with	
9 of		**10** of	

POINT 6-2 전치사 관용 표현: 동사 + 전치사

연습문제

1 of		**2** in	
3 for		**4** on	
5 to		**6** for	
7 after		**8** on	
9 for		**10** into	
11 with		**12** by	
13 at		**14** on	

연습문제 B

1 O		**2** on		**3** O	
4 in		**5** at		**6** O	
7 on		**8** O		**9** in	
10 O		**11** in		**12** on	

15 into	**16** for
17 in	**18** in
19 on	**20** into

POINT 6-3 전치사 관용 표현: 동사 + 명사 + 전치사

연습
문제

1 make use of	**2** take care of
3 get rid of	**4** took pity on
5 take part in	**6** pay attention to
7 had fun with	**8** makes a fool of
9 get rid of	**10** pay attention to

중간·기말고사 실전 문제

1 ③ **2** ④ **3** ② **4** ④ **5** (A) on
→ at (B) at → in (C) in → on **6** ⓐ from ⓑ during
ⓒ since ⓓ for **7** ④ **8** ③ **9** ②
10 ⑤ **11** ④ **12** ① **13** ③ **14** ②
15 ③ **16** (A) along (B) from (C) down (D) after
17 of **18** (1) ⓐ → in (2) ⓓ → on **19** ⑤
20 ④ **21** ⓐ with ⓑ as ⓒ near ⓓ in
22 turn the individual students into effective team
members **23** ① **24** ⑤ **25** ⑤

1 '그 곳은 새집처럼 느껴진다.'는 의미이므로 전치사 like(~처럼)를
쓴다.

2 ④ at → on

3 (A) '과거에'라는 의미로 in the past를 쓴다.
(B) '~ 동안'이라는 의미의 while은 접속사로 뒤에 완전한 문장이
온다.
(C) 특정 시점까지 어떤 행동이나 상황이 계속되는 것을 나타낼
때는 전치사 until을 쓴다.

4 'Michelle은 쇼핑몰에서 그녀의 여동생과 함께 재미있게 놀았
다.'는 의미이므로 ④ with(~와 함께)를 쓴다.

5 (A) '현재에'라는 의미의 at present를 쓴다.
(B) 아침(the morning) 앞에는 전치사 in을 쓴다.
(C) 기념일(Valentine's Day) 앞에는 전치사 on을 쓴다.

6 ⓐ '그 가게는 수리를 위해 화요일부터 금요일까지 닫았다.'라는
의미이므로 전치사 from(~부터)을 쓴다.
ⓑ '~동안'이라는 의미로 뒤에 명사(the winter)가 오므로
during을 쓴다.
ⓒ '~이후로'라는 의미의 전치사 since를 쓴다.
ⓓ '~동안'이라는 의미로 뒤에 숫자를 포함한 시간 표현(45
minutes)이 오므로 for를 쓴다.

7 ① of → for
② at → about

③ to → from
⑤ of → with

8 ③ '~을 할 수 있다'는 의미로 be capable of를 쓴다.

9 ⓐⓓ: in ⓑ: on ⓒ: with[to] ⓔ:for

10 ⑤: to
①②③④: on

11 (A) '서두르는'이라는 의미이므로 in a hurry를 쓴다.
(B) '~의 아래에'라는 의미이므로 at the bottom of를 쓴다.
(C) '위험에 빠진'이라는 의미이므로 in danger를 쓴다.

12 · '소방관들은 불타는 차량 밖으로 그 남자를 끌어냈다.'는 의미이
므로 전치사 out of(~밖으로)를 쓴다.
· leave와 함께 쓰여 가고자 하는 방향을 나타내고 있으므로 전
치사 for(~으로)를 쓴다.

13 첫 번째 빈칸: 요일(Saturday) 앞에는 전치사 on을 쓴다.
두 번째 빈칸: 비교적 넓은 장소(the city) 앞에는 전치사 in을 쓴
다.

14 밑줄 친 부분과 ②: '~에 찬성하는'
①③④⑤: '~을 위해'

15 · 요일(Sunday) 앞에는 전치사 on을 쓴다.
· 날짜(January 27, 1756) 앞에는 전치사 on을 쓴다.

16 (A) '고속도로를 따라서 아주 많은 표지판이 있다.'는 의미이므로
전치사 along(~을 따라서)을 쓴다.
(B) 'Dan은 캐나다부터 멕시코까지 운전했다.'는 의미이므로 전
치사 from(~부터)을 쓴다.
(C) 'Billy는 미끄럼틀을 타고 몇 번이고 아래로 내려갔다.'는 의미
이므로 전치사 down(~아래로)을 쓴다.
(D) 'Katie는 그녀의 아이 출생 후에 일을 잠시 쉬었다.'는 의미이
므로 전치사 after(~후에)를 쓴다.

17 · '~으로 이루어지다'는 의미로 consist of를 쓴다.
· '~으로 가득 차 있다'는 의미로 be full of를 쓴다.
· '~으로 죽다'는 의미로 die of를 쓴다.

18 (1) ⓐ '나의 가족과 나는 부산에서 호텔에 머물렀다.'는 의미이므
로 비교적 넓은 장소(Busan) 앞에는 전치사 in을 쓴다.
(2) ⓓ '우리는 TV에서 많은 영화를 보았다.'는 의미이므로 통신수
단 앞에는 전치사 on을 쓴다.

19 'Mark는 유명한 배우처럼 생겼다.'는 의미이므로 전치사 like
(~처럼)를 쓴다.

20 첫 번째 빈칸: '헬리콥터가 그 건물의 지붕 위를 날고 있었다.'는 의
미이므로 전치사 above(~ 위에)를 쓴다.
두 번째 빈칸: 'Sue는 그녀의 아픈 고모를 돌보기 위해 그녀의 고
모네 집 안으로 이사했다.'는 의미이므로 전치사 into(~ 안으로)를
쓴다.
세 번째 빈칸: 'Alice와 Nancy 사이의 자리에 앉아있는 소녀는
내 누나이다.'는 의미이므로 전치사 between(~ 사이에)을 쓴다.
네 번째 빈칸: '수영장에는 많은 사람이 있었다.'는 의미이므로 전
치사 in(~에)을 쓴다.
따라서 among은 어느 빈칸에도 들어갈 수 없다.

21 ⓐ '지난주, 우리 반은 학교의 나머지 사람들과 함께 조회에 갔다.'
는 의미이므로 전치사 with(~와 함께)를 쓴다.

ⓑ '그것은 성공하기 위해 팀의 일원으로 일하는 것에 관한 것이었
다.'는 의미이므로 전치사 as(~로)를 쓴다.

ⓒ '우리가 무대 가까이에 앉았으므로, 나는 우리가 발표자들을 들
을 수 있는 좋은 좌석을 가졌다고 생각했다.'는 의미이므로 전
치사 near(~ 가까이에)를 쓴다.

ⓓ '~에 참가하다'라는 의미이므로 take part in을 쓴다.

22 'A를 B로 바꾸다'라는 의미이므로 turn A into B를 쓴다.

23 · '오늘 밤, 나는 나의 가족과 몇몇 친구들과 함께 저녁을 먹으러
나갈 것이다.'라는 의미이므로 전치사 with(~와 함께)를 쓴다.

· '나는 내 용돈을 이용해서 새 가방을 샀다.'는 의미이므로 전치
사 with(~을 이용해서)를 쓴다.

· 'Ken의 이웃은 너무 시끄러운 소음을 만드는 사람들에 대한 문
제가 있다'는 의미이므로 전치사 with(~에 대해)를 쓴다.

24 ⑤ 동사(좋아하다)
밑줄 친 부분과 ①②③④: 전치사(~처럼)

25 '나는 부모님 없이, 혼자서 처음으로 비행기를 타기 때문에 조금 불
안하다.'는 의미이므로 전치사 without(~ 없이)을 쓴다.

CHAPTER 12
접속사
p.148

POINT 1 등위접속사: and, but, or, so

1 but	**2** and	**3** so
4 or	**5** but	**6** or
7 so	**8** but	**9** and
10 so		

POINT 2 상관접속사

1 O	**2** get
3 is	**4** are
5 O	**6** like
7 O	**8** have
9 are	**10** O

1 Both pasta and rice are

2 Not only English but (also) Chinese[Chinese as well as English] is

3 not Canada but the United States

4 Either he or she will write

5 Neither Chloe nor Jacob likes

6 not to talk but to listen

POINT 3-1 명사절을 이끄는 접속사: that

1 ⓑ	**2** ⓐ	**3** ⓒ
4 ⓐ	**5** ⓑ	**6** ⓐ
7 ⓒ	**8** ⓑ	

1 the news that his favorite band will release an album in May

2 the idea[thought] that kids should experience many different things

3 The thought[idea] that I might fail the exam

4 The suggestion that the students take longer vacations

5 The fact that the rival team won the match

POINT 3-2 명사절을 이끄는 접속사: if/whether

연습 문제

1 O		**2** whether	
3 whether		**4** O	
5 whether		**6** O	
7 Whether		**8** O	

POINT 3-3 명사절을 이끄는 접속사: 의문사

연습 문제

1 how she made	**2** when I will visit
3 why he didn't come	**4** How I got
5 who would win	**6** where they were

POINT 4-1 부사절을 이끄는 접속사: 시간

연습 문제 A

1 after		**2** as soon as
3 since		**4** as
5 till		**6** before
7 when		**8** until
9 as		**10** since
11 when		**12** as soon as

연습 문제 B

1 O		**2** tells
3 O		**4** rings
5 dust		**6** O
7 graduates		**8** O
9 become		**10** O

POINT 4-2 부사절을 이끄는 접속사: 이유

연습 문제 A

1 while	**2** as
3 since	**4** when
5 because	**6** as
7 now that	**8** since
9 now that	**10** Because
11 since	**12** now that

연습 문제 B

1 because of	**2** because
3 because	**4** because of
5 because	**6** because of
7 because	**8** because of
9 because of	**10** because

POINT 4-3 부사절을 이끄는 접속사: 조건

연습 문제 A

1 O	**2** unless
3 gets	**4** once
5 O	**6** if
7 O	

연습 문제 B

1 If you don't eat properly
　 Unless you eat properly
2 If you don't keep your promise
　 Unless you keep your promise
3 If you don't submit your application
　 Unless you submit your application
4 If you aren't responsible
　 Unless you are responsible

POINT 4-4 부사절을 이끄는 접속사: 양보

연습 문제 A

1 O
2 though[although/even though]
3 O
4 though[although/even though]
5 despite[in spite of]
6 O　　　　　　**7** O
8 though[although/even though]
9 O　　　　　　**10** O
11 Though[Although/Even though]
12 O

연습 문제 B

1 Although we had expected it
2 whereas his dad drank hot coffee
3 even though she is bad at directions
4 though she stayed up all night to study

POINT 4-5 부사절을 이끄는 접속사: so that ~

연습 문제

1 so that she could concentrate on her studying
2 so that people can understand what you are saying
3 so as to buy a gold necklace for her mom
4 so that you won't have any regrets afterwards
5 so that I could cook dinner
6 so as to join the school band
7 in order to get some fruit
8 so that we could play hide-and-seek

POINT 4-6 부사절을 이끄는 접속사: so ~ that …

1. so scary that no one could go in it
2. so exhausted that he couldn't move
3. too difficult to fully understand
4. too long for him to finish it in one day
5. so good at skiing that she always competes internationally
6. too short to ride the roller coaster
7. so noisy that they couldn't hear each other
8. so busy that he can't watch the movie tonight
9. so fast that I couldn't catch up with him
10. too greedily to enjoy the taste of the food
11. too heavy for me to lift it
12. so hungry that he ate an entire pizza

POINT 5 다양한 의미의 부사절을 이끄는 접속사

1	③	2	②
3	①	4	②

1. while I was waiting   2. since I was born
3. since the accident
4. while the show was going on
5. Since the girl was
6. while I was making breakfast

POINT 6 접속부사

1	However	2	For example
3	In fact	4	Moreover
5	Instead	6	Thus
7	For instance	8	In addition
9	Indeed	10	On the other hand

1. Therefore[Thus]
2. In contrast[However/On the other hand]
3. Otherwise

중간·기말고사 실전 문제

1. if I should have a sandwich or a salad   2 ③
3. so that she could memorize it   4 ③
5. ④   6 ③, ④   7 My passport as well as my wallet   8 what caused the experiment to fail   9 ①   10 Wear a seatbelt, and you

---

will reduce your risk of injuries.   11 ③
12. (1) The singer is so famous that he cannot go out in public alone.   (2) The fence was damaged so badly that it had to be replaced.   13 ⑤   14 get in trouble unless you follow school rules   15 ④
16. not only / but also   17 ②   18 ③
19. ①   20 ⑤   21 despite → though[although/even though]   22 (1) because (2) when
23. and she bought two pieces of bread   24 ⑤
25. ②, ⑤

1 명사절을 이끄는 접속사 if는 '~인지'의 의미이다. '샌드위치를 먹어야 할지 또는 샐러드를 먹어야 할지'라고 했으므로 '또는'을 의미하는 or를 쓴다.

2 · '지수는 두통 때문에 병원을 방문했다.'는 의미이므로 because of(~ 때문에)를 쓴다.
· '나는 점심 식사를 준비하는 동안 내 손가락을 베었다.'는 의미이므로 while(~하는 동안)을 쓴다.
· 'David는 그의 보고서에서 오류를 발견했기 때문에 그의 보고서를 다시 읽었다.'는 의미이므로 since(~이기 때문에)를 쓴다.
· '안전상 우려 때문에 우리는 비가 멈출 때까지 교실을 떠날 수 없었다.'는 의미이므로 until(~할 때까지)을 쓴다.
따라서 unless는 빈칸에 들어갈 수 없다.

3 so that은 '~하기 위해, ~할 수 있도록'의 의미로, 목적을 나타내는 부사절을 이끈다.

4 (A) while이 '~하는 동안'이라는 의미로 사용되었다.
(B) since가 '~한 이래로'라는 의미로 사용되었다.

5 · 접속사 that은 문장 안에서 주어 역할을 하는 명사절을 이끈다.
· 접속사 that은 문장 안에서 보어 역할을 하는 명사절을 이끈다.

6 ③, ④ that절이 목적어로 쓰였을 때 that은 생략할 수 있다.

7 'A뿐만 아니라 B도'라는 의미의 not only A but (also) B 구문은 B as well as A로 바꿔 쓸 수 있다.

8 의문사가 이끄는 명사절 안에서 의문사가 주어 역할을 하는 경우, 의문사 뒤에 동사를 바로 쓴다.

9 ① because of 뒤에는 명사(구)가 온다.

10 '만약 네가 안전벨트를 맨다면, 너는 너의 부상의 위험을 줄일 것이다.'는 의미이다. 따라서 '…해라, 그러면 ~'의 의미로 「명령문 + and ~」로 바꿔 쓸 수 있다.

11 ③ '~로서'라는 의미로 전치사 as가 쓰였다.
①②④⑤ '~이기 때문에'라는 의미로 접속사 as가 쓰였다.

12 (1) 「so + 형용사/부사 + that …」은 '너무 ~해서/~하게 …한'의 의미이며, 결과를 나타내는 부사절을 이끈다.
(2) 「so + 형용사/부사 + that …」은 '너무 ~해서/~하게 …한'의 의미이며, 결과를 나타내는 부사절을 이끈다.

13 첫 번째 빈칸: 앞 문장과 반대의 의미이므로 In contrast(그에 반해서)를 쓴다.
두 번째 빈칸: 앞 문장의 추가 설명을 하고 있으므로 Moreover

14 '만약 네가 학교 규칙을 따르지 않으면, 너는 곤란해질 것이다.'는 의미이고, If ~ not은 unless(만약 ~하지 않으면)로 바꿔 쓸 수 있다.

15 ④ so big plane that → so big that

16 'A뿐만 아니라 B도'라는 의미의 not only A but (also) B를 쓴다.

17 ② '~인지'의 의미의 명사절 접속사로 쓰였다.
①③④⑤ '만약 ~한다면'의 의미의 부사절 접속사로 쓰였다.

18 밑줄 친 부분과 ③: '~이기 때문에'의 의미로 쓰였다.
① '~할 때'의 의미로 쓰였다.
② '~하면서'의 의미로 쓰였다.
④⑤ '~처럼, ~듯이'의 의미로 쓰였다.

19 ① Now that은 '~이기 때문에'라는 의미이다.

20 ⑤ Besides → Therefore[Thus/As a result]

21 despite는 전치사이므로 뒤에 절이 아닌 명사(구)를 쓴다. '에어컨이 비록 틀어져 있었지만 그 방은 더웠다.'는 의미이므로 '비록 ~이지만'이라는 의미인 though[although/even though]를 쓴다.

22 (1) 밑줄 친 as가 '~이기 때문에'의 의미로 쓰였으므로 because(~이기 때문에)를 쓴다.
(2) 밑줄 친 as가 '~할 때'의 의미로 쓰였으므로 when(~할 때)을 쓴다.

23 '그리고'라는 의미의 and를 쓴다.

24 · '너의 빨래를 빨리 해라, 그렇지 않으면 너는 네가 가장 좋아하는 TV쇼를 놓칠 것이다.'라는 의미이므로 or를 쓴다. 「명령문 + or ~」는 '…해라, 그렇지 않으면 ~'의 의미이다.
· 'Rachel은 저녁 식사 후에 밥상을 차리거나 설거지를 한다.'는 의미이므로 either A or B를 쓴다.

25 '비록 Ivan은 친절했지만, 그는 낯선 사람 주위에서 초조해했다.'는 의미이므로 Although(비록 ~이지만)와 Though(비록 ~이지만)를 쓸 수 있다.

CHAPTER 13
관계사
p.166

POINT 1 관계대명사의 역할과 종류

1 which[that] / 주격
2 whom[who/that] / 목적격
3 whose / 소유격   **4** which[that] / 목적격
5 which[that] / 주격   **6** whose / 소유격
7 who[that] / 주격   **8** whose / 소유격
9 whom[who/that] / 목적격
10 who[that] / 주격

POINT 2-1 주격 관계대명사

1 got a new pair of glasses which are scratch proof
2 is the vase which is my mom's favorite
3 heard the surprising news which was about the famous movie star
4 went to an art exhibition with her friend who is interested in modern art
5 composed a song for his son who died in a car accident

POINT 2-2 목적격 관계대명사

1 want to apologize for our mistake which we made yesterday
2 made small talk with my old friend who[whom] I ran into on the street
3 have a lot of comic books which my younger brother wants to borrow
4 which the student needs to take will be here in a minute
5 who[whom] my friend used to be a fan of is now on TV

POINT 2-3 소유격 관계대명사

1 Can you see the mountain whose top is covered with snow?
2 Look at these coins whose sizes and shapes are different.

3 The lady whose daughter is in the hospital looks very sad.

4 We swam at the beach whose sand was white.

5 The team whose players have practiced the hardest will win.

POINT 3 관계대명사 that

1 is a student that Jaemin found hard working → who, whom

2 you want to go to the park that has many pine trees → which

3 respect the nurse that always helps people in need → who

4 is the restaurant that the locals recommend → which

5 you still talk to the woman that we used to work with → who, whom

1	ⓑ / 명사절 접속사	**2**	ⓓ / 관계대명사
3	ⓑ / 지시형용사	**4**	ⓐ / 명사절 접속사
5	ⓑ / 관계대명사	**6**	ⓒ / 지시형용사
7	ⓑ / 명사절 접속사	**8**	ⓑ / 지시형용사
9	ⓓ / 관계대명사	**10**	ⓑ / 지시대명사
11	ⓒ / 명사절 접속사		

POINT 4 관계대명사 what

1 what I just said

2 What most people believe

3 What you want to be

4 what he can do well

5 what the suspect had

6 what Cathy said to him

7 what you can do right now

8 what she offered

9 what she should do

10 what his friends said

POINT 5 전치사 + 관계대명사

1 which[that] Mr. Woods can sit on for a long time / on which Mr. Woods can sit for a long time

2 who[whom/that] my uncle is waving at / at whom my uncle is waving

3 which[that] many people were waiting for / for which many people were waiting

4 who[whom/that] I voted for / for whom I voted

5 who[whom/that] I went to school with / with whom I went to school

6 which[that] I live in / in which I live

7 which[that] I left my bike under / under which I left my bike

POINT 6 관계부사의 역할과 종류

1 when I became a doctor was the happiest day of my life

2 is the park where we run around every morning

3 you tell me (the reason) why you made this decision

4 was how the thief could come into the room

5 where they can have some coffee is a block away

1	where	**2**	how
3	when	**4**	why
5	where	**6**	how
7	where	**8**	when
9	how	**10**	when
11	why	**12**	how
13	when		

POINT 7 관계사의 계속적 용법

1 her dog, which barked

2 a song, which inspired me

3 the girl who[whom/that] we met

4 an older brother, who[whom] I often fight

5 the actor who[whom/that] I have always liked

6 the bus every morning, which comes

7 several rules, which you have to follow

1 visited the Colosseum, which was built around

2 loves her dog, which follows her

3 will travel to New York next year, where they can see the Statue of Liberty

4 went to the restaurant, where all customers had to dress up

POINT 8 복합관계사

1 Whichever you buy, you'll be satisfied.

2 I will support whatever you decide to do in the future.

3 Jackson watches action movies whenever he has nothing to do.

4 His parents don't care for whomever he hangs out with.

5 However tired Kenneth is, he needs to get his essay done by tonight.

6 Whatever she wants, I will buy it for her.

7 However rich you are, you shouldn't waste your money on useless things.

8 Whoever wants to participate, raise your hand.

9 Wherever he lives, we can go visit him.

10 However busy you are, you shouldn't skip meals.

11 Whatever you are saying, they won't be interested.

12 Becky always tries her best at whatever she does.

13 Wherever she goes, her fans gather around her.

중간·기말고사 실전 문제

1 ③　　**2** ①　　**3** The movie is about children who[that] discover a hidden cave.　　**4** ⑤
5 ④　　**6** ①　　**7** There were many advantages of Gutenberg's technique / which made it possible for everyone to buy books.　　**8** ⑤
9 ②　　**10** (1) which won an award　(2) which was based on a children's book　(3) whose plot was exciting　　**11** that　　**12** ⓐ which　ⓑ whom[who]
13 ③　　**14** ②　　**15** What you did was helpful to other students.　　**16** what　　**17** ⓒ → what
18 ⓑ → Jacob read about da Vinci, who painted the *Mona Lisa*.　　**19** ⓐ that　ⓑ what　　**20** ③
21 ⓐ → The chess player who[that] plans most effectively will win.　　**22** He studied the vocabulary words included on the test.　　**23** (A) whom　(B) which　　**24** ⑤　　**25** ①, ⑤

1 · 선행사(a phone)가 사물이므로 관계대명사 which를 쓸 수 있다.
· 선행사(someone)가 사람이므로 관계대명사 who를 쓸 수 있다.

2 ⓑ in that → in which
ⓔ the reason how → the reason why

3 두 번째 문장은 첫 번째 문장의 children에 대해 보충 설명하고 있고, 선행사(children)가 사람을 나타내므로 사람을 선행사로 하는 주격 관계대명사 who[that]을 쓴다.

4 (A) '그곳은 내가 평온과 고요를 위해 가는 장소이다.'는 의미로 장소를 나타내는 관계부사 where를 쓴다.
(B) '그 달은 내가 자전거 사고를 당했던 달이다.'는 의미로 시간을 나타내는 관계부사 when을 쓴다.
(C) '그들이 왜 기한을 지키지 않았는지 아는 사람이 있니?'라는 의미로 이유를 나타내는 관계부사 why를 쓴다.

5 · 관계대명사의 계속적 용법으로 선행사(the train)가 사물이므로 사물을 선행사로 하는 주격 관계대명사인 which를 쓸 수 있다. (that은 콤마 뒤에 쓸 수 없다.)
· 관계대명사의 계속적 용법으로 선행사(my teacher)가 사람이므로 사람을 선행사로 하는 주격 관계대명사인 who를 쓸 수 있다. (that은 콤마 뒤에 쓸 수 없다.)

6 ⓐ 선행사(the person)가 사람이므로 사람을 선행사로 하는 주격 관계대명사 who를 쓴다.
ⓑ 선행사(a new technique)가 사물이므로 사물을 선행사로 하는 목적격 관계대명사 that을 쓴다.

7 두 번째 문장은 첫 번째 문장의 Gutenberg's technique에 대해 보충 설명하고 있고, 선행사(Gutenberg's technique)가 사물을 나타내므로 사물을 선행사로 하는 주격 관계대명사 which를 쓴다.

8 · 선행사(my friend)가 소유하는 대상이 되는 명사(hair)가 있으므로 소유격 관계대명사 whose를 쓴다.
· 선행사(the passenger)가 소유하는 대상이 되는 명사(bag)가 있으므로 소유격 관계대명사 whose를 쓴다.

9 ② 소유격(Her microwave)이 쓰였으므로 소유격 관계대명사 whose를 쓴다.

10 (1) 선행사(a movie)가 사물이므로 사물을 선행사로 하는 주격 관계대명사 which를 쓴다.
(2) 선행사(a movie)가 사물이므로 사물을 선행사로 하는 주격 관계대명사 which를 쓴다.
(3) 선행사(a movie)가 소유하는 대상이 되는 명사(plot)가 있으므로 소유격 관계대명사 whose를 쓴다.

11 (A) 선행사(the box)가 사물이므로 사물을 선행사로 하는 목적격 관계대명사 which나 that을 쓴다.
(B) 선행사(the sports shoes)가 사물이므로 사물을 선행사로 하는 목적격 관계대명사 which나 that을 쓴다.
(C) 선행사(people)가 사람이므로 사람을 선행사로 하는 주격 관계대명사 who나 that을 쓴다.

12 ⓐ 선행사(a factory)가 사물이므로 사물을 선행사로 하는 목적격 관계대명사 which를 쓴다.
ⓑ 선행사(my dentist)가 사람이므로 목적격 관계대명사 who[whom]을 쓴다.

13 밑줄 친 부분과 ③: 관계대명사 that
①: 지시형용사　④: 지시대명사　②⑤: 명사절 접속사

14 ⓐⓓⓔ: Whenever
ⓑ: Whoever　ⓒ: However

15 관계대명사 what은 선행사를 포함하고 있으며, '~한 것'을 의미

한다.

16 · '나는 네가 무슨 말을 하는지 모르겠다.'는 의미이므로 관계대명사 what을 쓴다.
· 'Sarah는 그녀의 아빠에게 그녀가 돕기 위해 할 수 있는 것을 물었다.'는 의미이므로 관계대명사 what을 쓴다.

17 ⓒ 'John은 그 직원이 말한 것을 듣지 않았다'라는 의미이므로 관계대명사 what을 쓴다.

18 ⓑ 계속적 용법에서 관계대명사에 that은 쓸 수 없다.

19 ⓐ 선행사(the most dangerous animals)가 사물이고 선행사에 최상급이 포함되므로 관계대명사 that을 쓴다.
ⓑ '너를 놀라게 할 수 있는 것은 사람에게 가장 위험한 동물은 모기이고, 그것들은 많은 질병을 퍼뜨린다는 것이다.'라는 의미이므로 관계대명사 what을 쓴다.

20 (A) '내가 너에게 읽기를 추천하는 바로 그 책'이라는 의미이므로 book 뒤에 관계대명사가 필요하다. 선행사(the very book)가 동사 read의 목적어이므로 목적격 관계대명사 that을 쓴다. (목적격 관계대명사는 생략할 수 있다.)
(B) 'Antoni Gaudi에 의해 디자인된 대성당'이라는 의미이므로 the cathedral 뒤에 관계대명사가 필요하다. 선행사(the cathedral)가 관계절의 주어 역할을 하며 Antoni Gaudi에 의해 디자인되는 것이므로 주격 관계대명사와 함께 수동태의 동사 「be + p.p.」의 형태를 만드는 which was를 쓴다. (「주격 관계대명사 + be동사」는 생략할 수 있다.)

21 ⓐ 주격 관계대명사는 생략할 수 없다.

22 두 번째 문장은 첫 번째 문장의 the vocabulary words에 대해 보충 설명하고 있고, 선행사(the vocabulary words)가 사물을 나타내므로 사물을 선행사로 하는 주격 관계대명사 which[that]를 쓴다. 'He studied the vocabulary words which[that] were included on the test.'의 문장에서 「주격 관계대명사 + be 동사」는 생략할 수 있다.

23 (A) 관계대명사가 전치사의 목적어일 때, 전치사를 관계대명사 바로 앞에 쓸 수 있다. 선행사(a person)가 사람이므로 사람을 선행사로 하는 목적격 관계대명사 whom을 쓴다. 전치사 뒤에는 관계대명사 who나 that을 쓸 수 없다.
(B) 관계대명사가 전치사의 목적어일 때, 전치사를 관계대명사 바로 앞에 쓸 수 있다. 선행사(a city)가 사물이므로 사물을 선행사로 하는 목적격 관계대명사 which를 쓴다. 전치사 뒤에는 관계대명사 that을 쓸 수 없다.

24 빈칸은 to whom the package was이므로 ⓑ에는 whom이 들어간다.

25 ① 전치사 뒤에는 관계대명사 that을 쓸 수 없다.
⑤ 관계부사 where는 「전치사 + 관계대명사」이므로 on을 중복으로 쓸 수 없다.

CHAPTER 14
가정법

POINT 1 가정법 과거와 가정법 과거완료

1 wouldn't feel	**2** will pick
3 wouldn't have been	**4** could enter
5 were	**6** would talk
7 receives	**8** could join
9 had read	**10** were
11 had been	**12** hadn't made

1 I were not sick / I could go swimming with my friends
2 she had found out the truth / she would have been shocked
3 my phone had not broken / I could have called you
4 you had not told lies before / they would have trusted you

POINT 2 혼합 가정법

1 he hadn't missed / would be
2 Laura had hurried / could catch
3 she had corrected / wouldn't need
4 hadn't skipped / wouldn't be

POINT 3 가정법을 직설법으로 바꾸는 법

1 I didn't know to how to snowboard, I couldn't join the snowboarding club
2 the movie hadn't been boring, everyone in the theater wouldn't have fallen asleep
3 Ann doesn't play the violin well, she can't participate in the contest
4 you had asked me earlier, I could come shopping with you now
5 the supermarket is still open, I can go grocery shopping
6 Somin wore her watch, she could know the time
7 the novel weren't sold out, I could buy it from the bookstore

워크북 정답 및 해설 **Chapter 14** 가정법   **91**

POINT 4 if를 생략한 가정법

연습문제

1 Were I you
2 Were he a wise team leader
3 Were you good at cooking
4 Had Ian eaten breakfast
5 If Hyeju had been here
6 If I were as smart as Einstein
7 If the players had practiced harder
8 If Mr. Kim had been qualified
9 Were you interested in Egyptian art
10 If you had brushed your teeth every day
11 Had Jonathan not moved to Australia
12 If Sandra had told me she was upset

POINT 5 Without 가정법

연습문제 A

1 But for / it had not been for / it not been for
2 Without/ it were not for / it not for
3 Without / it not been for / it had not been for

연습문제 B

1 If it weren't for glasses
2 If it weren't for electricity
3 Had it not been for this workbook
4 But for the flowers
5 Without the spices
6 Had it not been for regular customers

POINT 6 I wish 가정법

연습문제 A

1 I wish my dad had fixed my computer.
2 I wish I knew how to answer that question.
3 I wish the patient had taken the pill on time.
4 I wish you had gone to the gym more often.
5 I wish we were allowed to drive a car.
6 I wish I had enough money to buy that dress.

연습문제 B

1 you didn't receive my e-mail
2 I could visit my uncle in New York
3 we don't have another day to finish this project
4 she didn't invite you to her birthday party
5 I had prepared for the presentation better
6 my favorite singer were more popular

POINT 7 as if[though] 가정법

연습문제 A

1 treated me as if I were a complete stranger

2 spoke as though he were a college student
3 talks as if he had known my mom for a long time
4 acted as though she had painted that portrait
5 feels as if it were spring already
6 looks as if it were recently built

연습문제 B

1 talked / had found something
2 acted / hadn't heard the news
3 looks / were five years old
4 speaks / were popular
5 talks / had been to Atlanta
6 acted / were in a good mood

중간·기말고사 실전 문제

1 ⑤ **2** we had bought tickets, we could attend the concert **3** I didn't apologize to Amy sooner **4** the public library doesn't have youth programs, it isn't attractive to them **5** the public library had interesting activities for them, it would attract more young people **6** ⑤
7 ② **8** ⑤ **9** ⑤ **10** ① **11** ④
12 ② **13** ① **14** I wish we had more space for the guests. **15** I wish I had taken swimming lessons. **16** ③ **17** (A) I wish I spoke French. (B) If I understood French, I would have more opportunities in the future. (C) English seems as if it were the most important language. **18** ①
19 ③ **20** ② **21** as if it were raining
22 as if it had been injured **23** (A) It would be nice / the weather were better (B) the rain stopped / we could play **24** everyone gave money to the charity / it could help more people **25** ②

1 첫 번째 빈칸: 가정법 과거의 주절에는 「주어 + 조동사의 과거형 + 동사원형」을 쓰므로 would를 쓴다.
두 번째 빈칸: 가정법 과거의 if절에는 「If + 주어 + 동사의 과거형」을 쓰므로 got을 쓴다.

2 혼합 가정법은 과거의 사실과 반대되는 일이 현재까지 영향을 미치는 상황을 가정할 때 쓰며 「If + 주어 + had p.p., 주어 + 조동사의 과거형 + 동사원형」을 쓴다.

3 「I wish + 주어 + had p.p.」는 「I'm sorry (that) + 주어 + 동사의 과거형」 형태의 직설법으로 바꿔 쓸 수 있다.

4 밑줄 친 (A)는 가정법 과거이므로 가정법 과거를 직설법으로 바꾸려면 if절과 주절의 과거 시제를 현재 시제로 바꾸고, 긍정·부정을 뒤바꾼다.

5 밑줄 친 (B)는 가정법 과거를 직설법 문장으로 바꿔 쓴 형태이므로 다시 가정법 과거로 바꾸려면 「If + 주어 + 동사의 과거형, 주

어 + 조동사의 과거형 + 동사원형」을 쓴다.

6 ① am → were
② will → would
③ asks → asked
④ won't → wouldn't

7 첫 번째 빈칸: 과거의 사실과 반대되는 일을 가정하는 가정법 과거완료를 쓴다. 가정법 과거완료에서 if절에는 「If + 주어 + had p.p.」를 쓴다. 가정법에서 if절의 동사가 조동사 had를 포함한 경우 if를 생략할 수 있다. 이때 if절의 주어와 had의 위치를 바꿔 「Had + 주어」의 형태로 쓴다.
두 번째 빈칸: 가정법 과거완료에서 주절에는 「주어 + 조동사의 과거형 + have p.p.」를 쓴다.

8 · 「I wish + 주어 + 동사의 과거형」은 '~하면 좋을 텐데'의 의미로 현재 실현 가능성이 매우 낮거나 없는 일을 소망할 때 쓴다.
· 「주어 + 동사의 현재형 + as if[though] + 주어 + 동사의 과거형」은 '마치 ~한 것처럼 …한다'의 의미이다.

9 첫 번째 빈칸: '만약 우리가 라이터를 가져왔다면, 캠프파이어를 시작할 수 있을 텐데.'의 의미이므로 혼합 가정법을 쓴다. 혼합 가정법의 if절에는 「If + 주어 + had p.p.」를 쓴다.
두 번째 빈칸: 주절이 「조동사의 과거형 + have + p.p.」이므로 가정법 과거완료 형태이며, 가정법에서 if절의 동사가 조동사 had를 포함한 경우 if를 생략할 수 있다. 이때 if절의 주어와 had의 위치를 바꿔 「Had + 주어」의 형태로 쓴다.

10 ① I'm sorry that you don't feel better.로 써야 두 문장의 의미가 같다.

11 ① can → could
② is → were
③ can → could
⑤ will not cancel → would not cancel

12 ② 현재의 사실과 반대되는 일을 가정하고 있으므로 가정법 과거 「If + 주어 + 동사의 과거형, 주어 + 조동사의 과거형 + 동사원형」을 쓴다.

13 현재의 사실과 반대되는 일을 가정하고 있으므로 가정법 과거 「If + 주어 + 동사의 과거형, 주어 + 조동사의 과거형 + 동사원형」을 쓴다.

14 「I'm sorry (that) + 주어 + 동사의 현재형」은 「I wish + 주어 + 동사의 과거형」으로 바꿔 쓸 수 있다.

15 「I'm sorry (that) + 주어 + 동사의 과거형」은 「I wish + 주어 + had p.p.」로 바꿔 쓸 수 있다.

16 「Without + 명사, 가정법 과거완료」는 '~가 없었다면 …했을 텐데'의 의미이다.

17 (A) 「I wish + 주어 + 동사의 과거형」은 '~하면 좋을 텐데'의 의미이다.
(B) 가정법 과거는 「If + 주어 + 동사의 과거형, 주어 + 조동사의 과거형 + 동사원형」을 쓴다.
(C) 「주어 + 동사의 현재형 + as if[though] + 주어 + 동사의 과거형」은 '마치 ~한 것처럼 …한다'의 의미이다.

18 ① 가정법 과거는 「If + 주어 + 동사의 과거형, 주어 + 조동사의 과거형 + 동사원형」을 쓰고, 주어진 문장은 현재의 사실과 반대되는 일을 가정하고 있으므로 지금 여분의 펜을 가지고 있지 않다는 것을 나타낸다.

19 ③ 현재의 사실과 반대되는 일을 가정하는 가정법 과거 「If + 주어 + 동사의 과거형, 주어 + 조동사의 과거형 + 동사원형」으로 바꿔 쓸 수 있다.

20 ② 과거의 사실과 반대되는 일을 가정하는 가정법 과거완료 「If + 주어 + had + p.p., 주어 + 조동사의 과거형 + have + p.p.」로 바꿔 쓸 수 있다.

21 주절의 시제(과거시제)와 같은 시점의 사실과 반대되는 일을 가정하는 「as if + 주어 + 동사의 과거형」을 쓴다.

22 주절의 시제(현재시제)보다 이전 시점의 사실과 반대되는 일을 가정하는 「as if + 주어 + had + p.p.」를 쓴다.

23 (A) 가정법 과거는 「If + 주어 + 동사의 과거형, 주어 + 조동사의 과거형 + 동사원형」의 형태로 쓴다.
(B) 가정법 과거는 「If + 주어 + 동사의 과거형, 주어 + 조동사의 과거형 + 동사원형」의 형태로 쓴다.

24 현재의 사실과 반대되는 일을 가정하고 있으므로 가정법 과거 「If + 주어 + 동사의 과거형, 주어 + 조동사의 과거형 + 동사원형」을 쓴다.

25 ⓑ didn't run → hadn't run

CHAPTER 15
일치와 화법

p.192

POINT 1-1 수 일치 I

1	is	2	like
3	show	4	is
5	O	6	is
7	O	8	O

POINT 1-2 수 일치 II

1	have	2	is
3	need	4	has
5	are	6	need
7	likes	8	do
9	enjoy	10	focuses
11	are		

POINT 2 시제 일치

A

1	O	2	would
3	O	4	had
5	O	6	had
7	O	8	O
9	couldn't		

B

1 My grandmother said that good health is more important than wealth.
2 The teacher taught the students that the Korean War began on June 25, 1950.
3 Josh said that he goes hiking with his parents every weekend.
4 Galileo believed that Earth goes around the Sun.
5 Owen told me that he usually gets up at 11 A.M. on Saturdays.
6 This book stated that the Parthenon was completed in 432 BC.
7 Elle said that empty vessels make the most noise.
8 We just learned that snakes sleep in winter.

POINT 3-1 화법 전환: 평서문

1 said, "I will visit my grandparents in Vancouver tomorrow."
2 said to his friend, "I studied hard last year."
3 said (that) he was very busy at that moment.
4 told me (that) she had received the package the previous Friday.
5 said (that) she wanted to go to the playground.

POINT 3-2 화법 전환: 의문사가 있는 의문문

1 said to me, "How did you solve these questions?"
2 asked where the nearest bank was.
3 asked why I hadn't come to class the previous day[the day before].
4 asked me when I was going to go to bed.
5 said, "Why are you in such a hurry?"
6 asked me what TV program I had watched the previous weekend.
7 said to the witness, "What did you see on the street?"

POINT 3-3 화법 전환: 의문사가 없는 의문문

1 said to me, "Do you want to play badminton with me?"
2 asked me if[whether] I liked watching horror movies.
3 asked me if[whether] I had met Tom before.
4 said to me, "Were there many people at the concert last night?"
5 asked if[whether] I was happy with the food there.

POINT 3-4 화법 전환: 명령문

1 ordered / not to use our cell phones in class
2 advised / to try to get enough sleep every night
3 instructed / to report the progress of the project
4 suggested / to say sorry to my friend first
5 told / to come back home before 9 o'clock
6 asked / to watch her bag while she was gone

---

1 ③　　**2** ②, ⑤　**3** ③　　**4** My younger sister asked who had taken the television's remote control.
5 ⑤　　**6** said / won't / tomorrow
7 ②　　**8** ③　　**9** ⑤　　**10** ④　　**11** The bus driver told me not to put my feet on the seat.
12 ③　　**13** ④　　**14** are → is　　**15** ③
16 ⑤　　**17** ③　　**18** said to / was injured / two days ago **19** ②　　**20** ⓐ are ⓑ is　　**21** where he had gone the previous weekend / (that) he had visited his cousin's house in the countryside
22 if[whether] there was anything he could do for her / to check her essay for errors　**23** ④　　**24** had bought　**25** could win

---

1 ⓑ ordered me wash → ordered me to wash
ⓓ we did have → we had
ⓔ what you wanted → what I wanted

2 '그 의사는 대기실에 환자가 더 있는지 물었다.'는 의미이다. 의문사가 없는 의문문은 if나 whether로 두 절을 연결한다.

3 ③ 금액은 단수동사를 쓴다. 우리말의 시제에 맞추어 현재시제를 쓴다.

4 전달동사가 과거시제이므로 said를 asked로 바꾸고, 의문사가 의문문의 주어이므로 「의문사 + 동사」의 어순을 그대로 쓴다. 전달동사가 과거시제이므로 종속절의 과거시제 took을 과거완료시제 had taken으로 바꾼다.

5 ⑤ don't leave → not to leave

6 첫 번째 빈칸: 간접 화법의 주절이 과거시제이므로 직접 화법의 주절도 과거시제 said를 쓴다.
두 번째 빈칸: 간접 화법의 종속절에 과거형 wouldn't가 쓰였으므로 직접 화법에는 현재형 won't를 쓴다.
세 번째 빈칸: 간접 화법의 the next day는 직접 화법에서 tomorrow로 쓴다.

7 (A) 주어가 국가명이면 항상 단수동사를 쓴다.
(B) 주어가 구면 항상 단수동사를 쓴다.
(C) 「a number of + 복수 명사」는 항상 복수동사를 쓴다.

8 ① have → has
② are → is
④ help → helps
⑤ are → is

9 평서문을 간접 화법으로 바꿀 때, 주절이 과거시제인 경우 종속절에는 현재시제 need를 과거시제 needed로 바꿔서 쓴다. 직접 화법의 this는 간접 화법에서 that으로 바꿔 쓴다.

10 ⓐ grows → grow
ⓔ are → is

11 부정 명령문의 간접 화법은 명령문의 Don't를 「not + to부정사」의 형태로 바꾸므로 not to put을 쓴다.

12 ③ 「the number of + 복수명사」에는 항상 단수동사를 쓴다.

13 전달동사 said to는 간접 화법으로 바꿀 때 시제를 일치시켜 told로 바꾼다.

14 every가 포함된 주어에는 항상 단수동사를 쓴다.

15 주절이 과거시제이고 종속절은 그 이전부터 지속된 일을 말하므로, 주절에는 과거시제를 쓰고 종속절에는 과거완료진행시제를 쓴다.

16 첫 번째 빈칸: 주절이 과거시제이므로 종속절에는 과거시제인 had를 쓴다.
두 번째 빈칸: 주절이 과거시제이므로 종속절에는 「조동사의 과거형 + 동사원형」인 would ask를 쓴다.

17 ③ 주절이 과거시제이므로 종속절에는 현재시제를 쓸 수 없다.

18 첫 번째 빈칸: 간접 화법을 직접 화법으로 바꿀 때, 전달동사 told를 said to로 바꾼다.
두 번째 빈칸: 간접 화법의 종속절의 동사가 과거완료시제 had been injured이므로 직접 화법에는 과거시제 was injured를 쓴다.
세 번째 빈칸: 간접 화법의 two days before는 직접 화법에서 two days ago로 바꿔 쓴다.

19 ② them they were enjoying → them if[whether] they were enjoying

20 ⓐ are: Both A and B는 항상 복수동사를 쓴다.
ⓑ is: 주어가 구면 항상 단수동사를 쓴다.

21 첫 번째 빈칸: 의문사가 있는 의문문의 간접 화법은 의문사(where)로 주절과 종속절을 연결하고, 종속절을 「의문사 + 주어 + 동사」의 어순으로 쓴다. 전달동사가 과거시제이므로 종속절의 과거시제 did ~ go를 과거완료 시제 had gone으로 바꾼다. 인칭대명사를 전달하는 사람의 입장에 맞게 바꿔야 하므로 you를 he로 바꾸고, 부사(구)를 전달하는 사람의 입장에 맞게 바꿔야 하므로 last weekend를 the previous weekend로 바꾼다.
두 번째 빈칸: 전달동사가 과거시제이므로 종속절의 과거시제 visited를 과거완료시제 had visited로 바꾸고, 인칭대명사를 전달하는 사람의 입장에 맞게 바꿔야 하므로 my를 his로 바꾼다.

22 첫 번째 빈칸: 의문사가 없는 의문문의 간접 화법은 if나 whether로 주절과 종속절을 연결하고, 전달동사가 과거시제이므로 종속절의 현재시제 Is ~ can do를 과거시제 was ~ could do로 바꾼다. 인칭대명사를 전달하는 사람의 입장에 맞게 바꿔야 하므로 I를 he로 바꾸고 you를 her로 바꾼다.
두 번째 빈칸: 명령문의 간접 화법은 동사원형을 to부정사로 바꾸고, 인칭대명사를 전달하는 사람의 입장에 맞게 바꿔야 하므로 my를 her로 바꾼다.

23 (A) 일반적 사실을 말하는 것이므로 주절의 시제와 상관없이 종속절에는 항상 현재시제를 쓴다.
(B) 현재의 습관을 말하는 것이므로 주절의 시제와 상관없이 종속절에는 항상 현재시제를 쓴다.

(C) 역사적 사실을 말하는 것이므로 종속절에는 항상 과거시제를 쓴다.

24 주절을 과거시제로 바꾸고 종속절은 현재완료시제이므로 과거완료시제 had bought로 바꾼다.

25 주절을 과거시제로 바꾸고 종속절은 현재시제이므로 과거시제 could win으로 바꾼다.

POINT 1-1 강조

1 much colder	**2** the very movie
3 did win	**4** does love
5 the very dish	**6** much dirtier
7 does look	**8** much nicer
9 did receive	**10** the very person
11 much harder	**12** the very house

POINT 1-2 강조: It is ~ that 강조 구문

1 It was Tina that played basketball on the court. → who

2 It was basketball that Tina played on the court. → which

3 It was on the court that Tina played basketball. → where

4 It is Jim that goes traveling to Europe next month. → who

5 It is next month that Jim goes traveling to Europe. → when

6 It was the diamond ring that the thief stole from the jewelry shop. → which

7 It was from the jewelry shop that the thief stole the diamond ring. → where

8 It was a play that I watched at the theater this afternoon. → which

9 It was at the theater that I watched a play this afternoon. → where

10 It was this afternoon that I watched a play at the theater. → when

11 It was he that saw Nancy on the street an hour ago. → who

12 It was Nancy that he saw on the street an hour ago. → who[whom]

13 It was on the street that he saw Nancy an hour ago. → where

14 It was we that ate dumplings in Chinatown. → who

15 It was dumplings that we ate in Chinatown. → which

16 It was in Chinatown that we ate dumplings. → where

POINT 2 부정

연습
문제

1 Not all of the questions
2 None of them
3 not always available
4 neither of them
5 never interested
6 Not all of the amusement parks
7 Neither of the cars
8 not always open
9 never stops
10 None of the movies
11 Not all of the vegetables
12 not always on

POINT 3 도치

연습
문제

1 could Julie
2 did he have any time to take a nap
3 are the books you wanted to borrow
4 does Mr. Smith buy flowers for his wife
5 do I
6 has the magician failed to please an audience
7 will you make use of the new features of the device
8 is the refrigerator cheap
9 slid the children
10 did my father complain about doing yard work
11 did Kara
12 ran the deer

POINT 4 생략

연습
문제

1 I listened to music with headphones while I was on the subway.
2 Though most people remained seated during the performance, some people didn't remain seated during the performance.
3 Let's go to the dessert place that[which] you told me about yesterday.
4 She drank a cup of coffee while she was reading the newspaper.
5 Jamie was looking at her younger sister who was sleeping on the couch.

POINT 5 동격

연습
문제

1 The idea of traveling around the world sounds wonderful.
2 Claude Monet, one of the most popular painters, is called the Father of Impressionism.
3 The news that David and Victoria got married surprised many fans.
4 Minji, my best friend since childhood, is the one I tell everything to.
5 His dream of opening his own café was realized.

POINT 6 병치

연습
문제

1 read   2 writing
3 to an Italian restaurant
4 jumped
5 for the general public
6 join   7 played
8 enjoyable   9 surprised
10 cloudy   11 to turn
12 gentle   13 order
14 to pick   15 warm
16 interesting   17 uncomfortable

중간·기말고사 실전 문제

1 ②   2 do gets → does get   3 ⑤
4 ③   5 ①   6 ③   7 ⑤   8 Your application will not be accepted unless accompanied by the required documents.   9 It was in 1939 that World War II broke out.   10 It is a French cooking class that[which]   11 It is in April that[when]   12 I did ask why Alice changed her mind about the gift.   13 California is much[even / still / far / a lot] larger than Florida.
14 This is the very ring that my grandfather gave to my grandmother.   15 ①   16 ②   17 ⑤
18 (1) ⓐ → does the zoo keep (2) ⓓ → jumped the kangaroo   19 ④   20 Into the darkness disappeared the thieves.   21 Seldom have I tasted such delicious food.   22 ⑤   23 ⑤
24 ③   25 ①

1   ② did needed → do[did] need

2   동사를 강조할 때는 동사원형 앞에 do를 주어의 인칭과 수, 시제

와 맞춰 쓴다.

3 ⓒⓔⓕ: 동사를 강조
ⓐ: 부가의문문 ⓑⓓ: 동사

4 ③ nobody는 '아무도 ~가 아니다'라는 의미로, 문장 전체를 부정할 때 쓴다.

5 비교급을 강조할 때는 비교급 앞에 much, even, still, far, a lot을 쓴다.

6 ③ 가주어 It
①②④⑤ 「It is ~ that …」 강조구문의 It

7 ⑤ where → when[that]

8 부사절의 주어가 주절의 주어와 같을 때, 부사절의 「주어 + be동사」는 생략할 수 있다.

9 「It is ~ that …」 강조 구문은 '…한 것은 바로 ~이다'의 의미로, 동사를 제외한 모든 문장 요소를 It was와 that 사이에 써서 강조할 수 있다. 이때 강조되는 말을 제외한 나머지 부분은 that 뒤에 쓰며, 기존 문장의 시제에 일치시킨다.

10 대답의 목적어인 a French cooking class를 강조하는 문장을 쓴다. 강조하는 대상이 사물이므로 that 대신 which를 쓸 수 있다.

11 대답의 부사구인 in April을 강조하는 문장을 쓴다. 강조하는 대상이 시간이므로 that 대신 when을 쓸 수 있다.

12 동사 asked를 강조할 때는 동사원형 ask 앞에 did를 쓴다.

13 비교급을 강조할 때는 비교급 앞에 much, even, still, far, a lot을 쓴다.

14 명사 ring을 강조할 때는 명사 앞에 the very를 쓴다.

15 ② speak → speaks
③ safe → safely
④ calling → call
⑤ sing → singing

16 ② There is he → There he is

17 ⑤ 부정의 의미를 가진 부사 seldom이 강조되어 문장의 맨 앞으로 올 때, 주어와 동사를 도치시켜 「부사(구) + 조동사 + 주어 + 동사 ~」를 쓴다.

18 (1) ⓐ keeps는 단수동사이므로 도치시킬 때는 주어 앞에 does를 쓰고 주어 뒤에 동사원형인 keep을 쓴다.
(2) ⓓ 방향을 나타내는 부사구 over the fence가 강조되어 문장의 맨 앞으로 올 때, 주어와 동사를 도치시켜 「부사(구) + 동사 + 주어 ~」를 쓴다.

19 ④ 주절과 종속절을 연결하는 콤마(,)이다.
①②③⑤ 동격을 나타내는 콤마(,)이다.

20 방향을 나타내는 부사구 into the darkness가 강조되어 문장의 맨 앞으로 올 때, 주어와 동사를 도치시켜 「부사(구) + 동사 + 주어 ~」를 쓴다.

21 부정의 의미를 가진 부사 seldom이 강조되어 문장의 맨 앞으로

올 때, 주어와 동사를 도치시켜 「부사(구) + 조동사 + 주어 + 동사 ~」를 쓴다.

22 ① going → go
② to exercise → exercising
③ intense → intensely
④ read → reading

23 '~도 아니다'는 의미로 neither를 사용할 때 주어와 동사를 도치시켜 「neither + 동사 + 주어 ~」를 쓴다.

24 ⓑ 목적격 관계대명사 that은 생략할 수 있다.
ⓒ 목적격 관계대명사 who는 생략할 수 있다.
ⓔ 「주격 관계대명사 + be동사」는 생략할 수 있다.

25 '~도 그렇다'는 의미로 so를 사용할 때 주어와 동사를 도치시켜 「so + 동사 + 주어 ~」를 쓴다.

MEMO

MEMO

최신 개정 교과서 완벽 반영

기출로적중
해커스
중학영문법

3학년

해설집

기출로 적중

해커스
중학영문법

3학년

핵심만 담았다!

문법 암기리스트

단어 암기장

기출로적중

해커스
중학영문법
3학년

핵심만 담았다!

문법 암기리스트

＋

단어 암기장

해커스북 중·고등
www.HackersBook.com

핵심만 담았다!

문법 암기리스트

CHAPTER 1 문장의 형식

4형식: 3형식으로 바꿀 때 전치사 to/for/of를 쓰는 동사

to를 쓰는 동사	give, send, bring, pass, show, teach, tell, write, read, lend, sell, pay, offer 등	I **showed** the security guard my ID card. → I **showed** my ID card **to** the security guard. 나는 보안요원에게 나의 신분증을 보여줬다.
for를 쓰는 동사	buy, cook, find, make, get, build 등	I **made** Janet a cup of coffee. → I **made** a cup of coffee **for** Janet. 나는 Janet에게 커피 한 잔을 만들어줬다.
of를 쓰는 동사	ask 등	The reporter **asked** her many questions. → The reporter **asked** many questions **of** her. 그 기자는 그녀에게 많은 질문을 했다.

POINT 4-1 ~ 4-4 **5형식**

1. 명사/형용사를 목적격 보어로 쓰는 동사

call ~를 -이라고 부르다   make ~를 -로/하게 만들다   keep ~을 -한 상태로 유지하다
think ~를 -이라고 생각하다   believe ~를 -라고 믿다   consider ~을 -이라고 여기다
find ~가 -이라는 것을 알게 되다

2. to부정사를 목적격 보어로 쓰는 동사

want ~가 -하기를 원하다   ask ~에게 -하라고 요청하다
encourage ~가 -하는 것을 격려하다   tell ~에게 -하라고 말하다
expect ~가 -하는 것을 기대하다   permit ~가 -하는 것을 허락하다
advise ~에게 -하라고 조언하다   allow ~가 -하는 것을 허락하다
force ~가 -하도록 강요하다   get ~가 -하게 시키다 (준사역동사)

3. 동사원형을 목적격 보어로 쓰는 동사

사역동사 make   have   let

4. 동사원형/to부정사를 목적격 보어로 쓰는 동사

준사역동사 help

5. 동사원형/V-ing형을 목적격 보어로 쓰는 동사

지각동사 see   watch   hear   listen to   smell   feel

CHAPTER 3 조동사

POINT 5 조동사 + have + p.p.

약한 추측	may[might] + have p.p.	~했을 수도 있다
강한 추측	must + have p.p.	~했음이 틀림없다
	can't + have p.p.	~했을 리가 없다
후회·유감	should + have p.p.	~했어야 했다 (하지만 하지 않았다)
	could + have p.p.	~했을 수도 있었다 (하지만 하지 않았다)

POINT 6 조동사 관용 표현

would like + 명사 ~을 원하다	I **would like a room** with a balcony. 나는 발코니가 있는 방을 원한다. (Tip) 부정형: wouldn't like
would like to + 동사원형 ~하고 싶다	I **would like to play** tennis. 나는 테니스를 치고 싶다. (Tip) 부정형: wouldn't like to
would rather + 동사원형 (차라리) ~하겠다	I **would rather visit** Spain than France. 나는 프랑스보다 차라리 스페인을 방문하겠다. (Tip) 부정형: would rather not
may well + 동사원형 (~하는 것도) 당연하다	They **may well think** so. 그들이 그렇게 생각하는 것도 당연하다. (Tip) 부정형: may well not
may as well + 동사원형 ~하는 편이 좋다	You **may as well try** the new program. 너는 새로운 프로그램을 시도해보는 편이 좋다. (Tip) 부정형: may as well not
had better + 동사원형 ~하는 것이 낫다	You **had better save** the money. 너는 돈을 저축하는 것이 낫다 . (Tip) 부정형: had better not

CHAPTER 4 수동태

POINT 9 수동태 관용 표현

be known as	~으로서 알려져 있다	be made of	~으로 만들어지다 (재료 성질이 변하지 않음)
be known to	~에게 알려져 있다	be made from	~으로 만들어지다 (재료 성질이 변함)
be known for	~으로 유명하다	be interested in	~에 흥미가 있다
be filled with	~으로 가득 차 있다	be remembered for	~으로 기억되다
be covered with	~으로 덮여 있다	be disappointed at	~에 실망하다
be pleased with	~에 기뻐하다	be used to + 동사원형	~을 하는 데 사용되다
be satisfied with	~에 만족하다	be supposed to + 동사원형	~을 하기로 되어 있다

CHAPTER 5 부정사

POINT 2-2 to부정사를 목적어로 쓰는 동사

want	promise	fail	wish	plan	choose
decide	agree	learn	need	hope	expect
refuse	aim	manage			

CHAPTER 6 동명사

POINT 4 동명사를 목적어로 쓰는 동사

enjoy	avoid	finish	keep	mind	admit	practice	suggest
quit	deny	imagine	resist	dislike	postpone	consider	recommend

POINT 5   동명사와 to부정사를 모두 목적어로 쓰는 동사

1. 동명사와 to부정사를 목적어로 쓸 때의 의미가 같은 동사

start	begin	love	like	hate	continue	prefer	intend

2. 동명사와 to부정사를 목적어로 쓸 때의 의미가 다른 동사

forget	동명사	(과거에) ~한 것을 잊다	He **forgot taking** the medicine. 그는 약을 먹은 것을 잊었다.
	to부정사	(미래에) ~할 것을 잊다	He **forgot to take** the medicine. 그는 약을 먹을 것을 잊었다.
remember	동명사	(과거에) ~한 것을 기억하다	I **remembered calling** her. 나는 그녀에게 전화한 것을 기억했다.
	to부정사	(미래에) ~할 것을 기억하다	I **remembered to call** her. 나는 그녀에게 전화할 것을 기억했다.
regret	동명사	~한 것을 후회하다	I **regret informing** you of the problem. 나는 너에게 그 문제를 알린 것을 후회한다.
	to부정사	~하게 되어 유감이다	I **regret to inform** you of the problem. 나는 너에게 그 문제를 알리게 되어 유감이다.
try	동명사	(시험 삼아) ~해보다	She **tried lifting** the box. 그녀는 시험 삼아 그 박스를 들어올려 보았다.
	to부정사	~하려고 노력하다	She **tried to lift** the box. 그녀는 그 박스를 들어올리려고 노력했다.

POINT 6   동명사 관용 표현

1. 전치사의 목적어로 동명사를 쓰는 관용 표현

be afraid of + V-ing ~하는 것을 두려워하다
be good at + V-ing ~을 잘하다
be interested in + V-ing ~하는 것에 흥미가 있다
be used to + V-ing ~하는 것에 익숙하다
be tired of + V-ing ~하는 것에 싫증이 나다
be sorry for + V-ing ~하는 것에 대해 유감이다
feel like + V-ing ~하고 싶다
by + V-ing ~함으로써, ~해서

How[What] about + V-ing? ~하는 게 어때?
look forward to + V-ing ~하는 것을 기대하다
end up + V-ing 결국 ~하게 되다
thank … for + V-ing ~에 대해 …에게 감사하다
when it comes to + V-ing ~하는 것에 관한 한
dream of + V-ing ~하는 것을 꿈꾸다
on + V-ing ~하자마자

2. 동명사를 쓰는 관용 표현

be worth + V-ing ~할 가치가 있다
be busy + V-ing ~하느라 바쁘다
cannot help + V-ing ~하지 않을 수 없다
have difficulty[trouble] + V-ing ~하는 것에 어려움[문제]이 있다

go + V-ing ~하러 가다
It is no use + V-ing ~해도 소용 없다
spend + 시간/돈 + V-ing ~하는 데 시간/돈을 쓰다

CHAPTER 7 분사

POINT 3 감정을 나타내는 분사

현재분사(~한 감정을 느끼게 하는)		과거분사(~한 감정을 느끼는)	
surprising	놀라게 하는	surprised	놀란
amazing	놀라게 하는	amazed	놀란
disappointing	실망스럽게 하는	disappointed	실망스러워하는
boring	지루하게 하는	bored	지루해하는
confusing	혼란스럽게 하는	confused	혼란스러워하는
embarrassing	당황스럽게 하는	embarrassed	당황해하는
shocking	충격을 주는	shocked	충격을 받은
depressing	우울하게 하는	depressed	우울해하는
exhausting	지치게 하는	exhausted	지친
amusing	즐겁게 하는	amused	즐거운
exciting	신나게 하는	excited	신이 난
thrilling	흥분하게 하는	thrilled	흥분한
worrying	걱정하게 하는	worried	걱정하는
pleasing	기쁘게 하는	pleased	기뻐하는
satisfying	만족스럽게 하는	satisfied	만족스러워하는
frightening	겁나게 하는	frightened	겁이 난
impressing	감동하게 하는	impressed	감동한
moving	감동하게 하는	moved	감동한
relaxing	편하게 하는	relaxed	편안한
interesting	흥미롭게 하는	interested	흥미로워하는
fascinating	황홀하게 하는	fascinated	황홀해하는

POINT 7	분사구문 관용 표현		
Generally speaking	일반적으로 말하면	Judging from	~으로 판단하건대
Strictly speaking	엄밀히 말하면	Considering	~을 고려하면
Frankly speaking	솔직히 말하면	Speaking of	~에 관해서 말한다면

CHAPTER 8 명사와 대명사

POINT 1	셀 수 있는 명사의 복수형: 불규칙변화

불규칙 변화	man – men tooth – teeth ox – oxen	woman – women goose – geese mouse – mice	child – children deer – deer sheep – sheep

POINT 4	재귀대명사의 관용 표현

by oneself 혼자서, 홀로
in itself 그 자체가, 본래
talk[say] to oneself 혼잣말을 하다
help oneself (to ~) ~을 마음껏 먹다

for oneself 스스로, 혼자 힘으로
enjoy oneself 즐거운 시간을 보내다
between ourselves 우리끼리의 이야기(지만)
make oneself at home (집에서처럼) 편히 쉬다

CHAPTER 9 형용사와 부사

POINT 7	타동사 + 부사

bring up ~을 꺼내다
call off ~을 취소하다
check out ~을 확인하다
fill in ~을 작성하다
find out ~을 알아내다
give up ~을 포기하다, 그만두다
hand in ~을 제출하다

look up ~을 찾아보다
make up ~을 만들어내다, 정하다
pick up ~을 줍다, 태우러 가다
put off ~을 미루다
put on ~을 입다, 쓰다
take off ~을 벗다
throw away ~을 버리다

try on ~을 입어보다
turn down ~을 거절하다
turn in ~을 제출하다
turn off ~을 끄다
turn on ~을 켜다
wake up ~을 깨우다
write down ~을 적다

CHAPTER 11 전치사

POINT 6-1 ~ 6-3 전치사 관용 표현

1. 형용사 + 전치사

be good/bad at ~을 잘하다/못하다
be frightened at[by] ~에 놀라다, 겁먹다
be surprised at[by] ~에 놀라다
be ashamed of ~을 부끄러워하다
be capable of ~을 할 수 있다
be full of ~으로 가득 차있다
be jealous of ~을 시기하다
be proud of ~을 자랑스러워하다
be short of ~이 부족하다
be tired of ~에 싫증이 나다
be based on ~에 기초하다, 근거하다
be crazy about ~에 빠져 있다

be known for ~으로 알려져 있다
be ready for ~할/~에 준비가 되다
be responsible for ~에 책임이 있다
be accustomed to ~에 익숙하다
be born to ~이 될/~을 할 운명을 타고 나다
be likely to ~을 하기 쉽다, ~을 할 것 같다
be married to ~와 결혼하다
be similar to ~와 비슷하다
be crowded with ~으로 붐비다
be filled with ~으로 가득하다
be satisfied with ~에 만족하다
be absent from ~에 결석하다

2. 동사 + 전치사

apologize for ~에 대해 사과하다
apply for ~에 지원하다
ask for ~을 요구하다
stand for ~을 나타내다
concentrate on ~에 집중하다
decide on ~으로 정하다
depend on ~을 의존하다/믿다
focus on ~에 초점을 맞추다
spend A on B A를 B에 쓰다
consist of ~으로 이루어지다
die of ~으로 죽다
laugh at ~을 비웃다

belong to ~에 속하다
prefer A to B B보다 A를 더 선호하다
believe in ~을 믿다
result in (결과적으로) ~을 낳다, 야기하다
succeed in ~에 성공하다
divide A into B A를 B로 나누다
run into ~와 우연히 만나다
turn A into B A를 B로 바꾸다
come up with ~을 제안하다, 생각해내다
talk with/to ~와 대화를 나누다
look after ~를 돌보다
live by (신조/원칙)에 따라 살다

3. 동사 + 명사 + 전치사

get rid of ~을 제거하다
make a fool of ~를 바보 취급하다
make use of ~을 이용하다
take care of ~를 돌보다

take pity on ~를 불쌍히 여기다
take part in ~에 참가[참여]하다
pay attention to ~에 관심을 갖다, ~에 주목하다
have fun with ~와 즐거운 시간을 보내다

CHAPTER 13 관계사

POINT 1 관계대명사의 역할과 종류

선행사 \ 격	주격	목적격	소유격
사람	who	who(m)	whose
사물, 동물	which	which	whose
모두 적용	that	that	–

POINT 6 관계부사의 종류

	선행사	관계부사
장소	the place, the city, the house 등	where
시간	the time, the year, the day 등	when
이유	the reason	why
방법	the way	how

해커스북 중·고등
www.HackersBook.com

핵심만 담았다!
단어 암기장

- 단어 리스트
- 단어 테스트

• 잘 외워지지 않는 단어는 박스에 체크하여 복습하세요.

🎧 3학년_단어암기장_CH1.mp3

☐	1	arrive	동 도착하다	☐	31 roof	명 지붕
☐	2	popular	형 인기 있는	☐	32 blow	동 불다
☐	3	appear	동 나타나다, ~하게 보이다	☐	33 hallway	명 복도
☐	4	nervous	형 긴장한	☐	34 emergency	명 위급상황
☐	5	recently	부 최근에	☐	35 cheek	명 뺨, 볼
☐	6	communication	명 의사소통	☐	36 explain	동 설명하다
☐	7	relationship	명 관계	☐	37 contact	동 연락하다
☐	8	comfortable	형 편안한	☐	38 whisper	동 속삭이다
☐	9	role	명 역할	☐	39 specialist	명 전문가
☐	10	awful	형 지독한	☐	40 permit	동 허락하다
☐	11	ripe	형 익은	☐	41 engineer	명 기술자
☐	12	discuss	동 ~에 대해 논의하다	☐	42 temperature	명 기온
☐	13	resemble	동 ~와 닮다	☐	43 trick	명 묘기
☐	14	attend	동 ~에 참석하다	☐	44 fair	명 박람회
☐	15	security	명 보안	☐	45 mention	동 언급하다
☐	16	reporter	명 기자	☐	46 ability	명 능력
☐	17	simple	형 간단한	☐	47 prepare	동 준비하다
☐	18	carpenter	명 목수	☐	48 principal	명 교장
☐	19	daily	형 매일의	☐	49 rise	동 오르다
☐	20	consider	동 여기다	☐	50 memorize	동 외우다
☐	21	allow	동 허락하다	☐	51 unusual	형 특이한
☐	22	disagree	동 반대하다	☐	52 career	명 직업
☐	23	silent	형 조용한	☐	53 audience	명 관객
☐	24	speech	명 연설	☐	54 foreign	형 외국의
☐	25	energetic	형 활기찬	☐	55 ordinary	형 평범한
☐	26	advise	동 조언하다	☐	56 participate	동 참가하다
☐	27	remind	동 상기시키다	☐	57 curious	형 호기심 있는
☐	28	truth	명 사실	☐	58 environment	명 환경
☐	29	director	명 감독	☐	59 stadium	명 경기장
☐	30	share	동 공유하다	☐	60 tap	동 톡톡 두드리다

CHAPTER 2 시제

• 잘 외워지지 않는 단어는 박스에 체크하여 복습하세요.

🎧 3학년_단어암기장_CH2.mp3

☐	1	peanut	몡 땅콩	☐	31	documentary	몡 다큐멘터리
☐	2	underground	뷔 지하에	☐	32	volcano	몡 화산
☐	3	soothe	툉 달래다	☐	33	abroad	뷔 해외로
☐	4	twist	툉 삐다	☐	34	poem	몡 시
☐	5	biology	몡 생물학	☐	35	university	몡 대학교
☐	6	exhausted	혱 지친	☐	36	research	툉 조사하다
☐	7	lately	뷔 최근에	☐	37	novel	몡 소설
☐	8	noodle	몡 국수	☐	38	fundraising	몡 모금
☐	9	graduate	툉 졸업하다	☐	39	company	몡 회사
☐	10	ceremony	몡 기념식	☐	40	various	혱 다양한
☐	11	international	혱 국제적인	☐	41	reasonable	혱 합리적인
☐	12	artist	몡 예술가	☐	42	national	혱 국가의
☐	13	statue	몡 조각상	☐	43	mayor	몡 시장
☐	14	forest	몡 숲	☐	44	hum	툉 흥얼거리다
☐	15	record	툉 녹화하다, 기록하다	☐	45	semester	몡 학기
☐	16	search	툉 찾다	☐	46	volunteer	툉 자원 봉사하다
☐	17	treasure	몡 보물	☐	47	regret	툉 후회하다
☐	18	carve	툉 깎다	☐	48	decorate	툉 꾸미다
☐	19	pirate	몡 해적	☐	49	receive	툉 받다
☐	20	assignment	몡 과제	☐	50	breaktime	몡 (짧은) 휴식시간
☐	21	countryside	몡 시골	☐	51	interrupt	툉 방해하다
☐	22	treat	툉 치료하다	☐	52	as usual	여느 때처럼
☐	23	gain	툉 얻다	☐	53	tear	툉 찢다
☐	24	overcome	툉 극복하다	☐	54	captain	몡 (스포츠팀의) 주장
☐	25	difficulty	몡 어려움	☐	55	lunch box	몡 도시락
☐	26	realize	툉 깨닫다	☐	56	seem	툉 ~처럼 보이다
☐	27	ill	혱 아픈	☐	57	fix	툉 고치다
☐	28	focus	툉 집중하다	☐	58	model	몡 모형
☐	29	photographer	몡 사진작가	☐	59	solar system	몡 태양계
☐	30	painter	몡 화가	☐	60	origin	몡 기원

• 잘 외워지지 않는 단어는 박스에 체크하여 복습하세요.

🎧 3학년_단어암기장_CH3.mp3

☐	1	**miracle**	명 기적	☐	31 **elderly**	형 연세가 드신
☐	2	**possible**	형 가능한	☐	32 **reveal**	동 폭로하다, 밝히다
☐	3	**flu**	명 독감	☐	33 **sunburn**	동 햇볕에 태우다
☐	4	**tricky**	형 까다로운	☐	34 **lift**	동 들어 올리다
☐	5	**change**	동 변경하다	☐	35 **oversleep**	동 늦잠 자다
☐	6	**turn in**	동 제출하다	☐	36 **heavily**	부 심하게
☐	7	**overseas**	부 해외에	☐	37 **lower**	동 낮추다
☐	8	**upcoming**	형 다가오는	☐	38 **recommend**	동 추천하다
☐	9	**kindergarten**	명 유치원	☐	39 **teenager**	명 십 대
☐	10	**law**	명 법	☐	40 **request**	동 요청하다
☐	11	**traffic**	명 교통	☐	41 **especially**	부 특히
☐	12	**follow**	동 지키다, 따르다	☐	42 **sneeze**	동 재채기하다
☐	13	**competition**	명 대회	☐	43 **uncertain**	형 확실하지 않은
☐	14	**skip**	동 빼먹다, 거르다	☐	44 **row**	명 열, 줄
☐	15	**mess**	명 엉망인 상태	☐	45 **electric**	형 전기의
☐	16	**participant**	명 참가자	☐	46 **thick**	형 짙은
☐	17	**form**	명 양식	☐	47 **fog**	명 안개
☐	18	**insist**	동 주장하다	☐	48 **musician**	명 음악가
☐	19	**courtroom**	명 법정	☐	49 **extra**	형 추가의
☐	20	**product**	명 상품	☐	50 **feed**	동 먹이를 주다
☐	21	**conservation**	명 보호, 보존	☐	51 **increase**	명 증가
☐	22	**shoulder**	명 어깨	☐	52 **allowance**	명 용돈
☐	23	**adopt**	동 입양하다	☐	53 **detergent**	명 세제
☐	24	**palace**	명 궁전	☐	54 **superstitious**	형 미신을 믿는
☐	25	**physical**	형 신체의	☐	55 **complete**	동 완성하다
☐	26	**blind**	형 맹인인	☐	56 **appointment**	명 약속
☐	27	**compete**	동 출전하다	☐	57 **purchase**	동 사다
☐	28	**exhibit**	명 전시품	☐	58 **demand**	동 요구하다
☐	29	**choir**	명 합창단	☐	59 **allergic**	형 알레르기가 있는
☐	30	**filter**	동 거르다	☐	60 **show up**	동 나타나다

단어 테스트 p.33

• 잘 외워지지 않는 단어는 박스에 체크하여 복습하세요.

🎧 3학년_단어암기장_CH4.mp3

☐	1	lighthouse	명 등대	☐	31	direction	명 방향
☐	2	divide	동 나누다	☐	32	evidence	명 증거
☐	3	operate	동 운영하다	☐	33	elect	동 선출하다
☐	4	ranch	명 목장	☐	34	representative	명 대표(자)
☐	5	nanny	명 유모	☐	35	look down on	~을 무시하다
☐	6	donate	동 기부하다	☐	36	put off	동 미루다
☐	7	unfortunate	형 불행한	☐	37	frequently	부 자주
☐	8	unexpectedly	부 뜻밖에	☐	38	prevent	동 예방하다
☐	9	garage	명 차고	☐	39	spirit	명 영혼
☐	10	disappear	동 사라지다	☐	40	praise	동 칭찬하다
☐	11	provide	동 제공하다	☐	41	humid	형 습한
☐	12	necessary	형 필요한	☐	42	hut	명 오두막
☐	13	estimate	동 추정하다	☐	43	distribution	명 배급
☐	14	researcher	명 연구원	☐	44	revise	동 수정하다
☐	15	mail	명 우편물	☐	45	supply	동 공급하다
☐	16	sort	동 분류하다	☐	46	opportunity	명 기회
☐	17	strike	동 치다	☐	47	region	명 지역
☐	18	salesclerk	명 점원	☐	48	equal	형 평등한
☐	19	disease	명 병	☐	49	delay	동 지연시키다
☐	20	resident	명 주민	☐	50	blood	명 피
☐	21	compose	동 작곡하다	☐	51	employee	명 직원
☐	22	release	동 개봉하다	☐	52	recover	동 복구하다
☐	23	conduct	동 하다	☐	53	commit	동 저지르다
☐	24	generation	명 세대	☐	54	translate	동 번역하다
☐	25	experiment	명 실험	☐	55	magnificent	형 훌륭한
☐	26	committee	명 위원회	☐	56	delicate	형 섬세한
☐	27	location	명 위치, 장소	☐	57	turn down	동 거절하다
☐	28	inquire	동 묻다	☐	58	embarrassed	형 창피한
☐	29	make use of	~을 사용하다	☐	59	preserve	동 보존하다
☐	30	outdated	형 구식인	☐	60	install	동 설치하다

• 잘 외워지지 않는 단어는 박스에 체크하여 복습하세요.

🎧 3학년_단어암기장_CH5.mp3

☐ 1 **mood**	명 기분
☐ 2 **fence**	명 울타리
☐ 3 **tax**	명 세금
☐ 4 **concern**	명 걱정
☐ 5 **annoying**	형 짜증스러운
☐ 6 **encourage**	동 격려하다
☐ 7 **effort**	명 노력
☐ 8 **aim**	동 ~을 목표로 하다
☐ 9 **specific**	형 구체적인
☐ 10 **detail**	명 세부 사항
☐ 11 **astronaut**	명 우주비행사
☐ 12 **refuse**	동 거절하다
☐ 13 **assemble**	동 조립하다
☐ 14 **support**	동 지지하다
☐ 15 **respect**	동 공경하다
☐ 16 **be destined to**	~할 운명이다
☐ 17 **intend**	동 ~하려고 하다
☐ 18 **competitor**	명 경쟁자
☐ 19 **entrance**	명 입구
☐ 20 **machine**	명 기계
☐ 21 **sign up for**	~을 신청하다
☐ 22 **creative**	형 창의적인
☐ 23 **solution**	명 해결책
☐ 24 **spoil**	동 상하다
☐ 25 **orphanage**	명 보육원
☐ 26 **politician**	명 정치인
☐ 27 **tongue**	명 혀
☐ 28 **slogan**	명 표어, 슬로건
☐ 29 **election**	명 선거
☐ 30 **silly**	형 어리석은

☐ 31 **confidence**	명 자신감
☐ 32 **thoughtful**	형 사려 깊은
☐ 33 **shallow**	형 얕은
☐ 34 **desirable**	형 바람직한
☐ 35 **vote**	동 투표하다
☐ 36 **explore**	동 탐험하다
☐ 37 **sunscreen**	명 선크림, 자외선 차단제
☐ 38 **expand**	동 확대하다
☐ 39 **cage**	명 우리
☐ 40 **continue**	동 계속하다
☐ 41 **minimize**	동 최소화하다
☐ 42 **decide**	동 결정하다
☐ 43 **handle**	동 다루다
☐ 44 **careless**	형 부주의한
☐ 45 **disaster**	명 재해, 참사
☐ 46 **colony**	명 군집
☐ 47 **laundry**	명 빨래
☐ 48 **nest**	명 둥지
☐ 49 **trial**	명 재판
☐ 50 **reach**	동 도달하다
☐ 51 **critical**	형 중대한
☐ 52 **flight attendant**	명 승무원
☐ 53 **impossible**	형 불가능한
☐ 54 **deserve**	동 ~을 누릴 권리가 있다
☐ 55 **campsite**	명 캠프장
☐ 56 **stressed**	형 스트레스를 받는
☐ 57 **admit**	동 인정하다
☐ 58 **deal with**	처리하다
☐ 59 **complain**	동 항의하다
☐ 60 **firework**	명 불꽃놀이

• 잘 외워지지 않는 단어는 박스에 체크하여 복습하세요.

🎧 3학년_단어암기장_CH6.mp3

☐	1	meaningful	형 의미 있는	☐	31	baker	명 제빵사

☐	1	**meaningful**	형 의미 있는
☐	2	**ruin**	동 (건강을) 해치다
☐	3	**persuade**	동 설득하다
☐	4	**trophy**	명 트로피
☐	5	**aware**	형 알고 있는
☐	6	**grateful**	형 고마워하는
☐	7	**failure**	명 실패
☐	8	**represent**	동 대표하다
☐	9	**college**	명 대학
☐	10	**deny**	동 부인하다
☐	11	**postpone**	동 연기하다
☐	12	**adjust**	동 적응하다
☐	13	**resist**	동 반대하다
☐	14	**notify**	동 알리다
☐	15	**dislike**	동 싫어하다
☐	16	**drawer**	명 서랍
☐	17	**wrist**	명 손목
☐	18	**entertaining**	형 재미있는
☐	19	**plenty of**	많은
☐	20	**press**	동 누르다
☐	21	**notice**	동 알아채다
☐	22	**weird**	형 이상한
☐	23	**indoor**	형 실내의
☐	24	**prefer**	동 선호하다
☐	25	**downtown**	형 도심지의
☐	26	**diverse**	형 다양한
☐	27	**astronomer**	명 천문학자
☐	28	**hopefully**	부 바라건대
☐	29	**childhood**	명 어린 시절
☐	30	**charge**	동 충전하다

☐	31	**baker**	명 제빵사
☐	32	**volleyball**	명 배구
☐	33	**worry**	동 걱정하다
☐	34	**come true**	이루어지다
☐	35	**chore**	명 허드렛일
☐	36	**garbage**	명 쓰레기
☐	37	**repeatedly**	부 되풀이하여
☐	38	**analyze**	동 분석하다
☐	39	**hide**	동 숨다
☐	40	**budget**	명 예산
☐	41	**fabric**	명 천, 직물
☐	42	**talent**	명 재능
☐	43	**freezer**	명 냉동실
☐	44	**purpose**	명 목적
☐	45	**accomplish**	동 달성하다
☐	46	**limit**	동 제한하다
☐	47	**authority**	명 권한
☐	48	**abuse**	명 남용
☐	49	**impact**	명 영향
☐	50	**spread**	동 퍼지다
☐	51	**snore**	동 코를 골다
☐	52	**beat**	동 이기다
☐	53	**criticize**	동 비난하다
☐	54	**quit**	동 그만두다
☐	55	**break into**	침입하다
☐	56	**stroll**	동 산책하다
☐	57	**worth**	형 ~할 가치가 있는
☐	58	**preference**	명 선호
☐	59	**relocate**	동 이동하다
☐	60	**compare**	동 비교하다

• 잘 외워지지 않는 단어는 박스에 체크하여 복습하세요.　　🎧 3학년_단어암기장_CH7.mp3

☐ 1	look after	~를 보살피다	☐ 31	border	몡 경계
☐ 2	wrap	동 싸다	☐ 32	serve	동 제공하다
☐ 3	exhibition	몡 전시회	☐ 33	recall	동 생각해내다
☐ 4	rescue	동 구조하다	☐ 34	remains	몡 유해
☐ 5	mash	동 으깨다	☐ 35	relative	몡 동족, 친척
☐ 6	own	동 소장하다	☐ 36	prove	동 입증하다
☐ 7	publish	동 출간하다	☐ 37	dwell	동 살다
☐ 8	behavior	몡 행동	☐ 38	marine	혱 해양의
☐ 9	confused	혱 혼란스러운	☐ 39	bend	동 구부리다
☐ 10	headline	몡 주요 뉴스	☐ 40	innocent	혱 무죄인
☐ 11	journal	몡 일기	☐ 41	depart	동 출발하다
☐ 12	rainforest	몡 열대우림	☐ 42	rob	동 도둑질하다
☐ 13	efficiently	붸 효율적으로	☐ 43	injure	동 부상을 입히다
☐ 14	frightened	혱 무서워하는	☐ 44	auction	몡 경매
☐ 15	scream	동 비명을 지르다	☐ 45	charity	몡 자선 단체
☐ 16	improvement	몡 향상, 개선	☐ 46	cheat	동 부정행위를 하다
☐ 17	public transportation	몡 대중교통	☐ 47	influence	동 영향을 주다
☐ 18	valuable	혱 가치 있는	☐ 48	local	혱 지역의
☐ 19	precious	혱 소중한	☐ 49	thief	몡 도둑
☐ 20	scratch	동 긁다	☐ 50	archaeologist	몡 고고학자
☐ 21	discover	동 발견하다	☐ 51	theory	몡 이론
☐ 22	pot	몡 항아리	☐ 52	identify	동 알아내다
☐ 23	distracted	혱 산만해진	☐ 53	telescope	몡 망원경
☐ 24	sprain	동 삐다	☐ 54	destination	몡 목적지
☐ 25	store	동 보관하다	☐ 55	achieve	동 성취하다
☐ 26	crowded	혱 붐비는	☐ 56	reputation	몡 평판
☐ 27	wizard	몡 마법사	☐ 57	approach	동 다가가다
☐ 28	silence	몡 침묵	☐ 58	inspiration	몡 영감
☐ 29	bandage	동 붕대를 감다	☐ 59	safety	몡 안전
☐ 30	cheer	동 환호하다	☐ 60	incredible	혱 굉장한

• 잘 외워지지 않는 단어는 박스에 체크하여 복습하세요.

🎧 3학년_단어암기장_CH8.mp3

☐	1	cradle	몡 요람	☐	31 concentrate	동 집중하다
☐	2	chase	동 뒤쫓다	☐	32 bathe	동 목욕시키다, 씻다
☐	3	sculpture	몡 조각품	☐	33 warranty	몡 품질 보증서
☐	4	blame	동 ~을 탓하다	☐	34 improve	동 향상하다
☐	5	respond	동 대답하다	☐	35 treaty	몡 조약
☐	6	graduation	몡 졸업	☐	36 basement	몡 지하층
☐	7	ignore	동 무시하다	☐	37 starve	동 매우 배고프다
☐	8	peel	동 껍질을 벗기다	☐	38 flavor	몡 맛
☐	9	dangerous	형 위험한	☐	39 motto	몡 좌우명
☐	10	develop	동 개발하다	☐	40 challenging	형 도전적인
☐	11	idiom	몡 관용구	☐	41 frozen	형 얼어붙은
☐	12	folk	형 민속의	☐	42 swan	몡 백조
☐	13	affect	동 ~에 영향을 주다	☐	43 massive	형 거대한
☐	14	lounge	몡 휴게실	☐	44 earthquake	몡 지진
☐	15	crack	몡 금	☐	45 cucumber	몡 오이
☐	16	pursue	동 추구하다	☐	46 uniform	몡 교복
☐	17	lend	동 빌려주다	☐	47 unwell	형 아픈
☐	18	get along with	~와 잘 지내다	☐	48 update	동 갱신하다
☐	19	presentation	몡 발표	☐	49 enter	동 들어가다
☐	20	flashlight	몡 손전등	☐	50 auditorium	몡 강당
☐	21	topic	몡 주제	☐	51 policy	몡 방침, 정책
☐	22	hard-working	형 열심히 하는	☐	52 step on	~을 밟다
☐	23	survive	동 생존하다	☐	53 harsh	형 혹독한
☐	24	goal	몡 목적	☐	54 Arctic	몡 북극 (지방)
☐	25	pill	몡 알약	☐	55 migrate	동 이동하다
☐	26	relieve	동 완화하다	☐	56 fur	몡 털
☐	27	method	몡 방법	☐	57 temperature	몡 기온
☐	28	attention	몡 관심	☐	58 terrifying	형 무서운
☐	29	character	몡 등장인물	☐	59 knowledge	몡 지식
☐	30	unusual	형 이례적인	☐	60 sentence	몡 문장

• 잘 외워지지 않는 단어는 박스에 체크하여 복습하세요.

🎧 3학년_단어암기장_CH9.mp3

☐	1	**parade**	명 퍼레이드	☐ 31	**closely**	부 주의하여, 면밀히
☐	2	**crowd**	명 군중	☐ 32	**blanket**	명 이불
☐	3	**passenger**	명 승객	☐ 33	**remember**	동 기억하다
☐	4	**crash**	명 사고	☐ 34	**invitation**	명 초대
☐	5	**cave**	명 동굴	☐ 35	**avoid**	동 피하다
☐	6	**survey**	명 설문 조사	☐ 36	**investigation**	명 조사
☐	7	**despite**	전 ~에도 불구하고	☐ 37	**astonishing**	형 정말 놀라운
☐	8	**bone**	명 뼈	☐ 38	**positive**	형 긍정적인
☐	9	**expect**	동 예상하다	☐ 39	**ashamed**	형 부끄러운
☐	10	**shelter**	명 보호소	☐ 40	**manager**	명 관리자
☐	11	**rat**	명 쥐	☐ 41	**memorable**	형 기억할 만한
☐	12	**fantastic**	형 환상적인	☐ 42	**summarize**	동 요약하다
☐	13	**workout**	명 운동	☐ 43	**article**	명 기사
☐	14	**production**	명 생산	☐ 44	**opinion**	명 의견
☐	15	**surround**	동 둘러싸다	☐ 45	**consumption**	명 소비
☐	16	**tourist attraction**	관광 명소	☐ 46	**absolutely**	부 굉장히
☐	17	**competitive**	형 경쟁적인	☐ 47	**ancestor**	명 조상
☐	18	**order**	동 주문하다	☐ 48	**consume**	동 소비하다
☐	19	**hesitation**	명 망설임	☐ 49	**qualified**	형 자격이 있는
☐	20	**application**	명 지원서	☐ 50	**student council**	명 학생회
☐	21	**entire**	형 전체의	☐ 51	**take part in**	~에 참여하다
☐	22	**turn down**	동 ~을 거절하다	☐ 52	**narrowly**	부 가까스로
☐	23	**call off**	동 ~을 취소하다	☐ 53	**make up one's mind**	결정하다
☐	24	**dictionary**	명 사전	☐ 54	**suggestion**	명 제안
☐	25	**meaning**	명 뜻	☐ 55	**forecast**	명 예측
☐	26	**predator**	명 포식자	☐ 56	**value**	명 가치
☐	27	**marble**	명 대리석	☐ 57	**frequent**	형 빈번한
☐	28	**prediction**	명 예측	☐ 58	**fault**	명 잘못
☐	29	**attempt**	동 시도하다	☐ 59	**quality**	명 품질
☐	30	**admire**	동 칭찬하다	☐ 60	**giant**	형 거대한

• 잘 외워지지 않는 단어는 박스에 체크하여 복습하세요.

🎧 3학년_단어암기장_CH10.mp3

☐	1	center	명 중심	☐	31 anxious	형 불안한
☐	2	surface	명 표면	☐	32 argument	명 논쟁
☐	3	entertaining	형 재미있는	☐	33 lifestyle	명 생활 방식
☐	4	passionately	부 열렬히	☐	34 complicated	형 복잡한
☐	5	human	명 인간	☐	35 dramatic	형 극적인
☐	6	schedule	명 일정	☐	36 empire	명 제국
☐	7	rent	동 빌리다	☐	37 planet	명 행성
☐	8	repairman	명 수리공	☐	38 highway	명 고속도로
☐	9	effective	형 효과적인	☐	39 neatly	부 깔끔하게
☐	10	calculation	명 계산	☐	40 nutritious	형 영양가가 높은
☐	11	leather	명 가죽	☐	41 recycling	명 재활용
☐	12	costly	형 많은 돈이 드는	☐	42 skillful	형 숙련된
☐	13	cheerful	형 밝은, 쾌활한	☐	43 airport	명 공항
☐	14	advance	동 진전시키다	☐	44 lazy	형 게으른
☐	15	pleasant	형 기분 좋은	☐	45 usual	명 평상시
☐	16	frequently	부 자주	☐	46 logically	부 논리적으로
☐	17	grocery store	명 식료품점	☐	47 development	명 발달
☐	18	tragic	형 비극적인	☐	48 measure	동 측정하다
☐	19	athlete	명 운동선수	☐	49 question	명 문제, 질문
☐	20	holiday	명 휴일	☐	50 traffic jam	명 교통체증
☐	21	shout	동 소리치다	☐	51 ladder	명 사다리
☐	22	rely on	~에 의존하다	☐	52 impressed	형 감명을 받은
☐	23	Antarctica	명 남극 대륙	☐	53 commonly	부 흔히
☐	24	unhealthy	형 건강하지 못한	☐	54 durable	형 내구성이 있는
☐	25	rare	형 희귀한	☐	55 population	명 인구
☐	26	up to	전 ~까지	☐	56 accurate	형 정확한
☐	27	brilliant	형 훌륭한	☐	57 organize	동 체계화하다
☐	28	writer	명 작가	☐	58 dense	형 밀집한
☐	29	literature	명 문학	☐	59 ambitious	형 야심에 찬
☐	30	repeat	동 반복하다	☐	60 stressful	형 스트레스가 많은

• 잘 외워지지 않는 단어는 박스에 체크하여 복습하세요.

🎧 3학년_단어암기장_CH11.mp3

☐	1	**slope**	몡 경사면	☐	31	**promotion**	몡 홍보 (활동)

☐ 1 **slope**	몡 경사면	☐ 31 **promotion**	몡 홍보 (활동)
☐ 2 **community**	몡 지역 사회	☐ 32 **period**	몡 시간, 기간
☐ 3 **hand out**	동 ~을 주다	☐ 33 **absent**	형 부재한
☐ 4 **thunder**	몡 천둥	☐ 34 **spare**	형 여분의
☐ 5 **sink**	동 가라앉다	☐ 35 **get rid of**	~을 제거하다
☐ 6 **economic**	형 경제의	☐ 36 **lunar**	형 달의
☐ 7 **loss**	몡 손실	☐ 37 **depend**	동 의존하다
☐ 8 **occur**	동 발생하다	☐ 38 **return**	동 반납하다
☐ 9 **connect**	동 연결하다	☐ 39 **double**	동 두 배로 되다
☐ 10 **convincing**	형 설득력 있는	☐ 40 **destruction**	몡 파괴
☐ 11 **fold**	동 접다	☐ 41 **extinct**	형 멸종된
☐ 12 **envelope**	몡 봉투	☐ 42 **coin**	몡 동전
☐ 13 **luxury**	형 고급의	☐ 43 **well**	몡 우물
☐ 14 **in the middle of**	~의 중앙에	☐ 44 **pole**	몡 막대기
☐ 15 **run into**	우연히 만나다	☐ 45 **import**	동 수입하다
☐ 16 **thrilled**	형 아주 신이 난	☐ 46 **clerk**	몡 점원
☐ 17 **private**	형 개인의	☐ 47 **professional**	형 전문적인
☐ 18 **fundraiser**	몡 모금 행사	☐ 48 **exactly**	부 정확히
☐ 19 **collect**	동 모으다	☐ 49 **distinguish**	동 구별하다
☐ 20 **urgent**	형 긴급한	☐ 50 **electricity**	몡 전기
☐ 21 **hop**	동 껑충껑충 뛰다	☐ 51 **equipment**	몡 장비
☐ 22 **psychological**	형 심리적인	☐ 52 **astronomer**	몡 천문학자
☐ 23 **stool**	몡 의자	☐ 53 **manufacturer**	몡 제조사
☐ 24 **tunnel**	몡 터널	☐ 54 **vehicle**	몡 차량
☐ 25 **preparation**	몡 준비	☐ 55 **capable**	형 ~을 할 수 있는
☐ 26 **environmental**	형 환경의	☐ 56 **consist of**	~으로 이루어지다
☐ 27 **medical**	형 의학의	☐ 57 **flour**	몡 밀가루
☐ 28 **except**	전 ~을 제외하고는	☐ 58 **construction**	몡 공사
☐ 29 **upcoming**	형 다가오는	☐ 59 **carving**	몡 조각
☐ 30 **tuna**	몡 참치	☐ 60 **stray**	형 길을 잃은

• 잘 외워지지 않는 단어는 박스에 체크하여 복습하세요.

🎧 3학년_단어암기장_CH12.mp3

☐	1	immediately	부 즉시	☐	31	difference	명 차이
☐	2	normally	부 보통	☐	32	recognize	동 인식하다
☐	3	honor	명 명예	☐	33	get used to	~에 익숙해지다
☐	4	train	동 훈련시키다	☐	34	whistle	동 휘파람을 불다
☐	5	vision	명 시력	☐	35	lay	동 (알을) 낳다
☐	6	celebrity	명 유명 인사	☐	36	staff	명 직원
☐	7	accept	동 받아들이다	☐	37	breeze	명 산들바람
☐	8	scare	동 겁먹게 하다	☐	38	conversation	명 대화
☐	9	downtown	부 시내에	☐	39	arrange	동 정리하다
☐	10	soldier	명 군인	☐	40	spontaneous	형 즉흥적인
☐	11	attack	명 공격	☐	41	tough	형 힘든
☐	12	guilty	형 유죄의	☐	42	counselor	명 상담 교사
☐	13	bother	동 신경 쓰이게 하다	☐	43	mess up	어지럽히다
☐	14	replace	동 대신하다	☐	44	symbolize	동 상징하다
☐	15	rush	동 서두르다	☐	45	responsible	형 책임이 있는
☐	16	farming	명 농업	☐	46	submit	동 제출하다
☐	17	wealthy	형 부유한	☐	47	funding	명 자금
☐	18	examine	동 검사하다	☐	48	shellfish	명 조개류
☐	19	report card	명 성적표	☐	49	jealous	형 질투를 느끼는
☐	20	volcanic	형 화산의	☐	50	courage	명 용기
☐	21	emotional	형 감정적인	☐	51	sibling	명 형제자매
☐	22	line up	동 줄을 서다	☐	52	brick	명 벽돌
☐	23	wag	동 (꼬리를) 흔들다	☐	53	sightseeing	명 관광
☐	24	drill	명 훈련	☐	54	obvious	형 분명한
☐	25	desire	명 바람	☐	55	instruction	명 설명서
☐	26	stay away	떨어져 있다	☐	56	posture	명 자세
☐	27	eruption	명 폭발	☐	57	ban	동 금하다
☐	28	photography	명 사진술	☐	58	lava	명 용암
☐	29	breath	명 호흡	☐	59	metal	명 금속
☐	30	invest	동 투자하다	☐	60	shortage	명 부족

CHAPTER 13 관계사

• 잘 외워지지 않는 단어는 박스에 체크하여 복습하세요.

🎧 3학년_단어암기장_CH13.mp3

☐ 1	sail	동 항해하다	
☐ 2	neighborhood	명 동네	
☐ 3	feature	명 특징	
☐ 4	suit	동 맞다, 편리하다	
☐ 5	renovate	동 개조하다	
☐ 6	cover	동 덮다	
☐ 7	get away	탈출하다	
☐ 8	donation	명 기부	
☐ 9	make sense	타당하다	
☐ 10	patient	명 환자	
☐ 11	stationery	명 문방구	
☐ 12	public	형 공공의	
☐ 13	waterfall	명 폭포	
☐ 14	stuff	명 물건	
☐ 15	factory	명 공장	
☐ 16	come across	동 우연히 마주치다	
☐ 17	found	동 설립하다	
☐ 18	retire	동 은퇴하다	
☐ 19	convenience store	명 편의점	
☐ 20	drone	명 무인 항공기	
☐ 21	expired	형 기한이 지난	
☐ 22	due to	전 ~ 때문에	
☐ 23	excited	형 신이 난	
☐ 24	violence	명 폭력	
☐ 25	acceptable	형 용납되는, 받아들여지는	
☐ 26	current	명 전류	
☐ 27	benefit	명 이로움	
☐ 28	technology	명 기술	
☐ 29	adopt	동 입양하다	
☐ 30	owner	명 주인	

☐ 31	unexpected	형 예기치 않은	
☐ 32	result	명 결과	
☐ 33	shell	명 껍데기	
☐ 34	creature	명 생물	
☐ 35	bucket	명 양동이	
☐ 36	impress	동 깊은 인상을 주다	
☐ 37	generous	형 관대한	
☐ 38	motivational	형 동기를 주는	
☐ 39	politics	명 정치	
☐ 40	dormitory	명 기숙사	
☐ 41	clinic	명 병원	
☐ 42	star	동 주연을 맡다	
☐ 43	spot	명 장소	
☐ 44	naturally	부 자연스럽게	
☐ 45	propose	동 청혼하다, 제안하다	
☐ 46	lead to	~로 이어지다	
☐ 47	bush	명 덤불	
☐ 48	platform	명 승강장	
☐ 49	match	동 어울리다	
☐ 50	trousers	명 바지	
☐ 51	cause	동 ~을 야기하다	
☐ 52	gorgeous	형 아주 멋진	
☐ 53	be supposed to	~하기로 되어 있다	
☐ 54	wife	명 아내	
☐ 55	reason	명 이유	
☐ 56	historic site	유적지	
☐ 57	require	동 필요로 하다	
☐ 58	confident	형 확신하는	
☐ 59	humble	형 겸손한	
☐ 60	last	동 오래가다	

• 잘 외워지지 않는 단어는 박스에 체크하여 복습하세요. 🎧 3학년_단어암기장_CH14.mp3

☐	1	**drown**	동 익사하다	☐	31	**masterpiece** 명 걸작
☐	2	**data**	명 자료	☐	32	**in trouble** 난처하여
☐	3	**couch**	명 소파	☐	33	**restriction** 명 규제
☐	4	**streetlight**	명 가로등	☐	34	**shame** 명 아쉬운 일, 창피
☐	5	**blackout**	명 정전	☐	35	**adorable** 형 사랑스러운
☐	6	**breathe**	동 숨을 쉬다	☐	36	**growl** 동 으르렁거리다
☐	7	**out of shape**	건강이 안 좋은	☐	37	**location** 명 위치
☐	8	**sew**	동 바느질하다	☐	38	**stuck** 형 꼼짝 못 하는
☐	9	**transfer**	동 갈아타다, 이동하다	☐	39	**apology** 명 사과
☐	10	**free of charge**	무료로	☐	40	**underwater** 부 물속에서
☐	11	**faded**	형 빛깔이 바랜	☐	41	**teleport** 동 순간 이동하다
☐	12	**afford**	동 ~을 할 형편이 되다	☐	42	**sticky** 형 끈적거리는
☐	13	**architect**	명 건축가	☐	43	**extend** 동 연장하다
☐	14	**punish**	동 처벌하다	☐	44	**compass** 명 나침반
☐	15	**get lost**	길을 잃다	☐	45	**stay in touch** 연락을 유지하다
☐	16	**gravity**	명 중력	☐	46	**proof** 명 증거
☐	17	**lecture**	명 강의	☐	47	**access** 동 ~에 접근하다
☐	18	**explanation**	명 설명	☐	48	**performance** 명 공연
☐	19	**rush hour**	명 혼잡 시간대	☐	49	**describe** 동 묘사하다
☐	20	**formula**	명 공식	☐	50	**outfit** 명 옷
☐	21	**give up**	동 포기하다	☐	51	**nightmare** 명 악몽
☐	22	**manual**	명 설명서	☐	52	**meow** 동 야옹거리다
☐	23	**stay over**	자고 가다	☐	53	**unaware** 형 알지 못하는
☐	24	**billionaire**	명 억만장자	☐	54	**tropical** 형 열대 지방의
☐	25	**fairy**	명 요정	☐	55	**paradise** 명 낙원
☐	26	**economics**	명 경제학	☐	56	**lush** 형 우거진
☐	27	**brag**	동 자랑하다	☐	57	**reply** 동 답장하다
☐	28	**chemistry**	명 화학	☐	58	**uncomfortable** 형 불편한
☐	29	**occupy**	동 거주하다	☐	59	**suffer** 동 고통받다
☐	30	**discussion**	명 논의	☐	60	**wing** 명 날개

• 잘 외워지지 않는 단어는 박스에 체크하여 복습하세요.   🎧 3학년_단어암기장_CH15.mp3

☐	1	major	몡 전공 분야	☐	31	physics	몡 물리학
☐	2	sharply	뷔 급격하게	☐	32	option	몡 선택권
☐	3	available	혱 이용할 수 있는	☐	33	banquet	몡 연회
☐	4	quarter	몡 4분의 1	☐	34	mechanic	몡 정비공
☐	5	education	몡 교육	☐	35	motorcycle	몡 오토바이
☐	6	skill	몡 기술	☐	36	illegally	뷔 불법적으로
☐	7	master	동 ~에 통달하다	☐	37	dynasty	몡 시대
☐	8	position	몡 자세	☐	38	suddenly	뷔 갑자기
☐	9	roll	동 구르다	☐	39	useful	혱 유용한
☐	10	wound	몡 상처	☐	40	flood	몡 홍수
☐	11	previous	혱 이전의	☐	41	capital	몡 수도
☐	12	vocabulary	몡 어휘	☐	42	heal	동 치유하다
☐	13	instrument	몡 악기	☐	43	perform	동 공연하다
☐	14	stove	몡 가스레인지	☐	44	coach	몡 코치, 감독
☐	15	garlic	몡 마늘	☐	45	instruct	동 지시하다
☐	16	guard	몡 경비 요원	☐	46	beg	동 간청하다
☐	17	track	몡 선로	☐	47	geography	몡 지리학
☐	18	significantly	뷔 상당히	☐	48	trainer	몡 훈련사
☐	19	distance	몡 거리	☐	49	clearly	뷔 분명히
☐	20	price	몡 가격	☐	50	president	몡 회장
☐	21	oxygen	몡 산소	☐	51	medicine	몡 약
☐	22	be made up of	~으로 구성되다	☐	52	clothing	몡 옷
☐	23	hydrogen	몡 수소	☐	53	be covered with	~으로 뒤덮이다
☐	24	claim	동 주장하다	☐	54	go up	동 올라가다
☐	25	copy	동 베끼다, 복사하다	☐	55	rainy	혱 비가 많이 오는
☐	26	bitter	혱 맛이 쓴	☐	56	story	몡 (건물의) 층
☐	27	championship	몡 선수권 대회	☐	57	tourist	몡 관광객
☐	28	attendee	몡 참석자	☐	58	take off	동 이륙하다
☐	29	utensil	몡 도구	☐	59	nap	몡 낮잠
☐	30	license plate	몡 자동차 번호판	☐	60	injury	몡 부상

CHAPTER 16 특수구문

단어 테스트 p.45

• 잘 외워지지 않는 단어는 박스에 체크하여 복습하세요.

🎧 3학년_단어암기장_CH16.mp3

☐	1	climate	명 기후	☐	31	amusing	형 재미있는

☐ 1 climate 　명 기후
☐ 2 threaten 　동 위협하다
☐ 3 survival 　명 생존
☐ 4 appreciate 　동 고맙게 생각하다
☐ 5 charismatic 　형 카리스마가 있는
☐ 6 fountain 　명 분수
☐ 7 photograph 　명 사진
☐ 8 excellent 　형 훌륭한
☐ 9 slide 　동 미끄러지다
☐ 10 decision 　명 결정
☐ 11 lab 　명 연구실
☐ 12 register 　동 등록하다
☐ 13 on time 　제때에
☐ 14 relaxing 　형 편안한
☐ 15 path 　명 길
☐ 16 be fond of 　~을 좋아하다
☐ 17 hearing 　명 청각, 청력
☐ 18 event 　명 행사
☐ 19 yell 　동 소리치다
☐ 20 send off 　퇴장시키다
☐ 21 field 　명 경기장
☐ 22 predictable 　형 예측할 수 있는
☐ 23 composer 　명 작곡가
☐ 24 announcement 　명 소식, 발표
☐ 25 gear 　명 기구, 기어
☐ 26 fear 　명 두려움
☐ 27 unlikely 　형 있을 법하지 않은
☐ 28 suburb 　명 교외
☐ 29 extremely 　부 극도로
☐ 30 inspiring 　형 영감을 불러일으키는

☐ 31 amusing 　형 재미있는
☐ 32 hardly 　부 거의 ~ 아니다
☐ 33 host 　명 주인
☐ 34 venue 　명 장소
☐ 35 dig 　동 파다
☐ 36 dirt 　명 흙
☐ 37 slippery 　형 미끄러운
☐ 38 hang out with 　~와 시간을 보내다
☐ 39 design 　동 설계하다
☐ 40 disagreement 　명 의견 충돌
☐ 41 search 　동 수색하다
☐ 42 be accused of 　~으로 고발당하다
☐ 43 intention 　명 의도
☐ 44 flock 　명 무리
☐ 45 suitable 　형 적합한
☐ 46 familiar 　형 익숙한
☐ 47 fancy 　형 화려한
☐ 48 renovation 　명 수리
☐ 49 cancel 　동 취소하다
☐ 50 device 　명 기구, 장치
☐ 51 maintain 　동 유지하다
☐ 52 sweaty 　형 땀에 젖은
☐ 53 interest 　명 이자
☐ 54 army 　명 군대
☐ 55 artwork 　명 예술 작품
☐ 56 rate 　명 요금, 비율
☐ 57 discounted 　형 할인된
☐ 58 domestically 　부 국내에서
☐ 59 mental 　형 정신의
☐ 60 expense 　명 비용

• 영어는 우리말로 쓰고, 우리말은 영어로 쓰시오.

1	rise	31	뺨, 볼
2	recently	32	박람회
3	contact	33	익은
4	reporter	34	반대하다
5	trick	35	지붕
6	unusual	36	활기찬
7	resemble	37	도착하다
8	permit	38	경기장
9	discuss	39	속삭이다
10	comfortable	40	참가하다
11	ordinary	41	관객
12	tap	42	능력
13	career	43	매일의
14	remind	44	조언하다
15	consider	45	교장
16	specialist	46	외국의
17	attend	47	위급상황
18	silent	48	허락하다
19	appear	49	의사소통
20	blow	50	환경
21	mention	51	기술자
22	security	52	공유하다
23	awful	53	목수
24	prepare	54	설명하다
25	memorize	55	역할
26	nervous	56	호기심 있는
27	relationship	57	기온
28	truth	58	연설
29	popular	59	간단한
30	director	60	복도

*정답은 HackersBook.com에서 확인할 수 있습니다.

• 영어는 우리말로 쓰고, 우리말은 영어로 쓰시오.

1	receive	31	국가의
2	assignment	32	깎다
3	volcano	33	후회하다
4	twist	34	땅콩
5	statue	35	시
6	breaktime	36	보물
7	fix	37	회사
8	painter	38	흥얼거리다
9	ceremony	39	숲
10	lately	40	아픈
11	origin	41	어려움
12	university	42	국제적인
13	seem	43	예술가
14	countryside	44	도시락
15	fundraising	45	모형
16	interrupt	46	녹화하다, 기록하다
17	pirate	47	태양계
18	search	48	학기
19	abroad	49	국수
20	focus	50	졸업하다
21	research	51	소설
22	various	52	지하에
23	reasonable	53	생물학
24	gain	54	(스포츠팀의) 주장
25	exhausted	55	꾸미다
26	treat	56	극복하다
27	soothe	57	다큐멘터리
28	tear	58	사진작가
29	as usual	59	깨닫다
30	mayor	60	자원 봉사하다

*정답은 HackersBook.com에서 확인할 수 있습니다.

• 영어는 우리말로 쓰고, 우리말은 영어로 쓰시오.

1	conservation	31	증가
2	insist	32	늦잠 자다
3	especially	33	재채기하다
4	lift	34	엉망인 상태
5	kindergarten	35	완성하다
6	show up	36	입양하다
7	purchase	37	빼먹다, 거르다
8	follow	38	어깨
9	thick	39	알레르기가 있는
10	extra	40	다가오는
11	competition	41	음악가
12	request	42	독감
13	demand	43	안개
14	exhibit	44	맹인인
15	appointment	45	연세가 드신
16	detergent	46	낮추다
17	uncertain	47	교통
18	physical	48	추천하다
19	courtroom	49	기적
20	tricky	50	참가자
21	reveal	51	궁전
22	compete	52	햇볕에 태우다
23	row	53	십 대
24	turn in	54	변경하다
25	superstitious	55	가능한
26	filter	56	전기의
27	choir	57	양식
28	product	58	먹이를 주다
29	allowance	59	법
30	overseas	60	심하게

*정답은 HackersBook.com에서 확인할 수 있습니다.

• 영어는 우리말로 쓰고, 우리말은 영어로 쓰시오.

1	frequently	31	방향
2	make use of	32	공급하다
3	revise	33	등대
4	garage	34	연구원
5	employee	35	기부하다
6	turn down	36	습한
7	strike	37	주민
8	inquire	38	우편물
9	look down on	39	위치, 장소
10	praise	40	사라지다
11	operate	41	구식인
12	preserve	42	번역하다
13	disease	43	작곡하다
14	recover	44	설치하다
15	embarrassed	45	증거
16	representative	46	선출하다
17	estimate	47	배급
18	conduct	48	점원
19	magnificent	49	뜻밖에
20	unfortunate	50	유모
21	put off	51	피
22	provide	52	세대
23	hut	53	필요한
24	divide	54	목장
25	sort	55	위원회
26	delay	56	지역
27	prevent	57	평등한
28	opportunity	58	영혼
29	release	59	저지르다
30	delicate	60	실험

*정답은 HackersBook.com에서 확인할 수 있습니다.

• 영어는 우리말로 쓰고, 우리말은 영어로 쓰시오.

1	concern	31	해결책
2	sign up for	32	투표하다
3	handle	33	재해, 참사
4	critical	34	세부 사항
5	desirable	35	우주비행사
6	silly	36	불가능한
7	aim	37	~하려고 하다
8	competitor	38	둥지
9	stressed	39	창의적인
10	colony	40	자신감
11	annoying	41	노력
12	deserve	42	계속하다
13	admit	43	선거
14	careless	44	선크림, 자외선 차단제
15	spoil	45	불꽃놀이
16	trial	46	얕은
17	cage	47	최소화하다
18	politician	48	빨래
19	assemble	49	세금
20	campsite	50	울타리
21	thoughtful	51	구체적인
22	be destined to	52	혀
23	mood	53	확대하다
24	encourage	54	공경하다
25	deal with	55	표어, 슬로건
26	complain	56	지지하다
27	orphanage	57	승무원
28	decide	58	기계
29	refuse	59	입구
30	reach	60	탐험하다

*정답은 HackersBook.com에서 확인할 수 있습니다.

• 영어는 우리말로 쓰고, 우리말은 영어로 쓰시오.

1	ruin	31	어린 시절
2	break into	32	걱정하다
3	preference	33	숨다
4	press	34	싫어하다
5	beat	35	제한하다
6	garbage	36	냉동실
7	diverse	37	알리다
8	postpone	38	비교하다
9	accomplish	39	실내의
10	adjust	40	예산
11	persuade	41	코를 골다
12	charge	42	실패
13	notice	43	산책하다
14	represent	44	배구
15	authority	45	퍼지다
16	repeatedly	46	~할 가치가 있는
17	criticize	47	도심지의
18	hopefully	48	제빵사
19	college	49	손목
20	entertaining	50	재능
21	resist	51	의미 있는
22	astronomer	52	허드렛일
23	plenty of	53	분석하다
24	purpose	54	트로피
25	quit	55	남용
26	come true	56	선호하다
27	grateful	57	천, 직물
28	weird	58	서랍
29	deny	59	알고 있는
30	relocate	60	영향

*정답은 HackersBook.com에서 확인할 수 있습니다.

• 영어는 우리말로 쓰고, 우리말은 영어로 쓰시오.

1	distracted	31	경계
2	own	32	전시회
3	recall	33	삐다
4	innocent	34	부정행위를 하다
5	precious	35	이론
6	identify	36	보관하다
7	mash	37	붕대를 감다
8	serve	38	안전
9	prove	39	영향을 주다
10	reputation	40	효율적으로
11	valuable	41	항아리
12	depart	42	도둑질하다
13	journal	43	향상, 개선
14	achieve	44	자선 단체
15	destination	45	경매
16	frightened	46	구부리다
17	discover	47	긁다
18	cheer	48	붐비는
19	approach	49	싸다
20	dwell	50	망원경
21	look after	51	영감
22	behavior	52	대중교통
23	remains	53	주요 뉴스
24	confused	54	동족, 친척
25	silence	55	해양의
26	archaeologist	56	마법사
27	rescue	57	부상을 입히다
28	incredible	58	출간하다
29	scream	59	열대우림
30	local	60	도둑

*정답은 HackersBook.com에서 확인할 수 있습니다.

• 영어는 우리말로 쓰고, 우리말은 영어로 쓰시오.

1	massive	31	조약
2	flavor	32	교복
3	concentrate	33	혹독한
4	pursue	34	발표
5	unusual	35	위험한
6	hard-working	36	갱신하다
7	sculpture	37	손전등
8	develop	38	지식
9	migrate	39	졸업
10	swan	40	등장인물
11	terrifying	41	문장
12	affect	42	주제
13	fur	43	지하층
14	lend	44	껍질을 벗기다
15	attention	45	북극 (지방)
16	relieve	46	방침, 정책
17	auditorium	47	~을 탓하다
18	crack	48	품질 보증서
19	starve	49	생존하다
20	respond	50	방법
21	goal	51	오이
22	chase	52	관용구
23	improve	53	알약
24	folk	54	휴게실
25	step on	55	좌우명
26	unwell	56	기온
27	get along with	57	요람
28	ignore	58	얼어붙은
29	enter	59	목욕시키다, 씻다
30	challenging	60	지진

*정답은 HackersBook.com에서 확인할 수 있습니다.

• 영어는 우리말로 쓰고, 우리말은 영어로 쓰시오.

1	marble	31	예측
2	admire	32	쥐
3	investigation	33	설문 조사
4	competitive	34	조상
5	ashamed	35	소비하다
6	crash	36	이불
7	workout	37	퍼레이드
8	consumption	38	환상적인
9	production	39	피하다
10	despite	40	관리자
11	call off	41	품질
12	take part in	42	잘못
13	order	43	지원서
14	suggestion	44	가치
15	absolutely	45	둘러싸다
16	turn down	46	보호소
17	frequent	47	기사
18	tourist attraction	48	포식자
19	expect	49	군중
20	memorable	50	뼈
21	entire	51	기억하다
22	attempt	52	뜻
23	forecast	53	초대
24	narrowly	54	긍정적인
25	make up one's mind	55	동굴
26	astonishing	56	거대한
27	summarize	57	학생회
28	hesitation	58	승객
29	closely	59	사전
30	qualified	60	의견

*정답은 HackersBook.com에서 확인할 수 있습니다.

• 영어는 우리말로 쓰고, 우리말은 영어로 쓰시오.

1 brilliant	31 고속도로
2 argument	32 스트레스가 많은
3 commonly	33 계산
4 grocery store	34 운동선수
5 advance	35 극적인
6 up to	36 문학
7 nutritious	37 사다리
8 entertaining	38 효과적인
9 usual	39 제국
10 ambitious	40 가죽
11 shout	41 게으른
12 development	42 휴일
13 schedule	43 반복하다
14 impressed	44 재활용
15 measure	45 교통체증
16 organize	46 작가
17 anxious	47 희귀한
18 neatly	48 행성
19 costly	49 비극적인
20 rely on	50 표면
21 pleasant	51 생활 방식
22 Antarctica	52 인간
23 logically	53 수리공
24 accurate	54 인구
25 durable	55 숙련된
26 unhealthy	56 중심
27 passionately	57 자주
28 dense	58 공항
29 complicated	59 밝은, 쾌활한
30 rent	60 문제, 질문

*정답은 HackersBook.com에서 확인할 수 있습니다.

• 영어는 우리말로 쓰고, 우리말은 영어로 쓰시오.

1 capable	31 멸종된
2 promotion	32 의학의
3 except	33 참치
4 occur	34 천문학자
5 thrilled	35 봉투
6 distinguish	36 가라앉다
7 clerk	37 고급의
8 run into	38 전기
9 psychological	39 천둥
10 depend	40 긴급한
11 private	41 조각
12 return	42 두 배로 되다
13 construction	43 차량
14 collect	44 동전
15 manufacturer	45 접다
16 fundraiser	46 수입하다
17 hand out	47 시간, 기간
18 equipment	48 달의
19 spare	49 연결하다
20 professional	50 우물
21 convincing	51 지역 사회
22 destruction	52 ~의 중앙에
23 preparation	53 깡충깡충 뛰다
24 stool	54 다가오는
25 get rid of	55 경제의
26 consist of	56 부재한
27 slope	57 막대기
28 environmental	58 손실
29 stray	59 밀가루
30 exactly	60 터널

*정답은 HackersBook.com에서 확인할 수 있습니다.

• 영어는 우리말로 쓰고, 우리말은 영어로 쓰시오.

1	sibling	31	시력
2	sightseeing	32	(알을) 낳다
3	funding	33	휘파람을 불다
4	tough	34	명예
5	immediately	35	훈련시키다
6	ban	36	용암
7	submit	37	대화
8	desire	38	줄을 서다
9	bother	39	부족
10	get used to	40	유죄의
11	replace	41	(꼬리를) 흔들다
12	drill	42	금속
13	recognize	43	투자하다
14	eruption	44	직원
15	obvious	45	벽돌
16	stay away	46	질투를 느끼는
17	wealthy	47	감정적인
18	spontaneous	48	호흡
19	normally	49	사진술
20	examine	50	공격
21	arrange	51	유명 인사
22	instruction	52	차이
23	symbolize	53	산들바람
24	mess up	54	화산의
25	scare	55	성적표
26	posture	56	군인
27	accept	57	시내에
28	rush	58	농업
29	responsible	59	조개류
30	courage	60	상담 교사

*정답은 HackersBook.com에서 확인할 수 있습니다.

• 영어는 우리말로 쓰고, 우리말은 영어로 쓰시오.

1	violence	31	청혼하다, 제안하다
2	expired	32	껍데기
3	naturally	33	정치
4	found	34	오래가다
5	impress	35	문방구
6	neighborhood	36	무인 항공기
7	spot	37	결과
8	historic site	38	공장
9	renovate	39	기숙사
10	due to	40	덮다
11	excited	41	이유
12	gorgeous	42	공공의
13	generous	43	주인
14	require	44	입양하다
15	lead to	45	승강장
16	get away	46	이로움
17	acceptable	47	덤불
18	current	48	환자
19	be supposed to	49	편의점
20	unexpected	50	주연을 맡다
21	suit	51	항해하다
22	match	52	물건
23	feature	53	기술
24	humble	54	타당하다
25	donation	55	아내
26	clinic	56	~을 야기하다
27	motivational	57	폭포
28	come across	58	양동이
29	confident	59	은퇴하다
30	trousers	60	생물

*정답은 HackersBook.com에서 확인할 수 있습니다.

• 영어는 우리말로 쓰고, 우리말은 영어로 쓰시오.

1	location	31	걸작
2	stay in touch	32	혼잡 시간대
3	formula	33	아쉬운 일, 창피
4	give up	34	바느질하다
5	adorable	35	익사하다
6	performance	36	길을 잃다
7	free of charge	37	화학
8	out of shape	38	요정
9	explanation	39	끈적거리는
10	discussion	40	야옹거리다
11	access	41	가로등
12	brag	42	사과
13	in trouble	43	묘사하다
14	lush	44	소파
15	manual	45	물속에서
16	restriction	46	정전
17	proof	47	경제학
18	reply	48	나침반
19	faded	49	자료
20	occupy	50	열대 지방의
21	uncomfortable	51	으르렁거리다
22	punish	52	날개
23	outfit	53	건축가
24	teleport	54	악몽
25	billionaire	55	숨을 쉬다
26	stuck	56	중력
27	transfer	57	알지 못하는
28	afford	58	강의
29	stay over	59	고통받다
30	extend	60	낙원

*정답은 HackersBook.com에서 확인할 수 있습니다.

• 영어는 우리말로 쓰고, 우리말은 영어로 쓰시오.

1	banquet	31	선택권
2	be covered with	32	코치, 감독
3	utensil	33	베끼다, 복사하다
4	story	34	약
5	previous	35	교육
6	skill	36	유용한
7	president	37	낮잠
8	championship	38	선로
9	mechanic	39	가스레인지
10	instrument	40	구르다
11	wound	41	홍수
12	license plate	42	맛이 쓴
13	be made up of	43	관광객
14	perform	44	마늘
15	beg	45	부상
16	dynasty	46	산소
17	hydrogen	47	4분의 1
18	sharply	48	가격
19	attendee	49	전공 분야
20	suddenly	50	지리학
21	available	51	비가 많이 오는
22	instruct	52	거리
23	significantly	53	오토바이
24	physics	54	어휘
25	claim	55	치유하다
26	illegally	56	수도
27	position	57	이륙하다
28	clothing	58	경비 요원
29	go up	59	~에 통달하다
30	clearly	60	훈련사

*정답은 HackersBook.com에서 확인할 수 있습니다.

• 영어는 우리말로 쓰고, 우리말은 영어로 쓰시오.

1	announcement	31	미끄러지다
2	host	32	교외
3	extremely	33	의견 충돌
4	be accused of	34	분수
5	mental	35	등록하다
6	photograph	36	기후
7	venue	37	이자
8	field	38	미끄러운
9	domestically	39	할인된
10	send off	40	연구실
11	expense	41	위협하다
12	fancy	42	무리
13	composer	43	편안한
14	intention	44	수색하다
15	device	45	흙
16	appreciate	46	파다
17	yell	47	카리스마가 있는
18	suitable	48	결정
19	hang out with	49	설계하다
20	predictable	50	땀에 젖은
21	be fond of	51	행사
22	renovation	52	취소하다
23	unlikely	53	두려움
24	rate	54	군대
25	excellent	55	영감을 불러일으키는
26	path	56	생존
27	amusing	57	기구, 기어
28	hardly	58	청각, 청력
29	on time	59	익숙한
30	maintain	60	예술 작품

*정답은 HackersBook.com에서 확인할 수 있습니다.

MEMO

MEMO

MEMO

기출로적중

해커스
중학영문법

3학년

절취선

핵심만 담았다!

문법 암기리스트

+

단어 암기장